readings in Russian history and culture

readings in
Russian history
and culture

edited by Ivar Spector, UNIVERSITY OF WASHINGTON

and Marion Spector, PH.D.

Pacific Books, Publishers
Palo Alto, California

First published 1965 by Allyn and Bacon, Inc.
Reissued 1968 by Pacific Books, Publishers.

Library of Congress catalog card No. 65-18891.
Manufactured in the United States of America.

PACIFIC BOOKS, PUBLISHERS
P. O. Box 558
Palo Alto, California 94302

preface

THE MAIN PURPOSE OF THIS WORK is to provide collateral readings, not available elsewhere in one volume, for students in Russian history and culture. It includes also selections of interest to students of Russian literature, science, sociology, and political science. Since the arrangement is chronological and the book covers significant aspects of Russian history and culture from the earliest times to the present, it can be read as an entity in itself.

This collection is based on many years of teaching courses in Russian history and civilization at the University of Washington. A substantial number of the selections has been translated into English for the first time by the editors. They have also provided an appropriate, up-to-date introduction to each selection.

Because of the wide interest today in modern and contemporary Russian history and culture, this book has been divided into two parts, the first covering the period from ancient times to the end of the nineteenth century, and the second devoted to the twentieth century.

I.S. & M.S.

acknowledgments

ACKNOWLEDGEMENT IS MADE to the following sources for material reprinted in this collection of readings. The numbers refer to the number of the reading in which the reprinted material is found.

3. Excerpts from *The Russian Primary Chronicle* by permission of the Medieval Academy of America.

15. Excerpts from Georges Florovsky, "The Problem of Old Russian Culture" (March, 1962) and D.S. Likhachev, "Further Remarks on the Problem of Old Russian Culture" (March, 1963) by permission of *Slavic Review*.

18. Aleksandr Nikolaevich Radishchev, *A Journey from St. Petersburg to Moscow*, translated by Leo Wiener, edited by Roderick Page Thaler. Cambridge, Mass.: Harvard University Press, Copyright, 1958, by the President and Fellows of Harvard College.

20. Reprinted by permission of the publishers from Richard Pipes, ed., *Karamzin's Memoir on Ancient and Modern Russia* (Cambridge, Mass.: Harvard University Press, 1959), pp. 162-63; 165-67.

32. Reprinted with permission of The Macmillan Company from *History of the National Economy of Russia to the 1917 Revolution* by Peter I. Lyashchenko. Copyright 1949 by the American Council of Learned Societies.

33. Excerpts from *The Memoirs of Count Witte* by permission of Avrahm Yarmolinsky.

34. Reprinted from "Sergei Witte and the Industrialization of Imperial Russia," *Journal of Modern History*, XXVI, No. 1 (March, 1955), pp. 64-74, by permission of The University of Chicago Press.

39. Reprinted from *Features and Figures of the Past* by V.I. Gurko, edited by J.E. Wallace Sterling, Xenia J. Eudin and H.H. Fisher; translated by Laura Mateev with permission of the publishers, Stanford University Press. Copyright 1939 by the Board of Trustees of the Leland Stanford Junior College.

41. Excerpts from Maurice Paléologue, *An Ambassador's Memoirs* reprinted by permission of The Hutchinson Publishing Group, London.

42. From Alexander Kerensky, *The Crucifixion of Liberty* by permission of The John Day Company.

43. From *The Real Situation in Russia* by Leon Trotsky, translated by Max Eastman, copyright, 1928, by Harcourt, Brace & World, Inc.; ©1956, by Max Eastman. Reprinted by permission of the publishers.

44.   From Ivar Spector, *The First Russian Revolution: Its Impact on Asia.* ©1962, by permission of Prentice-Hall, Inc., Englewood Cliffs, New Jersey.

54.   Article by H.J. Muller reprinted by permission of H.J. Muller and *Saturday Review.* ˒

Current Digest of the Soviet Press, published weekly at Columbia University by the Joint Committee on Slavic Studies appointed by the American Council of Learned Societies and Social Science Research Council. The following articles are reprinted from the *Digest* by permission: 52, 56, 61, 62, 63.

Soviet Press Translations published by the Far Eastern and Russian Institute, University of Washington. The following articles translated by Ivar Spector are reprinted by permission: 50, 51, 57.

contents

I. The Russian Past: From Earliest Times to 1905

II. Revolutionary Russia: 1905-1963

I. The Russian Past: From Earliest Times to 1905

1. the Khazars and the formation of the Russian state

THE KHAZARS, ACCORDING TO THE CONSENSUS OF SCHOLARS, were a Turkic people, related to the Bulgars, who came from the steppes of Central Asia. After 720 A.D. they established their political center at Atil [Itil] on the Caspian Sea, in the vicinity of the Volga delta, later the site of Saray-i-Batu, the first capital of the Golden Horde. They extended their sway over the Georgians, Armenians, and Avars, until their lands bordered those of the Byzantine Empire, and for a time Kiev came under their domination. In the ninth century, the Khazar rulers and some of their subjects were converted to Judaism. For more than three hundred years, from the seventh to the eleventh century, they formed an important bulwark on the steppes of Eastern Europe and from the Urals to the Crimea against invaders from the south and east. In the eighth century, they fought their greatest battles against Muhammed Marwan II (744-750), the last of the fourteen Ummayad caliphs of Damascus. This struggle provided a breathing spell for the Slavonic tribes and enabled them to lay the foundations of the Kievan state.

The passages presented below are translated from *Istoriya Khazar,* by M. I. Artamonov (Leningrad: Izdatel'stvo Gosudarstvennogo Ermitazha, 1962).

i. The Khazars

Khazaria was the first state with which Kievan *Rus* came into contact, following the appearance of the latter on the historical arena. This is an historical fact which cannot be denied and which is indispensable to a correct understanding of the historical development, not only of *Rus,* but of all Eastern Europe. Three centuries of Khazar rule could not have passed without a trace, and to belittle the significance of the Khazars is as bad, if not worse, than exaggerating the role they played.

3

The Russian chronicles contain very meager historical data about the Khazars, although the beginning of Russian history was so closely connected with them. This can be explained by the fact that the Khazars had already disappeared from the historical arena by the time Russian historiography began, and oral reminiscences about them had not been preserved in any detail.

It is to be assumed that by the seventies of the seventh century the power of the Khazars extended not only across the steppes between the Azov and Caspian seas, but also along the entire northern Black Sea littoral, including the greater part of the Crimea. Thus, the middle decades of the seventh century not only mark the rise of an independent Khazar state, but also the expansion of its power throughout the greater part, if not the whole, of the steppes of Eastern Europe, thereby accounting for its international significance from the eighth to the ninth centuries.

The Khazar people was an unusual phenomenon of the Middle Ages. Surrounded by savage and nomadic tribes, it nevertheless had all the attributes of a civilized state: an established government, an extensive, flourishing trade, and a regular army. The Khazar state was renowned for justice and tolerance, and those who were persecuted on religious grounds came from all directions to take refuge there. Like a luminous meteor the Khazar state shone brightly on the dark horizon of Europe and then vanished without a trace.

The Khazar state was ruled by an old Turkut dynasty, and the Khazars who pursued a nomadic life in the eastern coastal lands of the Caspian between the Volga and the Terek rivers constituted the core of the state. Their nearest neighbors were the Bulgars of the Kuban river valley and the Sabirs (also known as Huns) of northern Daghestan, who were under Khazar supremacy. The Sabirs were beginning to profess Christianity, whereas Judaism penetrated Khazaria from Iran.

The conversion of the Khazar Kagan and his attendants to Judaism, which elevated Judaism to a state religion, is a phenomenon unprecedented in the history of the Middle Ages. As early as the thirties of the eighth century Judaism was adopted by a Khazar prince in northern Daghestan, but this did not affect the inner life of the Khazar kingdom, where all who professed Christianity, Islam, or even worshipped the old Turkic god Tengri-khan, continued to enjoy complete freedom of religion. At the beginning of the ninth century, however, the Jewish Khazars increased their influence at the Khazar court, seized power, and instituted the dual kingship, which reduced the Kagan, the descendant of the Turkut dynasty, to the role of a sacred king without political power. A political and religious *coup d'état* carried out by Obadiah, founder of the Jewish Khazar dynasty, was followed by the religious persecution of Christians and Muslims. An uprising against the usurper, followed by a long civil war in Khazaria, led to the decline of the state and paved the way for the Magyars (Hungarians) to enter Europe. Then came the Pechenegs, who appeared for the first time on the stage of history.

The important position of Khazaria in international trade and the heterogeneous population of the capital led the Jewish Khazars to abandon their policy of religious persecution for one of complete freedom for all creeds. Since Judaism was not essentially a proselyting faith and remained the religion of the ruling class only, this contributed to the division rather than to the unity of the Khazar population. Among the religions which were extensively practised, old Turkic paganism was particularly popular. Hebrew learning flourished only at the court, where it led to the appearance of historical works, such as local geneologies and chronicles. The Khazars failed to create any material culture of their own, but developed old Sarmat-Alan traditions, supplemented by some borrowings from Central Asia and Iran and the Arab East. Ethnographically, there was very little difference between the Khazars and the Bulgars, both of whom were regarded as descendants of the Alans remaining in the Central Caucasus and along the northern outskirts of the steppes between the Don and the Donets rivers. The Magyars carried the elements of the same culture to Hungary.

The center of the Khazar Empire of the ninth and tenth centuries was the town of Atil [Itil],[1] located on both banks of the Volga. On the same site, Saray-i-Batu, the first capital of the Golden Horde, was subsequently established. The eastern part of Atil was inhabited by merchants and craftsmen from various countries, the western part being reserved for the pure-bred Khazars, and for the king's paid bodyguard comprised chiefly of Muslims. The Khazars remained in town during the winter. In the spring they went out to the steppes, where they stayed until autumn pasturing their flocks. Lands formally assigned to separate clans were in fact the feudal possession of the clan and military aristocracy to which the actual producers paid duties.

After the conversion of the Khazars to Judaism, Byzantium continued to maintain friendly relations with Khazaria for some time, even assisting in 834 the construction of Sarkil, a fortress on the Don. No further mention was made, however, of intermarriage between the ruling families of the Khazars and Byzantium. The basic alliance between these two states was founded on common interest. Both countries were beset at this time by domestic problems of such magnitude that they were forced to subordinate foreign policy, especially territorial expansion, to the preservation of peace at home. Moreover, both had common enemies, the Arabs and other Muslims, which was greatly instrumental in the continuation of their friendly relations.

The campaign of Muhammed Marwan II (744-750) was the last great military undertaking of the Arabs against the Khazars. Khazaria was on the brink of destruction, from which it was saved only by the depletion of the Arab forces. Had it not been for this, the history of Eastern Europe would have taken a different course from the one with which we are

[1] Near the site of modern Astrakhan.

familiar. Thanks to the Khazars, the spread of Islam was halted for several centuries at the Caucasus on the threshold of Europe. These centuries provided sufficient time for the establishment in Eastern Europe of a strong Russian state, with all its cultural traditions connected with the European world. . . . The role of the Khazars in stemming the tide of Muslim penetration of Eastern Europe cannot be questioned, and this alone assures their universal historical significance.

The Arabs found the Khazars worthy opponents, who were not only able to contain their advance north of the Caucasus, but also forced them to expend a great deal of energy to retain their conquests in the Transcaucasus. The military power of the Khazars was particularly important to Byzantium. Thanks to the Khazars, Byzantium was able, not only to hold out against the Arabs, but also to inflict a series of telling blows upon them.

II. The Khazars and Kievan *Rus*

The reign of Tsar Joseph,[2] who corresponded with the Spanish dignitary, Khasdai ibn Shafrut, was marked by the continuation of the struggle of Khazaria with Byzantium, and also by its encounter with a new power that emerged in Eastern Europe, which brought catastrophe to the Khazars, namely Kievan *Rus*.

Already by the end of the eighth and the beginning of the ninth century, the Polyane had liberated themselves from the Khazar yoke. Around Kiev an independent Russian state began to develop, which immediately proclaimed itself by devastating raids on the Crimea, the south coast of the Black Sea, and the Aegean islands. Information about these raids has been preserved in the biographies of Stefan Surozhsky, St. George of Amastris, as well as in the life of Saint Athanasius in the *Prolog*. However, the leader of the *Rus,* according to one of these sources, was Prince Bravlin of Novgorod, which would lead us to believe that the attacks on Byzantine and Khazar territories in the first half of the ninth century were undertaken by Novgorod-Varangians, instead of originating from Kievan *Rus*. However, the name *Rus* is connected, not with the north but with the south, that is, with the Middle Dnieper political formation, and this alone testifies that the main active force in the aforementioned events was not the Varangians, and not even the Novgorod Slavs, but the population of the Middle Dnieper. In fact, as substantiated by archeological data, Novgorod did not even exist in the ninth century. Moreover, the title of the *Rus* ruler—Kagan—was not used by the northern Slavs, but was in vogue among the Slavs of the Middle Dnieper, which was under Khazar suzerainty. By their adoption of this title, the Kievan princes declared

---

[2] A Khazar ruler of the tenth century.

their independence from the Khazars and their equality with the Khazar state. It is known that even later, from the tenth to the twelfth centuries, the grand princes of Kiev called themselves "Kagans."

In all probability, in the campaigns against Byzantium in the first half of the ninth century, there took part both the Slavs of the Middle Dnieper —the *Rus*—as well as the northerners—the Novgorodians—and together with the latter, the Varangians. The opening of the great route from the Varangians to the Greeks occurred precisely at this time.

That in the middle of the ninth century Slavic *Rus* represented an impressive force of international reputation may be concluded from the information presented by Yakubi[3] concerning the appeal for help made by the Transcaucasian feudalists, 854-855, to the rulers of Byzantium, Khazaria, and the Slavs. There is divergence of opinion as to which Slavs were meant. However, taking into consideration general historical conditions existing at that time, one must admit that the most accurate conclusion was that reached by J. Marquart,[4] who interpreted them to be the Kievan *Rus,* because of their devastating attacks in the Black Sea area, which were well known in the Transcaucasus.

No matter which Slavs were involved, in 860 *Rus* appeared capable of organizing a campaign against Constantinople, which placed the capital of the Empire in a very precarious situation. The strong impression this *Rus* attack made upon the contemporary population of Byzantium was indicated in a circular letter from Patriarch Photius: "A people of no distinction (prior to this attack on us); a people of no importance whatsoever; a people no better than slaves; unknown, but who became famous as a result of this campaign against us; insignificant, but who became significant thereby; downtrodden and poor, but who rose to great heights and incalculable riches; a people who lived somewhere far away . . .", etc.—this is the way Photius writes about the *Rus*. He notes especially that the *Rus* turned their weapons on Byzantium only after they had conquered the peoples around them. Although the *Rus* withdrew as unexpectedly as they came, nevertheless the campaign of 860 was not merely a raid for loot and booty, but had a definite political purpose; and this, as well as later campaigns, was connected with the trade interests of *Rus* in Byzantium—a fact substantiated by Photius in one of his letters— and subsequent relations between them, as a result of which a certain part of the *Rus* adopted Christianity.

The *Chronicle* attributes the campaign of 860, which it incorrectly dates 866, to the Kievan princes, Askold and Dir. The Arab geographer, Mas'udi, calls Dir the first Slavic prince: "The first Slavic tsar is Tsar Dir, who has large cities and many inhabited lands; Muslim merchants come to the capital of his kingdom with a variety of wares."

---

[3] Ninth century Arab writer.
[4] Author of *Osteuropäische und ostasiatische Streifzüge* (1903).

Taking these facts into consideration, and also the scope of the military enterprise of 860, in which, according to the *Chronicle,* there took part 200, and according to the Venetian chronicler, Joannes Diaconus, even 360 ships, it must be assumed that in the middle of the ninth century Dnieper *Rus* was already a significant political power with definite trade interests. The high level of *Rus* culture at that time is attested by the spread of Christianity there. A circular letter of Patriarch Photius in 867 refers to the establishment of Christianity in *Rus* and to the dispatch of a bishop there. According to legend, Askold was among those converted to Christianity, and the *Chronicle* indirectly confirms this by pointing out that the church of Nikola (Nicholas) in Kiev stood on his grave. In this connection, the Gospels and Psalter written in the Russian language, discovered in the Pannonsky Lives by Konstantine Kirill in Kherson, must also be taken into consideration. The cultural and social level requisite to the translation of the most important Christian books into the Russian language in the middle of the ninth century could only have existed in Kiev—the center of an already established, independent Russian state. In the final quarter of this century, after union with the Novgorod state, *Rus* became even stronger.

The Russian *Chronicle* states that the Novgorod prince, Oleg, after having assembled a multitude of warriors composed of Varangians, Chudians, Slavs, Merians, Vesians, and Krivichians, that is, of the Normans and all the Slavic and Finnish tribes over which his power extended, subdued Smolensk and Liubech, and thereafter moved toward Kiev. Having treacherously seized Askold and Dir, the rulers of the city, he killed them and took possession thereof. In the *Chronicle,* this event is said to have occurred in 882. Having subdued the Polyane along with Kiev, Oleg in the following year fought against the Drevlianians and levied tribute on them, and in 884 and 885 he extended his authority over the Severians and Radimichians, who had heretofore paid tribute to the Khazars. "And Oleg ruled over the Polyane, and Drevlianians, and Severians, and Radimichians, and fought the Ulichians and Tivercians." Thus ends the description in the *Chronicle* of the first years of Oleg's reign in Kiev. Oleg's state became so powerful that the united forces of the Eastern Slavs, which he could command, aroused terror in Byzantium. In Oleg's campaign against Tsargrad (Constantinople) there took part, according to the *Chronicle,* 2000 ships, that is, ten times as many as those of *Rus* when Constantinople was attacked in 860. Now the Russian state was not afraid of the Khazars. On the contrary, it was the Khazars who feared *Rus.*

We know nothing of the resistance of the Khazars to Oleg when he freed the Severians and Radimichians. It did not amount to much. However, the Vyatichians subsequently remained under the Khazar yoke, which may explain the serious obstacles that confronted Oleg when he united into one Russian state all the Slavs under the jurisdiction of the Khazars. Whether the Khazars were responsible for this, or the Vyatichians themselves, or both, remains unknown.

One thing is certain. After Oleg's victorious campaign on Constantinople, the Khazar Tsar was in such fear of *Rus* that he was ready to accept any terms whatsoever. In the struggle that developed with Byzantium, the Khazars were at least interested in keeping *Rus* neutral. These circumstances should explain the fact that the Khazars permitted an appreciable *Rus* force to get through to the Caspian Sea to loot the coastal areas, already well known to Russian merchants.

Ibn Khurdadhbih, whose work is a product of the ninth century, says that Russian merchants sailed not only on the Black Sea, but also on the Caspian. "They land on any coast. . . . Upon occasion, they use camels to transport their wares from the Caspian to Baghdad." Sometimes the merchant retainers formed robber bands. The first marauding act of the Rusy on the Caspian was known to have occurred in the second half of the ninth century (864-884), although exact information about it has not been preserved. In 909 the Rusy, using sixteen ships, reached the island of Abesgun in Astrabad Bay and laid it waste. In the following year, 910, the Rusy burned the city of Sary in Mazendaran, but were overtaken at sea and defeated. These attacks were committed by small bands of men—part merchant and part brigand. The campaign of *Rus* in the Caspian, 913-914, was of an altogether different character. From the very beginning, it, too, was ostensibly an act of brigandage, but it was carried out by huge, highly organized, and well-armed forces.

According to Mas'udi, the Russian armed force, on 500 ships, each of which contained 100 men, entered what is known today as Kerch Strait. Here the Khazars possessed a strong fortress, which guarded the road to the water, as well as the crossing over the frozen Strait. Mas'udi notes that the Guzy (Pechenegs?) often crossed the Strait on horseback on the ice. When the Khazar guard was unable to block their attack on Khazaria, the Tsar himself came out to meet them. When the Rusy arrived at the fortress, they dispatched from there a letter to the Khazar Tsar, in all probability to Benjamin, with a request that they be permitted to cross his country to the Caspian Sea. They promised to give him half of the booty on their return. Undoubtedly, it was precisely at this time that the Khazars were hard pressed to defend themselves against a coalition of the Pechenegs, Guzy, and Asians (As), organized by Byzantium. Only with the help of the Alans did the Khazars succeed in defeating their enemies, as a result of which the Asians who dared to rise against their rulers suffered severely. Confronting such a serious struggle, the Khazars could not turn down the request of *Rus*, and in order not to acquire a new and dangerous enemy, they had to accept its demand and permit the *Rus* army to cross their territory. When permission was granted, the Rusy portaged from the Don to the Volga, dragging their ships, and descended the Volga to the Caspian, where they broke up into detachments and began to devastate the coastal areas of Gilan, Tabaristan, Azerbaijan, and Shirvan. The islands located near Baku served as their base. The local population, which customarily encountered only merchants and fishing boats from the sea, was helpless in the face of the unexpected enemies. The Rusy killed, burned, and seized booty with impunity, until finally the ruler of Shirvan assembled the people, loaded them into boats and merchant vessels, and moved against the islands. Without difficulty the Rusy quickly routed the assembled militia, and for many months plundered at will. Finally, having obtained much loot, they set out on their return journey.

Having arrived at the mouth of the Volga, the Rusy sent to the Khazar Tsar the share of the booty agreed upon. Then the Muslim guard *(arsii)* demanded the blocking of the route to *Rus,* in retaliation for the evil inflicted on their co-religionists. "Permit us," they said to the Tsar, "to make short shrift of these people. They have plundered the lands of our Muslim brothers; they have shed blood and enslaved women and children." The Tsar could not oppose their demands, and perhaps he did not wish to do so; the political conditions which had forced him to make concessions to the demands of the Rusy might have changed by the time they returned; the guard was located at Atil; hence there was no war at the time. However, in the event of a possible defeat of the Muslims, the Tsar took the precaution to leave a loophole for agreement with the Rusy: he warned them about the danger threatening them. This precaution appeared to be superfluous. The Rusy, having violated trade connections with the Caspian, aroused such resentment on the part of the inhabitants of Atil that not only the Muslims but many of the Christians who lived there turned against them. Almost 15,000 horsemen were assembled. The Rusy disembarked from their ships and hurled themselves against their enemies. The battle lasted three days. The Rusy were routed; those who escaped the sword were drowned in the river. About 30,000 men were killed on both sides. Only 5000 Rusy succeeded in reaching their ships and escaped up the Volga. When they disembarked on the bank, probably with the intention of portaging to the Don, their previous route, the Burtas attacked and killed some of them. The Rusy had no alternative but to proceed along the Volga toward the Bulgars, who annihilated them completely.

It appears that this *Rus* campaign to the Caspian was not an official enterprise of the Russian state, but was organized, so to speak, at their own risk by the Varangian-*Rus* retainers, hired for war with Byzantium, and dismissed by the Kievan prince when they were no longer needed. Nevertheless, the tragic end of the campaign could not help but worsen relations between *Rus* and Khazaria, although it does not seem to have resulted in war.

We have already seen that Khazar religious tolerance represented one of the myths, created by ill-informed historians inclined toward the idealization of the Khazar state. In reality, the attitude of the Khazars toward religion was the same as that of other peoples in the Middle Ages—it was contingent upon political conditions. This can also be substantiated, in part, by the persecution of Muslims and Christians in Khazaria in the tenth century. As the above-mentioned events of 913 to 914 demonstrated, among the urban population of Atil there were·many Muslims, and even the Khazar Tsar's bodyguard was composed of them. Nevertheless, when it was necessary, the Khazar government had no scruples about persecuting the Muslim religion in its own capital.

In 922, an embassy from the Baghdad caliph arrived in Bulgaria on the Volga. Bulgaria at this time was in the process of formation as a feudal state. To strengthen it ideologically, the Bulgars introduced Islam. The Tsar and his entourage not only adopted this religion, but also strove to disseminate it throughout the entire country. In addition to internal causes, the veering toward Islam was dictated by very important external political factors. The economic interests of the Bulgars were irreconcilably opposed to the interests of the Khazars, whose supremacy they were forced to recognize and to whom they paid tribute. The son of the Bulgar Tsar was a Khazar hostage, and, in addition, the Khazar Tsar asked for his daughter in marriage. The Bulgars, in the hope of liberating themselves from the Khazar yoke, sought a rapprochement with the Muslim countries, especially with Khorezm, with which there existed permanent and direct trade and cultural connections. But Khorezm was allied with the Khazars. Therefore the Bulgars turned for help to the old opponent of the Khazars—the Baghdad caliph, who enjoyed great spiritual authority among the Muslims. To consolidate the projected alliance and to build fortresses for the Bulgars against the Khazars, an Arab embassy was dispatched to the Volga.

It stands to reason that the Khazars could not view with indifference the political activity of the Bulgars against them, especially when the conversion of the Bulgars to Islam aroused great sympathy among the Khazar Muslims. The strengthening of the Muslims presented a serious threat to the Khazar government, which professed the Jewish religion. It is not known what steps the Khazars took to thwart the Bulgars, but within their own country, probably to put and end to Muslim propaganda and to demonstrate the power of the government, the Khazar Tsar, on the pretext of the destruction of a synagogue in a certain place known as Dar-al-Babundzh, ordered the destruction of the minaret of the mosque in Atil and the execution of the muezzins. In this connection, he is supposed to have said: "Indeed, if I were not afraid that in the countries of Islam not one synagogue would remain, I would positively destroy the mosque also." Apparently the repression was sufficient to silence the Khazar Muslims. Evidently, the real forces of the Khazar Tsar, which confronted the Muslims were quite sufficient to hold the latter within appropriate bounds. It is possible that the repression of the Muslims in Atil had an effect also upon the course of events in Bulgaria. In any event, the Arab embassy produced no basic changes.

About 932 Byzantium had already instigated the North Caucasian Alans against the Khazars. This ended in the defeat of the former and the expulsion of the Christian church of the Empire from Alania. Several years later, according to information in the letter of the Khazar Jew, "Roman the Wicked" (Roman Lekapin [Roman I] 929 [920?]-944) instigated severe persecution of the Jews, which to a certain extent was also directed against the Khazars. Many Jews flocked to Khazaria. Tsar Joseph responded to the persecution of his coreligionists by repression of the Christians. Then the Byzantine government turned to the Russian prince and sent him rich gifts to encourage the Rusy to come out against the Khazars. *Rus* had no friendly feelings toward the Khazars and was ready to retaliate for the treacherous massacre of its clansmen by the Khazars in 913-914. According to the letter of the Khazar Jew, the Rusy fell upon the Khazar city of Samkerts, which V. Moshin[5] regarded as a suburb of Kerch, but which actually was the contemporary Taman. This was precisely the Khazar fortress which blocked passage from the Black Sea to the Sea of Azov, and the crossing of the Strait when it was frozen. It was well known to the Russian merchants, who reached the Crimean coast by way of the Dnieper. It was by this route, according to Constantine Bagryanorodny, that the Rusy went through to Black Bulgaria, Khazaria, and Syria (?).

The Rusy craftily seized Samkerts and, having acquired rich booty there, departed. The Khazar ruler of that area, which included Kerch Strait ("the Cimmerian Bosporus"), who bore the title "Bulshitsy"— known in Byzantine sources as "Balgitsii"—apparently was a Bulgar prince, the head of the pri-Kuban and Black Bulgars, who already in the seventh century were subjugated by the Khazars but preserved their tribal independence.

The Khazars conquered three cities and a multitude of settlements, and thereafter besieged Kherson. How the siege ended is unknown; but it appears to have been a failure. After that, the Khazars turned against the Russian prince, Helgi [Oleg]. The Rusy, according to the Jewish document, were routed by the Khazars and were compelled at the insistence of the Khazars, to fight against their own ally, Byzantium. "Then," concludes the author of this letter, "the Rusy became subject to the power of the Khazars."

Of course, it is impossible that in the tenth century *Rus* could have been subjugated by the Khazars. Here we have a completely obvious distortion of facts, which is understandable, since it emanated from the

---

[5]Author of "Kristianstvo v Rossii do sv. Vladimira," in *Vladimerskii Sbornik,* 1938.

mouth of a Khazar Jew whose purpose was to extol Khazaria. But with this reservation, there is no particular reason to distrust the facts stated in this letter. *Rus* could have intervened in the struggle between Byzantium and the Khazars, and, depending on circumstances, could have veered first to one side and then to the other.

In regard to the *Rus* attack against Byzantium, allegedly directed by the Khazars, the Khazar Jew in his letter undoubtedly had in mind the famous campaign of Igor against Constantinople in 941. It is more than likely that in beginning the great war against Byzantium, Igor took the precaution of protecting his rear by an alliance with Khazaria, which was never reconciled to the loss of its possessions in the Crimea and was greatly interested in securing the assistance of *Rus* against its stubborn and perfidious enemy. As is known, Igor's campaign was a failure; the Russian boats were destroyed by Greek fire and the Rusy were also routed on land. According to Lev Diakon,[6] Prince Igor with the pitiful remnants of his fleet fled to the Cimmerian Bosporus, that is, to the Kerch Strait, and the remainder of the Russian army returned to the coast of Thrace.

Byzantine information about the escape of Igor to the Kerch Strait, into Khazar lands, could serve as a good substantiation of the Khazar Jew's statement about the connection of the unsuccessful Russian enterprise with the Khazars. . . . It is quite likely that the *Rus* campaign against Constantinople in 941 was organized with the knowledge and sympathy of the Khazars.

The Khazars obviously feared the might of *Rus,* and in order to prevent a *Rus* attack on them were in certain cases forced to open the route to the Caspian Sea, although this could not help but have some effect on the trade interests of Khazaria. Thus the Khazars were compelled to choose the lesser evil: In order to deflect the Russian menace from their own people, they were at times compelled to violate their trade relations with Transcaucasia and Iran. These were exceptional occurrences, since ordinarily Khazaria exercised strong control over all movements through its country and strictly enforced a tithe on all wares, including those of the Russians.

Indeed, it is probable that Khazaria made every effort, as Joseph says, to prevent *Rus* bands of marauders, which seem, for the most part, to have been Norsemen, from reaching the Caspian Sea.

Yet the campaigns of the *Rus* to the Caspian in 913 and 914 convincingly substantiate the fact that in the tenth century Khazaria was no longer strong enough to oppose *Rus*. It was Svyatoslav, the heir of Igor, who took advantage of this situation and inflicted the death blow, which put and end to the existence of Khazaria as an independent state.

[6] *Lev Diakon Kolokiiskii (A History.* Trans. D. Popov, St. Petersburg, 1920, Vol. VI, Ch. 10).

2. the Rus on the Volga (according to Ibn-Fadhlan)

AHMED IBN-FADHLAN (DATE OF BIRTH AND DEATH UNKNOWN) was an Arab traveller and writer of the first half of the tenth century. He took part in Caliph Muqtadir's embassy to Bukhara, Khorezm, and Volga Bulgaria, 921-922. In his book about his travels, which constitutes an important source for the history of the Volga and the Urals in the first half of the tenth century, he told of the life and religious customs of the Eastern Slavs, Khazars, Bulgars, and Bashkirs. Prior to 1923 only excerpts of Ibn-Fadhlan's work were available. In that year a more complete manuscript was discovered in Meshed, Iran.

The translated excerpt below is taken from A. P. Kovalevskii, *The Book of Ahmed Ibn Fadhlan About His Travels on the Volga, 921-922* (Kharkov, 1956), pp. 141-146. See *Khrestomatiya po Istorii* SSSR, Vol. I. (Moscow, 1960), 130-136.

... I saw the *Rus,* when they arrived to trade and camped at the River Atil (Volga). I have never seen (people) with more perfect bodies than they had. They were like palm trees, blonde, with ruddy cheeks, and white skin. They wore neither jacket nor caftan; but the man wore a *kisa,*[1] which he wrapped around one shoulder off to one side so that one of his arms protruded from it. And each of them had an axe, sword, and knife, from which he was inseparable. The swords were broad, undulating, and French. And from his nails to his neck he had green trees, figures, and other things painted on his body.

As regards their women, each wears on her breast a little box, either of iron or silver, copper, gold, or wood, corresponding to the wealth and position of her husband. And each little box has a ring, to which a knife is likewise fastened on the breast. Around their necks were chains of gold and silver. If the man possessed ten thousand *dirhems,*[2] he

---

[1] A primitive dress of coarse material, which clothed him, and in which he slept.
[2] A medieval Arab silver coin.

bestowed on his wife one chain *(ryad),* and if he possessed twenty thousand, he bestowed on her two necklaces; and similarly, for each additional ten thousand *(dirhems)* he gave his wife a necklace, so that some of them had many rows of them.

The most magnificent decorations, from the viewpoint of the *Rus,* are green beads of ceramic, which is on the ships. They make exceptional efforts to acquire them, buying one such bead for a *dirhem* and stringing them as necklaces for their wives.

The *Rus dirhem* is a grey squirrel without fur, brush, front and back paws and head; and the same goes for sables. If something was missing, the monetary value of the skin was less. They also use them for trade transactions and they cannot be exported because they exchange them for wares. They do not have scales, only standard metal bars. They use a measuring cup for buying and selling.

As soon as their ships anchor, they all disembark, carrying a loaf of bread, meat, onions, milk, and an intoxicating beverage, with which they approach a high pillar of wood set in the ground, which bears an image resembling a human face, and around it are small decorated figures; and behind these figures are high pillars set in the ground. Thus he approaches the big pillar and bows to it and says: "Oh, my god, I have come from a far-away country and have with me such and such a number of girls and so many heads and so many sable skins," and so on, until he has enumerated everything he has brought. "And I come to thee with this gift." Thereupon he leaves all he has with him before this pillar. "I wish that thou wouldst send me a merchant who has an abundance of dinars and *dirhems,* who would buy all that I want to sell and would not object to my prices." And then he leaves.

If the sale proves difficult and his sojourn there is prolonged he will return bearing a second and a third gift; and if it still proves difficult for him to achieve what he seeks, he will present each one of the little figures a gift and ask for their intercession, and say: "These are the wives of our god, his daughters and his sons." Thus he continues his requests, now to one figure, now to another, asking them to intercede for him, and bowing very low before them. Sometimes, however, the sale is easy. Then he says: "My god has fulfilled my need and therefore I must compensate him." Then he takes a certain number of sheep or cattle, slaughters them, and gives away part of the meat to the poor; and the rest he carries and leaves before the big pillar and the small ones that surround it, and he hangs the heads of the cattle or sheep on the pillars planted behind. When night comes, the dogs gather and devour all of this. And he who has done this says: "My god was gracious to me and has eaten my gift."

If anyone becomes ill, they erect a tent off to one side, put him in it, and leave with him a certain amount of bread and water; but they neither approach him nor speak to him, especially if the person in

question is a poor man or a slave. But if he has a multitude of
relatives and servants, the people visit him every day and inquire about
him. Thus, when he convalesces and rises, he will rejoin them; but if
he dies, they will cremate him. If he had been a slave, they would
have left him where he was, so that dogs or birds of prey would devour
him.

If they catch a thief or robber, they take him to a tall and heavy
tree, and tie a strong rope around his neck, and let him hang until
his body decomposes.

More than once I have been told what they do with their leaders
when they die, which at least involves cremation. I had always wanted
to witness this, when I was informed of the death of one man very
prominent among them. Thus they put him in his grave and covered
him with planking for a period of ten days, until they finished cutting
out and making his clothes.

For instance, if this is a poor fellow, they build a small vessel, place
him in it, and burn it. As regards a rich fellow, they collect all he
has, divide it into three parts: one-third for his family, one-third for
his clothes, and the other third to prepare an intoxicating beverage,
which they drink until the day his girl kills herself and is cremated
together with her master. They over-indulge themselves, drinking day
and night, so that one of them dies with a goblet in his hand.

During those ten days, they drink and join their women and play the
caza.[3] And the girl who will be cremated with him drinks and makes
merry during these ten days, decorates her head and herself with various
ornaments and clothes, and thus decorated she surrenders herself to the
people.

If a leader dies, his family will say to his girls and boys: "Who
among you will die with him?" Someone says "I." And if he says that,
it is obligatory. He cannot retract. Even if he wished to do so, they
would not permit it. The majority of those who sacrifice themselves thus
are girls. When the man mentioned above died, they said to his girls:
"Who will die with him?" One of them said: "I." Thus they handed her
over to two girls to guard her and remain with her wherever she went.
They even washed her feet with their hands. And they (the relatives)
began to cut the clothes and to make the necessary arrangements. And
every day the girl drank and sang and made merry, happily looking
to the future.

When the day arrived on which they were to cremate him and his
girl, I came to the river where his boat was located. He had already
been brought to the river bank, and in his honor were erected four
foundations of *khadang* (pine?) and *khalandzh* (birch?) and a wooden
scaffold was placed around them. Then the boat was hauled up and

---

[3] Pizzicato musical instruments.

placed on this structure, and they walked back and forth and made comments which I did not understand. And the dead man was still in his grave, since they had not yet removed him.

In the middle of this vessel they erected a wooden hut and covered it with various kinds of good material. Then they brought a bench and placed it on the boat; and they covered it with quilts and Byzantine brocade and pillows, also covered with Byzantine brocade. And there came an old woman called the angel of death. And she spread these things out on the bench and covered it and prepared everything; and she also kills the girls. And I saw that she was an old female Hercules, robust and dour.

When they reached his grave, they first removed the earth from the planks, then the planks, and brought him out in the spread in which he died. I saw that he had already turned dark from the cold in that country. In his grave they had previously placed *nabiz,* some kind of fruit, and a musical instrument. Now they removed all these things. And he did not stink. No change had taken place in him, except his color. Then they clothed him in *sharovary* (wide trousers), *getry* (foot covering), boots, jacket, and a brocaded caftan with gold buttons. They put a hat made of brocade on his head, with a sable, and they bore him to the hut on the vessel, where they placed him on the quilt, supported him with pillows, and brought *nabiz,* fruits, various kinds of flowers, and sweet-smelling plants, and placed them near him. And then they brought bread, meat, and onion, and set them before him. And they brought a dog and cleft it in half with a sword, and threw it into the boat. Next they brought all his weapons and placed them beside him. Then they took two horses and drove them until they began to perspire. After this, they cleft the horses with swords and threw the meat into the vessel. Then they brought two cows, likewise cleft them, and also threw them into the boat. Then they brought a rooster and a hen, killed them, and left them there.

Many men and women gathered, played the *caza,* and each of the relatives of the deceased erected a hut at some distance from that of the dead man. And the girl, who wanted to be killed, went in all her regalia from one hut to the other of the relatives of the deceased, and visited the master. After he had had intercourse with her, he said in a loud voice: "Tell your master that I have done this because of love and friendship to you." Thus she went from hut to hut, where the same procedure was followed.

When this was finished, having divided the dog in half, they threw it into the ship, and having also cut off the head of the rooster they threw it to the right and left of the boat.

At sunset on Friday, they brought the girl to a structure they had made earlier, resembling an arch. She put her feet on the men's palms and was raised to the top of the arch, and looking down from above she uttered some words in her language, after which they lowered her. Then they raised her a second time and repeated the action. They lowered her and raised her a third time, and she did the same thing again. Then they gave her the hen. She cut off its head and hurled it (the head) away. They took the chicken, however, and threw it into the boat. I asked the interpreter about her actions, and he said: "The first time they lifted her she said: 'Behold, I see my father and my mother!'—and the second time, she said: 'Here are all my dead relatives seated.'—and the third time, she said: 'Here I see my master sitting in the garden; and the garden is beautiful and green and with him are men and lads, and he is calling me, so please lead me to him.'"

So they walked with her toward the boat. And she removed two bracelets from her arm, and gave them to the old woman known as the angel of death, who was going to kill her. And she removed two foot rings, and gave them to the two girls who had served her, who were the daughters of the woman known as the angel of death.

After that the men whom she had visited in their huts made a ramp for her with their hands, so that she could walk onto the ship, but they did not yet bring her into the hut. Then came the men, carrying shields and canes, and they gave her a goblet of *nabiz*. She began to sing over it and drank it up. The interpreter told me that thereby she said goodbye to her girl friends. Then they gave her another goblet. She took it and sang at length, while the old woman pressed her to drink it up and enter the hut of her master.

And I saw that she became confused. She intended to enter the hut, but she stuck her head between it and the boat. Thereupon the old woman seized her head and pushed her into the hut and entered with her; and the men began to beat their shields with their sticks, so that her cries would not be heard, because this would disturb the other girls, who would cease to ask to die with their masters. After that six men who were relatives of her husband entered the hut and all of them had relations with the girl in the presence of the dead man. Then they placed her beside her master. Two seized her feet, two her hands, and the old woman who was called the angel of death came and put a rope around her neck, and two men took the two ends and pulled. Then she began her job, holding in her hand a huge knife with a wide blade. She repeatedly stabbed the girl between her ribs, while the two men choked her with the rope until she died.

Then the nearest relative of the deceased appeared, took a stick and kindled the fire. Then he backed away, facing the people, holding in one hand the burning stick and in the other his bare anus, in order to kindle the wood under the boat. Then there appeared people with kindling and wood. Each one of them had a stick, the tip of which he lighted. Then he threw it into the wood piled up under the vessel. And the fire caught the wood, then the vessel, then the hut, and the man and the girl and everything that was in it. Then a very strong wind began to blow. The flames grew stronger. Next to me was a certain man from *Rus*. And I heard him converse with my former interpreter and asked the latter what he had been told. He said: "Indeed, he said: 'You Arabs are stupid!' I asked him why. He said: 'You take the most beloved man among you and the most respected, and you leave his remains to be eaten by insects and worms; but we burn him in the twinkling of an eye, so that he immediately enters into paradise.'" Then he began to laugh up-roariously. I asked him what he meant by that, and he said: "Because his god loved him, he sent the wind, so that it would take him within an hour." And indeed barely an hour passed when the ship, the wood, the girl, and the master were reduced to fine ashes.

Then they erected a mound on the spot where they had dragged the boat from the river and planted in the middle of it a big pine (?) pillar and wrote on it the name of this man and that of the Tsar of *Rus* and they departed.

3. excerpts from The Russian Primary Chronicle

The Russian Primary Chronicle, also known as *The Tale of Bygone Years* (*Povest' Vremennykh Let*), based on local tradition, is among the earliest written native sources of Russian history. It covers the period from the traditional origin of *Rus* (862) to the early twelfth century. Originally attributed to the monk Nestor of the Crypt Monastery in Kiev, contemporary scholars believe it to be a compilation from several annals of earlier date. In 1722 Peter the Great called for the collection and copying of all the early Russian annals. It was not until 1846, however, that the *Full Collection of Russian Chronicles* was printed. Critical study of the text of these annals belongs mainly to the twentieth century.

As indicated below, the *Chronicle* distinguished the *Rus,* as Scandinavians, from the Slavs, a distinction still made by most Western historians. Soviet historians contend, however, that the Russian state was established prior to the coming of the Norsemen.

The passages below are from *The Russian Primary Chronicle,* Laurentian Text. Trans. and ed., Samuel Hazzard Cross and Olgerd P. Sherbowitz-Wetzor (Cambridge, Mass.: The Medieval Academy of America, 1953), pp. 59-60, 110, 111. Reprinted by permission.

i. The Traditional Origin of the Russian State

. . . 6368-6370 (860-862). The tributaries of the Varangians drove them back beyond the sea and, refusing them further tribute, set out to govern themselves. There was no law among them, but tribe rose against tribe. Discord thus ensued among them, and they began to war one against another. They said to themselves, "Let us seek a prince who may rule over us and judge us according to the Law." They accordingly went overseas to the Varangian Russes: these particular Varangians were known as Russes, just as some are called Swedes, and others Normans,

English, and Gotlanders, for they were thus named. The Chuds, the Slavs, (20), the Krivichians, and the Ves' then said to the people of Rus', "Our land is great and rich, but there is no order in it. Come to rule and reign over us." They thus selected three brothers, with their kinsfolk, who took with them all the Russes and migrated. The oldest, Rurik, located himself in Novgorod; the second, Sineus, at Beloozero; and the third, Truvor, in Izborsk. On account of these Varangians, the district of Novgorod became known as the land of Rus'. The present inhabitants of Novgorod are descended from the Varangian race, but afore-time they were Slavs.

After two years, Sineus and his brother Truvor died, and Rurik assumed the sole authority. He assigned cities to his followers, Polotsk to one, Rostov to another, and to another Beloozero. In these cities there are thus Varangian colonists, but the first settlers were, in Novgorod, Slavs; in Polotsk, Krivichians; at Beloozero, Ves', in Rostov, Merians; and in Murom, Muromians. Rurik had dominion over all these districts.

With Rurik there were two men who did not belong to his kin, but were boyars. They obtained permission to go to Tsar'grad [Byzantium] with their families. They thus sailed down the Dnieper, and in the course of their journey they saw a small city on a hill. Upon their inquiry as to whose town it was, they were informed that (21) three brothers, Kiy, Shchek, and Khoriv, had once built the city, but that since their deaths, their descendants were living there as tributaries of the Khazars. Askold and Dir remained in the city, and after gathering together many Varangians, they established their dominion over the country of the Polyanians at the same time that Rurik was ruling at Novgorod. . . .

II. Conversion to Christianity

. . . 6495 (987). Vladimir summoned together his boyars and the city-elders, and said to them, "Behold, the Bulgars came before me urging me to accept their religion. Then came the Germans and praised their own faith; and after them came the Jews. Finally the Greeks appeared, criticizing all other faiths but commending their own, and they spoke at length, telling the history of the whole world from its beginning. Their words were artful, and it was wondrous to listen and pleasant to hear them. They preach the existence of another world. 'Whoever adopts our religion and then dies shall arise and live forever. But whosoever embraces another faith, shall be consumed with fire in the next world.' (107) What is your opinion on this subject, and what do you answer?" The boyars and the elders replied, "You know, O Prince, that no man condemns his own possessions, but praises them instead. If you desire to make certain, you have servants at your disposal. Send them to inquire about the ritual of each and how he worships God." ...

... Vladimir then announced the return of the envoys who had been sent out, and suggested that their report be heard. He thus commanded them to speak out before his retinue. The envoys reported, "When we journeyed among the Bulgars, we beheld how they worship in their temple, called a mosque, while they stand ungirt. The Bulgar bows, sits down, looks hither and thither like one possessed, and there is no happiness among them, but instead only sorrow and a dreadful stench. Their religion is not good. Then we went among the Germans, and saw them performing many ceremonies in their temples; but we beheld no glory there. Then we went to Greece, and the Greeks led us to the edifices where they worship their God, and we knew not whether we were in heaven or on earth. For on earth there is no such splendor or such beauty, and we are at a loss how to describe it. We only know that God dwells there among men, and their service is fairer than the ceremonies of other nations. For we cannot forget that beauty. Every man, after tasting something sweet, is afterward unwilling to accept that which is bitter, and therefore we cannot dwell longer here." Then the boyars spoke and said, "If the Greek faith were evil, it would not have been adopted by your grandmother Olga who was wiser than all other men." Vladimir then inquired where they should all accept baptism, and they replied that the decision rested with him. ...

4. the clergy: white and black

THE EXCERPTS BELOW ARE REPRINTED FROM *The Towns of Ancient Rus,* by M. Tikhomirov (2nd ed., Moscow: Foreign Languages Publishing House, 1959), pp. 176-195.

With the establishment of Christianity, the Orthodox clergy became a potent force in the towns of Kiev Rus. It was more or less sharply divided into two sections: the white and the black. Each of these had its own peculiarities and special privileges. . . .

I. White Clergy

The number of white clergymen in Kiev is indicated by the figure of 600 ("near six hundred") churches on Gora and Podol affected by the 1124 fire. Such a figure is almost fantastic for a single town, but it should be remembered that it includes the numerous monasterial and private chapels as well as the countless altars in the chantries, and so forth. Most of the princes, princesses and boyars had their private chapels. When on the verge of death, princesses often took the veil in their "own" churches. It well may be that the abundance of churches in Kiev gave rise to the fantastic figure of several hundreds, like the well-known Moscow "sorok sorokov" ("two score of two scores"). In any case, the number of Kiev churches ran into the hundreds.

Other major Russian towns reckoned their churches by the dozen, at least. In the terrible fire of 1185, when almost the entire town of Vladimir Zalessky was razed to the ground, 32 churches were destroyed, and 27 were burnt down in 1227 when half the town was razed by fire. Fifteen churches were destroyed in a great Rostov conflagration, while 17 churches were burnt to the ground in Yaroslavl by another fire.

These figures appear to be incomplete. It seems that the chronicler deals only with the parish churches, in contrast to the 600 in Kiev, and this accounts for such a great difference in the number of churches in Kiev and Vladimir Zalessky.

Every church was a special establishment with a staff of its own who

23

were much more numerous than they were in Russia at a later date. The clergy consisted not only of priests and deacons, who, it should be added, were not to be found in every church, but also of sextons. The "church regulations" list the following among the churchmen; the priest, the deacon, the priest's wife, their children, "those in the choir" (i.e., the deacons, sextons and others), and the woman wafer-baker. "These are people of the church, and servants of God." The church charter of Vladimir Svyatoslavich has a similar list with a few additions: the pope, his wife, and their children, the deacon, his wife, the wafer-baker, and "those in the choir": the sexton, the scribe, and all the clergy and their children. To this we should add the mendicants, who were a kind of permanent fixture at many churches (the widows, the halt, the blind), as well as several groups of people indentured to the church on a permanent or temporary basis (*proshchenniks, zadushniye lyudi*, etc.). The number of people varied greatly with every church, but almost every one of them was supposed to have several courtyards inhabited by churchmen, who made up a special neighborhood. On the whole, the churchmen with all their children and domestics comprised a goodly portion of the urban population, possibly somewhat greater than is commonly believed. An interesting report about the preparations to arm the Novgorod home guard in 1148 gives indirect evidence about the number of churchmen in the town. The Novgorodites decided to mobilize even the sextons, who were awaiting to be ordained. This act would have been absurd if there were only a few of these unordained churchmen. Actually there are reports of priests being killed in battle. The Sarai Bishop Feognost sent the following query to the Constantinople Patriarchal Congress: "If a priest kills a man on the field of battle, is he eligible for church service after that?" Their reply was: "Not forbidden by the sacred canons." The publishers of Feognost's questionnaire note that this answer was contained in the best and earliest transcripts and was the one originally given, whereas the later versions read: "This is forbidden by the sacred canons." Thus, Peresvet and Oslyabya, who fought the Tatars at Kulikovo Polye, were no exceptions among priests in Ancient Rus.

The staff of churchmen expanded for various reasons, both secular and ecclesiastic. The Church of St. John the Baptist on the Opoki, which served as a headquarters for the wax-dealers in Novgorod, had a permanent staff which included at least two priests, a deacon, a sacristan and the watchmen. "The churchmen of St. John" were a prominent ecclesiastical corporation on whom it was incumbent to read daily services ("to sing at St. John's daily"). Such a church must have been the centre of a small neighborhood inhabited by churchmen and mendicants, a peculiar but almost inevitable appendage to the clergy.

The importance of a church and its clergy increased perceptibly when it was a repository of some hallowed object such as icons or relics.

Belief in miracles was so commonplace in medieval times that the chroniclers are sincere in their reports about "God's mercy" or "forgiveness" granted to the sick and the halt by some holy object, since disease was regarded as a punishment. It was "forgiven" after the most ardent supplications.

We are aware of a number of churches in big towns which kept relics revered with particular devotion.

The Church of Boris and Gleb in Vyshgorod was a place to which the poor and the halt flocked and where the sick were brought and laid at the foot of royal relics.

Apart from their purely ecclesiastical functions, most of the urban churches, particularly those made in stone, were used to store goods and property in time of fire, strife and insurrection. The citizens who were accustomed to live in wooden houses willingly spent great sums to build stone churches, which served as refuge from fire and plunder.

Big churches were usually turned into *sobors*. Popes and deacons "daily" read vespers, mass and liturgies in these *sobors*. The *sobor* was headed by an "elder" who was appointed by the bishop. Priest Lazar was the "elder" of the *klirics* at the Church of Boris and Gleb in Vyshgorod. Lazar's son was apparently also intending to become a clergyman and, at the behest of his father, served as night watchman at the church.

The Greek word *klir* ($\chi\lambda\eta\varsigma o\varsigma$)—a body of churchmen—was used in Rus in a special sense with respect to great cathedrals, whose *kliroshane* made up an ecclesiastical association with aims and tasks similar to those of West-European chapters. That this was so was suggested long ago but merely as a thesis: *"Penes Episcopos et Metropolitas erat juxta indubitata testimonia annalium Ruthenorum distinctus Clerus, constituens sic dictum Krylos, cui in Ecclesia latina correspondent Capitulum."*

In episcopal centres, the *sobors* were under the personal charge of the bishop. But *sobors* existed at a distance from the cathedral in such towns as Vyshgorod, Belgorod and Bogolyubovo. There too the *kliroshane* made up compact associations headed by their elders. One of the chroniclers calls the *kliroshane* of the Church of the Assumption in Vladimir "Luka's *chad*," after Luka, their elder.

Cathedral churches were granted numerous privileges and holdings, and became clerical urban centres. The earliest report of a charter being granted dates back to 996. A *desyatina*, or a tithe, was granted to the Church of the Tithes by Vladimir Svyatoslavich to be collected from his estate and his towns. Later, Andrei Bogolyubsky granted the Cathedral of the Assumption in Vladimir, "suburban estates with tributes, and the best manors, and a tithe of his flocks, and a tithe of his trade." Thus, the cathedral owned suburban estates and manors with the right of immunity ("with tributes") and, besides, collected dues from one in every ten fairs. Our sources indicate that cathedrals also owned "tithe towns." The Church of the Tithes in Kiev owned the town of Polonny with the surrounding volosts, while the Cathedral of the Assumption in Vladimir-on-Klyazma owned the town of Gorokhovets.

Cathedral churches had libraries which were staffed with scribes. The chronicle mentions books which belonged to the Cathedral of the Assumption in Vladimir. The church treasury was located in the gallery *(polati)* and was regarded as civic property. The people of Vladimir were incensed when they heard that their new princes had seized the gold and silver of the Cathedral of the Assumption and got hold of the keys to the vestry. This act on the part of the princes was regarded as proof that the Rostislavichi were disloyal to the people of Vladimir, whom they treated not as their subjects but as the people of a conquered volost. That same church had a *terem* where money, books, sacred vessels and precious fabrics were kept. When a town was sacked the first thing the conquerers did was to loot the church. When the Poles captured Vladimir Volynsky, they tried to break into the Cathedral of the Mother of God and failed only because the cathedral doors proved to be extremely stout and withstood the onslaught until aid came.

Besides, urban cathedrals situated in commercial towns had a purely secular function: they were repositories of weights and measures. Under the article "on civic measures," the bishop was responsible for their remaining intact. Under Smolensk's treaty with the Germans the standard weight was kept at the cathedral on the hill. The Church of the Tithes in Kiev and St. Sophia's Cathedral in Novgorod took part in keeping the weights and measures.

The white clergy made up a substantial part of the urban population and enjoyed considerable prestige in the towns, particularly among the richer part of the community. This gave rise to a peculiar type of clergyman, a yesman who indulged his flock. The sermon of a certain Novgorod bishop of the 12th century (presumably Ilya-Ioann) describes the Novgorod priests as conniving at such practices as bearing false witness in church *(rotitsya)*. Nevertheless, the practice became widespread and was profitable to the clergy.

The close association of the white clergy with their parishioners, against a background of generally rude morals and manners, made the priests and their clergy regular participants of feasts and carousals. Even the strict bishop had no objections to priests taking part in feasts arranged by the laity, but what made him furious was the excessive drinking and the desire to get the guests drunk at all costs: "You see, there is a custom in this town to make one drunk by all means." One gets an idea of clerical participation in such carousals from the description in *Ipaty Annals* of the capture of Belgorod in 1150, at that time the seat of Prince Boris Yuryevich. When the enemy appeared near Belgorod, Boris was drinking in the gallery of the royal palace with his men-at-arms and the Belgorod priests.

The above-mentioned sermon of the Novgorod bishop reveals yet another purely mundane aspect of the white clergy's activities. It was at variance with ecclesiastical ideals but was highly typical of the behaviour of medieval clergy. The bishop hurled invective at priests who engaged in usury: "I have also heard of priests who take *rezas* (interest)." He does not wish to countenance such practices and announces strict punishment for such misdemeanour.

The incessant philippics of church writers directed against the priests, who were overtly engrossed in mundane affairs, were futile. Medieval practices demanded that the white clergy be in the thick of civic activities. In the late 11th century, Metropolitan Ioann II in his canonic replies even legalized the state of things which later aroused the indignation of the strict Novgorod bishop. The metropolitan wrote that priests who attended the feasts of the laity had to accept what they were offered with dignity and benediction, departing only when dances, games, music and quarrels arose and there was "great temptation." None the less, the picture of the drunken clergyman persisted in the mind's eye of the metropolitan, who demanded that priests "desist from drunkenness" under pain of being unfrocked.

This gives us a typical picture of the Ancient Rus town: numerous churches surrounded by church neighbourhoods inhabited by priests, deacons, watchmen, waferwomen and mendicants. The church was not only a place of devotion, it was also a place where public acts were certified and promulgated: the taking of oaths *(rota)*, proclamations by the authorities, etc. The popes were called upon to act as witnesses *(poslukhi)* in the drawing up of wills. Reflecting the aspirations of the townsfolk, the clergy frequently interfered in major political events. When Mstislav Vladimirovich decided to swear on the cross, the superior of the Andrei Monastery and the body of the Kiev priests interfered and took upon themselves the sin of Mstislav's perjury. The latter gave in to the priests, although "he bewailed it for the rest of his days." In order to get a comprehensive picture of the towns of Ancient Rus we must reckon with the white clergy as an important element of the urban population.

II. Black Clergy (Monks)

The white clergy, as we have seen, were in a measure allied with the craftsmen and merchants. But the black clergy, the monkhood, was the part of the clergy that lent the church its feudal features. Of course, it had its own hierarchy and contradictions, for the gulf between the common monk and the bishop was immeasurable. But it should be remembered that every monk was a member of the cloisteral community which vigorously defended their rights against infringement by the lay authorities and even the bishops.

The emergence of the monkery is traced as far back as the period of Rus's baptism. According to highly inaccurate chronicle reports, there were 70 cloisters in the 11th-13th centuries. Golubinsky says that they were distributed as follows: 17 in Novgorod, 17 in Kiev, 6 in Vladimir, 5 in Smolensk, 5 in Galich, 3 in Chernigov, 3 in Polotsk, 3 in Rostov, 2 in Pereyaslavl Yuzhny, and one each in Vladimir Volynsky, Pereyaslavl Zalessky, Suzdal, Murom, Pskov, Staraya Rusa, Nizhny Novgorod, Yaroslavl and Tmutarakan. The inaccuracy of these figures becomes evident from the fact that the very rich city of Vladimir Volynsky and Galich are shown to have had a single monastery, whereas, according to the chronicle, the Tatars in 1237, destroyed "monasteries" (not a monastery) in the small town of Moscow. Apart from the 17 cloisters mentioned in Kiev, there were others in the surrounding countryside. The foundations of a number of stone churches have been discovered in the vicinity of Galich. It may be presumed that these foundations were mainly of monasterial churches since the parish churches outside the town walls in Kev Rus were rarely built of stone.

In the early days of the Russian church, the monkery were closely connected with the towns.

For example, Golubinsky makes the observation in his *History of the Russian Church* that urban monasteries predominated in Rus in the period before the Mongol invasion. It is only from the late 14th century that monasteries were built in North-Eastern Rus more or less outside the urban centres. In the 11th-13th centuries, cloisters were still clustered around the town walls. Evidently, one of the reasons for this is that Christianity was not very widespread at the time. Ditheism and paganism gave way to Christianity very reluctantly, while the incessant feudal wars jeopardized the security of the cloisters situated in the sparsely populated areas. The chronicles repeatedly inform us that it was not only the Polovtsy but the Russians as well who readily looted monasteries and churches. It was only when the cloisters secured landholdings and became feudals that they settled in the countryside. From then on, they exerted the greatest efforts to acquire land, thus giving rise to an ideology of monasterial "covetousness" which was sharply at variance with monachal vows and precepts.

The number of monasteries was directly proportional to the size and economic welfare of the town. Kiev, as we have seen, had 17 cloisters, of which the biggest was the Kiev Pechera Monastery, founded around the mid-11th century. Most of the Kiev cloisters were built by princes and boyars. Such was the Kiev Pechera Monastery, which arose near Berestovo, a favourite manor of the princes. The founder of the cloister, Antony, was visited by Prince Izyaslav, and as a consequence "the great Antony became widely known and honoured by all." However, the selfsame Izyaslav had to build a new cloister, St. Dmitry's, because he was annoyed with the independent policy of the Pechera monks.

By that time, the several princely branches sought to build monasteries of their own. "Vsevolod's cloister on the Vydobych" is first mentioned in 1070. It sprang up close to Pechera Monastery, possibly very near Vsevolod's suburban residence. In the 12th century, the Monomakh family had their own cloister—St. Feodor's. They called it *otny*—father's, while the Oleg family had a similar attitude toward Kirill Monastery.

Convents in Kiev were also built by members of the princely family. In 1086, Vsevolod built the Church of St. Andrew together with a cloister in which his daughter, Princess Yanka, took the veil. Subsequently, the cloister was called Yantsin after its foundress. The Monastery of the Assumption in Vladimir Zalessky was founded by Grand Princess Maria, wife of Vsevolod Bolshoye Gnezdo.

The first monasteries built by prominent and rich men who were not of royal blood began to make their appearance in the 12th century. It seems that such cloisters first sprang up in Novgorod with its opulent boyars and merchants, although Novgorod's first big monastery, Yuri, was built by Prince Mstislav Vladimirovich who erected a huge cathedral within its walls. St. Antony's Monastery emerged almost simultaneously, and was apparently founded by a merchant. Khutyn Monastery was built in the late 12th century by Alexei Mikhailovich, the son of a Novgorod boyar.

The total number of monks in the towns was very indefinite and cannot even be estimated. But it may be said, without departing from the truth, that in such towns as Kiev and Novgorod they were numbered by the hundreds, rather than by the score. Pechera Monastery had 180 monks, apart from the bondmen who worked in the monastery. In the 13th century, Avraamy Monastery had 17 monks.

The *Pechera Paterik* tries to create the impression that there was complete equality within the orders, but that ideal was a far cry from reality. Stefan, the second superior of Pechera Monastery, was forced to leave the cloister because the monks rebelled against him and expelled him without allowing him to take his property. The *Paterik* describes the dissatisfied and ambitious monk who is meek one day and "furious and angry" the next. He keeps his peace for a short while and then resumes his grumbling against the superior.

The *Pechera Paterik* gives us the best account of the structure of the monastic order. The only fact it reports about Antony, the founder of the monastery, is that he was a pious man from the town of Lyubech. But he was no commoner, since he undertook a long voyage to the Athos which involved considerable expenditure. We learn much more about Superior Feodosy. His parents were nobles from Kursk. Feodosy went "with his slaves to the manor to work with great diligence." Nikola Svyatosha, the son of the Chernigov Prince Davyd

Svyatoslavich, was among the most renowned members of Pechera Monastery. It was in the lifetime of Superior Feodosy that the monastic vows were taken by the boyar Varlaam, the son of the boyar Ioann, "who was the first boyar of the Prince." Yefrem, who was "beloved of the prince and was his right-hand man," entered the cloister at the same time. Friar Erazm possessed great riches which he spent on decorating the church. Arefa, another monk, kept great riches in his cell and was a notorious miser. Moisei Ugrin, whose touching and woeful tale is told in the *Paterik,* was a favourite of Prince Boris, who was murdered at the order of Svyatopolk. Isaaky Zatvornik hailed from Toropets, where he was a rich merchant before he took the monastic vows. Finally, Nikon, the monk, was "one of the great men in the town."

Even these scanty reports show that there was a considerable number of former nobles and rich men among the monks of Pechera Monastery. It may be presumed at least that it was these men who headed the monkery and guided its activities.

The situation was similar in the Novgorod monkeries. Antony Rimlyanin was the founder of the famous St. Antony's Monastery. The byname "Rimlyanin" could scarcely have meant that Antony actually came from Rome. It may have appeared later, or could have been an old legend. The Novgorod memorials of the 12th-13th centuries sometimes used the words "Roman country" to designate a country in which Catholicism held sway. Thus, the *Life of Alexander Nevsky* even calls Birger a king "of the Roman parts." But what is beyond doubt is that Antony was a very rich man, because it took him only a short time to build a big stone cathedral and then a stone refectory in the cloister he founded. Antony's will reveals that the monastery was built without any assistance from either the prince or the bishop: "I did not accept any property either from the prince or from the bishop." Varlaam, the founder of another well-known cloister in Novgorod, was the son of the boyar Mikhail (Mikhal). Before taking the vows he was called Alexa Mikhailovich.

The general tendency in Russian monasteries to induct rich monks with an eye to their contributions explains why the aristocratic section of the monkery enjoyed such prestige in the cloisters.

In Novgorod, the monachal aristocracy was concentrated at Khutyn Monastery, whose founder, Varlaam, was a childhood friend of the boyar Dobrynya Yadreikovich ("his coeval"). The latter was not only a rich noble but was also a scholar who described his voyage to Constantinople, which he visited in 1204, shortly before it was sacked by the crusaders. Later, Dobrynya took the vows at Khutyn Monastery under the name of Antony. He subsequently became the archbishop of Novgorod. Proksha Malyshevich, who became friar Porfiry, and his brother Fyodor took the monastic vows in that same cloister. The

Novgorod *tysyatsky* Vyacheslav, the son of Proksha, also took the vows at Khutyn Monastery, which in the early 13th century was active in defense of the interests of the big boyars. Arseny, who was twice appointed archbishop of Novgorod and who aroused the hatred of the "common *chad*," was also a former Khutyn monk.

The close ties existing between the monkery and the aristocracy were evident in many cloisters. Superior Stefan, who was expelled from Pechera Monastery, immediately secured the support of many boyars who "gave him from their estates what he needed for himself and for other purposes."

The *Paterik* tells of the assistance extended to Pechera Monastery by some "lovers of Christ." Barrels of wine and oil, cartloads of grain, cheeses, fish, peas and millet, and vats of honey, contributed by the gentry, were frequently seen entering the cloister gates. The cenoby in Rus was just as aristocratic as that of medieval Catholic Europe. It was not the retreat for hermits it was made out to be.

The upper layers of the cenoby, in which such a prominent role was played by aristocrats, constantly supplied dignitaries for the church hierarchy. In the early 13th century, one of the monks of Pechera Monastery asserted with pride that "many bishops were appointed from that monastery of the Virgin Mary." According to his list, which is unquestionably incomplete, 15 bishops came from the ranks of the Pechera monkery within the relatively short period of one and a half or two centuries. Among them were such famous people as Metropolitan Ilarion, the Pereyaslavl bishop Yefrem, the Rostov bishops Leonty and Isaiya, the Novgorod bishop Nifont, and the Chernigov bishop Feoktist. It should be borne in mind, however, that the incumbency of an episcopal cathedra in Ancient Rus involved the expenditure of large sums of money which often came to as much as 100 *grivnas* of silver. That is why Ancient Rus literature abounds in invective against "conceited people" who sought fame "from man rather than from God." Simony is a frequent topic in Ancient Rus MSS [manuscripts].

Monasteries began to acquire real estate at an early date. In the lifetime of Feodosy, its founder, Kiev Pechera Monastery already possessed manors and villages. The administrators of monasterial estates were *tiuns* and servants, a fact made clear by Feodosy's instructions on his deathbed as reported by the *Pechera Paterik*: "He then ordered the fraternity to be gathered, including those who were in the manors or away on some other job, and having gathered all, gave instructions to his servitors as to how they should each of them do their duty."

The monks engaged in a number of handicrafts and offered the local craftsmen stiff competition in the local markets. There were craftsmen among the monks of Pechera Monastery. The transcribing of books was a permanent occupation among its monks. The *Paterik* singles out friar Ilarion who was "skilled in the writing of books." Among other famous

Pechera monks were the iconographer Alimpy, who learned his art from the Greeks, the physician Agapit, and others.

But even at that time, the bulk of monasterial wealth consisted of land holdings and pecuniary contributions. Monetary contributions at the reading in of novices apparently became a tradition almost with the appearance of monkeries in Rus. Nestor tells a naive tale of the peregrinations of young Feodosy who, wishing to take the orders, roamed from cloister to cloister begging for admission. The monks, however, seeing an ill-clad youth and taking him for a commoner, rebuffed the neophyte.

In the 12th century, the major monasteries as a rule possessed land. A typical monasterial manor is described in the donative deed of Varlaam of Khutyn, which is unquestionably an authentic memorial of the late 12th and early 13th century. Varlaam donated to his cloister "land and vegetable gardens, and fisheries and fowling grounds, and meadows." Two settlements stood on this Khutyn land. Otrok Volos and his wife, maid Fevronya with two nephews, and Nedach lived in one of them. There were six horses and a cow in that village. The other village with its Church of St. Georgy stood on the Sludnitsa. The princes were wont to donate to the monasteries manors and whole volosts "with tributes, and wergild, and *prodazhas.*"

Some of the cloisters began to extend their holdings beyond the limits of their towns and even principalities, and to set up their own baileys and church branches. Thus, Pechera Monastery in Kiev owned a bailey in Suzdal. In vain do the authors of the index to the *Ipaty Annals* believe that the bailey belonged to some Pechera Monastery in Suzdal itself, for it was owned by the Pechera Monastery of Kiev to which it was donated "even with manors" by the Bishop Yefrem of Suzdal, who was a neophyte at the Kiev cloister.

In the 12th century, the death of Gleb Vseslavich's widow was marked, the chronicle reveals, by an enormous contribution of land and money to Pechera Monastery. Her father, Yaropolk Izyaslavich, who died in 1087, gave the monastery the volosts of Nebl, Derevskaya and Lutsk, and those "near Kiev." Gleb himself together with his princess donated to the monastery 600 *grivnas* of silver and 50 *grivnas* of gold. When he died, the princess gave the cloister another 100 *grivnas* of silver, bequeathing to it five manors "with *chelyad,* and everything even unto the *povoi.*"

Disputes would often flare up between the cloisters for the possession of some church or sanctuary. The chronicler hurls invective at the Pechera monks, who succeeded in winning "through great sin and wrong" a litigation over the Church of St. Dmitry.

The potent effect which the monkery had on all sections of the community was largely due to the cloisters having been the centres of writing and learning. A more or less rich monastery usually had a good library. It was there that scribes who were engaged in transcribing books got their initial training. They were also the source of literary memorials such as hagiographies, lays and chronicles. Of course, the art of writing in Ancient Rus was not monopolized by the clergy, but the writing of books was a labour-consuming process and demanded particular attention and much time. Besides, the materials used in writing (parchment, ink and paints) were much too expensive for the art to have become very popular. That is why the transcriptions of books and the composition of literary memorials was largely the work of the clergy, and primarily the monkery. The Pechera Monastery was famed for this and produced a few talented men of letters. A number of sermons and discourses which have been preserved in MSS. are ascribed to Feodosy, its founder. Nestor, traditionally known as "the Chronicler" and the author of the *Chronicle of Ancient Years,* the greatest historical work of the Kiev Rus period, calls himself a pupil of Feodosy. Bishop Simon of Vladimir and friar Polikarp, whose writings are included in the *Pechera Paterik,* were also trained at Pechera Monastery in the early 13th century. One may even say that Pechera Monastery produced a literary school, which had a powerful effect on the literature of Kiev Rus.

There was yet another literary centre at Kiev. It was the Vydubitsky Monastery which tried to be independent in the 12th century. Silvester, its superior, was rather successful in his reproduction of *Chronicle of Ancient Years* compiled at Pechera Monastery. It immortalized his name and earned him the title of Silvester the Great as early as the 16th century. This literary tradition prevailed at Vydubitsky Monastery at least until the early 13th century, according to the naive but highly curious *Discourse About the Laying of a Stone Wall Under the Church of St. Mikhail in Vydubitsky Monastery.*

Other monasteries had their own writers. Yuri Monastery was a major cultural centre in Novgorod. The monk Kirik was a famous Novgorod scholar renowned for his *Inquiry* and paschal calculations. Khutyn Monastery produced Antony, who wrote an account of his voyage to Constantinople. The well-known Kliment Smolyatich came from Zarub Monastery which was also of some literary importance in the 12th century.

Many of our chronicles were written by monks. Their part in this work was so great that many of the chronicle reports and stories have retained a rather monkish tenor, particularly those in the *Lavrenty Annals* of the second half of the 12th century.

The monasteries had libraries which were staffed with scribes. The cathedral at the Kiev Pechera Monastery had a collection of Greek books brought there, according to legend, by the architects who erected that remarkable 11th century memorial. Greek books were kept in the galleries, where the libraries were usually organized. The *Life of Avraamy of Smolensk* hints at the existence of a relatively rich library at his cloister.

Naturally, the Ancient Rus cloister was not entirely detached from the townsfolk. *The Discourse of Daniil Zatochnik* presents a striking picture of the monk steeped in the vanity of the world. "Many," he declares, "after leaving the world return to it, like a cur to its retchings; like whining curs, they attend the manors and houses of the powers that be. Wherever weddings and feasts occur, there you will find monks and nuns, and every kind of lawlessness; they look like angels, but their souls are corrupt; they wear the cloth but are obscene in their practices." There is scarcely need to elaborate on the greed of the monkery and its craving for honours and wealth, for that is common knowledge. But these discourses and sermons are of unquestionable value in that they reveal the close ties between the cenoby and the townsfolk at large. This explains why the chroniclers were so well informed of civic events. On the one hand, temporal interests often strangely combined with typically monkish reasoning and quotations from ecclesiastical books. On the other, monasterial disputations found their way into the street, as the *Life of Avraamy of Smolensk* informs us. The black-surpliced monk was often to be seen in squares and streets, while the cloisters with their stone churches stood out sharply against the wooden structures of the laity.

By that time, neighbourhoods inhabited by bondmen had emerged around the cloisters. Among them were diverse categories of people whose station scarcely differed from that of serfs. Among them we find *proshchenniks* and "*zadushniye* people." Without going into the substance of their status, rather, the way in which they fell into the feudal bondage of the churchmen, I wish to note the following according to Dal *zadushye* was the alms given for the dead, while *proshchenniks* were people who had been cured and remained in cloisters and churches to work off the cure. Common *kholops* and serfs also lived in these monasterial neighbourhoods, as is made clear by the donative deed of Varlaam of Khutyn dating from the late 12th or early 13th century. These feudal churches and monasteries were veritable strongholds. The medieval "house" of the Kiev or Novgorod Sophia was a kind of feudal state.

5. three medieval towns: Kiev, Novgorod, Moscow

THE EXCERPTS BELOW ARE REPRINTED FROM *The Towns of Ancient Rus,* by M. Tikhomirov (2nd ed., Moscow: Foreign Languages Publishing House, 1959), pp. 305, 310-314; 397, 399-400, 404-406; 432-434.

I. Kiev

Kiev, the centre of that land [Kiev Land], was at the same time the biggest and most beautiful town in Rus and is situated below the confluence of the Dnieper and the Desna, its last major tributary. The mighty Dnieper, with the Berezina, the Pripyat, the Sozh and the Desna, forms a huge basin to which Kiev was the key, commanding the vast territories bordering on the above-mentioned rivers. No wonder the chronicler, in his original and picturesque language, calls Kiev "the mother of Russian cities."

The first settlements on its site are traced back to the earliest times by the finding of coins in various parts of the city dating from the period of the later Roman emperors at the beginning of the Christian era. In any case, Kiev is one of the most ancient, if not the oldest of Rus towns. Its name is derived from the Slav word *kiy* or *ky*, meaning a stick, a hammer. It could have been a personal name, in which case Kiev is the town of Kiy, which is how the ancient chronicler explains the origin of the Rus capital. The story of Kiy who founded the town is very plausible.

As early as the 9th-10th centuries, Kiev was a major centre which united Eastern Slav tribes. It remained an important town until its destruction by Batu's hordes. . . .

A most curious fact in Kiev's history is the existence of an extensive suburb known as Podol. Many scholars have reiterated Petrov's opinion that Podol was built up with wooden structures only and that even its churches were usually made of wood. But that is a misunderstanding which was due to the fact that Podol churches have not been preserved because that part of the city was poorly defended and was subjected to terrible devastation. The same Petrov says that the chronicles make mention of at least three churches in Podol. One of them (Boris and Gleb) was subsequently called a "heavenly church." One should imagine that the Cathedral of the Assumption in Podol was a magnificent building since it was the repository of the famous icon of the Mother of God Pirogoshchaya mentioned in *The Lay of Igor's Host*. Podol had a motley population. No wonder we discover that it had a Novgorod "chapel" as well as a Roman Catholic Church built somewhere "overlooking the Dnieper" around 1228. It was among Podol's motley population that the Dominican monks, who settled in Kiev, sought fertile soil for Catholic propaganda.

Podol's site was conducive to the development of a number of crafts which depended on the water supply (tanners, potters, etc.). The Kiev landing-stage on the Dnieper was nearby. Prince Gleb who fled from Kiev from his brother Svyatopolk, "went to the river where a vessel was waiting for him." In it he reached Smolensk. The fact that the Kievites had persevered in the part of ship-building is revealed in the story of Izyaslav's warships in the mid-12th century. It was there too that a big bridge was built across the Dnieper in 1115 which was apparently soon destroyed. In the 12th century the north of Podol was protected by a paling *(stolpye)* which ran from the Dnieper to the hills. Beyond that paling lay the swampy common pasture.

Kiev was the centre of miscellaneous industries—forging, armour-making, jewellery, glass-making, etc. New workshops built of "11th-century bricks (halves), clay and slate," have recently been discovered near the Kiev Pechera Monastery. These produced mainly mosaics.

This gives substance to the vivid story in the *Pechera Paterik* about Alimpy the iconographer, who studied mosaics under the Greeks.

Kiev soil is virtually saturated with household utensils, ornaments and the remains of Ancient Rus weapons.

Kiev was one of the richest of medieval cities with a large handicraft and merchant population. According to *The Lay of Igor's Host,* the unsuccessful campaign against the Polovtsy was bewailed by the Czechs and Moravians, the Germans and the Venetians. The *Pechera Paterik* gives us a colourful account of the disputes between the Pechera monks and the Armenians, Syrians, Jews and Latins (Catholics). The legend of Agapit, "the charitable doctor," is a story of an Armenian doctor ("an Armenian by birth and creed, who was skilful in doctoring") and his co-religionists and, consequently, of an entire Armenian colony. The Armenian doctor was received in exclusive feudal society and treated Vladimir Monomakh and his boyars. In his reply to a question by Prince Izyaslav concerning the Latins, Feodosy tells of the spread of the Catholic faith: "The Varangians are all over the land; and the Orthodox Christians who live among them suffer great oppression from them. . . ."

Several major monasteries stood around Kiev. The biggest of them was Pechera Monastery which was founded in the 11th century and very soon became a rich landowner. Vydubitsky Monastery, called "Vsevolod's," since it was the family monastery of Vsevolod Yaroslavich and his children, stood nearby. Their contribution to the letters of the Kiev period is well known and requires no comment. The *Pechera Paterik*, that major literary composition dating from between the 11th and 13th centuries, was written chiefly by the monks of Pechera Monastery. The monks of both cloisters were also engaged in editing the annals. . . .

II. Novgorod

Novgorod itself was a giant city in comparison with the other towns in the northern part of Ancient Rus.

Its rapid growth was due primarily to its central position on the ramified water system of Lake Ilmen and the Volkhov. It was on the route "from the Varangians to the Greeks" at a point where that route is nearest to the upper reaches of the Volga, so that it was a juncture of the two greatest waterways in the East-European Plain. . . .

A network of lakes and rivers connected Novgorod with the north of Rus. There was a route to Lake Beloye, the Sukhona, the Onega and the White Sea.

The *Lavrenty Annals* date its emergence to high antiquity and ascribe its construction to the Slovenes, who "sat near Lake Ilmer, were called by their own name and made a *grad* and called it Novgorod." *Ipaty Annals* ascribe its construction to Ryurik, a doubtful suggestion, since nothing is said of this in the *Novgorod Annals* which are based on the primary chronicle that precedes the *Chronicle of Ancient Years*. In any case, Novgorod should be regarded as one of the earliest Rus towns which was already in existence in the 9th century. In the next century it was regarded as being second only to Kiev and as a consequence usually ruled by the sons of the grand princes. Under Igor, according to Constantine Porphyrogenitus, it was his son Svyatoslav and later Vladimir. . . .

Novgorod was the centre of the most diverse industries; its territory abounds in miscellaneous remains. It had a developed tanning, pottery, armour-making and jewellery industry. . . .

Novgorod's wealth was emphasized by the large-scale stone construction in the 11th-13th centuries. One important fact should be noted: parallel to the construction of stately buildings by the princes, such as the Sophia Cathedral, the Nikola Cathedral in Dvorishche, and the Yuri Cathedral, similar undertakings were launched by prominent Novgorod citizens. A magnificent memorial of that period is the Antony Monastery whose cathedral was built in 1119 and decorated with frescoes in 1125. It was built by Anton, a rich merchant, as a subsequent biography reveals. The chronicler knew who that Anton was and did not elaborate on his personality. No wonder the chronicler notes the year of his installation as superior of the monastery and the year of his death. In splendour, Antony's Monastery matched the royal Yuri Monastery and this proves that great wealth accumulated in the hands of individuals in Novgorod.

I must also note the existence in Novgorod of the Gothic and German counters, the Varangian chapel, the churches of merchants' patron saints (Pyatnitsa of the overseas merchants, and John the Baptist of the wax-dealers). This completes the picture of Novgorod as a rich and densely populated town. It is not surprising, therefore, that it was in Novgorod that we find a system that later resulted in the emergence of an original state called "Lord Great Novgorod."

In the history of Rus culture, Novgorod holds a place equal to that of Kiev. It produced the comprehensive chronicles whose origins are traced back to the 11th century. The *Concise* and *Extensive* versions of *Russkaya Pravda* are also connected with Novgorod, for their earliest versions came from there. The bulk of ancient MSS. originated in Novgorod, for it preserved and multiplied the cultural riches of Ancient Rus. In the whole of its history it was devastated only once—by the Nazis during the Great Patriotic War.

Russian epic lore describes Novgorod as a most important cultural centre. The *bylinas* of the "Novgorod cycle" about Vasily Buslayev, the rich *gost* Sadko, etc., make up a part of the thesaurus of Rus folk literature.

Novgorod appears to have engulfed all the urban settlements over a territory with a 200-kilometre radius. Other towns of the Novgorod Land, with the exception of Pskov, never rose to great prosperity and independence. The other major centres in that land were Ladoga, Torzhok and Staraya Rusa. . . .

III. MOSCOW

Moscow is first mentioned in April 1147 as the meeting place of Yuri Dolgoruky and the Chernigov Prince Svyatoslav Olegovich. It is not known whether it was a *gorod,* a royal estate or a manor. The *Tver Annals* report in 1156 that "Grand Prince Yuri Vladimirovich founded the *gorod* of Moscow at the mouth of the Neglinnaya, above the Yauza River." This report is often questioned as being of later origin, but does not in substance arouse particular suspicion, for the information that a *gorod* was built in Moscow and the approximate date of its founding could have been remembered or recorded although the chronology may not be precise.

The story of Moscow's beginnings mentions the manors on its site belonging to boyar Kuchka who was killed by Yuri Dolgoruky. This story connected Moscow with its other name—Kuchkovo. Consequently, the legend which reached us in a 17th-century record has a measure of truth in it. Besides, the young men of the Kuchkov family have gone down in history as Andrei Bogolyubsky's assassins. The latter fact is explained by Yuri Dolgoruky's action against their father, the wealthy boyar Kuchka. The question is whether Kuchkovo was a village or a *gorod*. Legends of the 16th-17th centuries say nothing of the *gorod* but only describe the "beautiful manors of boyar Kuchka."

Rabinovich, who made excavations in Zaryadye, an ancient Moscow quarter at the foot of Kitai-Gorod Hill, has arrived at highly interesting conclusions. He says that Moscow had a *posad* as early as the 10th-11th centuries. "We managed to determine the outlines of a *posad* which stretched in a narrow strip along the bank of the river." It had a developed metal-working industry, jewellery, tanning and bootmaking industries, and had extensive trade ties reaching as far as Germany in the West, and Central Asia and Armenia in the East. But the author has allowed himself a few arbitrary conclusions. Does the discovery of dirhems in a place prove it to be necessarily connected with Central Asia? These may have been traces of trade in the upper reaches of the Volga. The dirhems may have arrived in Moscow by a long and devious route. The same applies to a seal which Rabinovich dates to the late 11th century in spite of the fact that the writing on it has not been deciphered. It is very doubtful that in the late 11th century a cargo of goods with that seal was shipped directly from, say, Köln to Moscow. Another surprising fact is that Rabinovich dates all his finds in Moscow to the 10th-11th centuries. Only a bootmaker's shop is dated to the 12th century, and there seem to be no finds at all dating from the 13th century. It transpires that Moscow was much richer in the 10th-11th centuries and that some kind of inexplicable regress had set in in the 12th-13th centuries. I think that the dating of the archaeological finds will have to be checked.

Rabinovich has done much to study ancient Moscow, but I think he was wrong in divorcing the *posad* from the town, for a *posad* was merely a part of a town inhabited by craftsmen and merchants, and in the 12th century, it could not have existed without the *gorod,* the citadel. The chronicles and legends are unanimous in indicating Yuri Dolgoruky as the founder of Moscow although this does not at all imply that there were no settlements or fortified hamlets around Moscow before him.

None the less, the excavations in Zaryadye shed new light on the history of Moscow. But the "industrial *posad* with its developed metal-working, jewellery, tanning and bootmaking industries," should be dated to the 12th-13th centuries. The chronicle report of the Mongolian devastation of the town in 1237 describes it as rich and flourishing. At all events, the discoveries made by Rabinovich call for a revision of the idea that Moscow was a shabby Rus town.

In the early 13th century, Moscow became a separate appanage vied for by the senior princes. In 1214, the annals mention the "Muscovites" as a group apart from the royal men-at-arms, while the story of the Tatar invasion in 1237 describes Moscow as a big and densely populated town. The Tatars "set fire to the *grad* and the holy churches and burnt the monasteries and the manors and, after taking much property, left." However, even during the time of Daniil, the founder of the Moscow royal house, its kremlin occupied only a corner of the present-day Kremlin, while the *posad*, called Podol, stretched on in a narrow strip under the Kremlin into what was later known as Zaryadye.

6. Andrei Rublëv: icon painter, 1360?-1430?

THE ART OF ICON PAINTING was one of the great cultural achievements of medieval Russia. It reflected the religious and cultural impact, first of Byzantium and second of Kievan Russia. The centers of icon painting were the workshops of Russian monasteries, two of the best known being the Troitse-Sergievsky Monastery [Zagorsk] about seventy kilometers from Moscow and the Andronikov Monastery in Moscow, both of which were renowned for book learning and artistic attainments. The tradition of icon painting has been preserved in the workshops of the villages of Palekh and Mtsery, mainly in the form of exquisite miniatures, painted on lacquered boxes of papier maché. During the Soviet period the preservation and restoration of many of the works of the great icon painters have been undertaken. Below is an account of the life and work of Andrei Rublëv acknowledged to be the greatest of all Russian icon painters, whose 600th anniversary was celebrated in the USSR in 1960. Rublëv exerted a profound influence on the development of Russian art.

Reprinted from *Andrei Rublëv,* by V. N. Lazarev (Moscow: Sovetskii Khudozhnik, 1960), pp. 22-23.

Andrei Rublëv lived in a period of national uplift. The rout of the Tatar hordes at Kulikovo in 1380—cogent proof of what a people could achieve when it rose as one man against its foe—radically changed the mood of Russian people, brought them new hopes for the future. It was now the Moscow princes who headed the long, hard struggle against the Mongols; and Moscow thus advanced to leadership among the numerous feudal principalities.

Rublëv was born between 1360 and 1370. He became a monk, and spent his youth and young manhood at the Troitsa (Trinity) Monastery [Zagorsk], some seventy kilometers from Moscow. Much of his painting was done either in Moscow or at the monastery. He worked repeatedly for the Grand Prince of Moscow, son of Dmitry Donskoi—hero of the Kulikovo Battle—and also for Yuri of Zvenigorod, Dmitry's second son, a brilliant military leader. Rublëv was closely associated, too, with Sergius of Radonezh, the founder of the Troitsa Monastery, a sworn foe of the dissensions among the Russian princes which hampered the unification of the national forces.

Coming into such contact with the finest Russians of the period, the most active participants in the struggle against the Mongol invaders, Rublëv keenly sensed the need for new forms of art, suitable to this new age of national uplift. And in this quest for such new forms he was so notably successful that his name soon came to be a synonym of perfection in the art of icon painting.

The Moscow school of painting, in the traditions of which Rublëv was trained, had been strongly influenced by Byzantine art. As early as 1344, at the invitation of the Metropolitan Theognostus, Greek painters came to work in the Moscow Kremlin; and later on many works of Byzantine art, mostly icons, were brought to Moscow. In the 1390's, the famed Theophanes the Greek arrived in Moscow—a personality of tremendous power, who greatly influenced Rublëv. Following in the footsteps of Theophanes and of the elder generation of Moscow artists, among these Prokhor of Gorodets—his teacher, possibly—Rublëv rapidly advanced into the ranks of the leading masters.

His earliest works were done at Zvenigorod, the residence of Prince Yuri, who was not only a god-son, but one of the greatest admirers of Sergius of Radonezh. A frequent visitor at the Troitsa Monastery, Yuri was evidently well impressed by the young monk and painter Andrei, and he invited him to Zvenigorod to decorate the churches he had founded there. In the Zvenigorod Cathedral of the Dormition, built at the turn of the fourteenth and fifteenth centuries, there is a fresco of St. Laurus which may be ascribed to Rublëv. The saint's expression is frank and pleasant. In the painter's free technique, in his rich highlights, we clearly sense the influence of Theophanes. Rublëv was the author, also, of three beautiful icons—Christ, The Apostle Paul, and The Archangel Michael, now the pride of the Tretyakov Gallery in Moscow, but originally part of a Deesis which adorned the altar screen of the Cathedral of the Nativity in the Monastery of St. Sabbas built about 1404. Particularly attractive in these icons is the serenity of their expression, the remarkable beauty of their cool, light tones, witness to Rublëv's outstanding talent as a colourist.

In 1405 Rublëv worked with Theophanes the Greek and the aged Prokhor of Gorodets on the decoration of the Cathedral of the Annunciation in the Moscow Kremlin. On the iconostasis of this church there are several icons that may be ascribed to Rublëv: The Annunciation, The Nativity, The Presentation in the Temple, The Baptism, The Raising of Lazarus, The Entry into Jerusalem, and The Transfiguration. Though their state of preservation is very bad, these icons still retain their remarkable beauty of colouring, their delicate compositional rhythm.

In 1408 Rublëv and his friend Daniil decorated the Cathedral of the Dormition in Vladimir. All that remains today on the walls of the church are the frescos in its western part—fragments of a large composition depicting the Last Judgment. In these frescos one can easily distinguish the work of two artists, an elder and a younger. The younger, whom we have every reason to identify as Rublëv, is notable for the strict precision of his brush. He avoids bold asymmetrical displacements, and favours smooth, parabolic lines. To all other compositional effects he prefers the circle, as the most lucid and the most tranquil. All of his work is highly artistic. His elongated figures are imbued with grace and charm, their outlines highly expressive; in their faces we read incomparable gentleness and nobility.

Besides the frescos in this church, Rublëv and his assistants painted the icons for the iconostasis. Twenty-seven of these icons have been preserved, and are now in museums: the Tretyakov Gallery in Moscow, and the State Russian Museum in Leningrad. Figures over three metres high, grouped around the Saviour, the Virgin, and the Baptist, comprised a grand and monumental composition, distinctly outlined against the gold background. Entirely flat, the figures depended for effect chiefly on their outlines. And the painters, understanding this perfectly, simplified and generalized these outlines to the utmost, thus attaining a rare power of expression.

Rublëv's finest work, his famed Trinity icon, now at the Tretyakov Gallery, was dedicated to the memory of Sergius of Radonezh, and dates, most probably, to the year 1411, when a wooden church was erected at Sergius' burial place. Of the three angels depicted on this icon, the central angel symbolizes Christ, the angel on the left—God the Father, and the angel on the right—the Holy Ghost. Christ, with bowed head, is blessing a cup with the head of the sacrificial calf. Since the calf, in the interpretation of the church, is the Old Testament prototype of the New Testament lamb, the cup is to be considered as a symbol of the Eucharist. By the gesture of blessing Christ declares his readiness to sacrifice himself. The angel on the left, with deep sadness in his look, is also blessing the cup. The icon thus represents what is regarded in the Christian religion as the supreme sacrifice of love—the father sending his son to death, and the son expressing his willingness to suffer and die in expiation of the sins of man. But Rublëv breathed new content into this old theme. His three angels personify the longing of the Russian people for the peace and harmony so vainly to be sought in the life of those times. And how happy the forms in which this longing is expressed, enchanting in their amazing unity, their essentially musical harmony! The circle—there we have the leitmotif of the entire composition. We find it in the bowed figure of the angel on the right, in the outlines of the mountain and the tree, in the inclination of the central angel's head, in the parabolic lines prevailing in the figure of the angel on the left, in the placing of the pedestals. The wonderful compositional rhythm of the icon is enhanced by the colouring, which is musical beyond all words. Amity—such would be the most appropriate term for the colour scheme of the icon, so clear, so lucid, so transparent; for it expresses with remarkable force the amity, the harmony among the three angels.

Rublëv's later years were spent at the Andronikov Monastery, in Moscow. Here he decorated the Church of the Saviour; but all that has been preserved of these frescos are a few fragments of the ornament.

The latest of Rublëv's works that have come down to us date to the late 1420's, when the painter was already an old man. Again in company with his friend Daniil, Rublëv worked on the icons for the iconostasis of the Church of the Trinity at the Troitse-Sergievsky Monastery (Zagorsk). The time assigned them being very limited, Rublëv and Daniil took on several assistants, of both the elder and the younger generations—whence the disunity in style of the icons. Only three of these—The Baptism, The Archangel Gabriel, and The Apostle Paul—can be ascribed to Rublëv, and that none too certainly. Very reminiscent of the style of the later Rublëv are two small icons now at the Tretyakov Gallery—The Saviour Among Seraphims and the Evangelistic Symbols, and a half-length figure of the Saviour—notable for the splendid preservation of their colours, bright as precious enamel.

Rublëv died between 1427 and 1430, and was buried at the Andronikov Monastery, now site of the Rublëv Museum—one of the chief centres studying the heritage of this famed master.

Andrei Rublëv was not merely one of the representatives of the Moscow school of painting. He was one of the greatest artists of early Russia. In his works, lucid and serene, we find no trace of the grim sternness of Byzantine painting. Through the canons of the Byzantine school of the fourteenth century his artist's soul discerned the grace and beauty of the art of ancient times, its music of motion, its delicate balance, bare of adornment and attractive in its austere and noble simplicity. And by this creative perception of the Byzantine heritage he overcame its contemporary influence. In place of the nervous modelling by colour of the Byzantine school we find in Rublëv's works calm, smooth, even colour surfaces; in place of the uneven, vibrating Byzantine contours—restrained and laconic outlines that render the silhouette of his figures perceptible at a glance; in place of the intricate Byzantine system of highlights—a clear-cut graphic treatment. His choice of colours is guided not by the traditional canons, but by the colouring of nature in the Russian countryside, to the beauty of which he was very sensitive. It was by these colours, and by his amazingly rhythmic lines, that he expressed his soul, the soul of a contemplative and keenly perceptive artist. And as that soul was noble and untainted, his art became one of the loftiest achievements of the artistic culture of the Middle Ages.

7. Ivan Grozny's defence of autocracy

THE CORRESPONDENCE OF IVAN IV (Grozny, 1530-1584) with Prince Andrew Kurbsky is an important contribution, not only to Russian literature of the sixteenth century, but to Russian history and political thought. Ivan IV's drive to substitute his own autocratic authority for the power of the feudal boyars alienated the influential and intelligent Kurbsky, one of his leading boyars and generals, who fled to Lithuania. From his refuge abroad, he addressed five angry epistles to his erstwhile ruler and friend. The translated passages below reveal Ivan Grozny's unbridled response in defence of autocracy, and his opposition to the interference of the church in state affairs.

See *Poslaniya Ivana Groznogo,* Ed. D. S. Likhachev and Ya. S. Lur'ye (AN, SSSR), 1951. For a complete translation of the letters, see *The Correspondence Between Prince A. M. Kurbsky and Tsar Ivan IV of Russia, 1564-1579.* Ed. with Translation and Notes by J. L. I. Fennell (Cambridge: Cambridge University Press, 1955).

... The Autocracy of this truly Orthodox Russian kingdom, by the will of God, can be traced back to the great Tsar Vladimir, who enlightened the whole Russian land with holy baptism, and to the great Tsar Vladimir Monomach [1113-1125], who received the highest honor from the Greeks, and to the brave and great sovereign, Alexander Nevsky, who won a victory over the godless Germans [1240], and to the great and praiseworthy sovereign, Dimitry, who won a mighty victory beyond the Don over the godless Hagarites,[1] and even to that avenger of injustice, our grandfather, the Grand Prince Ivan [Ivan III], and to our father of blessed memory, the great sovereign, Vasily, who retrieved lands belonging to our forefathers from time immemorial—and it has come down

[1] The sons of Hagar, or Ishmaelites, the term used to denote Muslims, including the Tatars. Reference here is to the Battle of Kulikovo, 1380, when Dimitry Donskoy defeated Mamai, khan of the Golden Horde.

45

even to us, the humble scepter-bearer of Russian tsardom. And we give praise for His great mercy bestowed upon us, since He has not permitted our right hand to become stained with the blood of our own people; for we have not seized the kingdom from anyone, but, by the grace of God and with the blessing of our forefathers and fathers, as we were born to rule, so have we been educated and grown up and ascended the throne by the grace of God, and with the blessing of our parents we have taken what is our own, and have not seized what belongs to others. From this truly Orthodox Christian autocrat, who rules over many dominions, comes a command; this is our Christian and humble answer to the former boyar and adviser and *voevoda* of our autocratic state who was once of the true Christian Orthodox faith, but who is now the betrayer of the unblemished and life-giving Cross of the Lord and the destroyer of Christianity, and the servant of those enemies of Christianity who have abandoned the worship of the divine icons and trampled on all the divine and sacred commandments and destroyed the holy temples and befouled and trampled on the sacred vessels and images, as did the Isaurian and the *Gnoeteznyi* (the Putrefied) and the Armenian[2]—to him, who has cast his lot with all these, to Prince Andrey Mikhailovitch Kurbsky, who with his traitorous ways wished to become master of Yaroslavl;[3] let it be known. . . .

. . . But as for the Russian autocracy, from the beginning the rulers themselves, and not the boyars and not the notables, have governed their entire realms. And according to your understanding, would it be dishonest to refuse to subordinate the power given us by God to govern by ourselves and not to be subject to the authority of a certain priest or to your nefarious schemes? . . .

. . . Many other things too will you find in the reigns of the tsars. They have restored their kingdoms under every kind of disorder and they have frustrated the designs and evil deeds of the wicked. And it is always fitting for tsars to be discerning, sometimes very meek, sometimes wrathful; mercy and gentleness for the virtuous; for the evil—wrath and torture. Moreover, if a tsar does not possess these qualities, then he is no tsar, for the tsar "does not strike fear in those who do good deeds, but in those who do evil. . . ."

. . . Or do you consider it "pious illustriousness" for a kingdom to be ruled by an ignoramus of a priest, by evil, traitorous men, and for a tsar to take orders from others? And is this "contrary to reason and the sign of a leprous conscience" for an ignoramus to be silenced, for evil men to be opposed and for a tsar to rule by divine right? For no kingdom ruled by priests has ever escaped disaster. But what are you

[2] Reference is made to the so-called "iconoclast" Emperors: Leo III (717-741), Constantine V (741-775), and Leo V. (813-820).

[3] Yaroslavl had belonged to the Kurbsky family since the end of the thirteenth century, but was annexed by Moscow in 1463.

after? Do you want to follow the Greeks, who destroyed their kingdom and became subjects of the Turks? Do you also advocate this ruination for us? Rather may this destruction descend upon your own head! . . .

Or do you call this "light," for a priest and arrogant, cunning servants to rule and the tsar to be respected only by virtue of his chairmanship, with power no greater than that of a servant? And do you call this "darkness," for the tsar to rule and govern his kingdom, and for his servants submissively to obey his orders? How can one be called an autocrat if he himself does not build? . . . But we, by the grace of Christ, have reached the age of maturity set by our father, and it is not fitting that we should remain under governors and tutors. . . .

Behold then and consider what sort of rule is established in various powers and governments, when their tsars listen to eparchs and counsellors, and how disastrous are the results. Is this what you advise for us, to bring about such a disaster? And is this piety, not to build up one's kingdom and not to restrain evildoers, and to submit to destruction by foreign races? Or do you say that such is your interpretation of the sacred teachings? Good and fitting! It is one thing to save one's own soul, but another to be responsible for many souls and bodies: it is one thing to practise fasting by one's self; it is another to live together in communal life [monasticism]. It is one thing to exercise spiritual authority; it is another to rule as a tsar. . . . Consider then the difference between the life of fasting and the coenobetic [communal], between religious and secular [royal] power. And is this befitting a tsar: when he is struck on one cheek, also to turn the other cheek? Is this then the most perfect commandment? For how can a tsar govern his kingdom if he himself is not respected? . . .

8. the beginning of book printing in Russia (1564)

IN 1964 THE USSR CELEBRATED THE FOURTH CENTENARY of book printing in Russia, with emphasis on Ivan Fyodorov, who printed *The Acts of the Apostles* in 1564.

The following article, "The Fourth Centenary of Book Printing in Russia," by Alexei Sidorov, Corresponding Member of the USSR Academy of Sciences, is from *Soviet Literature* (No. 3, 1964), pp. 158-160.

Four hundred years ago, on March 1, 1564, *The Acts of the Apostles,* part of the New Testament of the Bible, appeared in Moscow, in Slavonic script. The afterword to this book containing information about where and when it was printed, and by whom—an altogether unusual practice in Russian ecclesiastical works. The afterword stated that the book was printed by Ivan Fyodorov and his assistant Pyotr Mstislavets, and that the print-shop concerned had been opened one year earlier, in 1563. In addition it gave the purpose for which the book was intended—to spread enlightenment in the newly settled areas along the Volga. Prominence was given to the fact that the print-shop had state backing—funds for it were lavishly donated by the Tsar (Ivan Grozny). In analyzing the essence of this information given to the reader one cannot help being struck by a remarkable new development. The publisher-printer was himself addressing the people, telling them what he was doing and explaining his motives to them. He was acting as a publicist. In another ten years, in 1574, when he published a second edition of his *Apostles* in Lvov, Ivan Fyodorov included another afterword, this time a fuller one, an excellent autobiography of a man who had suffered considerable ordeals, including being driven from Moscow as a result of the intrigues of his enemies. Despite all this he remained faithful to his chosen vocation which was the enlightenment of the people. When the first printed Russian grammar was brought out in the same year Fyodorov dedicated it to his "beloved Russian people."

Our people have the utmost respect for the work done by the first Russian printer, and a memorial has been erected to him in Moscow. In the past few years Soviet scholars have done a great deal to elucidate the origin of Russian printing. From a study of all sources, above all of the very copies of the oldest Russian printed books, we know now that printing developed independently in Moscow, that after seeing examples of works from abroad printed at that time, primarily Southern Slav, German, Czech and Italian, the Russians worked out their own technique of two-colour printing (black and red), and devised their own type and system of ornamentation based on the tradition of the old Russian hand-written books. When the Russian craftsmen working in this sphere—they were of an inquisitive turn of mind, with considerable knowledge and experience—studied works printed in the West, they approached the matter in a creative way, the Renaissance techniques and motifs being subordinated to their own specifically Russian artistic outlook. We know that before Fyodorov's *Apostles* was published in 1564, there existed a print-shop in Moscow which printed several books without giving any indication of the publisher. Its technique was ingenious (it printed simultaneously in two colours), but on the whole the quality of its production was inferior to that of the *Apostles*. This was the print-shop in which Ivan Fyodorov learned his craft.

So we have chosen March 1, 1564, as the date for celebration. After all we celebrate the day of victory rather than that on which the battle began.

What does this book look like? *The Acts of the Apostles* is a volume without a title page; it has a rather large woodcut frontispiece—there were none of this kind in the old manuscript books and few in subsequent printed books. It has no engraved illustrations but many beautiful headpieces.

The frontispiece is the most striking feature of the publication. It portrays the Evangelist Luke, the alleged author of the book, framed in an archway. The treatment is vigorous and capable—this is certainly a realistic three-dimensional figure. The artist has depicted Luke from a point somewhere above eye-level, which is a typical Russian style of dealing with foreground perspective. The engraving is done by cutting the wood with a knife, and the use of this technique (for the curly hair on Luke's head, for example) must have presented considerable difficulties. The thickness of the lines is varied in a masterly way—in some places the line, stark black on white, seems as though done with a stroke of the pen. It is a triumph for this particular medium.

But even more interesting than the technique is the humanist conception of the composition, the fact that there is no usual spatial perspective, and no background details focus the onlooker's attention on the man himself. There is no conventional ecclesiasticism about the way Luke is portrayed. Any miniature taken from earlier books might serve as an ikon: the gold background, unrealistic colouring and elegant lettering of miniatures in such works as the 1531 manuscript of the Gospels are all points of resemblance to ikons. But this woodcut of

Luke could not possibly take its place in a church, its realism being entirely incompatible with the art of ikon painting. Furthermore, it is impossible to imagine this first printed Luke in colour.

The Moscow apostle is a large-scale work of monumental character. The figure is part of a carefully designed composition, being placed within the frame of a triumphal arch. Why did this have to be a classical arch, in fact an interpretation of a Western woodcut done in 1524? There is only one answer. This was something deliberately done. The progressive trend of the ideological policy of the time in which the *Apostles* was printed was to reveal the links connecting Russian culture with antiquity, and to show that the culture of the Russian state had roots deep in the past. The idea of this frontispiece was to connect the image with the ancient glory associated with the triumphal arch. Some of our scholars have, incidentally, pointed to a connection between this arch and the portals of Russian churches.

Apart from the frontispiece, the magnificent headpieces, initials and lettering in this edition enjoy deserved repute. The headpieces have a definite, very vital beauty. Striking in their diversity, they nevertheless retain a general uniting principle—branches and leaves of some plant spread out from the centre (fruit is incorporated in the design—pomegranates or cedar cones). The foilage has great variety, and the lines are graceful and fluid. At the same time the two-dimensional quality necessary in this case is preserved.

While the headpieces undoubtedly have certain associations with the West (fluidity of line and classical patterns not hitherto seen in Russian books), in composition, in outer form—they stretch along the horizontals of a rectangle—they are purely Russian, and as regards their role on the page derive from the methods of illumination used in earlier Russian manuscripts. It is interesting to note that pomegranates appeared in Russian printed fabrics in the 16th century as well.

The *Apostles* and all subsequent editions produced by Fyodorov are done by the dual-process technique in red and black instead of using the old simultaneous process. But his method of printing was quite different from that used in the West. The Russian craftsmen first printed the red lettering (although there was far less red than black on a page) and only afterwards printed the main body of the text in black. Not only was the book design specifically Russian—so also were the techniques employed.

Ivan Fyodorov was a great Russian craftsman—publisher, printer, engraver and book designer all in one. When in his afterwords he referred to himself as a *maker* of books he had full justification.

On March 1 this year [1964] the Soviet Union celebrates the fourth centenary of Fyodorov's *Apostles,* paying tribute to him in the knowledge that his work laid the basis for the development of the art of book production in our country to its present level.

9. the life of the Archpriest

Avvakum, 1621-1682

THE ARCHPRIEST AVVAKUM WAS THE CENTER of the dispute within the Russian Orthodox Church which produced the *Raskol* or Schism (1666). He was a leader of the opposition to the reforms of the Patriarch Nikon (1653-1660). Avvakum and his followers were especially hostile to certain changes in church ritual involving, among other things, the use of three instead of two fingers in making the sign of the cross, and the triple instead of the double Alleluia. They were successful in securing a wide popular following on these issues which were understood even by the illiterate masses. Because of his intransigence, Avvakum spent many years in exile in Siberia, where he assiduously preached his "subversive" doctrine. In an attempt to reconcile him to the official position of the Church, Tsar Alexis brought him back to Moscow. When all these efforts failed, he was tried and condemned by an Ecumenical Church Council in Moscow in 1666, and exiled to Pustozersk on the Arctic coast. It was here, in the midst of a community of Old Believers as they were called, that Avvakum wrote his autobiography. When the Schism threatened the unity of Church and State, on April 14, 1682 Avvakum was condemned to death at the stake by the *ukaz* of Tsar Fyodor Alexeyevitch.

Avvakum's autobiography, written as he himself indicates in the simple but vigorous colloquial Russian of his day, was an outstanding Russian literary contribution of the seventeenth century—a bridge, according to Prince D. S. Mirsky, between *The Lay of the Host of Igor* (twelfth century) and the Odes of Lomonosov and Derzhavin (eighteenth century). Alexei N. Tolstoy, in an attempt to recreate the atmosphere of the late seventeenth and early eighteenth centuries for his historical novel, *Peter I,* appears to have drawn heavily upon the literary style and vocabulary of Avvakum's autobiography.

The translated excerpts from the autobiography presented below are from *Zhitie Protopopa Avvakuma im samin napisanoe* (*The Life of the Archpriest Avvakum by Himself*), ed. N. K. Gudzy. USSR (n.d.).

With the blessing of my father confessor, Epiphanius, I, Archpriest Avvakum, have written this with my sinful hand and if what is said is expressed simply, I beseech you for the Lord's sake, you who read and listen, not to despise our simple speech. I love my Russian mother tongue and I am not accustomed to embellishing my speech with philosophical verse, for God listens not to flowery words. He looks for our deeds. And Paul writes: "Though I speak with the tongues of men and angels and have not charity, I am nothing." Why argue so much about this? It is not Latin, or Greek, or Hebrew, or any other language that God expects from us. He wants love and other good deeds; for this reason, I therefore do not concern myself with oratory, nor do I belittle my Russian language. Forgive me, then, a sinner, and may God forgive and bless you all, servants of Christ. Amen. . . .

I was born within the limits of Nizhegorotsk, beyond the River Kudma, in the village of Grigorovo. My father was a priest, named Peter; my mother was Mary, who as a nun was called Martha. My father was addicted to strong drink; my mother fasted and prayed, and always instructed me in the fear of God. Now one time at a neighbor's I saw a dead beast, and that night, rising from my bed, I wept abundantly for my soul before the ikon, pondering over death and how I too must die; and from that time I made a habit of praying every night. Then my mother was widowed, and I, young as I was, was an orphan, and we were driven out by our own kinsmen. It was my mother's wish that I should marry. And I prayed to the most holy Mother of God that she would give me such a wife as would help me to attain salvation. And in that same village there was a maiden, also an orphan, who was wont to go regularly to church, and her name was Anastasia. Her father was a blacksmith named Marko, extremely rich, but when he died all his substance was exhausted. She therefore lived in poverty and she prayed to God that He might so arrange it that she should be joined to me in matrimony; in accordance with the will of God, this came to pass. Thereafter my mother went to be with God, having first taken the veil. And I, because I was exiled, settled in another place. At the age of twenty I was ordained deacon and, after two years, a priest; and when I had been a priest eight years, I was raised to the rank of archpriest by orthodox bishops—this was twenty years ago. And for all of thirty years I have been connected with the priesthood. . . .

. . . In Lent he [Nikon] sent a pastoral letter to St. Basil's Minister, Ivan Neronov. Now he was my spiritual father and I lived all the time in his church; and when he was absent I was in charge of the church; and at the time they talked of making me the successor of the deceased Silas at St. Savior's, but God willed it not and I myself was not very anxious for it. I was well content to continue at St. Basil's. I used to read books to the people and a great many would come. In his instruction, Nikon wrote: "The year and the date. According to the tradition of the holy Apostles and the holy Fathers, it is not fitting to make obeisance in church to the knee; it should be no lower than the waist, and moreover, it behoves you to sign yourselves with three fingers." We thought this over and met together. It was as if Winter were about to come; our hearts froze and our limbs trembled. Neronov entrusted his church to me and secluded himself in the Chudov monastery. He spent a week praying in a cell, and there a voice came from the ikon during prayers: "The hour of tribulation has come; it behoves you to suffer and show no weakness." And, weeping, he repeated these words to me and to Paul, the Bishop of Kolomna, the same whom Nikon eventually burned at the stake in the Novgorod country, and then to Daniel, the Archpriest of Kostroma, and also to all the brethren. Daniel and I copied excerpts from the books concerning the manner to be used in crossing oneself and making obeisances, and we submitted them to the Emperor. And we copied a great deal. But he hid them, we know where; it seems to me that he gave them to Nikon. . . .

And I, too, while I was celebrating vespers, was arrested by Boris Neledinsky and his *streltsy,* and along with me they arrested about sixty men and took them off to prison, and me they fastened with a chain for the night in the Patriarch's court. And when Sunday dawned they placed me in a cart and spread out my arms and drove me from the Patriarch's court to the monastery of Andronicus. There they put me in chains and flung me into a black cell, dug into the earth, where I spent three days, and I neither ate nor drank; while sitting in the darkness, I bowed, in my chains, without knowing which was east and which was west. No one came to me but mice and black beetles, and crickets chirped, and of fleas there was abundance. . . . In the morning came the Archimandrite with the brethren, and they took me out; they rebuked me because I did not submit to the Patriarch, but I scolded them from the Scriptures and railed at them. . . . I remained there four weeks. . . .

So then they sent me to Siberia with my wife and children, and of the many and great privations on the way, had I the time there would be much to tell. Only a small part can be related. The Archpriestess bore a sickly child in the cart and we brought it as far as Tobolsk; it was a journey of 3000 versts, and for some thirteen weeks we dragged along in carts and by water and half of the way in sledges. . .

Then from the Nercha River we returned again to Russia. For five weeks we travelled in sledges over the bare ice. I was given two worn-out nags for the children and our belongings, and the Archpriestess and I trudged along on foot, injuring ourselves on the ice. The country was barbarous, the natives hostile, and we did not dare to lag behind the horses, but hungry and exhausted as we were, we could not keep up with them. My poor Archpriestess tramped on and on, and at times she even fell—it was quite slippery! Once as she stumbled, she fell and another man as weary as she was tripped and fell on her; both screamed, but could not get up. The *muzhik* yelled: "Matushka, my lady, forgive me!" And the Archpriestess cried: "What are you trying to do, old man, crush me to death?" I came up, and the poor woman complained to me, saying: "How long, Archpriest, will this suffering last?" And I said: "Markovna! till death!" She sighed and replied: "So be it, Petrovich, let us be on our way." ...

Then I arrived by boat at Russian settlements and I learned that the church was making no progress whatsoever; but there is more talk here than action. I was sad, and as I sat, I began to ponder: What can I do? Am I to preach the Word of God or where do I hide myself? For my wife and children tied me down. And seeing that I was sad, my Archpriestess came to me, neatly dressed, and asked: "What is it, my lord, that disturbs you?" And I told her the news in detail: "Wife! What shall I do? The winter of heresy is at the door. Am I to speak or to keep silent? You tie my hands!" She said to me: "Lord, have mercy! What are you saying, Petrovitch? I have heard—you have read the words of the Apostles: *Art thou bound unto a wife? Seek not to be loosed. Art thou loosed from a Wife? Seek not a wife.*[1] I and the children give you our blessing. Make bold to preach the Word of God as heretofore, and don't worry about us; until God wills otherwise, we'll live together; and when we separate, do not forget to pray for us; Christ is strong, and He will not abandon us! Go! Go to the church, Petrovitch—Expose the lechery of heresy!" I bowed low before her and shaking off my grievous blindness, began as before to preach and teach the Word of God in the towns and everywhere, and continued my bold exposure of the heresy of Nikon.

I wintered in Yeniseisk, and having sailed again in the summer, I spent the winter in Tobolsk. And en route to Moscow, in every town and in every village, in churches and in the market-place, I preached and taught the Word of God, and exposed the flattery of the ungodly. Then I reached Moscow [1664]. Three years did I travel from Dauria, and five years I travelled upstream. We journeyed eastward among the native [foreign] hordes and habitations. Much could be said about that! At times, we fell into the hands of the natives. On the great river Ob, in

---

[1] Paul's *Epistle to the Corinthians*, VII, 27.

my presence, twenty Christian men were slain, and they intended to do the same to me, but they let me go. Again on the Irtysh River we encountered a group of them. They lay in wait for our men of Berezov to slay us with clubs. But I, not knowing that, went up to them, and having reached them I put in to the river bank. They surrounded us with their bows. I tell you, I went forth to embrace them as if they were monks, and I said: "Christ be with me, and with you also!" And they were kind to me and they brought their wives to my wife. My wife likewise dissembled, as in the world people resort to flattery; and the women became well-disposed. And we always know that when the women are good, all is well for Christ. The *muzhiks* put aside their bows and arrows and began to trade with me. I bought some bear's meat from them, and they set me free. Having arrived at Tobolsk, as I was saying, some people were surprised to see us, since at that time the Bashkirs were fighting the Tatars all over Siberia. . . .

Thereupon I arrived in Moscow, and as though I were an angel of God the Tsar and all his boyars received me gladly. I called upon Theodore Rtishchev. He rushed out of his cell, received my blessing and began to speak of many things. For three days and three nights he would not let me go home, and thereafter he informed the Tsar about me. The sovereign forthwith issued a command that I be brought to him and he spake kindly to me. "How art thou, archpriest?" said he. "God bade me to see thee again." And I in response kissed his hand and pressed it, and myself said: "God lives and my spirit lives, Your Majesty! But what lies ahead of us, that God will ordain." And he sighed softly and went where he had to go. And other things happened, but why should I talk much about that? It too has passed! He bade them put me in the guest house of a monastery in the Kremlin, and when he passed my door going out on expeditions he often greeted me, bowing low, and would say: "Bless me, and pray for me." And once he took his fur cap from his head and dropped it as he was riding past on horseback. He used to slip out of his carriage to come to me and then all his boyars kept bowing and scraping, crying, "Archpriest, bless us and pray for us." How shall I not grieve for such a Tsar and such boyars? It grieves me to think how good they were! Even now they are not unkind to me. The devil is badly disposed toward me, but all people are kind to me. Even now they offered me any place I wished, and they named me their confessor, that I might be united with them in the faith. But I regarded all these things as dung. And I gained Christ and was conscious of death, and how all these things pass away.

I will tell you still more of my wanderings. How they brought me out of the Paphnutiev monastery in Moscow and put me in the guest house, and after many wanderings I found myself in the Chudov monastery, where they brought me face to face with the ecumenical Patriarchs, and all of ours sat there like so many foxes. I spoke with the Patriarchs of many things in the Scriptures. God opened my sinful mouth and Christ put them to shame. The last word they spoke to me was this: "Why are thou stubborn? Our whole Church, including the Serbs, Albanians, Wallachians, Romans, and Poles, all these cross themselves with three fingers, only thou standest out in thine obstinacy and dost cross thyself with two [five] fingers;[2] it is not proper." And I answered them on behalf of Christ thus: "O you ecumenical Teachers! Rome has long since fallen and lies prostrate, and the Poles likewise have perished along with them, being to the end the enemies of Christianity. And your Orthodoxy has become heterogeneous, because of the brute force of the Turkish Muslims. Small wonder you act so, because you are weak, and henceforth it is you who should learn from us. By the gift of God we have autocracy. Till the time of Nikon, the apostate, in our Russia under our pious princes and tsars the Orthodox faith was pure and undefiled, and in the Church there was no sedition. Nikon, the wolf, together with the devil, ordained that the cross should be made with three fingers, but our first shepherds themselves made the sign of the cross with two [five] fingers and blessed men as of old with two [five] fingers, according to the tradition of our holy fathers, Meletina of Antioch, Theodoret, the blessed Bishop of Cyrene, Peter of Damascus, and Maxim the Greek; and so too did our own Moscow *Sobor,* in the reign of Tsar Ivan, bid 'iem, putting their fingers together in that wise, make the sign of the cross and give the blessing as taught in olden times by the holy fathers Melety and others. Then in the reign of Tsar Ivan there were at the *Sobor* the standard bearers, Gury and Varsanophii, wonder-workers of Kazan, and Philip, the Abbott of the Solovetskii Monastery, among the Russian saints." And the Patriarchs fell to pondering, and our people jumped up and began to howl like wolf-cubs and to vomit out words against their fathers, saying: "Our Russian holy men were ignorant, and they did not understand, they were not scholars. How can one trust them? They were illiterate." O Holy God! How hast Thou suffered Thy Holy Ones to be so maligned? I, miserable one, was bitter, but I could do nothing. I abused them, I abused them as much as I could, and my last word was as follows: "I am pure, and the dust that cleaves to my feet I shake off before you, as it is written—'better one who does the will of God than a multitude of the lawless.'" Then louder than before they began to cry out against me: "Seize him, seize him! He hath dishonored us all!" And they began to push me and to beat me. And the patriarchs themselves threw themselves on me. About forty of them I think there must have been. Great was the army of Antichrist that assembled. . . .

. . . After that the authorities again came to me and began to talk with

[2] Actually, the text says five fingers. For an explanation, see *Zhitie Protopopa Avvakuma im samim zapisanoe.* Ed N. K. Gudzy (N.D.), p. 373.

me about the Alleluias. Christ put it in my mouth and I put them to shame for their Romish lie, through Dionysius the Areopagite, of whom mention has been made previously. And Euphemii, the cellarer of the Chudov monastery, spake: "Right art thou. We have nothing more to say to thee." And they led me away in chains.

Then the Tsar sent an officer with the Streltsy and they took me to the Vorobiev hills. . . .

Then again they brought me to Moscow, to the Nikolsky guest house, and they obtained from us another statement of the true faith. After that there were sent to me many times gentlemen of the bed-chamber, Artemon and Dementii. And they spoke to me in the name of the Tsar: "Archpriest! I see that thy life is pure and uncorrupted and God-like. I and the Tsarina and our children, we beseech thee to bless us and pray for us." The messenger bowed as he spake, and I weep for him always. I was exceeding sorry for him. And again he spake: "I beg thee, listen to me. Join with the Patriarchs. Make at least some concession to them." And I said: "Even if God wills that I should die, I will not be joined together with apostates." I said: "Thou art my Tsar, but they, what have they to do with thee?" I said: "They have lost their Tsar and they have come here to gobble you up—I—say I—will not cease to lift my hands to heaven until God delivers you to me." And there were many such messages, which had something to say. The last word he said was: "Wherever thou art, do not forget us in thy prayers." And I, sinful one, as far as I can, now pray to God for him.

After executing my brethren, but not me, they banished me to Pustozersk. . . .

10. Semyon Dezhnev and the discovery of Bering Strait (1648)

IN THE CENTURY FOLLOWING THE SEIZURE OF KAZAN (1552) and Yermak's expedition beyond the Urals (1582), Russians developed great interest in Siberia. Merchants, Cossacks, and artisans travelled widely and contributed much to Russian geographical knowledge about Asiatic Russia. Exploration, as in the case of Dezhnev, was often a by-product of the search for tribute in furs from Siberian native tribes, a business which carried collectors ever farther afield. One result of the expeditions of Dezhnev and others of his time was the preparation on orders from Tsar Alexis of a map of Siberia (1667).

Soviet interest in the Northern Sea Route has led to substantial research on geographical explorations of earlier centuries. The article translated below, "The Three Hundredth Anniversary of the Discovery of Bering Strait by Semyon Dezhnev (1648-1948)," was written by Academician L. S. Berg, an outstanding Soviet geographer. It appeared in *Viestnik Academii Nauk SSSR* (No. 10, October, 1948), with an English translation in *Soviet Press Translations,* Vol. IV (No. 6, March 15, 1949), 178-184.

This marks the three hundredth year since the Yakutsk Cossack, Semyon Dezhnev, rounded the northeastern tip of Asia and passed through Bering Strait from the Arctic Sea to the Pacific Ocean. On the anniversary of this remarkable geographic discovery it is fitting to commemorate it by once again relating its history in the pages of our press.

I. The Strait of Anian

If we glance at a map of Asia in any of the geographic atlases of the end of the sixteenth century or of the entire seventeenth century we see the Strait of Anian instead of the present Bering Strait between Asia and

America. It was retained on some maps right up to the beginning of the nineteenth century, when Bering Strait was already well known.

The Italian cartographer, Gastaldi, was the first to mention the Strait of Anian in 1562. In his book *La universale descrittione del mondo,* referring to a map of the world that has not come down to us, he states that Asia is bounded on the east by the Strait of Anian *(il stretto detto Anian)*, and further that the boundary runs through the Gulf of Hainan *(Cheinan)*, the sea of Mangi *(Manzi)*, etc.

Of the maps that have come down to us, the earliest showing the Strait of Anian is a map of North America published by the Italian cartographer Zaltieri in 1566. Here the *Stretto di Anian* is located between northeastern Asia and northwestern America, and farther south are the Gulf of Hainan and the Sea of Mangi, already known to us.

How did a strait between Asia and America—a strait located in the very place where the Bering Strait should be—come to be represented on the maps? Can we suppose that the idea of a Strait of Anian was based upon real data, and that some European had sailed in these localities or in neighboring localities in the middle of the sixteenth century?

We must answer all these questions very emphatically: Prior to Dezhnev (1648) no European had sailed in the region of Bering Strait and the conjecture as to a strait between Asia and America was an armchair fabrication that accidentally anticipated the truth. The origin of the word "Anian" affords evidence that this is the case.

In Marco Polo's *Travels,* which are dated 1271-1295, reference is made to a province of *Anin,* situated in southeastern Asia, on the coast of the Gulf of *Cheinan,* with which we are already familiar; this same gulf washes the shores of the above mentioned Province of *Manzi* (or *Mangi).* Ordinarily, by Anin is to be understood northern Annam, Hainan is the name of the island of Hainan (Hainang), while Manzi, or Mangi, is one of the names for southern China.

As we see, all the places enumerated are situated in southeastern Asia and bear no relation to the region of the Bering Strait. On the ancient maps the province of Anin was located in various places. Thus, it is situated between northern China and Tibet on Behaim's famous globe of 1492. And it was only the careless Gastaldi who took it into his head to locate this province in northeastern Asia.

Now the question arises: Where did the *Gulf* of Anian spring from? On one of Gastaldi's maps of 1561, Ania pro(vincia) is inscribed in extreme northeastern Asia, while on a map of 1562, Asia is bounded on the east by the Gulf of Anian, as we mentioned above. It must be said that even before Gastaldi the early cartographers had represented the route from northern Europe to China and India around eastern Asia as unobstructed. This is the case in a portolano of 1502 from the Ami Collection by an unknown author. We see the same thing in an atlas of Ptolemy, published in 1513. And so forth.

As soon as the Gulf of Anian made its appearance on the maps of Gastaldi, this concept received immediate general acknowledgement. We find this gulf in the atlases of Mercator in 1569 and of Ortelius in 1570 and in many others—right up to the beginning of the nineteenth century. In January 1725, shortly before his death, Peter I said to Lord High Admiral Apraxin: "I recently recalled something that I have long had in mind and that other affairs prevented my undertaking, that is, a route through the Arctic Sea to China and India. The route called the *Anian*, sketched on this naval map, was not put there by accident."

Certain scholars, even in the twentieth century, have also thought that the Gulf of Anian was not located "by accident" on the maps of those days. The hypothesis has been advanced that knowledge of the Bering Strait could have been brought by Spanish navigators of the first half of the sixteenth century, when several expeditions were sent from Mexico to the northern Pacific. But this possibility is completely excluded. As we stated, the Gulf of Anian appeared on the maps for the first time in 1562, while it was not until 1595 that the Spanish ascended to a latitude of 41½° north (i.e., almost 25 degrees south of Bering Strait.)

Thus, the Gulf of Anian is a cartographical fantasy—the result of the conjectures of the Italian cartographers of the second half of the sixteenth century. This error was based upon the imperfectly understood data given by Marco Polo on southern China.

II. The Northern Sea Route

In 1525 the Muscovite envoy Dmitry Gerasimov was in Rome. In the same year an *Account of the Embassy of Vasily, the Great Prince of Moscovy, to Pope Clement VII* was published in his own words in Latin (of which, by the way, Gerasimov had a fluent knowledge). In this treatise Gerasimov advances the following remarkable and prophetic opinion:

> It is quite well known that the Dvina, carrying with it innumerable rivers, flows in a raging stream to the north and that the sea there is of such vast extent that it may be very reasonably supposed that, by keeping to the right shore, it might be possible to reach the country of China by ship if no land is encountered in the interval.

These few lines contain the entire program of exploration for the mastery of the northern sea route. This task was not concluded until Soviet times, after four hundred years of effort, when the ship *Sibiryakov,* commanded by Captain V. I. Voronin and having a scientific staff of distinguished polar explorers headed by Professor V. Y. Vize and Academician O. Y. Schmidt, proceeded from the White Sea along the coast of Siberia to the Pacific Ocean in one voyage in 1932.

Thus, the discovery of a northeastern passage from Europe to the Pacific Ocean required enormous labors and effort. Such outstanding Russians as Dmitry Gerasimov, Semyon Dezhnev, Peter I, Bering and Tchirikov, Prontchishchev, the brothers Laptev, Lomonosov, Voyeikov, Kropotkin, Makarov, Mendeleyev, V. I. Voronin, V. Y. Vize, O. Y. Schmidt, and many others worked at the solution of this task. In all fairness, the idea of a northern route must be termed a national Russian idea, since it was both conceived (in 1525) and finally realized (in 1932) by Russians.

By the middle of the seventeenth century the entire northern coast of Siberia had been explored by Russian seamen and overland travelers, and it had been proved that there was no land between the White Sea and the Pacific Ocean that might obstruct the route to the East, as Dmitry Gerasimov had feared. In 1619 or 1620, Russian traders from the West skirted Vilkitsky Strait and rounded Cape Tchelyuskin, apparently bound for the mouth of the Khatanga. This did not become known until 1940, when a detachment of the Central Board of Administration of the Northern Sea Route discovered, on the east coast of the Taimyr Peninsula, remains of a boat and various articles, including more than 3,400 Russian silver coins dating from the time of Vasily III to Mikhail Fyodorovitch. By 1646 the Russians had gone east by sea as far as the Gulf of Tchaunsk.

A further step in the conquest of the northern sea route was achieved by Dezhnev in 1648.

III. Semyon Dezhnev

Biographical data concerning this remarkable man are extremely meager. It is known that Semyon Ivanovitch Dezhnev was from Ustyug Veliki. Like other enterprising citizens of Ustyug, he set out to seek his fortune in Siberia. He served in Tobolsk and Yeniseisk. In 1638 we find him at the recently founded (1632) Yakutsk Ostrog, where he was recorded as a Cossack. There is reason to suppose that Dezhnev was about thirty years old at this time; thus, he was probably born in the early years of the seventeenth century.

In 1640 Dezhnev was ordered to the Yana River to levy tribute in furs. While bringing back the furs collected to Yakutsk, he was attacked by the Tungus on the way, and was wounded in the leg, but repelled the attack "with musketry." Two years later we encounter Dezhnev at Oimekon on the upper course of the Indigirka. Here he was again attacked by the Tungus, but he and his small detachment succeeded, with the help of other loyal Tungus and Yakuts, in overcoming the attackers, although Dezhnev received two wounds in the fight. Shortly thereafter, he descended the Indigirka with twelve Cossacks to the sea, and from there reached the Alazei River by land, where he came upon the Yukaghirs from whom tribute in furs had not been collected. From the Alazei, Dezhnev crossed over to the Kolyma and there met another famous overland explorer, Mikhailo Stadukhin, to whom belongs the honor of discovering (in 1644) the "unknown river" Kolyma and of founding the Nizhnekolymsk blockhouse on it.

In 1647 the highlander Fedot Alexeyevitch Popov, a clerk of the Usovs, Ustyug merchants, fitted out a party from Nizhnekolymsk, which was to make a voyage by sea eastward in search of walrus or "fish" bone (walrus tusks), highly valued at that time. The ultimate goal of the party was the Anadyr River. Dezhnev, who was known for his experience and daring, was invited to be a member of the party. He was to take care of levying tribute in furs and of discovering new peoples from which this tribute had not been collected. In the summer of 1647 the party set out from the mouth of the Kolyma in four *kotchi*.[1] But the voyage proved unsuccessful: they were soon obliged to turn back due to ice.

But this failure did not stop the energetic Dezhnev. The voyage was repeated the following year. Six *kotchi* were fitted out, in which ninety men set out. Here is how Dezhnev describes his expedition in a report to the Governor of Yakutsk in April 1655:[2]

On June 20 [O.S.], 1648,

> I, Semeika, was sent from the Kovyma [Kolyma] River to the new Anandyr River to discover new peoples from whom tribute in furs had not been collected.

In the same year of 1648

> on the twentieth of September, en route from Kovyma River by sea, the trader Fedot Alexeyev [Popov] was wounded by Tchuktchi in a fight at a haven, and Fedot and I, Semeika, lost sight of each other at sea, and I, Semeika, was carried willy-nilly everywhere on the sea and was cast up on shore on the fore point beyond the Anandyr River. And there were twenty-five of us in all in the *kotch,* and we all started uphill, not even knowing the way, cold, hungry, naked, and barefoot. And I, poor Semeika, and my comrades took exactly ten weeks to get to the Anandyr River and reached the Anandyr River down near the sea, and we could catch no fish, there was no wood, and our poor ranks had been dispersed by hunger . . . . And of the twenty-five of us there remained but twelve and we twelve set up the Anandyr River in boats and came to the Anauls [the Anauls are one of the tribes of the Yukaghirs] and in the fight they carried off two men and dealt me a deadly wound and carried off the furs collected as tribute. . . .
>
> And one can go from the Kovyma River by sea to the Anandyr River,

---

[1] A type of vessel in use at that time.
[2] We use the revised text published by G. A. Knyazev and B. Malkevitch in *Izvestia Vsesoyuznogo geografitcheskogo obshchestva*, 1948.

and there is a headland [Cape Dezhnev], which extends far out into the sea . . . , and opposite this headland are two islands [Diomede or Gvozdev], and on these islands live Tchuktchi [actually Eskimos], and they have teeth in slits in their skins and their lips are pierced with fish bone [walrus tusks]. And this cape lies between north and *polunoshnik* and the features of the cape of the Russian [western] side are the mouth of a stream, an encampment made by the Tchuktchis with towers of whale bone. And the cape bends around to the Onandyr River.[3] And it is a good three days' march, but no more, from the cape to the Onandyr River, while it is not far to go from the coast to the river, because the Anandyr River empties into the bay.

On the 162nd day of last year [1654] I, Semeika, walked by the sea and I, Semeika, on the way retrieved from the Koryaks a Yakut woman belonging to Fedot Alexeyev, and this woman told how Fedot and his serving-man Gerasim, as she said, had died of scurvy, and how our other comrades had been killed, and how only a few men remained who took to the boats to save themselves, and I do not know where they went.

To this meager report may also be added the following facts from the report made by Semyon Dezhnev and Nikita Semyonov to the Yakutsk governor in April 1655:

Mikhailo [Stadukhin] did not reach the Great Rocky Headland [Cape Dezhnev], which headland extends very far into the sea, and on it live a great many Tchuktchi people, while opposite this headland live a people called the *Zubaty,* because they pierce their lips with two large bone teeth, but it is not that first Holy Cape from the Kolyma [Cape Shelagsky at the entrance to Tchaunsk Bay] that I, Semeika, and my comrades know, but the Great Headland, because the boat of the serving-man Yerasim Onkudinov and his comrades was wrecked at that headland, and I, Semeika, and my Comrades took those shipwrecked people aboard our boats and saw those *Zubaty* people on the island, and the Anandyr River and the reef [Russian Cat] is far from that headland.

And this is all the material that we have at our disposal for judging the famous voyage that proved, for the first time, the existence of an unbroken route from the Arctic Sea to the Pacific.

Reading the terse account of this historic voyage from the Kolyma to the Anadyr, accomplished in the middle of the seventeenth century, one cannot but be astonished at the daring of the Russian navigators and their knowledge of their task. Even in our time such a passage is no easy matter (let us only remember the hardships that the ship *Tchelyuskin* had to undergo in 1933-1934 in the same regions), while in the seventeenth century the navigators sailed the Arctic Sea in *kotchi* —small flat-bottomed sailboats, which could proceed only with the wind.

The authenticity of Dezhnev's reports is beyond the slightest doubt, although formerly there were skeptics that disputed the truth of the accounts of the overland traveler. Nevertheless, indisputable proof of

---

[3] *Podlegly*—according to Dal's dictionary, "subordinate," "dependent," "subject." It is possible, however, that here it is a verb.

the authenticity of Dezhnev's discoveries (the glory of which, incidentally, he did not at all attempt to secure for himself) may be drawn
from his own descriptions, short as they are. Indeed, let us recall the
description of Bering Strait given by Dezhnev. There are actually
Tchuktchi living on the Great Rocky Headland, or Cape Dezhnev. Opposite this cape there are actually two islands—Ratmanov and Kreuzenstern.
The inhabitants of these islands—*Zubaty* Tchuktchi, according to Dezhnev—are Eskimos, who, until recent times, wore ornaments of walrus
tooth, stone, or bone in slits in their lower lips. The wearing of these
"plugs," or *kolyuzhini,* as our ethnographers call them, was also prevalent among the Eskimos of Alaska. For this reason, the Tchuktchi, who
have never made use of such ornaments, gave the Eskimos of the Dio-
mede Islands and Alaska the nickname of big-mouths, while the Russians
called them *Zubaty*.

Skeptics have also pointed out that nothing was known of Dezhnev's
expedition either in Siberia or in Moscow until G. F. Müller found his
reports in Yakutsk in 1736. But this is not true. Dezhnev's expedition
was known both in Siberia and abroad. Yury Krizhanitch, a Croatian
Catholic priest, who spent the years 1661-1676 in exile in Tobolsk,
wrote an extensive account in 1680 entitled *Historia de Sibiria.* In this
account he posed the question of whether the Arctic Sea was connected
with the Eastern Sea which bounds Siberia and China on the east, or
whether these seas were separated from one another by some mainland,
and answered that "this doubt was resolved in very recent times by
soldiers of the Lena and Nertchinsk Region; they, while collecting tribute
from the natives, traversed this whole country to the very ocean and
proved that there is no solid land to the east and that the seas referred
to are not separated from each other by anything, but that Siberia . . .
and China are washed on the east by one continuous ocean." These
facts can only refer to Dezhnev's voyage of 1648, although Krizhanitch
represents the matter as if the problem had been solved by explorations
on land.

A Swedish prisoner taken at Poltava, Filipp Tabbert, who subsequently
assumed the name of Stralenberg in his native land, lived in Siberia
from 1709 to 1722 and traveled widely there. In 1715 he prepared a
map of Siberia at Tobolsk, which was published with corrections in
1730 at Stockholm. Opposite the mouth of the Indigirka this map bears
an inscription in Latin:

From here the Russians, traversing a sea blocked with ice, which the
north wind drove to the shore and the south wind drove back, reached
the region of Kamtchatka with enormous effort and peril to their lives.

In the summer of 1725 Bering reported from Yeniseisk:

If a voyage were commissioned from the mouth of the Kolyma to the
Anadyr, to reach which is in every way possible, as the new maps of

Asia testify and the inhabitants tell that a trip was made by this route heretofore, the desired [i.e., the solution of the problem of whether Asia is connected with America] would be attained at the smallest cost, that is, with more dispatch than via Okhotsk and Kamtchatka.

In 1711 a Yakutsk serving-man, Pyotr Popov, was ordered to Cape Dezhnev to levy tribute in furs among the local ("headland") Tchuktchi. But the hostile Tchuktchi living on the cape declared to Popov: "Russians came before this to the Tchuktchi in *kotchi* by sea, and that time the Tchuktchi did not pay any tribute in furs to the Russians, and they will not pay now." The words of the Tchuktchi confirm beyond a doubt the fact of Dezhnev's voyage.

Finally, Y. I. Lindenau, a translator with the Kamtchatka Expedition, relates, in his *Description of the Land of the Tchuktchi and Its Location* [1742], the words of the Tchuktchi of Cape Dezhnev to the effect that some seventy years before more than twelve *kotchi* containing Russians from Srednekolymsk had crossed, one party to Kamtchatka, and the other landing due to bad weather "on the island called the Great Land (Alaska)"; here the Russians intermarried with the inhabitants of the Great Land. There is no doubt that one of the episodes from Dezhnev's voyage is meant.

As we see, Dezhnev's expedition in Siberia was known even before Müller. The authenticity of the voyage is fully confirmed by the words of the Tchuktchi. But to Academician G. F. Müller, a member of Bering's expedition, belongs great credit for immortalizing Dezhnev's historic exploits. In 1737 he found genuine reports and petitions by Dezhnev in the local archives at Yakutsk, the value of which he appreciated at once. This discovery was immediately reported to Petersburg. In the journal of the Admiralty College of December 20, 1737, it is noted that "there has been received from Bering an opinion by the corresponding professors there [at Yakutsk], who report that a voyage by sea, not only from the Lena to the Kolyma, but from the latter around the Tchukotsk Headland to the Anadyr River, took place previously."

The first printed information about Dezhnev's voyage was published in an anonymous article, "Information Concerning the Northern Voyage of the Russians from the Mouths of Certain Rivers Emptying into the Arctic Sea." This article, which appeared in an "Appendix to the St. Petersburg Gazette" of June 21, 1742, stems from the pen of Academician G. F. Müller, as has been established by F. A. Knyazev, director of archives of the Academy of Sciences of the USSR. And then Dezhnev's reports are printed in their entirety in *Addenda to Historical Records* (IV, 1851). Certain new materials were reported by N. Ogloblin in 1890.

Let us return to Dezhnev's journey. Thus, subsequent to October 1, 1648, Dezhnev's *kotch* was cast up on shore by the storm somewhere to the south of the mouth of the Anadyr. Dezhnev's detachment, consisting of twenty-five men, set out for the mouth of this river and constructed winter quarters there. By summer only twelve men remained of Dezhnev's detachment; the rest had perished from hunger and from insupportable hardships. In the summer of 1649, those who remained alive built a *kotch* and ascended the Anadyr, on the middle course of which they encountered the Yukaghir tribes—the Anauli, Tchuvantsi, and Khodyntsi. Here they built the Anadyr winter quarters, where they spent the winter of 1649-1650. In the spring of 1650 Semyon Motora's detachment arrived here, coming from Nizhnekolymsk across the mountains.

During his sojourn on the Anadyr, Dezhnev mapped this river from its headwaters to its mouth, as well as a portion of the Anyui River (a tributary of the Kolyma).

In his reports he gave a short, but detailed description of the natural features of the Anadyr territory. "The Anadyr River," writes Dezhnev, "is unforested and there is little sable along it." Six or seven days' journey from the headwaters grows the *maly listvyak,* i.e., thin larch woods of the genus *Larix dahurica.* This observation is quite correct: larch is distributed only on the upper course of the Anadyr, not extending farther south than a latitude of 65° north (a little above Markov). "And of other deciduous forest there is none, except birch and aspen groves, and from Maly Mayen [Main] there is no forest at all besides willow groves." By birch groves are meant clumps of white birch *(Betula Cajanderi),* encountered on elevated locations in the valleys. Dezhnev gave the name of aspen groves to woods of aromatic poplar *(Populus suaveolens)*; even today this tree is called aspen among the inhabitants on the Anadyr. It is strange that Dezhnev does not mention the Korean willow *(Salix macrolepis),* which is incorrectly called poplar on the Anadyr today.

Further on, Dezhnev writes: "And the forest does not extend far from the banks; all is tundra and rock." This is also a true observation: with the exception of the larch forest on the upper course of the Anadyr, forests of Korean willow, aromatic popular and, in places, white birch are encountered exclusively in the river valleys in the basin of this river; the valley of the Anadyr itself in its middle and lower part is treeless[4] as Dezhnev correctly notes.

"And there are many red fish, and this fish comes in great numbers from the mouth of the Anadyr, and is found in small numbers on the upper river, because this fish dies on the upper Anadyr, and does not swim back to the sea." Here is meant the Siberian salmon of the genus *Oncorhynchus (Oncorhynchus keta),* which enters the Anadyr in great

[4] V. B. Sotchaba, "Forest Boundaries in Extreme Northeastern Asia," *Priroda Magazine,* No. 12, 1929, p. 1070.

numbers from the sea. And in fact it invariably dies following spawning.

Dezhnev did not return to Yakutia until 1662. From here he was shortly thereafter ordered to Moscow with "ivory" (i.e., walrus tooth). Here Dezhnev submitted a petition, in which he reported that he had received no wages either in money, bread, or salt from 1643 to 1661. One hundred twenty-six rubles, twenty kopecks in all, were credited for payment to him. It was decreed that Dezhnev be given, from the Siberian *Prikaz,* a third in money and two-thirds in cloth. Finally, in February 1665, Dezhnev received 38 rubles and 67 kopecks in money and 97 arshins of cloth—cherry colored and green—and in addition it was ordered that "for his, Senka's, service and for his discovery of fish tooth and bone and for his wounds he should be made an ataman." Thereupon Dezhnev was sent back to Yakutsk "with state treasure in money." En route Dezhnev visited his native Ustyug.

In 1670 the Yakutsk governor, Prince Baryatsky, commissioned Dezhnev to take back revenue in sable and various official documents from Yakutsk to Moscow. Dezhnev delivered all this in its entirety, the trip requiring one year and five months. He was already over sixty. The wounds and hardships that he had undergone in remote districts told on his health and in 1673 this outstanding man died in Moscow.

The name of Dezhnev will remain forever in the history of the great geographic discoveries. He was the first to confirm the conjecture of Dmitry Gerasimov concerning the possibility of a northern sea route.

Fifty years ago, in 1898, Dezhnev's name was assigned to the "Great Rocky Headland" or "East Cape" of the old maps at the request of the Geographical Society. Today it is proposed to immortalize Dezhnev's exploit by erecting monuments to him in Veliky Ustyug, Vologda, as well as on Cape Dezhnev (in the form of a lighthouse).

IV. The Discovery of the American Coast of Bering Strait by Fyodorov and Gvozdev

Neither Dezhnev nor Bering (1728) saw the American coast of Bering Strait. The honor of discovering both shores of this strait belongs, not to Cook (1778), as is commonly thought, but to second mate Ivan Fyodorov and his assistant, the surveyor Mikhail Gvozdev. Setting out from the mouth of the Kamtchatka River on July 23, 1732, they headed for the region of the cape that today bears the name of Dezhnev. Having inspected the islands of Ratmanov and Kreuzenstern in Bering Strait, they set out for the American shore towards the cape which today bears the name of Cape Prince of Wales, and in December 1732 sent a detailed report of the voyage to their superior in Anadyrsk, Captain

Pavlutsky. In 1741 a map of this remarkable voyage was prepared at Okhotsk, which was long considered lost, but which was recently found in Moscow by A. V. Yefimov, corresponding member of the AS of the USSR.

The discoveries of Fyodorov were well known in Petersburg in the middle of the eighteenth century, and on the map, *Nouvelle carte des decouvertes faites pas des vaissaux russiens aux côtes inconnues de l'Amerique septentrionale avec les pays adjacents,* prepared by Academician G. F. Müller in 1754 and printed in 1758, the gulf between Asia and America bears the inscription on the American shore: "Côte decouverte par le Geodesisre Gwosdew en 1730" (actually, the coast was discovered in 1732).

Thus, Ivan Fyodorov, who saw both shores of the Bering Strait and who supplied material for the preparation of a map, completed the work of Dezhnev[5] in a fitting manner.

[5] For details and bibliography on Dezhnev, see: L. S. Berg, *The Discovery of Kamtchatka and the Expeditions of Bering, 1725-1742,* third ed., Leningrad, 1946, pp. 379; V. A. Samoilov, *Semyon Dezhnev and His Time, with an Appendix of Reports and Petitions by Semyon Dezhnev Concerning His Expeditions and Discoveries,* Publishing House of the Central Board of Administration of the Northern Sea Route (in part, according to a previous work), Moscow, 1945, p. 150.

11. Kliuchevsky: the reforms of Peter the Great

VASILI OSIPOVITCH KLIUCHEVSKY (1841-1911), is Russia's most famous historian. Son of a village priest, he succeeded Sergei Soloviev as professor of history at the University of Moscow in 1879, remaining there until his death. His primary interest was the social and economic history of Russia. Kliuchevsky's historical masterpiece was the monumental *Kurs Russkoi Istorii* (*Course of Russian History*), based on his highly popular lectures, which was published from 1904 to 1910. A fifth volume based on his notes appeared in 1921. One volume of this work was devoted to the social and administrative changes undertaken by Peter the Great, of whom Kliuchevsky is still one of the best interpreters.

The excerpts on Peter's reforms presented below have been translated from *Kurs Russkoi Istorii* (2nd ed., Part IV. Moscow: State Publishing House, 1923), pp. 273-283.

... This is not all that Peter did. But this is precisely what he wanted to do with the help of Western Europe. Peter called on the Western European to work and teach the Russians in the broad area of military technique, national economy, financial, administrative, and technical knowledge. He did not want to adopt from the West the ready-made fruits of their technique, but to master it, to transplant to Russia the industrial production itself, together with the skill and technical knowledge. The thought that dimly glimmered in the best minds of the seventeenth century was the necessity, first of all, to increase the productive capacity of the people by directing it with the help of technical knowledge toward the exploitation of the untapped natural resources of the country, in order to enable it to carry out the increased responsibilities of the state. This is the idea with which Peter was imbued, and which he carried out as no one ever did before or since his time. In this respect, he is unique in our history. Likewise in foreign policy he concentrated all the national strength on the solution of the task that seemed to him most important for the national economy—the Baltic question.

He introduced into the national economy so many new productive enterprises that it is difficult to evaluate them. The tangible evidence of this increased wealth was not manifested in an over-all rise in the national standard of living, but in the state treasury. The war, with its consequences, drained off all the increased earnings. The reform of the national economy was transformed into a financial reform and it resulted in financial success, not in a successful national economy. When Pososhkov[1] wrote to Peter in 1724 that it is easy to fill the national treasury, but "it is a great and very difficult task to enrich all the people," he expressed not merely a truism of political economy but the sorrowful observation of thoughtful contemporaries about what was taking place before their very eyes. The workers to whom Peter fell heir worked not for themselves but for the state, and, after more intensive and better work than their fathers ever accomplished, in the end they emerged even poorer. Peter did not leave the state one kopeck in debt, nor did he spend one single working day at the expense of future generations. On the contrary, he bequeathed to his successors abundant reserves, on which they subsisted for a long time but to which they added nothing. His superiority over them lies in the fact that he was not a debtor, but a creditor of the future. However, this pertains to the results of the reform, of which we shall speak later. Summing up Peter's activities, exclusive of foreign defence and the international position of the state, but with reference to the improvement of the national welfare, it can be said of Peter's broad plans for the national economy —the basis of his reform—that his failure was inherent in the course which this reform took; its main result was expressed in terms of financial successes.

Thus Peter took from old Russia state power, supreme authority, the law, and the class structure, but from the West he adopted the technical know-how for the building up of the army, the navy, the state and national economy, and government institutions. Where then, you might ask, was the upheaval which renewed or distorted the Russian way of life from top to bottom, which gave it not only new forms but new principles, good or evil, as the case may be? This was the impression of Peter's contemporaries, nevertheless, who transmitted it to the next generation. The reform, if it did not renew, at least stirred up Russian life profoundly, not so much by its innovations as by certain methods; not by its character, but by its temperament, if one may say so. The results of the reform were directed for the most part to the future, and

---

[1] Ivan T. Pososhkov (1670-1726), a highly articulate trader and small businessman, an admirer of Peter the Great, whose major work, *A Book on Poverty and Wealth,* led to his imprisonment after Peter's death. (Eds.)

its essence was far from being understood by everyone, but its methods were felt, first of all, by Peter's own contemporaries. They had a direct impact, with which Peter had to reckon. These methods were the product of Peter's personal character, of the conditions under which his reform took place, and of the situation with which he had to cope vis-à-vis the mode of life, concepts, and customs of the people. The reform was conditioned by foreign war and internal strife. Although the war served as the mainspring of the reform movement, it had a most adverse effect on its course and success. The reform took place in an atmosphere of confusion, the usual concomitant of war. The requirements and difficulties which war entailed at every step forced Peter to do everything in a hurry. The war lent to the reform a nervous and feverish tempo and an unhealthily accelerated pace. . . .

Moreover, the reform took place in the midst of blind and stubborn domestic strife which often burst into violence. There were four terrible uprisings and three or four conspiracies, all of which were aimed against the innovations and all of which were based on the appeal to the past, its concepts and prejudices. Hence Peter's hostile attitude toward his country's past, toward the people's mode of life, his tendentious persecution of certain outward features which expressed these concepts and prejudices. Peter's attitude was a direct product of his political education. His political concepts and feelings were an outgrowth of trouble, of the struggle engendered by two trends which split Russian society in the seventeenth century: the advocates of change who turned for help and instruction to the West, and who clashed with the political and religious Old Believers. The beards, clothes, etc., of the latter were the outward symbols which distinguished the old Russian from the Western European. These outward distinctions did not in themselves, of course, obstruct the reform, but the sentiments and convictions of those who wore them did serve as a serious obstacle: they were the signs of opposition, the symbols of protest. Having taken the side of the innovators, Peter hotly attacked these trivialities, which served as a cover for old traditions dear to the Russian. . . .

All this might have been amusing if it were not contemptible. For the first time Russian legislation, abandoning its serious tone, degraded itself by dealing with trifling matters better left to hairdressers and tailors. How much irritation and hostility were generated by these caprices! And this needless legislation also hampered the cause of the reform. Such trivialities and numerous difficulties explain the relatively modest results achieved by Peter in the domestic system, successes not commensurate with the cost and sacrifices involved. It is astonishing how much labor was invested in the course of the reform to produce even modest successes. Even such an ardent supporter as Pososhkov had to admit this and beautifully described how badly Peter handled this affair, pulling uphill alone, while millions pulled downhill. . . .

A reforming zeal and reliance on autocracy—these were Peter's two hands, which did not work in harmony, but rather one obstructed and paralyzed the energy of the other. . . .

Thus, without exaggerating or belittling the work of Peter the Great, we can express its significance, as follows: The reform itself was an outgrowth of the daily needs of the state and the people, instinctively felt by a powerful and talented man with a sensitive mind and strong character, . . . such a man as for no apparent reason mankind produces from time to time. With these features, animated by a sense of duty and a determination "not to spare his own life in the service of the fatherland," Peter took his place at the head of a people which, as compared with other European nations, was, historically speaking, at a disadvantage. This people had found the strength toward the end of the sixteenth century to build a great state, one of the largest in Europe; but in the seventeenth century it began to feel that it lacked the material and spiritual attributes to maintain its 800-year-old structure. The reform carried out by Peter the Great was not aimed directly at rebuilding the political, social, or moral order already established, nor was it aimed at refashioning Russian life in accordance with an unaccustomed Western European pattern, or at the introduction of newly adopted principles. It was limited to arming the Russian state with ready-made Western European intellectual and material resources, thus placing the state on a level commensurate with its position in Europe, and at raising the productive capacity of the people to full strength. . . .

In conclusion, let us attempt to provide our own estimate of Peter's reform. The contradictions in his work, the mistakes and vacillation, at times giving way to obstinacy, his weakness in civic affairs, his inhuman cruelty over which he exercised no restraint and, along with these traits, his wholehearted love for the fatherland, his unflagging devotion to his work, his broad, enlightened view of his own tasks, his bold plans, conceived with creative genius and executed with incomparable energy, and finally the successes achieved by the incredible sacrifices of the people and by the great efforts of the reformer—such a variety of features do not lend themselves to creation of a unified image. The prevalence of lights or shades in the impressions of those who studied him either led to unqualified praise or unqualified criticism; but the criticism prevailed because even the good deeds were carried out by obnoxious force.

Peter's reform represented a struggle of despotism with the people's inertia. He hoped by the threat of his power to arouse independent initiative in a serf society, and strove with the help of the slaveholding nobility to introduce into Russia European science and national education as the indispensable prerequisite to social initiative. He wanted the serf, while remaining a serf, to act consciously and freely. The conjunction of despotism and freedom, enlightenment and serfdom, amounted to a political squaring of the circle, to a riddle which people have tried without success to solve during the two centuries since Peter's time. Moreover, the people of the eighteenth century have already tried to find some means of reconciling Peter's reforms with humanitarianism. Prince Shcherbatov,[2] an enemy of autocracy, devoted an entire treatise ("conversation") to the explanation and even justification of Peter's absolutism and vices. He recognized the enlightenment introduced into Russia by Peter the Great as a personal good deed and attacked Peter's critics, who themselves received from the autocracy the very enlightenment which helped them to understand the evil inherent in it.

Peter's faith in the miraculous power of education, with which he was imbued, and his reverence for the cult of science, forcefully kindled in the minds of the serfs a spark of enlightenment, which gradually flared up into an intelligent striving for truth, that is, for freedom.

Autocracy in itself is repugnant as a political principle. It will never receive recognition from the civilian conscience, but we can reconcile ourselves to a person in whom this unnatural power is combined with self-sacrifice, when the autocrat, without sparing himself, stops at nothing to promote the general welfare, risking destruction by hurling himself against obstacles which cannot be overcome, including those of his own making. Thus we reconcile ourselves to the impetuous spring storm which, while breaking down century-old trees, freshens the air and with its downpour helps the new seed to sprout.

---

[2] Mikhail M. Shcherbatov (1733-1790), historian and writer, author of the seven-volume *History of Russia from Ancient Times* (to 1610). (Eds.)

12. the first Russian newspaper:

Vedomosti

Vedomosti (*Record, Register*), the first printed Russian newspaper, appeared in Moscow, January 2, 1703, in the reign of Peter I. Its full title was "A Record of Military and Other Affairs Worthy of Knowledge and Recording, which Have Occurred in the Moscow State and Other Adjacent Countries." Thirty-nine issues appeared in 1703, with a circulation of one thousand copies. This newspaper was published without interruption until 1727, when the Academy of Sciences introduced the *St. Petersburg Vedomosti*.

A translation of the first number of *Vedomosti,* January 2, 1703, is given below. See *Khrestomatiya po istorii SSSR,* Vol. II (Moscow, 1953), 115-116.

In Moscow 400 bronze cannon, howitzers, and mortars have recently been cast for 24, 18, and 12-pound shells. The howitzers are for bombs weighing a pood [40 Russian pounds] and a halfpood [20 Russian pounds]. The mortars are for nine, three, and two-pood bombs, and less. There are also many big and medium-sized molds prepared for casting cannon, howitzers, and mortars. And now at the arsenal over 40,000 poods of copper await further casting.

By order of His Majesty, the Moscow schools are multiplying; forty-five men are enrolled in philosophy and have already completed dialectics.

In the Mathematics and Navigation School over 300 men are enrolled and they are doing well in their studies.

From November 24 to December 24, there were 386 births, male and female, in Moscow.

Dispatch from Persia. The Indian Tsar has bestowed upon our great sovereign an elephant and many other gifts. The elephant has travelled overland from the city of Shemakha to Astrakhan.

Dispatch from Kazan. Along the river Sok a great deal of oil and copper ore have been discovered; from this ore a handsome amount of copper has been smelted, which is expected to provide a substantial profit for the Moscow state.

Dispatch from Siberia. In the Chinese Empire the Jesuits are greatly disliked for their cunning, and some of them have been put to death.

Dispatch from Olonets [east of Lake Ladoga]. The priest, Ivan Okulov, of the city of Olonets, having assembled thousands of our volunteers, has crossed the Swedish border and has defeated the Swedes at the posts of Rugozensk, Gipponsk, Sumersk, and Kerisursk. At these posts a large number of Swedes has been killed and a cavalry banner, drums, and swords, as well as a substantial number of muskets and horses, have been taken. The priest has distributed to his soldiers the supplies and belongings that were seized. All the rest of the things, even the grain supplies that he could not take with him, he burned. He also burned Solovsky manor and many other nearby manors, and about a thousand village houses. According to the tales of the prisoners at the above-mentioned posts, 50 Swedish cavalrymen were killed and 400 foot soldiers; 50 horsemen and 100 foot soldiers escaped. Of the priest's troops, only two were wounded.

Dispatch from Lvov. December 14. The Cossack forces under Colonel Samusem are increasing daily. In Nemirov, they cut down the commandant together with his warriors, seized the city, and already intend to take Belaya Tserkov, since Palei will join forces with their troops; already it is reported that they have joined forces, and will have altogether an army of 12,000 men. The Lithuanian Hetman is en route to his army near Brest-Litovsk. Part of the Swedish army, according to secretary Orukho, is in Kazimir, part is stationed in Sandomir, and it is reported to be en route through great Poland to Prussian territory. . . .

From Nien [Nienshantz] *in Ingermanland* [Ingria], October 16. We are living here under poor circumstances, since Moscow treats this region very badly, and for this reason many people, out of fear, are leaving for Viborg and Finland, taking the best of their possessions with them.

The high fortress of Oreshek [Schlusselburg] forty versts from here, which is surrounded by water, is besieged in force by Moscow troops; already more than four volleys from about 20 guns have been fired and more than 1500 bombs thrown. Nevertheless, the damage to date has been slight, and it will be very difficult for them to capture this fort.

From Narva, October 13. On September 26, a Moscow army of ten thousand men advanced on this side of the river Neva near Notenburg between the Russian and Ingermanland borders. It stopped there and began to dig trenches, 500 steps from the fortress on its side of the river. Our troops under General Kroniort are located on the far side of the river, between it and Notenburg. Not all of them have infantry and cavalry and shells, but they prevent the Russian troops from crossing the river Neva, whenever they attempt to do so. They intend to shell the fort at Notenburg, but it is constructed entirely of stone and the troops besieged there are good. Recently 400 were brought in, and so at present there is nothing to fear.

From Amsterdam, November 10. From the city of Archangel, September 20, comes the report that after his Imperial Majesty dispatched his troops in several ships to the White Sea, he himself followed them, and sent the vessels back to the city of Archangel, where 15,000 soldiers are stationed, and 600 men are working on the new fortress on the Dvinka.

13. St. Petersburg: the new capital

THE EXCERPTS BELOW are from the notes of a contemporary, a member of the Polish embassy. They include a description of the new capital of Peter I and a short account of its history. The notes are dated 1720.

From *Russkaya Starina,* (No. 6, 1879), pp. 265-267.

Whoever wishes to describe St. Petersburg properly should have been there prior to its founding and seen what this place, where a large stone city has now been constructed, was like then. The broad and deep river Neva with its tributaries flows through it. The city is uniformly settled along the banks of the wide canals which traverse it.

In this place, as I learned, there were formerly no more than fifteen huts, in which Swedish fishermen lived. After Moscow occupied this country, the village was burned, and the Tsar ordered the construction here of a small two-room house, in which he himself lived. This little house is still standing. It is covered with tiles, but has no windows. For its better protection, it has been fenced. It is located on the river bank between the Senate and the palace of Gagarin. While living in it, the Tsar laid out the plan of the city, measured the river's banks, its tributaries, and the canals. Already this is a big city, and if the Tsar lives he will make it huge. On the other side of the river, on the road to the monastery, there used to be a fort, where ships anchored en route by sea from Moscow state via Lake Ladoga. This fort has now been demolished and in its place were built many small, ordinary izbas and a windmill. Now there are many buildings here.

. . . Near St. Petersburg the Tsar has reinforced the banks of the river, built a dam and lock, and dug canals, in order to dispose of the surplus waters borne in by the wind from the sea. If this had not been done, the waves would have flooded the buildings. The locks above were covered with boards, so that people could cross them on horseback. The closer it comes to the sea, the wider flows the Neva; and it divides into several tributaries, which branch out in various directions. On the banks of these tributaries, piles have now been driven, and in other places the banks have been levelled so that vessels could make their approach. Whenever necessary, the river bed has been widened, raised, and deepened.

This city, where any senator, minister, and boyar must have a palace, sprawls over a tremendous area; one person even built three palaces when so ordered. Fortunate was the man who was allocated a dry spot; but the one to whom fell marsh and swamp perspired, while he built a foundation and cleared the land, since the closer to the sea the more swampy and boggy the soil. Even now, although houses have been built, they shake whenever a carriage passes nearby. This is the result of a jerry-built foundation. This part already has the aspect of a city. There are homes here, locks, and huge buildings with wings and conveniences. Further in the direction of Kronstadt, there are many places where construction has already begun and where several thousand persons of the lower middle class have already settled right on the seacoast.

Here there are churches, colleges, palaces, and so-called shops where one can get everything. This is a four-cornered structure, in which merchants live on every side. The palaces are tremendous stone buildings, with wings, kitchens, and conveniences; only they were built hastily, so that even with a little wind the tiles fall. They must be of poor material or were built in winter, since summer does not last long here. Half of this city has not yet been built.

On this side of the Neva, homes are located, extending right up to the Tsars' palaces, of which there are three: two for summer and one for winter. The gardens are beautiful. I heard the Tsar himself say: "If I live three years, I'll have a better garden than the French King's Versailles." And, indeed, a host of marble statues and columns has been brought here from Venice, Italy, England, and Holland; even an entire arbor of alabaster and marble has been brought from Venice for the garden located right on the river between the canals.[1] There are a great many remarkable things here: arbors, galleries, pumps, and unusually beautiful trees. On the side of the river near the garden a stone wall has been erected; the galleries lead to the river, where one can go sailing in a small boat, galley, yacht, or ice-boat, or can stroll along the canal and the big, wide river. There is an island in the river, on which houses are being constructed, and to which a museum (*Kunstkamere*) will be moved.

---

[1] Reference is made to the St. Petersburg Summer Garden.

14. the founding of the Academy of Sciences

PETER THE GREAT, after his tour of Western Europe, was determined to transform backward Russia into a modern, industrial state, in which science and learning flourished. He sought, among other things, to establish a learned society after the pattern of the Royal Society of London, the Académie des Sciences in Paris, and the Berlin Academy of Sciences. The initiative came from the monarch, for there was as yet no university in Russia. It was for this reason that Peter sought to combine a learned scientific society with a university. Peter consulted scholars inside Russia and abroad in connection with this project. In January, 1724, a detailed plan for the St. Petersburg Academy of Sciences (to which were attached an academic university and a gymnasium) was sent to the Senate. Of necessity, the new Academy was at first staffed by foreign scholars, principally by Germans, and for some years largely by foreign students. Peter's death (January 28, 1725) occurred before his plans were brought to fruition. His wife and successor, Catherine I, formally established the Academy by a decree of December 7, 1725. Emphasis was placed on the sciences, especially on mathematics, since more than half of the sixteen original members of the Academy were specialists in that field.

The excerpt below is translated from the decree of Peter I, January 28, 1724. See *Khrestomatiya po istorii SSSR*, Vol. II (Moscow, 1953), 128-129.

... To set up an Academy for instruction in languages, other sciences, and the well-known arts, and for the translation of books. ... There shall be allocated for its maintenance the income from customs and licence fees collected from the cities of Narva, Derpat, Pernov, and Arensburg, amounting to 24,912 rubles. ...

As regards the arts and sciences, two different types of institution are in general use: the first is called a university, the second an academy or "society" for the arts and sciences. . . .

Since at present no institution for the cultivation of the arts and sciences exists in Russia, it is therefore impossible to follow here the accepted pattern of other states; but in view of the status of our empire, it is proper for the intellectual development of teachers and students that such an institution be set up as will not only redound to the glory of this state through the dissemination of science in our times, but will also be of advantage to our people in the future through training and the acquisition of learning.

The founding merely of an academy of sciences would not fulfill both purposes; for although under these conditions the promotion and dissemination of the arts and sciences would be achieved, they would not bear fruit quickly among the people; and the organization of a university would accomplish still less. When we realize that there are as yet no ordinary schools, *gymnaziya,* and seminaries in which young people would begin their education and then proceed to more advanced sciences to equip themselves fully with knowledge, it is clearly impossible for a university to be of any use in such a situation.

And so it would be best of all for us if a society were set up, comprised of the best scholars capable of 1) advancing and perfecting science, as well as 2) teaching young people publicly and 3) instructing some persons individually, who in turn would teach young people the elements of all the sciences.

In this fashion, one institution at little expense would accomplish as much as three separate societies in other countries.

Reference

VUCINICH, ALEXANDER, *Science in Russian Culture. A history to 1860.* Stanford: Stanford University Press, 1963, pp. 65-74.

15. the problem of Old Russian

culture: a discussion

THE DISCUSSION ON "The Problem of Old Russian Culture," from which the following excerpts have been taken, appeared in the *Slavic Review,* Vol. XXI (No. 1, March, 1962), 1-15; and Vol. XXII (No. 1, March, 1963), 115-120. Father Florovsky, author of the first excerpt, is a professor of Eastern church history at Harvard Divinity School. D. S. Likhachev, author of the last two sections, is a Corresponding Member, Academy of Sciences, USSR, and professor at Leningrad University. For the balance of this discussion, see Vol. XXI (No. 1, March, 1962), 16-42. Reprinted by permission.

> Die wahre Kritik liegt im Verständnis.
> *Bachofen,* Antiquarische Briefe

GEORGE FLOROVSKY

I. The Pattern of Interpretation

There was, in Russian historiography of the last century, an established pattern of interpretation, and, to some extent, it is still commonly used. It was traditional to divide the history of Russia into two parts, and to divide it sharply and rigidly: the Old and the New, Ancient and Modern. The time of Peter the Great was regarded as the Great Divide, as the decisive turning point in the total process. Of course, it was much more than a chronological demarcation. Passionate value judgments were implied therein. Kliuchevsky has rightly stated: "The whole philosophy of our history was often reduced to the appraisal of Peter's reform; by a certain scholarly foreshortening, the whole problem of the meaning of Russian history was condensed into one single question—about the deed of Peter and the relation of his new reformed Russia to the old." The

81

Old Russia was regarded and evaluated in the perspective of the New, in the light of "the Reform." In fact, this approach was itself an integral part of the Reform, and its most ponderous legacy. This pattern of interpretation was first invented by the pioneers of the Reform in order to justify the break, which was intended to be radical and definitive, and then it was maintained in its defense. The story of Old Russia had to be presented in such a way as to show that the Reform was inevitable, necessary, and just. "The Old" meant in this connection the obsolete, sterile and stagnant, primitive and backward. And "the New" was depicted, by contrast, in the brightest colors as a great achievement and a glorious promise. The whole history of Old Russia, before Peter, was usually treated as a kind of prehistory—a dark background against which the whole splendor of the new cultural awakening could be spectacularly presented; or as a protracted period of infancy and immaturity, in which the normal growth of the nation was inhibited and arrested; or else as a lengthy preparation for that messianic age which had finally descended upon Russia, under Peter and by his sovereign will, from abroad if not from above. "History," in the proper sense of the word, was supposed to have begun in Russia only with Peter. It was assumed that only at his time did Russia enter the stage of history and civilization—indeed as a belated newcomer, sorely delayed in development, and thereby destined to tarry for a long time in the humble position of a learner, in the commonwealth of cultured nations.

There were manifold variations on this basic theme in Russian historiography. For our immediate purpose it would suffice to quote but one of them. Sergius M. Soloviev had the reputation of a sober historian, and he well deserved the praise. His monumental *History of Russia from the Oldest Times* is still the most reliable survey of the subject, well documented and skillfully arranged. It is highly significant that Soloviev simply loses his temper when he comes to the times of Peter, to the Reform. About Peter he writes in a very special style, passionate, nervous, and pathetic, at once elevated, ornate, and excited. It is the style of heroic legend. Indeed, for Soloviev, Peter was *the* hero of Russian history, probably the only hero, and the last one. "Only Christian faith and the nearness in time saves us—and still incompletely—from the cult of this demigod and from the mythical conceptions about the exploits of this Hercules." Peter was almost a supernatural being. "The period of heroes comes to its end with the coming of civilization." Peter concludes the epic period of Russian history and opens the era of civilization for Russia. It means that for Soloviev there was no civilization in Russia before Peter, even if there was an enormous dynamic potential—in the state of chaotic fermentation. The change under Peter was most radical: from epic to history—from prehistory to history proper. Only since Peter has Russia become an "historic" nation.

There is in this interpretation a striking discrepancy between the political and the cultural course of the process. The political history of Russia was continuous from the very beginning, through the Reform—in spite of its cataclysmic character—up to the present. Old Russia was just a stage in the formation of the definitive Russian Empire. The unity of Russian history is seen precisely in the history of the Russian state. On the other hand, there is a radical discontinuity in the history of Russian culture. The culture of Old Russia has been simply dismissed, and it is assumed that it had to be dismissed and discarded, and replaced by another. It was not a link in the continuous chain. There was rather no such continuous chain at all. The true Russian culture had to be created afresh; actually, it had to be imported. As Soloviev phrased it himself, "It was the turn of the Russian people to serve a foreign principle." The true history of Russian culture is, from this point of view, the history of Western culture in Russia. Old Russia was contrasted with the New as a "primitive society" with the "civilized." Many Russian historians of the last century were using these and similar phrases. Theodore I. Buslaev, one of the great founders of Russian historical philology, could not find in Old Russia any trace of genuine culture: no intellectual curiosity, no aesthetic vision, no literary skill. There was no dynamism, no advance whatever. In the same vein, A. N. Pypin would contend that actually there was almost no "chronology" in the history of Old Russian literature. For Buslaev the whole period of Russian history up to Peter could be characterized by two words: "primitivism" *(pervobytnost')* and "stagnation" *(velikoe kosnenie russkago naroda).* From this point of view, Old Russian culture was to be studied by archaeologists, not by historians. Indeed, it was under the guise of "Russian antiquities" that the history of Old Russian culture was studied in the last century. The term "culture" is often used in a wider sense to include "primitive cultures." In that sense one could also speak of Old Russian culture, but only in that sense. It was a field for antiquaries, not for historians.

The line of Russian cultural development was not merely bent but really broken. The old order had passed away. Old Russia was a dead world. It had to be admitted, however, that the Reform, as radically as it had been conceived from the beginning, was not accomplished at once. The old world was terribly shaken, but it did not disappear. Much of the old order survived, but only beneath the level of "civilization" in those strata of the nation which resisted the Reform and attempted an escape. But these strata were, in a sense, outside history, and it had to be hoped that finally, with the spread of "enlightenment," they would also be dragged in. What remained from the old order was no more than "survivals." As Pypin said, "The life of the small civilized class was surrounded by the element of old custom." All survivals were actually in the realm of customs and routine, in that realm which is denoted by the untranslatable Russian word, *byt.* But *byt,* at its best, is no more than a dead mask of culture. The Reform had split the nation into two parts:

the civilized elite and the masses. It was in the masses that relics of Old Russia had been preserved. It was assumed that in good time they would be completely discarded. . . .

The vision of the contemporary historian has been drastically enlarged in recent decades. The fiction of "unchanging Russia," ever the same for several centuries, in which many historians of older generations were still able to believe, has crumbled. One is bound to distinguish ages and stages. "Old Russia" appears to be an artificial and unhistorical concept. One must speak rather of various local cultures—of Ancient Kiev, of Novgorod, Tver, Moscow, and the like, and of Western Russia. These local cultures were, of course, interrelated and ultimately integrated into one great national culture. But first of all they must be understood in their distinctive characters. Some regional studies in the field of Old Russian culture were initiated already in the last century, and a number of provocative observations were accumulated. But much has been left undone. On the other hand, there was in these regional studies a tendency to overstress local distinctions. In any case, it is still too early to attempt a synthetic description of Old Russia as a whole. Obviously, there were deep internal tensions within the realm of Old Russian culture. The cultures of all societies are more or less stratified: there are always different levels and high culture is always kept and promoted by a minority, the leading and creative elite. The problem is much more intricate and complex than was admitted by the historians of earlier generations.

The time has come when the story of Old Russia must be carefully revised and probably rewritten. This time it must be written as a history in its own right, and not just as a preamble to the history of New Russia. Of course, historical interpretation is inevitably retrospective—that is the very heart of the historical method. It was inevitable to look back at Old Russia. What was wrong in the traditional pattern was not the retrospection itself but the unfortunate selection of the observation point— and also the lack of congeniality with the subject of study. . . .

II. The Ways of Old Russia

Old Russia stood in a very definite cultural succession. She was in no sense isolated in the cultural world. She entered the commonwealth of civilized nations when she was christened by the Byzantine. She received then, together with the Christian faith, an impressive cultural dowry— a complex of cultural values, habits, and concerns. The Byzantine inheritance of ancient Kiev was conspicuous. The city itself was an important cultural center, a rival of Constantinople, an adornment of the empire. It was not the only center: Novgorod in any case must be mentioned. The literary production of the Kievan period was intense and diverse.

Russian art was also taking shape. Behind the documents of the time we cannot fail to discern cultural activity, cultural forces. We discern groups and individuals eagerly committed to various cultural tasks. The movement of ideas has already begun.

The Kievan achievement must be regarded in a wider perspective. It was an integral part of the incipient Slavic culture. V. Jagic once suggested that in the tenth century there was a chance that Slavic civilization might have developed as a third cultural power, competing with the Latin and the Greek. The Bulgarian literature of the Simeonic age was already so rich and comprehensive as to stand comparison with the Byzantine. Indeed, it was the same Byzantine literature, but already indigenized. This cultural promise was curtailed and frustrated. The great cultural impetus was checked. Yet the promise was real, and the actual achievement was by no means negligible. Of course, this incipient Slavic civilization was deeply rooted in the Byzantine tradition, just as Western culture was rooted in the traditions of the classical world. But it was more than a repetition or an imitation. It was an indigenous response to the cultural challenge. And it was mainly from Bulgaria that a rich supply of literary monuments was transferred to Kiev and other centers. Cultural taste and skill were formed. Cultural interests were aroused. Kievan Russia was not isolated from the rest of the Slavic world, as it was not separated from Byzantium and the West, or from the East. Kievan Russia was able to respond conscientiously to the cultural challenge. The ground was already prepared. . . .

. . . Quite recently the late Professor George Fedotov suggested that the cause of Old Russian backwardness, and indeed the tragedy of Russian culture at large, was precisely the attempt at indigenization. He had serious doubts about the benefits of the use of the Slavic vernacular. Having received the Bible and a vast amount of various religious writings in their own language, the Slavs had no incentive to learn Greek, for translations once made were sufficient for immediate practical needs. They were enclosed, therefore, within the narrow limits of an exclusively religious literature. They were never initiated into the great classical tradition of Hellenic antiquity. If only our ancestors had learned Greek, speculated Professor Fedotov, they could have read Homer, could have philosophized with Plato, could have reached finally the very springs of Greek inspiration. They would have possessed a golden key to classical treasures. But this never happened. Instead they received but *one* Book. While in Paris, a poor and dirty city as it was in the twelfth century, the Schoolmen were already discussing high matters, in the golden and beautiful Kiev there were but monks engaged in writing chronicles and lives of saints. In other words, the weakness and backwardness of Old Russia depended upon that narrow foundation, exclusively religious, on which its culture had been built. The charge is by no means new. The lack of classical tradition was often emphasized as one of the peculiar and distinctive features of Old Russian culture. Fedotov's imaginary picture is pathetic, but is his argument fair and sound? The West seems to have had the golden key of Latin. How many in the West, however, were using that key for the purpose of which Fedotov speaks? And was the Latin known at that time sufficient for the task? Classical values were transmitted rather indirectly through Christian literature. Platonism was accessible through Augustine, Pseudo-Dionysius, Origen, and Gregory of Nyssa. It could be no less readily discovered in Byzantine ecclesiastical sources. The Christian Hellenism of Byzantium neither impresses nor attracts Fedotov. He has a twisted picture of Byzantium: Byzantine Christianity appears to him to be a "religion of fear," of *phobos*; human values were suppressed in it. Anyhow, Fedotov contended that Kievan Russia never accepted this grim version of Christianity and developed its own conception: humanitarian and kenotic. And, in fact, that picture of Kievan Russia which Professor Fedotov himself has given us in his impressive book, *The Russian Religious Mind,* is bright and moving. Kievan Christianity, in his appraisal, has perennial value: "that of a standard, a golden measure, a royal way," in his own phrase. Indeed, we are given to understand that its attainments were so high because the Russians did not follow either the Byzantines or the Bulgarians, because they created their own Christian vision and way. In any case, it appears that Kievan Russia was vigorous and creative—at least in one field. What is more significant, basic human values were firmly established, high ethical standards acknowledged, and personal initiative disclosed and encouraged. There was strong human impetus in the Kievan culture. One has to assume, as was indeed Fedotov's own contention, that cultural growth and advance were impeded at a later stage. The absence of the classical tradition probably was not so tragic and fatal.

There is an increasing tendency in modern historiography to idealize the Russian beginnings. The Kievan period is depicted as a kind of golden age, a golden legend of Russia. Dark times came later—after the Mongolian conquest. There was a visible decline in literary production, and there were no outstanding personalities in this field. A closer scrutiny of extant sources, however, corrects this first impression. Writers of that time, from the twelfth century to the fifteenth, are aware of problems with which they are wrestling—the problems of the artistic craft: problems of style and representation, problems of psychological analysis. There were in Russia at that time not only scribes and *nachetchiks,* but true writers. There were not only skillful craftsmen but real masters in art. The recent studies of D. S. Likhachev are very suggestive, especially his analysis of the problem of man in the literature and art of Old Russia. Behind the stylistic devices used by the artists one can detect their spiritual vision, and this vision was the fruit of reasoning and contemplation. The new wave of the "South Slavic" impact did not mean just a transfer of new literary documents, mainly translations, of spiritual and hagiographical content. It was a wave of inspiration, a deep spiritual movement, stemming from the great Hesychast tradition, revived at that time both in Byzantium and in the restored Bulgarian kingdom. Both writers, chroniclers and hagiographers, and painters, including the iconographers, were fully aware of the problem that they had to wrestle with—the presentation of human personality. It may be true that their concept of personality and character was different from the modern view, and probably at this point their insight was deeper. They did not depict fixed characters; they saw men in process obsessed and confronted with problems, in the state of decision and indecision. One may speak almost of the "existentialist" approach to the problem of man. One may contend that psychology based on the concept of temptation, inner struggle with the passions, conversion and decision, was a deeper psychology than that which would deal with the fixed character. In any case, it is more dynamic and less in danger of falling into schematism of characteristic types. In the great Russian art of the fourteenth and fifteenth centuries one discovers not only a high level of artistic mastery but also deep insights into the mystery of man. And this art was not only produced at that time but appreciated. Obviously, there was both a demand for this high art and an understanding of it, in circles which could not have been very narrow. It would not be an exaggeration to assume that the aesthetic culture of that time was refined and profound. It was still a religious culture, but artistic methods were adequate to the problem of revealing and interpreting the ultimate mysteries of human existence in all its unruly and flexible complexity. The challenge probably came from outside—from Byzantium once more—but the response was spontaneous and creative. There was more than dependence or imitation. There was real response. . . .

The most disquieting question in the history of Old Russian culture is this: What was the reason for what can be described as its intellectual silence? There was a great art, and there was also an intensive creative activity in the political and social field, including ideological speculation. But surely nothing original and outstanding has been produced in the realm of ideas, theological or secular. It was easier to answer this question when it was assumed that Old Russia was simply primitive, slumbering and stagnant. But now we know that in many other respects Old Russia was able to attain a high level. Still one may be tempted by easy answers. It may be suggested, and actually has been suggested more than once, that the "Russian soul" was, by its inner constitution, rather speculative or intuitive than inquisitive, and that therefore the language of art was the only congenial idiom of self-expression. It may be suggested, on the other hand, that the "Russian soul" approached the mystery of Christian faith by way of charity and compassion and was therefore indifferent to the subtleties of theological speculation. It does not help very much if we try to collect scattered data indicating that a certain amount of philosophical information was available to people of Old Russia. A solid amount of patristic writings was indeed in circulation, but there is no proof that theological interest had been awakened. All easy formulas are but evasions. And the riddle remains. Moreover, all speculations that operate with the precarious concept of the "Russian soul" are utterly unsafe. Even if "national souls" do exist, they are made, shaped, and formed in history. For that reason they cannot serve as a principle of interpretation. Again, the character of the "Russian soul" has been so diversely described and defined as to require a thorough re-examination. It has been usual to emphasize the irrational aspect of Russian mentality and its constant lack of form. There is enough evidence to the contrary. With adequate reason it has been contended that the "Russian soul" had always a strong feeling and understanding for order and form, and this specific insight was the root of its great aesthetic achievements. In its extreme expression it led to ritualism, to the worship of external forms. Kliuchevsky had much to say about the thrill of rite and habit when he attempted to explain the genesis of the great Russian *raskol*. And the same striving after orderliness has created in Russia what we call *byt*. Of course, it may be claimed that underneath the *byt* there was always chaos. Finally, we are left with an antinomy, with an unresolved paradox.

In the total perspective of Russian historical development the paradox is even more spectacular. In the later period, after the Reform, Russians have appeared to be probably one of the most intellectual nations in Europe, inwardly troubled by all "damned problems" of religion and metaphysics. Exercise in philosophy, of various shapes and shades, and commitment to theory and speculation were the distinctive mark of the Russian mind in the last two centuries. This striking phenomenon was usually explained by Western influence, direct and indirect. It was suggested that dormant curiosity had been awakened by the challenge of Western thought. One should ask at this point why this intellectual curiosity was not awakened by the challenge of Byzantine civilization, which was renowned and notorious for its unquenchable commitment to speculation, in a measure offensive for the sober taste and mind of the West. Byzantium was not only dogmatic, but ever searching and rather unquiet in its heart. Indeed, Byzantium knew the mystery of harmony and cosmic order. But it also knew the thrill of search and the "clouds of unknowing." But Byzantine challenge did not awaken the alleged Russian soul.

The tragedy of Old Russia, which led to its inner split and impasse, was not a tragedy of primitivism or ignorance, as has been contended more than once. It was a tragedy of cultural aberration. One may suggest that Byzantium had offered too much at once—an enormous richness of cultural material, which simply could not be absorbed at once. The charm of perfection was tempting: should not the whole harmony be transplanted? The heritage was too heavy, and too perfect, and it was thrilling in its harmony, in its accomplishment. Art also requires training, but in this case training is probably more formal—the acquisition of technical skill. In the realm of the mind, training is indissolubly bound with the essence of the task. In this realm questions are no less important than answers, and unresolved problems, the "perennial questions," are the real stimulus and token of mental advance. Old Russia seems to have been charmed by the perfection, completeness, and harmony of Byzantine civilization, and paralyzed by this charm. Once more it must be stressed that Russian Byzantium was not just a servile repetition but a new and peculiar version of Byzantine culture, in which one can discern a true creative power. . . .

The crisis became conspicuous in Moscow in the seventeenth century, in that great age of changes, shifts, and troubles in the Russian state and society. It was an age of great cultural confusion. Certain elements of Byzantine achievement were strongly challenged, including the traditional "symphony" of state and church. Moscow was moving hesitantly toward an increasing secularization of its political order. The impact of Western mentality was growing, first in the form of the new Kievan learning, which itself was an unfortunate hybrid of Polish and quasi-Byzantine factors. The spread of this pseudomorphic culture was felt at Moscow more as a shock or offense than as a challenge, and provoked only resistance along with blind imitation. There was a search, but it was a search for ready solutions. Probably it was a blind alley. And then came the Reform.

The ultimate tragedy was that the Reform itself was promoted in the same old manner. There was again the thrill of accomplishment or achievement. The spirit of the Reform was intrinsically utilitarian. There was again a charm—a charm of Western achievement, of Western habits and forms. Curiosity was aroused, but was it a sound and sober intellectual curiosity? The new civilization was accepted in its ready form, into which the life of the nation could not be fitted. There was an effect of astonishment, but no real awakening. The new culture was much less organic than the old one, and therefore even less spontaneous and creative. It is instructive that it was possible to present the whole history of Russian literature, including its ideological content, as a story of Western influence, as a story of consecutive waves of imported ideas and forms. Was the cultural initiative really awakened? One may have very grave doubts. It is not surprising that a paradoxical resistance to culture as such has been one of the vigorous trends in the new culture; though it was to some extent provoked also by the thought of a Westerner, Rousseau, it was deeply rooted in the psychology of "reformed" Russians. Was not the way of simplicity higher than the way of culture? Technical culture has indeed been transplanted. But did Reform promote any disinterested concern for higher culture? Was it a real advance in comparison with the culture of Old Russia? During the whole modern period complaints were loudly voiced on this theme: there was no genuine *will for culture,* although admiration and even respect for culture were rather widespread. The root of the trouble was still the same: Culture was still regarded as an order, as an achievement, as a system. For that reason one could propagate the acceptance of foreign forms; they were finished and ready to hand. Indeed, there was sometimes much vigor and also much obstinacy in this endeavor of adaptation, and it could instill vitality into the products. The thrill of the modern Russian culture is in its scattered explosions—the deeds of individuals. But there was no general culture. Moreover, the larger part of the nation was not yet involved in the process, and was much more outside the culture, and thus outside history, than it had been in the days of Old Russia. This was the sharpest objection against the new order in comparison with the old, as Kliuchevsky has so eloquently phrased it.

So much can be said about the old "society." Did this "unsuccess," to use the term of Wladimir Weidlé,[1] discredit that system of cultural values to which Old Russia was pledged and committed? Did this system crumble also? It is not for the historian to answer this question. It is a question for the philosopher. But the historian must insist that there are perennial achievements in the inventory of Old Russian culture. The greatness of the Old Russian religious art is in our day widely acknowledged, with understanding or simply by fashion. The vigor and freshness and the profundity of the Russian religious quest, although it seems to be often disguised by ritual formalism, is also increasingly recognized. There were profound human values in this old culture, as detached, as archaic, as exotic as it may appear to those trained in the Western ways. And it becomes more and more evident that Old Russian culture did, from its very inception, belong to the wider circle—to the circle of that civilization which had been built, on the composite basis of ancient classical culture, under the creative impact, and often under direct guidance and deep inspiration, of Christian faith and mission.

Old Russia, indeed, left a precious legacy, at least in the realm of art. At this point its "culture" survived its "paternal society," and must be studied as a perennial treasure in its own right.

D. S. Likhachev

1. On the Continuity in the Development of Russian Culture

... It is inaccurate to see a territorial break between Muscovite and Kievan Rus. "Kievan Rus" is a conventional designation. Kievan Rus was

[1] Wladimir Weidlé, *Russia: Absent and Present* (New York, 1952), pp. 15 ff.

not limited to Kiev and its immediate surroundings. The great political and cultural role of Novgorod, first in Kievan Rus and later in Muscovite Rus, is well known. In the twelfth century the Vladimir-Suzdalian land—the land in which Moscow developed—acquired outstanding importance in Kievan Rus. The architecture of Vladimir-Suzdal was perhaps the best in Kievan Rus, and the literature, composition of chronicles, and painting of Vladimir in the twelfth and thirteenth centuries were not inferior to that of Kiev proper. Despite political fragmentation, in the realm of culture Kievan Rus constituted an amazing cultural unity—from Ladoga in the north to Tmutorokan in the south, from Yaroslavl in the east to Galich and Polotsk in the west. The majority of literary works were produced in the most remote parts of this broad territory. Nikon the Great wrote his chronicle in Kiev and in Tmutorokan. The *Kievo-Pecher-skii Paterik* was produced in Kiev and in Vladimir. Serapion of Vladimir wrote in Kiev and in Vladimir. The entire composition of the Russian chronicles was based on the exchange of chronicle evidence among the different regions. Cases are known in which manuscripts written in Novgorod were bound in Kiev.

The "intelligentsia" of Kievan Rus possessed very great mobility, and constantly traveled from principality to principality. Bands of builders, fresco-painters, and churchmen were continually moving from one principality to another, even in the years immediately following the Tatar-Mongol invasion. The cultural ties Alexander Nevsky had with Galician-Volynian Rus are known. Moscow grew up on the territory of the Vladimir-Suzdalian principality, which was culturally one with Kiev; it arose on the territory of Kievan Rus. Gradually including in its domains Rostov, Tver, Yaroslavl, Novgorod, Pskov, and so forth, it all the more broadly embraced domains with the rich cultural tradition of Kievan Rus. Thus it is clear that Moscow Rus was territorially linked with Kievan Rus.

But did not Moscow Rus perhaps forget the cultural traditions of its own land, breaking with them and striking out on its own path? Of course, history does not remain fixed on the same spot; the life of society develops, and culture also develops. However, in regard to Moscow Rus it must be said that in it there existed a quite distinct version of the traditions of Kievan Rus. The proverbial Muscovite conservatism of the sixteenth and seventeenth centuries, the effort to judge everything "according to antiquity and duty" (according to the customs of olden times) arose on the basis of the peculiar revival of Kievan antiquity in all realms of cultural life in the fourteenth and fifteenth centuries.

It is noteworthy that at the time of the struggle for national independence in the fourteenth and fifteenth centuries, the Russians turned to their own national past. The heightened interest of Muscovite Rus in old Kiev, old Vladimir, old Novgorod can be observed in ecclesiastical and political life. It was expressed in intensified effort in historical thought, in the compilation of numerous and extensive collections of chronicles, of historical works, in increased attention to the works of the eleventh to the beginning of the thirteenth centuries: the *Discourse on Law and Grace* by Metropolitan Hilarion of Kiev, the *Tale of Bygone Years,* the *Tale of the Host of Igor,* the *Kievo-Pecherskii Paterik.* They were copied and imitated. The restoration of pre-Mongol buildings and frescoes was being carried on in Vladimir and Novgorod. The Muscovite princes were tracing their genealogies to the "old prince Vladimir," and Russian *byliny* were being unified into a single Kievan cycle. It is clear that Muscovite Rus did not simply follow Kievan traditions, but consciously cultivated them. The struggle for the Kievan heritage—territorial, political, and cultural—inspired Moscow in the course of three whole centuries. Kievan Rus played the role of "its own" ancient times, in the cultural revival after the Tatar-Mongol invasion. The Ukraine and Belorussia in the same period also continued Kievan traditions, but being included in the make-up of foreign states they were not in this period capable of reviving Kievan traditions on such a large scale.

The question of the links of post-Petrine culture with the culture of Old Rus is more complex. In contrast to the effort of Muscovite Rus to emphasize its continuity with Kievan Rus and to revive the traditions of the epoch of independence, Petrine Russia consciously broke the links with Old Rus and "broke through a window onto Europe." This conscious endeavor at rupture with traditions, however, ought not to confuse us. The more we study concretely the history of Russian art, Russian literature, and Russian science in the seventeenth to the nineteenth centuries, the clearer it becomes that the rupture was more external than internal. The flowering of Russian literature, music, and architecture in the later period has deep roots in the millennium-long development of Russian culture. In Russian literature and social thought one may observe a striking continuity of themes, models, and ideas. The whole of Russian literature, both old and new, from the eleventh to the twentieth century, is filled with civic pathos, the effort at education—in which moral themes play a role of first importance. This may be said in general; as for the particulars, take for example the work of genius, the *Tale of Woe and Misfortune,*[1] and you will be convinced that in it there is much that gives rise to the heritage of the humanist themes of Russian literature of the nineteenth century.

The principles of design of Russian architecture of the seventeenth century were expressed in the planning of Petrine Petersburg. The ensembles of the Russian kremlins and monasteries were reflected in the architecture of the eighteenth and the beginning of the nineteenth century (compare the building of the Zakharov Admiralty in Leningrad). The palette of Russian icon painting was repeated in individual pictures of

[1] Alexander S. Griboyedov (1795-1829), Eds.

the eighteenth century and inspired the Russian painting of the beginning of the twentieth century. The tormented themes of the social thought of the sixteenth and seventeenth centuries in a new fashion but within the boundaries of continuity agitated the Russian social thought of the nineteenth century. . . .

II. On the "Intellectual Silence" of Old Rus

The discovery, at the beginning of the twentieth century, of the aesthetic value of the Old Russian icons occurred simultaneously with the discovery of the culture of Old Rus. For a long time the icons were its most notable representatives. They spoke the voiceless language of color and line, but they were in consequence no less intellectual. The speculative side of the icon was as astonishing as its aesthetic side.

After the icon, Old Russian architecture was discovered. I remember that the remarkable scholar to whom the honor of discovering the icon fundamentally belongs, Igor Grabar, who had been a not less remarkable painter, assigned first place not to the painting but to the architecture of Old Rus. I. Grabar wrote, "Summarizing everything that Russia achieved in the realm of art, one comes to the conclusion that she was above all a nation of architects. A flair for proportions, an understanding of outline, a decorative instinct, an inventiveness with forms—in a word, all the architectural virtues are encountered so constantly and universally in the course of Russian history that they lead to the idea of the absolutely exceptional architectural gifts of the Russian people."

Of course, architecture was also a "silent" art, but no less intellectual than icon painting. If the medieval Gothic cathedrals of Western Europe may be termed philosophical and historical encyclopedias in stone, then Russian churches with their complex systems of fresco paintings deserve this characterization no less. Those who speak of the "intellectual silence" of Old Rus evidently leave completely out of the reckoning the literature of Old Rus. By its very nature literary art is not silent in its message. Consequently, Old Russian literature seems to them unworthy of attention.

Old Russian literature indeed is little known and as yet is far from completely evaluated from the aesthetic standpoint. Often one hears reproaches of Old Russian literature for having no Dante or Shakespeare! However, Dante and Shakespeare cannot serve as measures for the literature of Old Rus. It was a literature of a folkloristic type, and not at all of a personal sort. We cannot demand of an embroideress of the people that she with her threads should create a picture that would raise her name to the level of that of the genius Rembrandt. In Old Russian literature one finds another kind of art, high and one which delights us, but not one of a personal type. Old Russian composers of books (I refrain from calling them "writers") engaged in "the embroidery of words," combined verbal stitches and popular themes, and created productions of astonishing verbal richness and refinement. I refer merely to the writings of Epiphanius the Wise, to his golden art of weaving words, his art of "wickerwork of the word." The great themes that excited the Old Russian composers of books for the most part were not worked out by them in writing, but were only transferred to writing out of the life of society. The productions of Old Russian literature must be compared not with the works of Dante or Shakespeare, but with the great epic poems of the past, with the *byliny,* the lyrics of folklore, the ritual poetry of the people. When in the seventeenth century the literary art began to change its folkloristic character, there appeared works of a new type: the *Life of Avvakum,* the *Life of Epiphanius,* in part the *Tale of Woe and Misfortune,* and many others.

In the culture of Old Rus there are many other peculiarities of its intellectual type. In Old Rus theological thought was little developed, but to make up for it publicistics and especially historical thought attained a broad and deep development. The interest in history permeated all sides of the culture of Old Rus. Thousands of manuscripts of chronicles, chronographies, "books of degrees," historical tales and legends, have been preserved. Each principality, each episcopate, sometimes municipal chancelleries, monasteries, individual churches carried on their own writing of chronicles, in which local events are set in the framework of the events of general Russian history and at times world history. Historical argumentation predominated in Old Russian diplomacy, publicistics, the deciding of juridical disputes, and so forth. The whole of Russian life was filled with the spirit of history. I remember, for example, that Russian churches of the eleventh to seventeenth centuries were often erected in commemoration of one historical event or other. Saint Sophia in Kiev was built on the spot of the victory of Yaroslav the Wise over the Pechenegs. The Uspensky Cathedral in Kolomna is a monument to the victory of the Russians at Kulikovo. The Church of the Ascension in Kolomenskoe was built in honor of the birth of Ivan IV. The Church of Basil the Blessed is a monument to the annexation of the state of Kazan. The cathedral of the Novodevichi monastery in Moscow was founded in remembrance of the liberation of Smolensk, and its paintings are devoted to the glory of Russian arms and of the Russian state. Very much could be written on the historicism of Old Russian culture; this topic is one of the most interesting.

Finally, one last remark. In Old Russian culture the aesthetic monument notably predominated. The philosophical and social thought for the most part was clothed in artistic form. In some measure this continued to be true in the nineteenth century; the unaccustomed artistic form prevents one from noticing the existence of great Russian philosophy. The reproach to Russian culture in the nineteenth century for an absence of philosophy has now ceased; it is time also to cease to reproach Old Russian culture for its alleged "intellectual silence," which is directed at it only because its world view was clothed in the form of art and not in the form of scientific treatises.

16. M. V. Lomonosov and the

founding of Moscow University

MIKHAIL VASILIEVITCH LOMONOSOV (1711-1765), a renowned scholar of peasant origin, has been acclaimed for his contribution to Russian language, poetry, history, philosophy, and science. Not until the twentieth century, however, did his scientific work receive special recognition, based on the studies of his foremost biographer, Boris Menshutkin. Under the Soviet regime Lomonosov's versatility and intellectual prowess have received lavish praise, and the University of Moscow has been renamed in his honor. Soviet interpretation of the founding of this university tends to exalt Lomonosov at the expense of Count I. I. Shuvalov. The latter, however, was himself a linguist, well versed in the literary and philosophical ideas of the French Enlightenment. It was he who commissioned Voltaire's *Histoire de l'empire de Russie sous Pierre le Grand* (1759-1763), and who promoted the founding in Russia in 1757 of the Academy of Arts.

Moscow University was established by the *ukaz* of the Empress Elizabeth of January 12, 1755. Its founders regarded it as an important step toward the training of Russian scientific, technical, and administrative personnel, which would reduce the country's dependence on foreigners. The Academy of Sciences established by Peter I in St. Petersburg, with its emphasis on research, had failed to meet Russia's need for professional manpower. Although Moscow University, which included two gymnasiums, opened with one hundred students and accorded priority to teaching over research, its development was slow. This was due in part to the postponement of Catherine II's plans for a public school system to provide a sound background for higher learning. Of its original faculty of eight members, only two were Russian, the rest German.

In commemoration of the two hundredth anniversary of the founding of Moscow University in 1955, a two-volume history of the institution was published. The passage below represents a Soviet effort to substantiate the significance of Lomonosov's role, as compared to that of Shuvalov, in the founding of Russia's first university in Moscow. It is translated from *Istoriya Moskovskogo Universiteta*, Vol. I (Moscow University: 1955), 15-20.

There were special factors that favored the founding of a university in Moscow, which were absent in St. Petersburg. Having taken the lead in the history of our country by initiating the unification of the Russian people into one state and organizing its struggle for liberation from a foreign yoke, Moscow in the middle of the XVIIIth century was the largest Russian city, situated in the center of the most populated and cultured region of the country. The ancient capital had retained its significance as the center of all Russia. This was underlined by the existence in Moscow of a special Senate office for on-the-spot decision of administrative and legal affairs. One feature of Moscow was the existence there of a significant number of factories and handicraft shops. The biggest enterprise was the Moscow cloth court, in which hundreds of workers were employed.

According to the record of the 1771 plague, prepared by Shafonskii, there were in Moscow 113 factories, in which nearly 13,000 workers were employed. Moscow had also retained its significance as the biggest trade center in Russia, connected with the remote parts of the country by numerous river and land routes.

An important feature of the cultural life of Moscow was the presence there of several educational institutions, whose doors were open to the *raznochintsy*.[1] The "Spasskii schools" were filled with *raznochintsy* and had long served as the main source of schoolboy and student recruits for the academic university in St. Petersburg.

As a former graduate of the Slavonic-Greek-Latin Academy,[2] Lomonosov was well versed in the reasons for the creation of the first Russian university in Moscow. This was reflected in the "report" on the establishment of a university in Moscow, which was introduced in the Senate, undoubtedly on the basis of data obtained from Lomonosov. The "report" pointed out the following advantages of Moscow as a university site: 1) The large number of noblemen and *raznochintsy* living there. 2) The location of the capital in the heart of the Russian state. 3) The low cost of maintenance. 4) Students and pupils having all sorts of relatives and acquaintances there. 5) A large number of private tutors supported by the landowners in Moscow.

[1] Plebeians, or intellectuals not belonging to the gentry.
[2] This Academy, located at the Zaikonospassky Monastery, was founded in 1684.

It is characteristic that the "Report" indicated the large number of noblemen and *raznochintsy* living in Moscow, as well as the location of Moscow in the center of Russia. The establishment of a university was regarded in the "report" as one of the necessary measures for the training of educated people, not only from the ranks of the nobility, but also from the *raznochintsy*. Thus, in the project for the creation of a university in Moscow, the very same provisions were introduced which Lomonosov advocated with such persistence for the university in St. Petersburg. This at once and indubitably reveals that the author of the project for the creation of a university in Moscow was Lomonosov.

An enthusiastic advocate of education, irrespective of class, for all strata of the population, Lomonosov, a peasant by birth, sought the opening in Moscow not of a privileged, scholarly institution, but of a higher school of learning accessible to all strata of the population. The reference to the "large number of private tutors supported by the land-owners in Moscow" likewise indicates that the university was mainly oriented toward students and *raznochintsy*, since the nobility never held jobs as private tutors, considering such an occupation beneath their dignity and unprofitable.

The "report" in the Senate was presented in the name of Ivan Ivanovitch Shuvalov, a favorite of the Empress Elizabeth Petrovna. This circumstance permitted authors from the gentry and middle class to create a legend about the Empress and her favorite as the founders of the University of Moscow. One should note that in the imperial *ukaz* [decree] on the creation of Moscow University "the author of that useful enterprise" was designated as I. I. Shuvalov, which was entirely understandable in view of the special position he occupied at Elizabeth's court. In the eyes of the aristocratic and middle-class historians, I. I. Shuvalov became the founder of Moscow University, pushing into the background its real founder—the brilliant Russian scholar, Mikhail Vasilevitch Lomonosov.

In a special work published in connection with the celebration of the one hundredth anniversary of Moscow University in 1855, several pages in all were devoted to the circumstances under which that institution came into being. The author—one of the reactionary ideologists of the "theory of official nationality," Professor Shevyrev—attributed the creation of the first Russian university to three persons: the Empress Elizabeth Petrovna, her favorite, Ivan Ivanovitch Shuvalov, and Mikhail Vasilevitch Lomonosov, having put the last-mentioned in third place. After making a few comments about Lomonosov, Shevyrev makes no further reference to him, as if his entire activity was confined solely to the initial discussion with Shuvalov.

Shevyrev's view of Shuvalov as the founder of Moscow University assumed in Tsarist Russia the character of "an official opinion." During that same 1855 jubilee there appeared a small book, written by the great Russian historian, S. M. Solovëv, under the characteristic title, "A Word of Thanks to Ivan Ivanovitch Shuvalov." Not until the celebration of the two hundredth anniversary of Lomonosov's birth at Moscow University in 1911 did Professor M. N. Speranskii make bold to speak of the two founders of Moscow University—Lomonosov and Shuvalov, putting Lomonosov in first place.

Nevertheless, in an article dedicated to the 185th anniversary of Moscow University, Shuvalov was again represented as the founder of Moscow University.

The services of Lomonosov in the creation of Moscow University were duly recognized only with the publication of his correspondence under the editorship of Academician S. I. Vavilov. "If the legal founder of the university," he said in his commentaries on the correspondence, "by virtue of his special position at the court of the Empress, was I. I. Shuvalov, its real initiator and inspirer was Lomonosov, who was also responsible for working out the detailed program of the future university, as well as its internal structure, and the organization of instruction.

The real founder and creator of Moscow University was Mikhail Vasilievitch Lomonosov. He calls himself "a participant in the establishment of Moscow University," saying that he advanced "the first reason for the establishment of the above-mentioned body." In a letter to Shuvalov dated 1760, Lomonsov claims that "even prior to this he gave advice about Moscow University."

Behind the back of I. I. Shuvalov was concealed the whole group of his kinsmen, headed by Count Peter Ivanovitch Shuvalov. The rise of Shuvalov undermined the position at court of the Razumovskys, the oldest of whom, Count Alexei Grigorovitch, was at one time as great a favorite of the Empress as I. I. Shuvalov became. The younger Razumovsky, Kiril Grigorovitch, was president of the Academy of Sciences, and was not well disposed toward Lomonosov. Under these circumstances, it is quite understandable that Lomonosov turned to I. I. Shuvalov for help in regard to the creation of a university in Russia.

The founding of Moscow University entered into the plans of Shuvalov, as one of the enterprises which met the needs of numerous and influential members of the Moscow and provincial nobility. In the capacity of curator of Moscow University, I. I. Shuvalov made his way to a place of honor in the state equal to that held by the president of the Academy of Sciences. Shuvalov's new position was quickly taken cognizance of by the president of the Academy of Sciences—K. G. Razumovsky. He and his protégé, Teplov [G. M. Teplov,] wholly indifferent to the fate of the university at the Academy of Sciences, were busy with plans for the creation of a university in Baturin, the residence of K. G. Razumovsky, a Ukrainian hetman. According to the project worked out by Teplov in 1760 for a university in Baturin, the Ukrainian hetman—in this instance, K. G. Razumovsky—was to hold for life the title of founder and protector of Baturin University. The project failed to materialize, but it indicates clearly enough what kind of political interests were back of it.

Lomonosov understood that without the support of influential personages he would have no chance of realizing his project for the founding of a university in Moscow, and therefore he was compelled to act through Shuvalov.

The possibilities of founding a university in Moscow were finally cleared up by Lomonosov during his visit to Moscow in 1753, when the Empress and court were there. The arrival of Lomonosov in Moscow was, in all probability, connected with the preparation for the founding of the university, although the immediate object of his journey was the business of the mosaic factory.

The difficulty of Lomonosov's position derived from the fact that he was the real organizer and creator of higher education in Russia, and was forced to yield the semblance of this honor to Shuvalov, who, at any cost, wanted to be regarded as "the founder" of Moscow University.

At the decisive moment of the preparation of the "report" in the Senate, Lomonosov revealed himself as a great citizen and patriot. He did not put his own personal interests ahead of those of the people at large. It is impossible, without emotion, to read his letter to Shuvalov, written in May, 1754, concerning the project of the "report" in the Senate: "Under this circumstance, I am gratified to see how great a contribution your innate, incomparable talent can make and how it can promote the reading of many books. However, advice to Your Excellency from those who have not only seen universities but have studied in them for several years will not be superfluous, so that their institutions, regulations, ceremonies, and customs may be represented clearly and vividly, as in a picture. Inasmuch as you intend to establish Moscow University on foreign models, which is quite justifiable, I should wish to see you prepare the plan. But if, due to shortage of time or for other reasons that is not feasible, placing my hopes in Your Excellency's fatherly grace and magnanimity toward me, I make bold to offer my opinion in brief about the founding of Moscow University."

The great Russian scholar was forced to write about the "fatherly grace" of the young favorite toward him. Lomonosov's letter introduces us, as it were, to the situation that prevailed prior to the founding of Moscow University. Knowing that Shuvalov acts without any clear plan and without knowledge and understanding of the enterprise, Lomonosov, under the guise of admiration of his "talents," in essence set forth the principles which should be laid down as a basis for the code of regulations of the future university. He concluded his short letter with the words: "My advice is to take your time about the *ukaz,*

Your Excellency, so as not to have to alter it later. If it could wait a full ten days then I could submit an all-embracing plan." Without confining himself to that, Lomonosov had already in the letter given a rough outline of the faculties and future chairs of Moscow University. This rough outline is comparable to Lomonosov's note submitted to the Academy of Sciences in 1743; that is, it was written ten years before the "report" of Shuvalov. Lomonosov projected the same three faculties —law, medicine, philosophy—which were indicated in the letter to Shuvalov. He particularly insisted on the necessity of establishing a gymnasium (secondary school) at the university, saying that a university without a gymnasium was "like ploughed land without seed."

Lomonosov's note served as the basis of the academic program of the newly opened Moscow University. In the university three faculties were set up—law, medicine, and philosophy (but the number of professors was slightly reduced). The number and specialization of the professors of Moscow University corresponded to Lomonosov's letter, coinciding almost identically with it. Thus, in the law faculty three chairs were established: general jurisprudence, Russian jurisprudence, politics. In the medical faculty likewise three chairs were established: chemistry, natural history, anatomy. The curtailment was carried out only in the faculty of philosophy, where instead of the six professors proposed we find only four, but in the same disciplines as in Lomonosov's plan: philosophy, physics, rhetoric (in which was included oratory), and history, with antiquity and heraldry included.

A comparison of the regulations for Moscow University with those which Lomonosov repeatedly proposed for the university at the Academy of Sciences in St. Petersburg indicates that it was his proposals that formed the basis of the creation of Moscow University. Thus, with complete justification, we may say that the real founder of Moscow University was Lomonosov.

Lomonosov's original letter to Shuvalov, of which there is a phototype reproduction in the present work, indicates that Shuvalov made use of the Lomonosov plan but curtailed its requirements. Thus, Shuvalov, using brackets, combined in one person the professors of philosophy and physics, the same type of brackets are placed opposite the professors of oratory and poetry, and they also combine the professors of history, antiquity, and criticism. Shuvalov's own creativity was expressed only by the addition to history of "heroldry," that is to say, heraldry, a typically aristocratic science about coats of arms, mottoes, and other heraldic insignia of the nobility. The range of Shuvalov's "scientific" knowledge was proved by his combination in one chair of philosophy and physics. Later he had to establish four chairs in the philosophy faculty, having separated physics from philosophy.

It must be said that Shuvalov assiduously concealed the participation of Lomonosov in the creation of Moscow University. In contrast to the other letters of Lomonosov, the one referred to above was not printed during Shuvalov's lifetime and first appeared in print only in 1825.[3] But that Lomonosov took a most active part in working out the statutes of Moscow University is demonstrated in the memoirs of I. F. Timkovskii who, on the basis of conversations with Shuvalov, directly affirmed that Lomonosov together with Shuvalov "worked out the project and code of regulations of Moscow University. Lomonosov then strongly persisted in his own opinions and wanted to retain the complete image of Leyden, with liberties incompatible [in Russia]." The information from Timkovskii leads us to the essence of the disagreement between Lomonosov and Shuvalov.

The great Russian scholar sought for the university in Moscow freedom for the teaching of the sciences, which was incompatible with the order of serfdom in XVIIIth century Russia. Freedom of entry for the representatives of all classes into the university, Lomonosov did not achieve; but he was able to obtain the right of instruction in Moscow University for representatives of the non-noble classes. His own views on the necessity of education for all classes Lomonosov expressed with complete clarity, pointing out that "in a university the student who works more is respected more, but whose son he is is immaterial." The founding at the university of two separate gymnasia, one for the nobility and one for the *raznochintsy,* was the work of Shuvalov.

While Lomonosov fought for the accessibility of education to all strata of the population, the aristocratic government tried as much as possible to impede the access of peasants, who comprised the overwhelming majority of the population of Russia in the middle of the XVIIIth century, to the newly created university. Therefore the first university regulations confirmed by the Empress, Elizabeth Petrovna, categorically prohibited the landlords' peasants from entering the university.

In contrast to Lomonosov's proposals on the training of educated people for practical work, the *ukaz* on the establishment of the university gave no consideration whatsoever to this question.

Culture, science, and education were placed at the service of the nobility by the *ukaz* of Elizabeth Petrovna. This feature of the *ukaz* safeguarded more easily the entry into government circles, where the interests of the nobility were identified with the interests of the state. The chief authors who restricted and tightened the Tsarist *ukaz* on the founding of Moscow University are known. They are the brothers Alexander and Peter Shuvalov, who were at this time in power, and especially Peter Shuvalov.

---

[3] It was published in the journal *Moskovskii Nablyudatel'* in 1825, and in an edition of *Speeches and Poems,* produced in honor of the founding of Moscow University (Moscow, 1832).

The Tsarist government in every respect watched over the interests of the nobility, whereas Lomonosov believed:

> That the Russian land
> Can produce its own Platos
> And keen-minded Newtons.

Lomonosov did not cease his efforts on behalf of Moscow University even after its establishment. Thus, he sought professors for it in Germany, which is obvious from one letter of December, 1756. Later he solicited university privileges, "which could be of some service to Moscow University."

Reference

MENSHUTKIN, B. N., *Russia's Lomonosov: Chemist, Courtier, Physicist, Poet.* Tr. from the Russian by J. E. Thal and E. J. Webster. Princeton, N.J.: Princeton University Press, 1952.

17. Russian commerce

in the age of Catherine II

WILLIAM TOOKE, F. R. S., AN ENGLISHMAN who lived in Russia during the greater part of the long reign of Catherine the Great, was a member of the Russian Academy of Sciences and of the Free Economic Society of St. Petersburg. As a close friend of two heads of the Russian Academy, M. Domashnev and the Princess Dashkov, he enjoyed free access to its libraries and collections. As an Englishman, Tooke was seriously concerned about the potential threat of Russian commerce to British interests in India.

The excerpts below on Russian trade and commerce at the close of the eighteenth century have been taken from William Tooke's three-volume study of Russia, entitled, *View of the Russian Empire during the Reign of Catherine the Second, and to the Close of the Eighteenth Century,* Vol. III (London: T. N. Longman and O. Rees, 1800), pp. 432-434; 440-442; 445-446; 450; 455-457; 469-471.

Archangel. Soon after this[1] tzar Ivan Vassilievitch caused the harbour of the archangel Michael to be constructed, granted several privileges to the english nation, and thereby at length grew up the trading port of Archangel, since become of such consequence. The commerce here soon increased; and in 1655 the exports from this port alone to England were to the value of 660,000 rubles; from 1691 to 1701, on a yearly average, to the amount of 112,251 pounds sterling; whereas the imports from England were estimated at only 58,884 pounds sterling. The revenue of the crown at Archangel amounted annually to about 100,000 rubles, a sum which, according to the then value of money, may be deemed very considerable. The principal articles of export at that time were: potashes, caviar, tallow, wax, hides,[a] hemp, feathers, tar, yarn, beef, rhubarb, silk

---

[1] Following the voyages of Sir Hugh Willoughby (1553) and Richard Chancellor to the Arctic to open trade between England and Russia.

(probably chinese or persian), cork, bacon, cordage, furs, bristles, &c. all rough commodities.[b]—But during the reign of Peter I a great revolution took place in this trade; for, having built the city of St. Petersburg, he drew thither the commerce of Archangel, and it became thence-forward the chief mart of the russian empire. However, the commerce of Archangel has not entirely gone to ruin; nay, since the alteration and debasement of the value of money, it amounts at present to a far greater sum than formerly, as we may safely venture to state the exports at two millions, while we can only reckon the imports at one fourth of that sum, or half a million of rubles. To the former articles of exportation, others of various importance are now added, as corn[c] [grain], linseed, iron, flax, trail-oil, sail-cloth and other coarse linens, tobacco, &c.

St. Petersburg. The commerce of St. Petersburg began in a short space of time to be of great consequence. Even in the year 1742, the exports amounted to about two millions and a half, and the imports to two millions of rubles. At present the former are estimated at from 32 to 37, and the latter at from 19 to 26 millions of rubles. The chief articles of the Petersburg exports are: iron, hemp, yusts, tallow, tobacco, wax, kaviar, cordage, soap, tar, hemp-oil, sail-cloth and coarse linens, furs, salt-petre, &c.

Riga. The commerce of Riga is likewise of no slight consequence, amounting, if we include that of Arensburg and Pernau, as belonging to to the same government, with it, to an object of between six and seven millions of rubles, whereof the exports may be between four and a half and five, and the imports one and a half or two millions annually. The chief articles of export are hemp, flax, cordage, potash, linseed, hempseed, ship-timber, tobacco, corn, brandy, &c. . . .

Mr. Hermann in 1790 calculates the total of the exports from all these ports to amount annually to from four and a half to five millions, and the imports from one and a half to two millions of rubles: and the whole of the commerce, active and passive, of that government might then amount annually to between six and seven millions. . . .

The Black Sea and the Caspian. The commerce of the Euxine, or Black sea, since its revival, is, in a manner, still in its infancy. However, we may estimate the exportation, from all the ports there belonging to Russia, at about one million; and the importation at one million and a quarter. The principal articles that find a vent here are, cannon, furs, salted beef, butter, cordage, sail-cloth, kaviar, corn, and a variety of russian manufactures, especially iron, linen, cotton stuffs, &c. The imports are, wine, fruit, coffee, silks, rice, and all kinds of turkish commodities.

Over the Caspian, commerce, indeed, is of very ancient date; but at present is not so very considerable as it might be made. The exports amount to somewhere about 1,200,000, and the imports to 1,000,000 rubles. The articles of exportation here are nearly the same with those that find purchasers on the Euxine, whereas we take in return scarcely any thing but silk.

As early as the fourteenth century the Venetians and the Genoese, by the way of the Caspian, brought the indian, persian, and arabian commodities, with which they supplied the southern parts of Europe over Astrakhan, to their magazines at Azof and Keffa. From Astrakhan the goods went up the Volga, then by land as far as the Don, on which river they were next forwarded to Azof. Even the northern parts of Europe were furnished with the same asiatic commodities by the russian traders, over Astrakhan, who sent them to their principal magazine at Visbey [Wisby], a hanse-town on the isle of Gothland. The devastations occasioned by the wars of Timur, towards the end of the fourteenth century, caused the transfer of this trade from Astrakhan to Smyrna and Aleppo; and the arabian commerce, for which these places, besides, lay more convenient, never returned again to Astrakhan; but a part of the persian trade was, some time afterwards, turned into its former channel. . . .

. . . The principal commodities that are brought from Astrakhan to the ports of the Caspian, are dutch, french, silesian, and english cloths, vitriol, soap, alum, sugar, russian leather, needles, russia linens, velvet, glass ware, paper, some few furs, hides, a small matter of tea, corn, butter, wine, brandy, wooden vessels for household uses, sea-horse-teeth, iron, copper, tin, lead, iron ware, clocks, indigo, cochineal, &c. The most material articles of importation are silk (mostly raw) from Shirvan and Ghilan, lamb-skins from Bukharia, rice, dried fruits, spices, saffron, a trifling matter of salt, sulphur, and naptha. The Indians and the merchants of Khiva bring occasionally gold and silver in ingots and bars, golddust, precious stones, and pearls, to Astrakhan. —In the year 1770, the exports and imports of the whole commerce, both by sea and land, to and from the Caspian sea, amounted only to about 400,000 rubles; in the year 1768, already to upwards of 800,000, and in 1775, to more than a million of rubles; without reckoning the contraband trade. At present it is undoubtedly at the same amount. . . .

. . . The revival of the trade of the Krim [Crimea] or rather of Taurida, was reserved for the brilliant reign of Catherine II when, on the re-acquisition of Azof and Taganrok [Taganrog] in 1774, and with them the fortresses of Kinburn, Kertch, and Yenicali, and a great stretch of country between the Bogue [Bug] and the Dnieper, it began again to rear its head; but it did not thoroughly revive till 1782, when this commerce was settled on a firm and lasting basis, and the grandest prospects opened to it, by the obtention of the whole Krimea. This commerce, however, cannot be pushed to any considerable degree of consequence, till the navigation of the Euxine is entirely free to Russia, and till Taurida and the neighbouring regions, have greatly increased in population. . . .

. . . Enlightened by science, improved by arts—and by an extensive and lucrative commerce, rising fast to opulence, she [Russia] is now become a mighty nation; and it may be considered as certain, that in the period of a very few years she will greatly injure the british trade to India—for it is known to be a fact, that the Russians carry on a very lucrative trade on the Caspian. For a long time, indeed, it suffered very serious losses from the kozak [Cossack] hordes, who often interrupted and plundered the russian caravans, on their way to Astrakhan; but at length these robbers were completely subdued, the roads became safe, and the commerce of Persia again revived and centered in Astrakhan; and we find merchants flocking thither from Bulgaria, Krimea, Armenia, Hindostan, and various parts of India, to traffic with the Russians.

A company was formed by Peter I to which he granted an exclusive privilege of trading to Astrakhan and Persia; however the empress Catharine II annulled this exclusive right granted by Peter, and allowed all her subjects to participate in that trade. Factories, at a great expense, were built at Astrakhan, and consuls settled at Baku and Sinfili: this commerce is, however, greatly injured by a contraband trade carried on in Shamakia, and other persian inland towns, by the armenian merchants; who, knowing the country and the language, have a considerable advantage over the Russians. The city of Astrakhan is built on an island formed by the Volga, at its discharge into the Caspian; and as through the Volga all articles of commerce from the Baltic ports are carried thither, with great ease and safety, the city of Astrakhan is in consequence become one of the most considerable marts of the globe, and is inhabited by Russians, Turks, Armenians, Persians, Tatars, and Jews, not to mention emigrations from Kabul and the province of Oude.

At Rascht [Resht], the Russians have also a factory, with a body of soldiers, and a church of their own: they carry thither european goods, which sell at a great advantage, and bring from thence silks and stuffs, manufactured at Ghilan, which are esteemed the best in Persia; but the trade to China is certainly the most lucrative and important branch of their commercial intercourse with Asia. The principal mart at present is Kiachta, situated on the frontiers of the two empires, and the Russians take care to supply it with all kinds of european goods, which the Chinese buy up with avidity.

The amount of this trade to Russia, in exports and imports, is valued at one million pounds sterling annually; and to this circumstance alone we may in a great measure attribute the present cramped and humiliated state of the company's trade in China; for so long as the Chinese can be furnished with every article that Europe affords, they will never suffer the English, whom they call "a restless discontented set of people," or indeed any other european nation, to exceed the present prescribed limits, which are confined to Canton. Various have been the schemes and plans submitted to the directors for extending the export of british articles into China; and many experiments had actually been tried with the mandarines, which, after producing humiliation, imprisonment, a great loss to the company, and personal insult to their supercargoes, proved abortive. . . .

Commerce by Land. The commerce by land with the Poles, Prussians, &c., is considerable. Russia takes from these countries commodities for about two millions of rubles, and carries to them for scarcely 500,000. The principal objects of importation are, scythes, cloths, linens, hemp, flax, &c., the two last of which products are again sent off from Riga.

The commerce by land with Persia passes over Kitzliar and Mosdok, and Russia receives principally, by the same way, silk. The exports amount to about 100,000 and the imports to 200,000 rubles.

The commerce with the Kirghises is mostly carried on in the way of barter, and this chiefly in the siberian fortresses of Orenburg, Troitzk, Peterpavlovsk, Yamisheva, Semipalat, and Ust-kamenogorsk. Goods to about a million and a half rubles are exported, and imported to just the same amount. The Kirghises bring principally horses, horn-cattle, sheep, and very costly sheep-skins, receiving from Russia in return woolen cloths, iron, and a great quantity of household goods and other european commodities.

The chinese commerce (which, however, is at present interrupted) is likewise a mere barter, but very considerable. We may admit, without much danger of mistake, that Russia, of late years, has thence received articles from two millions, and returned them for nearly as much. The chief of the matters that come to Russia from China, are tea, silk, and kitaika (nankeen), and of what are carried thither, the valuable siberian furs.

The aggregate total then of the whole commerce of Russia by land, comes to near 9,800,000 rubles; which gives a balance of about 1,600,000 rubles against the empire. . . .

Internal Commerce—Siberia. . . . The Siberian commerce is of great consequence; but must be understood peculiarly of the governments of Irkutsk, Kolhyvan, Tobolsk, Perme, and Ufa. All the products of these parts, not consumed in the country itself, or not (as at present, when the commerce is interrupted) disposed of to China or to the Kirghises, go by the interior districts and ports of Russia. The major part, at least of the heaviest commodities, are brought almost entirely from the eastern regions of Siberia, to St. Petersburg. This navigation proceeds from the Selenga to the Baikal, and from the Angara into the Yenissey, from that into the Oby [Ob], from the Oby into the Tobol; from here over a tract of land of about 400 versts, as far as the Tshussovaia, from this into the Kamma, from the Kamma into the Volga; from this, by the sluices at Vishney-Volotshok, into the Volkhof, from the Volkhof into the Ladoga-canal, and from this canal into the Neva. The most of the return or barter of european commodities against siberian furs, and against chinese commodities, is carried on in the town of Irbit, in the government of Perme, where a famous fair[d] is held annually in the months of January and February. The products carried every year from Siberia to Russia, may be nearly estimated as follow:

	Rubles
Iron, for the amount of	3,000,000
Salt	2,000,000
Gold and silver	1,700,000
Furs and skins	1,000,000
Copper money	1,500,000
Copper in pieces	500,000
Tallow and leather	500,000
Marble, precious stones, &c	300,000
Chinese tea, &c. (or if the commerce be interrupted, so much the more furs instead)	1,500,000

All together therefore 12 millions of rubles drawn annually by Russia from Siberia; and therefore it has, not unjustly, been called the russian Peru. . . .

Author's Notes

[a] In the year 1674 the total amount of the exportation of yusts was somewhat above 100,000, but at present is near upon 200,000 poods.

[b] Bachmeister, on the arrival of the English in Russia. Petersb. journal, 1780, p. 248.

[c] Corn is indeed not properly a new article of exportation from Archangel; for even so early as the reign of tzar Ivan Vassillievitch, rye was carried from that port to England, Holland, Sweden, Denmark, and France.

[d] The chinese and siberian commodities come to this fair as well by land as by water. By land they go from the borders and the remoter districts, by Irkutsk, from thence by Tomsk, thence proceed by Tara, and from Tara by Tobolsk, and from thence over Tiumen to Irbit. They reckon from Kiachta to Irbit, by this road, to be 3914 versts. The way by water is that shewn above: namely, at Kiachta the goods are shipped on the Selenga, and by that brought into the Mare Baikal. Out of this sea they go upon the Angara into the Yenissey as far down as Yenisseisk, where they are unloaded and carried over a short track of land, into the Ket, and on this river into the Oby. From the Oby they then proceed up the Irtysh and the Tobol to Tiumen, where they lie till the season of sledge-ways; or, if they are designed for Russia, are carried by land to the Tshussovaia.

18. Fonvisin and Radishchev: two protests against the institution of serfdom

UNDER CATHERINE THE GREAT, the institution of serfdom reached its peak in Russia. The landowning nobility not only owned their serfs, but could do with them virtually what they pleased. It was at this time that two outstanding members of the nobility, endowed with literary talent, voiced strong protests against the plight of the serfs, each in a different manner. One was D. I. Fonvisin (1745-1792), the other Alexander Radishchev (1749-1802).

Denis Fonvisin, sometimes called the Russian Molière, expressed his views in the play *Nedorosl* (*The Minor*, or *The Teenager*, 1782). According to him, those landowners who abused their privileges vis-à-vis the peasantry were not true noblemen. He appears to have been the first Russian writer to differentiate between the Russian nobility (intelligentsia) and intellectuals. As stated in this play, not every intellectual can be classified *ipso facto* as a nobleman. Adroitly and tactfully he pointed out that noblemen, even if they did not free their serfs completely, would treat them humanely and improve their status. In brief, this play presents a definition of a nobleman in eighteenth-century Russia.

Alexander Radishchev, although he pursued the same objective as Fonvisin, was less discreet and much more belligerent in the forthright expression of his denunciation of the institutions of serfdom and autocracy. In his *Journey from St. Petersburg to Moscow* (1790), printed on his own private press, he not only blamed the landowning nobility for the abuses that prevailed, but claimed that such conditions could exist only under an autocratic system of government such as that in Russia. His *Journey* is a Russian version of *J'Accuse* (Zola). Fonvisin, being more tactful, emerged virtually unscathed from his effort to ameliorate the plight of the underprivileged. Catherine II, under the impact of the Pugatchev Revolt and the American and French revolutions, denounced Radischev's work as seditious, with the result that he was tried and sentenced to death, a sentence finally commuted to ten years of exile in Siberia. The pioneer efforts of Fonvisin and Radishchev strongly influenced Russian writers of the nineteenth century, especially Gogol, Belinsky, and Turgenev.

Below are excerpts from *The Minor,* by Denis Ivanovitch Fonvisin (George R. Noyes, ed., *Masterpieces of Russian Drama.* New York, 1933, Act IV, Scene II); and from Alexander Radishchev, *A Journey from St. Petersburg to Moscow* (Trans. Leo Wiener. Ed. Roderick Page Thaler. Cambridge: Harvard University Press, 1958). Reprinted by permission.

From The Minor: Act IV, Scene II

Starodum: Quite right, my dear! And I am willing to call a rich nobleman a happy man. But first let us decide who is noble and who is rich. I have my own reckoning. The ranks of nobility I count by the number of deeds which the distinguished man had performed for his fatherland, and not by the amount of work he has taken on himself because of his arrogance; not by the number of servants idling in his hall, but by the number of people pleased with his work and conduct. My nobleman is, of course, happy. And my rich man too. In my reckoning that man is not rich who counts his money merely to lay it away in his coffers—rather the man who sets aside his surplus in order to help those who are in want.

Sophia: Is it possible that such simple truths are not felt in every heart? Why does not everybody reflect on them? Where then is the intellect of which men are so proud?

Starodum: Why should one be proud of having intellect, my dear? Intellect, if it is naught but intellect, is merely a trifle. We see bad husbands, bad fathers, bad citizens endowed with acute intellects. The value of the mind depends upon virtue. Without virtue, without morals, a clever man is a monster. Virtue is incomparably higher than any acuteness of the mind. This is easily understood by anybody who really thinks about such things. There are many, many different kinds of intellect. A clever man may be easily excused if he lacks a certain quality of intellect; but an honorable man cannot be forgiven if any one property of soul is missing from his heart. He simply must have all of them. The merit of one's heart is indivisible. An honorable man must be absolutely honorable.

Sophia: Your explanation, Uncle, accords with my own inner feeling, which I have been unable to express. Now I vividly appreciate both the worth of an honorable man and his duty.

Starodum: Duty! Ah, my dear! That word is so often spoken, but so little understood! The word has become so familiar to us through constant use that when he utters it a man neither thinks nor feels anything whatsoever. And yet, if men only understood its true dignity, no one could ever utter it without profound respect. Only think what duty means! It is the sacred pledge by which we are bound to all those with whom we live and upon whom we depend. If men really did their duty in the way they assert, each class of men would abide within its own sphere of action, and would be completely happy. A nobleman, for instance, would deem it most dishonorable to do nothing when there is so much to be done, when there are people in need of help, when there is the fatherland which needs his service. Then there would be no nobleman whose nobility was buried, so to speak, with his ancestors. A nobleman! Unworthy of his name! I do not know anything in the whole world more vile!

From A Journey from St. Petersburg to Moscow

(*14) Lyubani

... A few steps from the road I saw a peasant ploughing a field. The weather was hot. I looked at my watch. It was twenty minutes before one. I had set out on Saturday. It was now Sunday. (*15) The ploughing peasant, of course, belonged to a landed proprietor, who would not let him pay a commutation tax.[1] The peasant was ploughing very carefully. The field, of course, was not part of his master's land. He turned the plough with astonishing ease.

"God help you," I said, walking up to the ploughman, who, without stopping, was finishing the furrow he had started. "God help you," I repeated.

"Thank you, sir," the ploughman said to me, shaking the earth off the ploughshare and transferring it to a new furrow.

"You must be a Dissenter,[2] since you plough on a Sunday."

---

[1] (*15) Commutation tax (*obrok*), money or produce which a serf gave to his master instead of working on the master's land. Although the master could demand obrok in whatever amount he pleased, the amount tended to remain relatively constant. Paying obrok was considered less burdensome than working on the master's land.

[2] (*15) Dissenter (*Raskol'nik*), one who refused to accept the decisions made at the Church council held in Moscow in 1654. The council had decided, among other things, that Christ's name should be spelled "Iisus," not "Isus,"

"No, sir, I make the true sign of the cross," he said, showing me the three fingers together.[3] "And God is merciful and does not bid us starve to death, so long as we have strength and a family."

"Have you no time to work during the week, then, and can you not have any rest on Sundays, in the hottest part of the day, at that?"

"In a week, sir, there are six days, and we go six times a week (*16) to work on the master's fields;[4] in the evening, if the weather is good, we haul to the master's house the hay that is left in the woods; and on holidays the women and girls go walking in the woods, looking for mushrooms and berries. God grant," he continued, making the sign of the cross, "that it rains this evening. If you have peasants of your own, sir, they are praying to God for the same thing."

"My friend, I have no peasants, and so nobody curses me. Do you have a large family?"

"Three sons and three daughters. The eldest is nine years old."

"But how do you manage to get food enough, if you have only the holidays free?"

"Not only the holidays: the nights are ours, too. If a fellow isn't lazy, he won't starve to death. You see, one horse is resting; and when this one gets tired, I'll take the other; so the work gets done."

"Do you work the same way for your master?"

"No, sir, it would be a sin to work the same way. On his fields there are (*17) a hundred hands for one mouth, while I have two for seven mouths: you can figure it out for yourself. No matter how hard you work for the master, no one will thank you for it. The master will not pay our head tax; but, though he doesn't pay it, he doesn't demand one sheep, one hen, or any linen or butter the less. The peasants are much better off where the landlord lets them pay a commutation tax without the interference of the steward. It is true that sometimes even good masters take more than three rubles a man; but even that's better than having to work on the master's fields. Nowadays it's getting to be the custom to let villages to tenants, as they call it. But we call it putting our heads in a noose. A landless tenant skins us peasants alive; even the

---

and that the sign of the cross should be made with three fingers, not with two. Those who refused to accept these decisions included many of the most devout members of the Church. The loss of these people greatly weakened the Church. Many of the Raskol'niki were the most oppressed and discontented of the peasants, and in peasant uprisings against the government and landlords, Raskol'niki often took the lead.

[3] (*15) Three fingers indicate that he is Orthodox.

[4] (*15) Work on the master's fields (*barshchina*), compulsory, unpaid labor of serfs on the manorial fields, that is, on the master's own demesne lands. Barshchina was generally considered the worst and most burdensome form of serfdom, and people generally thought of barshchina when they thought of serfdom.

best ones don't leave us any time for ourselves. In the winter he won't let us do any carting of goods and won't let us go into town to work; all our work has to be for him, because he pays our head tax. It is an invention of the Devil to turn your peasants over to work for a stranger. You can make a complaint against (*18) a bad steward, but to whom can you complain against a bad tenant?"

"My friend, you are mistaken; the laws forbid them to torture people."

"Torture? That's true; but all the same, sir, you would not want to be in my hide." Meanwhile the ploughman hitched up the other horse to the plough and bade me goodbye as he began a new furrow.

The words of this peasant awakened in me a multitude of thoughts. I thought especially of the inequality of treatment within the peasant class. I compared the crown peasants with the manorial peasants.[5] They both live in villages; but the former pay a fixed sum, while the latter must be prepared to pay whatever their master demands. The former are judged by their equals; the latter are dead to the law, except, perhaps, in criminal cases. A member of society becomes known to the government protecting him, only when he breaks the social bonds, when he becomes a criminal! This thought made my blood boil.

(*19) Tremble, cruelhearted landlord! on the brow of each of your peasants I see your condemnation written (pp. 46-48).

Peshki

... For the first time I looked closely at all the household gear of a peasant hut. For the first time I turned my heart to things over which it had only glided heretofore. The upper half of the four walls, and the whole ceiling, were covered with soot; the floor was full of cracks and covered with dirt at least two inches thick; the oven without a smoke-stack, but their best protection against the cold; and smoke filling the hut every morning, winter and summer; window holes over which were stretched bladders which admitted a dim light at noon time; two or three pots (happy the hut if one of them each day contains some watery cab-bage soup!). (*413) A wooden bowl and round trenchers called plates; a table, hewn with an axe, which they scrape clean on holidays. A trough to feed the pigs and calves, if there are any. They sleep together with them, swallowing the air in which a burning candle appears as though shrouded in mist or hidden behind a curtain. If they are lucky, a barrel of kvas that tastes like vinegar, and in the yard a bath house in which the cattle sleep if people are not steaming in it. A homespun shirt, the foot-wear given them by nature, and leggings and bast shoes when they go out. Here one justly looks for the source of the country's wealth, power, and might; but here are also seen the weakness, inadequacy, and abuse

[5] (*18) Crown and manorial peasants, those on lands belonging respectively to the crown and to individual landed proprietors.

of the laws: their harsh side, so to speak. Here may be seen the greed of the gentry, our rapaciousness and tyranny; and the helplessness of the poor. Ravening beasts, insatiable leeches, what do we leave for the peasants? What (*414) we cannot take from them, the air. Yes, and nothing but the air. We frequently take from them not only the gifts of the earth, bread and water, but also the very light. The law forbids us to take their life—that, is, to take it suddenly. But there are so many ways to take it from them by degrees! On one side there is almost unlimited power; on the other, helpless impotence. For the landlord is to the peasant at once legislator, judge, executor of his own judgments, and, if he so desires, a plaintiff against whom the defendant dare say nothing. It is the lot of one cast into fetters, of one thrown into a dismal dungeon: the lot of the ox under the yoke.

Hard-hearted landlord, look at the children of the peasants subject to you! They are almost naked. Why? Have you not imposed upon those who bore them—in pain and sorrow—a tax, in addition to all their work on your fields? Do you not (*415) appropriate the linen to your own use even before it is woven? And of what use to you are the stinking rags which your hand, accustomed to luxury, finds loathsome to touch? They will scarcely do for your servants to wipe your cattle with. You collect even that which you do not need, in spite of the fact that the unprotected nakedness of your peasants will be a heavy count against you. If there is no judge over you here, you will be answerable before the Judge Who is no respecter of persons, Who once gave you a good guide, conscience, whom, however, your perverse reason long ago drove from his dwelling place, your heart. But do not imagine that you will escape punishment. The sleepless watcher of your deeds will surprise you when you are alone, and you will feel his chastising strokes. Oh, if only they could be of some good to you and those subject to you!—Oh, if man would but look into his soul more frequently, and confess his deeds to his implacable judge, his conscience! (*416) Transformed by its thunderous voice into an immovable pillar, he would no longer dare to commit secret crimes; destruction and devastation would become rare—etc., etc., etc. (pp. 220-221).

The following is a Soviet interpretation of Radishchev's contributions on the occasion of the two hundredth anniversary of his birth:

"A Remarkable Russian Writer and Revolutionary" by V. Orlov in Literaturnaya Gazeta, August 10, 1949

... Radishchev belongs among those truly great and noble people of the Russian nation of whom the Soviet people are proud. His creative work represents the peak of eighteenth century social thought. Among the thinkers and writers of that time there is no one in the whole world who could equal Radishchev in the depth, resoluteness, and consistency of his revolutionary views.

The elemental struggle for liberation of the Russian people against the tyranny of landlords and the oppression of a feudal absolutist state, and above all, that most powerful manifestation of national wrath—the peasant war of 1773-1775, headed by Yemelyan Pugatchev, had a most profound influence on the formulation of Radishchev's world outlook. In his time, Radishchev was the only writer among the nobles who recognized the people's moral and historical right to overthrow autocracy by force and to abolish slavery.

His sympathetic attitude toward the Pugatchev uprising sharply distinguishes Radishchev from the other eighteenth century propagators of enlightenment. The French enlighteners and materialist philosophers who laid the ideological foundations for the bourgeois revolution of the eighteenth century were nevertheless quite moderate in their immediate political demands. As a rule, they compromised on "enlightened despotism." Radishchev flatly rejected the principle of absolutism. He did not have any illusions as to the "philosopher on the throne," and he exposed the demagogical falsehood of Catherine II's official "enlightenment," by which she tried to camouflage her despotism....

Radishchev was an extremely well-educated man, with truly encyclopedic learning, which was based not only on science and literature, but also on a superb knowledge of reality and rich personal experience. The range of his interests was unusually vast. The economic situation and the cultural condition of Russia, the arbitrary exercise of state power unchecked by law, the evil deeds of slave owners, the poverty and lack of rights of slaves, questions of civil ethics and public education, enlightenment, the press and the censorship, the reactionary role of the church and religious superstitions, the position of the writer in society, the special problems of philosophy, history, political economy, law, art, and literature, of the natural sciences, astronomy, chemistry, medicine, agronomy —all interested Radishchev; he commented on everything; he was armed with precise knowledge in every field, and he managed to strike a new note—the note of the materialist and revolutionary.

A profound faith in the creative abilities of the people, in their constructive energy, in their will to struggle for liberty, characterized the fiery patriotic feeling that possessed Radishchev. He said of the Russian people:

> Firmness in enterprises, and indefatigability in performance are the essential qualities distinguishing the people of Russia. . . . O people, born to greatness and fame, if only these qualities were to be directed toward all that could be achieved for the common happiness!

Jealous of the liberty and happiness of the Russian people, *born to greatness and fame* but humiliated and oppressed by tsars and landlords,

Radishchev subordinated his entire work to the clearly comprehended problems of the struggle for liberation.

In 1790 Radishchev published (anonymously and by his private press) *A Journey from St. Petersburg to Moscow*—a book which immortalized his name.

Radishchev was seized, thrown into the casemate of the Petropavlovsk Fortress, tried, and condemned to death. The sentence was thereafter "commuted," and he was exiled to the remote Ilimsk Prison in eastern Siberia.

In his preface to the *Journey* Radishchev said that when he looked "around him" at Russian reality, his heart "was torn by the sufferings of humanity." The sufferings of oppressed humanity and its struggle for liberation became Radishchev's main theme. Desiring to characterize Russian autocracy in metaphor, he inserted a line from Tredyakovsky's *Telemachiad* as the epigraph of his book: "A monster heavy, big, immense, hundred-mouthed, and barking." With remarkable courage and superb daring, he began to struggle alone against this huge monster and dealt him a crushing blow.

Radishchev, with great expository force and with clear and impressive examples, portrayed the terrible and repulsive image of serfdom.

With pain and anger Radishchev tells of the sale of whole families of peasants on the slave block, of the barbaric recruiting custom, of the tragic fate of the educated serfs—people who accidentally received an education because of a landowner's whim, but who remained slaves without rights—and of the robbery and extortion of the great lords, tsarist bureaucrats, and various worldly parasites living off the people and getting rich at their expense.

Consumed by a burning and irreconcilable hatred of serfdom, Radishchev flatly stated in his book that this horrible world of violence and oppression must be utterly destroyed and from its fragments a new world must be built, based on "personal liberty," inasmuch as "man is born entirely free" and "enslavement is a crime."

Radishchev not only spoke openly in defense of the people's interests, but he also depicted their greatness and nobility, their indestructible spiritual strength, heroism, and unselfishness. In the Russian peasant, bowed down by the landowners' yoke and beaten by landowners and officials, Radishchev discerned a man in the full and genuine sense of the word— a man whose moral qualities cannot be compared with the corrupt "morals" of the landowners, "who are unworthy of being called human."

Radishchev, discerning in the people a source of moral strength, also saw in them a guarantee of a better future. He understood that the people would obtain freedom only if they won it for themselves. In his *Journey* he declared flatly and unequivocally that the liberation of the serfs could be expected not from the "counsels" of liberal champions of the people who remain "great lords of the manor"... but only from "the burden of enslavement itself." This was a call for a peasant revolution, and this is precisely how Catherine understood Radishchev. In her remarks on the *Journey* she wrote in regard to the above-mentioned citation: "That is, he pins his hope on a peasant uprising." The tsaritsa called Radishchev himself "a worse rebel than Pugatchev."

Radishchev openly threatened the landowners with a new Pugachev. He wrote that the peasants are only "awaiting the occasion and the hour," and he predicted "sword and poison, fire and death" for the landlords as a just retribution for their "severity and inhumanity. . . ."

The author had profound faith in the constructive powers of the people. He expressed firm assurance in the fact that the eradication of the "tribe" of serfs would not do any damage to Russian statehood and culture, because the people, in gaining their freedom, would produce new and worthier leaders from their ranks:

> Oh, even if the slaves, weighed down by their heavy bonds, and enraged by their despair, would break with iron the heads of us who block their freedom, the heads of their inhuman masters, and stain their fields with our blood—what would the state lose thereby? Soon great men would be wrested from their ranks as replacements for the beaten tribe; but they would have a different opinion of themselves and would be deprived of their rights of oppression. This is not a dream, but a gaze that pierces the thick screen of time concealing the future from our eyes. I am looking through a whole century.

He actually "did look through a whole century." Radishchev's world outlook, of course, was limited by the patterns imposed by social and historical reality of his time. He did not and could not discern the whole depth of the controversies of the new social order, which was an outgrowth of feudalism and serfdom. But he guessed at these controversies. Responding with sympathy to the war of liberation in the North American colonies against English sovereignty, Radishchev at the same time discerned with remarkable insight the real form of the American "democracy," which left millions of Negroes as slaves, who "till the abundant fields of America under the heavy club of material progress."

In the famous ode *Liberty,* excerpts of which are published in the *Journey,* Radishchev set forth his political convictions. This ode is an inspired hymn to freedom, "the source of all great deeds." Its central theme—the theme of the people's revenge against tyrants—is embodied in a striking picture of a revolutionary uprising.

In the final verses of *Liberty,* Radishchev's imagination shifts to the inevitable (though remote, as he understands it) liberation of "the dear fatherland," when the power of despotism "will be dispelled in an instant," when "all misfortunes will vanish," and when the "day of days" will dawn over Russia.

For a whole century autocracy attempted to suppress Radishchev's thought, strictly prohibiting the reprinting of the *Journey.* Even as late as 1903 this seditious book was burned by order of the tsarist court.

But the truth uttered by Radishchev could not be silenced. The ideas of liberation which he proclaimed were inherited and developed by all the really progressive forces of Russian public opinion and literature. The radical democratic writers and journalists of the nineteenth century, the Decembrists and Pushkin, Griboyedov and Lermontov, Belinsky and Herzen, and Dobrolyubov and Tchernyshevsky perceived a vital and continuing bond between themselves and Radishchev.

19. Gerasim Lebedev: a pioneer of Russian oriental studies*

I HAPPENED TO ACQUIRE a most interesting book in one of Moscow's book stores—the *Asiatic Annual Register,* which was published in London in 1799. This compilation of about a thousand pages, which contains a great number of original documents on the history of English policy in India, long ago became a bibliographical rarity, not only here, but also in England.

In leafing through its yellowed pages, I saw handwritten notes along the borders, which were written in Russian in a hand characteristic of the eighteenth century. It was obviously the handwriting of the first owner of the book. Who, then, was this Russian who apparently had a good command of the English language and who was acquainted with the affairs of India? After turning a few more pages, I found the answer. Next to the extensive obituary of a certain Honorable John Hyde, Esquire, who was a member of the Supreme Court of Calcutta, there was written in Russian: "John Hyde. He was truly a most fair judge and a humanitarian. And that he was such, I hereby testify through my personal experience. Gerasim Lebedev."

So he is the one to whom this rare book belonged!

I recalled everything I knew about Gerasim Lebedev, that surprising self-made man of eighteenth-century Russia.

He was the son of an impoverished parish priest and did not learn to read until the age of fifteen. The church choirmaster, who was enraptured by the beauty and power of his voice, taught the boy to read notes.

In 1775 he obtained a position as choirboy in the Russian embassy en route to Naples, and left his motherland. He was then 25 years old.

The embassy was detained a long time in Vienna, and Lebedev began to journey through Europe alone, hoping to maintain himself by means of his musical art.

He mentions briefly that he had the opportunity of giving performances in many European households and of "earning the good will of great landowners and other important personages."

* By E. Steinberg, Professor, Doctor of Historical Sciences in *Ogonyok,* No. 10, March 1947

120

A certain rich Englishman invited him to enter his service. Lebedev accepted the offer and went first to London and later to East India. So here he is in Madras. The news of the Russian artist's musical talents quickly spreads through the local English colony. He is flooded with invitations to social balls and family celebrations. He is liberally remunerated for these appearances. The English Maecenas, having wound up his affairs, sailed for home. Lebedev remained in Madras.

He associated only casually with the residents of the European settlement. It was much more interesting to wander through the alleys of the ancient Hindu city or to sit in a tavern, where from morning till night a motley troop of people gathered, and where it was always possible to listen to wandering singers. He not only completely mastered the English language in two years, but also learned Tamil and Telugu, which are the two most widely used tongues of southeast India.

In 1787 Gerasim Lebedev moved from Madras to Bengal, and then to Calcutta. At that time the residence of the English Governor-General was still a small and quite slovenly little city, but already the outlines of the future sumptuous capital of the British eastern empire were beginning to appear. From here emanated those threads of English diplomacy and espionage which enveloped the households of Indian maharajahs, nabobs, and sultans. Hither poured golden rupees and pagodas, procured through blackmail, extortion, and direct looting by officers and officials of the East India Company. Here lucrative leases, charters, contracts, and profitable positions were obtained by means of fabulous bribes.

Having received a modest position as a translator, Gerasim Lebedev plunged into the study of Sanskrit, the ancient written language of India, and the study of contemporary Bengali. He translated several ancient literary manuscripts into Russian and English, compiled a grammar, dialogues, and a dictionary of the Bengalese language, and collected and prepared extensive materials on the ideology and mores of the Hindus. Lebedev's scholarly labors won deep respect among the educated Brahmins. Many came to Calcutta especially to talk with him.

But Lebedev could not remain a mere bookish scholar. His was a volatile and, above all, an artistic nature. He had a long-standing dream: to create a new Indian theatre. He translated into Bengalese the English comedy *Pretensions,* which was written in the spirit of Sheridan's plays, selected Indian actors, and trained them patiently. It was necessary that the actors understand the character of the persons in the European comedy and at the same time preserve the methods and traditions of Indian national art. Now the troupe is gathered and the play learned. Only a building is lacking. All suitable buildings had already been rented by the officials of the East India Company to English entrepreneurs presenting shows designed for the low tastes of newly rich colonial upstarts.

Lebedev began the construction of a building for his theatre. His modest savings quickly melted away, and it was necessary to have recourse to usurers.

The day of the first performance arrived. The hall, designed for 400 persons, was filled to overflowing. Everyone was curious to see how the Indian comedians would portray the gentlemen and fashionable ladies of London's West End. Their success surpassed Lebedev's fondest expectations. He was flustered, happy, and proud. Come what might, it was he who created the new Indian theatre!

Success having lent him wings, Gerasim Lebedev prepares for new presentations. Now he writes his own Russian play, translates it into Bengalese, and studies it with his actors.

Meanwhile, the entrepreneurs of Calcutta, alarmed by the triumph of Lebedev's theatre, unite to get rid of such a dangerous competitor. Lawsuits followed one after another. A lengthy, tiresome litigation ensues. Lebedev is naive and inexperienced, while his opponents are cunning money-makers who enjoy the patronage of the colonial authorities.

Only with the greatest of difficulty was Lebedev able to escape prison. But he finally emerged from this mess a ruined and broken man. He lost his position. No one wished to publish his compositions and translations.

Through an acquaintance, an English captain, Lebedev sends a letter to Count Semyon Romanovitch Vorontsov, the Russian Ambassador in London. This letter, which was published in 1880 in the 24th volume of the *Vorontsov Archieves,* gives a sufficiently clear picture of Gerasim Lebedev's personality.

In describing the misfortunes he had suffered, Lebedev complains that "due to the envy of theatrical producers, I was defrauded, robbed, and ruined, and in this matter I could not gain the favour of the guardians of justice. . . ." He tells of the baiting he received from competing translators who enjoyed the full patronage of the East India Company, noting bitterly: "The whole world knows that foreigners fare better in Russia. . . ."

He writes with contempt of the "Company's suckling pigs" in Calcutta who persecute him: ". . . they do not comprehend the glory of the Sanskrit alphabet, and peck as they may, they cannot ingest the pearls of Hindustan literature." He asks the Ambassador to defend him in "this foreign Far Eastern country" and to help him "in making known my achievements, which were written in Bengalese as a labor of love to my native land and translated with all possible regard for the truth."

The Ambassador apparently answered this appeal.

At the end of 1797 Lebedev left India. In London in 1801, with the help of Vorontsov, he succeeded in publishing his valuable scientific work in the English language: *Grammars of the Pure and Mixed East Indian Dialects with Supplementary Dialogues,* etc. In this book Lebedev gives a detailed analysis of the errors in the grammars of the Indian languages by various European authors, and he fearlessly criticizes the theories of such a scholarly authority of that time as William Jones. From London he finally returns to his motherland, and receives funds from the government for the establishment of a special publishing house with Sanskrit type. In 1805 he published his second work in the Russian language. This work, which was called *An Impartial Contemplation of the Brahmin System of Eastern India, Their Holy Rites, and National Customs,* was immediately translated into German and was highly esteemed in the scientific circles of Western Europe. This is all that is known of the works of Gerasim Lebedev. He lived about thirteen years longer, holding a position in the Ministry of Foreign Affairs, and published nothing else, in any event nothing which has come down to us; and he died in 1818, forgotten by his contemporaries.

Such is the fragmentary information extant concerning Gerasim Stepanovitch Lebedev—scholar extraordinary, traveler, artist, writer, and theatrical director, founder of the new Indian theatre, and progenitor of that most scintillating galaxy of Russian oriental scholars of the nineteenth and twentieth centuries.

20. Karamzin: serfdom and emancipation

NICHOLAS M. KARAMZIN (1766-1826) was an outstanding early nineteenth century historian of highly conservative views, best known for his *History of the Russian State* (to 1610) and his *Memoir on Ancient and Modern Russia* (written 1810-1811). Karamzin was a vigorous advocate of autocracy (as distinguished from despotism) as Russia's traditional form of government. Although he hailed the accession of Alexander I, which followed a period of extreme reaction under Paul I, he became increasingly disillusioned over Alexander's domestic and foreign policies. His *Memoir*, apparently inspired by the politically ambitious Grand Duchess Catherine, the Emperor's younger sister, included strong and by no means dispassionate criticism of the Tsar. At the time, however, the manuscript was known only to a handful of Russians. Until 1870, when the first complete edition appeared in Russia, handwritten copies of the manuscript were circulated.

Karamzin was a true representative of the Russian gentry which for economic reasons opposed some of Alexander's measures of "reform," especially those pertaining to serfdom. His views on emancipation, therefore, reflect not merely his personal opinions, but the thinking of a broad strata of Russian society in the early nineteenth century. In the excerpt from his *Memoir* reproduced below, he attacks two measures in particular: the Law of Free Agriculturists (1803), which permitted landlords to free their serfs individually or by entire villages on the basis of contractual agreements, with the proviso that the serfs were given an allotment of land; and the law forbidding the Sale and Purchase of Recruits, directed against the reprehensible practice indulged in by many of the gentry, burghers, and state peasants, who evaded military service by the substitution of serfs acquired from private landlords for the purpose. The Russian gentry feared these reforms as the precursor of general emancipation.

From *Karamzin's Memoir on Ancient and Modern Russia*. Translated and analyzed by Richard Pipes (Cambridge, Mass.: Harvard University Press, 1959), pp. 162-163; 165-167. Reprinted by permission.

... The act to which I want to turn next has offended many and gladdened no one, although the sovereign, when he issued it, was inspired by the most sacred humanitarianism. We have heard of monstrous landowners who engaged in an inhuman traffic with people. Having purchased a village, these men picked the peasants fit for military service, and then sold them without land. Let us assume that there still are such beasts today. Trade of this kind should then be outlawed by a strict decree, containing a proviso that the estates of the unworthy landowners engaging in it are to be placed under guardianship. The enforcement of such a law could be entrusted to the governors. Instead of doing this, the government outlaws the sale and purchase of recruits. In the past, the better farmer toiled gladly for ten, twenty years in order to accumulate 700 or 800 rubles with which to purchase a recruit, so as to keep his family intact. Now he has lost his most powerful incentive to engage in beneficent hard work and stay sober. Of what use is wealth to a parent if it cannot save his beloved son? Yes, innkeepers rejoice, but the heads of families weep. The state must have its recruits—it is better to draw them from miserable than from happy people, for the latter are incomparably worse off in the army than they were before. I would like to ask whether the peasants of a tyrannical landlord—one whose greed is such that he would be capable of selling them as recruits—prosper from the prohibition of such sales? If anything, their lot may be less miserable in the regiments! But as for the landowners of modest means, they have now lost an opportunity of ridding themselves of unsatisfactory peasants or household serfs, to their own and to society's benefit; under the old system the lazy, intemperate peasant would mend his ways in the strict military school, while the diligent, sober one would remain behind the plow. Moreover, the example itself exercised a salutary effect, and other peasants swore off the bottle knowing the master's rights to sell them as recruits. What means has a petty landowner nowadays with which to frighten his dissolute peasants when it is not his turn to furnish recruits? The cane? Backbreaking labor? Is it not more useful to have them frightened of the cane in the ranks of the military company? One may argue that our soldiers have improved as a result of this decree, but have they indeed? I inquired of generals—they have not noticed it. At any rate, it is true that the village peasants have deteriorated. The father of three or even two sons readies in good time one of them for the draft, and keeps him unmarried; the son, knowing what awaits him, drinks, because good behavior will not save him from military service. The legislator should view things from a variety of angles and not merely from one; or else, extirpating one evil, he may occasion yet greater evil.

Thus we are told that the present government had the intention of emancipating proprietary serfs. . . .

What does the emancipation of serfs in Russia entail? That they be allowed to live where they wish, that their masters be deprived of all authority over them, and that they come exclusively under the authority of the state. Very well. But these emancipated peasants will have no land, which—this is incontrovertible—belongs to the gentry. They will, there-fore, either stay on with their present landlords, paying them quitrent, cultivating their fields, delivering bread where necessary—in a word, continuing to serve them as before; or else, dissatisfied with the terms, they will move to another, less exacting, landlord. In the first case, is it not likely that the masters, relying on man's natural love for his native soil, will impose on the peasants the most onerous terms? Previously they had spared them, seeing in the serfs their own property, but now the greedy among them will try to exact from the peasants all that is physically possible. The landlords will draw up a contract, the tiller will renege—and there will be lawsuits, eternal lawsuits! In the second case, with the peasant now here, now there, won't the treasury suffer losses in the collection of the soul-tax and other revenues? Will not agriculture suffer as well? Will not many fields lie fallow, and many granaries stay empty? After all, the bread on our markets comes, for the most part, not from the free farmers but from the gentry. And here is one more evil consequence of emancipation: the peasants, no longer subjected to seignorial justice from which there is no appeal and which is free of charge, will take to fighting each other and litigating in the city—what ruin! . . . Freed from the surveillance of the masters who dis-pose of their own *zemskaia isprava,* or police, which is much more active than all the Land Courts, the peasants will take to drinking and villainy —what a gold mine for taverns and corrupt police officials, but what a blow to morals and to the security of the state! In short, at the present time, the gentry, dispersed throughout the realm, assist the monarch in the preservation of peace and order; by divesting them of this supervisory authority, he would, like Atlas, take all of Russia upon his shoulders. Could he bear it? A collapse would be frightful. The primary obligation of the monarch is to safeguard the internal and external unity of the state; benefiting estates and individuals comes second. Alexander wishes to improve the lot of the peasants by granting them freedom; but what if this freedom should harm the state? And will the peasants be happier, freed from their masters' authority, but handed over to their own vices, to tax farmers, and to unscrupulous judges? There can be no question that the serfs of a sensible landlord, one who contents himself with a moderate quitrent, or with labor on a *desiatina* of plowland for each household, are happier than state peasants, for they have in him a vigilant protector and defender. Is it not better quietly to take measures to bridle cruel landlords? These men are known to the governors. If the latter faithfully fulfill their obligations, such landlords will promptly become a thing of the past; and unless Russia has wise and honest governors, the free peasants will not prosper either. I do not know whether Godunov did well in depriving the peasants of their freedom since the conditions of that time are not fully known. But I do know that this is not the time to return it to them. Then they had the habits of free men— today they have the habits of slaves. It seems to me that from the point of view of political stability it is safer to enslave men than to give them freedom prematurely. Freedom demands preparation through moral improvement—and who would call our system of wine-farming and the dreadful prevalence of drunkenness a sound preparation for freedom? In conclusion, we have this to say to the good monarch: "Sire! history will not reproach you for the evil which you have inherited (assuming that serfdom actually is an unequivocal evil), but you will answer before God, conscience, and posterity for every harmful consequence of your own statutes."

I do not condemn Alexander's law permitting villages to gain their freedom with their masters' permission. But are many of them sufficiently rich to avail themselves of it? Will there be many prepared to surrender all they have in return for freedom? The serfs of humane landlords are content with their lot; those who serve bad landlords are impoverished— the situation of both categories renders this law ineffectual.

21. the Decembrists:

aristocrats revolt

THE DECEMBRIST UPRISING (December 14/26, 1825) is sometimes called the first Russian Revolution. It marked the first attempt in modern Russian history to overthrow the autocracy. Its leaders were aristocrats — complete amateurs in revolutionary theory and tactics — who were disillusioned by the failure of the monarchy to achieve basic political and social reforms following the Napoleonic Wars. The occasion of the uprising was the accession to the throne of Nicholas I, a known reactionary, in preference to his older and seemingly more liberal brother, Constantine. Poorly organized, the uprising amounted to little more than demonstrations of disapproval, which Nicholas I had no difficulty in suppressing. Five of its leaders were executed and over one hundred exiled to Siberia. The Decembrist revolt was nevertheless of profound significance, because it occurred in the Russian capital and because its leaders represented the flower of the Russian aristocracy. They were celebrated thereafter as martyrs to the cause of constitutional government.

The three excerpts below, the work of two leading Decembrists, A. A. Bestuzhev and Prince S. P. Trubetskoi, as samples of the voluminous amount of primary source material pertaining to the Decembrist movement, provide some understanding of the origins of the revolt and the aims of its leaders. Two useful secondary accounts are Anatole Mazour, *The First Russian Revolution, 1825* (Berkeley: University of California Press, 1937); and Mikhail Zetlin, *The Decembrists,* trans. George Panin (New York: International Universities Press, Inc., 1958).

i. Decembrist A. A. Bestuzhev to Emperor Nicholas I

In this extract of an undated letter to Nicholas I, A. A. Bestuzhev (1797-1837) outlines the causes of the Decembrist movement, naming Russia's international situation, the impact of the Napoleonic

Wars, and the conditions prevailing among the various social classes, in particular, the lower middle class, the merchants, and the nobility. The letter was written from Petropavlovsk prison, where the writer was already confined on December 15/27, 1825. Bestuzhev, a writer and literary critic, was exiled to Yakutsk. He and his brother, Nicholas, were the first exiles to open a school in Nerchinsk for vocational training. In 1829, Bestuzhev was transferred to the Caucasus, where he served as a common soldier and where, under the pseudonym of Marlinsky, he wrote a number of stories and novels which were best sellers in their time. As his letter reveals, Bestuzhev regarded serfdom as unethical and unwarranted.

The excerpt translated below is from *Khrestomatiya po istorii SSSR,* Vol. II (Moscow, 1953), 538-542.

Your Imperial Majesty!
Confident that you, the Sovereign, love the truth, I make bold to set before you the historical development of freedom of thought in Russia and, in general, of the many concepts which constitute the moral and political aspects of the events of December 14. I shall speak with complete frankness, without concealing the evil, likewise without toning down my expressions, for the duty of a loyal subject is to tell the monarch the unvarnished truth. I commence.

The beginning of the reign of the Emperor Alexander was marked by the most brilliant hopes for the well-being of Russia. The nobility had recuperated; the merchant class made no complaints about advancing credit; the army served without making trouble; scholars studied what they pleased; everyone said what he thought, and all who were doing well expected to do still better. Unfortunately, circumstances prevented that and hopes faded without fulfillment. The unsuccessful war of 1807[1] and many other things upset the finances; but this was lost sight of during preparations for the War of the Fatherland. Finally, Napoleon invaded Russia, and only then did the Russian people, for the first time, become aware of their strength; only then did there awaken in all hearts a feeling for independence, first political, and later also national. This marked the beginning of freedom of thought in Russia. The government itself uttered the words: "Freedom, Liberation!" It disseminated works about the abuses resulting from the unlimited power of Napoleon; and the cry of the Russian monarch resounded on the banks of the Rhine and the Seine. The war was not yet over, when the soldiers returning home first spread discontent among the masses. "We have shed our

[1] The War of Russia against Napoleon, 1806-1807, in alliance with Prussia, culminated badly for Russia in the Peace of Tilsit.

blood," they said, "and yet once again we are forced to sweat under the *barshchina*. We delivered the Fatherland from the tyrant, but once again the gentry tyrannizes over us." The army, from generals down to common soldiers, upon its return harped only on how good things were in foreign lands. The comparison with their own country naturally gave rise to the question: Why are things not the same here? At first, as long as they talked about this freely, their words were wafted away on the wind, for the mind, like gunpowder, is dangerous only under pressure. The ray of hope that the Tsar Emperor would grant a constitution, as he mentioned at the opening of the Seim[2] in Warsaw, and the attempts of some generals to liberate their serfs, still encouraged many. But after 1817 everything was changed. The people who witnessed evil, or who wished for better things, were compelled by the great number of spies to start conversing secretly, and this was the beginning of the secret societies. Oppression of deserving officers by the authorities inflamed men's minds. Then the military began to say: "Did we liberate Europe, only to assume her chains ourselves? Did we grant a constitution to France, only so that we dare not speak about it ourselves, and did we buy with our blood the first place among the nations, only to abase ourselves at home?" The destruction of the model schools and the persecution of education compelled us to think, in despair, about most important measures. And since the grumbling of the people, which stemmed from exhaustion and the abuses by rural and civil authorities, threatened bloody revolution, these societies intended to avert the greater evil by a lesser one, and to begin their activities at the earliest opportunity. Now I shall describe the situation, as we saw it in Russia.

Napoleon's troops, like locusts, for a long time left in their wake the seeds of destruction. Many provinces were impoverished and the dilatory measures or meager assistance given them by the government altogether destroyed them. Rain and drought brought famine to other areas. A system of jerry-built roads covered a third of Russia and grain rotted before it was cut. The abuses of the district police officers became more apparent to the improvished peasants, and those of the nobility more perceptible, because they began to understand the rights of the people. Forbidding distillation deprived many provinces of all means of marketing seed and the multiplication of saloons corrupted morals and ruined peasant life. The military colonies paralyzed not only the minds but also all the trade of the places in which they settled, and produced terror in the rest. The frequent marches of the regiments were an infinite burden to the inhabitants; shortage of money led the peasants into arrears that could not be repaid—in brief, everybody pined for the past, all grumbled about the present, and all craved something better than the empty rumor that places are being allotted on the Amu-Darya, which attracted thou-

[2] The representative assembly granted to Poland, and opened by the Tsar in 1818.

sands of residents of the Ukraine. Whither? They did not know themselves. Entire villages got under way and wandered at random, and much
resentment of the *barshchina* marked the last three years of Alexander's
reign.

The petty bourgeoisie [*meshchane*], a respectable and important class
in all other countries, is insignificant among us, is reduced to poverty,
burdened with obligations, and deprived of the means of subsistence. In
other nations, it inhabits the cities; with us, however, cities exist only on
the map, and freedom of trade hampers their shops, they roam from
place to place like gypsies, and busy themselves with the resale of trifles.
The decline of trade is reflected among them even more than among
the poor; for, as petty traders or factory workers, they depend on the
merchants.

The merchant class [*kypetchestvo*], restricted by the guilds and hampered in making deliveries, suffered a serious decline in 1812. Many
colossal fortunes were lost; others were shattered. Doing business with
the Treasury brought ruin to the majority of the merchants and con-
tractors, and along with them to their clients and warranters, due to
delayed payments, accounts and illegal pressure methods. Extortion made
itself felt everywhere. . . . Fraudulent bankruptcies multiplied and confidence collapsed. The instability of the tariff reduced to destitution many
manufacturers and frightened others, and both our own and foreign
negotiators lost confidence in our government. Consequently there was a
great decline in the value of our money abroad, because of state debts
and the general complaint that no cash was available. The illegal system,
which enriched the smugglers, did not increase the prices of our products
and, as was the fashion, all paid exorbitant prices for so-called confiscated
goods. Finally, a decree that the petty bourgeoisie and small traders
must either register with the police or pay fines would have inflicted a
decisive blow on trade, and the failure to execute it did not stop people
from complaining. Even without that, the decline in trade was so great
that at the principal fairs and at the ports exchange and exports abroad
were reduced by one-third. The merchants also complained justifiably
against foreigners, especially the English who, in spite of the law, had
their agents in the villages buying at the source raw materials for export
abroad, and thereby depriving small traders of business and the state of
the circulation of currency.

The nobility [*dvoryanstvo*] was likewise dissatisfied with the poor sale
of its products, high prices for luxury items, and protracted legal procedures. It is divided into three categories: the educated, of whom the
great part consists of people of rank; the literate, who either torture
others as judges or are themselves the victims of one lawsuit after
another; and finally, the hicks, who live in villages, serve as church
elders, or are already retired, having served, God knows, just as if they
were in the army. Of these, however, the small gentry constitutes the

ulcer of Russia; always guilty and always grumbling, and desiring to live beyond its means and in accordance with its pretentions, it tortures its poor peasants mercilessly. Others have ruined themselves at the chase, brawling (?), by riotous living in the capital, or by lawsuits. The greater part of the best nobility, which serves in the army or in the capitals, demanding luxury, entrusts its property to hirelings who rob the peasants and defraud their masters, and thus nine-tenths of the estates in Russia are disorganized and mortgaged. The village priesthood is in a sorry plight. Not having any fixed salary, its members are completely at the mercy of the peasants and are compelled to cater to them; and by so doing they lapse into vice, for which the law prescribes their removal. . . .

. . . The soldiers grumbled at exhausting drills, cleaning up, and performing guard duty; the officers, at their meager salaries and excessive discipline; the sailors at unskilled labor, aggravated by abuses; the naval officers at inactivity. People with talents complain that the road to advancement in the service is blocked to them, demanding from them nothing but unquestioning obedience; scholars that they are not allowed to teach; the youth at impediments to study. In brief, dissatisfied faces were to be seen everywhere; on the streets people shrugged their shoulders, everywhere they whispered rumors—everyone talked about where this would lead. All elements were in ferment. The government alone slumbered lightheartedly on the brink of a volcano; the tribunal alone was blissfully happy, because only for it was Russia the promised land. Their extortion reached an unprecedented degree of shamelessness. Scribes acquired horses, court clerks bought villages, and only the high cost of bribes distinguished people in high places, so that in the capital under the eyes of the police there was conducted an open traffic in justice. It wouldn't be so bad if payment were made for service, but they took it and did nothing. In all probability, Your Imperial Majesty is now familiar with these abuses, but they were concealed from the late Emperor. Lucrative positions were sold for a fixed fee and likewise required a kickback. The centralization of the courts, by luring each trifling matter to the top, encouraged appeals, inquiries, reviews, and decades elapsed before decisions were made, with the result that both sides were ruined.

In brief, in the treasury, in the courts, in the commissariats, at the governor's and at the governor-general's—everywhere, where interest was involved, whoever could, robbed, whoever lacked the courage, stole. Everywhere honest people suffered and pettifoggers and knaves rejoiced. . . .

II. Organization of the "Union of Salvation"

The Union of Salvation, a secret society, was founded in St. Petersburg, February 9/21, 1816, by a few close friends (named in the excerpt below) of widely divergent views, who formed the nucleus of the Decembrist movement. Its aims were vague and its members appear to have been inspired by patriotism and a desire for social reform. Later the program included the emancipation of the serfs and the substitution of a constitutional monarchy for Russia's autocratic regime. In the excerpt translated below, Prince S. P. Trubetskoi (1790-1860), one of the founders of the Union, tells of its origin, goals, and membership, and of the internal dissension that characterized it from the beginning.

Translated from *Zapiski knyazya S. P. Trubetskogo* (St. Petersburg, 1907), pp. 11-13.

Some young people, who formerly fought for the fatherland and its Tsar on the field of battle, wanted also to serve as the loyal bodyguard of their leader on the field of peace. They promised one another to assist the monarch by word and deed in all his plans for the welfare of his people. They were few in number, but they were confident that their circle would increase daily—that others, like them, would not want to confine themselves to feats of military glory, but would wish to evince their zeal and love for the fatherland, not solely by fulfillment of the service obligations imposed on them, but by the dedication of all their means and abilities to the promotion of all aspects of the general welfare.

For those who applied for membership in this small society, the requirements were, as follows: (1) Strict fulfillment of service obligations; (2) Honest, noble, and irreproachable conduct in personal life; (3) Corroboration, upon their word of honor, of all measures and propositions of the monarch for the general good; (4) Divulgence of praiseworthy deeds and censure of abuse by persons in any service whatsoever. The activities of the society must be based on the reasoning that many government employees and private persons would rise up against certain intentions of the Emperor (as, for instance, those concerning the liberation of the serfs), and, consequently, no matter how weak the voices of those who would justify this, the constant tendency in the society to speak about the subject in question and to justify it will convince many and will lend strength to the government to carry out its good intentions. In the beginning, the young people confined themselves solely to discussions. It was not yet known precisely what the monarch himself intended to do; but confident that he sincerely desired to promote the welfare of Russia, they decided to give form to the society and to define the course of action by which they intended to support and strengthen the monarch's proposals. On February 9, 1816, [Pavel] Pestel, Nikita Muravyev, Sergei Shipov, and [Sergei] Trubetskoi founded the society. Joining them were Alexander Nikolayevitch Muravyev, Nikolai Novikov (former director of the chancellery of Prince Repnin), Ilya Bibikov, Prince Ilya Dolgoruky, Fyodor Nikolayevitch Glinka, Sergei and Matvei Muravyev-Apostol, Prince Pavel Petrovitch Lopukhin, and [Ivan] Yakushkin. Pestel, Dolgoruky, and Trubetskoi were commissioned to write the constitution of the society. The last mentioned occupied himself with the rules for the admission of members and the procedures of the society. Dolgoruky devoted himself to the purpose of the society and the means of achieving it. Pestel was entrusted with the initiation ritual and internal organization. He had a predilection for the Masonic ritual and wanted to introduce something similar for purposes of solemnity. At the first general session for the reading and adoption of the constitution, Pestel gave some members reason to distrust him; in reading the preamble to them, he said that France flourished under the administration of the Committee of Public Safety. There was a general revolt against this and it left an unfavorable impression of him, which never could be eradicated, and which always led people to distrust him.

The Masonic ritual introduced in the sessions and for the admission of members impeded the activities of the society and led to secrecy, which was out-of-keeping with the characters of most of the members. They wanted open and above-board action, although provision was made to keep the objectives of the society secret, in order not to provide ammunition to those with malignant designs against the members. There was no requirement for general meetings, but only for private sessions for the communication of matters requiring the dissemination of information about the society to the public. And therefore it was decided, after a short time, to change the constitution in this respect, since it was admittedly impractical.

III. Trubetskoi's Manifesto to the Russian People, 1825

This Manifesto, drafted by the Decembrist "dictator," Prince S. P. Trubetskoi (1790-1860), was to have been issued on December 14, 1825, in the event of a successful uprising. Although hastily prepared, it is an important document, revealing the objectives of the Decembrists. Its author, a colonel in the Preobrazhensky Regiment established by Peter the Great, belonged to an old, aristocratic family. One of the founders of the Union of Salvation, Trubetskoi became leader of the Northern Society and its elected "dictator" in 1825. His failure to assume decisive command at the critical moment led to charges of cowardice and treason to the movement. Essentially a moderate, who favored reforms to prevent political upheaval, Trubetskoi was apprehensive of violent revolution and opposed to regicide. He distrusted Pavel Pestel, leader of the more radical Southern Society. Although Pestel was executed, Trubetskoi was sentenced to hard labor for life in the Nerchinsk foundries. In 1856 he was pardoned and returned to Russia. His *Notes* were published in London in 1864.

Translated from *Vosstanie dekabristov. Materialy,* Vol. I (Moscow-Leningrad, 1925), 107-108.

O God, save Thy people, and bless them!
The Senate Manifesto proclaims, as follows:
1. Abolition of the former regime.
2. Establishment of a Provisional Government until a permanent one is elected.
3. Freedom of the press, and therefore abolition of censorship.
4. Freedom to all faiths for the performance of public worship.
5. Abolition of the right to own people as property.
6. Equality of all classes before the law, and therefore abolition of military courts and all kinds of judicial commissions; from which all cases will go to the nearest civil courts.
7. Declaration of the right of every citizen to engage in any enterprise of his choice, and therefore the nobleman, merchant, petty bourgeois, and peasant all have equal rights to enter the military and civil services, and to follow a religious calling, wholesale and retail trade, provided they pay established taxes for such trade. To acquire all kinds of property, such as land and houses in villages and cities. To conclude all kinds of contracts among themselves, and to summon one another to court.
8. Removal of the per capita [poll] tax and arrears.
9. Abolition of monopolies; for instance, those on salt and the sale of alcoholic liquor, etc.; and therefore the institution of free distillation and procurement of salt, with payment commensurate to the quantity of salt and vodka procured.
10. Abolition of recruiting and of military colonies.
11. Reduction of the term of military service for the rank and file, to be followed by equalization of military service for all classes.
12. Retirement without exception of all who have served in the lower ranks fifteen years.
13. Establishment of *volost*,[3] county, *guberniya* [provincial], and regional administrations, and of procedures for the election of those members of the administration who must replace all officials previously appointed by the civil government.
14. Public trials.

[3] Small rural district (eds.).

15. Introduction of juries in criminal and civil courts. There shall be established an Administration of two or three persons, to which all parts of the highest administration shall be subject, that is, all the Ministries, the Council, the Committee of Ministers, the Army, and the Navy. In brief, the entire supreme executive power, exclusive of the legislative and judicial branches. For the latter, there remains the Ministry, subject to the Provisional Government, but for the judgment of cases not decided in the lower courts there will remain the department of the Senate for criminal cases and the department created for civil cases, which shall have final jurisdiction, and the members of which shall remain in office until a permanent government is established.

The Provisional Government is commissioned to carry out:

(1) Equalization of the rights of all classes.

(2) Formation of local *volost,* county, *guberniya,* and regional administrations.

(3) Formation of a National Guard.

(4) Formation of a judicial branch, with juries.

(5) Equalization of recruiting service among all classes.

(6) Abolition of the regular army.

(7) Establishment of procedures for the election of candidates to the House of the People's Representatives, which must ratify the future system of Government and the State Constitution.

22. S. S. Uvarov and the theory of official nationality

THE TERSE FORMULA OF THE OFFICIAL IDEOLOGY of Tsarism in the reign of Nicholas I (1825-1855)—"Orthodoxy, Autocracy, and Nationality"—was first confronted in the writings of Count Serge S. Uvarov (1786-1855). Uvarov presided at the intellectual helm in Russia as President of the Imperial Academy of Sciences (1818-1855) and as Minister of National Education (1833-1849), during an era of political reaction. Although he had received a liberal, Western education, Uvarov readily adapted himself to the climate of opinion under Nicholas I, and his main objective became the implementation of the doctrine of official nationality in Russian intellectual life and in the educational system. Brilliant as he undoubtedly was, he was distrusted and disliked by many of his contemporaries. S. Soloviev, in particular, denounced him for propagating Orthodoxy when he himself was an atheist, autocracy, when he was a liberal, and nationality, when he read French and German books rather than Russian. To his credit, Uvarov established an "Asian Academy" to promote research in Oriental studies.

See I. M. Solov'ev, *Russkie universitety v ikh ustavakh i vospominanniyakh sovremennikov,* ch. I. (SPB, 1914), str. 53-54.

Amid the rapid decline of religious and civilian institutions in Europe and the universal dissemination of destructive concepts, and in view of the sad occurrences surrounding us on every side, it became necessary to strengthen the fatherland on the firm foundations which are the basis of the prosperity, strength, and life of the people; to discover the principles that are the distinguishing marks of Russian character and that belong to it exclusively; to assemble into one whole the sacred remnants of its nationality and on them to anchor our salvation. Fortunately, Russia has preserved a warm faith in the salutary principles without which she cannot prosper, become strong, or live.

Sincerely and profoundly attached to the church of his fathers, the Russian from time immemorial has regarded it as the guarantee of social and family happiness.

Without love for the faith of its ancestors, a people no less than an individual must perish. The Russian, devoted to the fatherland, is no more likely to consent to the loss of one of the dogmas of our *Orthodoxy* than to the theft of even one pearl from the crown of Monomakh.

Autocracy constitutes the condition of Russia's political existence. The Russian colossus rests upon it as upon the cornerstone of its greatness. This truth is felt by the overwhelming majority of Your Majesty's subjects. They feel it in full measure, although they come from various walks of life and differ in education, as well as in their relations to the government.

The salutary conviction that Russia lives and is preserved by the spirit of a strong, humane, and enlightened autocracy must permeate the people's education and develop with it.

Along with these two national principles, there is a third, no less important, no less powerful—that of *Nationality*. The question of nationality lacks the unity of the former; but both emanate from the same source and are interwoven with every page of the history of Russian Tsardom. As regards nationality, the only difficulty consists in bringing into harmony the ancient and new concepts; but nationality does not compel us to retrogress or to stand still; it does not demand immobility in ideas. The governmental structure, like the human body, changes its outward aspect in proportion to its age; its features alter with the years, but its physiognomy must not change.

Reference

RIASANOVSKY, NICHOLAS V., *Nicholas I and Official Nationality in Russia, 1825-1855* (Berkeley and Los Angeles: University of California Press, 1959).

23. Belinsky's "letter to Gogol,"
July 3, 1847

VISSARION GRIGORYEVITCH BELINSKY (1811-1848), son of a country doctor, was the real founder of literary criticism in Russia. The Russian literary critic of the nineteenth century was much more than a reviewer of books on the Western model. His articles on Russian works served as a vehicle for the expression of his own ideas. The exclusive circle of Russian readers often paid as much attention to an outstanding critic as to the works he reviewed. From 1833, when his literary career began, Belinsky contributed to a number of well-known Russian magazines, including *Teleskop, Moskovski Nablyudatel (Moscow Observer), Otechestvennye Zapiski (Fatherland Notes),* and *Sovremennik (The Contemporary).*

During a sojourn abroad for his health, Belinsky in 1847 wrote his famous "Letter to Gogol" to upbraid that novelist for his "vile" book, *Selected Passages from the Correspondence with Friends,* and to explain why it angered him. It was this "Letter," which, according to Belinsky's contemporary, Alexander I. Herzen, became the "testament" for several generations of revolutionaries in Russia. The Russian novelist, Fyodor Dostoyevsky, was condemned to death, the sentence later commuted to penal servitude in Siberia, for having read Belinsky's "Letter" to the Petrashevsky circle of Utopian socialists in 1849. Herzen first published the "Letter" in London in *The Polar Star* in 1855. Although it was banned from the Russian press until the Revolution of 1905, generations of Russian teachers and students could recite it by heart.

The "Letter," reprinted below, reflected Belinsky's uncompromising opposition to extreme Slavophilism and called for the abolition of serfdom and corporal punishment, and for an end to the tyranny of police and government officials. Soviet writers have acclaimed Belinsky as "the pioneer of utopian socialism and revolutionary democracy in Russia."

From V. G. Belinsky, *Selected Philosophical Works* (Moscow: Foreign Languages Publishing House, 1948), pp. 503-512.

You are only partly right in regarding my article as that of an angered man: that epithet is too mild and inadequate to express the state to which I was reduced on reading your book. And you are entirely wrong in ascribing that state to your indeed none too flattering references to the admirers of your talent. No, there was a more important reason for this. One could suffer an outraged sense of self-esteem, and I would have had sense enough to let the matter pass in silence were that the whole gist of the matter; but one cannot suffer an outraged sense of truth and human dignity; one cannot keep silent when lies and immorality are preached as truth and virtue under the guise of religion and the protection of the knout.

Yes, I loved you with all the passion with which a man, bound by ties of blood to his native country, can love its hope, its honour, its glory, one of the great leaders on its path of consciousness, development and progress. And you had sound reason for at least momentarily losing your equanimity when you forfeited that love. I say that not because I believe my love to be an adequate reward for a great talent, but because I do not represent a single person in this respect but a multitude of men, most of whom neither you nor I have ever set eyes on, and who, in their turn, have never set eyes on you. I find myself at a loss to give you an adequate idea of the indignation which your book has aroused in all noble hearts, and of the wild shouts of joy which were set up on its appearance by all your enemies—both the non-literary—the Chichikovs, the Nozdrevs and the mayors ... and by the literary, whose names are well known to you. You see yourself that even those people who are of one mind with your book have disowned it. Even if it had been written as a result of deep and sincere conviction it could not have created any other impression on the public than the one it did. And it is nobody's fault but your own if everyone (except the few who must be seen and known in order not to derive pleasure from their approval) received it as an ingenious but all too unceremonious artifice for achieving a sheerly earthly aim by celestial means. Nor is that in any way surprising; what is surprising is that you find it surprising. I believe that is so because your profound knowledge of Russia is only that of an artist, but not of a thinker, whose role you have so ineffectually tried to play in your fantastic book. Not that you are not a thinker, but that you have been accustomed for so many years to look at Russia from your *beautiful far-away;* and who does not know that there is nothing easier than seeing things from a distance the way we want to see them; for in that *beautiful far-away* you live a life that is entirely alien to it, you live in and within yourself or within a circle of the same mentality as your own which is powerless to resist your influence on it. Therefore you failed to realize that Russia sees her salvation not in mysticism, nor asceticism, nor pietism, but in the successes of civilization, enlightenment and humanity. What she needs is not sermons (she has heard enough of them!) or prayers (she has repeated them too often!), but the awakening in the people of a sense of their human dignity lost for so many centuries amid the dirt and refuse; she needs rights and laws conforming not with the preaching of the church but with common sense and justice, and their strictest possible observance. Instead of which she presents the dire spectacle of a country where men traffic in men, without even having the excuse so insidiously exploited by the American plantation owners who claim that the Negro is not a man: a country where people call themselves not by names but by sobriquets, such as Vanka, Vaska, Steshka, Palashka; a country where there are not only no guarantees for individuality, honour and property, but even no police order, and where there is nothing but vast corporations of official thieves and robbers of various descriptions! The most vital national problems in Russia today are the abolition of serfdom and corporal punishments and the strictest possible observance of at least those laws which already exist. This is even realized by the government itself (which is well aware of how the landowners treat their peasants and how many of the former are annually done away with by the latter), as is proven by its timid and abortive half-measures for the relief of the white Negroes and the comical substitution of the single-lash knout by a cat-o'-three tails.

Such are the problems which prey on the mind of Russia in her apathetic slumber! And at such a time a great writer, whose beautifully artistic and deeply truthful works have so powerfully contributed towards Russia's awareness of herself, enabling her as they did to take a look at herself as though in a mirror—comes out with a book in which he teaches the barbarian landowner in the name of Christ and Church to make still greater profits out of the peasants and to abuse them still more.... And you would expect me not to become indignant?... Why, if you had made an attempt on my life I could not have hated you more than I do for these disgraceful lines.... And after this, you expect people to believe the sincerity of your book's intent! No! Had you really been inspired by the truth of Christ, and not by the teaching of the Devil you would certainly have written something entirely different in your new book. You would have told the landowner that since his peasants are his brethren in Christ, and since a brother cannot be a slave to his brother, he should either give them their freedom, or, at least, allow them to enjoy the fruits of their own labour to their greatest possible benefit, realizing as he does, in the depths of his own conscience the false relationship in which he stands towards them.

And the expression: "Oh, you unwashed snout, you!" From what Nozdrev and Sobakevich did you overhear this, to give to the world as a great discovery for the edification and benefit of the muzhiks, whose only reason for not washing is that they have let themselves be persuaded by their masters that they are not human beings? And your conception of the national Russian system of trial and punishment, whose ideal you have found in the foolish saying that both the guilty and innocent should be flogged alike? That, indeed, is often the case with us, though more often than not it is the man who is in the right who takes the punishment, unless he can ransom himself, and for such occasions another proverb says: *guiltlessly guilty!* And such a book is supposed to have been the result of an arduous inner process, a lofty spiritual enlightenment! Impossible! Either you are ill—and you must hasten to take a cure, or . . . I am afraid to put my thought into words! . . .

Proponent of the knout, apostle of ignorance, champion of obscurantism and Stygian darkness, panegyrist of Tatar morals—what are you about! Look beneath your feet—you are standing on the brink of an abyss! . . . That you base such teaching on the Orthodox Church I can understand: it has always served as the prop of the knout and the servant of despotism; but why have you mixed Christ up in this? What in common have you found between Him and any church, least of all the Orthodox Church? He was the first to bring to people the teaching of freedom, equality and brotherhood and set the seal of truth to that teaching by martyrdom. And this teaching was men's salvation only until it became organized in the Church and took the principle of Orthodoxy for its foundation. The Church, on the other hand, was a hierarchy—consequently a champion of inequality, a flatterer of authority, an enemy and persecutor of brotherhood among men—and so it has remained to this day. But the meaning of Christ's message has been revealed by the philosophical movement of the preceding century. And that is why a man like Voltaire who stamped out the fires of fanaticism and ignorance in Europe by ridicule, is, of course, more the son of Christ, flesh of his flesh and bone of his bone, than all your priests, bishops, metropolitans and patriarchs! Do you mean to say you do not know it! It is not even a novelty now to a schoolboy. . . . Hence, can it be that you, the author of *Inspector General* and *Dead Souls,* have in all sincerity, from the bottom of your heart, sung a hymn to the nefarious Russian clergy which you rank immeasurably higher than the Catholic clergy? Let us assume that you do not know that the latter had once been something, while the former had never been anything but a servant and slave of the secular powers; but do you really mean to say you do not know that our clergy is held in universal contempt by Russian society and the Russian people? Of whom do the Russian people relate obscene stories? Of the priest, the priest's wife, the priest's daughter and the priest's farm hand. Does not the priest in Russia represent for all Russians the embodiment of gluttony, avarice, servility, and shamelessness? Do you mean to say that you do not know all this? Strange! According to you the Russian people is the most religious in the world. That is a lie! The basis of religiousness is pietism, reverence, fear of God. Whereas the Russian man utters the name of the Lord while scratching himself somewhere. He says of the icon: *if it isn't good for praying it's good for covering the pots.*

Take a closer look and you will see that it is by nature a profoundly atheistic people. It still retains a good deal of superstition, but not a trace of religiousness. Superstition passes with the advances of civilization, but religiousness often keeps company with them too; we have a living example of this in France, where even today there are many sincere Catholics among enlightened and educated men, and where many people who have rejected Christianity still cling stubbornly to some sort of god. The Russian people is different; mystic exaltation is not in its nature; it has too much common sense, a too lucid and positive mind, and therein, perhaps, lies the vast scope of its historic destinies in the future. Religiousness with it has not even taken root among the clergy, since a few isolated and exclusive personalities distinguished for such cold ascetic reflectiveness prove nothing. But the majority of our clergy has always been distinguished for their fat bellies, scholastic pedantry and savage ignorance. It is a shame to accuse it of religious intolerance and fanaticism; rather could it be praised for an exemplary indifference in matters of faith. Religiousness with us appeared only among the Schismatic sects who formed such a contrast in spirit to the mass of the people and were so insignificant before it numerically.

I shall not dilate on your panegyric to the affectionate relations existing between the Russian people and its lords and masters. I shall say point-blank: that panegyric has met sympathy nowhere and has lowered you even in the eyes of people who in other respects stand very close to you in outlook. As far as I am concerned, I leave it to your conscience to admire the divine beauty of autocracy (it is both safe and profitable), but continue to admire it judiciously from your *beautiful far-away:* at close quarters it is not so attractive, and not so safe. . . . I would remark but this: when a European, especially a Catholic, is seized with a religious ardour he becomes a denouncer of iniquitous authority, similar to the Hebrew prophets who denounced the iniquities of the great ones of the earth. With us on the contrary: no sooner is a person (even a reputable person) afflicted with the malady which is known to psychiatrists as *religiosa mania* than he begins to burn more incense to the earthly god than the heavenly one, and so overshoots the mark in doing so that the former would fain reward him for his slavish zeal did he not perceive that he would thereby be compromising himself in society's eyes. . . . What a rogue our fellow the Russian is! . . .

Another thing I remember you saying in your book, claiming it to be a great and incontrovertible truth, that literacy is not merely useless but positively harmful to the common people. What can I say to this? May your Byzantine God forgive you that Byzantine thought, unless, in committing it to paper, you knew not what you were saying. . . . But perhaps you will say: "Assuming that I have erred and that all my ideas are false, but why should I be denied the right to err and why should people doubt the sincerity of my errors?" Because, I would say in reply, such a tendency has long ceased to be a novelty in Russia. Not so very long ago it was drained to the lees by Burachok and his fraternity. Of course, your book shows a good deal more intellect and talent (though neither of these elements is very richly represented) than their works; but then they have developed your common doctrine with greater energy and greater consistence, they have boldly reached its ultimate conclusions, have rendered full meed to the Byzantine God and left nothing for Satan, whereas you, wanting to light a taper to each of them, have fallen into contradiction, upholding for example, Pushkin, literature and the theatre, all of which, in your opinion, if you were only conscientious enough to be consistent, can in no way serve the salvation of the soul but can do a lot towards its damnation. . . . Whose head could have digested the idea of Gogol's identity with Burachok? You have placed yourself too high in the regard of the Russian public for it to be able to believe you sincere in such convictions. What seems natural in fools cannot seem so in a man of genius. Some people have been inclined to regard your book as the result of mental derangement verging on sheer madness. But they soon rejected such a supposition, for clearly that book was not written in a single day, or week, or month, but very likely in one, two or three years; it shows coherence; through its careless exposition one glimpses premeditation, and the hymn to the powers that be nicely arranges the earthly affairs of the devout author. That is why a rumour has been current in St. Petersburg to the effect that you have written this book with the aim of securing a position as tutor to the son of the heir-apparent. Before that your letter to Uvarov became known in St. Petersburg, wherein you say that you are grieved to find that your works about Russia are misinterpreted, then you evince dissatisfaction with your previous works and declare that you will be pleased with your own works only when the tsar is pleased with them. Now judge for yourself, is it to be wondered at that your book has lowered you in the eyes of the public both as a writer and still more as a man? . . .

You, as far as I can see, do not properly understand the Russian public. Its character is determined by the condition of Russian society in which fresh forces are seething and struggling for expression, but weighed down by heavy oppression and finding no outlet, they induce merely dejection, weariness and apathy. Only literature, despite the Tatar censorship, shows signs of life and progressive movement. That is why the title of writer is held in such esteem among us, that is why literary success is easy among us even for a writer of small talent. The title of poet and writer has long since eclipsed the tinsel of epaulettes and gaudy uniforms.

And that especially explains why every so-called liberal tendency, how-ever poor in talent, is rewarded by universal notice, and why the popu-larity of great talents which sincerely or insincerely give themselves to the service of orthodoxy, autocracy and nationality declines so quickly. A striking example is Pushkin who had merely to write two or three verses in a loyal strain and don the *kamer-junker's* livery to suddenly forfeit the popular affection! And you are greatly mistaken if you believe in all earn-est that your book has come to grief not because of its bad trend, but because of the harsh truths alleged to have been expressed by you about all and everybody. Assuming you could think that of the writing fraternity, but then how do you account for the public? Did you tell it less bitter, home truths less harshly and with less truth and talent in *Inspector General* and *Dead Souls*? Indeed the old school was worked up to a furious pitch of anger against you, but *Inspector General* and *Dead Souls* were not affected by it, whereas your latest book has been an utter and disgraceful failure. And here the public is right, for it looks upon Russian writers as its only leaders, defenders and saviours against Russian autocracy, orthodoxy and nationality, and therefore, while always pre-pared to forgive a writer a bad book, will never forgive him a pernicious book. This shows how much fresh and healthy intuition, albeit still in embryo, is latent in our society, and this likewise proves that it has a future. If you love Russia rejoice with me at the failure of your book! . . .

I would tell you, not without a certain feeling of self-satisfaction, that I believe I know the Russian public a little. Your book alarmed me by the possibility of its exercising a bad influence on the government and the censorship, but not on the public. When it was rumoured in St. Petersburg that the government intended to publish your book in many thousands of copies and to sell it at an extremely low price my friends grew despondent; but I told them there and then that the book, despite every-thing, would have no success and that it would soon be forgotten. In fact it is now better remembered for the articles which have been written about it than for the book itself. Yes, the Russian has a deep, though still undeveloped instinct for truth.

Your conversion may conceivably have been sincere, but your idea of bringing it to the notice of the public was a most unhappy one. The days of naive piety have long since passed, even in our society. It already understands that it makes no difference where one prays, and that the only people who seek Christ and Jerusalem are those who have never carried Him in their breasts or who have lost Him. He who is capable of suffering at the sight of other people's sufferings and who is pained at the sight of other people's oppression, bears Christ within his bosom and has no need to make a pilgrimage to Jerusalem. The humility which you preach is, first of all, not novel, and, secondly, it savours on the one hand of prodigious pride, and on the other of the most shameful degradation of one's human dignity. The idea of becoming a sort of abstract perfection, of rising above everyone else in humility, is the fruit of either pride or imbecility, and in either case leads inevitably to hypocrisy, sanctimoniousness and Chinaism. Moreover, in your book you have taken the liberty of expressing yourself with gross cynicism not only of other people (that would be merely impolite) but of yourself—and that is vile for if a man who strikes his neighbour on the cheek evokes indignation, the sight of a man striking himself on the cheek evokes contempt. No, you are not illuminated, you are simply beclouded; you have failed to grasp either the spirit or the form of Christianity of our time. Your book breathes not the true Christian teaching but the morbid fear of death, of the devil and of hell!

And what language, what phrases? "Every man hath now become trash and a rag"—do you really believe that in saying *hath* instead of *has* you are expressing yourself biblically? How eminently true it is that when a man gives himself wholly up to lies, intelligence and talent desert him. Did not this book bear your name, who would have thought that this turgid and squalid bombast was the work of the author of *Inspector General* and *Dead Souls*?

As far as it concerns myself, I repeat: you are mistaken in taking my article to be an expression of vexation at your comment on me as one of your critics. Were this the only thing to make me angry I would have reacted with annoyance to this alone and would have dealt with all the rest with unruffled impartiality. But it is true that your criticism of your admirers is doubly bad. I understand the necessity of sometimes having to rap a silly man whose praises and ecstasies make the object of his worship look ridiculous, but even this is a painful necessity, since, humanly speaking, it is somehow awkward to reward even false affection with enmity. But you had in view men who, though not brilliantly clever, are not quite fools. These people, in their admiration of your works, have probably uttered more ejaculations than talked sense about them; still, their enthusiastic attitude toward you springs from such a pure and noble source that you ought not to have betrayed them neck and crop to both your common enemies and accused them into the bargain of wanting to misinterpret your works. You, of course, did that while carried away by the main idea of your book and through indiscretion, while Vyazemsky, that prince in aristocracy and helot in literature, developed your idea and printed a personal denunciation against your admirers (and consequently mostly against me). He probably did this to show his gratitude to you for having exalted him, the poetaster, to the rank of great poet, if I remember rightly for his "pithless, dragging verse." That is all very bad. That you were merely biding your time in order to give the admirers of your talent their due as well (after having given it with proud humility to your enemies)—I was not aware; I could not, and, I must confess, did not want to know it. It was your book that lay before me and not your intentions: I read and reread it a hundred times, but I found nothing in it that was not there, and what was there deeply offended and incensed my soul.

Were I to give free rein to my feelings this letter would probably grow into a voluminous notebook. I never thought of writing you on this subject though I longed to do so and though you gave all and sundry printed permission to write you without ceremony with an eye to the truth alone. Were I in Russia I would not be able to do it, for the local "Shpekins" open other people's letters not merely for their own pleasure but as a matter of official duty, for the sake of informing. This summer incipient consumption has driven me abroad, [and Nekrasov has forwarded me your letter to Salzbrunn which I am leaving today with Annenkov for Paris via Frankfort-on-Main]. The unexpected receipt of your letter has enabled me to unburden my soul of what has accumulated there against you on account of your book. I cannot express myself by halves, I cannot prevaricate; it is not in my nature. Let you or time itself prove to me that I am mistaken in my conclusions. I shall be the first to rejoice in it, but I shall not repent what I have told you. This is not a question of your or my personality, it concerns a matter which is of greater importance than myself or even you; it is a matter which concerns the truth, Russian society, Russia. And this is my last concluding word: if you have had the misfortune of disowning with proud humility your truly great works, you should now disown with sincere humility your last book, and atone for the dire sin of its publication by new creations which would be reminiscent of your old ones.

Salzbrunn, July 15, 1847.

24. V. V. Stasov: the basic principles of the new Russian musical school, 1850-1870

VLADIMIR VASILYEVITCH STASOV (1824-1906), a leading Russian art and music critic and art historian, interprets here the basic objectives of the new Russian musical school, "the Mighty Five," to which belonged M. A. Balakirev (1836-1910), M. P. Mussorgsky (1839-1881), N. A. Rimsky-Korsakov (1844-1908), A. P. Borodin (1833-1887), and Ts. A. Cui (1835-1918). In 1872 Stasov became head of the art department of the St. Petersburg Public Library. He led the struggle for Russian national music and for the recognition of the composers who exemplified this musical trend. In particular, he ranks among the outstanding students and disseminators of the music of Mikhail Glinka (1804-1857), to whom he devoted more than thirty works.

Stasov's article, from which the abbreviated excerpts below were taken, was first printed in *Vestnik Evropy,* 1882-1883. From V. V. Stasov, *Sobr. soch.,* Tom. I (St. Petersburg, 1894), stolb. 645-646, 648, 649, 649-651, 651-652, 653. These passages were included in *Khrestomatiya po istorii SSSR,* Vol. III (Moscow, 1952) pp. 802-806.

... Glinka thought he was creating only Russian opera, but he was mistaken. He created the whole of Russian music, an entire Russian musical school, and a whole new system. In the course of the next fifty years, our music and our school have grown and developed in wonderful, original beauty, talented and strong. For a long time, they received no recognition. They were regarded with scorn and condescension. "How many first-rate experts we have," wrote Dargomyzhsky,[1] "even in 1860,

---

[1] A. S. Dargomyzhsky (1813-1869), composer of the operas *Rusalka* and *The Stone Guest.*

who question the possibility of the existence of a Russian school, not only in song, but even in composition! Meanwhile, obviously it has made its own way. It is already too late to suppress it. Its existence has already been engraved on the 'Tables of Art'." Yes, the Russian school has existed since the time of Glinka, with original features that distinguish it from other European schools.

What forces have created the special peculiarities of our school? What elements have given it its exclusive direction and its original character?

One such force and element is, above all, the absence of prejudice and blind faith. Beginning with Glinka, the Russian musical school has been distinguished by complete independence of thought and opinion in regard to music created earlier. It accepts no universally recognized authorities. It wants to verify everything for itself, to convince itself of everything, and only then agrees to recognize the greatness of a composer and the significance of what has been created. Such independence of thought is rarely encountered even now among European musicians, and it was still more uncommon fifty years ago. Only a few musicians, as, for example, Schumann, dared to express their own personal criticism of universally recognized and adored celebrities; the majority of Western musicians, however, believed blindly in all authorities and shared all the tastes and prejudices of the crowd. The new Russian musicians, on the other hand, are terribly "disrespectful." They do not want to believe in any tradition, until they have set their own standards as to what is significant. . . .

. . . Then, beginning with Glinka, all the best Russian musicians have had very little faith in school learning, and, in general, have not regarded it with that servile and superstitious esteem, with which it is still viewed in many parts of Europe. It is ridiculous to deny science or learning, irrespective of the field, including music; but only the new Russian musicians, not having behind them the historical tradition inherited from past centuries of the long chain of scholastic periods in Europe, boldly face up to science; they respect it, make use of its blessings, but without exaggeration and obsequiousness. They deny the need for its dull and pedantic excesses, deny its gymnastics, to which so much importance is attributed by thousands of Europeans, and refuse to believe that it is necessary to vegetate submissively for years over its pompous mystery.

. . . Later, the successors and comrades of Dargomyzhsky did not waste long years in vain, as do the Germans; they learned the grammar of music very quickly and simply, like any other grammar; but this did not prevent them from learning it well and thoroughly. Such an attitude to the "imaginary wisdom," so much revered by musical schools, saved the new Russian school from pedantic and routine compositions, which are althogether absent from it. This is one of the important features that distinguish it from earlier European schools.

Another outstanding feature of our new school is its urge for nationalism. This began even with Glinka and has continued uninterruptedly up to the present time. Such an urge can be found in no other European school. The historical and cultural conditions among other peoples were such that the folk song—the spontaneous expression of unsophisticated folk musicality—has almost wholly and long since vanished among the majority of civilized peoples. Who in the 19th century knows and listens to French, German, Italian, and English folk songs? They existed, of course, and once upon a time they were in vogue, but upon them has descended the levelling scythe of European culture, so hostile to the ordinary native elements, and now we need the efforts of musical archeologists or curious travellers to find in remote provincial corners fragments of old folk songs. In our fatherland, things are completely different. The folk song is still heard everywhere. Every peasant, carpenter, stonemason, yard-keeper, coachman, old woman, laundress and cook, every nurse and wet-nurse, brings it along to St. Petersburg, to Moscow, and to any city in his or her native land; and you can hear it from one end of the year to the other. It surrounds you always and everywhere. As thousands of years ago, no Russian worker, male or female, can do his work without singing a vast array of songs. The Russian soldier goes into battle with a folk song on his lips. It is an integral part of every one of us, and no archeological investigation is needed to understand and love it. Therefore every Russian, born with a creative musical soul, from the first days of his life grows up amid musical elements that are deeply nationalistic. It so happens, moreover, that nearly all the most outstanding Russian musicians were born, not in the capitals, but deep inside Russia, in provincial cities or on their fathers' estates; and there they spent their early years (Glinka, Dargomyzhsky, Mussorgsky, Balakirev, Rimsky-Korsakov). Others many years in their youth lived in the provinces, outside the city, in close and frequent contact with folk songs and folk singing. Their first and most basic musical influences were national. If for a long time we had no artistically developed folk music, the blame must be placed solely on the unfavorable conditions of Russian life in the 18th and 19th centuries, when all that came from the people was trampled under foot in the mud. Nevertheless, nationalism in music was so akin to all, was such a basic necessity for all, that even in Catherine's century, the age of court wigs and powder, first one of our musicians, then another, endeavored to introduce national melodies into his bad operas—copies of the bad European operas of that time. The same was true later even with Verstovsky.[2] The national elements appeared here in a very unfortunate light, but all the same they were present, they testified to demands which existed among no other peoples. But no sooner had times changed a little, no sooner had people begun to talk about life and literature,

---

[2] Verstovsky (1779-1862).

about national character, than once again sympathy for it flared up—at once talented people emerged, who sought to create music in those national Russian forms that were nearer and dearer to them. No doubt European composers (at least the strongest and most talented among them) would have followed the same road as ours did, beginning with Glinka, but such a road no longer existed for them. This is indicated very clearly by the eagerness with which they have always grasped at every expression of national music, even when it was foreign, even for one grain of it. Remember, for instance, how Beethoven more than once attempted to appropriate for himself the themes of Russian folk songs, Franz Schubert, the Slovakian, Liszt, the Hungarian; and yet, they created neither Russian, nor Slovakian, nor Hungarian music. Music is not solely a matter of themes. If it is to be national, if it is to represent the national spirit and soul, it must be addressed to the very root of the people's life. . . .

. . . Russian composers confronted different conditions. To begin with, they were not outsiders. They were "native" to that world from which emanated Russian and Slavic melodies in general, and therefore they have a mastery of it, enabling them to present in all truth and strength their coloring, mentality, and character. What Glinka has accomplished is universally known and universally recognized. He blazed a new trail, created a national opera in forms that exist nowhere else in Europe. The successors of Glinka have followed suit, supported by his brilliant example and initiative.

In connection with the Russian folk element, there is still another element which constitutes the distinguishing characteristic of the new Russian musical school. This is the Oriental (Eastern) element. Nowhere in Europe does it play any such leading role as with our musicians. . . . Some have themselves seen the Orient (Glinka and Balakirev, by living in the Caucasus); others, although they did not travel to the Orient, were surrounded all their lives by impressions of the East and therefore vividly and clearly gave expression to them. In this respect, they shared the common Russian sympathy for everything Oriental. Small wonder that such an accumulation of everything Oriental was always a part of all forms of Russian life, and gave them such a special, characteristic coloring. Already Glinka felt this when he stated in his *Notes:* "No doubt our Russian song is a child of the north, but, to some extent, it also came out of the Orient." As a result, many of Glinka's best works are imbued with elements of the East, as are those of all his heirs and successors. To see in this only the strange whim and caprice of Russian composers (as our musical critics often do) is comical and short-sighted.

Finally, another trait strongly characteristic of the Russian musical school, is its extreme propensity for "program music."

Having arrived in Paris and lived there for several months, Glinka suddenly wrote his friend, Kukol'nik, in April, 1845: "The study of the music of Berlioz and the local audience have led me to extremely important conclusions. I have decided to enrich my repertoire with some concert pieces for orchestra under the title, *Fantaisies Pittoresques*. It seems to me that it is possible to combine the requirements of art with those of the age and, having profited by the improvement of instruments and renditions, to write pieces for both the expert and the ordinary public. In Spain, I shall start work on the afore-mentioned *Fantaisies*. The originality of the local melodies will be of considerable help to me." Thus came into being *Jota* and *Night in Madrid,* and a little later— *Kamarinskaya.*

These works were not only highly talented, but they had another significance: they were the first prototypes of "program music" in Russia. In this respect, Glinka followed the general trend of the century, which first found expression in Beethoven, then in Weber, Berlioz, Mendelssohn, and later still in all the important new composers—Liszt, Wagner, etc.

. . . What was begun by Glinka was continued by his heirs and successors. Almost without exception, Russian symphonic music is program music. . . .

. . . Such were the main characteristic features of the Russian musical school. In taking note of them, it is not my purpose to put our school one bit ahead of other European schools. This would be a task both absurd and ridiculous. Each nation has its great people and its great works. To me it only seemed essential to outline the peculiar characteristics and trends of our school, which are, of course, very interesting and important.

25. N. N. Murav'ev-Amurskii on
the strengthening of Russia in
the Far East

NIKOLAI NIKOLAEVICH MURAV'EV (1809-1881) was governor-general of Eastern Siberia, 1847-1861. His main objective was the strengthening of Russian influence in the sparsely-populated and little-known lands of the Pri-Amur, the Ussri territory, and the Island of Sakhalin. These lands, the course of the Amur and Ussuri rivers, the islands and coastal waters of the Far East, were studied and described by courageous Russian travellers, often outfitted and supported by Murav'ev (the expeditions of Gavrilov, Orlov, Nevel'sky, and Mid-dendorf). At the same time, the settlement of the Far Eastern wilderness by Russian immigrants was begun. In May, 1858, Murav'ev concluded the Treaty of Aigun, acquiring for Russia the left bank of the Amur and the Ussuri territory, for which he received the title of Count and the addition of Amurskii to his family name.

The passages below are taken from his notes: "The Reasons for the Necessity of the occupation of the mouth of the River Amur and that part of the Island of Sakhalin which lies athwart it, and likewise of the left bank of the Amur." Memorandum of 1849-1850.

From Ivan Barsukov, *Graf N. N. Murav'ev-Amurskii (materialy dlya biografii)* (Kniga II, Moscow, 1891), str. 46-48.

I. Apprehension for the Eastern Boundary of
the Empire (1849)

For a long time rumors have been circulated in Siberia about the enterprises of the English at the mouth of the Amur River and on the Island of Sakhalin; and God preserve us, if they are firmly established there ahead of us! To assure complete control of trade into China, the English undoubtedly must have the mouth of the Amur and control navigation on this river. If the Amur were not the only river flowing from Siberia into the Eastern ocean, then we could afford to be lenient toward their enterprises; but the navigation of the Amur, as the only convenient route to the East, is the century-old dream of Siberians of every rank and station, perhaps instinctively, but none the less well-grounded.

After on the spot consideration of all the circumstances known to me, I can say that whoever possesses the mouths of the Amur will also be master of Siberia, at least as far as Baikal, and in firm possession; for control of the mouth of this river and of navigation there are sufficient to hold Siberia and especially the more populated areas where agriculture and industry flourish. It will remain a loyal tributary and also subject to whatever power holds that key.

II. Consolidation and Guarantee of the Possession of the Kamchatka Peninsula

Only through possession of the left bank of the Amur and control of navigation on that river can communication be established with Kamchatka, which makes it possible to insure continued possession of this peninsula for Russia; for the road through Yakutsk and Okhotsk or Ayan offers no means of providing Kamchatka with sufficient military aid, or with a substantial population, which in itself, under the protection of fortresses, would constitute the strength of this remote region and make it possible to supply the military forces there and the fleet with the necessary provisions. Through the establishment of steamship communications via the Amur, Kamchatka could be supplied from Nerchinsk with settlers and whatever else is necessary in no more than two weeks. The Amur River flows from our boundaries to the Island of Sakhalin, a little over 2000 versts away, and according to information available, it is navigable throughout.

III. The Maintenance of Our Trade with China

The decline of the Kyakhta trade already indicates that the enterprises of the English in China would not be to our advantage. In the years immediately following their war,[1] this could not be detected: for the Chinese, inspired by hatred toward the English, preferred to deal with us, as with good and lenient neighbors; but time and material benefits mitigate the gusts of hatred, and moderate even the warmth of a friendship which does not afford any basic advantages. I think that the only means of maintaining our trade with China is to transform it from a

[1] The Opium War, 1839-1842.

local affair to a delivery service, by using the Amur River to transport our manufactured products to all the northeastern provinces of China, which are more remote from the present activities of the English, whose competition would prove destructive to our trade.

IV. The Preservation of Our Influence in China

The English war and peace in China laid the foundation for the radical transformation of this populous empire, under the influence of the English; but we could still have hoped, during the lifetime of the late Chinese Emperor, that he, personally, having so to speak been insulted by them, would not be well disposed toward them and, consequently, would not permit the spread of English influence in his empire. Now, however, with the accession of his 18-year-old son, we can be sure that the English will hasten to take advantage of this favorable change, with their characteristic enterprise, speed, and persistence, in order to take over, not only the trade, but also the policy of China. I cannot judge whether we can prevent this, now that five Chinese ports are not only accessible to them, but have almost become English cities; I think, however, that it is at least necessary for us to insure for ourselves our boundaries with China in line with our vital interests before the English have become complete sovereigns there, and to take possession of the Amur. I also think that we ought to make use of the present situation in China to present our views to them, based on the common interests of both states, under which no one other than Russia and China should control navigation on the Amur—and the mouth of this river must be protected, of course, but not by Chinese.

The Voyage of G. I. Nevel'skii on the Amur

The outstanding Russian traveller-explorer, Captain of the first rank (later admiral) Gennadii Ivanovich Nevel'skii (1813-1876), completed in 1850 a remarkable voyage of navigation in the waters of the Far East, in the mouth of the Amur, and on the upper course of the Amur. The travels of Nevel'skii, which continued in the following years (1851-1853), were an important factor in the subsequent strengthening of Russia in the Far East.

Below are excerpts from the Notes of Governor-General of Eastern Siberia, N. N. Murav'ev-Amurskii, containing an account of Nevel'skii's activities. The Notes are dated 1850.

(Ivan Baruskov, *Count N. N. Murav'ev-Amurskii* (Materials for a Biography), Book II, Moscow, 1891, pp. 70-75, 78-79).

Captain of the first rank Nevel'skii reports that, accompanied by the Gilyaki, he returned at the beginning of July from Ayan to the harbor of Schastiya on the brig "Okhotsk," which was sent from Okhotsk by Major Karsakov with a crew of skilled workers of the 46th fleet and some Cossacks of the Yakutsk regiment, together with the appropriate weapons, cartridges, instruments, and materials for construction.

There, during his absence, lumber was prepared with the help of the Gilyaki, and the topographer made a survey of the coast of Schastiya harbor.

Having made a final check up of the new entrance into the mouth of the Amur River from the northern side of the estuary on whale boats and on the brig "Okhotsk" itself and given the appropriate orders for construction of winter quarters in Petrovsk, Nevel'skii found it necessary to go himself to the Amur River on a whale boat and kayak for observation and description of the localities, to find out how much farther up it was possible to go, and for personal verification of the disposition toward us of the Gilyaki tribes inhabiting both banks of this river.

At the peninsula of the great Prince Constantine, he left a topographer to produce a detailed survey, both of that peninsula and of the entire area on the left bank of the Amur located between this peninsula, the estuary, and the harbor of Schastiya, and he himself sailed farther. Everywhere the Gilyaki showed special confidence in him, coming en masse to his tents with their wives and children, and expressing their joy; and they told him that with the arrival of our ship in the village of Iskai (in Schastiya harbor) the negroes will be afraid to come to them, and the Manchurians are now more amiable. They call the commanders of the whaling ships "negroes," for among them there are indeed many dark-complexioned persons. In one of the villages he met three visitors from the Island of Sakhalin, living near the southern strait, who also told him about the arrival this spring of two big warships—one with 20, and the other with 14 guns; that these ships arrived even before the break up of the ice in the estuary, and remained in their vicinity a month and a half, surveyed the land and water in the strait itself, and anchored at the village of Pogobi, which is situated at the very entrance into the estuary from the south.

En route, he likewise assembled detailed topographical information about the course of the river Amur and about the direct, close connection with it of this harbor—de-Kastri, which is situated in Tatar Bay below 51.5 degrees latitude, and about other places in this part of the Gilyaki lands, about the population of the Island of Sakhalin itself, which, as proved by their own statements, includes a large part of the Gilyaki, and then toward the south the hairy Kuriltsy (Kuge), and, finally, those who inhabit the east coast of the island, that is, the Tungusi, who, of course, came from our boundaries, and whom the Gilyaki also consider as belonging to Russia; they said also that every year to the southern part of the island come the Japanese, with whom they, the Gilyaki, and the Kuge, trade.

Everywhere the Gilyaki repeatedly requested us not to abandon them but to protect them, and they brought him fresh fish, millet, and *arak* [a strong alcoholic beverage]. Nevel'skii treated them to kasha with butter, and tea, and made them gifts of earrings, rings, beads, knives, and so on.

In the village at Cape Ogi, on the right bank of the Amur, about 120 versts from the mouth, there came to visit him an elderly Gilyak, named Chedano, with all his family. Chedano brought rice, sterlet, and *arak,* and also told him how glad they were that the Russians trade with them and protect them, and that now the Manchurians will be afraid to mistreat them; and to the question: "What right have the Manchurians to mistreat you?"—the old man replied: "Only because they are stronger and we, the Gilyaki—the Neidal'tsi, and Samogiri, are foreign to them; yes, and they do not think about this." Chedano, by the way, told Nevel'skii that farther up the Amur, beyond the mouth of the Amguni, there is on the right bank of the river a special kind of stones, which, according to their legend, either fell from heaven, or were placed there by the *Locha,* i.e., by the Russians; the Gilyaki guard these stones, and when the Manchurians, sailing up to trade, wanted to throw them down, the Gilyaki paid them not to do it; for it is their superstition that if these stones are thrown into the river, then the river will become turbulent, and trade will be bad for them. Chedano entreated Nevel'skii to go without fail to see these stones, and volunteered to lead him there himself. Nevel'skii took him along and struck out for the mouth of the Amguni River, which flows into the Amur, on the left bank, 200 versts from the estuary. Here he met the Neidal'tsi, who had arrived from the upper reaches of the Amguni River; these people carried on trade with our Yakuts, but, unfortunately, the latter cheated them in barter, and they spread the most unfavorable rumors about us (which were even before known to me, and against which I had already taken measures last year in Yakutia), assuring them that the Russians will begin exacting the *yasak* from them and will beat them up; that from the Manchurians they could still escape, but not from the Russians. Nevel'skii convinced them otherwise, and advised that they go to trade in Schastiya harbor, gave them presents, and sailed up the Amguni nearly 15 versts to inspect the forests; and then, having returned again to the Amur, crossed the right bank to the village of Tyrs, where he encountered in the river eight big boats, about which Chedano told him with apprehension that they were Manchurians; and, indeed, on the bank there appeared a big crowd of people, nearly 80 men, with clean-shaven heads and pig tails, armed with bows and arrows, and others even with guns with slow-match.

This crowd, having seen Nevel'skii, approached him; and at its head was an elderly man with the appearance of a leader. Even before this,

Nevel'skii had ordered the oarsmen to remain on the sloop, to be ready for anything, but to spread out their wares, as if to display them for sale.

The elderly Manchurian, approaching Nevel'skii, asked him arrogantly who he was. Nevel'skii replied with the same question; and when the former answered that he was a Manchurian, the latter said he was a Russian.

The Manchurian scrutinized him with distrust, and after conversing with his people, asked: "Why are you here?" Nevel'skii, pointing to the wares, replied: "For the same reason you are here, don't you see!"—"We have come to trade with the Gilyaki," said the Manchurian. "You came from higher up," answered Nevel'skii, "and, with the same purpose, we have come from the sea."—"This is a foreign land," said the Manchurian. "Whose land is this?" asked Nevel'skii. The Manchurian, without replying, arrogantly stroked his mustaches and began to sit down on a stump covered with material, which was brought for him. Nevel'skii seized him by the breast and said: "We are both merchants and therefore should converse with both of us either standing or sitting." The Manchurian was taken aback and rose, and the Gilyaki also gave Nevel'skii a stump, and then both sat down; but meanwhile the crowd of Manchurians surrounded them. The Gilyaki, Neidal'tsi, and Samogiri melted away, and with Nevel'skii there remained only two Gilyaki and a Tungus interpreter. "Whose land is this?" repeated Nevel'skii. "We are trading here," replied the Manchurian.—"This is the land of the Gilyaki, so why are you here and who are you?"—and with this question, the Manchurians gazed intently at Nevel'skii's clothes and at the oarsmen on the boat, and conversed among themselves; and Nevel'skii answered the Manchurian: "We do not think this is the place or time to quarrel; we are both merchants, come to trade, and therefore must live in friendship and bring one another products to our mutual advantage." Then the Manchurian, insolently pointing to the crowd which closely surrounded Nevel'skii, said: "We are many, and you are few."

Two Gilyaki, formerly on either side of Nevel'skii, grabbed their knives. Nevel'skii produced from his pocket his double-barrelled pistol, and put it against the forehead of the Manchurian, and said: "Who dares to touch me now?"

The Manchurian, the leader and the whole crowd, jumped aside and began to bow; Nevel'skii put the pistol in his pocket, and the Manchurian asked him, already bowing from a distance: "Are you really a Russian, as the Gilyaki say? You are not a red head (that is, not English) from that vessel which was at Pogobi?" The Gilyaki all shouted that this is a *dzhengi*, the top Russian from Iskai; and Nevel'skii repeated his earlier statement that he was a Russian and trades with the Gilyaki, and sees to it that the red heads should not come to them; and then he went up to the Manchurian, and having seized his hand, calmed him down. The Manchurian told him his name, summoned one of his men who had been at Kyakhta, and showed him our silver coin; meanwhile, Nevel'skii's tent was set up and he invited some of the Manchurians into it to drink tea and wine with him. From this time on his relations with the Manchurians became quite friendly and frank, and their leader, who proved to be an official from the Manchurian city of Gotto, who had been sent there precisely to find out what ship was approaching from the south, told Nevel'skii:

1. That the lands of the Samogiri, the Neidal'tsi, and Gilyaki do not belong to the Manchurians.

2. That trade with these people was permitted by the Manchurian government only in the small town of "Mylka," near the city of Gotto, right on the Manchurian boundary; that in Mylka the Gilyaki, Neidal'tsi, and Samogiri, when they arrive, give presents to the chief and then they are permitted to carry on barter, but only at a certain place, which is fenced off.

3. That to the lands of the Samogiri, Neidal'tsi, and Gilyaki, the Manchurian merchants come without permission of the government on the pretext that they go to capture the women; for among them it is not considered reprehensible to seize the women of people whom they consider dogs, belonging to no one.

4. In the city of Gotto, it is known that a Russian ship was in the estuary last year, and that the Russians now trade at Iskar, but their administrator does not worry about this, for it is free land; but they were frightened by the arrival of ships from the south with red heads, fearing that they would enter the river Amur, reach them, and act with hostility, as was the case in other places. The red heads, as he described them, have big guns and they shoot fast. At the conclusion of the conversation, the Manchurian told Nevel'skii they'd be glad if the Russians permitted nobody on the Amur, for they themselves could not protect these places; and he explained to Nevel'skii that from where they stood the route into their lands is by water, and that from the end of navigation it takes only eight days' travel by camel to Bogdikhan (i.e., to Peking).

Nevel'skii spent almost 24 hours in conversation with the Manchurians, with the object of getting as closely acquainted with them as possible, and to find out various ways of communication on the Amur and its environs, and to tell them also about the mutual advantages of trade. The Manchurian fully agreed with this and promised next year to arrive without fail to barter at Iskai, asking for our wares, and especially for velveteen and cotton prints, which Nevel'skii had with him, and barter began there and then for lollipops, salt, and millet, from the Manchurian.

Right there, in the presence of the Manchurians, emissaries from the Neidal'tsi and Samogiri came to Nevel'skii, asking us to take them also under our protection; and Nevel'skii declared to the Manchurians that they must conduct trade honestly with these people, without violence, and without seizing their women.

Three versts from the village of Tyrs, on the right bank of the Amur, on the cliffs above the water, Nevel'skii found four columns, which Chedano pointed out to him. On two of these columns he found the years carved in stone—on the first, 1649, and on another, 1669, and the Slavic letter "b".

On these same columns Nevel'skii carved with a knife, 1850, and the monogram of Your Majesty.

Having returned to the village of Tyrs, he was again met by the Manchurians, who invited him to visit them and treated him to tea, etc. Once again there was conversation about trade with the Gilyaki, whom the Manchurians continued to call foreign dogs, and who confirmed what Chedano had said, that they threaten the Gilyaki, that they are going to throw down the columns into the water, and force them to pay them off not to do it. It was noticeable, however, that the Manchurians likewise feared the Daurtsi, living further up on the left bank of the Amur, and do not seize their wives, but buy them—and this costs them a great deal.

Nevel'skii made them promise not to offend the Gilyaki, Samogiri, and Neidal'tsi, and finally, having taken leave of them in very friendly fashion, and having inspected the valley of the river Tyrti on the right bank, he went back down the river and the Manchurians simultaneously sailed up the river to their boundaries. . . .

. . . Having thus given an account of the present state of our affairs in Kamchatka and the Sea of Okhotsk, I must turn to the most important matters dealt with by Captain Nevel'skii, which include: In the first place, that the Gilyaki tribes, inhabiting the banks of the River Amur, seek the protection and patronage of Your Imperial Majesty against the oppression they endure from their Manchurian neighbors and their fear of foreign visitors from the sea. 2. That the Manchurians themselves admit that the Gilyaki, living on both banks of the Amur River, do not belong to the Chinese Empire, and they conduct open trade with them at the Manchurian boundary post of Mylka, situated on the right bank of the Amur, nearly 600 versts from its mouth. 3. That the Island of Sakhalin is populated by these same Gilyaki and Tungusi, who have crossed from our domains on the mainland, and by the hairy Kuriltsi, the same tribe as those inhabiting our Kurile Islands, and that all these tribes carry on trade with the Japanese, who sail on whaling boats to the southern parts of this island; and most important 4. That foreign warships this spring made in the southern strait of the Amur estuary a detailed investigation of the passage, which was heretofore considered closed and which is shown on the maps as sandbars, of course, not without purpose and perspective, proving, by the way, many previous circumstances; and that not only the Gilyaki, but also the Manchurians themselves were uneasy about these visits; and the latter, fearing that the red heads (as they call the English) will penetrate the Amur and the navigable rivers in the interior of Manchuria which flow into the Amur, admit to the Russians that they themselves are not strong enough to block this penetration, and find it likewise advantageous to them for the Russians to protect the entrance to the Amur River, and also want very much to carry on trade with us in those areas.

All these facts not only confirm our previous information about these matters and about all the perils which I presented in 1848, but at the same time they point to the necessity of acting with all possible speed, in order not to be forestalled in the estuary and mouths of the Amur by foreigners, who are as dangerous in this case to us as to the Chinese Empire.

In view of all this, I make bold to think that it would not be to our disadvantage to enter without delay into formal, secret negotiations on this subject with the Chinese government, and, at the same time, to hasten to take advantage of the attitude of the Gilyaki to bring them under our protection, and to strengthen our posts wherever they have been established by every means the local administration will have at its disposal next summer in the Sea of Okhotsk, and to authorize those who are to implement this matter to enter into relations with the Chinese authorities on the other side of the border.

In conclusion, one may say that if, on the one hand, it is indispensable to act without delay, then, on the other hand, the most favorable consequences for us can be expected from all the above-mentioned conditions; and if the negotiations with the Chinese government are only conducted in accordance with the present state of affairs, and in ways basically and mutually advantageous, then perhaps, in this event, we shall achieve also our long-standing objective of navigation on the Amur, by pointing out to the Chinese that we must have the nearest and quickest communications with our posts at the mouth of the Amur.

I am not speaking of those advantages which we can derive from trade on the Amur with the Manchurians, which they so sincerely want, and about the possibility, in this event, also of beginning trade via Sakhalin with the Japanese.

Treaty of Friendship and Delimitation of Boundaries Between Russia and China

Signed at Aigun, May 16, 1858
Ratified by the Emperor of Russia, July 8, 1858
Ratified by His Majesty, the Bogdokhan of China,
June 2, 1858

Lieutenant-General Nikolai Murav'ev, Governor-General of Eastern Siberia, Adjutant-General of His Majesty, Emperor Alexander Nikolaye-vitch, on behalf of the Great Empire of Russia, and Prince I-Chan, Adjutant-General, "Grand de la Cour," and Commander-in-Chief on the Amur, on behalf of the Great Empire of Ta-Tsing, desiring to establish an eternal and very close friendship between the two Empires, and in the interest of their respective subjects, have reached a common accord:

Article I. The left bank of the Amur River, from the Argun River to the mouth of the Amur, shall belong to the Russian Empire, and its right bank, down to the Ussuri River, shall belong to the Ta-Tsing Empire; the territories and places located between the Ussuri River and the sea, as at present, shall be held jointly by the Ta-Tsing Empire and the Russian Empire, pending the demarcation of the frontier between the two states. The navigation of the Amur, the Sungari, and Ussuri is to be open exclusively to the ships of the Ta-Tsing and Russian Empires: the navigation of these rivers shall be prohibited to the vessels of any other State. The Manchu inhabitants located on the left bank of the Amur, from the river Zeya south to the village of Khormoldzin, shall retain in perpetuity the places of their ancient domicile under the administration of the Manchu Government, with the provision that the Russian inhabitants shall not in any way mistreat or oppress them.

Article II. In the interest of good mutual relations between their respective subjects, the settlers of both Empires shall be permitted to trade with one another along the Ussuri, Amur, and Sungari rivers, and the authorities must afford reciprocal protection to the traders on both banks.

Article III. The stipulations reached in the common accord by the Plenipotentiary of the Russian Empire, Governor-General Murav'ev, and by I-Chan, Commander-in-Chief on the Amur and Plenipotentiary of the Ta-Tsing Empire, will be strictly and inviolably executed in perpetuity; to this effect, Governor-General Murav'ev, for the Russian Empire, has submitted a copy of the present Treaty written in Russian and Manchu to Commander-in-Chief Prince I-Chan, for the Ta-Tsing Empire, and Commander-in-Chief Prince I-Chan, for the Ta-Tsing Empire, has submitted a copy of the present Treaty in the Manchu and Mongol languages to Governor-General Murav'ev, for the Russian Empire. All the present undersigned stipulations shall be published for the information of the inhabitants bordering on the two Empires.

> May 16, 1858, City of Aigun
> Signed   Nikolai Murav'ev
> Pierre Peroffsky
> I-Chan
> Dziraminga

26. the Eastern Question as interpreted by a soldier, a writer, and a diplomat

BELOW ARE THE VIEWS OF GENERAL R. A. FADEYEV, F. M. Dostoyevsky, and A. I. Nelidov on the Eastern Question. The first two deal with the Eastern Question on the eve of the Russo-Turkish War (1877-1878). The third reflects the official Russian outlook following the Congress of Berlin (1878), where Alexander II was forced by an anti-Russian coalition of European powers to abandon the "Greater Bulgaria" created by the Treaty of San Stefano (1877). Although the Congress deprived Russia, at least temporarily, of her sphere of influence in the Balkans and damaged her prestige in that area, it failed to end Russian plans for the control of the Dardanelles.

i. General R. A. Fadeyev on the Eastern Question

Major-General R. A. Fadeyev (1824-1883) was a military writer and conservative-aristocratic publicist. Below are excerpts from two of his Memoranda, which are of interest in connection with the preparation of Tsarist Russia for war with Turkey, 1877-1878: (1) Memorandum of May 28, 1876, submitted to the Ministry of Foreign Affairs for N. K. Girs, at that time Foreign Minister, and (2) Memorandum on the "Bulgarian Affair" of November 20, 1876, submitted to D. A. Milyutin, Minister of War. They were published in a Special Supplement to "A Description of the Russo-Turkish War, 1877-1878," 1st issue, St. Petersburg, 1899, pp. 53-55, and 6th issue, St. Petersburg, 1911, pp. 293-294. From *Krestomatiya po istorii SSSR,* Vol. III (Moscow, 1852), 612-614.

Memorandum Submitted to N. K. Girs

...Everybody understands that Constantinople alone is nothing, that the Eastern Question is the question of the Dardanelles and only of the Dardanelles, and that without exception everything connected with the great question—both the soundness of its solution and the procedure in regard to the Turkish line of succession—depends solely on who secures a firm footing at the Dardanelles.

Thinking people in the East, both official and private, understand distinctly that the age-old question is now drawing swiftly and inevitably to a head, that the very essence of it lies in the possession of the Dardanelles, that there are only two competitors for possession of it—Russia and the sea powers (who lay hands on the Straits in the name of Europe, but under the Greek flag—in other words, this kind of protection would become for them an eternal apple of discord), and that Russia cannot retreat in this matter without repudiating herself; they are also aware that possession of the Straits, separating Europe from Asia, at once decides the Eastern Question in one or another, but in a completely definite sense.

For us Russians, at least one side of the affair must be absolutely clear: We must have open communication with the southern seas, without interference from any direction whatsoever. Without it, we cannot exist. For 150 years since Peter the Great, history has compelled the Russian sovereign to solve in the south the very question which the first reformer solved in the Twenty Years' War in the north. At that time, Russia consisted basically of the northern half of the country, from the Oka to the Arctic Ocean, and therefore the vital question was the opening of the route to the Baltic Sea; now the center of gravity has shifted, and the majority of the Russian population and the greater part of our productive forces, lie between the Oka and the Black Sea, which, without possession of the Straits amounts to no more than the Caspian. Russia, deprived forever of free entry into the Mediterranean Sea, would come to resemble a bird with one wing.

We could somehow get along with the Bosphorus in foreign hands, as long as it remains in the hands of the Turks, deprived of justice and rights before every consular agent; but it is difficult to have even an approximate idea of those innumerable adversities and the periodically perilous and constantly humiliating situations which would fall to our lot in the event of the final transfer of the Straits into the hands of any other ruler, no matter how weak, who is protected by full European rights. We should be literally behind bars; and meanwhile the most durable occupation of the Straits, sufficient to oppose any alliance, requires no more than one-third of the forces necessary for the protection of the Black Sea coast from Poti to the Danube. The Dardanelles position is invincible under good artillery defence and with 60,000 troops in the field. But the occupation of the Straits can only be attained when the fall of Turkey is imminent, or never. . . .

Memorandum on the "Bulgarian Affair"

It is still necessary to regard the Bulgarian Affair[1] from the point of view of the final solution of the Eastern Question. England's desire for the transfer of Constantinople, together with the Straits, to some third party in the event of the final fall of Turkey would be a measure fundamentally hostile to us, on which no further comment is needed. But the elimination of this measure leaves only one way of solving the Eastern Question. . . . Our final goal could be nothing other than the completely decisive occupation of the Dardanelles, with or without the destruction of the sultanate, depending on circumstances.

The inevitability of this goal in the relatively near future, long understood by Russian representatives in the East, is beginning to enter into the consciousness of the majority of landowners and capitalists in the southern half of Russia, for whom the fortuitous closure of the Straits, or even the rumor of it, each time threatens complete ruin; and besides it constantly hampers them, paralyzing any nautical and coastal industrial enterprise on the Black Sea. Even the peasants of south Russia will grasp the necessity for the occupation of the Straits at all costs, since there will soon be a new political regime on the coast of the Sea of Marmora, as conceived by England, with its manifest consequences. For political and also for military people, it is impossible not to see the tremendous significance of such a dénouement, which permits the blocking of our southern boundary by one corps by turning its available forces to the western boundary. . . .

II. F. M. Dostoyevsky: "Constantinople Must Be Ours"

Fyodor Mikhailovitch Dostoyevsky (1821-1881) voiced the sentiments of the Slavophile camp on the Eastern Question. He is best known as the author of the novels *Crime and Punishment* (1866), *The Idiot* (1868), *The Possessed* (1871-1872), *The Brothers Karamazov* (1879-1880). It was in his *Diary of a Writer,* published irregularly from 1873-1881, that Dostoyevsky expounded his political philosophy on the issues of his time, including the future of Slavdom and the Eastern Question on the eve of the Russo-Turkish War,

---

[1] Bulgarian affair—the question of the possibility of making use of Bulgarian territory, which is on the Turkish boundary, for the purpose of bringing Tsarist Russia closer to the Straits of the Bosphorus and Dardanelles.

1877-1878. His articles on these topics in 1876 and 1877 are believed to have influenced the thinking of Alexander II and to have encouraged the enlistment of large numbers of Russian volunteers to aid the Serbs against the Turks. In some respects, they suggest a summons to a holy war against the Ottoman Empire.

The excerpts below are from his *Dnevnik Pisatelya (Diary of a Writer,* March, 1877, "Once Again on the Subject that Constantinople, Sooner or Later, Must be Ours"), *Sobr. Soch.,* Vol. XI (St. Petersburg, 1895), 73-85.

Yes, the Golden Horn and Constantinople—all this will be ours. . . . In the first place, this will come to pass of its own accord, precisely because the time has come, and even if it has not yet arrived, indeed it is already near at hand; all signs point to this. This is the natural solution, the word of nature herself, so to speak. If it has not occurred before this, it has been precisely because the time was not yet ripe. . . . No matter what happens there—peace, or new concessions on the part of Russia—sooner or later, Constantinople will be ours. . . .

Yes, it must be ours, not only because it is a famous port, because of the Straits, "the center of the universe," "the navel of the earth"; not from the standpoint of the long-conceived necessity for a tremendous giant like Russia to emerge at last from his locked room, in which he has already grown up to the ceiling, into the open spaces where he may breathe the free air of the seas and oceans. . . .

It is clear that all this can be avoided [Russian involvement in unpleasant Slavic-Greek disputes] only by timely firmness on the part of Russia on the Eastern Question and by her steadfast pursuit of the great traditions of our ancient, centuries-old Russian policy. In this matter, we must yield nothing, no matter what kind of Europe there may be and for no considerations whatsoever, because for us this is a matter of life and death. Sooner or later, Constantinople must be ours, if only to avoid the serious and unpleasant church dissensions which are so likely to arise among the young and inexperienced peoples of the East, and which have been demonstrated by the dispute between the Bulgarians and the ecumenical Patriarch, which ended so badly.

Once we take possession of Constantinople, nothing like this can occur. The peoples of the West, who are so jealously following every step taken by Russia, at this moment still do not know and do not suspect all these new, as yet visionary, but all too feasible future combinations. If they should learn of them now, they would not understand and would not attach to them any special significance. However, they will grasp them fully and attribute significance to them when it is already too late. The Russian people, who understand the Eastern question only as the liberation of all Orthodox Christendom, as the great future of a united church, should they observe, on the contrary, new dissensions and new discord, will be too shocked and perhaps any new solution of the matter would profoundly affect them and their whole mode of existence, especially if in the final analysis it should assume a predominantly ecclesiastical character. For this reason alone, under no circumstances can we relinquish or weaken the extent of our centuries-old participation in this great question. Not the splendid port alone, not only the route to the seas and oceans connects Russia so closely with the solution of the destinies of this fatal question, and not even the unification and rebirth of the Slavs. . . . Our task is much deeper, immeasurably deeper. We, Russia, are indeed also indispensable and inevitable to all Eastern Christendom, both to the whole future destiny of Orthodoxy on earth, and to its unity. Our people and their rulers have always understood this to be so. . . .

In brief, this dreadful Eastern Question constitutes almost our whole future destiny. Therein lie, as it were, all our problems, and what is most important—our only exit into the plenitude of history. Therein lies also our final conflict with Europe and our ultimate union with her, but only upon new, mighty and fruitful foundations. Oh, how can Europe at this time grasp the fateful, vital importance to us alone of the solution to this question?—In a word, no matter what may be the outcome of the present, perhaps quite indispensable diplomatic agreements and negotiations in Europe, nevertheless, sooner or later, *Constantinople must be ours,* even if it should take another century!

This all of us Russians must always and steadfastly bear in mind. This is what I wanted to announce, especially at the present European moment. . . .

II. Memorandum of A. I. Nelidov "On the Occupation of the Straits"

The Russian diplomat, A. I. Nelidov (1835-1910), served as chargé d'affaires in Constantinople, 1877-1878, and as Russian ambassador there from 1883-1897. The Memorandum, from which the excerpts below were taken, was drawn up by Nelidov in December, 1882, in Constantinople, when he was on a special mission for the Russian government. On the original, Tsar Alexander commented: "All this is very businesslike and to the point. God grant that we live long enough to experience this comforting and heartfelt moment. I do not cease to hope that sooner or later this will come to pass, and it must be so! The main thing is not to lose time and an opportune moment."

Nelidov's Memorandum dealt with the concrete circumstances at the beginning of the Eighties of the XIXth century, when Germany and Austria, having strengthened their claims in the Balkans and the Near East, joined England and France to block a Russian solution of the problem of the Straits.

From *Krasnyi Arkhiv,* Vol. 3(46), 1931, pp. 182-187. See also, *Khrestomatiya po Istorii SSSR, Vol. III* (Moscow, 1952), 647-649.

Since our last war [1877-1878], Turkey little by little is being deprived of her possessions by peaceful means. The European powers, one after another, have been taking away the provinces which were of advantage to them. Greece received from the Berlin Congress [1878] part of Thessaly and Epirus, Austria occupied Bosnia and Herzogovina, France seized Tunis, England haggled until she obtained Cyprus, and now, having taken advantage of propitious events, she is actually taking possession of Egypt. It is easy to foresee that in the future the disintegration of the Turkish Empire will be accomplished in the very same way as that of the Byzantine Empire, until the capital itself will be taken and the remnants of the dying regime will be transferred to finish its life somewhere in Asia.

This role of the conquered capital, it seems, was destined by fate and history to go to Russia, whose entire political, trade, and military interests urgently demand the occupation of the Straits. The inevitability of this event is so clearly obvious to everyone that it seems superfluous to put forward all the advantage, all the necessity for Russia to have under its power the Dardanelles and the Bosphorus. The question now is not the expansion of our limitless fatherland, not the annexation to it of new possessions, but the assertion of Russian power along the route of our southern, maritime communications with the open seas and ocean. Besides, our establishment on the Bosphorus will finally consolidate for us all our Transcaucasian possessions, will unite in one point our entire defensive line on the Black Sea coasts, and give us a decisive influence on the fate both of the Balkans and the peninsulas of Asia Minor. Finally, it will strengthen our defensive power on the western boundary, affording us the possibility of providing for its protection by all the military means which were heretofore immobilized on the Black Sea coasts. For us, this is what comprises the satisfactory and advantageous solution of the Eastern Question. . . .

Judging by local conditions, the possibility of the occupation of the Straits presents itself in three ways:

1. By outright force in time of war between us and Turkey.
2. By a surprise attack, with the help of internal conditions or external danger to Turkey.

3. By peaceful means—in the event of a close connection or alliance with the Porte, if he could be induced to seek for himself our good offices* . . . .

Under such conditions, the existence of the Ottoman Empire and the Turkish capital on the Bosphorus would not necessarily be brought to an end by our strong position on its coasts. For us, on the contrary, it would be more advantageous in many respects to have under our protection the semi-independent remnants of the Turkish Empire, and we could little by little help them to determine their own fate. In Constantinople, itself, however, we should never under any circumstances appear to be the sole master. As a city of world trade, of any number of historical memories, of religious faiths, and the most diverse nationalities, Tsargrad [Constantinople] must be and must remain an independent city, belonging only to itself. But it must be under our protection, protected by our troops, and for their maintenance perhaps they should pay us tribute in return for this protection. Its annexation to Russia would expand our boundaries tremendously, would set against us the local population, and would weaken us, whereas by their retention of political and administrative freedom the inhabitants of Byzantium and its small territory (with some points on the Dardanelles) would regard the Russian protectorate as the guarantee and source of their security and well-being. . . .

---

* At this point, Alexander III commented: "Of course, this would be the most desirable."

27. Emancipation Manifesto of

19 February (March 3), 1861

ALEXANDER II (1855-1881) signed the Emancipation Manifesto on February 19, 1861 (March 3, N.S.), the sixth anniversary of his coronation, and approximately one and one-half years prior to Lincoln's emancipation of the slaves in the United States. Because the Russian government feared that publication of the Manifesto on the eve of the customarily jubilant celebrations of pre-Lenten Carnival Week, beginning February 26, might give rise to serious public disturbances, it was not issued until Sunday, March 5, the day before Lent. The Manifesto, which announced the liberation of the serfs and summarized the chief provisions of the law (almost 400 printed pages) pertaining to this matter, was read in the churches, distributed throughout the country, and posted. Not until May did it reach some of Russia's remote villages. In St. Petersburg, however, March 5 was a day of great rejoicing and enthusiasm. According to Prince Kropotkin *(Memoirs,* pp. 133-135), crowds thronged before the Winter Palace and followed the Emperor's carriage through the streets of the capital. At the opera, the national anthem was sung over and over again.

It soon became evident, however, that the peasants were seriously dissatisfied over the Tsar's failure to grant them free land as well as personal freedom. Some even contended that landowners, priests, and corrupt officials had suppressed the true Manifesto. Confronted by the prospect of having to pay for the land they had used so long, of securing in some instances even less land than they had held as serfs, and of waiting for their freedom for as much as two years, the peasants on many estates reacted violently, spontaneously, but without organization. There were, it is estimated, 1,176 acts of insubordination in 1861, 400 in 1862, and 386 in 1863. The government, however, was prepared for this eventuality and ruthlessly suppressed the disturbances.

Translated from *Russia. Laws. Statutes, etc., 1855-1881* (Alexander II), "Polozhenie 19 Fevralya 1861 goda" (Moscow, 1916), pp. 4-8.

By the Grace of God, We, Alexander II, Emperor and Autocrat of All the Russias, Tsar of Poland, Grand Duke of Finland, etc., etc., etc.

Declare to all Our loyal subjects:

By God's Providence and the sacred law of the succession, having been summoned to the ancestral Throne of All the Russias, in conformity with this summons, We vowed in Our heart to encompass within Our Tsarist love and care all Our loyal subjects of every rank and station, from the nobleman who wields his sword for the defence of the Fatherland to the humble working craftsman who uses a tool, from him who performs the highest service to the state to him who turns a furrow in the field with a wooden or metal plow.

After careful consideration of the class strata of which the state is comprised, We discovered that the state legislation, well and efficiently organized for the upper and middle classes, defining their obligations, rights, and prerogatives, has not been equally well defined for the serfs, as they are called, due in part to the old laws, in part to custom and hereditary bondage under the power of the landowners, on whom also rests the obligation to improve their welfare. Until the present time, the rights of the landowners were broad and were not defined with the precision of the law, which was replaced by tradition, custom, and the good will of the landowner. Under the best of circumstances, this produced good patriarchal relations, sincere and just guardianship, philanthropy on the part of the landlord and good-natured obedience on the part of the peasant. But with the decline in the simplicity of customs, with increased diversity of relations, with a decrease in the direct, paternal relations of the landowners toward the peasants, sometimes with the fall of the landowners' rights into the hands of people anxious only for personal gain, good relations deteriorated, and the way was opened for arbitrary rule, burdensome to the peasants and unfavorable to their well-being, which was responsible for the slow progress of the peasants toward the improvement of their own daily lives. Our Eternally Remembered Predecessors took cognizance thereof and adopted measures for the improvement of the condition of the peasants; but these were in part half-measures, submitted for voluntary, freedom-loving action on the part of the landowners, and some were decisive only in certain localities, contingent upon demand, special circumstances, or were undertaken as experiments. Thus, Emperor Alexander I issued the decree concerning free tillers of the soil; Our late Father, Nicholas I, the decree about bonded peasants. In the western provinces, the allotment of land to the peasants and their obligations are defined by regulations governing the inventory. But the decrees about the free tillers of the soil and the bonded peasants were put into effect on a very small scale.

Thus We have become convinced that the matter of ameliorating the plight of the serfs is for Us a legacy from Our Predecessors and, due to the course of events, the lot assigned to Us by the hand of Providence.

We entered upon this business with an act demonstrating Our confidence in the Russian nobility, who have evinced in practice their great devotion to the Throne and their readiness to make sacrifices for the sake of the Fatherland. To the nobility itself We offered, in accordance with its own challenge, to draft a bill for the new structure of the daily life of the peasants, with the understanding that the nobility should limit its rights over the peasants and ease the difficulties of the transformation without reducing its prerogatives. And Our confidence was warranted. In the Provincial committees, the members of which are invested with the confidence of the entire aristocratic society of each province, the nobility voluntarily relinquished its rights over the persons of the serfs. In these committees, based upon essential information, were drafted proposals for the new structure of the daily life of those who were still in a state of serfdom and for their relations toward the landowners.

These suggestions, which, as might have been expected owing to the nature of the case, turned out to be diverse, collated, and in agreement, have been reduced to correct form, revised, and amplified in the Main Committee dealing with this matter, and thus were drafted these new regulations about the landowners' peasants and household serfs which were reviewed in the Council of State.

Having called upon God for help, We decided to put this into effect.

By virtue of the aforesaid new regulations the serfs will in due time receive the full rights of free rural inhabitants.

The landowners, preserving the right to ownership of all land belonging to them, allot to the peasants in perpetuity, in return for fixed obligations, the homesteads on which they were settled and, in addition, for the security of their daily lives and the fulfillment of their obligations to the Government, a definite amount of field and other lands, as defined in the "Regulations." In return for the use of the land allotments, the peasants, on their part, are duty bound to discharge for the benefit of the landowners the obligations defined in the "Regulations." In this situation, which is transitional, the peasants are designated as temporarily obligated.

In addition, they are given the right to redeem the homesteads on which they are settled, and by agreement with the landowners they can acquire ownership of the field and other lands allotted to them in perpetuity. By acquiring ownership of a definite amount of land, the peasants will be freed from obligations to the landowners on the land they have purchased and will acquire the definitive status of free peasant proprietors.

By a special regulation concerning household serfs, their transitional period is made contingent upon their occupations and requirements; at the end of a two-year term from the date of publication' of this Regulation they will receive complete freedom and immediate benefits.

On these main principles, in accordance with the Regulations as formulated, the future organization of the peasants and household serfs is defined, the system of the peasants' communal administration is established, and the rights granted to the peasants and household serfs and the obligations devolving upon them in respect to the Government and landowners are pointed out.

Although these same regulations, general, local, and special supplementary rules for certain particular localities, for the estates of small landowners, and for peasants working in the landowners' factories and foundries, have been adapted to local economic requirements and customs —nevertheless, in order to preserve the customary order where it is to mutual advantage to do so—We are leaving it to the landowners to make voluntary agreements with the peasants and to conclude agreements pertaining to the size of allotments to the peasants and the ensuing obligations for the same, in conformity with the regulations established to protect the inviolability of such agreements.

Inasmuch as the new system, due to the unavoidable complexity of the changes required, cannot be carried out suddenly, but requires time, approximately no less than two years, therefore, during this period, to prevent confusion and to guard the public and private interests, the system that has existed heretofore on the landowners' estates must be preserved until the necessary preparations have been completed, at which time the new system will be inaugurated.

For the proper accomplishment of this purpose, We have deemed it right to command:

1. The opening in each Province of a Provincial Council-Chamber for peasant affairs, to which will be entrusted supreme jurisdiction over the affairs of the peasant communes, established on the landowners' lands.

2. For the review of local misunderstandings and disputes which might arise during the execution of the new regulations, the appointment of district arbiters of the peace and the organization from them of District Peace Assemblies.

3. The formation thereafter on the landowners' estates of Mir administrations, retaining the present structure of the village communes, and the opening of Volost administrations in sizable villages, and the unification of small village communes under one Volost administration.

4. The drafting, verification, and ratification in each village commune or estate of a charter of rules, in which there will be enumerated, on the basis of local conditions, the size of the land allotments to the peasants for perpetual use in proportion to the obligations required of them

for the benefit of the landowner, both for the land, as well as for other benefits received from him.

5. These charters of rules are to be implemented in accordance with their confirmation on each estate, but final implementation throughout all the estates is to be carried out within two years from the date of publication of the present Manifesto.

6. Pending the expiration of this term, the peasants and household serfs are to remain, as they were previously, in subjection to the landowners and are to fulfill their former obligations without reservation.

7. The landowners are to retain supervision of law and order on their estates, with the right to administer justice and mete out punishment, pending the formation of the Volosts and the opening of Volost courts.

Taking into consideration the inevitable difficulties connected with the transformation We, first of all, pin Our hopes on God's All-Gracious Providence, which protects Russia.

Furthermore, We pin our hopes on the heroic zeal for the common good of the nobility, to whom we cannot but express for Ourself and for the entire Fatherland well-deserved gratitude for selfless action in the realization of Our plans. Russia will not forget that, induced solely by respect for the dignity of man and Christian love for his neighbor, it (the nobility) voluntarily rejected serfdom which has now been abolished and laid the foundation of a new economic future for the peasants. We undoubtedly expect that it will also demonstrate still more thoroughness in the execution of the new regulations in good order, in a spirit of peace and good will, and that each landowner will complete, within the bounds of his own estate, the great civil feat of the entire class, by organizing the daily life of the peasants and household serfs settled on his land under mutually profitable conditions, and will thereby set the village population a good example and offer encouragement for the precise and honest execution of the state decisions.

Having in mind examples of the generous trusteeship of the landowners with reference to the welfare of the peasants and the gratitude of the peasants for the beneficent guardianship of the landowners, Our hope is confirmed that by mutual, voluntary agreements there will be solved a large part of the difficulties inevitable in certain circumstances in the application of general regulations to the diverse conditions of the individual estates, and that in this way the transition from the old order to the new will be facilitated, and that good will and singlehearted striving for the common weal will be firmly established.

For the most convenient implementation of those agreements between the landowners and peasants, by which the latter will acquire ownership of property, together with homesteads and field lands, the Government will extend grants-in-aid based upon special regulations, will advance loans, and transfer estate debts.

We rely also upon the common sense of Our people.

When the Government's idea about the abolition of serfdom spread among peasants unprepared for it, some misunderstandings cropped up. Some thought about freedom and forgot about obligations. But the general common sense was not shaken in the conviction that, even by natural reasoning, one who enjoys freedom by the grace of society has an obligation to serve the welfare of society by fulfilling certain requirements, and in accordance with Christian law, *every soul must be subject unto the higher powers* (Romans, XIII, 1), *render to all their dues, tribute to whom tribute, custom to whom custom, fear to whom fear, and honor to whom honor* (*Romans,* XIII,7); the rights which were legally acquired by the landowners cannot be taken from them without proper remuneration or voluntary concessions; it would be contrary to all justice to make use of the landowners' land and not perform corresponding obligations in return.

And now we hopefully anticipate that the serfs for whom a new future has been opened up will comprehend and accept with gratitude the important sacrifice made by the nobility for the improvement of their daily lives.

They will be convinced that by receiving for themselves a firmer foundation of ownership and great freedom to manage their own possessions they have become obligated before society and before themselves for the soundness of the new law, which they will observe sincerely, loyally, and diligently, in return for the rights bestowed upon them. The most beneficial law cannot make people prosperous if they do not make an effort themselves to establish their own prosperity under the protection of the law. Contentment is acquired and increased only by unremitting labor, prudent application of one's efforts and means, strict economy, and, in general, by an upright life lived in the fear of God.

The executors of the preparatory action for the new structure of the peasants' daily life and for its very introduction into this system will require vigilant care, in order that this should be accomplished properly and without disturbance, also taking into consideration the matter of their convenience, so that the attention of the tillers will not be deflected from their urgent agricultural work. Let them assiduously till the land and gather its fruit, so that thereafter, out of a well-filled granary they will have seed to sow the land under perpetual use or the land acquired as their own property.

And now, make the sign of the cross, O Orthodox people, and call upon God to bless your free labor, which is the guarantee of your domestic well-being and of the common good.

Issued at St. Petersburg, on the nineteenth day of February, in the year of Our Lord eighteen hundred and sixty-one, in the seventh year of Our Reign.

The Original text in His Imperial Majesty's own hand— "Alexander"	Printed in St. Petersburg at the State Senate

28. D. I. Pisarev on the

education of women

EXCERPT FROM AN ARTICLE by the outstanding Russian literary critic, Dmitryi Ivanovitch Pisarev (1840-1868), "The Thoughts of Virkhov on the Education of Women" (1865).
From *Sotchineniya* D. I. Pisareva. Pln, sobr. v shesti tomakh, 4-e. izd., t. IV (St. Petersburg, 1903), stbl. 454-456.

Some intelligent and honest people have expressed in our periodical literature the idea that a woman should be an active and useful member of society, and consequently she must study and work. Others have disputed this, also in our periodical literature, maintaining that a woman has nothing to do in society, that her place is at the family hearth, that she should be exclusively a wife, mother, and mistress of the house. To me these objectors are unintelligent and unhappy people, because they pretend to be the protectors of something very respectable which nobody would ever venture to attack. When the problem of the serious scientific education of women was raised, they defended the chastity of young girls who were not exposed to the slightest danger. When the problem of team labor was raised, they defended husbands as family benefactors, although nobody had said a bad word against them. By such cheap means they contrived to cast improper aspersions on their literary opponents and succeeded in strengthening their own reputations as vigilant and well-meaning guardians of social morals. The public, before whom these superficial tricks were staged, as usual was complacent, looked blank, and let itself be duped. It stands to reason that the women's question, under such conditions, ran aground, and to refloat it became almost a dangerous business.

It seems to me, however, that the question "ran aground" simply because our progressives lacked quick wits and resourcefulness. Having at their disposal some doses of these priceless qualities, they could have derived the most tangible benefit for the question under consideration, even from the objections. Completely unexpectedly, they could have accepted the point of view of these sophists and defeated them utterly with their own weapons. These benefactors of our society assert *ad infinitum* that a woman should be exclusively a wife, mother, and mistress of the house. Fine. It is very good that they should express their own wishes, and express them so frequently, so loudly, and solemnly, that they can no longer disavow them. Now it only remains to ask them whether they want a woman to be a *good* wife, a *good* mother, and a *good* mistress of the house. If to this question they reply *no,* then perhaps even our complacent public will cease to drink champagne to their health. If, as is to be expected, they answer *yes,* then the progressives can consider that they have won their case and can read the hoaxers a very splendid and very edifying lesson. "Listen, you benefactors," the progressives will say, "do you know what a high level of development is necessary for this? Do you know what a radical transformation must be brought about in the whole system of women's education in order that it should actually provide society with *good* wives, *good* mothers, and *good* mistresses of the house? If you do not know this, then you are empty phrasemongers. If you do know this, then, having incessantly harped on the theme of women, mothers, and mistresses of the house, you should act in concert with us to seek even more diligently than we do seriousness and versatility in women's education. And since you yourselves strive to block everything that leads to the education of *good* wives, *good* mothers, and *good* mistresses of the house, then you are again nothing but empty phrasemongers and paltry hoaxers. Those persons to whom the well-being and perfection of the Russian family and Russian economy are really dear should reject your hypocritical chatter and lend an ear to what is said by honest citizens and thoughtful observers of social life."

By making use of such a philippic, the progressives could shut the mouths of those unrecognized guardians of the social virtues. Then, having snatched from their hands the banner of domestic benefactors and having convinced society that these benefactors are not exposed to the least danger, the progressives could unfold an educational program which actually develops women, mothers, and mistresses of the house. This program, by virtue of its obvious logic, would attract the sympathy and complete confidence of all unbiased, uncorrupted persons in our society. The most timid and short sighted minds would perceive without difficulty its obvious practical use, and the great idea of women's education and women's work would become an integral part of our society, precisely because of its modest, simple, and unpretentious appearance.

29. higher education for women
in the nineteenth century

KONSTANTIN DMITRIEVITCH USHINSKII (1824-1870) was an outstanding Russian pedagogue, who created his own original pedagogical system. Ushinskii first applied his progressive ideas in the reform of the Smol'ny Institute in St. Petersburg, 1859-1862, as an institution for the education of women.

Below are excerpts from the memoirs of E. N. Vodovozova (1844-1923), one of Ushinskii's Smol'ny students, who subsequently became a talented writer for young people and author of valuable pedagogical works. The first excerpt recounts Ushinskii's introductory lecture on pedagogy; the second his speech on the occasion of the liberation of the serfs, February 19 [March 3], 1861.

From E. N. Vodovozova, *Na zare zhizni i drugie vospominaniya.* Academiya edition. Vol. I (Moscow-Leningrad, 1934), 578-582, 599-601.

1. With great impatience we awaited Ushinskii's lectures; but, since instruction had not yet begun, we conceived the idea of asking him to lecture about something anyway. At the time of which I speak, he was especially overloaded with work and with numerous responsibilities connected with the reform of the institute. He nevertheless responded with enthusiasm to our request, declared that it just happened that he did have a free hour, and could proceed to lecture forthwith. Although at this time there were only a few persons in the class, he said that he would give his opening lecture on pedagogy.

He began it by pointing out all the banality, all the nonentity, all the harm, all the moral poverty of our expectations and vain aspirations for wealth, finery, splendid balls, and worldly amusements.

"You should, in fact you are in duty bound," said he, "to kindle in your hearts, not dreams of worldly vanity, which are the desires of empty, pitiful creatures, but a pure flame, an unquenchable, inextinguishable thirst for the acquisition of knowledge, and you must develop in yourselves, first and foremost, a love for work. Without this your lives will be neither worthy of respect, nor will they be happy. Work elevates your mind, ennobles your heart and vividly demonstrates to you all the illusiveness of your dreams. It will give you strength to forget sorrow, terrible bereavement, deprivations, and adversities, which so lavishly strew the path of life of every human being. It will bring you pure delight, moral contentment, and the consciousness that you do not live in the world in vain. Everything in life can deceive you, all dreams can prove to be empty illusions, only intellectual work—it alone—never betrays anyone. If you surrender yourself to it, it is always beneficial to you and to others. By constantly broadening your intellectual horizon, little by little it will open to you more and more new interests in life; it will compel you to love it more and more, and not for the sake of egotistical enjoyment and worldly pleasures. . . . Constant intellectual work develops in your soul the purest, highest love for your fellow man, and only such love provides honest, noble, and true happiness. And for this everyone can and should strive, if he is not a phrasemaker and a windbag, if he does not have a flabby nature, if in his breast there beats a human heart, capable of loving something other than himself. Everyone can achieve this greatest happiness on earth, therefore every person can be the blacksmith of his own happiness.

From the impassioned and elated apotheosis of work, Ushinskii passed on to a definition of maternal love and what it should be. Love for its offspring exists in the heart of every animal: Wild animals—the bear and the wolf—protect their cubs at the peril of their own lives, often dying in the struggle with the enemy; they fed them at their own breasts, warm them with their own bodies, throw dry grass and leaves into their lairs so that they may have a softer place to sleep. Is it possible that woman, a rational creature, is concerned like the wild animal only about the physical well-being and preservation of the life of her child? In addition to the natural concern, lodged in her heart by mother nature, of which she is instinctively conscious, a woman adds love, which she considers human, but in the vast majority of cases it should be called make believe, since it is the product of petty vanity. In this connection, he brought in the example of mothers who resort to every means to dress their children beautifully, to make them more attractive—they play with them, as a child with a toy. Already from an early age education must develop in a child the need to work, must instil in it the desire for education and self-education, and subsequently inspire in it the idea of its obligation to enlighten the simple people—your serfs, your so-called slaves, by whose grace you are here, receive an education, exist, have a good time, indulge in your own dreams; while he, this slave of yours, like a machine, like a beast of burden works for you indefatigably, without getting enough to eat and drink, submerged in darkness, ignorance, and poverty.

Now all these ideas have long ago become common knowledge, have seeped into the flesh and blood of educated people, but at that time [1860], on the eve of the liberation of the peasants, they were new to

Russian women in general, and the more so to us, institute students, who up to that time had not heard one intelligent word, and were contaminated by banal aspirations, which Ushinskii destroyed mercilessly.

Everything that I pass on about Ushinskii's first introductory lecture is but a pale, weak abstract of his speech, which at that time I outlined in brief, including only its general features.

In order to understand what an earth-shaking impression this opening lecture made upon me, it is necessary to bear in mind, not only the fact that the ideas expressed in it were completely new to us, but also that Ushinskii expressed them with fervent passion and expressiveness, with the unusual power and brilliant erudition, in which he so excelled. Small wonder that this speech was engraved on our hearts in letters of fire, so that at the time all of us had tears running down our cheeks!

Ushinskii's whole appearance contributed greatly to the profound impact of his words upon us. He was above medium height, thin, and extremely nervous. From beneath his heavy black, arched eyebrows his dark brown eyes sparkled feverishly. His expressive, delicate features, his finely moulded high forehead, bespeaking a remarkable intelligence, strikingly intensified his paleness within the frame of jet black hair and black side whiskers around his cheeks and chin, reminiscent of a short, thick beard. His thin colorless lips, his stern visage and his piercing look which, it seemed, penetrated through and through a person, bespoke the presence of a strong character and stubborn will. It seems to me that if the renowned Russian artist, V. M. Vasnetsov, had seen Ushinskii, he would have depicted him as some kind of inspired prophet-fanatic, whose eyes emitted sparks when preaching, and whose face became unusually severe and stern. Whoever saw Ushinskii even once always remembered the face of this man, whose outward appearance also sharply distinguished him from the crowd.

Many decades have elapsed since my active career came to an end and I stand on the threshold of the grave, but even now I cannot forget the impassioned speech of this great teacher, which first struck a human spark in our heads, made our hearts beat with human feelings, and awakened in us the noble virtues of the soul, without which it would have been extinguished. This lecture alone made it impossible for us to revert to our former outlook, at least in the sphere of elementary questions of ethics, and we listened to a whole series of his lectures, and talked with him regarding various social phenomena.

2.   The year 1861 arrived. When the Manifesto of February 19 [March 3] was promulgated, we celebrated with a thanksgiving service. Some hours after returning from church, Ushinskii came and stated that he wanted to clarify for us the significance of this great act. In a brilliantly popular, concise survey, he sketched the life of the landlords under serfdom, acquainted us with how they amused themselves, taking turns at feasting, hunting, and other lordly entertainment, and he pointed out the cruelty of many of them toward their serfs. He related how the landlords

themselves, who considered labor as a stigma, or through their managers, burdened their peasants with back-breaking toil, leaving them to eke out a miserable existence, full of cruel deprivations, submerged in the utter darkness of ignorance and degrading service. He concluded this brilliant speech by stating that the act of emancipation of the peasants placed on all of us an obligation to repay even an insignificant part of our indebtedness. For our education, for the opportunity to live comfortably, for happiness, acquired at the expense of the age-old servitude of the masses, we, in order to atone for the heavy sins of many generations, must devote all our strength to the enlightenment of the people. "And each one of you, in whose breast there is not a stone, but a heart, must in good faith respond to this summons." According to Ushinskii, from this moment everyone was obligated to bring to the people his work, knowledge, and talent, and on Russian women the beginning of the epoch of liberation imposed still another special obligation—their emancipation from the prejudices that weighed especially upon them. It was not so long ago that we did not consider it necessary to teach a woman even the three R's; and even now in the families of educated people, where it is considered essential to provide higher education for the son, the daughter is instructed willy nilly, in haphazard fashion. And everybody, even women themselves, accept this as the normal order of things. To be a tutor of the young generation is a great and noble task, but at the same time extremely difficult and complicated. To achieve success, a woman must be fully armed with serious knowledge. Consequently, women like men should receive a higher education. "You are in duty bound," said he, "to imbue yourselves with an aspiration for the conquest of the right to higher education, to make it the purpose of your life, to instil this aspiration in the hearts of your sisters, and to strive for the attainment of this goal until the doors of the universities, academies, and higher schools are thrown open to you as hospitably as to men." It must be remembered that Ushinskii said this as early as 1861.

During my acquaintance with Ushinskii after graduation, no matter what kind of conversations and discussions he conducted in the circle of his acquaintances, I never heard him express socialist or radical-democratic ideas. He was always and everywhere a passionate admirer, sympathizer, and propagandist for education in general and for its dissemination among simple people in particular, as well as a preacher of broad education for women. Only in women's attainment of higher education did he see the alpha and omega of equal rights for women, his ultimate purpose and goal. Only the most progressive members of the Russian intelligentsia were at that time imbued with such views on the women's question. Women themselves, even the most progressive among them, by equal rights meant at that time the same rights as men to higher education, as well as the right to independent earnings.

30. P. M. Tretyakov and his art gallery

PAVEL MIKHAILOVITCH TRETYAKOV (1832-1898) was a rich Moscow merchant, a passionate devotee and connoisseur of Russian art, who in 1856 began to acquire pictures by Russian artists. His brother, A. M. Tretyakov, also collected art works. Through the efforts of P. M. Tretyakov, there was established in his home in Lavrushinsky Lane in Moscow a national gallery of Russian art, which in quantity (upwards of 1,300 pictures) was the largest of Russian galleries and from the standpoint of strict selectivity the most valuable. Tretyakov collected works of art distinguished by their profound idea content, democratic trend, and realism, In this gallery were concentrated the best pictures of the Russian artists. I. E. Repin (1844-1930), V. I. Surikov (1848-1916), V. V. Vereshchagin (1842-1904), V. G. Perov (1832-1882), I. N. Kramskoi (1837-1887), V. M. Vasnetsov (1848-1926), M. V. Nesterov (1862-1942), I. I. Levitan (1861-1900), A. K. Savrasov (1830-1897), A. I. Kuindzhi (1842-1910), N. A. Yaroshenko (1846-1898), and others.

In 1892, Tretyakov transferred ownership of this collection of 1,840 works, together with the house in which it was situated, as a gift to the city of Moscow. On June 3, 1918, by the decree of V. I. Lenin, the Tretyakov Gallery was nationalized. Tretyakov's pictures provided the nucleus of a collection which, by 1956, the one hundredth anniversary of the founding of the gallery, numbered about 35,000 works. Today it is the most complete and most valuable collection of Russian national art and sculpture.

The excerpts given below are from the memoirs of Nikolai Andreyevitch Mudrogel' (1868-1942), whose father was a former serf and who was himself an employee of the Tretyakov Gallery for sixty years and an assistant to P. M. Tretyakov. These passages vividly depict P. M. Tretyakov and the Tretyakov Gallery in the last two decades of the nineteenth century.

183

From N. Mudrogel', "58 let v Tret'yakovskoi galeree. Vospominaniya," *Novyi Mir* (No. 7, 1940), pp. 139, 140-145, 146,
148-150, 152, 153, 156-159.

I was five or six years old when Pavel Mikhailovitch [Tretyakov] decided
to make the first annex to the house—a gallery for pictures only. He was
afraid that a fire might occur in the house and the pictures would then
be destroyed. The gallery was constructed by Tretyakov's son-in-law, the
architect Kaminskii. Part of the garden was cleared and in the course
of one summer the two-story building with two spacious halls was erected.
All the pictures were transferred from the living quarters to these halls.
Partitions were placed in the halls to serve as walls for pictures already
short of space.

... In 1873 the gallery was opened to the public, which was then as
formerly allowed to view the pictures only by permission of Pavel Mikhailovitch. And understandably it was inconvenient to permit everyone
to enter the family quarters.

Over the wicket gate, which separated the court from the garden,
there appeared the sign, "Picture Gallery." Each visitor went from
Lavrushinsky Lane first into the court, then through the gate into the
garden, and from the garden into the gallery. My father met the visitors
and admitted them to the halls....He was already fully occupied with
the pictures and did nothing else. And many pictures were purchased
during these years. On the lower story of the living quarters, Pavel
Mikhailovitch allocated one of his own three rooms for processing the
pictures before they were hung in the gallery. In this room the picture
was framed, glazed, and sometimes cleaned....

... At the close of the fall of 1880 an auction was announced in St.
Petersburg for the sale of the pictures of the artist, V. V. Vereshchagin.
To all such auctions Tretyakov went without fail and invariably brought
back pictures. Many of Vereshchagin's pictures were to be sold at this
time and the auction was publicized in the newspapers.

Some days after Pavel Mikhailovitch's departure for St. Petersburg my
father told me, smiling at my mother, that the paper had announced:
"Tretyakov has purchased the entire Vereshchagin collection. Nobody
else was able to buy a single picture." And my father fetched the newspaper, where Stasov described the auction: "Tretyakov slew all his rivals
with rubles. No matter what price his competitors set, he invariably
squeaked, just like a squeaking cart: 'One ruble higher.' And the picture
was his. Thus, the whole Vereshchagin collection—Turkestan and Indian
—passed to the Tretyakov Gallery in Moscow."

Soon Pavel Mikhailovitch himself arrived home, contented and happy.
And already we knew all about it: when he made a successful purchase in St. Petersburg, he returned to Moscow in good humor, and
everybody in the house, in the courtyard, in the office, likewise became
happy:

"Pavel Mikhailovitch has purchased good pictures!"

If he failed to purchase, he arrived stern, irritated, said little, and everyone in the house fell silent. The coachman, who met him at the station after the purchase of the Vereshchagin pictures, saw at once that this was a successful purchase. So at this time there was joy everywhere —and I recall that there was much amusement in the courtyard over the newspaper articles in which Pavel Mikhailovitch was called "a squeaking cart."

Tretyakov said to my father: "There are so many pictures that a big new annex will have to be made. And he went with him several times into the garden with a measure in order to plan where the new halls would be built. Many trees had to be cut down. Vera Nikolayevna[1] and their daughters greatly lamented that the garden would be ruined.

My mother said that the conversation of the Tretyakovs ran, as follows:

"Where will we go for a walk? Where will our children go for a walk?"

And Pavel Mikhailovitch said: "There is enough space, and we must think, not only of ourselves, but about society—build for all Muscovites and for all the Russian people.

"I am not trying to do this for myself alone. The time will come when I shall give this gallery to the city of Moscow. And for the children I shall make a smaller garden."

... In the summer of 1882, already as an employee, I first started work in the gallery.

... That very summer the next annex to the gallery was completed— six spacious halls, three on each story. Already there were many pictures, but I remember, in particular, "The Misalliance," by Pukirev, "Princess Tarakanova," by Flavitsky, "Return from the Crimean War," by Filippov, "The Halt of the Prisoners," by Yakoby, and "The Fountain of Hannibal," by Lagoriya. There were many of Perov's pictures. Here were "Troika" (apprentice-artisans carrying water), "The Arrival of the Governess at the Merchant's Home," "The Fowlers," and "The Wanderer." One room of the lower story was filled with portraits, the works of artists of the end of the XVIIIth and the beginning of the XIXth centuries—Antropov, Levitsky, Borovikovsky, Argunov, Rokotov, Matveyev, Tropinin, Venetsianov, Briullov, and also scenes of Rome, Naples, and Sorrento, the work of Sylvester Shchedrin.

In the new halls of the lower story were also accommodated the Vereshchagin collection.

I liked my new work very much. Visitors were still few at that time: ten to fifteen on weekdays and twenty to thirty on holidays. And here for six hours, from ten to four, I used to walk through the halls, neatly dressed, in new boots, my hair brushed, and around me on the walls was a marvellous life, faces, flowers, cities. In the rooms it was quiet

[1] The wife of P. M. Tretyakov.

and bright, and the air was pleasant. Fine! I gazed at the pictures, study-ing every detail in them. . . . What is a picture? The more you look at it, the more you see. Almost every artist gives many details in a picture, which at first glance you fail to notice. One must look a long time, intently, with love, to see everything. And also Pavel Mikhailovitch prodded me:

"Study the artists, Nicky. Study their manner of delineation. This is necessary, so that you can recognize immediately to what artist the picture belongs."

He used to pick up any sketch, show it from a distance, and ask: "Who painted it?"

. . . Pavel Mikhailovitch himself never went from the house to the gal-lery when the public was there, even if his friends or certain celebrities were there. During all my work in the gallery, such an event never occurred. Nor did he make his appearance even when members of the Tsar's family visited the gallery. It happened very often in those years when Sergei Alexandrovitch Romanov, the brother of Alexander III, was the Governor-General of Moscow. He was proud of the fact that in Moscow there was such a landmark—an art gallery—and he brought his own guests there—foreigners and his own relatives. And every time he used to ask: "Where is Tretyakov himself?" But Pavel Mikhailovitch gave us attendants, once and for all, a strict order: "If you are given notice beforehand that there will be a special royal guest, say that Pavel Mikhailovitch is out of town. If they should arrive without warning and ask for me, say that I am away from home, nobody knows where." To us, of course, this was astonishing. What an honor! The Tsar's brother, himself, various grand dukes and princesses, counts, and generals would arrive in formal dress, with stars, ribbons, decorations, in the richest carriages, the police would be stationed along the entire lane, beginning at the stone bridges, and all the yard workers were turned out of the houses to sweep and water the streets. But he: "Not at home!" He would sit in his study, occupy himself with his business, or read.

. . . At that time, there came to the gallery mainly the intelligentsia, students, and pupils from the secondary schools. There were very few workers, and Pavel Mikhailovitch was very glad when he saw that workers were also coming. In the evening he would question me in great detail about how the workers conducted themselves, what they said, in front of what pictures they stood especially long, what they passed by and paid little attention to.

"I am collecting this for the people, I must know the opinion of the people," he said to us frequently.

At that time people stopped most of all in front of the pictures of Perov, Vereshchagin, Shishkin, Makovsky, and later, as their pictures appeared, before Repin and Surikov. Many likewise stopped in front of Maksimov, Kozukhin, Savitsky, Kuindzhi, Aivazovsky. It is curious that in front of these pictures the stone floor was worn with age and hollows appeared because so many people thronged there.

Entry was free to all; we received everyone gladly. If they questioned us, we tried to give the most detailed and most courteous reply. Pavel Mikhailovitch impressed upon us that everyone who came to the gallery was his dear guest and we must meet him as such.

The fame of the Tretyakov Gallery began to grow, and even our neighbors, the Zamoskvorets merchants and the townsfolk became interested in it. At one merchant's, for instance, a guest arrived from the provinces, "with a smattering of knowledge," and asked to be shown where in Zamoskvoretchie was the gallery with very interesting pictures.

"Where is it? We have not heard of it"—ingenuously declared the master.

"Yes, somewhere here, the merchant Tretyakov collects. . . .

"Oh, Tretyakov, almost our neighbor, lives nearby! That is his house where some people are going. . . . We too should go there."

And with his guest the neighboring merchant pays his first visit to our gallery. . . .

. . . Tretyakov's enthusiasm over his art collection increased year by year. In the Eighties he acquired such masterpeices as "Ivan Grozny and His Son," by Repin, and "The Morning of the Execution of the Streltsy," by Surikov, and there appeared halls named for Repin and Surikov. All the best items from the exhibitions were transferred to our gallery forthwith. Tretyakov used to spend hundreds of thousands of rubles a year on the purchase of pictures. Every holiday he invariably visited the Moscow artists, trying to fish out of them whatever he could. He used to go to antique shops. He received many letters from Muscovites and people in other cities, with proposals to sell him their pictures. Tretyakov first corresponded with them, found out the size of the picture, and upon what material it was painted, what were the colors, and whence it came; then, depending upon the reply, he would either have the picture brought to the gallery, or, if it were large, he would send me to examine it on the spot. Every time he would ask me for details and, if the picture were interesting, he went himself to see it.

A year passed, a little over two, and no space was left in the rooms; no place to hang anything. Then Tretyakov began a new annex. . . . By the time of his death he had built twenty-five rooms, which now form the central part of the gallery.

The number of visitors greatly increased at the beginning of the Nineties. The gallery became known to wide circles of Muscovites, and many persons came even from other cities.

. . . Pavel Mikhailovitch Tretyakov was an unusual man. He had his shortcomings, of course, and perhaps even big ones, but in general his was an illustrious personality, of great benefit to our country. He was a merchant close with his money and economical, so that he would not spend even a ruble for nothing. Sometimes artists complained about him: "Tretyakov squeezes us." Truly, in these complaints there was an element of truth: during the years of my work I heard them more than once. However, all the artists sold their best works to Tretyakov. Very few pictures slipped by him.

And the employees also complained at times; there was too little pay. And there were rumors that at the Kostroma factory of the Tretyakov brothers the workers did not live well. In brief, in this respect, Pavel Mikhailovitch was a true son of his merchant class. But it must be noted that both Tretyakov's employees and workers generally lived very long and left very reluctantly. When I compare Pavel Mikhailovitch with other Moscow merchants and noblemen (and I saw much of them) then I see the difference. In Moscow there were merchants a thousand times richer than Tretyakov. And what did they do for their country and for our culture? Nothing! Again let us take the life of Pavel Mikhailovitch from childhood. . . . The man did not receive any education and reached the point where he was acquainted with all the foremost Russian artists, writers, scholars, actors, composers, and musicians; he carried on correspondence with them, and they were his guests. During the years 1880-1889 I did not know any other man in Moscow who was as widely acquainted with the best people of our country as he was. He was respected by all he came in contact with—by the painters, writers, actors, and various social figures. It must be assumed that everyone understood what a vast national undertaking this man was engaged in.

This, you see, everyone knew in our time: that one must live not only for himself, but also with and for all. But when Pavel Mikhailovitch's life began, such an awareness had barely begun to awaken. He mastered it, and lived precisely with and for all, and not merely for himself.

. . . I have said already how he avoided meetings with members of the Tsar's family. It looked as if he had no love for the bearers of power, either secular or spiritual. I recall once we were informed that "John Kronshtadtsky will be in the gallery tomorrow." At that time this priest was so famous that he had tens of thousands of followers. They considered him to be a saint, regarded it as a great honor to be "blessed" by him. But Tretyakov, as soon as he found out that such an honor was in prospect, immediately made up his mind to go off to Kostroma for a couple of days.

"Say that I have been called away on urgent business."

In 1893, after a visit to the gallery, Tsar Alexander III decided to confer nobility upon Tretyakov. Some important official told Tretyakov about it and Pavel Mikhailovitch replied:

"I am very grateful to His Majesty for the great honor, but the high rank of nobleman I decline. I was born a merchant and will die a merchant."

He was awarded medals, of course, and uniforms also; however, he neither wore the medals nor ever put on any uniform—only a tail coat when it was indispensable. Only one title did he accept: that of honorable citizen of the city of Moscow. He loved Moscow very much—and one must assume that the conferment of the title upon· him afforded him satisfaction, because he accepted it without any discussion.

When the gallery was given to the city, the artists decided to celebrate this event and arranged an all-Russian congress in Moscow. Tretyakov understood that he would be the central figure at this congress, that in his honor speeches would be made. . . . A week before the congress he urgently made up his mind and went abroad.

And he loved the artists most of all. Nevertheless, he declined their celebration in his honor.

. . . The basic occupation and passion of Tretyakov was, of course, the collection of pictures and the building of the gallery. Here he fussed and fumed, was proud, dreamed about the gallery day and night. All his great joys and sorrows were connected with the gallery.

I do not recall who it was that once called Tretyakov a maniac. If we accept the fact that a maniac is a man strictly haunted by one purpose— then Tretyakov actually was a maniac. His purpose—to collect a picture gallery for the people—he pursued with determination until he achieved it.

I do not know when Pavel Mikhailovitch conceived the idea of giving this gallery to the city. This was before my time. I already remember when he said definitely:

"The pictures will belong to all the people."

And he constantly instilled in us, the employees of the gallery, that we were guarding and taking care of the people's property.

In the first years, Tretyakov's collection also included the pictures of western artists, but later, having visited in St. Petersburg the well-known collector, Pryanishnikov, he was so struck by the beauty of Russian painting that he decided to collect only the works of Russian artists.

He collected the works of popular artists, such as Perov, Repin, Kramskoi, Surikov, Maksimov, and others. These artists portrayed the life of the Russian people, with its sufferings, griefs, and joys, or in their pictures they held up to ridicule priests, landlords, and merchants. Such pictures as, for instance, "The Procession of the Cross at Easter in the Village of Bol'shie Mytishchi," by Perov, or "The Procession of the Cross in Kursk Province," by Repin. Very few would have had the audacity to display them. But Tretyakov took them. And he took "Ivan Grozny and His Son," when there was a rumor that this picture was pernicious, directed against Tsarist power, and that it should be destroyed.

On the other hand, such pictures as Tsarist parades, various patriotic festivals, Tretyakov did not take. He loved the simple Russian life in all its manifestations.

Since the artistic life of that time was concentrated more in St. Petersburg than in Moscow, Tretyakov very often travelled there for exhibitions and auctions. He was acquainted with all the artists. And not only with the outstanding ones, but also with those of lesser fame. He tried not to let one good work escape him. Before an exhibition he made the rounds of the artists' studios and made note of what to buy. The first time in the studios he bought little. But usually by the day of varnishing he had bought everything that was of interest at the exhibition.

When the exhibition opened, all the best pictures already belonged to Tretyakov. For other collectors, there remained the tail end.

At that time there were already many collectors—Soldatenkov, Ostroukhov, the Botkins, Mamontov, Tsvetkov, and others. Due to Tretyakov's luck, collection then became fashionable. Collectors would come to an exhibition and there was nothing to buy, because all the best had been snatched up by Tretyakov.

Once at an Itinerants' exhibition[2] Tsar Alexander III arrived. He likewise collected Russian pictures. He went to the exhibition, looked—. He liked one. "I should like to acquire that." The organizers respectfully announced:

"Your Majesty, the picture has already been acquired by Tretyakov."

The Tsar frowned. "If that is the case, then I shall take this one."

"Your Majesty, this too has been acquired by Tretyakov."

"How about this one?"—"Likewise."—"And this?"—"Likewise."

The Tsar became very angry, and in a dissatisfied tone said to the organizers:

"I wanted to obtain something from you, but the merchant Tretyakov has beaten me to all of these."

The managers, of course, were trembling! And on that very day they came to the decision: "At an exhibition nothing was to be sold until the sovereign Emperor had visited it."

Tretyakov was very much disturbed.

Before the next exhibitions he proceeded as follows: He bought the pictures directly at the artists' studios, with the proviso that at the exhibition they were to be labelled: "Property of P. M. Tretyakov," or after the gallery had been turned over to Moscow—"Property of the Moscow gallery named after the brothers Tretyakov."

... If Pavel Mikhailovitch regarded pictures with so much respect and with such love, then with what feeling he must have regarded the artists! And indeed artists were for him a superior kind of people, the bearers of some great truth. Even as a small boy I remember that in the Tretyakov house everyone spoke of artists as the most deserving people in the world.

"An artist has come! An artist has arrived!"—they said with enthusiasm

---

[2] The Society of Itinerant Exhibitions, headed by Kramskoi, was supported and subsidized by Tretyakov (eds).

and trepidation all over the house, even the coachmen in the yard, the housemaids, and the office employees.

Always serious and reticent, Pavel Mikhailovitch himself became animated all of a sudden; he talked more amiably with an artist than he had ever done with anyone else. On meeting an artist, he usually kissed him three times.

In the beginning, I remember, he astonished all of us: to us in the gallery there were coming grand dukes, counts, and generals, who expressed a wish to see Pavel Mikhailovitch, to get acquainted with him, to talk with him, and he instructed us to say: "He is not at home. He has gone out, we know not where." But along comes an artist and there is no dearer guest than he. And he would invite him into his study (and very rarely did he invite other persons there), and led him into the house to the second story to his family, where Vera Nikolaevna treated him to breakfast.

The artist Nevrev [N. V. Nevrev, 1830-1904], as I recall, was the first and oldest friend in the Tretyakov house. As early as 1867 he painted "The Ward," in which he depicted a room in the Tretyakov house, where S. Shchedrin's picture, "Moonlight Night," was displayed. The picture even now is located in the exposition gallery, and whoever wants to know in what surroundings the Tretyakovs lived at that time, let him look at this picture.

Nevrev himself also lived not far from Lavrushinsky Lane, near Krasnokholmsky bridge. He was a dyed in the wool Muscovite, lived all his life in Zamoskvoretchie and Tretyakov must have liked the fact that Nevrev depicted a mode of life familiar to him. I recall that the artist often came to dinner at the Tretyakovs, that at dinner he used to tell jokes, and laughed out loud. Pavel Mikhailovitch himself he called "the bishop" and me "Nicky of the gallery."

. . . Another artist, close to the Tretyakov family, was V. G. Perov. As an artist, Tretyakov rated him extremely high, often went to his studio, followed all his works, trying not to let one of his pictures out of his own hands. Perov had near Moscow a favorite place, where he observed life and customs—this was the village of "Bolshie Mytishchi," located on the road to the Sergeyev Monastery. It was here that he painted "The Procession of the Cross at Easter," with a drunken priest and drunken gonfalon bearers. Tretyakov bought the picture and immediately placed it in his gallery. A rumor circulated in Moscow that "Tretyakov is displaying a blasphemous picture." The priesthood and officials began to get indignant. Finally, Tretyakov was ordered to remove the picture from exposition. Then he placed it in his own living quarters. For this picture Perov was arraigned. But he proved that what he depicted was only true to life: A drunken priest in fact arranged such a "procession of the cross" in Mytishchi. The authorities of necessity left the artist in peace.

It was also in Mytishchi that Perov painted "Tea-Drinking"—a fat bishop drinking tea, with his lay brother standing behind him, and a leg-less, invalided soldier begs for alms; here he likewise painted "At the Last Tavern," and "The Family Pilgrimage of the Chief of the Police Station from Moscow to the Troitse-Sergeyev Monastery," and many other works. All have been collected in our gallery. Tretyakov was on friendly terms, not only with the artist himself, but also with his family.

... All the artists understood that in selling pictures to Tretyakov, they were selling them to a national museum, and some therefore greatly reduced the price. Americans, for instance, offered Vereshchagin consid-erably more money for his pictures than Tretyakov, but nevertheless he let Tretyakov have them. And Victor Vasnetsov also let Tretyakov have his pictures for less than other art patrons paid him.

Of course, the personal friendship of Pavel Mikhailovitch with the artists had much significance in this respect.

There were few artists with whom Tretyakov was not on friendly terms. And if he was not on good terms with an artist, then there were serious grounds for it. For instance, he did not recognize Semiradsky. At that time, this artist was highly successful in Russia, but Tretyakov did not want to buy a single one of his pictures.

"Why do you not have Semiradsky?"—Tretyakov was often asked. And he replied:

"Semiradsky presented his best picture to the city of Cracow. Hence he regards himself as a foreigner amongst us. How shall I keep him in a Russian gallery?"

... Tretyakov's friendship with most artists was very close. I recall that Pryanishnikov and Vladimir Makovsky were very often guests of the Tretyakov family. They came to dinner without ceremony, often visited the gallery, examining closely each new picture. Both were merry and witty. Makovsky called Pryanishnikov Larioshka.

"Look, Larioshka, how this was done," he used to say, pointing out some picture to his friend.

Sometimes the Tretyakovs arranged large dinners for the artists, especially at the time of the opening of the Itinerants' Exhibition. It must be said that although artistic life flourished in St. Petersburg, Moscow played the chief role in this respect. Here lived the chief collectors of artistic works. Artists coming to Moscow without fail called upon Tret-yakov. I recall one big meeting of artists at the Tretyakov house, when almost all the Itinerants were there, headed by Kramskoi. With Kram-skoi were Repin, Yaroshenko, Nevrev, Maksimov.... They discussed the question of how to organize exhibitions better and how to improve the life of the artists.

... Of course, the artists, meeting with such care and attention on the part of Pavel Mikhailovitch, regarded him highly. They especially valued his ability to discover all the best, his skill in understanding a painting.

Here is, for instance, a letter from the artist Goravksy to Pavel Mikhailovitch:

"I shall not forget with what attention and satisfaction, at your place downstairs twenty years ago, you intently and lovingly examined the pictures in a quiet place, and having detached yourself from your business office, as a sincere, born amateur, listened with curiosity to my conversation on the collection of Pryanishnikov, who did not pursue great names, but found the best works, no matter who executed them. Look what has happened after twenty years to Pavel Mikhailovitch, who turned out to be more deserving than Pryanishnikov; of course, by collecting, the deceased also encouraged talent, but after having collected he sold to the government; but our most esteemed Pavel Mikhailovitch Tretyakov, after having collected gave his collection to the fatherland."

Tretyakov received many similar letters. With Vereshchagin and Perov, for instance, he carried on a very extensive correspondence, from which it is evident how highly the artists rated him. For a young artist, it was already a tremendous success to have his picture acquired by Tretyakov. The artist Pervukhin painted the picture "Winter" and sent it to an exhibition. When it reached the exhibition Tretyakov acquired it and, as in such circumstances, a label was immediately attached: "Sold to P. M. Tretyakov." When the author of this picture appeared, he saw this note and removed it: he did not believe it! The manager of the exhibition came, saw that there was no label and attached another. Pervukhin returned and for a second time saw the inscription: "Sold." He went to the manager to verify this and it turned out to be true.

And he lived, not in his own apartment, but at his uncle's. Evidently the surroundings were modest and with his canvas he disturbed his uncle, who often said to him: "Why are you doing this, Constantine? It would be better for you to do something else. Such pictures as Tretyakov buys we can never expect to get from you."

And when it happened that Tretyakov bought his picture, Pervukhin rushed back to the apartment and whirled around the room like a wheel. His uncle asked him in fright: "What has happened?" And he cried: "Tretyakov bought my picture!" So highly did the artists rate the Tretyakov Gallery.

31. Pobedonostsev and the Loris-Melikov "Constitution"

COUNT MIKHAIL LORIS-MELIKOV (1825-1888), general and statesman, commanded the Caucasian Corps during the Russo-Turkish War, 1877-1878. In 1880 Alexander II appointed him Minister of the Interior. In this capacity, he drafted a flimsy project for the reform of the Russian political structure. After the assassination of Alexander II in 1881 this project was discarded, Loris-Melikov was forced to retire, and spent the remainder of his life abroad.

Konstantin Petrovitch Pobedonostsev (1827-1907) was a leading exponent of reaction in Russia, 1880-1905. As tutor in law to Alexander III and Nicholas II, he was in a position to exert great influence over the last two Romanov Emperors. In 1868 he became a member of the Senate, in 1872 a member of the State Council, and from 1880 to 1905 he served as Procurator of the Holy Synod. With the granting of the Constitution of 1905, he was forced to retire from the political arena.

At the Council of Ministers, March 8, 1881, under the chairmanship of Alexander III, Pobedonostsev made a speech in opposition to the project drafted by Loris-Melikov and approved by Alexander II (February 17, 1881) for the establishment of committees for the preliminary consideration of bills, committees which were to include representatives elected from the Zemstvos and cities (the so-called Loris-Melikov "Constitution"). No definite decision was reached at the session of March 8, 1881, but Pobedonostsev's speech on that occasion was said to have convinced Alexander III to reject even the mild Loris-Melikov prescription for the restriction of autocratic power.

Below is an abbreviated version of Pobedonostsev's speech of March 8, 1881, as presented in *Dnevnik* (Diary) *E. A. Peretsa* (Moscow- Leningrad, 1927), pp. 38-40.

Your Majesty, my obligation under the oath of allegiance and my conscience require me to tell you what is on my mind. I find myself not only embarrassed, but in despair. As in former times, prior to the destruction of Poland, they said: "Finis Poloniae," so now it is quite fitting for us also to say: "Finis Russiae." The very consideration of the project presented for your approval wrings my heart. This project has a false ring—even more, it reeks of falsehood.

We are told that the best way to draft legislative projects is to invite people to participate who are familiar with the national life. It is necessary to hear the experts. I would have nothing to say against this, if it were all they wanted to do. Experts were invited in former times, but not as is now proposed. No. They want to introduce a constitution into Russia, and if not all at once, at least to take the first step in that direction.

. . . And what kind of constitution? Western Europe provides us with the answer to this question. The constitutions in effect there are the instrument of every kind of falsehood, the instrument of every kind of intrigue. . . .

. . . And this falsity, based upon a foreign pattern unsuited to us, to our misfortune and to our ruin they also want to introduce here. Russia has been strong, thanks to autocracy, thanks to the unlimited mutual confidence and close bonds between the people and their Tsar. Such a bond between the Russian Tsar and the people is of inestimable value. Our people are the custodian of all our valor and good qualities; it is possible to learn a great deal from them. The so-called representatives of the zemstvo only separate the Tsar from the people. Meanwhile, the government must look after the people, it must get to know their real needs, must try to cope with perpetual need. This is the goal toward which it must strive, this is the real task of the new reign.

But instead of this, they propose to set up for us a "debating society" like the French Estates-General. Even without that, we already suffer from chatterboxes who, under the influence of good-for-nothing journals, only arouse popular passions. Thanks to the empty prattlers, what happens to the lofty plans of a deceased, unforgettable ruler who has assumed at the very end of his reign a martyr's crown? Where did the great, sacred idea of the liberation of the peasants lead? . . . They were granted freedom, which failed to provide them with any proper authority, without which the dark masses of ignorant people could not manage. Moreover, saloons opened everywhere; the poor people, left to themselves and having remained without anyone to look after them, took to drink, got too lazy to work, and therefore became the unfortunate victims of tapsters, kulaks, Jews, and all kinds of usurers.

Thereafter, zemstvo and city social institutions were opened—"debating societies" in which no real business was accomplished, where people talked profusely and at random about the most important state problems for which they were not in any way responsible. Who does all this endless talking? Who runs these talkfests? Unqualified persons, immoral, some of whom occupy prominent positions, but who have never lived with their own families, who have abandoned themselves to debauchery, dream only about personal gain, yearn for popularity, and spread every kind of sedition.

Thereupon, new legal institutions were established—new "debating societies"—debating societies of lawyers, thanks to whom the most savage punishments—doubtless murder and other forms of heinous villainy—go unpunished.

Finally, they granted freedom of the press, this most terrible "debating society," which to every corner of this immense Russian land, for thousands and tens of thousands of versts, spreads disparagement and censure of authority; they sow among peaceful and honest people the seeds of dissension and dissatisfaction, arouse passions, and incite people to the most flagrant lawlessness.

And when, sire, do they propose that you establish a new supreme "debating society," based on a foreign model? . . . Now, only a few days after the commission of the most frightful crime ever perpetrated in Russia, when, on the other side of the Neva in Petropavlovsk Cathedral the remains of a kindly Russian Tsar, torn to pieces in broad daylight by Russians, still lie unburied. I shall not speak of the guilt of the villains who performed this terrible crime, unparalleled in history. But all of us, from first to last, must repent for regarding so very casually what has been perpetrated in our midst; we are all guilty in that, without taking cognizance of the constantly repeated attempts on the life of our common benefactor, we with our inertia and apathy failed to protect a righteous man. On all of us lies the stamp of the indelible shame which has befallen the Russian land. All of us must repent—must feel remorse! . . .

In such terrible times, sire, we must think, not about instituting a new "debating society," in which more depraved speeches will be made, but about deeds. We must act!

Khrestomatiya po istorii SSSR. Vol. III
(Moscow, 1953), 432-435.

32. Russian economic conditions, 1880-1900

PETER I. LYASHCHENKO (1876-   ), the USSR's top economic historian, produced a monumental work on the Russian national economy from prehistoric times to the Revolution of 1917. Although written from a Marxist viewpoint, it is a mine of economic information presented in scholarly fashion. Lyashchenko, a Corresponding Member of the Academy of Sciences, was a former professor at the First Moscow State University. The book was translated into English under the Russian Translation Project of the American Council of Learned Societies.

The three excerpts below are from Lyashchenko's *History of the National Economy of Russia to the 1917 Revolution* (New York: The Macmillan Company, 1949), pp. 532-534, 549-552, and 563-565. Reprinted by permission.

I. The Russian Labor Movement, 1880-1900

The historic 1885 strike of the workers of the Morozov factory at Orekhovo-Zuyev played an important role in awakening the class consciousness of the workers. While it began as an ordinary dispute involving a demand for a rise in wages and the improvement of conditions (against fines, and so forth), the strike eventually became a major political event that revealed the full extent of the political implications of the labor problem in Russia. The workers were ordered to appear in court. Here the whole amazing story of labor exploitation at the Morozov factory was told in full. Labor conditions at this factory, which employed about 8,000 workers, were deteriorating daily: wages were systematically being reduced, and the workers were persecuted by fines which reduced every ruble of wages by 30 to 50 kopecks. Eventually, the strike was stopped by military force, over 600 workers were arrested, and several dozens of workers were put on open trial.

The horrible tale of exploitation told in the courtroom was such that the court was compelled to acquit the defendants, who were thereupon

immediately arrested and sent into exile by administrative order. Nevertheless, after the Morozov strike the government was forced to undertake
some "regulation" of the labor problem, enacting at this time its decree
on fines, which, according to the new law, instead of being paid to
the owner, had to be collected in a special fund for the welfare of the
workers.

Altogether, about 80,000 workers took part in 48 strikes during the
five-year period of 1881-1886. The mass character of these strikes began
to change the elemental opposition to capital into a class-conscious
political struggle. The workers were beginning to understand that they
could not win except through organized struggle. In the course of the
nineties, leadership of the strike activities of the workers passed to the
party of the working class. The tasks arising in that struggle were clearly
formulated by Lenin, who soon became the head of the party's leadership of the workers' movement, uniting all Marxist labor circles in 1895
into the League of Struggle for the Liberation of the Working Class, thus
preparing the creation of a revolutionary Marxist labor party. During
this period of recurrent strikes, previously discussed and formulated
demands were presented, and the time and place of each strike were
determined in advance. These "systematic strikes already indicated a
beginning of the class struggle, but only a beginning," wrote Lenin in
his book *What Is to Be Done?*

In an article entitled "New Tasks and New Forces" (1905), Lenin
formulated the following sequence of stages in the advance of the labor
movement in Russia:

> The development of the mass labor movement in Russia parallel with
> the development of our social democratic activity is characterized by
> three notable transitions. The first transition was from narrow propa-
> gandistic circles to broad economic agitation among the masses; the
> second phase took us to political agitation on a large scale and to open
> street demonstrations; the third led to actual civil war and to insurrec-
> tion. Every one of these stages was duly prepared, on the one hand, by
> the direction of socialist thought toward one main objective, and on the
> other hand, by profound changes in the living conditions and in the
> psychological mood of the working class, and by awakening more and
> more strata of the laboring population to a more conscious and active
> struggle.

In time, the first of the three stages cited by Lenin coincided largely
with the 1890's. The height of the economic struggle of the workers
came after the famine of 1891-1892, when the acutely critical conditions
in the village evoked a new exodus into the cities and industry. At the
same time, with a mature labor movement, the industrial prosperity of
the middle nineties intensified the struggle of the workers, which had
now acquired more of a class-conscious political character.

After 1894-1895 a wave of strikes spread throughout the country,
beginning at the same time to fall under the express influence of the

social-democratic workers and under the direction of the League of Struggle for the Liberation of the Working Class. In 1894 occurred the clashes at the Semyannikov factory; in 1895 occurred the strike in the Petersburg harbor, at the Thornton factory (November, 1895), at the Laferme factory, at the mechanical shoe factory, at the Koenig cotton-spinning mill, at the Lebedev weaving mill, at the Putilov plant, at the factory of the brothers Karzinkin at Yaroslavl, and elsewhere. In January, 1896, a strike broke out at the Voronin spinning mill in Petersburg; in May, 1896, came the general strike of the Petersburg weavers and spinners. The strike spread from Petersburg to Moscow, to Ivanovo-Voznesensk, to the Vladimir region, again to the Morozov factory at Orekhovo-Zuyev, to the Tver plants, and to the mines and mills of the Urals.

The Petersburg strikes of 1896-1897 were of particular significance, encouraging the working class in all parts of the country to present its economic demands for a shorter workday, for higher wages, and for changing the methods of wage payment. Next came a series of purely political demands, which after 1898 were beginning to predominate in all labor demands. Through the League of Struggle Lenin began to achieve the *merging of socialism with the labor movement* and to link the struggle of the workers for economic goals with political struggle against tsarism, passing from propagandization of Marxism to political agitation among the broad masses of the working class. Thus, on May 1, 1898, occurred the first political strikes in celebration of May Day at Petersburg. In the same year, during a strike at the Maxwell and Pall factory, the workers not only presented purely political demands, such as freedom of assembly and the right to strike, but also offered organized resistance to the troops sent against the strikers by the tsarist government. A strike movement on an even larger scale and of a general character also spread during these years to Poland and the Baltics, where the workers similarly moved from economic to political demands.

The activities of Lenin and the League of Struggle which he created furnished a powerful impetus for the organization and unification of Marxist and labor groups in the other areas of Russia. During the middle nineties Marxist organizations arose in Transcaucasia, and in 1894 came the establishment of the Union of Workers at Moscow. During the same years similar Marxist social-democratic organizations came into existence in all major industrial centers of Russia and Siberia: at Yaroslavl, Kostroma, Orekhovo-Zuyev, Yekaterinoslav, and Rostov-on-the-Don. Finally, organizations of this type also extended to the non-Russian border lands and to Poland and Lithuania. At the first Social-Democratic Congress held in 1898 (by this time Lenin had been sentenced to exile, and was therefore absent from the congress) an attempt was made to unify all Marxist social-democratic organizations. The congress officially announced the formation of the RSDRP (Russian Social-Democratic Workers' Party—Ed.). In reality, however, the Marxist-Social Democratic Party did not begin to function as such. Owing to a number of causes, ideological dissension began to increase within the local organizations, resulting in the encouragement of an opportunist tendency toward "economism," which denied the necessity for creating an independent political party of the working class. From his place of exile, Lenin waged a bitter struggle against the champions of "economism." For the purpose of unifying the scattered Marxist organizations into one party, Lenin proposed and carried out his plan of launching the first all-Russian publication of the revolutionary Marxists, the well known *Iskra*. The first few issues were published abroad (1900-1901), and "served as a transition to a new period, a period of actual organization of a single Russian Social-Democratic Party from the scattered groups and circles."

II. Railroad Production as a Factor in the Industrial Upsurge of the Nineties

We stated earlier that the upsurge of the 1890's was due primarily to the expansion of railway building. Railroad construction was responsible for the fact that the production base of the industrial rise of the nineties included the various branches of heavy industry such as ferrous metallurgy, machine building, rail production, coal and petroleum, and, to a lesser degree, the brick, cement, and other industries vital to railway construction.

These industries, as we have seen above, were still in their early stages of development during the 1870's. A rapid expansion of these industries required the investment of large capital, which had become available during the nineties in the form of large-scale foreign corporation capital. To the extent to which the construction movement of the railways involved first the metallurgical and fuel industries, then the other branches of heavy industry, followed also by the light industries, railroad construction became the ultimate base of industrial upsurge as a whole, and of the expansion of the internal market for industrial capitalism.

After the railroad fever of 1870-1875, which augmented the Russian railway network by 7,500 versts, had subsided, new construction on the railways proceeded at a more moderate tempo during 1876-1890. By 1891-1895, however, a new surge of activity produced an additional 6,257 versts of new railway lines, while the subsequent five-year period (1896-1900) added 15,139 more versts, following which the total network increased to 56,130 versts in 1901. In other words 37 per cent of the entire network, or one-half as much as built during the preceeding fifty years, was constructed in the course of the single decade of 1890. After this, capitalist Russia did not experience another surge in railway construction on a scale similar to that of 1895-1900.

It should be pointed out, of course, that even despite this feverish period of railway construction Russia was still rather backward in the density of its railway network by the standards of the advanced capitalist nations: for each thousand of square kilometers of territory there were only 1.5 kilometers of railroad in Russia in 1895, of which the European half had 9.7 kilometers and the Asiatic half, 0.6 kilometers, whereas England had 106 kilometers, and Germany, 80.

The system of railway construction itself had also witnessed a number of important changes since 1870. Although the government did not forbid private construction and even encouraged private initiative, nevertheless, as a result of the unsuccessful experience of the Chief Company, the major share of new construction was borne by the government. According to the calculations by Schwanebach, during the second half of the nineties (the period of greatest activity in railroad construction), investment was almost evenly divided between private and government capital. But the financial participation of the government in railroad affairs was considerably greater, since in addition to the direct government railroad loans a system of "government-guaranteed" private loans came into practice during the nineties. For the latter loans the government guaranteed the profit on each loan, thereby making them essentially similar to ordinary government loans. Besides, the government authorized the treasury to buy from private railway companies either the more important or the heavily indebted roads. Consequently, the role of the government in the nation's railway construction, as well as in ownership, increased conspicuously during 1890-1900.

By 1890 the cumulative value of all railroad loans attained 1,363 million rubles; during the following ten-year period (under Minister Witte) a total of about one billion rubles of guaranteed loans (exclusive of the Chinese Eastern Railway) were contracted. Moreover, the direct expenses of the state for the construction of new lines and for the improvement of the network and the rolling stock amounted to about 1,350 million rubles (not including the 275-million ruble loan to the Chinese Eastern Railway). The total value of nonguaranteed loans floated by private companies amounted to 205 million rubles. Hence we may reckon the total value of the government share in the nation's railway business at 3.5 to 3.6 billion rubles during 1890-1900. At the turn of the century the entire capital of the railroads in the country amounted to 4.7 billion rubles, of which approximately 3.5 billion rubles belonged to the government. To provide this amount the state treasury during the last decade of the nineteenth century paid out 1,691 million rubles in direct capital expenditures (including the Chinese Eastern Railway), or about one-half of total government capital invested in the railways during the entire period of construction.

What were the sources of this immense volume of capital invested by the government in railway construction? Of the total amount mentioned above, foreign investment covered about 341 million rubles, while the bulk of the capital was raised within the country, chiefly through the general budgetary government resources. Thus, during the period of heavy railroad and industrial construction the state, by using its pressure, its direct and indirect taxes, the vodka monopoly, and customs taxes, extorted from the population an average of 120 million rubles a year, which was spent in building railways, and thus in subsidizing and supporting heavy industry by costly orders of rails, locomotives, and other equipment. How large a part in the business of railroad construction was played by the small savings of the population, drained from them through the system of the government's credit institutions, may be judged from the fact that the deposits in the state savings banks were utilized largely in support of railroad loans: as of January 1, 1901, 637 million rubles of the general balance of deposits in the state savings banks amounting to 752 million rubles, consisted of government interest-bearing notes, and 248 million rubles of this, or as much as 37 per cent, were in railroad loans.

III. Results of the Industrial Boom of the Nineties

During the last decade of the nineteenth century, industrial capital, displacing small-scale production, routine technology, and backward social relationships, was rapidly advancing Russian industry. To be sure, by volume of production in specific industries Russian industry still lagged far behind the advanced nations of the period. In the course of one decade, however, it had none the less progressed substantially, reaching a degree of industrial concentration much higher than the most advanced capitalist countries. With respect to its tempo of development during these years, Russian industry outstripped nearly all countries. The smelting of pig iron during this ten-year period, for example, increased in England by 18 per cent, in Germany by 72, in the United States by 50, and in Russia by 190, as a result of which Russia became the seventh ranking power in 1880, sixth in 1890, fifth in 1895, and fourth in 1900. The production of iron during this period increased in England by 8 per cent, in Germany by 78, in the United States by 63, and in Russia by 116. The coal industry of Great Britain expanded by 22 per cent, that of Germany by 52, of the United States by 61, and that of Russia by 131. Finally, in number of spindles operating in the cotton industry, England made a gain of 3.8 per cent in the course of the same decade, the United States, 25.6, the European continent, 33, and Russia, 76. By virtue of this number of spindles, Russia in 1890 owned 4 per cent of the world's total number of spindles and 14 per cent of the total spindles in use on the European continent, while by 1899 it accounted for 6 per cent of the world total and 18 per cent of the European total number of spindles.

Naturally, these relative figures present a somewhat inaccurate picture of actual conditions in that the high percentage of increase just cited was due entirely to the low initial level of production.

Hence, if we compare the scale and tempo of capitalist development during the nineties with the precapitalist era in Russia, we must admit that they are rather considerable. If, however, we compare this

rapid development with what could have been achieved with the aid of contemporary technology and civilization, then actual progress of capitalism in Russia must indeed be recognized as having been slow. And it could not have been anything but slow, since no other capitalist country retained altogether such an abundance of ancient institutions incompatible with capitalism, retarding industrial development, and hopelessly depressing the condition of the producers, who "suffer both from capitalism and from the inadequate development of capitalism." [1]

Yet the 1890's definitely brought the national economy of Russia into the world system of capitalist economy as a major national-capitalist entity with vast natural possibilities for development and with capitalist institutions penetrating deeply into the nation's economy. And whereas at the beginning of this period there were voices at home which considered it possible "to turn the wheel of history" away from capitalism, by the end of the century it was apparent even to the most convinced champions of precapitalist Russia that a retreat from capitalism with all its historically positive and negative elements was impossible. Russia had been decisively transformed into a capitalist country with its own peculiar "national system" of capitalism. The peculiarities of this system were such that, despite the rapid growth of capitalism during the nineties and the high degree of concentration of Russian industry, the nation suffered from technological and social-economic backwardness, a confusion of clearly expressed bourgeois-capitalist relationships with many survivals of medievalism, the supremacy of the serf-owning landed aristocracy, and a backward village where the most flagrant forms of exploitation continued to exist. This was enough to retard a progressive development of capitalism, and placed Russia in a position of semicolonial dependency upon western European capitalism, which only sought in Russia a supply of the raw materials it required, a market for the sale of its industrial goods, and an outlet for the profitable investment of its capital.

In Russia of the 1890's the capitalist seed was still growing within its old "autocratic" and semifeudal shell, which retarded capitalist development in every way possible. In the interest of the industrial bourgeoisie, it was necessary as quickly and as completely as possible to discard these feudal brakes on industrial development in the aspect of serfdom latifundia and

[1] Lenin, V. I., *Sochineniya*, Vol. III, p. 469.

the vestiges of semiserf relationships in the village which slowed rural differentiation, rapid increase in production for sale, and expansion in the capacity of the village market. But the interests of the dominant feudal-minded section of the landowning class consisted in preserving the social isolation of the peasantry, its land hunger, and proximity to the land, and the semifeudal methods of exploitation in the village. The latter tendencies, despite the considerable entrenchment of capitalism by this time, still proved predominant during the 1890's, succeeding not only in placing their characteristic imprint upon this era of Russian industrial capitalism but continuing also during the subsequent period of imperialism.

33. Serge Witte and the Trans-Siberian Railway

THE RAPID EXTENSION OF THE RUSSIAN RAILWAY SYSTEM owed much to the energy and financial acumen of Count Serge Julievitch Witte (1849-1915). Having distinguished himself during the Russo-Turkish War (1877-1878) by his excellent management of troop transportation on the Odessa Railroad, he shortly thereafter became director of the South-Western Railway and a member of the imperial commission for the study of railroad construction and management. In 1888 his career as a government official began as director of the Department of Railroad Affairs in the Ministry of Finances. In 1892 Alexander III in quick succession made him Minister of Ways of Communication and Minister of Finances (succeeding I. A. Vyshnegradsky). Witte was a strong advocate of the use of foreign capital for the inauguration of a program of public works, railroads, harbors, and industrial enterprises that would increase Russian economic self-sufficiency. As Minister of Finance, one of the major projects under his jurisdiction was the construction of the Trans-Siberian Railway (1891-1904), including the negotiations with Li Hung Chang for the Chinese Eastern cut-off via Manchuria to Vladivostok.

The excerpts below are from *The Memoirs of Count Witte,* translated and edited by Avrahm Yarmolinsky (Garden City, New York: Doubleday, Page and Company, 1921), pp. 52-54, 86-87, 89-90, 91, 94-95. Reprinted by permission.

... It will not be an exaggeration to say that the vast enterprise of constructing the great Siberian Railway was carried out owing to my efforts, supported, of course first by Emperor Alexander III, and then by Emperor Nicholas II. The idea of connecting European Russia with Vladivostok by rail was one of the most cherished dreams of Alexander III. He spoke to me about it in the course of one of my first conferences with him following my appointment as Minister of Ways of Communication. As is known, Czarevitch Nicholas, the present Emperor, during his trip through the Far East, inaugurated, on May 19, 1891, the construction of the Ussurian Railroad, connecting Vladivostok with Khabarovsk. The Emperor complained that in spite of his efforts, which extended over ten years, his dream had failed to materialize owing to the opposition of the Committee of Ministers and the Imperial Council. He took my promise that I would bend my energies to the accomplishment of his desire.

In my capacity of Minister of Ways of Communication and later as Minister of Finances, both during the reign of Alexander III and afterwards, I persistently advocated the idea of the necessity of constructing the great Siberian Railway. As much as the former Ministers thwarted the plan, so I, remembering my promise to the Emperor, sought to advance it. As Minister of Finances, I was in a peculiarly favorable position with regard to furthering the project, for what was most needed for the construction of the railway was money. Had I remained Minister of Ways of Communication, I would have had to face the opposition of the Minister of Finances.

I devoted myself body and soul to the task, yet Emperor Alexander III did not live to see the realization of his dream, and it was only under Nicholas II that the immense railroad was completed. I was aided by the circumstance that the young Emperor took a personal interest in the matter. At my instance, while his father was still alive, he was appointed head of the Siberian Railroad Committee, which I had formed to promote the construction of the railroad. This committee was empowered to eliminate all manner of unnecessary delay and had the authority over both the administrative and the legislative matters involved in the construction. For the young heir-apparent this task was something in the nature of a preparatory school of statesmanship. He worked under the guidance of the vice president of the committee, Bunge, who was also his tutor. This was a very happy arrangement. The future ruler took his appointment in earnest and worked with enthusiasm. When he became Emperor, he retained the title of President of the Siberian Committee and did not lose his interest in the matter. This enabled me to complete the work within a few years. . . .

In the meantime the great Trans-Siberian Railway, which was under construction, had reached Transbaikalia and the question arose as to the further direction which the railroad should follow. I conceived the idea of building the road straight across Chinese territory, principally Mongolia and Northern Manchuria, on toward Vladivostok. This direction, I calculated, would considerably shorten the line and facilitate its construction. Considering the enormous mileage of the Trans-Siberian, it was natural to seek to shorten the route. Technically the Amur section presented great difficulties. Besides, the road would run along the Amur River and would thus compete with the Amur steamship companies. The

Manchurian route would save 514 versts. In comparison to the Amur region this section also possessed the advantage of a more productive soil and a more favourable climate. The problem was how to get China's permission for this plan, by peaceful means based on mutual commercial interests. The idea appealed to me strongly and I found occasion to draw His Majesty's attention to it. The court physician, Badmayev, a Buriat by birth, who wielded a considerable influence over the Emperor, on the contrary, stood for the Kyakhta-Peking direction. I could not sympathize with his project, first, because I considered Vladivostok as the most desirable terminus for the Trans-Siberian, and, second, because I believed that a railroad to Peking would arouse the whole of Europe against us. It must be borne in mind that the great originator of the Trans-Siberian had no political or military designs in connection with the road. It was an enterprise of a purely economic nature. Alexander III wished to establish communication by the shortest possible route between the distant Maritime Province and Central Russia. Strategically, both Alexander III and his successor attributed a strictly defensive importance to the road. Under no circumstance was the Trans-Siberian to serve as a means for territorial expansion. . . .

In my conferences with Li Hung Chang I dwelt on the services which we had recently done to his country. I assured him that, having proclaimed the principle of China's territorial integrity, we intended to adhere to it in the future; but, to be able to uphold this principle, I argued, we must be in a position, in case of emergency, to render China armed assistance. Such aid we would not be able to render her until both European Russia and Vladivostok were connected with China by rail, our armed forces being concentrated in European Russia. I called to his attention the fact that although during China's war with Japan we did dispatch some detachments from Vladivostok, they moved so slowly, because of the absence of railroad communication, that when they reached Kirin the war was over. Thus I argued that to uphold the territorial integrity of the Chinese Empire, it was necessary for us to have a railroad running along the shortest possible route to Valdivostok, across the northern part of Mongolia and Manchuria. I also pointed out to Li Hung Chang that the projected railway would raise the productivity of our possessions and the Chinese territories it would cross. Finally, I declared, Japan was likely to assume a favourable attitude toward the road, for it would link her with Western Europe, whose civilization she had lately adopted.

Naturally enough, Li Hung Chang raised objections. Nevertheless, I gathered from my talks with him that he would agree to my proposal if he were certain that our Emperor wished it. Therefore, I asked His Majesty to receive Li Hung Chang, which the Emperor did. It was practically a private audience and it passed unnoticed by the press. As a result of my negotiations with the Chinese statesman, we agreed on the following three provisions of a secret pact to be concluded between Russia and China:

1. The Chinese Empire grants us permission to build a railroad within its territory along a straight line between Chita and Vladivostok, but the road must be in the hands of a private corporation. Li Hung Chang absolutely refused to accept my proposal that the road should be either constructed or owned by the Treasury. For that reason we were forced to form a private corporation, the so-called Eastern Chinese Railroad Corporation. This body is, of course, completely in the hands of the Government, but since nominally it is a private corporation, it is within the jurisdiction of the Ministry of Finances.

2. China agrees to cede us a strip of land sufficient for the construction and operation of the railway. Within that territory the corporation is permitted to have its own police and to exercise full and untrammelled authority. China takes upon herself no responsibilities with regard to the construction or operation of the road.

3. The two countries obligate themselves to defend each other in case Japan attacks the territory of China or our Far-Eastern maritime possessions.

I reported the results of my negotiations to His Majesty and he instructed me to take up the matter with the Foreign Minister. I explained to Prince Lobanov-Rostovski that I had come to an oral agreement with Li Hung Chang regarding the provisions of a secret Russo-Chinese pact, and that the only thing left now was to embody the agreement in a formal written instrument. After listening to my statement of the terms of the agreement, the prince took a pen and wrote the text of the treaty. The document was drafted so skilfully that I approved it without the slightest reservation. The prince told me that the following day he would submit the document to His Majesty and return it to me if it was approved by the Emperor...

In Moscow I devoted much time and attention to Li Hung Chang, for I considered it a matter of primary importance to the State to bring our negotiations to a successful consummation. The Russo-Chinese alliance meant two things: first, a great railroad extending as far as Vladivostok on a straight line without curving northward along the Amur River; and, second, firmly established peaceful relations with our neighbor, the Chinese Colossus. . . .

Not the slightest information penetrated into the press regarding our secret agreement with China. The only thing Europe learned was the bare fact that China had agreed to grant the Russo-Chinese Bank a concession for the construction of the Eastern Chinese Railway, a continuation of the Trans-Siberian. The concession was drawn up under my instructions by the Assistant Minister of Finances, Piotr Mikhailovich Romanov, in consultation with the Chinese Minister in St. Petersburg, who was also China's envoy to Berlin. Winter and spring he usually spent in St. Petersburg, while the rest of the year he stayed in Berlin. Since it was then summer-time, Romanov went to Berlin and it was there that the terms of the concessions were drafted. The project was subsequently ratified by the two contracting Governments. At the time it was rumoured in Europe, I remember, that Li Hung Chang had been bribed by the Russian Government. I must say that there is not a particle of truth in this rumour.

The terms of the railroad concession granted by China were very favourable for Russia. The agreement provided for China's right to redeem the road at the expiration of 36 years, but the terms of the redemption were so burdensome that it was highly improbable that the Chinese Government would ever attempt to effect the redemption. It was calculated that should the Chinese Government wish to redeem the road at the beginning of the 37th year, it would have to pay the corporation, according to the terms of the concession, a sum not less than 700 million rubles. . . .

34. Witte's "five-year plan" for the industrialization of Russia

THE SECRET MEMORANDUM OF COUNT SERGEI WITTE, Minister of Finance, to Nicholas II, dated March 22 (O.S.), 1899, called for economic national planning by the government as a prerequisite to the speedy transformation of underdeveloped, agrarian Russia into a leading industrial power. This "Manifesto of Economic Nationalism," as it has been called, inspired by Friedrich List's *National System of Political Economy,"* prescribed a policy of high tariff protectionism, increased taxation, and the import of foreign capital. The serious condition of the Russian economy, worsened by the crop failures of 1897 and 1898, impelled Witte to recommend drastic measures to promote industrialization over the next five years. By 1904, he hoped that the Russian economy, like that of the United States, would be based on two pillars—agriculture and industry. Witte, who had placed Russia on the gold standard in 1895 to improve the country's credit abroad, had aroused the hostility of powerful agrarian and extreme Slavophile interests. Although the Emperor sustained his program for several years, they finally secured Witte's removal from office in August, 1903. The sense of urgency with which Witte's program was imbued, its emphasis on sacrifices and hard work to insure future benefits, as well as on the exploitation of Russia's vast mineral wealth and of her position in Asia, are in some respects reminiscent of the Soviet Five-Year Plans.

This "Report of the Minister of Finance to His Majesty on the Necessity of Formulating and Thereafter Steadfastly Adhering to a Definite Program of a Commercial and Industrial Policy of the Empire" is from T. H. von Laue, "A Secret Memorandum of Sergei Witte on the Industrialization of Imperial Russia," *Journal of Modern History,* XXVI (March, 1954), 64-74. Reprinted by permission.

REPORT OF THE MINISTER OF FINANCE TO HIS MAJESTY ON THE NECESSITY OF FORMULATING AND THEREAFTER STEADFASTLY ADHERING TO A DEFINITE

PROGRAM OF A COMMERCIAL AND INDUSTRIAL POLICY OF THE EMPIRE.
EXTREMELY SECRET

The measures taken by the government for the promotion of national trade and industry have at present a far deeper and broader significance than they had at any time before. Indeed, the entire economic structure of the empire has been transformed in the course of the second half of the current century, so that now the market and its price structure represent the collective interest of all private enterprises which constitute our national economy. Buying and selling and wage labor penetrate now into much deeper layers of our national existence than was the case at the time of serf economy, when the landlord in his village constituted a self-sufficient economic little world, leading an independent life, almost without relation to the market. The division of labor; the specialization of skills; the increased exchange of goods among a population increasingly divided among towns, villages, factories, and mines; the greater complexity of the demands of the population—all these processes rapidly developed in our fatherland under the influence of the emancipation of the serfs, the construction of a railroad network, the development of credit, and the extraordinary growth of foreign trade. Now all organs and branches of our national economy are drawn into a common economic life, and all its individual units have become far more sensitive and responsive to the economic activities of the government. Because of the extremely interlaced network of contemporary economic relationships, any change in the conditions of one or the other industry, of one or the other branch of trade, credit, or communications, touches and influences, often in hidden ways, the fate of a considerable majority of our enterprises.

As a result of such fundamental transformation of the economic interests of the country, every major measure of the government more or less affects the life of the entire economic organism. The solicitude shown to various branches of industry, a new railroad, the discovery of a new field for Russian enterprise, these and other measures, even if partial and of local application only, touch the entire ever more complicated network and upset the established equilibrium. Every measure of the government in regard to trade and industry now affects almost the entire economic organism and influences the course of its further development.

In view of these facts, the minister of finance concludes that the country, which in one way or the other is nurtured by the commercial and industrial policy of the government, requires above all that this policy be carried out according to a definite plan, with strict system and continuity. Isolated and un-co-ordinated acts of encouragement can never offset the pernicious and painful shocks which the economic organism suffers from a change of the guiding policy. Even the most beneficial measures of the government in the realm of economic policy during the first years of their operation often seem to impose a hardship on the population. It is a difficult matter; years, even decades, must pass before the sacrifices can bear fruit. Wise statesmanship requires, then, that these difficult years be suffered patiently, as the experience of other peoples shows that the sacrifices demanded by the coherent and steadfast adherence to a firm and just economic system are always rewarded a hundred fold. Any change of basic policy before the fruits of sacrifice have had time to mature leads to the complete loss of all capital invested in the previous system, or it leads to new sacrifices in the pursuit of a new system. A government with an unsteady commercial and industrial policy is like a businessman who constantly reorganizes his production without producing anything. No matter how great the technical perfection of such a business, it always ends in ruin.

When I became minister of finance, I acted on the conviction that the government, no matter which commercial and industrial system it follows, is guided by the property interests of the entire people and that in order to compensate them for their losses one has merely to wait for the positive results of the government's economic system. This lasts years and sometimes decades. In taking over the ministry of finance in 1892, I felt obliged to make clear to myself the foundations of the commercial and industrial policy of my predecessors and to bend all efforts toward continuing and finishing what they had begun or had taken over from their predecessors. The necessity of such succession and continuity seemed to me so paramount that I relinquished my own personal views. I realized, of course, that there were weighty arguments against the protectionist system and against high tariffs. But I supposed that even the proponents of free trade must be aware that it would be extremely harmful from the government view point to repudiate the protective system before those industries had been securely established for whose creation whole generations had paid by a high tariff. I assumed that an absolutely perfect tariff system did not exist and that each system had positive and negative features. And I furthermore concluded that in making a choice one should throw one's weight in favor of the system already existing, for which the people bore such heavy sacrifices and to which the country's economy is already adapted. Besides, it was clear to me that any commercial and industrial policy touching very directly the property interests of the population would always have its defenders and opponents. I considered it my duty to listen attentively to the latter, and I recognized the necessity of alleviating the measures which inevitably brought temporary damage to some. Nevertheless, I did not waver in my fundamental aim to complete in detail what was so boldly begun in the reign of Alexander III and of Your Imperial Highness. The results of state policy in economic matters are the work of decades, and the most harmful of all commercial and industrial systems is that which is inconstant and wavering.

These conclusions find special confirmation in the facts· of our industrial development. The absence of a strictly enforced plan and sudden changes from protectionism to almost unlimited free trade did not permit our industry to develop calmly. What was created yesterday was destroyed today; and only by the will of Emperor Alexander III was a customs tariff established which gave positive protection to our industries. His wise command was realized in the tariff of 1891, which was worked out while I was still one of the directors of the departments in the ministry of finance. It has been the starting point of our industrial system.

Now, as the attacks on the existing commercial and industrial policy continue and even increase in bitterness, I consider it my duty to review once more its chief foundations and to submit them to Your Imperial Highness. In order to be the true executor of Your Imperial Majesty's will, I must have instruction not for individual measures but for a comprehensive commercial and industrial policy. The country needs, above all, a firm and strict economic system.

In Russia at the present moment the protectionist system is in force. Its principal foundations were laid down in the tariff of 1891.

What are the tasks of the protectionist system?

Russia remains even at the present essentially an agricultural country. It pays for all its obligations to foreigners by exporting raw materials, chiefly of an agricultural nature, principally grain. It meets its demand for finished goods by imports from abroad. The economic relations of Russia with western Europe are fully comparable to the relations of colonial countries with their metropolises. The latter consider their colonies as advantageous markets in which they can freely sell the products of their labor and of their industry and from which they can draw with a powerful hand the raw materials necessary for them. This is the basis of the economic power of the governments of western Europe, and chiefly for that end do they guard their existing colonies or acquire new ones. Russia was, and to a considerable extent still is, such a hospitable colony for all industrially developed states, generously providing them with the cheap products of her soil and buying dearly the products of their labor. But there is a radical difference between Russia and a colony: Russia is an independent and strong power. She has the right and the strength not to want to be the eternal handmaiden of states which are more developed economically. She should know the price of her raw materials and of the natural riches hidden in the womb of her abundant territories, and she is conscious of the great, not yet fully displayed, capacity for work among her people. She is proud of her great might, by which she jealously guards not only the political but also the economic independence of her empire. She wants to be a metropolis herself. On the basis of the people's labor, liberated from the bonds of serfdom, there began to grow our own national economy, which bids fair to become a reliable counterweight to the domination of foreign industry.

The creation of our own national industry—that is the profound task, both economic and political, from which our protectionist system arises. The advantages derived from the successful completion of this system are so numerous that I select here only the principal ones.

National labor, which at present is intensively employed only for a short agricultural season, will find full application and consequently become more productive. That, in turn, will increase the wages of the entire working population, and that again will cause an improvement of the physical and spiritual energy of the people. The welfare of Your Empire is based on national labor. The increase of its productivity and the discovery of new fields for Russian enterprise will always serve as the most reliable way for making the entire nation more prosperous.

The demand not only for raw materials but also for other articles will be met to a considerable extent by the work of the people themselves. And consequently the payment to foreigners, which at present consumes a considerable part of our national revenue, will be reduced. The import of foreign goods will then be determined not by the weakness of our industry but by the natural division of labor between nations, by which an industrially developed nation buys abroad only what it cannot advantageously produce at home; purchase abroad then enriches rather than exhausts it. Thanks to that, the accumulation of new capital from national savings is considerably facilitated, and that, in turn, promotes a further growth of productivity.

Within the country, exchange between the products of the soil and of labor will expand and give greater purchasing power to the grain market, which then can afford to pay higher prices for agricultural goods, thanks to which export prices also will rise. As a result, the income derived from land will also increase. And that, in turn, will make it possible for land cultivators, small and large, to improve their agricultural techniques and to raise the productivity of the land. The improvement of agricultural techniques will inevitably reduce the extreme fluctuation of harvests, which at present imposes such a heavy strain upon our national prosperity.

The gradual growth of industry in the country, always accompanied by falling prices for manufactured goods, will make it possible for our export trade to deal not only in raw materials, as at present, but also in industrial goods. Our present losses in the European trade can then be converted into profits in the Asiatic trade.

Popular welfare and state finance will find firm support not only in agriculture but also in industry and will gain considerably greater steadfastness and strength thereby.

Such are the great tasks of the protectionist system, which was steadily applied to Russia, beginning with the reign of Alexander III. But a great task also demands heavy sacrifices.

A new industry cannot arise on short order. Protective duties must, therefore, be continued for decades in order to lead to positive results. Meanwhile, in the course of the long preparatory period, the population will need the products of industry. And as domestic production cannot yet satisfy the domestic demand, the consumers are forced to buy foreign goods at increased prices because of the customs duties; and they have to pay almost as much for the goods of domestic origin. So, for instance, an Englishman pays for a pood of pig iron 26 kopecks, an American 32 kopecks, but a Russian up to 90 kopecks.

Of all charges against the economic policy of Russia, the minister of finance is most keenly aware of the following: that because of the tariff a Russian subject pays for many items considerably more than the subjects of other countries; that the costs of production rise in proportion as they are determined by the value of capital goods; that the cost of living also grows for both rich and poor; and that the paying powers of the population are strained to the utmost, so that in many cases consumption is directly curtailed. The minister of finance recognizes that the customs duties fall as a particularly heavy burden upon the impoverished landowners and peasants, particularly in a year of crop failure. These imposts are a heavy sacrifice made by the entire population, and not from surplus but out of current necessities. Naturally, the question is asked: Are there no ways to avoid or to reduce those sacrifices which have such an enervating effect on our economy?

It must be stated first of all that the system, because it is coherently carried out, is already beginning to show results. Industry numbers now more than 30,000 factories and mills, with an annual production surpassing 2,000,000,000 rubles. That by itself is a big figure. A widespread and tight net of economic interests is linked to the welfare of that industry. To upset it by a shift to free trade would undermine one of the most reliable foundations of our national well-being; such a shock would adversely affect its general level. In several branches, our industry grew very rapidly. Thus the smelting of pig iron, not exceeding 10,000,000 pood at the beginning of the century, rose to 36,000,000 pood in the last decade and to 114,000,000 pood in 1897, i.e., it trebled in ten years. And if it did not meet the demand, it was only because the demand itself rose from 102,000,000 pood in 1893 to 166,000,000 pood at present. In 1893, 131,000,000 pood were smelted. Still more characteristic was the development of the cotton industry, which produces goods of wide popular consumption. That industry formerly used foreign raw materials exclusively; at the present, thanks to the protective tariff, it obtains up to 30 per cent of the required cotton inside the empire. Its annual productivity grew from 259,000,000 rubles in 1885 to 531,000,000 rubles in 1896, i.e., more than double. The import of yarn from abroad fell from 296,000 pood to 127,000 pood. Now the value of imported cotton fabrics does not exceed 5,000,000 rubles, and that is accompanied by a noticeable increase of exports from Russia to Persia, Bokhara, Middle Asia, China, etc. That export, which amounted to 3,500,000 rubles in the past decade, now attains 12,000,000 rubles.

In this way the sacrifices of the population are not borne in vain. Industry has grown very considerably as compared with the condition in which the tariff of 1891 found it. Russian enterprise has found itself new outlets; internal trade has developed. But much remains still to be done before we can say that the building is finished. Domestic production grows, but the consumption of the population grows still more rapidly. It can be satisfied only with the very considerable help of the import of foreign goods, which, therefore, is growing despite the development of domestic production. Thus for the years 1886-90 an average of 410,000,000 rubles worth of foreign goods was imported; from 1891 to 1895, 585,000,000 rubles; and in 1897, 560,000,000 rubles worth. We pay the foreigners for their goods almost as much as the government takes annually from the people in the form of indirect taxes. And if we talk about the heavy burden which the government budget imposes upon a considerable part of the population of the empire—that additional tribute paid to foreigners represents an almost unbearable burden, particularly for the agricultural population. One cannot, therefore, ignore the fact that even goods which we are beginning to produce at home are still imported from abroad. Thus, although the metallurgical industries grew considerably after the tariff of 1891, their extent is still insufficient. In 1897 we imported metals (crude or in finished goods) for 152,000,000 rubles. The natural conditions of our economy are such that all this could be extracted and processed inside the country. The same is true of other industrial commodities, woolens, cotton textiles, hides, pottery, furniture, etc., of which we import from abroad 62,000,000 rubles worth, only because our domestic industry cannot catch up quickly with our growing domestic demand. Among raw materials and semifinished goods, of which we import 250,000,000 rubles worth, one can find many like wool, cotton, fat, hides, anthracite, etc., which could be produced in greater quantity at home. The extensive import of so many commodities which could be, or which are already, produced in the country serves as a true indication that our domestic production, despite its great successes in recent years, is not yet large enough to satisfy the needs of the population. Under these conditions our industries are not only unable to free the population from the heavy duties imposed by the tariff, but they also charge, at the same time, highly monopolistic prices for their own goods. It is one of the most irrefutable economic laws that only such industries work cheaply as produce their goods in such large quantities that the supply of goods either equals the demand or even exceeds it and finds its outlet in foreign markets. If the conditions of production are what we see in Russia, i.e., if only part of the goods is produced at home and the remainder abroad, then the consumer, i.e., the entire population, is compelled to pay dearly for both foreign and domestic products.

It is obvious that our domestic industry, no mater how extensively it has developed, is quantitatively still small. It has not yet reached such proportions as to give birth to the creative forces of knowledge, the mobility of capital, and the spirit of enterprise. It has not yet attained the pitch of healthy competition which would enable it to produce cheaply and repay the population for its sacrifices by the cheapness and abundance of its products. It is not yet an equal partner of agriculture in providing goods for export and bearing the tax burden. But that partnership must be accomplished, and in the shortest time possible. Economic conditions in the past years have become very complex, and the protective tariff has borne down extremely heavily upon the population. It has been too difficult for the population to provide for both itself and an almost monopolistic industry. The task of our present commercial and industrial policy thus is still a very difficult one. It is necessary not only to create industries but to force them to work cheaply; it is necessary to develop in our growing industrial community an energetic and active life—in a word, to raise our industries, qualitatively and quantitatively to such a high level that they cease to be a drain and become a source of prosperity in our national economy.

What do we need to accomplish that? We need capital, knowledge, and the spirit of enterprise. Only these three factors can speed up the creation of a fully independent national industry. But, unfortunately, not all these forces can be artificially implanted. They are mutually interconnected; their own proper development depends upon the very growth of industry.

The accumulation of capital is possible only to the extent that the productivity of an enterprise yields an unused surplus. In Russia, where the great majority of the population is still engaged in agriculture, that surplus of income over expenditure is insufficient for the accumulation of new capital. Actually, the savings of which account is kept—those which go into banks and savings institutions—amount to about 200,000,-000 rubles a year. And a considerable part of them (about 130,000,000 rubles) is spent for the purchase of mortgages from land banks, i.e., they are consumed by the needs of rural and urban economy. The creation of larger funds—say, for the construction of railways—always requires the help of the government in our country. Only the industrial regions of Your Empire show a real ability to create new capital for economic application. This capital appears also as the chief promoter of our industrial progress. But, as the influence of these industrial regions in our vast national economy is relatively small, these savings seem insufficient for the quick creation of an independent national industry.

We have thus neither capital, nor knowledge, nor the spirit of enterprise. The extension of popular education through general, technical, and commercial schools can have, of course, a beneficial influence; and Your Majesty's government is working on that. But no matter how significant the promotion of enlightenment, that road is too slow; by itself, it cannot realize our goal. The natural school of industry is first of all a lively industry. Institutions of learning serve only as one aid toward that end. The first investment of savings awakens in man the restlessness of enterprise, and with the first investment in industry the powerful stimulus of personal interest calls forth such curiosity and love of learning as to make an illiterate peasant into a railway builder, a bold and progressive organizer of industry, and a versatile financier.

Industry gives birth to capital; capital gives rise to enterprise and love of learning; and knowledge, enterprise, and capital combined create new industries. Such is the eternal cycle of economic life, and by the succession of such turns our national economy moves ahead in the process of its natural growth. In Russia this growth is yet too slow, because there is yet too little industry, capital, and spirit of enterprise. But we cannot be content with the continuation of such slow growth. No matter how great the results attained by the present protectionist system, to accomplish what is still ahead and what the entire country so impatiently waits for is by all accounts the most difficult matter. We have to develop mass-production industries, widely dispersed and variegated, in which not customs duties but the more powerful and beneficial laws of competition play the dominant role. We must give the country such industrial perfection as has been reached by the United States of America, which firmly bases its prosperity on two pillars—agriculture and industry. In order to reach these ultimate goals, we must still pass through the most difficult stretch of the road we have chosen. We have not only to direct the flow of capital into this or that field or to find new spheres for its investment, but we have to have above all a great abundance of capital, so that by its natural competition it undermines its own present monopoly position. But not even the most powerful government can create capital.

What, then, must we do?

We cannot wait for the natural accumulation of capital in a country in which the majority of the population is experiencing hard times and which surrenders a considerable part of its surplus to the government in the form of taxes. And we cannot continue to make the population pay dearly for what it buys—that is too much of a burden for the population and for agriculture, its primary occupation. Neither can we repudiate the protectionist system and grant free or at least easier access to foreign goods; we cannot thus give up the industries which the people created with such heavy sacrifices—for that would mean to deprive the country, already so destitute of capital, of the industries which it has protected by the sweat of its brow.

This dilemma would be fatal to our economy, if the government, powerless to create new capital in sufficient quantity, were not in a position to hasten the influx of capital into the empire from states which have a surplus of it.

The influx of foreign capital is, in the considered opinion of the minister of finance, the sole means by which our industry can speedily furnish our country with abundant and cheap goods. Each new wave of capital, swept in from abroad, knocks down the immoderately high level of profits to which our monopolistic entrepreneurs are accustomed and forces them to seek compensation in technical improvements, which, in turn, will lead to price reductions. Replenishing the poor store of popular savings by foreign capital makes it possible for all capital in the country to flow more freely over a broader field and to work up not only the fat but also the leaner sources of profit. Hence the natural riches of the Russian land and the productive energies of its population will be utilized to a considerably greater extent; our economy will begin to work with greater intensity. It will be difficult to say then whether foreign capital or our own productive forces, invigorated and given a chance by foreign capital, will have the greater influence over the further growth of our industries.

But in recent times objections have been raised against the influx of foreign capital. It is said that this influx is detrimental to basic national interests, that it tries to siphon off all profits from our growing Russian industries, that it will lead to the sale of our rich productive forces to foreigners. It is no secret, of course, to the minister of finance that the influx of foreign capital is disadvantageous primarily to entrepreneurs, who are harmed by any kind of competition. Not only our own, but also foreign, capitalists who have already obtained an advantageous place in Russian industry join in these heart-rending complaints and thus try to guard their monopolistic profits. But, as frequently happens in the public discussion of economic problems, the interested voices are hiding behind impartial but little-informed representatives of public interests; and what is undesirable for private groups is, by a misunderstanding, eagerly interpreted as harmful to our economy as a whole.

The extent of the influx of foreign capital into Russia is usually much exaggerated. The foreign corporations formed in 1896 numbered twenty-two, with a basic capital of 80,000,000 rubles. In 1897 their number was fifteen, with 55,000,000 rubles capital. Even if one adds foreign capital invested in Russian corporations (12,000,000 rubles in 1896 and 22,000,000 in 1897) one finds that, all together, foreign capital does not amount to more than one-third of the capital of all joint-stock companies formed annually. One should also remember that the corporation is still something very strange and unpopular with Russian entrepreneurs. The organization which they prefer is the personal enterprise or at least the family partnership. A considerable part of Russian capital is invested in such enterprises; the number of these formed every year equals that of the joint-stock companies. It would seem, then, that of the total amount of capital invested every year in the further development of our industries, foreign capital scarcely constitutes more than one-fifth or one-sixth.

Ninety-two million rubles in 1896; 77,000,000 rubles in 1897; 376,-000,000 rubles all together since 1887—do these statistics prove that there is a danger for our vast Russian economy? Can our productive forces be sold at such a figure? That much foreign capital is no more than a leaven, which derives its significance not from its size but from the energy which it sets free in our sluggish industrial community. Foreign capital, five times smaller than Russian, is nonetheless more visible; it arouses attention because it carries with it better knowledge, more experience, and more initiative. But it deposits these cultural forces in Russia, and with that we really cannot find fault.

There are complaints that our protectionist system obstructs the import trade, that we do not bring in many foreign goods but instead open our doors wide to foreign capital. As a matter of fact, we imported foreign capital to the amount of 92,000,000 rubles in 1896 and 77,000,000 rubles in 1897, but foreign goods to the amount of 585,000,000 rubles and 560,000,000 rubles, respectively, i.e., six or seven times more than capital. But, on the other hand, if we look more deeply into the character of foreign capital, we find that in the last analysis it flows to us not in the form of money—our currency is furnished with a sufficient quantity of tokens—but, by a complex exchange process, in the form of useful goods. The import of foreign capital constitutes a part of the import of foreign goods, but with the difference that it is not spent for immediate consumption by the population but saved for productive purposes, for constructive investment in industry.

If we compare our import from abroad for the past years (1896 and 1897) with the average for the years 1888-90, we see that the import of pig iron, iron ore, steel, machines, apparatus iron and steel products, iron ships—in a word, of capital goods which have long been protected and are necessary not for the consumer but for the producer—amounted to 98,000,000 rubles in 1896 (when 92,000,000 rubles of foreign capital was imported). In 1897 it amounted to 82,000,000 rubles (when 77,000,-000 rubles of foreign capital was imported). In the woolen and silk industries the import of thread fell off and was replaced by the import of raw wool and silk, as the processing of these raw materials for the domestic consumer was done more and more by our own industries. In the cotton industry the import of finished goods, thread, and even raw cotton declined. It is obvious that the very character of our import changes; consumers' goods are replaced by producers' goods. And it seems hardly understandable to the minister of finance when it is said in the same breath that it is advantageous for the country to buy abroad, say, cotton fabrics year after year and yet that it is harmful for the same country to buy abroad the machines which could produce such fabrics inside the country. Why does everybody wholeheartedly approve if a country does not consume all its income but spends part of it for further production, and why should they at the same time consider it a danger if it practices equal thrift with its foreign purchases?

Apparently such falsehoods grow from dissatisfaction with the fact that the revenue from these new enterprises will go to the foreign capitalists and that the owners of the imported machinery which is set to work in the country will also be foreigners. But then the factories which produce abroad for the Russian consumer also belong to foreigners and are also founded by foreign capital; their revenue does not go to Russia, either. But there is a basic difference: the machinery imported into Russia and set to work here, even though it belongs to a foreigner, operates in a Russian setting. And it will not work by itself. It demands raw materials, fuel, lighting, and their auxiliary materials, and it demands human labor. All that, its owner must buy in Russia. Taking all this into account, it seems that the greater part of a ruble spent for any product of foreign enterprise at work on Russian territory goes for the payment of various ingredients of production bought inside the country; and only the remaining part goes to the foreign capitalist as a reward for his capital, knowledge, enterprise, and risk. How much of the price of a given commodity goes to the worker and how much to the entrepreneur may be seen, for instance, from analyses published by the American department of labor about the relationship between wage, entrepreneurial profit, and the price of goods. In the cotton industry 30 per cent goes to the workers, but only 6½ per cent to the entrepreneur; in the glass industry 38 per cent goes to the workers, but only 9 per cent to the entrepreneur; in metallurgy and machine-building, 35 per cent to the worker and 10 per cent to the entrepreneur; in railway companies, 34 per cent to the workers and less than 3 per cent to the entrepreneurs. In this manner, out of one ruble paid for the finished commodity produced with the help of foreign capital, approximately 25-40 kopecks accrue to the Russian worker. Another considerable part is spent for raw materials and other auxiliary items, and only 3-10 kopecks is left as the entrepreneur's profit. But in paying for an imported commodity, the entire ruble leaves the country; and neither the producers of raw materials and fuel nor the worker receives a single kopeck. The complaint about the exodus of part of the income as reward for the application of foreign capital would have full weight only if we had a choice between Russian capital and foreign capital and only if we could hope that the former could fulfil not only its own present function but also that now performed by foreign capital. As that is not the case, one has to compare the merits of the following two propositions. Which is better, to import finished goods or to draw from abroad foreign capital, which enables our Russian productive forces to manufacture them here at home? Either way we have to pay the foreigner, but obviously in the case of imported capital that payment will be considerably less than in the case of imported goods.

One has to consider also the fact that it is generally held advantageous to sell finished goods and dangerous to sell productive forces. The buyer obviously must be guided by the contrary principle. If in our present situation we cannot satisfy all our demands from our own resources and have to resort to purchasing abroad, it will be more advantageous for us to buy not finished goods but capital, which is one of the most necessary productive forces, particularly in industry. This consideration apparently is lost sight of by those who look so apprehensively at the prospect of paying dividends to foreigners.

What is that percentage, that outflow abroad of a part of our national income, which is so threatening to our future? Foreign capital comes to us from countries in which the capitalists are not spoiled by the fat profits to which our Russian capitalists are accustomed. It gravitates to us because in these countries capitalists are used to small profits. It works its way into our industry only because it is satisfied wherever it goes with smaller profits than its Russian predecessors. A new hundred million, flowing into the country from abroad during a given year, lowers by the laws of competition the rate of interest of all capital previously invested in Russian industry, which amounts to billions. If the country pays for these new hundred million rubles ten million in dividends, it gains still a considerably larger sum from the lower interest rates for the capital already invested in its economy. As the billions of national capital become cheaper, the prices of all industrial products will also fall considerably. We have at our disposal cheap labor, tremendous natural riches, and only the high price of capital now stands in the way of getting cheap goods. So why not let foreign capital help us to obtain still more cheaply that productive force of which alone we are destitute? Then we will be able to raise our industry to such a level that it can provide us with cheap goods in sufficient quantity not only for domestic consumption but also for export. Even at present we are getting closer to that goal. By bringing the transformation which is occurring under our eyes to its natural conclusion, we will eventually be able to pay the interest charges for capital received from Europe out of the profits of our Asiatic trade.

The entire country could be brought to that level if, with the help of new capital, the products of our industries could be made more cheaply and their productive forces could work more intensively for both domestic consumption and export. As history shows, these are the conditions under which a people rapidly becomes able to save and begins to accumulate its own capital. Only the first steps on that road are difficult. One has to take them, however, even with the help of foreign capital. Any further accumulation proceeds naturally by the laws of geometric progression. According to the experience of other industrially developed nations, millions give rise to billions. The fact that quantitatively the amount of foreign capital is small serves as the best indication that our economic policy does not aim at founding our further industrial growth primarily on foreign capital. We admit only a little of it, no bigger than a seed, which, embedded in our own thrift, should in the very near future produce national capital. In a way, obeying the laws of economic circulation, foreign capital against its will raises its own competitors. Tempted into Russia by higher dividends, it brings with it industrial energy, knowledge, a willingness to take risks, and in the end it will lower its dividends and amass so much native capital as to reduce imperceptibly its own influence. The presence of foreign capital will thus stand out only at the beginning of the process of industrialization.

It must also be stated that the influx of foreign capital does not proceed so easily and freely as is necessary to assure its continuation until the demands of the country no longer require the help of foreign savings. On the contrary, there are in our country such obstacles to its influx as exist in no other civilized country. We do not have the corporation laws which are in effect in the majority of civilized countries. Under such laws, everyone who wishes can form a joint-stock company by fulfilling certain conditions stipulated by law. In Russia a foreign company can be opened only by a special decree of the Committee of Ministers, which requires the confirmation of Your Imperial Highness. Russian joint-stock companies in which foreigners are shareholders are permitted to have only a minority of foreigners on their board of directors. In ten provinces of tsardom Poland, in eleven provinces of the western regions of Russia, in Turkestan, the Steppe regions, and the Amur district, neither foreign companies nor Russian companies with foreign participation are permitted to acquire property or exploit natural resources. A new company is admitted into Russia only with the permission of the local administration, and the acquisition of the right to exploit natural resources for a stated period is decided entirely on an individual basis and then only after preliminary investigation by the local administration into the actual needs of such enterprise. All foreign companies are subject to Russian laws and regulations as well as to ordinances and rules *which may be subsequently issued*. In permitting the activities of foreign companies in Russia, the government retains *the right to revoke at any time that permission and to demand the liquidation of any company*. Obviously, every detail of the influx of foreign capital into Russia is kept under strictest control by the central and local government. Whether this influx will be increased, decreased, or stopped altogether depends on their estimate and their interpretation of public welfare. Under these circumstances, one should rather speak of an excess of government control of foreign capital, which takes its chances in going to Russia, and of unnecessary limitations imposed upon its freedom of investment. One should not forget that in a country which has the right at any time to close down foreign companies there are no safeguards against the harmful effects of sudden closure. Furthermore, because of such difficulties and tribulations which a foreign entrepreneur has to go through in Russia, because of all kinds of petitions and applications which he has to submit to provincial and central authorities, and because of constant interference not only by the law but also by administrative regulations, the influx of foreign capital into Russia is not yet copious enough. That, despite the invigorating effects which foreign capital has upon the productive resources of our entire national economy!

Considering the fact that the influx of foreign capital is the chief means for Russia in her present economic condition to speed up the accumulation of native capital, one should rather wish that our legislation concerning foreigners might be simplified. Historical experience shows that those human energies which accompany foreign capital are a useful creative ferment in the mass of the population of the most powerful nation and that they become gradually assimilated: mere economic ties change into organic ones. The imported cultural forces thus become an inseparable part of the country itself. Only a disintegrating nation has to fear foreign enslavement. Russia, however, is not China!

I have now analyzed the chief bases of the economic system which has been followed in Russia since the reign of Alexander III.

Its starting point is the protective tariff of 1891, somewhat lowered by the subsequent trade treaties with France, Germany, Austria-Hungary, and other governments.

That protective sysem has for its aim the creation of a Russian national industry, which would contribute to the growth of our economic, and consequently also our political, independence and would make possible more favorable terms for both international and domestic trade.

That task, demanding great sacrifices from the population, has in some respects already been fulfilled. Russia has now an industry of tremendous size. The interests of our entire economy are closely tied to its future.

This industry, however, has not yet reached such an extent and such technical perfection as to furnish the country with an abundance of cheap goods. Its services cost the country too dearly, and these excessive costs have a destructive influence over the welfare of the population, particularly in agriculture. They cannot be sustained much longer.

We cannot possibly count on an adequate growth of our industry out of our own national resources, because our store of capital, knowledge, and the spirit of enterprise is altogether insufficient to provide us with cheap industrial goods.

To obtain cheaper goods, of which the population stands in such urgent need, by a substantial tariff reduction would be too expensive. It would forever deprive the country of the possible results of the protective system, for which a whole generation has made sacrifices; it would upset the industries which we have created with so much effort just when they were ready to repay the nation for its sacrifices.

It would be very dangerous to rely on the competition of foreign goods for the lowering of our prices. But we can attain the same results with the help of the competition of foreign capital, which, by coming into Russia, will help Russian enterprise to promote native industry and speed up the accumulation of native capital. Any obstructions to the influx of foreign capital will only delay the establishment of a mature and all-powerful industry. The country cannot afford to defer that goal for long. The burden of expensive manufactured goods so oppresses the population that, unless we resort to the help of foreign capital for the quick development of our industry, it would be better to give up the tariff of 1891 altogether. Without the help of foreign capital, which can create an industry in a country surrounded by high tariff barriers, a tariff is merely preventive and not creative; such a tariff can destroy a country. The tariff of 1891 was a beneficial measure only because of the subsequent trade treaties and of the influx of foreign capital. One cannot give up these logical corollaries and not run the risk of rendering the original measure harmful to national welfare.

As our industries grow with the help of foreign capital, it will be possible gradually and in strict accordance with the course of our industrial development to lower our tariffs. Such reduction, however, ought to be timed to the renewal of our trade treaties, because, without a cautious reduction adjusted to the conditions of our industry, we will not be able to defend the interests of our foreign trade. The coming renewal of our trade treaties on favorable terms will be a difficult matter economically as well as politically. In dealing with countries which buy our agricultural exports, we should insist on their lowering their tariffs for our goods. But this time the conflict with the interests of native agriculture in these countries with whom we must deal may be even more bitter than at the time of the memorable tariff war with Germany. It will be possible to obtain from them better conditions for our exports only if we, on our part, are in a position to offer them lowered tariffs for their industries. A trade agreement is nothing but a mutual exchange of such tariff reductions. If we voluntarily reduce our tariff before 1904 without receiving compensation from foreign governments, then we cannot induce them to reciprocate at the time of the conclusion of a new treaty. They not only will not agree to making concessions to our exports but under pressure from their native agrarians might even raise their barriers. That is the reason why our protective tariff should stand unchanged until 1904.

If we carry our commercial and industrial system, begun in the reign of Alexander III, consistently to the end, then Russia will at last come of age economically. Then her prosperity, her trade and finance, will be based on two reliable pillars, agriculture and industry; and the relations between them, profitable to both, will be the chief motive power in our economy. Russia will move closer to that goal with the help of foreign capital, which, anyway, is required to make the protective tariff of 1891 effective.

Your Imperial Highness may see from the foregoing that the economic policy which the Russian government has followed for the last eight years is a carefully planned system, in which all parts are inseparably interconnected. Other persons, perhaps, can devise a better system to establish the needed equilibrium more successfully in a different way. Upon assuming the direction of the ministry of finance, I found a protective system almost in full operation. This system seemed to me then, and still seems to me now, completely justified. I bent all my efforts to speed its beneficial results and to alleviate, principally with the help of foreign capital, the hardships of the transition period. It is possible that we could have pursued a different policy. But in following the directives of Your Imperial Highness in such an intimately interdependent matter as our national economy, I believed it my duty as minister of finance to ask Your Majesty to consider this point: even if it were possible to follow a different economic policy, it would, no matter how beneficial its ultimate results, produce in the immediate future a sharp break. Such an unnecessary shock would aggravate the hardships now existing. Only by a system strictly sustained, and not by isolated measures, can a healthy development be guaranteed to our national economy.

Pledging all my efforts to fulfil still better the will of my sovereign, I make bold to ask that it may please Your Imperial Highness to lend your firm support to the foundations of our economic system as I have analyzed them. They form, in essence, the following program:

1. To keep the tariff of 1891 unchanged until the renewal of our trade treaties.

2. To work in the meantime by all means for reducing the prices of industrial goods, not by increasing the import of goods from abroad but by the development of our domestic production, which makes mandatory the influx of foreign capital.

3. To postpone a lowering of our tariff until the time of the renewal of our trade treaties, so that, in turn, we can insist upon favorable terms for our agricultural exports.

4. Not to impose in the meantime new restraints on the influx of foreign capital, either through new laws or new interpretations of existing laws or, *especially, through administrative decrees.*

5. To maintain unchanged our present policy toward foreign capital until 1904, so that with its help our domestic industries can develop in the meantime to a position of such strength that in the renewal of trade treaties we may be able to make genuine reductions on several of our tariff rates.

6. To review in 1904, at the time of the renewal of the trade treaties, the problem of foreign capital and to decide then whether new safeguards should be added to existing legislation.

In submitting this program to favorable consideration by Your Imperial Highness, I respectfully ask that it may please you, my sovereign, to make certain that it may not be endangered henceforth by waverings and changes, because our industries, and our national economy in general, require a firm and consistent system carried to its conclusion.

If this program does not find the support of Your Imperial Highness, then, pray, tell me which economic policy I am to pursue.

STATE SECRETARY S. IU. WITTE

II. Revolutionary Russia:

1905-1963

35. the Russian Revolution

of 1905 and Asia *

In the life of the Asian peoples, the Russian Revolution (of 1905) played the same tremendous role as the great French Revolution formerly played in the lives of Europeans.

M. PAVLOVITCH

TWO DEVELOPMENTS DURING THE OPENING YEARS of the twentieth century had significant repercussions in the Near East, the Middle East and throughout Asia. These were the Russo-Japanese War and the Russian Revolution of 1905.

The Russo-Japanese War was geographically an Asian conflict in which Japan, a rising Asian power, defeated backward European Russia. It had a profound impact on many Asians, making them conscious of events in Tsarist Russia to an extent that might not otherwise have been the case. From the safe vantage point of Western Europe, the still relatively unknown Lenin grasped the significance for Asia of the Tsarist defeat. Writing in *Vperyod* (Forward) for January 1, 1905, on "The Fall of Port Arthur," he hailed the triumph of Japan as the triumph of Asia over Europe: "A progressive and advanced Asia has inflicted an irreparable blow on a backward and reactionary Europe."[1]

Japan's victory over Russia in 1905—her second Asian triumph within a decade—electrified the Japanese nation. By the defeat of China (1894-1895), Japan had enhanced her prestige in Asia. Her defeat of Russia, a European nation, now transformed Japan from an Asian into a world power. The repercussions of her victory were felt throughout Asia. As Sun Yat-sen pointed out, Japan's success gave the nations of Asia "unlimited hope" and "raised the standing of all Asiatic peoples" *(San Min Chu I,* tr. Price, Shanghai, 1927, p. 15). What Japan had achieved in 1905, Chinese, Indians, Iranians, Turks, and other Asian peoples dared to hope they could achieve in the foreseeable future.

* From Ivar Spector, *The First Russian Revolution: Its Impact on Asia.* © 1962, by permission of Prentice-Hall, Inc., Englewood Cliffs, New Jersey.

[1] For a more detailed analysis, see M. Pavlovitch, *Revolyutsionnyi Vostok,* Part I, "SSSR i Vostok," (Moscow-Leningrad, 1927), pp. 21-35.

The defeat of Russia by Japan proved to be as much of a stimulus to China as to Japan. In one respect the war, which was fought mainly on Chinese soil, accentuated the helplessness of the Manchu dynasty before foreign encroachment. On the other hand, the Japanese victory over a first-rate Western power eased for China the sting of her earlier defeat in the Treaty of Shimonoseki (1895). At least temporarily, it raised the prestige of Japan in Chinese eyes, gave impetus to the migration of Chinese students to Japan, and encouraged the belief that China, too, by adopting Western tools, could achieve independence from Western imperialism.

It is not always possible to distinguish between the impact on Asia of the Russo-Japanese War and the impact of the Russian Revolution of 1905, which took place concurrently. Western scholars, with few exceptions, have been prone to attribute to Japanese victory the subsequent national and constitutional upsurge in Asian countries from Turkey to China, often ignoring completely the revolution in Russia. The Russo-Japanese War, by and large, appears to have underlined the possibility of the overthrow of Western imperialism in Asia. The Russian Revolution of 1905 indicated the feasibility of the overthrow of autocracy, native or foreign, and the establishment of constitutional regimes. In most Asian countries, where the two objectives were fused, the fact of Russia's defeat and the example of Russia's revolution together produced a resounding and durable impact.

The Revolution of 1905, which was national in scope, had a strong appeal, both inside Russia and abroad, perhaps stronger in some respects than the October Revolution of 1917. With its focus on political freedom and constitutional government for Russia, it appealed to many parties and classes, whereas the Bolshevik Revolution, which stressed social transformation, called for the dictatorship of one class, the proletariat, and of one party, the Communist. The real strength of the Revolution of 1905 lay in the absence of any messianic zeal on the part of its leaders to disseminate ideas abroad. It was the example of Russia that counted.

In Western Europe, where the labor and socialist movements already were well established and their members were politically conscious, the revolution served as a tonic, especially to Social Democrats and Socialists, for the promotion of social unrest. In the blow to Russian autocracy, German and Austro-Hungarian Social Democrats and French and Italian Socialists saw, as in a mirror, the ultimate success of their own struggle against the ruling classes and reactionary forces in their own societies. French Socialists heralded the revolution in Russia as the most significant event since the Paris commune of 1871. An epidemic of labor meetings and conferences occurred throughout Western Europe, their leaders paying tribute to the achievements of Russian workers and excoriating Tsarist policies. From 1905 to 1906 the Governments of Germany, France, Austria-Hungary, and Italy were plagued by a wave of strikes organized by miners, textile workers, and railroad employees. In Hungary, where agrarian conditions most closely resembled those in Tsarist Russia, widespread peasant disorders occurred, as well as political ferment among the Slavic minorities in favor of national liberation. Even in the Balkan States of Bulgaria, Serbia, and Rumania the pattern of events in revolutionary Russia was reproduced on a smaller scale. Although these various manifestations of social, national, and political unrest were essentially an outgrowth of local conditions, the Russian Revolution of 1905 served to increase the tempo and broaden the scope of the demonstrations.

In Asia, the Russian Revolution contributed to political and national, rather than social, unrest. Western influence already had made the politically conscious elements in Asian lands adjacent to Russia constitution-minded. It was the Revolution of 1905, however, which afforded a practical demonstration to them that a constitution could be won from an autocratic ruler in a country that was still agrarian rather than industrial, and where the masses were both heterogeneous in origin and largely illiterate. These conditions were part of Asian experience and had their counterparts in every Asian country, whereas Western industrial democracy was still largely alien to them. The Russian demonstration on their very doorsteps, so to speak, of the establishment of a constitutional regime could not fail to make a profound impression. The contemporary parallel of the rapid industrialization of Soviet Central Asia and the "liquidation" of illiteracy there within the span of a single generation has had a comparable impact in Asia since World War II.

Soviet scholars themselves admit that the impact of the 1905 Revolution was not the same throughout Asia. In every instance, its impact was greater and more direct in countries contiguous to Tsarist Russia, where cross-border communications were commonplace, as in Iran, Turkey, and China. For example, in December 1905, a revolution started in Iran that continued until the close of 1911. In 1905 there was a resurgence of the revolutionary movement in the Ottoman Empire, the outcome of which was the Young Turk Revolution of 1908. In 1905, under the leadership of Sun Yat-sen, anti-Manchu activities in China and abroad were coordinated in Japan into one effective organization, the T'ung-meng Hui, the main objectives of which were achieved in the Chinese Revolution of 1911. From 1905 to 1908 in India there developed a strong anti-imperialist movement, manifested chiefly by strikes and internal disorders.

Maurice Baring, writing from the Near East in 1909, was keenly aware of the impact of the Russian Revolution on the Muslim population of the British Empire.

The British Empire includes large dominions inhabited by Moslims, and ever since the Russo-Japanese War, in all the Moslim countries which are under British sway, there have been movements and agitations in favour of Western methods of government, constitutionalism, and self-government. There has been a cry of "Egypt for the Egyptians," and of

"India for the Indians," and in some cases this cry has been supported and punctuated by bombs and assassinations.[2]

As Soviet writers are prone to point out, Russia as an imperialist power differed from England, France, and Germany in that she had within her own borders Persians, Turks, Armenians, Georgians, Chinese, Koreans, and Mongols. Whatever happened inside Russia, therefore, was bound to have its repercussions across Asia. In some instances, as in Iran and China, the Russian Revolution of 1905 helped to galvanize into action revolutionary groups which successfully overthrew a long-established autocracy and substituted, at least temporarily, a new constitutional regime. In Turkey, the very example of Russia was an important factor in accelerating the movement of the Young Turks for the restoration of the constitutional regime of 1876, abandoned long since by the Sultan.

This is why Communist writers, such as M. Lentzner,[3] called the Russian Revolution of 1905 "l'avant-coureur des revolutions nationales d'Orient. . . ." Writing for a French audience in the mid-Twenties, at a time when Communists were highly conscious of the importance of the Orient, he elaborated on this point:

> La revolution de 1905 ouvrit des mouvements nationaux revolution-naires en Orient. Les rapports sociaux et economiques, la lutte des classes en Orient rappelle beaucoup ceux de la Russie. C'est pourquoi la revolution russe devait éveiller les peuples opprimés de Chine, de Perse, de Turquie, et donner le signal de la revolution en Orient.[4]

Of all the minorities of Asian origin within the borders of Tsarist Russia, the Muslims were the most significant from the standpoint of the Orient. They constituted around twelve per cent of the population. In 1905 there were approximately 20,000,000 Muslims of Turkic origin in Russia, divided as follows: (1) eastern Muslims—Siberian Tatars, Chinese Uighurs, (2) southern Muslims—Othmans, Azerbaijanians, and Turkmenians, and (3) central Muslims—Tatars, Kirghiz, Bashkirs, and Nogai. For purposes of administration the Muslim population was organized in sixteen regions.

The sixteen regions, and their administrative centers, were: the Caucasus (Baku), the Crimea (Simferopol), Moscow-St. Petersburg (St. Petersburg), Lithuania (Minsk), the Lower Volga (Astrakhan), the Upper Volga (Kazan), Ufa (Ufa), Orenburg (Orenburg), Turkestan (Tashkent), Siberia (Irkutsk), the Steppe (Uralsk), Omsk (Omsk), Semipalatinsk (Semipalatinsk), Semiretchensk (Vernyi), Akmolinsk (Petropavlovsk), and the Transcaspian (Ashkhabad).[5]

[2] Maurice Baring, *Letters from the Near East 1909 and 1912* (London, 1913), pp. 12-13.

[3] M. Lentzner, *La Revolution de 1905* (Paris, 1925), p. 2.

[4] *Ibid.*, p. 48.

[5] See I. D. Kuznetsov, *et al.*, "Musul'manskoe dvizhenie v period revolyutsii i reaktsii," *Natsional'nye dvizheniya v period pervoi revolyutsii v. Rossii* (Tcheboksary, 1935), pp. 215-76.

According to Russian sources, the Tsarist Government had expropriated the richest Muslim lands in Siberia, Kazan, the Volga area, the Caucasus, the Transcaucasus, the Crimea, and Turkestan. It is claimed that, during the two centuries prior to the Bolshevik Revolution of 1917, the Tsarist rulers deprived the Muslims of 41,675,000 *desyatinas* of land, as well as other forms of wealth. The Crimean Tatars, in particular, bore the brunt of Tsarist persecution, with the result that on several occasions there was a mass exodus to Turkey. At the time of the Russian annexation of the Crimea, Catherine the Great (1762-1796) bestowed hundreds of thousands of acres of land on her favorites—Potëmkin, Bulgakov, Zubov, Zotov, Katchioni (a Greek)—on the ground that the Crimean Tatars, not being members of the nobility, had no right to hold land. In 1791, as a result, approximately one hundred thousand Crimean Tatars left Russia for the Ottoman Empire. Following the Crimean War, about 1861, several thousand more escaped to Turkey. In 1901, due to the Government's Russification policy which the Muslims regarded as a threat to their Islamic faith and heritage, more than fifty thousand Crimean Tatars left Russia. Not content with the expropriation of the private property of the Crimean Tatars, the Russian Government took over the *waqf* lands and institutions, thus depriving these Muslims of their community centers, schools, and so forth. On the eve of World War I, the streets of Turkish cities were literally teeming with Tatar refugees, commonly referred to as *Urus-muhadjiry* (Russian refugees).[6] Not all Russian Muslims, however, were persecuted as relentlessly as were the Crimean Tatars.

Under the impact of the Revolution of 1905, several attempts were made to organize the Russian Muslims. The first Muslim Congress was held on August 15, 1905, in Nizhni-Novgorod, and was followed by a second congress in St. Petersburg, January 13-26, 1906. Whatever the original motives of the Muslim leaders, the two congresses indicated clearly that, in spite of a wide divergence of opinion on many issues, there was no disposition toward secession from the Russian Empire. Moreover, delegates to the second congress, instead of establishing a separate Muslim party, expressed their readiness to join the Constitutional Democrats (Kadets).

In the first Imperial Duma, where there were twenty-five Muslim deputies, no Muslim faction existed. In the second Duma, when their numbers increased to thirty-five, after much effort a Muslim faction was organized under the chairmanship of Ali Mardan bey Toptchibashev, a Baku oil industrialist and leader in the two Muslim congresses. The dwindling of their representation to ten in the third Duma and to six in the fourth Duma rendered any perpetuation of the Muslim faction impractical.

Many Muslims, especially the more articulate leaders, had a vested

[6] Alexander Tamarin, *Musul'mane na Rusi* (Moscow, 1917), No. 52, pp. 5-6.

interest in the regime, some having acquired wealth and titles, others having become army officers during the Russo-Japanese War. These Muslims had no desire to organize a radical political opposition, especially one that veered toward atheism and revolution. This disposition toward conservatism was characteristic of the military, clerical, and business elements among the Muslims. In 1905, the majority of the Muslims in Russia appear to have been concerned primarily with the attainment of local cultural and religious autonomy. Police records indicate the existence of Muslim secret societies which attracted a radical minority, but did not represent the leading spokesmen of the Muslim population.[7] Such societies were especially prevalent in Kazan, the virtual capital of Russian Islam.

The intensification of Turkic political and national activity, however, during the years 1905 to 1907, was a source of grave concern to the Russian Government. Although there was no appreciable demand for secession, the Tatars made a strong bid for leadership of all the Turkic peoples inside Russia. This drive for unity found expression in efforts to promote a common language and in the resurgence of Islam. Thus, the third All-Muslim Congress resolved to introduce the Ottoman Turkish language in all Russian Muslim schools. Islamic missionary zeal during this period led to the wholesale defection to Islam of 49,000 Muslim converts to Christianity in the Volga Region.[8]

The political, religious, and cultural ferment among the Muslims inside the Russian Empire, stimulated and articulated by the Russian Revolution of 1905, had widespread repercussions among the followers of Islam beyond the Russian borders, especially in the adjacent Islamic country of Iran and in the Ottoman Empire. These "Russian" Muslims were instrumental in transmitting the ideas and objectives of the 1905 Revolution to their co-religionists abroad. According to Friedrich-Wilhelm Fernau,[9] Turkish national consciousness emerged first among the Turkish-speaking peoples of the Tsarist regime, some of whom were educated in Russian universities, and was transmitted by them to the Ottomans, when, at the beginning of the twentieth century Constantinople became "the national center" for Turks.

[7] See I. D. Kuznetsov *et al., op. cit.,* p. 225. See also A. Arsharuni and Kh. Gabidullin, *Otcherki Panslavizma i Panturkizma v Rossii* (Moscow, 1931), pp. 35-38.

[8] See Serge A. Zenkovsky, *Pan-Turkism and Islam in Russia* (Cambridge, Mass., 1960), p. 106. See also E. Fedorov, "1905 god i korennoe naselenie Turkestana," *Novyi Vostok,* Vols. 13-14, 1926, pp. 132-57; and V. Apukhin "Revolyutsionnoe dvizhenie 1905 g. sredi gortsev severnogo kavkaza," *Ibid.,* pp. 158-78.

[9] "The Birth of the Turkish Nation," *New Outlook,* III, No. 6 (28), Tel Aviv, May 1960, pp. 24-25.

36. the October Manifesto (1905)

IN 1903, COUNT SERGEI WITTE became president of the Committee of Ministers, nominally, at least, the highest office in the government of Nicholas II. He strongly opposed the drift toward war in the Far East and urged the Emperor to make political concessions, first to allay domestic discontent and later to quell the Revolution of 1905. Although Nicholas II reluctantly agreed, he did not follow Witte's advice *in toto*. He issued both the October Manifesto and made public Witte's Report. Witte became the first prime minister and ironically enough negotiated the large foreign loan with France which left the government independent of the new constitutional regime.

Below are a translation of the October Manifesto (by the editors), and Witte's Report to the Emperor, together with his evaluation of the Manifesto. The Report and the evaluation are from *The Memoirs of Count Witte,* translated and edited by Avrahm Yarmolinsky (Garden City, New York: Doubleday, Page, and Company, 1921), pp. 234-235, 310-313. Reprinted by permission.

I. The Manifesto of October 17/30, 1905
By the Grace of God

We, Nicholas II, Emperor and Autocrat of All the Russias, Tsar of Poland, Grand Duke of Finland, &c, &c, &c.

Declare to all our loyal subjects: Unrest and disturbances in the capitals and in many parts of Our Empire fill Our heart with great and heavy grief. The welfare of the Russian Sovereign is inseparable from the welfare of the people, and the people's sorrow is His sorrow. The unrest, which now has made its appearance, may give rise to profound disaffection among the masses and become a menace to the integrity and unity of the Russian State. The great vow of Tsarist service enjoins Us to strive with all the might of Our reason and authority for the speediest cessation of unrest so perilous to the State. Having ordered the proper authorities to take measures to suppress the direct manifestations of disorder, rioting, and violence, and to insure the safety of peaceful people

238 · readings in Russian history and culture

who seek to fulfill in peace the duties incumbent upon them, We, in order to carry out more successfully the measures designed by Us for the pacification of the State, have deemed it necessary to coordinate the activities of the higher Government agencies.

We impose upon the Government the obligation to carry out Our inflexible will:

1. To grant the population the unshakable foundations of civic freedom based on the principles of real personal inviolability, freedom of conscience, speech, assembly, and association.

2. Without halting the scheduled elections to the State Duma, to admit to participation in the Duma, as far as is possible in the short space of time left before its summons, those classes of the population which at present are altogether deprived of the franchise, leaving the further development of the principle of universal suffrage to the newly established legislature (i.e., according to the law of August 6, 1905, to the Duma and Council of State).

3. To establish it as an unbreakable rule that no law can become effective without the sanction of the State Duma and that the people's elected representatives should be guaranteed an opportunity for actual participation in the supervision of the legality of the actions of authorities appointed by Us.

We call upon all the loyal sons of Russia to remember their duty to their country, to lend assistance in putting an end to the unprecedented disturbances, and together with Us to make very effort to restore peace and quiet in our native land.

Issued at Peterhof on the seventeenth day of October in the year of Our Lord, nineteen hundred and five, in the eleventh year of Our reign. The original text signed in His Imperial Majesty's own hand.

Nicholas

II. Witte's Report to the Emperor

The unrest which has seized the various classes of the Russian people cannot be looked upon as the consequence of the partial imperfections of the political and social order or as the result of the activities of organized extreme parties. The roots of that unrest lie deeper. They are in the disturbed equilibrium between the aspirations of the thinking elements and the external forms of their life. Russia has outgrown the existing régime and is striving for an order based on civic liberty. Consequently, the forms of Russia's political life must be raised to the level of the ideas which animate the moderate majority of the people.

The first task of the Government is immediately to establish the basic elements of the new order, notably personal inviolability and the freedom of the press, of conscience, of assemblage, and of association, without waiting for the legislative sanction of these measures by the Imperial Duma. The further strengthening of these foundations of the political life of the country must be effected in the regular legislative procedure, just as the work of equalizing all the Russian citizens, without distinction of religion and nationality, before the law. It goes without saying that the civic liberties granted to the people must be lawfully restricted, so as to safeguard the rights of the third persons and peace and the safety of the State.

The next task of the Government is to establish institutions and legislative principles which would harmonize with the political ideals of the majority of the Russian people and which would guarantee the inalienability of the previously granted blessings of civic liberty. The economic policy of the Government must aim at the good of the broad masses, at the same time safeguarding those property and civil rights which are recognized in all the civilized countries.

The above-outlined foundations of the Government's activity will necessitate a great deal of legislative and administrative work. A period of time is bound to elapse between the enunciation of a principle and its embodiment in legislative norms or, furthermore, the introduction of these norms into the life of the people and the practice of the Governmental agents. No Government is able at once to force a new political régime upon a vast country with a heterogeneous population of 135 million, and an intricate administration brought up on other principles and traditions. It is not sufficient for the Government to adopt the motto of civic liberty to inaugurate the new order. Alone the untiring and concerted efforts of a homogeneous Government, animated by one aim and purpose, will bring it about.

The situation demands that the Government should only use methods testifying to the sincerity and frankness of its intentions. Consequently, the Government must scrupulously refrain from interfering with the elections to the Imperial Duma, and also sincerely strive to carry out the reforms outlined in the decree of December 12, 1904. The Government must uphold the prestige of the future Duma and have confidence in its work. So long as the Duma's decisions are not out of keeping with Russia's grandeur, the result of the age-long process of her history, the Government must not oppose them. In accordance with the letter and spirit of his Majesty's manifesto, the regulations relating to the Imperial Duma are subject to further development, in proportion as the imperfections of that institution come to light and as new demands arise. Guided by the ideas prevalent among the people, the Government must formulate these demands, constantly striving to satisfy the desires of the masses. It is very important to reconstruct the Imperial Council on the basis of the principle of elected membership, for that alone will enable the Government to establish normal relations between that institution and the Imperial Duma.

Without enumerating the other measures to be taken by the Government, I wish to state the following principles which, I believe, must guide the authorities at all the stages of their activity:

1. Frankness and sincerity in the establishment of all the newly granted rights and privileges.
2. A firm tendency toward the elimination of extraordinary regulations.
3. Coordination of the activities of all the Governmental agents.
4. Avoidance of measures of repression directed against acts which do not threaten either Society or the State, and
5. Firm suppression of all actions menacing Society or the State, in strict accordance with the law and in spiritual union with the moderate majority of the people.

It goes without saying that the accomplishment of the outlined tasks will only be possible with the broad and active coöperation of the public and on the condition of peace, which alone will enable the Government to apply all its forces to fruitful work. We have faith in the political tact of the Russian people. It is unthinkable that the people should desire anarchy, which, in addition to all the horrors of civil war, holds the menace of the disintegration of the very State.

Witte's Evaluation of the October Manifesto

The manifesto was drawn up hastily and until the last moment I did not know whether His Majesty would sign it. Had it not been for Grand Duke Nikolai Nikolaievich, he would not perhaps have done it. It is noteworthy that immediately upon the promulgation of the manifesto the Grand Duke embraced the creed of the Black Hundreds. Prince A. D. Obolensky, one of the authors of the manifesto, was in a state of neurasthenia at the time when he took part in its composition. Several days after the publication of the act this earnest advocate of the manifesto declared to me that his participation in the movement for the manifesto had been the greatest sin of his life. In the days immediately preceding the publication of the manifesto, His Majesty conducted two parallel sets of conferences. I participated in one, Goremykin—in the other. This extreme duplicity at such a critical time greatly discouraged me.

As a matter of fact, I was rather opposed to the publication of a constitutional manifesto, and I gave much thought to the alternative plan of setting up a military dictatorship. The original text of the document was drafted against my will and behind my back. Seeing, however, that the high spheres were intent upon issuing the manifesto, I insisted that my own version of it should be adopted, if I was to be appointed Prime Minister.

The effect of the act of October 17th was in many respects salutary.

Thus, for instance, the manifesto destroyed that unity of front which made the camp of the opposition so formidable. It sobered the country down, so that the voice of patriotism was heard in the land again, and the propertied people girt their loins and arose in defence of their possessions. But it also had its serious drawbacks. The manifesto came as a bolt from the blue. Most of the provincial authorities did not understand what happened, and many were clearly out of sympathy with the new course of policy. As the manifesto came unexpectedly, the regions which had already been in a state of tension were thrown into a fever by its sudden appearance. Violent outbreaks, both revolutionary and counter-revolutionary, took place all over the country, the reactionary manifestations involving, of course, pogroms. The latter were organized or, at least, encouraged by the local authorities. Thus the manifesto actually stimulated disorder. That was what I feared, and that was why I opposed the idea of issuing a manifesto. Furthermore, it laid the imprint of undue haste upon all the other acts of the Government.

I did not for a moment doubt the necessity of a parliamentary régime for the country. In those days even the conservatives advocated a constitution. In fact, there were no conservatives in Russia on the eve of October 17, 1905. The manifesto cut Russia's past from her present as with a knife. The historical operation was surely necessary, but it should have been performed with greater care and more precautions. Yet, I thank the Lord that the constitution has been granted. It is far better that the past has been cut off, even though somewhat roughly and hurriedly, than if it had been slowly sawed off with a blunt saw wielded by a bungling surgeon.

Everybody understood that the act of October 17th marked an historical turning-point of great significance. The truly enlightened element, which had preserved its faith in the political decency of the ruling powers, perceived that the dream of several generations, to which, beginning with the Decembrists, so many noble lives were sacrificed, had come true. As for the embittered and the unbalanced, they felt that the chief representatives of the old order, above all the Monarch himself, should have gone into the scrap-heap with the ancient régime. For did not Nicholas II actually ruin Russia and cast her off the pedestal on which she had stood? Many also suspected—and their suspicions proved eminently true—that the constitution had been granted by the Emperor in a fit of panic and that as soon as his position improved he would so manipulate the constitution as to annul it and turn it into a ghastly farce.

In October, 1905, a feeling of profound dejection reigned at the court. The following incident will plainly show how deep that feeling was. In those days we used to go to Peterhof by steamer to attend the official sessions, for the railway workers were on strike. Once, Adjutant General Count Benckendorf, a brother of our ambassador in London, happened to be with us on board the steamer. A sensible, educated man, very much devoted to the Emperor, he belongs to the few noblemen who lend the splendour of their culture to the throne. Count Benckendorf regretted, he said among other things to N. I. Vuich, who accompanied me, that their Majesties had five children (four princesses and the poor heir Alexis, a very nice boy, they say). Should the Imperial family have to leave Peterhof by steamer to seek shelter abroad, he explained, *the children would be a great hindrance.*

37. Lenin: "The Lessons of the Moscow Uprising" (1905)

LENIN TOOK NO DIRECT PART in the early stages of the Revolution of 1905. Following his return to Russia in November, he instigated the general strike and actively prepared for the Moscow uprising. The December uprising marked the climax of the Revolution. It was ruthlessly suppressed by Tsarist forces brought from St. Petersburg, Tver, and other centers in European Russia. The Mensheviks denounced the resort to arms, but Lenin contended that the uprising should have been conducted more resolutely and aggressively. On the basis of the 1905 experience, Lenin instructed his followers on how to plan for the next revolution. The tactics of the Bolsheviks in the October Revolution of 1917 demonstrated that they had learned the lessons of the Moscow uprising of 1905. Lenin's article, translated below, appeared in *Proletarii* (No. 2, August 29, 1906).

From V. I. Lenin, *Polnoe Sobranie Sotchinenii,* Fifth edition, Vol. XIII (Moscow, 1960), 369-377.

The appearance of the book, *Moscow in December 1905* (Moscow, 1906), could not have been more timely. Assimilation of the experience of the December uprising is an essential task of the workers' party. Unfortunately, this book is like a barrel of honey with a spoonful of tar. The material is most interesting, in spite of its incompleteness, but the conclusions are incredibly slovenly, incredibly banal. We shall deal with these conclusions elsewhere; at present we shall turn to the contemporary political issue of the day, to the lessons of the Moscow uprising.

The principal form of the December movement in Moscow was the peaceful strike and demonstrations. The overwhelming majority of the working masses actively participated only in these forms of struggle. But the December action in Moscow proved clearly that the general strike has ceased to be effective as an independent and principal form of struggle, that the movement is extricating itself from these narrow bounds with spontaneous and irresistible force and is giving birth to a higher form of struggle, the uprising.

In declaring the strike, all the revolutionary parties, all the Moscow unions, recognized and even felt the inevitability of its transformation into an uprising. On December 6 [19] the Soviet of Workers' Deputies resolved "to strive to transform the strike into an armed uprising." In reality, however, none of the organizations were prepared for this. Even the Coalition Soviet of Combat Units (December 9 [22]!) referred to an uprising as something remote. The street fighting undoubtedly took place against its will and without its participation. The organizations failed to keep pace with the growth and scope of the movement.

The strike grew into an uprising, first and foremost, under the impact of the objective conditions that took shape after October. The government could no longer be taken by surprise by a general strike: it had already organized the counter-revolution which was ready for military action. The general course of the Russian revolution after October, and the sequence of events in Moscow in the December days, also afforded striking corroboration of one of the most profound theses of Marx: revolution progresses by creating a unified and strong counter-revolution, *i.e.,* it compels the enemy to resort to more and more extreme measures of defence and thus devises more powerful means of attack.

December 7 [20] and 8 [21]: a peaceful strike, peaceful mass demonstrations. The evening of the 8th [21st]: the siege of the Aquarium. The morning of the 9th [22nd]: the crowd on Strastnaya Square is massacred by the dragoons. In the evening: Fiedler's house is wrecked. The mood changes for the worse. The unorganized street crowds, absolutely spontaneously, but diffidently, set up the first barricades.

The 10th [23rd]: the beginning of artillery fire on the barricades on the streets and into the crowd. Barricades are set up with greater assurance, and not just isolated ones, but on a really mass scale. The entire population is in the streets; all the principal centers of the city are covered by a network of barricades. For several days a stubborn partisan struggle unfolds between the insurgent detachments and the troops, a struggle that exhausted the troops and forced Dubasov[1] to beg for reinforcements. Not until December 15 [28] did the government completely gain the upper hand and on December 17 [30] the Semenov regiment destroyed the Presnya district, the last stronghold of the uprising.

From strike and demonstrations to isolated barricades. From isolated barricades to the mass erection of barricades and street fighting against the troops. Over the heads of the organizations the mass proletarian struggle passed from a strike to an uprising. Therein lies the greatest historical achievement of the Russian revolution by December, 1905, and like all previous achievements, it was purchased at the cost of enormous sacrifices. The movement was raised from a general political strike to a higher level. It compelled the reaction to *go to the limit* in its

---

[1] Military Governor-General of Moscow.

resistance and thereby vastly accelerated the moment when the revolution will also go to extremes in the adoption of the means of attack. The reaction cannot *go beyond* artillery bombardment of the barricades, houses, and street crowds. But the revolution can go ever so much further than the Moscow combat units did; in fact, it can go ever so much wider and deeper. And the revolution has made great progress since December. The base of the revolutionary crisis has become immeasurably broader—the blade must now be sharpened still more.

The proletariat felt sooner than its leaders the change in the objective conditions of the struggle and the need for a transition from the strike to an uprising. Practice, as always, preceded theory. A peaceful strike and demonstrations immediately ceased to satisfy the workers, who asked: What comes next?—They demanded more resolute action. The instructions to build barricades reached the districts after a tremendous delay, when barricades were already being erected in the center. The masses of the workers got busy, but dissatisfied even with this, they asked: What comes next?—They demanded more action. In December we, the leaders of the Social Democratic proletariat, proved to be like the commander-in-chief who had arranged the disposition of his regiment in such an absurd way that most of his troops failed to participate actively in the battle. The masses of the workers demanded but failed to obtain instructions for resolute mass action.

Thus, nothing could be more short-sighted than Plekhanov's viewpoint, which is seized upon by all opportunists, that the untimely strike should never have been started and that "it was unnecessary to resort to arms." On the contrary, they should have taken up arms more resolutely, energetically, and aggressively; the impossiblity of peaceful strikes alone and the necessity for a fearless and ruthless armed struggle should have been explained to the masses. And now we must at last openly and publicly admit that political strikes are inadequate; we must carry on the widest propaganda among the masses in favor of an armed uprising and make no attempt to obscure this issue by talk about "preliminary stages," or by casting a veil over it. To conceal from the masses the necessity for a desperate, sanguinary war of extermination as the immediate task of future action means deceiving both ourselves and the people.

This is the first lesson of the December events. The other lesson concerns the character of the uprising, the methods of conducting it, and the conditions under which the troops are won over to the side of the people. In the Right wing of our Party, an extremely biassed view prevails on this matter. It is said to be impossible to fight modern troops, that the troops must first become revolutionary. Of course, unless the revolution assumes a mass character and also affects the troops themselves, there is no use talking about a serious struggle. Work among the troops is, of course, necessary. But we must not imagine that the troops will be won over to our side at one stroke, as it were, as a result of persuasion, on the one hand, or of their own consciousness, on the other. The Moscow uprising clearly demonstrates how trite and ghastly this view is. As a matter of fact, the vacillation of the troops, which is inevitable in every really popular movement, leads to a real contest for the troops between the reaction and the revolution. Dubasov himself declared that only five thousand out of fifteen thousand Moscow troops were reliable. The government held on to the waverers by the most varied and most desperate measures: it persuaded them, flattered them, bribed them, presented them with watches, money, etc.; it made them drunk with vodka, it deceived them, intimidated them, confined them to barracks, and disarmed them; and the soldiers suspected of being most unreliable were removed by treachery and violence. We must have the courage to confess frankly and openly that in this respect we lagged behind the government. We failed to utilize the forces at our disposal to wage an active, bold, enterprising, and aggressive struggle for the vacillating troops, as did the government. We have prepared and we will still more stubbornly prepare for the ideological "indoctrination" of the army. But we shall prove to be sorry pedants if we forget that at the moment of the uprising a physical struggle for the army is also necessary.

In the December days the Moscow proletariat taught us magnificent lessons in the ideological "indoctrination" of the troops, as, for example, on December 8 [21] on Strastnaya Square, when the crowd surrounded the Cossacks, mingled with them, fraternized with them, and persuaded them to depart. Or on December 10 [23] in the Presnya district, when two working girls, carrying a red flag in a crowd of 10,000 people, rushed towards the Cossacks and cried: "Kill us! We shall not surrender this flag while we live!" And the Cossacks were disconcerted and galloped off to the cries of the crowd: "Long live the Cossacks!" These instances of courage and heroism must forever leave an indelible impression on the consciousness of the proletariat.

But here are some examples of how we lagged behind Dubasov. On December 9 [22], some soldiers were marching down Bolshaya Serpukhovskaya Street to join the insurgents singing the *Marseillaise*. The workers sent delegates to meet them. Malakhov[2] himself galloped at breakneck speed towards them. The workers were too late, Malakhov arrived in time. He delivered a fiery speech, made the soldiers vacillate, surrounded them with dragoons, marched them off to the barracks, and locked them up. Malakhov reached them, we did not, although two days later 150,000 men rose at our summons, who could and should have organized the patrolling of the streets. Malakhov surrounded the soldiers with dragoons, whereas we failed to surround the Malakhovites with bomb-throwers. We could and should have done this; and long ago

---

[2] Chief of Staff of the Moscow military area.

the Social Democratic press (the old *Iskra*) pointed out that in the event of an uprising the ruthless extermination of the civil and military chiefs is our duty. What took place on Bolshaya Serpukhovskaya Street was apparently repeated, in the main, in front of the Nesvizhsky barracks and in front of the Krutitsky barracks, and when attempts were made by the proletariat to "call off" the Ekaterinoslav regiment, and when delegates were sent to the sappers in Alexandrov, and when the Rostov artillery en route to Moscow was turned back, and when the sappers were disarmed in Kolomna, etc. At the moment of the uprising we did not measure up to the task in our struggle for the wavering troops.

December graphically confirmed another of Marx's profound tenets, forgotten by the opportunists, which states that revolt is an art, and that the principal rule of this art is that there must be a desperately bold and irrevocably determined *offensive.* We have not sufficiently mastered this truism. We have not sufficiently learned it ourselves, nor have we taught the masses this art and this rule of attacking no matter what happens. We must make up for this omission now with all our energy. Alignment on the matter of political slogans is not enough; we stand in need of still another alignment on the matter of an armed uprising. Those who are opposed to it, those who do not prepare for it, must be ruthlessly evicted from the ranks of the supporters of the revolution and sent back to its enemies, to the traitors or cowards; for the day is approaching when the force of events, when the conditions of the struggle will compel us to separate enemies from friends according to this principle. We must not preach passivity, nor must we just keep "waiting" for the troops to "come over." No! We must proclaim far and wide the need for a bold offensive and an armed attack, the necessity at such times of wiping out those in command, and of a most energetic struggle for the wavering troops.

The third great lesson taught by Moscow concerns tactics and the organization of forces for the uprising. Military tactics depend on the level of military technique.—Engels assimilated this truism and put it into the mouths of the Marxists. Military technique today is not what it was in the middle of the nineteenth century. For crowds to go into action against artillery and to defend barricades with revolvers would be folly. Kautsky was right when he wrote that it is high time, after Moscow, to reappraise Engels' conclusions, and that Moscow inaugurated *"new barricade tactics."* These tactics were the tactics of guerilla warfare. The organization required for such tactics was that of mobile and exceedingly small units, units of ten, three, or even two persons. We often meet Social Democrats now who snicker whenever five-men and three-men units are mentioned. But snickering is just a cheap way of shutting one's eyes to the *new* problem of tactics and organization called forth by street fighting under contemporary military technique. Read carefully the story of the Moscow uprising, gentlemen, and you will understand the connection between "five-men units" and the question of "new barricade tactics."

Moscow advanced them, but did not develop them far enough, did not expand them on a broad, truly mass scale. There were few combat units, the slogan of bold attack was not issued to the masses of the workers, nor did they make use of it. The character of the guerilla detachments was too humdrum, their arms and methods were inadequate, their ability to lead the crowd was practically undeveloped. We must make up for all this and we are making up for it by learning from the experience of Moscow, by disseminating this experience among the masses, and by rousing the creativeness of the masses themselves for the further development of that experience. And the guerilla warfare, the mass terror which has been going on in Russia everywhere and almost continuously since December will undoubtedly help to teach the masses the correct tactics to be used during an uprising. Social Democracy must recognize and incorporate this mass terror into its own tactics, organizing and controlling it, of course, subordinating it to the interests and conditions of the labor movement and the general revolutionary struggle, by eliminating and ruthlessly lopping off the "hobo" perversion of this guerilla warfare which was so magnificently and so ruthlessly suppressed by the Muscovites in the days of the uprising and by the Letts in the days of the notorious Lettish republics.

Military technique has made new progress of late. The Japanese war produced the hand grenade. The small arms factories have put automatic rifles on the market. Both these weapons are already being successfully adopted in the Russian revolution, but to an inadequate extent. We can and must take advantage of improvements in technique, teach the workers' units to make bombs on a mass scale, help them and our combat units to stock up the essential explosives, fuses, and automatic rifles. If the masses of the workers participate in city uprisings, if there are mass attacks upon the enemy, if there is a determined and skillful struggle to win over the armed forces, which since the Duma, since Sveaborg and Kronstadt, are vacillating even more, if the participation of the rural districts in the general struggle is assured—victory will be ours in the next all-Russian armed uprising!

Let us then more extensively develop our work and more boldly set our tasks, while assimilating the lessons of the great days of the Russian revolution. At the base of our work lies the correct estimate of the class interests and the requirements of nationwide development at the present time. Around the slogan—overthrow of the tsarist regime and convocation of a constituent assembly by a revolutionary government—we are rallying and shall continue to rally an increasingly large section of the proletariat, the peasantry, and the army. The development of the consciousness of the masses remains, as heretofore, the basis and the chief content of our entire work. But let us not forget that in addition to this general, constant, and fundamental task, times like the present in Russia impose other and special tasks. Let us not become pedants and philistines, let us not excuse ourselves from these special tasks of the moment, these special tasks of the given forms of struggle, by meaningless references to duties which are permanent and immutable, irrespective of time and circumstances.

Let us remember that the great mass struggle is approaching. This will be an armed uprising. It must, as far as possible, be simultaneous. The masses must know that they are entering upon an armed, sanguinary, and desperate struggle. Contempt for death must spread among the masses and thus insure victory. The offensive against the enemy must be most energetic; attack and not defence must become the slogan of the masses; the ruthless extermination of the enemy will be their task; the organization of the struggle will become mobile and flexible; the wavering elements of the troops will be drawn into active struggle. The party of the class-conscious proletariat must fulfill its duty in this great struggle.

38. the opening of the

First Duma (1906)

MAURICE BARING (1874-1945) was an English man of letters and a journalist. For the English newspaper, *Morning Post,* he covered the Russo-Japanese War in Manchuria, 1904-1905. He spent the year 1905-1906 in Russia, at which time he recorded his impressions of the opening of the First Duma. Baring later edited the *Oxford Book of Russian Verse* (1924).

The excerpt below is from Maurice Baring, *A Year in Russia,* Second Edition (New York: E. P. Dutton and Company Publishers, 1917), pp. 178-181, 188-189.

St. Petersburg, May 14 [1906]
I had the good fortune to gain admission to the Duma yesterday afternoon. I think it is the most interesting sight I have ever seen. When you arrive at the Tauris Palace, which outside has an appearance of dignified statelinesss, the stateliness of the end of the eighteenth century, you walk through a spacious front hall into what looks like a gigantic white ballroom built in the late Louis XVI style. This is the lobby; beyond it is the Hall of the Duma itself. In this long gallery members and visitors were already flocking, walking up and down, talking, and smoking cigarettes and throwing away the ashes and the ends on the polished floor. One saw peasants in their long black coats, some of them wearing military medals and crosses; popes [priests], Tartars, Poles, men in every kind of dress except uniform. When the sitting began, I went up into the gallery. The Hall of the Duma itself is likewise white, delicate in decoration, an essentially gentlemanlike room. The sitting began about three o'clock. The members go to their appointed places, on which their cards are fixed, and the impression of diversity of dress and type becomes still stronger and more picturesque.

You see dignified old men in frock coats, aggressively democratic-looking "Intelligents," with long hair and pince-nez; a Polish bishop dressed in purple, who looks like the Pope; men without collars; members of the proletariat, men in loose Russian shirts with belts; men dressed by

250

Davies or Poole, and men dressed in the costume of two centuries ago. The President walked into his seat under the portrait of the Emperor, which is a rather shiny study in blue and white. . . .

The President, C. A. Muromtsev, strikes one as dignity itself. He exercises his functions with perfect serenity and absolute fairness. After reading congratulatory telegrams from various parts of the Empire, he proceeded to read a motion proposed by a workman of the Government of Moscow that before proceeding further a telegram should be sent to the Emperor asking for a general amnesty for political offenders, and another motion asking for an immediate amnesty, proposed by a peasant. A debate ensued. The speeches were sensible and moderate. Most of the members spoke against the motion, and it seemed as if the matter was settled in the sense that the question of amnesty would be dealt with in the Reply to the Address and not before, when Professor Kovolievsky proposed a third course—that the President of the Duma should inform the Emperor of the unanimous desire of the Duma for a general amnesty. What struck me most in the speeches I heard was the naturalness of their tone and the absence of declamatory emphasis. Several of the speeches were eloquent; only one was tedious. Professor Kovolievsky began speaking in his seat, and went on with his speech quietly and in the most natural manner conceivable, as he walked up to the tribune, where he continued it, just as if he were engaged in a quiet talk with a few intimate friends. A second thing which struck me was the respect and the instantaneous obedience shown to the President; when he called to order by ringing his bell, the silence was immediate and complete. Soon after four o'clock there was an *entr'acte,* and the Duma proceeded to elect the thirty-three members by whom the Reply to the Address is to be drawn up. The members poured into the gallery, and everywhere small groups collected discussing various matters; some carried on their discussions in the adjacent lobbies and rooms; many went to drink tea or have some food in the dining-room, where the accommodation is excellent.

Many of the small groups where the discussion was being carried on were interesting. One heard violent ideas and wild words being bandied about. One peasant said to a friend of mine: "When I look upon this palace my blood boils; it was built out of the blood and the sweat of the poor." So it was. "Then you are a person who nurses hatred," said my friend. "Yes," he answered. "I hate, hate, hate the rich!" Another man told a lady of my acquaintance that he was a Socialist. She asked him if he was in favour of the land being made over to the State. He said "No." He explained his views, which were really rather those of an extreme Radical than of a Socialist, clearly and with intelligence, and at the end she said to him: "But you are not a Socialist?" "Yes, I am," he answered; and asked her who she was. She said that she was the daughter of a Count who is a member of the Duma. "I am very pleased to have spoken with a Countess," he answered, perfectly simply. I saw a big landed proprietor; he came up to me and said: "This is very amusing for you; but to me it is life and death." After the interval the sitting was continued. At 6:45 p.m. the result of the election of the thirty-hree members was read out, and Professor Kovolievsky's motion was debated shortly and rejected. After this the question of closure was discussed and referred to a committee. Then I left. The sitting came to an end shortly afterwards. . . .

May 23rd

Every time I pay a fresh visit to the Duma I am struck by the originality of the appearance of its members. There is a Polish member who is dressed in light-blue tights, a short Eton jacket, and Hessian boots. He has curly hair, and looks exactly like the hero of the "Cavalleria Rusticana." There is a Polish member who is dressed in a long white flannel coat reaching to his knees, adorned with an intricate pattern of dark crimson braid, and he also wears a long, soft, brown sleeveless cloak hanging from his shoulders, bordered with vermilion stripes. There are some Socialists who wear no collars, and there is, of course, every kind of head-dress you can conceive. The second, and what is to me the principal impression of the Duma, is the familiar ease with which the members speak; some of them speak well, and some of them speak badly, but they all speak as if they had spoken in Parliament all their lives, without the slightest evidence of nervousness or shyness. The sittings of the Duma are like a meeting of acquaintances in a club or a *café*. There is nothing formal about them. The member walks up to the tribune and sometimes has a short conversation with the President before beginning his speech. Sometimes when he is called to order he indulges in a brief explanation. The last sitting I attended they did their work in a most business-like manner and got through it fairly quickly and without many speeches. The peasants think there is too much speaking altogether. One of them said to me: "There are people here who have no right to be here." "Who?" I asked. "Popes, for instance," he said. "Why shouldn't popes be members?" I asked. "Because they get 200 roubles a year," he answered; "what more can they want?" If this principle were carried out in England, there would be no members of Parliament at all. . . .

39. V. I. Gurko on the

First Duma (1906)

VLADIMIR IOSIFITCH GURKO (1862-1927), scion of a distinguished family, and a brilliant, energetic public servant of conservative persuasion, was an Assistant Minister of the Interior and Member of the State Council during the reign of Nicholas II. He published several works on Russia's agrarian problems, a field in which he was a specialist, and in 1902 served as Manager of the Peasant Section of the Ministry of the Interior under Plehve. It was Peter Stolypin, however, who carried out some of Gurko's ideas for the creation of a strong peasantry freed from the domination of the *Mir*. One of the highlights of Gurko's public career was his appearance before the First Duma as government spokesman on the agrarian question. Gurko was noted for his trenchant comments on the people and events of his time. Following the Revolution, he joined the Whites in opposition to the Bolsheviks.

The passage presented below is from V. I. Gurko, *Features and Figures of the Past. Government and Opinion in the Reign of Nicholas II*. Edited by J. E. Wallace Sterling, Xenia Joukoff Eudin, and H. H. Fisher; translated by Laura Matveev (Stanford: Stanford University Press, 1939), pp. 469-485. Reprinted by permission.

... The First Duma was dominated by the Cadets, who did not even take the trouble to conceal the fact that they intended to use the Duma not for the good of the country but as an instrument to overthrow the government. Their attitude is illustrated by an interesting incident. On the occasion of the opening of the State Duma, it was suggested in the Moscow municipal Duma that felicitations be sent to the new national representative body; but the Cadet members of the municipal Duma (twenty-six out of one hundred and fifty) opposed the suggestion. Their leader, Professor A. A. Manuilov, even went so far as to say privately to Mayor N. I. Guchkov: "You wish the Duma to do good work, but we desire only to overthrow the government."

This Cadet attitude was certainly known to Nicholas II, as is revealed by what he said to Witte. On December 6, 1905, when Witte presented the statute on the elections to the Duma for the Tsar's signature (in the presence of S. E. Kryzhanovsky, author of the statute, whom he had taken along in case the Tsar should ask technical questions to which Witte would have no ready answer), he said to the Monarch: "The Duma will be as an assistant to Your Majesty in your difficult work." "Oh, come now, Sergei Yulevich!" the Tsar answered, "I know perfectly well that I am agreeing to the establishment of an institution which will be my enemy. Yet I am thinking of the future; I am thinking of my son. I wish to create a new center of authority in the country to insure the strength of the country at large."

The attitude of the underground revolutionary elements toward the Duma was one of opposition. This was no secret. They feared that the bourgeois elements in the Duma would realize that their main enemy was not the government but the revolutionists—the militant Socialists who dreamed of overthrowing the entire social structure—and that they would therefore come to some understanding with the government and ally with it in war upon the really revolutionary movement. But, alas, neither the government nor the progressive public realized that their mutual conflicts profited only that *tertius gaudens* which, eleven years later, was to seize power, overthrow the political regime, undermine the social structure, and ruin that same progressive public.

The hostility of the majority of the First Duma toward the throne was shown clearly on the first day of its sessions. All the Duma members attended the Imperial reception in the throne room of the Winter Palace dressed in a deliberately careless fashion. Be it said, however, that there was a certain lack of tact on both sides. The court had decided that this reception was to be particularly solemn and brilliant. The Imperial regalia had been brought from Moscow, and these were to be borne by the highest officials, ranged on both sides of the throne. The throne was draped in the Imperial ermine mantle; it was said that the Tsarina herself had draped the mantle so that it would hang in artistic folds. Velvet ropes down the center of the room formed a sort of corridor through which the Imperial suite was to pass. On one side of this corridor were members of the State Duma and on the other members of the State Council, senators, and the other higher civil and military officials. The contrast was striking. The court and the government, flourishing gold-laced uniforms and numerous decorations, was set opposite the gray, almost rustic group representing the people of Russia. Naively believing that the people's representatives, many of whom were peasants, would be awed by the splendor of the Imperial court, the ladies of the Imperial family had worn nearly all their jewels; they were literally covered with pearls and diamonds. But the effect was altogether different. This Oriental method of impressing upon spectators a reverence for the bearers of supreme power was quite unsuited to the occasion. What it did achieve was to set in juxtaposition the boundless Imperial luxury and the poverty of the people. The demagogues did not fail to comment upon this ominous contrast. Nor did the Tsar's address of welcome improve matters. It was intelligently composed and clearly delivered with a certain Imperial dignity, but the Tsar especially emphasized the fact that he was welcoming *the best* representatives of the people.

In the Duma itself, the leaders of the people's representatives, who had outlined in their minds the whole program of their proposed attack upon the government, turned the Duma tribune into a pulpit for the preaching of revolution. This began when I. I. Petrunkevich, one of the most malicious enemies of the government and the existing order, touchingly demanded of the government an immediate and general amnesty for all political prisoners, including those who had committed civil crimes from political motives. If I remember correctly, Petrunkevich's motion was adopted unanimously. Then the Duma composed an address to the Tsar stating all the points of the Cadet program and demanding their immediate acceptance. These points included political amnesty, universal suffrage in elections to the State Duma, and the expropriation of state, udel, church, and private lands in favor of the peasantry.

Unwilling as Goremykin was to have anything to do with the Duma, the government was obliged to break its silence and make some sort of answer. But the preparation of this answer produced extensive wrangling in the Council of Ministers.

The sessions of the Council were held in the Ministry of the Interior building near the Tsepnoi Bridge, in the residence occupied bv Goremykin. Here in the large study, with which I was so familiar in Plehve's time, the ministers met daily. At first the sessions lacked organization. The members did not sit around a common table but distributed themselves about the room; this gave the sessions the air of a social gathering. Nor did the members attend the sessions too punctually. Izvolsky, for instance, was late almost every day as he came from dinner at some foreign embassy, wearing a dress coat, *une fleur à la boutonnière.* For some unknown reason he preferred to sit astride his chair, facing its back, a position not altogether in harmony with the tone of the gathering and the seriousness of the discussion. His face reminded one of a pug dog, and he wore a monocle. He was anxious to pass as an authority on parliamentary practice and procedure; but his influence was negligible. Kokovtsov made lengthy and seemingly businesslike speeches, but evidently had not yet come to any definite decision concerning what attitude the government should assume toward the Duma; certainly it was very difficult to follow the trend of his ideas. Stolypin maintained an obstinate silence. Discussion went from one topic to another, as there was no prepared government program and, generally speaking, the opinions expressed were not clearly thought out. Only Stishinsky and Shirinsky had definite views concerning the State Duma, and these could be summed up thus: the State Duma was a revolutionary institution; therefore, it would be well to dismiss it, or still better, to abolish it completely. Goremykin did not appear to be master of the situation at all. He presided over the sessions without giving them direction, and with an air which seemed to say: "Babble as you will, for I shall act as I see fit."

In discussing the Duma's address to the Tsar, Izvolsky suggested that it be answered by an address from the throne, as was done in Western states. The objection was made that this would bring the Tsar directly into conflict with the people's representatives. Goremykin was inclined entirely to disregard the Duma's address, but some ministers protested that that would only embarrass the government in the long run. Stolypin was still silent. It was finally decided that the government would stand between the supreme power and the people's representatives and answer the Duma's address in its own name. The Duma's address was discussed in summary fashion, and it was decided which of the Duma's demands might be realized even partially; then the Council charged Shcheglovitov and myself each to compose an answer. I suppose that I was chosen for this task because I had urgently advised that the government break its silence and express its real opinion.

The Council examined our drafted answers on the next day. Shcheglovitov read his first. It was humble, ingratiating, and remarkably vague. Then, with no intervening discussion, I was asked to read mine. The answer I had prepared was written in the language of authority; it stated definitely the government's views on all issues mentioned in the Duma's address. Goremykin generally took a long time to make up his mind, but once he had made a decision he carried it out with unwavering resolution. On this occasion he decided for my project, which was then discussed in detail. A few unimportant changes were made in it, which softened its tone; then I was given the task of re-editing it and sending copies to all members of the Council of Ministers, so that they might make whatever objections and observations they might have. I was then to check these observations and prepare the final edition for printing and for forwarding to the members of the Duma. All this had to be done within twenty-four hours.

As usual the session of the Council of Ministers lasted until a late hour; but with the aid of a typist with a hectograph I sent out the copies of the revised draft and by about five the next afternoon these copies had been returned with comments. I have to trust to memory to recall these comments, but if I am not mistaken they were made mostly by V. N. Kokovtsov and A. S. Stishinsky, who, with their customary thoroughness, had read and commented upon my text. Happily, their remarks were not at variance, so that it was easy to incorporate them into the text and prepare the final edition, which Goremykin read the next day from the tribune of the Duma.

When Goremykin rose to deliver the government's answer there was dead silence in the Duma; but he had a feeble voice and hardly anyone heard what he said. Fortunately and wisely copies of the government's reply were distributed among the Duma members. Only once did Goremykin raise his voice, and that was when he read the passage regarding the impermissibility of expropriating privately owned lands in order to increase the land allotment of the peasants; then he even lifted his finger as a threat.

The leaders of the Duma were infuriated not so much by the ministers' disagreement with their program—they had had a premonition on that score—as by the finality of its tone. Concluding, with reason, that the government intended actively to resist their pretentions, they raised their own demands according to the adage: "Behold the lap dog! What a mighty animal he must be to bark thus at the elephant."

The tone of the government's answer was all the greater surprise since all previous statements by individual members of the government had been remarkably humble in spirit. Shcheglovitov had been especially meek before the Duma.[1] His readiness to make concessions to the revolutionary public was revealed in the legislative projects which he was going to present to the people's representatives. One of them dealt with the responsibility of government officials, and the other proposed the abolition of capital punishment even as a sentence of courts-martial. The former was essentially just. The existing order of things by which officials could not be indicted for civil-service offenses without the approval of their chiefs was quite intolerable. Shcheglovitov's remark to me when the Council of Ministers was debating this project was quite sound. He whispered in my ear: "Well, if even this reform is impermissible, then we had better return to the practices of Genghiz-Khan." I do not recall whether or not this project was adopted; if it was, nothing definite came of it, for the existing order of indicting officials for civil-service offenses remained unchanged until the end of the old regime.

Shcheglovitov's other project—the abolition of capital punishment—found no support in the Council, if I remember correctly. Although Stolypin had voted for Shcheglovitov's other project, he opposed this one because he considered it untimely. He left the further elaboration of his attitude to his assistant, A. A. Makarov, a typical prosecuting magistrate, whom I met now for the first time. Other members of the Council of Ministers argued that it would be strange indeed to abolish capital

---

[1] Later, in the Third Duma and as Chairman of the State Council, when he had sensed that the government had gained the upper hand, Shcheglovitov changed his attitude and became insufferably harsh and insolent in addressing the legislative chambers. Like all cowards, he was insolent when he considered himself invulnerable and humble when he was not sure of his position.

punishment at a time when the revolutionists were making a system of murdering state officials and employees.

Since various projects were being advanced I tried to persuade the Council of Ministers to present to the Duma the project of a statute allowing the peasants freely to leave their land communes, a project which had been rejected by the State Council for formal reasons during Witte's ministry. Stolypin placed this project before the Council of Ministers, but Goremykin took a definite stand against it. Stolypin did not utter a word in its defense, and it was again rejected. But inasmuch as the project was at variance with the desires of the Cadet party and therefore would have been turned down by the Duma, Goremykin's stand was probably the right one at that time.

While the Council of Ministers was thus discussing projects but approving none, the Duma continued its attack upon the government. This attack was concentrated on the agrarian issue. The main points of the agrarian reform it proposed were stated in a document signed by thirty-three Duma members. These points were set forth very briefly as in a proclamation. They were designed simply to increase public unrest and to risk nothing, since their authors were sure that neither the government nor the State Council would agree to them. They were not accepted even by all the Duma members. Such progressive public men as N. N. Lvov and Prince Volkonsky opposed them.

Nevertheless, these demands provoked the Council of Ministers to break its silence on the agrarian issue. The ministers decided to take exception to the essential points of the proposed reform. They even selected Stishinsky and myself to expound these exceptions from the tribune of the Duma, but they gave us no instructions concerning the nature of the remarks we were to make. I had not been present at the session where this decision was taken and learned of it from Stishinsky. I asked him what was the government's positive program on the agrarian question, for I considered it impossible merely to criticize and reject the Duma's suggestions. Stishinsky replied that this matter had not been discussed. "You are to go to the Duma in the morning," he said, "but it is for you to decide what you will say."

What was I to say? I was bound by no instructions, but I could not ignore the fact that a few days previously the Council of Ministers had summarily declined to present to the Duma a project permitting each member of the commune freely to leave it. But inasmuch as this project had been presented to the Council of Ministers over Stolypin's signature, thus making official his agreement to it, I resolved to end my speech to the Duma by pointing out that the only means of improving peasant well-being was not to abolish private landownership but to strengthen it by abolishing communal landownership. I worked almost the entire night on my speech and at about eleven o'clock the next morning went to the Taurida Palace. News of the governmental move had traveled far and wide, so that almost all members of the Duma were present. In the ministers' room (the ministers' pavilion was built much later) Stolypin accosted me. "Please, do not speak today in the Duma," he said. His agitation showed through his habitual calm and composure, and I was completely dumfounded by his words. In the first place, I was vexed to think that I had spent the entire night to no purpose; and, in the second place, I was anticipating with pleasure a chance to pit my-self against those dilettantes who had spoken on this subject in the Duma. The land question was highly complicated and I was sure that I should not meet with any serious refutation of the material I had collected. This material proved beyond doubt that the transfer to the peasants of all fertile lands of European Russia would not improve their well-being, since it would not increase to any perceptible degree the amount of land already in their possession; for the majority of the peasants such an increase would be expressed in fractions of a desiatin per capita. I asked Stolypin why he wanted me not to speak.

"Because the land question and all suggestions connected with its final solution must come from me, the Minister of the Interior. In this basic and most important question I cannot allow any person but myself to speak in the Duma."

"You must address your objection, Petr Arkadievich, not to me but to the Council of Ministers, which has charged me to speak today. I cannot comply with your wishes unless the Council, or at least its chairman, advises me to do so."

"Yet you cannot act contrary to my desire."

"I have already explained my stand and I cannot change it. Here is a telephone. Call up Goremykin, and if, after talking with you, he himself tells me not to speak today, I shall not do so."

But Stolypin would not agree to call Goremykin. For some time we continued to walk back and forth. Stolypin continued to state reasons why I should not appear, and I replied stubbornly: "Here is the telephone! Call up Goremykin."

At last, seeing that he could not prevail upon me, he said: "Well, in any event, please keep to the facts and make no generalizations." But I paid no heed to this admonition. My speech was written out and I had no desire to change it. But Stolypin had also asked me to speak in my own name and not in that of the Minister of the Interior, and with this request I felt obliged to comply—with what results we shall see later.

The session opened about midday. Prince Petr Dolgorukov, a vice-chairman, was presiding. He was reputedly a specialist in peasant problems; but his knowledge of the subject was elementary, and his treatment was that of a Russian intellectual who absolutely ignored the economic consequences of the measure proposing the expropriation of private lands. Unlike the majority of the Cadets, however, he was sincerely persuaded that this measure would be beneficial to the state and he supported it even though it would injure his own interests. At about four in the afternoon the land question was taken up. The long hours since the session had begun not only had proved trying but also had increased the agitation which I naturally felt at making my first appearance before the representatives of the Russian people.

Stishinsky spoke first, for about an hour. His speech, smoothly and calmly delivered as usual, was essentially a formal report, full of many references (as the press was quick to note) to prove that neither the existing laws nor the decisions of the Senate permitted the allotment of any additional land to the peasants. Then came my turn. As I was beginning to speak I noticed Stolypin leave the assembly; but in view of his request I said to the assembled Duma: "Permit me to step outside the boundaries of the ministry in which I have the honor to work and to explain the matter as far as my intelligence and abilities allow, as one who has made the study of it his specialty." I ended the speech with these words: "Not by abolishing private ownership, not by repealing the right of private ownership of land, but by giving the peasants full possession of that land which they are now using shall the State Duma—a gathering of state-minded persons—earn the deep gratitude of the Russian people."

I had spoken in a voice clear and strong and commanding. It was the voice of a representative of the government, and the Duma had listened very attentively. If I may say so, my speech made a tremendous impression. However, the data I had used were just as important as the manner of speaking in making the speech effective. The leaders of the Duma, and especially the leaders of the Cadet party, saw immediately that their task of overthrowing the government was not to be so easy—that the government was still able to fight for itself. I believe they realized then the futility of their attempts to lower the prestige of the government, to overthrow it, and to take power into their own hands. From this realization it was but one step to personal hatred of the ministers comprising the government, and against these ministers they decided to concentrate their attacks.

After I had spoken, a Trudovik (the name adopted by the Socialist-Revolutionists in the Duma) requested the Chairman of the Duma not to permit speeches by "outsiders." Dolgorukov evidently did not understand what I had said to evoke this remark, for he answered in a puzzled tone that as far as he was aware no outsider had been permitted to speak.

The next speaker was Herzenstein (if I remember rightly), a Cadet. His arguments were so very weak and based upon intentional perversions of points I had made that I was eager to answer him. But as I waited for an opportunity to do so I became increasingly excited. My head went suddenly empty, and despite every mental effort I could not decide what I should say or how I should deliver my counter-attack. I was seized with a premonition of certain failure, and such failure would have destroyed completely the impression made by my first speech. It would seem, however, that the Duma leaders feared what I might say in rebuttal to Herzenstein, lest it should ruin them completely in the eyes of the many peasant representatives. Fortunately for me, therefore, they proposed and carried a motion of adjournment, although it was quite early and the sessions usually ended much later. My lucky star and my adversaries had saved me from failure. The land question was not discussed again in the Duma till four days later, and by then I had recovered my composure.

Because my speech had made an impression upon the Duma, Stolypin was displeased with me for making it and considered himself insulted. He went directly from the Duma to see Goremykin and announced that he wished to tender his resignation, since he could not permit that his assistant and not himself should appear before the Duma in matters under his direction. He was especially hurt, as Goremykin explained to me the next day, because the Council of Ministers had chosen me to speak on the land problem over Stolypin's opposition. In my opinion Stolypin had some grounds for feeling as he did. In the first place, Stishinsky, the other person who addressed the Duma on the land question, was the head of the Chief Administration of Land Management, that is the head of a ministry and not its second ranking representative; second, Stolypin himself had not yet spoken from the tribune of the Duma; third, the land problem was the most important problem of the time. Goremykin did not accept Stolypin's resignation; he managed to pacify him in some way and, in speaking of the matter to me, asked me to do all in my power to smooth over the misunderstanding.

Meanwhile the State Duma had learned of the incident and had decided to permit representatives of the ministries to speak only as acknowledged spokesmen of the ministers. The leaders of the Duma probably intended by this regulation to prevent me from speaking and answering criticism. I learned of this turn of affairs in the Duma itself from a clerk of the Ministry of the Interior who was on duty in the Duma during its sessions. He also told me that Stolypin would not attend that particular session and charged me to speak for the ministry.

My first speech had been published, and in the intervening three days the leaders of the Duma had had a chance to study it and to prepare their replies. Even so the criticism of it by Petrunkevich, a Cadet leader, was neither clever nor eloquent. For my own part, I had remembered my previous confusion when faced with speaking impromptu and had prepared my answers to speeches as yet unmade. In this I had been unexpectedly helped by one of my former colleagues in the Peasant Section, Baron A. F. Meyendorff (later Vice-Chairman of the Fourth Duma), who sent me a magazine containing a speech Herzenstein had made at a zemstvo convention in Moscow in April. This speech had dealt with the agrarian question, and in it Herzenstein had tried to prove the patent absurdity of expropriating private lands; he had pointed out that the presence of representatives of landowners in legislative institutions was important, since it facilated the fight against representatives of capital and industry. In further preparing myself I had made use of petitions to the Peasant Land Bank from some Cadet members of the Duma who were in favor of land expropriation; the petitioners had requested the Bank immediately to purchase their lands. One of these petitions was especially insistent. It had been sent in by D. D. Protopopov, a member of the Duma and marshal of the nobility of one of the uezds of Samara Gubernia; his signature was conspicuous among the thirty-three who had signed the Duma project for agrarian reform. Thus armed, I faced the Duma with confidence.

When I mounted the tribune, I was greeted with cries of "Retire!". (Stishinsky was usually accorded a similar welcome.) I can still see the member Zhilkin in one of the upper seats shouting, "Retire! Retire! Retire!" and, as he finished, hiding his head under the desk with which all seats were supplied. His shouts let loose a terrific din and yelling, so that I was obliged to fold my arms and make it apparent that I would wait until quiet was restored. I was just as little inclined to renounce my right to speak as I was willing to speak while they were so noisy. In the end I was given a good hearing. My remarks were brief but successful. When confronted with the fact that he had changed his views, Herzenstein declared that at the zemstvo convention he had been discussing theories, whereas now the Duma was engaged in practical work. He sought a way out of his dilemma by saying something to the effect that at any rate his writings were read, which in itself was a victory.

After the debates on the agrarian question the Duma changed its methods of carrying out its program. At first it had acted with a measure of outward decency and propriety toward the government. After the government's answer to the Duma address, the Duma's attitude had become hostile. But now, after the debates on the land question, it adopted definitely a revolutionary course of action. This was undoubtedly due to the fact that the Duma had become convinced that by opposition alone it would not be able to seize power from the crown and that in order to force the Monarch to make further concessions, the events which had led up to the Manifesto of October 17 would have to be repeated. In short, the Cadet party wanted to have the Socialists pull its chestnuts out of the fire. The Cadets did not realize that once the revolution began it would not stop until it had run to extremes which would claim them and the entire bourgeois intelligentsia for its victims. This was proved by the Revolution of 1917.

So the Trudoviks came to the fore—as did persons of shady reputation, such as Aladin, once a guide in the low dives of London and later, during the war and the Revolution of 1917, a hireling of the English secret service. This individual, who spent much of his time in flagrant, open debauchery, made fiery speeches from the tribune of the Duma, denouncing the government and going so far as to say: "Blood is flowing in the shadow of the Imperial mantle." But even this did not cause the chairman of the session to call the speaker to order.

It is difficult to say what the government should have done. Anything, I suppose, but play the silent game it played. Not being a minister, I was unable to do anything except to laugh openly in the faces of orators who stormed from the tribune of the Duma. It was quite convenient to do so, as the government's seats were right next to the tribune. On one occasion, before the opening of the session, I said to a minister sitting next to me, and loudly enough so that several Duma members in the passage separating the government seats from the places of the deputies could hear me: "Let us listen, to the ravings of these hooligans." This, together with my speech on the agrarian question, made many members of the Duma, especially their leaders, hate me. I was aware that neither Goremykin nor Stolypin approved of this course of action. They, especially Stolypin, thought that the government should preserve an Olympian calm toward the Duma; but I could not bear to conduct myself in that way. I continued to act as I saw fit, especially since no member of the government said anything to me about it.

Soon after the debates on the agrarian question the Duma debated the government's suggested appropriation of funds to provide relief for regions suffering from famine. On this issue the Duma was placed in a difficult position: it had either to approve the appropriation—that is, to agree with the government—or to risk arousing the discontent of the population by refusing the appropriation for relief and for assistance in sowing the winter crops. Stolypin decided to speak to the Duma in person on this matter, and thus I was deprived of a chance of giving the Duma a piece of my mind.

I confess that I had some misgivings regarding Stolypin's success before the Duma. He was not too well acquainted with the organization of relief and, besides, I suspected him of being a poor orator because of a certain defect in enunciation, if for no other reason. But I was mistaken. From the tribune, Stolypin spoke loudly, distinctly, and masterfully. Also his appearance was a great asset: he was tall and slender and looked not only dignified but even majestic.

His speech was somewhat deficient in factual material, but was permeated by an inner conviction and sincerity and contained some happy phrases and figures of speech. He endeavored to separate the Socialist orators from the Cadets, with whose leaders he was at that time on friendly terms. He created no ill feeling on the part of the Duma toward himself. All this certainly must be construed as marking a successful speech. The suggested appropriation was granted, even though accompanied by several resolutions denouncing the government.

But things could not go on as they were. The government had either to come to some agreement with the Duma or to dismiss it altogether.

On this issue the members of the government entertained different views. The minority, including Izvolsky and D. F. Trepov, were inclined to compromise with the Duma, but for different reasons. Izvolsky, for instance, was completely ignorant of conditions in Russia, largely as a result of prolonged sojourns abroad. He was fascinated by Western European customs and was openly sympathetic to parliamentary forms of government. In the interest of such a form of government he conducted conversations with the Cadet leaders and workers—Miliukov and Company—and tried to persuade the Tsar that the only sound course of action was to transfer all authority to the Cadets. When the question of dissolving the Duma was discussed by the Council of Ministers he opposed the measure, as was to be expected, and pointed out that, in the West, legislative chambers had been dissolved because of a refusal to approve budgets or legislative projects considered necessary by the government but that no legislative body in the West was ever dissolved because of its members' speeches or resolutions. However, as the Duma became more and more radical and increased its revolutionary propaganda, thus demoralizing the country, and as Izvolsky saw more clearly that he was likely to lose his ministerial portfolio under a Cadet regime, he experienced a change of mind. One evening he appeared in the Council of Ministers, late as usual, and, getting astride a chair, solemnly announced that he now considered the dissolution of the Duma possible in principle, since "a few days ago the Portuguese legislature was dissolved for no reason except its general revolutionary spirit." This incredible reasoning made the action of tiny Portugal a criterion of political procedure. According to this logic Russia was permitted to adopt this or that measure only on condition that an analogous measure had been adopted by a foreign country, no matter how insignificant. Yet such reasoning did not provoke even a smile in the Russian Council of Ministers. Those who favored the dissolution of the Duma were evidently so glad that Izvolsky had at last been able to see their point of view that they were willing to overlook the reason for his change of opinion.

Goremykin's behavior in this matter was peculiar. Openly, he neither opposed nor supported the dissolution, and gave the general impression that he would take no action. Secretly, however, he painstakingly prepared the ground at Peterhof for such a move.

Stolypin also kept his own counsel. He had no direct dealings with the Cadet leaders but was apprised of the steps which Izvolsky had undertaken. Also, through the Duma members from Saratov Gubernia (mainly through N. N. Lvov), he tried to persuade the Cadets that he personally held liberal ideas and ideals.

The Cadets, headed by Miliukov, were perfectly sure that they had won their game. They thought it was no longer a question of securing power but only of becoming sole masters of the situation. Accordingly they announced that they would not have Stolypin as a member of their government; his portfolio would be given to one of their own men, the famous Prince Lvov, who in 1917 became the head of their government and used his position to effect the destruction of all authority in the country.

Meanwhile the Right wing of the Council of Ministers used every means in its power to hasten the dissolution of the Duma. It endeavored to enlist the assistance of D. F. Trepov, who continued to enjoy the confidence of the Tsar; but all its efforts in this direction were in vain. Trepov's political convictions were founded not on reason but on sentiment and were therefore unstable. He was concerned with only one thing: to protect the person of the Tsar and his family. He belonged not to the government but to the court, and considered himself beyond the reach of any political party as long as the Tsar's power existed. Trepov was no longer interested—or so he thought—in leaving state power in the hands of the bureaucrats. Hence he negotiated with the Cadet leaders. This circumstance caused the Cadet party leaders, who overestimated the importance of Trepov, to believe that very soon complete power would fall into their hands. Meanwhile the Duma continued its government baiting. Prince Shirinsky and Schwanebach were most anxious to have it dissolved. They called on me one day and suggested that I go with them to Goremykin. We found Goremykin at home and, as usual, unengaged. What means he used to prevent anyone from disturbing him I do not know, but the fact remains that he was usually alone.

It was a hot day in July. Goremykin was sitting on a sofa near a window looking out on the Fontanka on whose other bank stood the Engineer Palace. He was dressed in a pongee suit but was wet with perspiration. His smooth, round, pale face and his pale, protruding, expressionless eyes really reminded one of a whitefish; in fact, in some senatorial circles he was so nicknamed. On a small table at his elbow stood a dish of milk curds which he was eating lazily and mechanically. He listened with the greatest indifference to the expostulations of Shirinsky and Schwanebach to the effect that the Duma had to be dissolved immediately. He did not even trouble to argue the point. In vain did Shirinsky unleash his favorite incomprehensible metaphors. In vain did Schwanebach proudly quote examples from the history of the French Revolution. Goremykin remained unmoved.

I was sitting aside near the window. Goremykin's impassivity made me furious. I had a great desire somehow to ruffle his calm.

"Ivan Logginovich," I suddenly exclaimed, pointing outside, "do you see that?"

"Where? What?" Goremykin woke up, evidently supposing that I had detected some danger from which he was not entirely protected.

"Over there, on the other bank."

"Well, what about it?"

"The Engineer Palace."

"What of it?" asked Goremykin, composed again.

"This of it! Had the event which took place there on March 11, 1801 (the assassination of Emperor Paul I), been postponed until March 12, it would not have taken place at all, for on the 12th Arakcheev, especially called to St. Petersburg by Paul, was already at the gates of the city and would have been able to break up the plot. The same holds true of the Duma. Today it may be possible to dissolve it. Whether this will be possible in a week's time, we do not know."

"You are right," said Goremykin, slightly moved.

I doubt if what I said had any influence on bringing Goremykin to a decision, for he was a man who arrived at decisions quite independently and as a result of his own deliberations. However, on the next day the Council of Ministers adopted a resolution calling for the dissolution of the State Duma, and on the day following Goremykin went to Peterhof with the minutes of the Council of Ministers.

When the members of the Council learned of this they (with the exception of Stolypin) assembled at Goremykin's house to await his return. About eight o'clock he arrived. He entered the room, in which the ministers were waiting, with a notably cheerful air and quoted a sentence from a letter of Madame de Sévigné to her daughter: " 'Je vous le donne en cent, je vous le donne en mille, vous n'avez pas idée de la nouvelle que je vous apporte!' I am no longer Chairman of the Council." Then he announced that the ukase dissolving the Duma had been signed and that the new Chairman of the Council was to be Stolypin, who was then at the palace but was expected any moment. Shortly after Goremykin's announcement Launits, Governor of St. Petersburg, arrived and announced that no demonstrations were expected when the Duma was dissolved but as a precaution he had recalled several cavalry regiments of the guards from their summer quarters to St. Petersburg. He also suggested that some of the ministers, such as Stishinsky, who resided in private houses, should move for the time being to official buildings in order to make easier the work of the police. Stolypin soon arrived, but as he had no further news the ministers dispersed.

This is what had happened. Goremykin had twice reported to the Tsar on the necessity of dissolving the Duma and had twice secured the Tsar's approval. But when he had eventually presented the text of a ukase for the Tsar's signature, he had learned that the Tsar had changed his mind. When he left for Peterhof on July 8 Goremykin had resolved to get the Tsar's signature at any cost. So he took with him the text of a ukase dissolving the Duma and also his own resignation, which he intended to tender to the Tsar should the latter refuse to sign the ukase. Somewhere on the way he learned that it had already been decided that he should resign in favor of Stolypin, and that Stolypin had had orders to appear at Peterhof....

40. Peter Stolypin (1862-1911):

a characterization

by Alexander Izvolsky

ALEXANDER IZVOLSKY (1856-1919), who held the post of Russian Foreign Minister in Peter Stolypin's cabinet, 1906-1910, was a strong supporter of the Franco-Russian Alliance and the Anglo-Russian Entente. In his capacity as Russian ambassador in Paris, 1910-1914, he shared the responsibility for the outbreak of World War I. Although Izvolsky voiced his unqualified approval of the oft-maligned Peter Stolypin's agrarian program, he disapproved his high-handed methods of implementing it. Stolypin was misunderstood by his contemporaries, especially by the Cadets, partly because of his ruthless suppression of violence during the Revolution of 1905-1907. In disposing of the *Mir*, it was his objective to create in Russia a nation of farmers instead of landless peasants. His agrarian policy provoked widespread resistance among the large landowners of the Right and the Social Revolutionaries of the Left. It nevertheless proved highly successful, and had Stolypin not been assassinated in 1911, Russia might have had a substantial agrarian middle class. Soviet historians, particularly conscious of this implication of his agrarian policy, have conducted serious research in this area in recent years. Their unqualified hostility toward Stolypin is based in part on the acknowledgment that the success of his program would have forestalled in Russia a social revolution of Bolshevik vintage.

The characterization of Stolypin presented below is from *Recollections of a Foreign Minister (Memoirs of Alexander Izvolsky)*, translated by Charles Louis Seeger (Garden City, New York: Doubleday, Page and Company, 1921), pp. 87-94.

Pierre Stolypin was of gentle origin and belonged by birth and relationship to the high society of St. Petersburg; his father had occupied one of the great positions at Court and his mother was the daughter of General Prince Gortchakoff, who was commander-in-chief of the Russian Army at Sebastopol. From my youth upward I was in cordial relations with his family, and I became acquainted with him when we were finishing our studies, he at the University and I at the Imperial Lyceum. We were of about the same age, and I remember him as a charming young man, greatly loved and respected by his comrades, a little awkward and timid on account of a slight deformity; his right hand was stiff, as the result of an accident, and he made use of it with some difficulty. He married when very young, and in romantic fashion, the fiancée of his elder brother, who was killed in a duel and who on his death-bed placed his brother's hand in that of the young girl whom he tenderly loved. Instead of entering the military or civil service of the State, as was the custom of young men of his station in life, he retired to his properties, situated in one of the western provinces of Russia, and led the life of a rich country gentleman. After some time he accepted the duties of Maréchal de la Noblesse of his district. The marshals of the nobility—who were elected in the central provinces of Russia, or appointed by the Government in those provinces where the Russian elements were in conflict with the Polish—were not only expected to care for the interests of their body, but were clothed with general administrative functions of considerable extent. Having shown talent and energy in the performance of his duties, M. Stolypin was offered by the Government the post of Prefect of the Province of Saratoff, which was disturbed at that period by the revolutionary agitation. He decided to accept, in a spirit of duty to his country and his sovereign rather than of ambition, and during the time that he occupied that difficult position he proved himself to be an excellent administrator, as well as a man of remarkable courage and *sang-froid*. Like most of the governors of provinces at that time, he was subjected to the danger of assassination, and on one occasion he seized and disarmed a revolutionary who had fired several shots at him without effect.

An anecdote is told of his presence of mind and his domination over a crowd. A mutiny had broken out in one of the quarters of the town at the instigation of certain revolutionary leaders, whose chief had lately been a soldier in one of the regiments of the local garrison, and M. Stolypin knew that he had been an officer's servant. Before resorting to force, the Governor resolved to try persuasion; he arrived at the scene of the disorders, and perceiving in the front row of the crowd the aforesaid ringleader, he walked straight toward him and, before haranguing the mutineers, tossed him quickly his cloak as it slipped from his shoulders, and ordered him to hold it. The ex-orderly, accustomed to passive obedience, did as he was told before he realized it, and so lost in an instant, by the mere performance of a servile act, all prestige in the eyes of the mob, who presently became docile and yielded to the injunctions of the energetic Governor.

It was this very reputation for energy that commended M. Stolypin to the Emperor's choice for the office of Minister of the Interior. Totally out of his element in the bureaucratic world of the capital, this country gentleman of a rather provincial aspect appeared at first to play an insignificant part at the meetings of the Council of Ministers, but very soon his robust and original personality imposed itself strongly upon the routine functionaries who composed the majority of the Cabinet. As for me, I fell a victim to his charm at once, and was happy to find among my chance companions a man to whom I felt drawn by a communion of ideas and political convictions, for at that time M. Stolypin appeared to me to be an especially sincere partisan of the new order of things, resolved to collaborate with the Duma in every way possible. Like him, for reasons which I will explain later, I was a stranger to the bureaucratic environment of St. Petersburg, and felt more in sympathy with the members of the provincial nobility and the zemstvos, who had sent to the Duma some of their best representatives. The more M. Goremykin, sustained by the reactionary Ministers, emphasized his hostile attitude toward the assembly, the more closely I drew to M. Stolypin, with whom I formed, so to speak, the left wing of the Cabinet.

M. Stolypin was gifted with a very clear and healthy turn of mind that enabled him to comprehend the general significance of matters submitted to him for decision, and to master them in their details as well; his capacity for work and his physical and moral power of endurance were prodigious. Accustomed as he was to the duties of a landowner, engaged in the development of vast properties, and, afterward, to the activity in practical affairs that was requisite for the efficient administration of a province, he had little patience with bureaucratic routine and astonished everyone by the simplicity and good sense with which he attacked the most arduous problems of State, that had been the subject of many discussions at the meetings of the Council of Ministers.

A quality which was lacking, unfortunately, in M. Stolypin's character —and he was conscious of this himself—was a broad culture, in the European sense of the word. I do not mean to say that he was devoid of education, for he had pursued serious studies at the University, was well-read and well-informed in a general way; but his opinions on the great political and social questions which he was called upon to consider had not passed through the sieve of modern scientific criticism, and his state of mind was strongly influenced by certain intellectual currents which prevailed in Russia during his youth, and which may be summed up in what, by common consent, albeit improperly, is termed "Slavophilism."

Reserving for further and more detailed discussion a theory that has had so great an influence on the foreign and domestic policies of Russia, it will suffice for the present to say that Slavophilism condemns European civilization *en bloc*, as being corrupted by atheism and an excess of individualism. It attributes to the Russian nation the providential mission of creating a superior culture; in the domain of religion the Slavophiles proclaim that the Russian Orthodox Church alone has remained faithful to the precepts of Christ; and in the political domain they denounce the reforms which Peter the Great borrowed from the Occident and demand a return to the "national" systems of the Muscovite period. One of their principal doctrines has for its basis a claim that the commune, or *Mir,* is an original invention of Russian genius, and they find in communal proprietorship the essential foundation for the social and economic organization of Russia.

I will tell how, and thanks to what influences—after having been attracted by the arguments of the Slavophiles, together with almost all the other men of my generation and M. Stolypin's—I freed myself from their obscure teachings at a comparatively early period; as for M. Stolypin, without professing their faith to excess, he remained an adherent in many respects. If he had enjoyed the opportunity, as I did, to study the political and social life of Western Europe, I am certain that his clear and vigorous mind would have rejected all their errors ultimately. In dealing with one of the questions most vital to Russia—that of agrarian organization—he did not hesitate to abandon the fatal theory of the *Mir,* cause of so many evils, and to adopt, against violent opposition, the system of small individual ownership. On the other hand, unfortunately, he was never able to rise superior to certain particularly dangerous conceptions of the Slavophiles, and so it was that, in spite of all my efforts to dissuade him, he veered toward a narrow and even exaggerated nationalism, which had the most lamentable consequences, and finally caused the rupture of our political relations.

But that which constituted the incontestable and undisputed superiority of M. Stolypin and established from the outset his ascendancy over his colleagues was a rare *ensemble* of qualities, both of heart and character. I have referred already to the reputation that he had acquired for courage and *sang-froid,* of which he gave example later in a still more striking manner. These two traits were the expression of a vital energy that I have seldom seen equalled, especially in an individual of my race; however, when meeting him for the first time, one was impressed and attracted by a simplicity and a sweetness which gave to his personality an irresistible charm, and, upon further acquaintance, one discovered in him a high-mindedness and a nobility of soul that the exercise of a power, which, at certain times, became even dictatorial, never in the least affected. His exalted and chivalrous conception of duty made of him a servant, devoted to the point of martyrdom, of his sovereign and his country, but, at the same time, he was so proud of his name and jealous of his liberty that he ever maintained, toward a court and a bureaucracy which regarded him in the light of an intruder and were more or less hostile to him from the beginning, an attitude of reserve and independence to which one was little accustomed in that sphere, and which,

I am sorry to say, was never appreciated at its worth by the Czar and his intimates.

The portrait which I have essayed to draw of this distinguished man would be incomplete were I to omit to mention his marvellous gift of oratory; in his first address to the Duma he revealed himself as a public speaker of extraordinary power. I used the word "revealed" because, up to that moment, no one had the slightest knowledge of his talent, for, prior to the meeting of the first Duma, there was no school in Russis in which parliamentary oratory could be acquired. We have seen that the debates in the assemblies of the zemstvos were of a rather familiar and informal character, unfavourable to the cultivation of an oratorical style. The Russian, as we have since discovered, especially during the period following the fall of the monarchy, is not only endowed with a natural gift of eloquence, but is, alas, too much inclined to abuse this gift to the detriment of action. I have no hesitation in repeating that the use of the rostrum produced an unhealthy effect upon the debates of the Duma, but, in the case of M. Stolypin, it became a mighty instrument of government. In the assemblies of the zemstvos, in which he had taken part before he became a Minister, he had been trained to speak without preparation, and the most remarkable speeches pronounced by him in the Duma were purely *extempore*. Oftener than not he mounted the tribune on the spur of a sudden impulse, without manuscript and even without notes, and for more than an hour held his hearers spell-bound by his fiery eloquence, accentuated by an irresistible sincerity; at such times a slight fault of enunciation, common to his mother's family, disappeared completely, and it was with a clear and vibrant voice that he pronounced those "winged words" with which he was so often inspired, and which became a rallying cry for thousands of Russians who read his speeches. It was an invaluable advantage for the Government to be able to oppose orators of the strength of M. Stolypin, and the clearness of M. Kokovtzoff, to their adversaries, who, although they counted among their number some very notable speakers in the first Duma, could boast of none that were superior or even equal to those two eloquent Ministers.

41. Maurice Paléologue on the Revolution

MAURICE GEORGES PALÉOLOGUE, French diplomat and writer, was France's ambassador in St. Petersburg, 1914-1917. His mission was to consolidate the Franco-Russian Alliance, and, following the outbreak of World War I, to secure effective military action by Russia on the Eastern Front. Paléologue was intimately acquainted with Russian leaders, both civilian and military. Below is an account of his conversation on June 2, 1915, with Putilov, head of the largest munitions plant in Russia, who prophetically described the coming of revolution and the certain violence of its course. An acute observer of contemporary events, Paléologue has also left an eye-witness account of the opening months of the Revolution.

From *An Ambassador's Memoirs,* by Maurice Paléologue, Vol. I, (4th ed., New York: George H. Doran Company, 1925), 348–350; Vol. III: pp. 213-215, 217, 221-223, 228, 232-233, 272-273, 295-296, 322-324. Reprinted by permission.

Forecast of Revolution

Wednesday, June 2, 1915

I dined quite privately this evening with the most important metallurgist and financier in Russia, the multi-millionaire Putilov. I always derive great pleasure and profit from my meetings with this business man whose psychology is most original. He possesses in a high degree the dominating characteristics of an American business man, the creative instinct and spirit of initiative, the craving for vast undertakings, a strict sense of reality and the feasible, values and forces. But he is none the less a Slav in certain intimate sides of his nature and the most pessimistic outlook I have yet met with in Russia.

He is one of the four industrials who are members of the Munitions Council, established at the War Ministry. His first impressions were simply deplorable. It is not merely a technical problem, a question of labour and output, which has to be solved. The whole administrative system of Russia must be reformed from top to bottom. We had not exhausted the subject when dinner was over.

The moment the cigars were lit champagne was brought and we discussed the future; he almost revelled in describing the fatal consequences of the imminent catastrophes and the silent work of decadence and dislocation which is undermining the Russian edifice:

"The days of Tsarism are numbered; it is lost, lost beyond hope. But Tsarism is the very framework of Russia and the sole bond of unity for the nation. Revolution is now inevitable; it is only waiting for a favourable opportunity. Such an opportunity will come with some military defeat, a famine in the provinces, a strike in Petrograd, a riot in Moscow, some scandal or tragedy at the palace. It doesn't matter now! In any case, the revolution isn't the worst peril threatening Russia. What is a revolution, strictly speaking? It is the substitution of one political system for another by violence. A revolution may be a great benefit to a nation if it can reconstruct after having destroyed. From that point of view the English and French Revolutions strike me as having been rather salutary. But with us revolution can only be destructive because the educated class is only a tiny minority, without organization, political experience, or contact with the masses. To my mind *that* is the greatest crime of Tsarism: it will not tolerate any centre of political life and activity outside its own bureaucracy. Its success in that way has been so great that the day the *tchinovniks* disappear the whole Russian State will dissolve. No doubt it will be the bourgeois, intellectuals, "Cadets" who give the signal for the revolution, thinking that they're saving Russia. But from the bourgeois revolution we shall at once descend to the working class revolution and soon after to the peasant revolution. And then will begin the most frightful anarchy, interminable anarchy, . . . ten years of anarchy! . . . We shall see the days of Pugatchev again, and perhaps worse!"

Eyewitness to Revolution

Tuesday, March 6, 1917

Petrograd is short of bread and wood, and the public is suffering want.

At a bakery on the Liteïny this morning I was struck by the sinister expression on the faces of the poor folk who were lined up in a queue, most of whom had spent the whole night there.

Pokrovski, to whom I mentioned the matter, did not conceal his anxiety. But what can be done! The transport crisis is certainly worse. The extreme cold (43°) which has all Russia in its grip has put more than twelve hundred engines out of action, owing to boiler tubes bursting, and there is a shortage of spare tubes as a result of strikes. Moreover, the snowfall of the last few weeks has been exceptionally heavy and there is also a shortage of labour in the villages to clear the permanent way. The result is that at the present moment fifty-seven thousand railway wagons cannot be moved.

Thursday, March 8, 1917

There has been great agitation in Petrograd all day. Processions have been parading the main streets. At several points the mob shouted for "Bread and peace!" At others it sang the Working Man's *Marseillaise*. In the Nevsky Prospekt there have been slight disorders. . . .

Friday, March 9, 1917

This morning the excitement in industrial circles took a violent form. Many bakeries were looted, especially in the Viborg Quarter and Vassili-Ostrov. At several points the Cossacks charged the crowd and killed a number of workmen.

Pokrovski has been confiding his anxieties to me:

"I should regard these disorders as of minor importance if my dear colleague at the Interior still retained a shred of common sense. But what can you do with a man who has lost all idea of reality for weeks, and confers with the shade of Rasputin every night? This very evening he's been spending hours in conjuring up the ghost of the *staretz!*"

Saturday, March 10, 1917

The hair-raising problem of food supplies has been investigated to-night by an "Extraordinary Council," which was attended by all the ministers (except the Minister of the Interior), the President of the Council of Empire, the President of the Duma and the Mayor of Petrograd. Protopopov did not condescend to take part in the conference; he was no doubt communing with the ghost of Rasputin.

Gendarmes, Cossacks and troops have been much in evidence all over the city. Until four o'clock in the afternoon the demonstrations gave rise to no untoward event. But the public soon began to get excited. The *Marseillaise* was sung, and red flags were paraded on which was written: *Down with the Government! . . . Down with Protopopov! . . . Down with the war! . . . Down with Germany! . . .* Shortly after five disorders began in the Nevsky Prospekt. Three demonstrators and three police officers were killed and about a hundred persons wounded. . . .

Sunday, March 11, 1917

. . . In spite of the warning of the Military Governor, the mob is becoming increasingly disorderly and aggressive; in the Nevsky Prospekt it is getting larger every hour. Four or five times the troops have been compelled to fire to escape being brushed aside. There are scores of dead.

Towards the end of the day, two of my secret informers whom I had sent into the industrial quarters returned with the report that the ruthless measures of repression adopted have taken the heart out of the workmen, who were saying that they had "had enough of going to the Nevsky Prospekt to be killed!"

But another informer tells me that the Volhynian Regiment of the Guard refused to fire. This is a fresh factor in the situation and reminds me of the sinister warning of October 31. . . .

Monday, March 12, 1917

At half-past eight this morning, just as I finished dressing, I heard a strange and prolonged din which seemed to come from the Alexander Bridge. I looked out: there was no one on the bridge, which usually presents such a busy scene. But, almost immediately, a disorderly mob carrying red flags appeared at the end which is on the right bank of the Neva, and a regiment came towards it from the opposite side. It looked as if there would be a violent collision, but on the contrary the two bodies coalesced. The army was fraternizing with revolt.

Shortly afterwards, someone came to tell me that the Volhynian regiment of the Guard had mutinied during the night, killed its officers and was parading the city, calling on the people to take part in the revolution and trying to win over the troops who still remain loyal.

At ten o'clock there was a sharp burst of firing and flames could be seen rising somewhere on the Liteïny Prospekt which is quite close to the embassy. Then silence.

Accompanied by my military attaché, Lieutenant-Colonel Lavergne, I went out to see what was happening. Frightened inhabitants were scattering through the streets. There was indescribable confusion at the corner of the Liteïny. Soldiers were helping civilians to erect a barricade. Flames mounted from the Law Courts. The gates of the arsenal burst open with a crash. Suddenly the crack of machine-gun fire split the air: it was the regulars who had just taken up position near the Nevsky Prospekt. The revolutionaries replied. I had seen enough to have no doubt as to what was coming. Under a hail of bullets I returned to the embassy with Lavergne who had walked calmly and slowly to the hottest corner out of sheer bravado. . . .

One piece of bad news followed another. The Law Courts had become nothing but an enormous furnace; the Arsenal on the Liteïny, the Ministry of the Interior, the Military Government building, the Minister of the Courts' offices, the headquarters of the Detective Force, the too, too famous Okhrana, and a score of police-stations were in flames; the prisons were open and all the prisoners had been liberated; the Fortress of SS. Peter and Paul was undergoing a siege and the Winter Palace was occupied. Fighting was in progress in every part of the city. . . .

March 13
... I have successively learned that Prince Golitzin, (President of the Council) the Metropolitan Pitirim, Sturmer, Dobrovolsky, Protopopov, etc., have been arrested. The livid glow of fresh fires can be seen at various points. The Fortress of SS. Peter and Paul has become the headquarters of the revolt. Fierce fighting is taking place around the Admiralty, where the War Minister, the Naval Minister and several high officials have taken refuge. In all other parts of the city the insurgents are ruthlessly tracking down "traitors," police officials and gendarmes. The shooting has sometimes been so brisk in the streets round the embassy that my *dvorniks* have refused to take my telegrams to the General Post Office, the only one which is still working; I have had to rely on a petty officer of the French Navy who is on leave in Petrograd and is not afraid of bullets.

About five o'clock, a high official, K————, came to tell me that the executive committee of the Duma is trying to form a "provisional government," but that President Rodzianko, Gutchkov, Shulgin and Maklakov are utterly taken aback by the anarchical behaviour of the army.

"They never imagined a revolution like this," my informer added; "they hoped to direct it and keep it within bounds through the army. The troops recognize no leader now and are spreading terror throughout the city...."

March 14, 1917
... Shortly afterwards the Potemkin Palace was the scene of another and equally melancholy spectacle. A body of officers and men, who had been sent by the garrison of Tsarskoïe-Selo, signified its adherence to the revolution.

At the head were the Cossacks of the Escort, those magnificent horsemen who are the flower of the *Kasatchesvo,* the proud and privileged élite of the Imperial Guard. Then came the Regiment of His Majesty, the *légion sacrée* which is recruited by selection from all the units of the Guard and whose special function it is to secure the personal safety of their sovereigns. Next came His Majesty's Railway Regiment which has the duty of conducting the imperial trains and watching over the safety of their Majesties when travelling. At the end of the procession marched the Police of the Imperial Palaces, chosen satellites who have to guard the imperial residences from within and thus participate daily in the intimate, private life of their masters. All of these men, officers and privates alike, have vowed their devotion to the new authority—whose very name they do not know—as if they could not embrace the chains of a new servitude too soon.

While this shameful piece of news was being told him, my mind went back to the grave Swiss who let themselves be cut to pieces on the steps of the Tuileries on August 10, 1792, though Louis XVI was not their sovereign and when they greeted him they did not call him: *Tsar batiushka,* "Our Little Father the Tsar!"

In the course of the evening Count S——— called on me to ask for information about the situation. I told him incidentally of the humiliating submission of the Tsarskoïe-Selo garrison at the Tauride Palace. At first he would not believe me. After long and mournful reflection he continued:

"What a horrible, horrible thing. The Guard troops who took part in that demonstration have disgraced themselves for ever. But perhaps the fault is not entirely theirs. In their continual attendance on Their Majesties they've seen too many things they ought not to have seen; they know too much about Rasputin. . ."

As I wrote yesterday when on the subject of Kchechinskaïa, a revolution is always more or less a summary and a sanction. . . .

Monday, March 26, 1917

Alexander Nicolaïevitch Benois, the painter and historian of art and a friend of whom I see quite a good deal, has given me an unexpected call.

Descended from a French family which settled in Russia somewhere about 1820, he is the most cultivated man whom I know here, and one of the most distinguished.

I have spent many a delightful hour in his Vassili-Ostrov studio, talking with him *de omni re scibili et quibusdam aliis.* Even from a political point of view, his conversation has often been valuable to me, as he is on terms of close friendship not only with the élite of the artists, men of letters and university professors but also with the chief leaders of the liberal opposition and the "Cadet" party. Many a time have I obtained from him interesting information about those circles the éntrée to which was formerly very difficult, and in fact almost closed to me. His personal opinions, which are always judicious and far-sighted, are all the more valuable in my eyes because he is eminently representative of that active and well-informed class of professors, savants, doctors, artists, men of letters and publicists which is styled the *intelligentzia.*

He came to see me about three o'clock, just as I was preparing to go out.

He looked grave and sat down with a weary sigh:

"Forgive me if I inconvenience you, but yesterday evening some of my friends and I were indulging in such gloomy reflections that I couldn't help coming to tell you about them."

Then he gave me a vivid and, alas, only too accurate picture of the effects of anarchy on the people, the prevailing apathy of the governing classes and the loss of discipline in the army. He ended with the observation:

"However painful such an admission must be to me, I feel I'm only doing my duty in coming to tell you that the war cannot go on. Peace must be made at the earliest possible moment. Of course, I realize that the honour of Russia is involved in her alliances, and you know me well enough to allow that I appreciate the full meaning of that aspect. But necessity is the law of history. No one is compelled to do the impossible!". . .

Wednesday, April 11, 1917

I had the leader of the "Cadet" party, Basil Maklakov, Princess Dolgoruky, Prince Scipio Borghese and Alexei Nicholaïevitch Benois, the painter and art critic, to lunch with me to-day.

Maklakov, who has seen as much of the revolution at close quarters as anyone, told us all about its beginnings.

"Not one of us," he said, "foresaw the immense scale of the movement; no one expected such a cataclysm. Of course we knew that the imperial regime was rotten; but we never suspected that it was as rotten as it has proved to be. That's why nothing was ready. I was discussing it only yesterday with Maxim Gorky and Cheidze; they haven't recovered from the shock even yet."

"So this combustion of all Russia has been spontaneous?" asked Borghese.

"Yes, absolutely spontaneous." . . .

Monday, April 30, 1917

The forces of anarchy are swelling and raging with the uncontrollable force of an equinoctial tide.

All discipline has vanished in the army. Officers are everywhere being insulted, ragged and—if they object—massacred. It is calculated that more than 1,200,000 deserters are wandering over Russia, filling the stations, storming the carriages, stopping the trains, and thus paralysing all the military and civil transport services. At junctions in particular they seem positively to swarm. A train arrives: they make its occupants get out, take their places and compel the stationmaster to switch the train off in any direction they like. Or it may be a train laden with troops for the front. The men get out at some station, arrange a meeting, confer together for an hour or two, and wind up by demanding to be taken back to their starting point.

In the Civil Service there is no less disorder. The heads have lost all authority over their subordinates, who in any case spend most of their time in speechifying in the *Soviets* or demonstrating in the streets.

Of course the food shortage shows no sign of improvement, if indeed it is not getting worse. And yet there are in the stations of Petrograd four thousand wagons loaded with flour. But the lorry drivers refuse to work. Then the *Soviet* publishes an eloquent appeal:

"Comrade Lorry-drivers!
"Do not imitate the infamies of the old regime! Do not let your
brothers die of hunger! Unload the wagons!"

The comrade lorry-drivers answer as one man: "We will not unload the wagons, because it is not our pleasure to do so. We are free!"

Then when the day comes in which it pleases the comrade lorry-drivers to unload the wagons of flour, it is the turn of the bakers to refuse to work. Then the *Soviet* publishes an eloquent appeal:

"Comrade Bakers!
"Do not imitate the infamies of the old regime! Do not let your
brothers die of hunger! Make bread!"

The comrade bakers answer as one man: "We will not make bread, because it is not our pleasure to do so. We are free!"

In the streets many of the *izvochtchiks* are refusing to keep to the left, because they are free. But as they are not agreed about it, the result is continual collision.

The police, which was the main, if not the only, framework of this enormous country, has simply ceased to exist, for the "Red Guard," a kind of municipal militia instituted in some of the large cities, is nothing but a hoard of outcasts and apaches. And as all the prisons have been opened, it is miraculous that more attacks on persons and property have not been reported.

Yet agrarian disorder is greatly on the increase, particularly in the districts of Kursk, Voronej, Tambov and Saratov.

One of the oddest signs of the general derangement is the attitude of the *Soviets* and their following towards the prisoners of war.

At Schlusselburg the German prisoners are allowed to go about unattended in the town. Within a distance of five versts from the front one of my officers has seen bodies of Austrian prisoners walking about without let or hindrance. To crown everything, a regional conference of German, Turkish and Austro-Hungarian prisoners has demanded—and successfully—that the "eight-hour day should be applied to them!"

42. Kerensky: the Provisional

Government and the Allies

ALEXANDER F. KERENSKY (1881-   ) served as a "Trudovik" (Labor Group) delegate in the Third and Fourth Dumas, in the Provisional Government successively as Minister of Justice, War Minister and Prime Minister, and in the Petrograd Soviet as Vice-President. His works include *The Prelude to Bolshevism, The Catastrophe,* and *The Crucifixion of Liberty.* Together with Robert Paul Browder, Kerensky collected and edited the documents of the first period of the Russian Revolution in *The Russian Provisional Government, 1917* (3 Vols., Stanford University Press, 1961).

Kerensky emerged as one of the most controversial figures of the Russian Revolution, highly popular in the beginning, especially with the army, but cursed by conservative elements ever since for the failure of the Provisional Government and the triumph of the Bolsheviks. Although critical of Allied policy toward the new Russia, he conceived and carried out the unsuccessful "July offensive" against the Central Powers to strengthen the position of his government vis-à-vis the Allies. Following that episode, he was responsible for the appointment as military commander of General Kornilov, whose conspiracy contributed substantially to the downfall of the Provisional Government.

Asked in recent years what action he would take if he could retrace his steps, Kerensky told the editors that the only way he could have retained power was to have done what the Bolsheviks did —make a separate peace with Germany and establish a dictatorship, neither of which he was constitutionally capable of doing. Defending himself against his enemies' allegation that he was "weak," Kerensky justifiably pointed out that Kolchak and Denikin, who were thought to be "strong," who were backed by disciplined armies and substantial Allied aid, were likewise defeated by the Bolsheviks.

Kerensky was understandably bitter toward Russia's Allies for their failure to lend outright support to the Provisional Government. The excerpts below, which explain his difficulties with the Allies, are from *The Crucifixion of Liberty* (New York: The John Day Company, 1934), pp. 333-360. Reprinted by permission.

Without a clear understanding of the fact that the February Revolution happened during a war, that the war went on, and that, apart from the enemy troops at the front, we were bombarded from the rear with human bombs loaded by the external enemy and by Lenin with poisonous propaganda—without a clear understanding of this situation, it is impossible to see in its true light the tragic story of Russia's fight for her liberty, internal and external, from the day the monarchy fell and even to the present time. The fate of our revolution was not decided in the usual way, by an internal struggle between parties, but on the battlefields and in the foreign offices of *all* the warring countries.

There is an absurd story current that the Allies had helped in the making of the February Revolution or even actually made it themselves. By the method of exclusion the role of its chief organizer is usually allocated to the English Ambassador, Sir George Buchanan. The Italian Ambassador, the jovial and mobile, Marquess Carlotti, looked on rather than acted and moreover always ranked third in importance, well behind Buchanan and Paléologue. As for the latter it was impossible to accuse him of helping any opposition movement whatever, still less a revolution. He was a society snob who never left the grand ducal drawing-rooms, especially that of the Grand Duchess Maria. . . .

Under the Provisional Government every foreign diplomat went where he wished—visited members and the Soviets, attended meetings and met any one who interested him. Some continued in the old way, visiting a particular *salon* on a particular day of the week. Others hastened to make the acquaintance of the Siberian convicts of yesterday—the revolutionaries. As regards the Provisional Government, most of the Allied representatives took up a critical attitude, and even one of opposition: we were accused of weakness, lack of determination, and all the other mortal sins of rulers. Nevertheless the diplomats themselves soon learned—no less than any ordinary workman or soldier—to abuse their "excessive freedom." . . .

. . . Was it to be wondered at—in view of their own political leanings and their old connections in St. Petersburg—that the majority of the members of the Allied Embassies and Military Missions very soon came to a mutual understanding, both in the capital and at Headquarters, with people who were opposed to the Provisional Government? . . .

I have hitherto been very reserved in my writings about the true attitude of Paris and London to Russia after the revolution in general, and to the Provisional Government in particular. I feel that it is now time to establish the truth, as it really was.

Although Paléologue was recalled from St. Petersburg, it was his point of view, on the whole, that carried the day in the capitals of Russia's allies. The revolution seemed to have excluded Russia from the full and equal membership of the Entente. Needless to say, they would do all they could to keep the Russian armies at the front, and they would listen to the diplomatic babble of the inexperienced ministers. But in essence they would wage the war on their own, without inviting Russia to participate and without any regard for her needs. . . .

It is often said nowadays that the offensive of the Russian armies in July, 1917, was a reckless adventure, embarked upon at the instance of the Allies. True, Paris and London were very keen to see our army resume active operations at the front. It is also true that since it was a coalition war, and since we were very friendly and loyal to our Allies, we considered the interests of the alliance as well as those of Russia. Still, the resumption of military operations at the front was prompted primarily by the interests of Russia and by the logic of revolution: having been born to a great extent of the opposition to separate peace, the revolution could establish liberty and democracy on a firm foundation only in the event of a successful conclusion of the war. Moreover, in view of the attitude of our allies to Russia, it was clear that only the strengthening of the army, a demonstration of a certain amount of *force,* would make the Allies a little more circumspect about pigeonholing the notes of the Provisional Government, or would at least remind them that at the inter-Allied conferences the Russian delegates sat in their own right and expected to find a seat ready for them when they entered the conference room. . . .

Coming back to it, however: where was the source of the unfriendliness and sometimes unconcealed hostility of the Allied Cabinets to the Provisional Government? First and foremost, in the extremist mentality common to all the warring Western States at that time. The public opinion of Europe was just warming up, in Germany to the Brest-Litovsk Treaty, in Paris to the Versailles demands. And suddenly, at the beginning of the crucial 1917 campaign, there came the "absurd," quixotic Provisional Government proclamation of some new, democratic war aims! *"The free Russian nation, while defending its frontiers, has no wish to conquer foreign lands, has no wish to extract tribute from any one, and desires only the earliest conclusion of an equitable universal peace on the basis of the self-determination of nations."* . . .

. . . The hostile reaction of the Allies to the war policy of revolutionary Russia was quite natural: they were still in the old world of prewar ideas, whereas we, the first in Europe, had crossed the boundary of that world and felt the new spirit in international relations hinted at, but not realized, by the League of Nations. It is doubtful whether to-day, in 1933, the words of the Provisional Government's manifesto can strike any one in Europe as particularly outrageous and unacceptable; but they were written scarcely a fortnight after Paris had wired its consent to the Czar's wish to include all Poland, Austrian, German and Russian, within the boundaries of the Russian Empire—though admittedly as an autonomous unit. This telegram, again, was sent in return for the Czar's consent to the formation of a buffer state under the protectorate of France on German territory along the left bank of the Rhine.

However, the strenuous fight between the Provisional Government and the Allied Cabinets throughout the course of the February Revolution had less to do with the actual war aims than with the motives of their revision. The Provisional Government had no wish whatever to quarrel with its allies over sharing the lion's skin before the beast was killed. We wanted simply to win the war. To do so we had to have an army that could fight. To make the army fight we had to give it new war aims, which to the rank and file would fit in with its new spirit born of the revolution. At least it was essential to speak a new, different, diplomatic language which would not be reminiscent of the old "imperialist" language of Czarism, so bitterly hated in the trenches. In peace time the army is the last resort of diplomacy; but when war is on, diplomacy is only a servant of the army. "Say what you like," appealed V. N. Guchkov to the Minister for Foreign Affairs, Miliukov, at Cabinet meetings, "so long as your words are such that they strengthen the army.". . .

I am glad to be able to say that Sir George Buchanan and Albert Thomas understood the war diplomacy of the Provisional Government to perfection. They realized that the wordy imperialism of Miliukov simply strengthened the hands of the defeatists in the trenches, roused the ire of the Soviets against the government, and broke up the unity of the nation, so necessary to the success of the war. They both understood, therefore, that the change of ministers at the Foreign Office which occurred early in May, Miliukov being replaced by Tereshenko, was not the result of any intrigue of the foreign socialist delegation which came to St. Petersburg after the revolution—as the adherents of Miliukov asserted—but an essential move in the restoration of the Russian army to active service.

In a way, the time when Miliukov was leaving the Foreign Office was the happiest moment in the relations between the Allies and the Provisional Government. Alas, it was due to a misunderstanding! The fact is, the diplomatic spheres of London and Paris at first understood the personal change at the Foreign Office as indicating the decision of the Provisional Government to limit its new diplomatic policy to the one-sided renunciation of all the benefits which were to accrue to Russia in the event of a victory. London and Paris were particularly whole-hearted in their approval of our renunciation of Constantinople, because the military necessity to concede it to Russia had been a very sore point with Paris and went equally against the grain in London. The tried statesmen of the Entente regarded the leaders of revolutionary Russia as pleasant simpletons who were dying to pull the Allied chestnut out of the fire of the World War, quite unselfishly, for the sake of their revolutionary ideals, as it were. I remember how at the very beginning of the revolution —while Miliukov was still defending Sazonov's war aims, though on his own initiative and against the wishes of the rest of the Cabinet—one of the Allied representatives said to me: "Ah, well! If Russia will forsake Constantinople it will be all the better for us: it will bring the end of the war nearer."

But was it reasonable to turn to the overtired Russian soldier and tell him in so many words: we have renounced all materialistic objects of victory and all Polish territory, so that from now on we shall be fighting only that England should get the German colonies and her fleet, that France should get Alsace-Lorraine, the "Rhenanie," and a huge money tribute, Italy, the Slav Dalmatia, and so forth? Such an interpretation of the democratic war policy would have been sheer madness! Tereshenko, Prince Lvov nor I had ever imagined that the war aims of the Provisional Government could find such a rough-and-ready interpretation in London and in Paris. The misunderstanding was soon cleared up by the new minister. Translated into the language of diplomacy the Provisional Government manifesto concerning the new war aims meant that the Provisional Government was suggesting that all the allied countries should together reconsider their war aims; for itself, it announced that with a view to the earliest possible termination of war it was prepared to forsake its own share of military gains, commensurably with the concessions made by the other Great Powers of the alliance.

Right through the summer we were trying to get London and Paris to convoke, without delay, an inter-Allied conference for the revision of the war aims. Right through the summer London and Paris delayed the conference in every possible way. Even their consent to calling a conference at all was obtained only after our offensive. Tiresome and mutually annoying conversations dragged on for months. They simply could not understand, or rather would not acknowledge, in the Allied capitals, that a revolution is not merely the act of overthrowing a monarch, but also a long process of radical change in the entire outlook of a country. To-day, after a storm of revolutions and counter-revolutions all over Europe, statesmen and politicians have a better understanding of the meaning of revolution. But at that time the Allies assumed the attitude that an event of such immeasurable importance as the disappearance of the monarchy could not and should not have made any difference to the international policy of Russia. If it did the fault lay entirely with the feeble and weak-willed new government, a prisoner in the hands of the Soviets.

In the meanwhile the Germans, before our very eyes, were bombarding the Russian trenches with the poison-gas bombs of peace proposals and appeals attuned to the new mentality of revolution-stunned soldiers. These continuous moral attacks gave Berlin some excellent results. It was up to us to open an immediate moral counter-offensive if we were to preserve the front; and it was the duty of the Allies to help us. Did not the Fourteen Points of Wilson's peace policy in 1918 have a tremendous psychological effect in paving the way for the surrender of Germany? In urging the publication of new and democratic war aims, the Provisional Government was merely proposing to the Allies to open the "Wilsonian" offensive against Germany eighteen months earlier. Such an attack, boldly and unanimously launched, would have given dazzling and decisive results.

I base this assertion on our own experience. When the Provisional Government renounced Constantinople, the result was quite like winning a great battle on the Turkish Front. After the Russian Revolution, the feeling in the ruling spheres of Stamboul began to change rapidly and drastically: in the autumn Turkey was quite ripe for dropping out of the war. The ground for this move was fully prepared by Tereshenko and the American diplomatic representatives in Constantinople (The U.S.A., it will be remembered, never did declare war against either Turkey or Bulgaria.) Peace with Turkey would probably have been concluded in November.

Bulgaria, also, was preparing to drop out of the war. Free Russia had at one stroke morally disarmed the Bulgarians. The Austro-Hungarian army on the Russian Front was likewise rapidly disintegrating under the influence of the Russian Revolution. . . .

What was the task before our armies for the military campaign of 1917? Were we to attempt offensive operations to capture Constantinople, Budapest or Berlin? Obviously not. Military objectives which had not been attained by the Russian army during the course of the war previous to the revolution could not be expected with the country in a general revolutionary turmoil. The Provisional Government chose a more modest strategic aim, but one which was commensurate with its strength. Our objective was to restore the army so far as possible to a fighting condition, and so keep the maximum amount of enemy troops on the Russian Front.

The reason for this was, firstly, to prevent General Ludendorff from being free to maneuver on the Western Front; and secondly, to postpone by this means the final clash between the two military coalitions until the spring of 1918. This postponement alone would enable the United States to join in the war *effectively* and to give the Allies their decisive help, as they did, in 1918. . . .

I am not absolutely clear to this day as to the motives which had urged certain prominent and influential Englishmen and Frenchmen, alike Generals and civilians, to give active support to the Generals' rebellion against the Provisional Government at the very moment when it was carrying out military operations of the utmost importance both to Russia and to the Allies themselves. . . .

. . . In August, shortly before his rebellion, General Kornilov received a letter from London, brought by a well-known soldier of fortune, Aladin, once a Trudovik member of the First Duma. This letter was from a very prominent statesman, and conveyed his wholehearted approval of General Kornilov's intentions. It is not improbable that this message was the deciding factor in the destiny of that unsuccessful Russian Napoleon.

In spite of the obvious and abject failure of General Kornilov's move, the people who determined the military policy of England remained true to the end to their policy of interference in Russian military affairs and of giving support to the men who opposed the democracy while it was fighting the Lenin-Ludendorff alliance. . . .

The annoyance felt at Russia's new military-diplomatic policy found a very good justification: why, the true patriots of Russia themselves desired nothing better than the overthrow of the Provisional Government and the setting up—by the hand of a military dictator—of a truly national strong government! It was clearly the duty of every sincere friend of Russia to help such patriots! Could there be the slightest infringement of the allied obligations in helping these Russian patriots to overthrow the semi-bolsheviks? Of course not! . . .

. . But apart from that: how could the Provisional Government be overthrown and the revolutionary elements subdued by a General who had not a single soldier among his adherents and who could not move a step in the army without my commissars?

The Allies proved to be poor punters in backing such a very feeble horse. But this experience taught them nothing. When, within a few hours, the game was lost, their attitude to the Provisional Government remained the same. It seemed as though some one in London and Paris was hastening to help the Ludendorff-Lenin combination to sink the Russian Government which was still supporting the Allies on the battlefields in spite of the incredibly difficult internal situation.

One day early in September, soon after the Generals' mutiny was quashed, Tereshenko told me, sulkily enough, that the three Allied Ambassadors, the British, the French and the Italian, wanted to make me a joint verbal representation. . . . Indeed, the joint verbal note was perfectly outspoken: it was a threat of withdrawing all military aid to Russia unless . . . unless the Provisional Government took immediate drastic steps to restore order in the country and at the front. . . .

In fact, it amounted to this: I was being presented with an ultimatum to restore order after it had been undermined through the folly of General Kornilov. . . .

43. Trotsky and the October

Revolution

LEON TROTSKY (Lev Davidovitch Bronstein), 1897-1940, a former Menshevik, returned to Russia from the United States in May, 1917, following the establishment of the Provisional Government. He joined the Bolshevik Party in July of the same year, and became President of the Petrograd Soviet in October, when the Bolsheviks gained control of it. As Commissar of Foreign Affairs he entered into peace negotiations with the Germans, but disapproved the subsequent Treaty of Brest-Litovsk, March 3, 1918. Outside the USSR, Trotsky's name is associated with the organization in 1918 of the Red Army and with its early achievements. He came out in opposition to the New Economic Policy (NEP) in *The Lessons of October* (1924). After Lenin's death, Trotsky, an exponent of world revolution and militant communism, led the opposition to Stalin's policy of achieving socialism in one country. The decline of Trotsky in Soviet Russia, which began in 1925 with his expulsion from the post of War Commissar, ended in his banishment from the USSR in 1929. Inside the USSR, Trotsky was henceforth disowned, his name became the subject of bitter invective, and his role in the Revolution was belittled.

Below is Trotsky's own defence of his position of leadership alongside Lenin in the preparation of the October Revolution. From *The Real Situation in Russia,* by Leon Trotsky, translated by Max Eastman (New York: Harcourt, Brace and Company, 1928), pp. 219-225. Reprinted by permission.

II. My Part in the October Revolution

As to my participation in the October Revolution—in the notes to Volume XIV of the *Complete Works* of Lenin, you read:

"After the majority of the Petersburg Soviet passed into the hands of the Bolsheviks, Trotsky was elected its president and in that position organized and led the insurrection of October 25."

How much is true here, and how much false, let the Bureau of Party History decide—if not the present one, then some future Bureau. Comrade Stalin has lately categorically denied the truth of this assertion. Thus:

"I have to say that Comrade Trotsky played no particular rôle in the October insurrection and could not do so, that being president of the Petrograd Soviet, he merely fulfilled the will of the corresponding party authority, which guided his every step."

And further:

"Comrade Trotsky played no particular rôle either in the party or the October insurrection, and could not do so, being a man comparatively new to our party in the October period."

In giving this testimony, Stalin forgot what he himself said on the sixth of November, 1918; that is, on the first anniversary of the revolution, when facts and events were still too fresh in the minds of all. Even then Stalin had already begun that work in relation to me which he has now developed on such a grand scale. But he was then compelled to conduct it far more cautiously and underhandedly than he is now. Here is what he wrote then in *Pravda* under the title, "The Rôle of the Most Eminent Party Leaders":

"All the work of practical organization of the insurrection was conducted under the immediate leadership of the President of the Petrograd Soviet, Comrade Trotsky. It is possible to declare with certainty that the swift passing of the garrison to the side of the Soviet, and the bold execution of the work of the Military Revolutionary Committee, the party owes principally and above all to Comrade Trotsky."

Those words, spoken by no means for the purpose of laudatory exaggeration—on the contrary, Stalin's goal was then wholly different, but I will not dwell on that—those words sound absolutely incredible today as coming from the lips of Stalin.

It was said long ago: A truthful man has this advantage, that even with a bad memory he never contradicts himself. A disloyal, unscrupulous, and dishonest man has always to remember what he said in the past, in order not to shame himself.

Comrade Stalin, with the help of the Yaroslavskies, is trying to construct a new history of the organization of the October insurrection based on the fact that the party created a "practical center for the organizational leadership of the insurrection," of which, it appears, Trotsky was not a member. Lenin was not a member of that committee. That fact alone demonstrates that the committee had only a subordinate organizational significance. It played no independent role whatever. The legend about this committee has been created today for the simple reason that Stalin was a member of it. Here is the membership: "Sverdlov, Stalin, Dzerzhinsky, Bubnov, Uritzky." However unpleasant it is to dig in the rubbish, it seems necessary for me, as a sufficiently close participant and witness of the events of that time, to testify as follows:

The role of Lenin, of course, needs no illumination. Sverdlov I often met, and I often turned to him for counsel and for people to help me. Comrade Kamenev, who, as is well known, occupied then a special position, the incorrectness of which he himself has long ago acknowledged, took nevertheless a most active part in the events of the revolution. The decisive night, from the twenty-fifth to the twenty-sixth, Kamenev and I spent together in the quarters of the Military Revolutionary Committee, answering questions and giving orders by telephone. But stretch my memory as I will, I cannot answer the question in just what consisted, during those decisive days, the rôle of Stalin. It never once happened that I turned to him for advice or cooperation. He never showed the slightest initiative. He never advanced one independent proposal. This fact no "Marxist historian" of the new style can alter.

A Supplementary Insertion

Stalin and Yaroslavsky, as I said above, have wasted much effort these last months in proving that the organizational center created by the party consisting of Sverdlov, Stalin, Bubnov, Uritzky, and Dzerzhinsky guided, so to speak, the whole course of the insurrection. Stalin has emphasized, every way he can, the fact that Trotsky was not a member of that center. But alas! through sheer carelessness on the part of Stalin's historians, in *Pravda* for Nov. 2, 1927—that is, after the present letter was written—there appeared an accurate excerpt from the report of the Central Committee for the sixteenth to the twenty-ninth of October, 1917.

"The Central Committee creates a military revolutionary center with the following members, Sverdlov, Stalin, Bubnov, Uritzky, and Dzerzhinsky. *This center is to be a constituent part of the Revolutionary Soviet Committee.*"

The Revolutionary Soviet Committee is the Military Revolutionary Committee created by the Petrograd Soviet. No other Soviet organ for the leadership of the insurrection existed. Thus these five comrades, designated by the Central Committee, were required to enter as a supplement into the staff of that same Military Revolutionary Committee of which Trotsky was the president. Superfluous, it would seem, for Trotsky to be introduced a second time into the staff of an organization of which he was already the president! How hard it is, after all, to correct history after it is finished!

Nov. 11, 1927

I wrote at Brest a short outline of the October Revolution. This book went through a great number of editions in various languages. Nobody ever told me that there is a flagrant omission in my book—namely, that it nowhere points out the chief guide of the insurrection, "the military revolutionary center," of which Stalin and Bubnov were members. If I so badly remembered the history of the October insurrection, why did not somebody clear me up? Why was my book studied with impunity in all the party schools in the first years of the revolution?

Even in the year 1922 the Organization Bureau of the party seemed to think that I understood fairly well the history of the October Revolution. Here is a small but eloquent confirmation of that:

No. 14302   Moscow, May 24, 1922.

"To Comrade Trotsky:

"Excerpt from the report of the session of the Organization Bureau of the Central Committee for May 22, 1922. No. 21.

"Commission Comrade Yakovlev by the first of October to compose, under the editorship of Comrade Trotsky, a textbook of the history of the October Revolution.

"*Signed,* Secretary of the Sub-department of Propaganda."

That was in May 1922. And my book about the October Revolution and my book about the year 1905, having appeared before that time in many editions, were well known to the Organization Bureau—the head of which, at that period, was already Stalin. Nevertheless, the Organization Bureau considered it necessary to lay upon me the task of editing the school book of the history of the October Revolution. How does this happen? It happens because the eyes of Stalin and the Stalinists were opened to "Trotskyism," only after the eyes of Lenin were closed forever.

44. the impact of the October

Revolution on the Orient

SOVIET POLITICAL LEADERS AND SCHOLARS have never ceased
to stress the influence of the October Revolution of 1917 on the countries and peoples of the East.

Below is a kind of symposium of Soviet thinking on this issue,
presented at a session of the Pacific Institute, November 17-19, 1947,
as the Civil War in China approached its climax.

From *Viestnik Academii Nauk USSR,* No. 1, January, 1948.
Translated in *Soviet Press Translations,* edited by Ivar Spector and
published by the Far Eastern and Russian Institute, University of
Washington, Vol. III (No. 9, May 1, 1948), 272-277.

On November 17-19 a convention was held in the Pacific Institute devoted
to the problem of the influence of the Great October Socialist Revolution
on the countries of the East. The victory of socialism in one-sixth of the
world has dealt imperialism a terrific blow, declared Corresponding
Member of the AS of the USSR E. M. Zhukov, Director of the Pacific
Institute, in his opening address. The last thirty years have been marked
not only by the victory of the great ideas of Lenin and Stalin, which
insured a decisive victory for socialism in our country, but also by the
development of a general crisis in the capitalistic system. Changes on an
enormous scale have taken place in dependent and colonial countries. On
the shores of the Pacific Ocean the countries that were regarded as
preserves for cruel exploitation became the focal points of progressive
movements.

The people of the colonies no longer wish to live in the old way, and
the dominating classes of the metropolis cannot administer the colonies
as heretofore. The attempts of the imperialists to suppress the powerful
upsurge of the national movement are leading to protracted colonial
wars. A most important result of the mass movement in the colonies and
semicolonies under the influence of the October Revolution is the
emergence there of communist parties, steadily expanding their influence

among the masses and coming forward as a real directing force in the struggle for national liberation.

The convention heard a report by A. S. Perevertailo, Candidate in Economic Sciences, on "The Great October Socialist Revolution and China."

Having briefly analysed the position of China in the 19th century and the beginning of the 20th century, the speaker noted that the October Revolution had severed the solid chain of imperialism that fettered China. The peoples of revolutionary Russia supported the Chinese people in their struggle for liberation. Comrade Stalin formulated a sound and profound theory of the Chinese Revolution at its present stage as a revolution of the bourgeois-democratic type, having a dual antifeudal and anti-imperialist character.

From the very start the Soviet Government took a stand against the predatory policy of the imperialistic bourgeoisie, which built its welfare on the enslavement of the workers of Asia. It supported the revolutionary Government of Sun Yat-sen, and renounced treaties that did not offer equal rights. Sun Yat-sen studied the experience of the October Revolution with profound attention and took much from it, without being himself a Marxist. He reorganized the Kuomintang Party as a party of the masses, and accepted communists in it. It became the Party of the bloc of all the revolutionary forces of the country. Sun Yat-sen pursued a policy of close cooperation with the USSR.

Revolutionary China achieved a victory over the militarists. Since the treachery of the Chinese bourgeoisie, however, the Kuomintang was transformed into a headquarters of reaction; it made a deal with the foreign imperialists and capitulated to them, having severed its relations with the Soviet Union in 1917. Four years after the counter-revolutionary coup d'etat of the Kuomintang, at the height of internal civil war, the Japanese imperialists attacked China.

Having described in detail the struggle against the Japanese usurpers, the speaker pointed out that from the very beginning of its existence the Soviet Union had made a resolute stand against the Japanese imperialists, and that the struggle against them had become the common historic task of the peoples of the USSR and of China. The Soviet people supported consistently and with warm sympathy, the struggle for the liberation of the Chinese people from the Japanese aggressor. The Soviet Union, having concluded a nonaggression pact with China, extended the latter practical aid even during the most critical moments of the Great Patriotic War.

As a result of World War II, the authority and influence of the Chinese Communist Party increased. The defeat of German fascism and Japanese imperialism facilitated the struggle of the Chinese people for the liberation of their country and for its democratic reorganization. The forces of reaction, however, are striving to impede the creative work of the Chinese people. Following the capitulation of Japan the USA has been attempting, with the aid of the Kuomintang bosses, to enslave China and seize the positions lost by Japan. Having extended China loans and credits to the sum of $2,000,000,000, it has placed China's economy in servile dependence upon the USA and is attempting to convert China into a military and strategic base of operations in the struggle for world domination. Now the Chinese people are obliged to defend themselves against American imperialism with the weapons at hand. The conditions of the struggle of the Chinese people have changed, however; the experience of the laboring masses has increased; and the forces of Chinese democracy and its leading detachment—the Communist Party of China—have multiplied. The People's liberation army of China is extending, with more and more success, the struggle against reaction, headed by Chiang Kai-shek, H. H. Kung, T. V. Soong, and the Chen brothers, robbers and betrayers of their own people.

G. V. Astafev, Candidate in Economic Sciences, delivered a report, entitled "The New Democracy in China."

The speaker noted that the Chinese Revolution, like the Communist Party of China, was a product of the October Revolution, since the ideas of the Lenin-Stalin revolutionary doctrine have had a decisive influence on their development. It was by orienting themselves in the works of Lenin and Stalin that the Chinese communists, headed by Mao Tse-tung, worked out the principles for the contemporary policy of the Chinese Communist Party. At the present stage of the popular democratic revolution in China the Communists are striving for the achievement of a minimum program—the overthrow of foreign imperialistic oppression and the construction of a free, democratic China, based on the support of a majority of the people, and on a coalition of the democratic parties and groups.

Having emphasized that since the war all the democratic forces of the country have united around the Chinese Communist Party, the speaker analyzed the achievements of Chinese democracy in the military, political, economic, and cultural fields. A characteristic of the new democracy in China is the solidarity of the broad masses of the Chinese people for the purpose of solving the most difficult military, political, and economic problems confronting them. The basis for this solidarity was the extension to the people of broad political rights, and their inclusion in the administration of the country, the election of all those in authority, and the achievement of an extensive program of political, cultural, educational, and sanitation measures, aimed at raising the cultural level of the whole population. A basic economic reform was the destruction of the economic basis of feudalism in China through the achievement of an agrarian reform, which handed over the manorial lands to the peasants without remuneration, and which freed the peasantry from usurious and enslaving debts. State and cooperative ownership of the means of production has been developed in industry in the regions liberated from the Kuomintang authorities. New relations have grown up between labor and capital; they are expressed in the safe-guarding of the rights of the workers as regards duration of the working day, minimum wages, and social insurance; the workers are being encouraged to supervise production and to share the profits.

In conclusion the speaker noted that the new democracy in China is a manifestation of the world-wide process of formation of a new transitional order in the capitalistic world, in which elements of socialism in the shape of public ownership and a collective form of labor are growing up side by side with a retention of capitalistic ways under the control of the people.

A. M. Dyakov, Doctor of Historical Sciences, delivered a report on "The Great October Socialist Revolution in India."

The speaker noted that since the October Revolution in Russia a new stage in India's development has begun. The social base of the national liberation movement of the peoples of India is being extended, and its character, demands, and program are being radically changed. India's working class is being transformed into an independent force in the vanguard of the Indian national liberation movement. The Indian national liberation movement is joining ranks with the national liberation struggle of the working class against world imperialism.

Following World War II during which India's working class, under the leadership of the Communist Party, emerged in the vanguard of the anti-imperialistic national liberation movement, it was the workers who gave weight and effectiveness to the struggle against the use of India's resources for the suppression of the liberation movement in Indonesia and Indo-China. The Communist Party is playing a leading role in the Indian trade-union movement.

The influence of the October Revolution on India has not been confined to the workers' movement alone. A peasants' movement in India has also begun to grow under the influence of the development of the workers' movement.

The entire character of the national movement, its extent, demands, and program, was changed following the October Revolution. Until 1929 the program of the National Congress was confined solely to the demand for the extension of self-government in India. In 1929 the Congress stated that its goal was the achievement of full independence for India. The agrarian question arises not only in the program of the Indian Communist Party, but also in the programs of the National Congress, and in the pre-election manifesto of the Congress a demand is being advanced for the confiscation of manorial lands and their transfer to the use of the peasants. The idea of a planned national economy enjoys even greater popularity in India. In its economic program the National Congress provides for the nationalization of key industries.

"The Great October Socialist Revolution in Indonesia" was the subject of the report by A. A. Guber, Doctor of Historical Sciences.

The speaker set himself the task of tracing the origin of the struggle of the Indonesian people for their independence and a democratic régime, which evolved under the direct influence of the Great October Socialist Revolution. As a result of Dutch colonial policy in Indonesia the prerequisite conditions were present for the formation of a broad anti-imperialistic front on a democratic basis. This opportunity, however, was utilized for the first time as a result of the influence of the October Revolution. The Communist Party of Indonesia, one of the first in the colonial countries, which emerged and was finally organized in 1921, appeared from the very start as a revolutionary force uniting the broad masses of the Indonesian people.

An expression of the all-national, anti-imperialistic front in the years after World War I was the Party of Sarakhat Islam the revolutionary wing of which, headed by the Communists, played a decisive role until the 1923 split. The program of Sarakhat Islam, in particular the program of its Fifth Congress, clearly reflected an attempt to combine the struggle for independence with the struggle for genuine democracy. The bourgeois elements in the leadership of Sarakhat Islam succeeded in achieving a split in the Party. The masses, however, followed in the train of its revolutionary wing. And in the years of the most violent terror, from 1926 to World War II, the struggle of the Indonesian people did not cease, just as attempts did not cease to create national revolutionary parties struggling for independence and social and economic reforms.

In this struggle, just as in the demands in the programs of such parties and organizations as the National Party, the Indonesia Party, and others, the ideas of the Great October Revolution were unquestionably reflected.

Following the defeat of Japan a real opportunity arose for declaring independence and for the struggle of the Indonesian people for the new democracy. Today Indonesia is joining the anti-imperialistic front; the ideas of Lenin and Stalin are directing the Indonesian people in the struggle for independence and genuine democracy.

A. M. Zorina, Candidate in Historical Sciences, delivered a report on "The Great October Socialist Revolution and Latin America."

The speaker noted that the great ideas of the October Revolution were not unknown to the nations of Latin America, which, in spite of their formal independence, are actually subordinate to the interests of Anglo-American monopolistic capital and provide an arena for the grim struggle of the capitalistic powers.

The influence of the October Revolution on the countries of Latin America has been marked by the upsurge of a mass workers' movement. A tempestuous wave of strikes and peasant commotions has swept over all the countries. The proletariat, the urban poor, and the petit bourgeois with revolutionary sentiments have expressed their sympathy with the ideas of the Great October Socialist Revolution in numerous meetings and street demonstrations. In Chile (1931-1932), and in Cuba (1933) Soviets of workers' and peasants' deputies were even set up.

The influence of the ideas of the Great October Socialist Revolution, the general world crisis of capitalism, and the subsequent upsurge of the mass movement have contributed to the emergence of communist parties in such countries of Latin America as Mexico (1919), Argentina (1920), Chile (1921), and Brazil (1922). In succeeding years communist parties were formed in almost all other Latin American countries. The emergence of communist parties has contributed in a considerable degree to the political development of Latin America, and has formed a basis for an independent revolutionary proletarian movement, based on the ideas of Marxism and Leninism. In spite of terror and persecution (in Chile, Argentina, and Brazil), the communist parties have begun to achieve an ideological and political hegemony over the revolutionary proletariat in the all-democratic national liberation movement. During World War II, taking into account the growth of sympathy toward the Soviet Union, the majority of the Latin-American Governments were obliged to recognize the Soviet Government *de jure* and to exchange diplomatic representations with the latter. The severance by Brazil and Chile of diplomatic relations with the Soviet Union, which merely indicates that these Governments are tools of foreign imperialism, met with general condemnation among the democratic circles of the Latin-American countries as a reactionary and anti-democratic act.

M. S. Alperovitch, a postgraduate student in the Pacific Institute, delivered a report on "The October Revolution and the struggle of the Mexican People Against Imperialism and Reaction."

Having shown by concrete facts the enormous revolutionary influence of the October Revolution on Mexico, the speaker specially emphasized the extraordinary popularity that the idea of Soviets had won among the masses of the people and cited a number of examples characterizing the attempts to set up Soviets in the course of the revolutionary demonstrations and strikes of 1920-1921. The Mexican people managed to make Mexico the first of the states of the American continent to establish diplomatic relations with the USSR. The severance by the Mexican Government of diplomatic relations with the USSR (1930) was dictated by North American imperialism. The growth of the mass movement in Mexico in the beginning of the thirties and the formation of a people's anti-imperialistic front (1936) were accompanied by the development of an extensive campaign for the restoration of relations with the Soviet Union. The progressive and antifascist forces of Mexico, however, were unable to achieve this until World War II (1942).

Having pointed out that the world-wide historic successes of the Soviet

Union exerted an influence on certain measures of the Government of progressive President Cardenas (1934-1940), the speaker showed the failure of the attempts undertaken by the latter to plan the economy of the country (the so-called Six-year Plan) and to introduce elements of cooperation in agriculture. These experiments served only to strengthen the position of the Mexican national bourgeoisie.

Having emphasized that in the postwar period the reactionary circles of Mexico have subordinated their policy more and more to the aggressive goals of American imperialism, the speaker noted that the example of the Soviet Union was inspiring the Mexican people in their struggle against imperialism and reaction.

O. I. Zabozlayeva, junior scientific associate of the Pacific Institute, delivered a report on "The Ideas of the Great October Socialist Revolution and the Anti-imperialistic Struggle in the Philippines."

Having pointed out that the democratic anti-imperialistic movement in the Philippines is an attempt at practical application of the ideas of the October Revolution, the speaker noted that the struggle for independence in the Philippines has taken a course different from that in other colonies. The Philippine landowners are closely allied with the export industry, which processes agricultural products, and is in the hands of American, Spanish, English, and Japanese capitalists. For this reason the American imperialists permitted themselves the luxury of encouraging the landowning nationalism, by preparing a reliable champion of their interests in the form of the bourgeois landowners' party.

The author pointed out how difficult was the struggle conducted by the Communist Party of the Philippines in the fight for the liberation of the worker and peasant masses from the influence of the bourgeois "National Party." The workers and the peasants are uniting in unions, and a workers' and peasants' front has been created in the struggle for the improvement of the material and legal position of the workers, a front that became particularly strong in the last decade before World War II. Following a number of peasant uprisings, cruelly suppressed by the Americans, the Philippines were granted autonomy in 1934, with the promise of full independence in 1946. With the creation of an autonomous national government, class conflicts in the Philippines became more intense.

In January 1942 the United Front of Progressive Political Parties was completely organized as a political group having as its goal the expulsion of the Japanese from the Philippines, cooperation with the United Nations with a view to the successful conclusion of the war, the achievement of full independence for the Philippines, liberation from American domination, the creation of a democratic government, and the annihilation of the betrayers of the Philippine people. The People's anti-Japanese army, struggling against the Japanese usurpers, numbered up to 60,000 soldiers.

Three reports at the convention were devoted to the Great October Socialist Revolution and the Mongol People's Republic.

F. S. Tsaplin, a postgraduate student in the Pacific Institute, delivered a report on "The Mongol Revolutionary Party as the Inspiration and Organizer of the Victories of the Mongol People."

The speaker emphasized that the Mongol People's Revolution was bound up with the victory of the October Revolution in Russia, which proclaimed the principle of emancipation of enslaved nations. The speaker showed how the Mongol People's Revolutionary Party had grown and increased in strength, and how with the support of the USSR it had fought for the democratization of the country and for the eradication of the feudal régime.

P. P. Staritsina, lecturer in the Institute of Oriental Studies, delivered a report on "The State Organization of the Mongol People's Republic."

The speaker noted that according to the Constitution of the Republic the direction of the economic policy of the country was concentrated in the hands of the state, the budget was centralized, a monopoly of domestic trade was introduced, and national economic planning was provided for. The land and its deposits, the forests, and the waters have been declared state property; and private ownership of the land is not allowed. A number of figures cited in the report showed convincingly what economic and cultural progress has been achieved by the Mongol People's Republic, thanks to the genuine democratization of its régime.

Professor I. N. Ustyuzhaninov delivered a report on "The Great October Socialist Revolution and the Mongol People's Republic."

The report pointed out how the progressive leaders of Mongolia have used the teaching of Lenin and Stalin in the organization of the Mongol People's Revolutionary Party, in the struggle against intervention and against feudalism and serfdom, as well as in economic and cultural reforms in the country. By relying on the friendly help of the Soviet people, the Mongol People's Republic has confidently taken the course predicted as early as 1920 by V. I. Lenin, who pointed out that with the help of the proletariat of the most progressive countries, backward countries could proceed to a Soviet régime, and through definite stages of development likewise to communism, bypassing the capitalistic stage of development.

F. I. Shabshina delivered a report on "The Great October Socialist Revolution and the Peasants' Movement in Korea."

The speaker noted that in the national liberation struggle of the Korean people, which developed under the influence of the October Revolution in Russia, the peasantry always represented a basic force, since Korea was an agrarian country. Having annexed Korea, the Japanese imperialists took over all its resources, and especially the land. They separated the peasants from the land and robbed them. From year to year the number of tenants increased, and the number of peasant proprietors was reduced. The numerous taxes on the peasants increased steadily. In spite of all his efforts the peasant could never get on his feet. As early as 1935 the total sum of indebtedness of the Korean rural areas exceeded 1,000,000,000 yen.

Following the October Revolution the Korean masses entered the struggle against the Japanese imperialists. The speaker traced all the stages of this struggle, beginning with the events of 1919, when nearly 1,700,000 persons took part in the movement, and the ringleaders of the movement, intimidated by the rebellious people, turned to the Japanese for aid. This mass movement suffered defeat as a consequence of its spontaneous character and lack of organization. After 1919 the national liberation struggle in Korea entered a new stage, and organizations of workers and peasants were set up. In 1929 the workers' and peasants' unions formed united centers, and in 1924 the "General Korean Workers' and Peasants' Organization" was set up. The reformers, however, took over the leadership of the unions and directed their activities along a legal path, and, inasmuch as they were basically anti-Japanese, the unions did not become mass fighting organizations. In 1925 the Communist Party of Korea was organized far underground and a *volte-face* began in the revolutionary movement of workers and peasants. The qualitative and quantitative growth of the peasants' movement dates from 1929.

The most cherished dreams of the Korean peasant were answered by the revolutionary solution of the agrarian question in Russia. The successes of the socialist reorganization of the Soviet village inspired him in the struggle against the Japanese colonizers.

Following the capitulation of Japan in 1945, Korea awaited the arrival of the Soviet armies. The Korean masses understood that only the army of the USSR would bring them a guarantee of independence.

In its zone of responsibility the Soviet Army, having liberated Korea, aided the Korean people to obtain both land and democratic freedom. The agrarian reform law of 1946 liquidated both Japanese and Korean manorial landowning. Today the free labor of the peasant is well remunerated, the agrarian reform has unleashed political activity on the part of the peasantry, and admitted the latter to state leadership. The working conditions of laborers and employees have been radically changed, and rapacious colonial exploitation has been liquidated. In South Korea, however, in the American zone of responsibility, the peasant, as before, does not have the right to dispose of the harvest that he gathers, and reaction predominates there.

The Soviet proposal to withdraw foreign troops from Korea at the beginning of 1948 met with the warm approval of the Korean people, who know that only the policy of the USSR, based on the principle of the self-determination of people, has laid the foundation for the creation of a united democratic Korean state.

The convention heard a report by B. G. Sapozhnikov, Candidate in Historical Sciences, on "The Role of the USSR in the Defeat of Japanese Imperialism."

The report noted that the Great October Revolution in Russia was greeted with enthusiasm by the Japanese workers, who understood perfectly the significance of the Russian Revolution. Herein lay one of the reasons why the Japanese imperialists came forth as one of the first and most mortal enemies of revolutionary Russia. During World War II Japan was plainly and openly preparing for war against the Soviet Union; did not cease its anti-Soviet attacks; and hindered mutual Soviet and American trade relations. In the name of hatred toward all progressive humanity, Japanese statesmen sacrificed to expediency the strict observance of the conditions of the neutrality pact between Japan and the USSR. The speaker showed that the USSR played a decisive role in the task of liquidating the citadel of war in the Far East by defeating the Kwantung Army, which constituted the most powerful unit in the armed forces of Japan.

A. B. Kozorovitskaya, senior bibliographer of the Pacific Institute, delivered a report on "The Great October Socialist Revolution and the Progressive Movement Among Advanced Elements of Japanese Society."

The speaker traced all the stages of the development of the struggle by the workers of Japan, and primarily by the working class, for their democratic rights against the capitalists and the Japanese reactionary Government. The treacherous policy of the Japanese reformers, who entered into an alliance with the Japanese bourgeoisie, impeded the formation of a united fighting proletarian party in Japan and facilitated the struggle of Japanese reaction against the proletariat.

The convention demonstrated how great are the tasks that confront our scientists in the concrete study of the influence of the Great October Socialist Revolution on the development of the countries of the East and of the Pacific.

45. the Communist blueprint

for the Arab countries

FOLLOWING THE FAILURE OF THEIR INITIAL EFFORT to Bolshevize the Near and Middle East, 1917-1921, the Communist International (Comintern) drafted secret programs for the new Communist Parties of the East (Turkey, the Arab Countries, Egypt, and Palestine). These documents were published by the Marx-Engels-Lenin Institute of the Central Committee of the All-Russian Communist Party (Bolshevik) in Moscow in 1934. In 1955 a copy of these documents was located by the editors of this volume at the Library of Congress and translated into English.

The significance of these documents is that they reveal a Communist blueprint for the Near East, which is still basically valid. They envisage a Communist takeover by three stages: 1. The elimination of the "imperialist" power and the establishment of national independence. 2. The overthrow of the "bourgeois" regime of the newly independent state by the "workers and peasants." 3. The establishment of a Communist regime. The Communist programs emphasize that a political revolution (national independence) is not enough. It must be accompanied or immediately succeeded by a social revolution, which, they claim, can only be achieved under Communist leadership.

Below is a translation of the Communist program for "The Arab Countries," from *The Soviet Union and the Muslim World,* by Ivar Spector (Seattle, Washington: University of Washington Press, 1959), pp. 127-140.

The Arab Countries

In 1920 a Socialist party was organized in Egypt. In 1923 it changed its name to "The Communist Party of Egypt," and became a section of the Communist International. In 1924 it carried out (with the aid of

301

the revolutionary federation of labor, which was under its influence) a number of mass strikes and demonstrations in Alexandria. In the same year, the National Reform government of Zaghlul Pasha, which came to power, banned the party, arrested and tried its leaders. The Party was driven underground. In subsequent years, the work of the Party was weak, limited to the publication of Party organs, leaflets, and desultory action; and partly because until 1931 there were in the Party leadership undesirable elements, who occupied themselves with intrigues and squabbles, and who were subsequently excluded from the ranks of the Party and Communist International, it achieved no success in the area of work among the masses.

The program of action of the Communist party of Egypt, published after the removal of the old leadership, gives an analysis of the class forces in Egypt and lists the most important tasks of the anti-imperialist revolution in the country, pointing out the close connection of this struggle with the antimonarchist and antifeudal revolution in Egypt, and calling upon the masses to break away from the national reformists and traitorous Wafd by exposing this basic party of the Egyptian bourgeoisie and landowners.

The program of action points out a whole series of partial demands, around which it is necessary to weld the workers of Egypt, and it lists the basic demands of the peasantry. It gives the objectives of the Party on most important questions confronting the trade-unions and the agrarian movement. The program of action of the Communist party of Egypt plays a great role in restoring and improving the Party and serves as a lever for the development of its work among the masses.

The Communist party of Syria was founded in 1924, but was not taken into the Communist International as a section until 1928. The Party did not openly enter the political arena until 1930. However, during its brief existence, it has already achieved some success. The Party actively participated in the strikes of the Syrian workers and in the mass movement against French imperialism; and, of late, it has become active among the trade-unions. In particular, the Party demonstrated its great revolutionary activity in the strikes of the chauffeurs and printers (1933).

A resolution adopted at a joint session of the Syrian and Palestinian Communist parties on "The Work of the Communists in the Arab National Revolutionary Movement" sets forth the slogan of unification of the Arab countries in their struggle for independence. The resolution shows that the persecution of the Arab countries by imperialism is accompanied by their dismemberment, in which they are parceled out by force among the imperialist powers. Analyzing the causes of this partition and the necessity of the participation of the Communist party in the national revolutionary movement, the resolution sets forth the slogan of unification of the workers' and peasants' republics of the Arab countries. It has great significance, not only for the program of Palestine and Syria, but for all the Arabic countries in general.

The Communist party of Palestine was founded in 1919. In the beginning it experienced a prolonged factional struggle. It was taken into the Communist International in 1924. The Party, by carrying out a whole series of anti-imperialist and anti-Zionist activities, assumed a basically erroneous position on the Palestine national question, that is, on the question of the role of the Jewish national minority in Palestine with regard to the Arab masses. As a result, the Party did not carry out practical work among the Arab masses and remained a particularistic section, which worked only among the Jewish workers. This isolation was reflected in the position of the Party during the Arab revolt of 1929, when the Party was cut off from the mass movement.

After two appeals to the Party by the Executive Committee of the Communist International, at the end of 1930 the seventh Congress of the Communist party of Palestine convened. This Congress adopted a number of resolutions, which corrected the errors previously permitted and served as a basis for the reorganization and Arabization of the Party.

The Tasks of the Communists in the All-Arab National Movement*

1. One of the most important tasks of the revolutionary struggle for liberation against imperialism in the huge area of the Near East is the solution of the Arab national question. The masses of the people in all Arab countries are under the yoke of imperialism. In one form or another, to one degree or another, all the Arab countries are deprived of political independence. Palestine, Transjordania, and Iraq are mandates wholly subject to the domination of English imperialism; Syria is governed by French imperialists; Egypt is under the heel of British domination, and the "independence" of that country, declared in 1921, is an insult to real independence, due to the fact that the most important, key political positions are in the hands of English imperialists; moreover, the English remain the dictators of the Sudan; Tripoli is a colony of the Italian imperialists; the French regime dominates Tunisia and Algeria, and as for Morocco, it is partitioned between French and Spanish imperialists. Yemen, Hijaz, and the Nadj, although they are not directly subjected to imperialist domination, are deprived of the prerequisites for an independent existence, and, encircled and hounded by the colonies of the imperialists, are forced to submit themselves to the dictates of imperialism.

* Resolution adopted at the Conference of the Communist parties of Palestine and Syria in 1931.

The entire system of imperialist domination over the Arab peoples is based, not only on their outright enslavement and subjugation, but on the fact that they have been split up arbitrarily into parts at the command of world imperialism. This division of the Arab peoples among the English, French, Italian, and Spanish imperialists reflects the prevailing balance of power among these imperialists and is so adjusted as to perpetuate their domination. It is the most crying contradiction to the vital interests of the Arab peoples. The political boundaries dividing them have been established and maintained forcibly by the imperialists, who thus carry out the principle of "divide and rule." These boundaries artificially weaken the masses of the Arab peoples in their struggle against the foreign yoke for their political independence and national unification in accordance with the free decision of the masses of the people.

The gist of the Arab national question consists in the fact that the English, French, Italian, and Spanish imperialists have dismembered the living body of the Arab peoples, hold the Arab countries in a state of feudal fragmentation, deprive each and every one of these countries of the prerequisites for an independent economic and political development, and block the national political unification of the Arab countries.

Syria is arbitrarily broken up into five parts, each with a different government, different laws, etc. The English have seized the Sudan by force. By converting all the Arab countries into agrarian and raw material appendages to corresponding metropolises, and by distorting and hampering the development of the productive forces and their general development, imperialism thereby strives to preserve and to perpetuate their enslavement. The feudal elements thus become predominant, whereas the development of the capitalist elements, for the most part, is confined to the creation of a business bourgeoisie, which is more or less tied to the feudal landowners, its function being to dispose of the products of the metropolis and to pump out the raw materials for the metropolis. Thus imperialism preserves the medieval feudal monarchies (Egypt, Morocco, and Tunisia), creates new semifeudal monarchies (Iraq, Transjordania), relying upon various petty "dynasties," or creates its own imperialist colonial regime without the aid of its monarchial agents (Palestine, Syria, Tripoli, Algeria), combining oppression and plunder with mandatory government in the name of the League of Nations.

2. What is general and decisive for all Arab countries is the fact that, alongside the key political positions occupied by the imperialists, foreign and financial capital holds in its hands all the decisive key economic positions. The biggest banks, factories, railroads, ports, navigation, mines, the most important irrigation systems, the key positions in foreign trade, the state debts, etc., are in the hands of foreign financial capital. Moreover, the majority of the imperialist plunderers of the Arab countries have seized the best lands (in Morocco, Algeria, Tunisia, Tripoli, Egypt, Syria, Palestine), and the English imperialists have employed counter-

revolutionary Zionism to seize and plunder the lands in Palestine. The Arab fellahin and the Bedouins[1] are crowded onto the poorer land and are deprived of land and pasture. Imperialism makes use of its key political and economic positions for the merciless exploitation of the Arab masses.

In oppressing and exploiting the workers, the imperialists rely on reactionary monarchial cliques, on feudal and semifeudal landowners and sheikhs,[2] on native bourgeois compradores, and on the higher clergy. What is characteristic, general, and decisive for the agrarian system of the Arab countries is that a large part of the land, livestock, and pasture, not yet seized by the foreign owners of *latifundium,* planters, banks, colonists, or the state, are in the hands of feudal and semifeudal landowners, sheikhs, and the church. The fellahin and Bedouins are subjected to the worst forms of feudal exploitation (khamis,[3] *metayage*). Against the background of feudal exploitation of the peasantry, under conditions of the development of goods and money relations, imperialistic plunder of the land, the disintegration of the communities, the plunder of communal lands by landowners and by the imperialist colonial regime, and the crowding of the Bedouins from their pasture, usury flourishes on a grand scale. Extremely high taxes, which, in part, are still in kind (ashar in Syria, Palestine, etc.) constitute an additional burden on the already unbearable situation of the basic masses of the people. The various areas of the Arab countries are at different stages of economic development and class struggle. In Syria, Palestine, and Egypt, the struggle for national independence and national unification of the Arab peoples, on the basis of people's governments, inevitably is fused with the struggle for an agrarian peasant revolution, directed against the imperialist usurpers and their agents (Zionists in Palestine) and simultaneously against the local feudal landowners. In Iraq, there still prevails feudal, tribal, and patrimonial ownership, which is being subjected to seizure on the part of plantation companies of the top local feudal lords and business bourgeoisie, acting under the control of imperialism. Here the center of gravity of the agrarian movement lies in the mobilization of the masses of the people for the struggle against the usurpers, against the background of the struggle with imperialism and its immediate assistants. To a still higher degree this applies to such countries as Tripoli and Morocco, where the basic mass of the population is still chained to the nomadic mode of life and to the feudal patrimonial system, and where the urban centers cannot extend their revolutionary influence. In northern Algeria there exists, more or less, an established colonial domination, with cruel exploitation of

[1] Fellahin—peasants; Bedouins—pastoral tribes, eds.
[2] Sheikh—the head of a tribe, village, etc., combining spiritual and civil power, eds.
[3] Ostensibly a fifth, but actually a larger part of the crop, exacted by the landowners for their benefit, eds.

the local sedentary population and a relatively important development of the cities and capitalist relations. In southern Algeria, there are still nomadic tribes, not yet subdued by the French imperialists. Under a backward social economic order, the peasants often begin to constitute an independent force only during the process of the disintegration of semi-primitive communities and patrimonies. An exact account of all the specific variations of these conditions is absolutely necessary for an accurate statement of the problem of the relationship between the anti-imperialistic and agrarian peasant revolutions of the Arab peoples. The Communist parties and groups of the Arab countries must devote special attention to the study of these conditions and make use of them in the interest of the revolutionary struggle.

3. The struggle for the liberation of the Arab peoples and for the destruction of the imperialist yoke, which dominates in the most diverse forms, in accordance with the various stages of development in different countries, has already enveloped all the Arab countries. In Morocco, and in southern Algeria and Tripoli, the national liberation struggle manifests itself in almost continuous armed uprisings of the tribes against French, Italian, and Spanish imperialism. In Tunisia the Destour,[4] meanwhile, succeeded in heading the mass indignation and then left it leaderless. In Egypt, the postwar development is characterized by a wave of national struggle, which has led more than once to mass outbreaks. In Syria, the armed uprising of 1925 was crushed, but by 1929 there was a new wave of anti-imperialist struggle. In Palestine, mass indignation against British imperialism and its agency, counterrevolutionary Zionism, has more than once resulted in armed uprisings against the British imperialists and Zionists. In Iraq, the national movement against the English mandate does not subside. In the struggle of the Wahhabis[5] under a peculiar religious guise there were certain elements of struggle against the agents of British imperialism, etc., etc.

What is characteristic of all these movements is that they have evoked the most lively response and sympathy all over the Arab East. In spite of the artificial political boundaries, in spite of the feudal fragmentation, and in spite of the fact that the movement was directed now against English, now against French, now Italian or Spanish imperialism, the national struggle in any one Arab country reverberated, in one degree or another, in all the Arab countries from Palestine to Morocco.

The striving of the Arab masses toward national unification with political boundaries established, not at the command of the imperialists, but on the basis of their own free decision, is inseparable from their endeavor to liberate themselves from the yoke of English, French, Italian, and Spanish imperialism. The Arab masses feel that in order to cast off the yoke of

---

[4] Reform Party of Tunisia, eds.
[5] A militant Arab tribe under the leadership of Ibn Saud, eds.

imperialism they must unite their forces, relying on a common language, historical conditions, and a common enemy. Their fusion in the revolutionary struggle against imperialism and the scope of the struggle indicate that the Arab peoples have all the prerequisites to cast off the imperialist yoke, to achieve national political independence, and to create a number of Arab states, which, thereafter, of their own free will, could unite on the basis of federal principles.

4. The conversion of the Arab countries into agrarian and raw material appendages to the metropolis and the divergence of their economic systems results in the fact that the formation of the classes of capitalist society and the development of the elements of national sovereignty proceed very slowly and irregularly. The imperialists take complete advantage of this situation in their own interests, by grouping under their leadership the reactionary feudal elements and by attempting to make of the Arabic countries strong bases for their imperialistic and aggressive policy of usurpation. In particular, the English imperialists make use of their domination of Iraq, Palestine, and Egypt, to protect the approaches to India, to prepare for a war against the U.S.S.R., and to develop their interests in the eastern Mediterranean. The French imperialists endeavor to convert the Arab population of their colonies into cannon fodder for a future imperialist war and intervention against the U.S.S.R. The feudal landowners and the top feudal lords in all areas of sedentary population finally have gone over, more or less, to the side of imperialism. In the ranks of the Arab bourgeoisie and of the landowners tied up with it, national reformism prevails, and assumes more openly the character of counterrevolution and capitulation. The bourgeoisie and the bourgeois-landowning elements are incapable of a revolutionary struggle against imperialism. They veer more and more in the direction of a counter-revolutionary deal with it within the framework of limited pseudoconstitutional concessions, which only disguise the imperialist domination. The mass movement in the summer of 1930 in Egypt quite clearly revealed the traitorous essence of the Wafd, which removed the slogan of "independence" and tries only to obtain a constitution, which demonstrates that it fears the awakening of the peasant masses more than complete capitulation to imperialism (agrees to sign an Anglo-Egyptian treaty). The position of the Kutlat el Watani[6] in Syria is determined by playing the role of the opposition, absolutely refusing to take part in any revolutionary activities and in any real struggle. Many of the former leaders in the uprising of 1925 are now sitting quietly at the feet of the French generals. The Kutlat el Watani is preparing a deal with the French oppressors. In Palestine, the Arab Executive Committee has entered upon the road of traitorous competition with Zionism in bargaining for concessions from English imperialism in exchange for a guarantee of "peace and

[6] "The National Bloc," the National Reform party of Syria, eds.

quiet" for the Arab masses. National reformism turns more and more to counterrevolution and capitulation, in proportion as, on the one hand, especially under the influence of the world industrial and agrarian crisis, the dissatisfaction and indignation of the toiling masses increase; the more so, that it (i.e., national reformism) does not meet with adequate opposition to the traitorous national interests on the part of the broad masses of the Arab workers and peasants, who, as yet, have been unable to organize themselves adequately and to oppose their bourgeois and bourgeois-landowning reformism with their own revolutionary platform. In Iraq, the National party appeals to the League of Nations, but actually it does not wage a struggle against the English usurpers, but confines itself only to phrases. In Tunisia, the remnants of the Destour went over to the French imperialists. In Algeria, bourgeois-landowning national reformism demands only the granting of French citizenship to the Arabs. The bourgeois and bourgeois-landowning national reformism opposes imperialist domination only within the framework of the exploiting interests of the local bourgeoisie and landowners. They themselves want to exploit the masses of workers and peasants. However, in so far as their immediate exploiting interests, especially in a situation of crisis and imperialistic pressure on the colony, are at variance with the general national interests, they openly betray the general national interests and help imperialism in its struggle against the masses. The traitorous counterrevolutionary nature of national reformism has not as yet been adequately revealed to the broad masses of workers, peasants, and urban *petite bourgeoisie*. National reformism in the Arab countries does not go beyond the political boundaries, established by imperialism, which artificially divide the Arab peoples. It capitulates before the feudal monarchs, who are tools of imperialism, and refuses to struggle against imperialism on an all-Arab scale. The peculiarity of the present stage is that, whereas in all Arab countries national reformism openly capitulates to imperialism, the masses of the workers, peasants, and urban *petite bourgeoisie* are more and more energetically drawn into the struggle for their everyday interests, into the national liberation struggle. The fact that counterrevolutionary national reformism has not been exposed before them to any appreciable extent thereby threatens grave consequences, since this would make it easier for new counterrevolutionary treason and for blows from an ambush. Now, as never before, over against the capitulation and counterrevolution of national reformism there must be juxtaposed an *all-Arab revolutionary anti-imperialist front* of the broad masses of workers, peasants, and urban *petite bourgeoisie,* a front which relies on the development of the workers' and peasants' movement, and which draws from it its strength.

5. In a number of Arab countries, the working class has played and is playing an increasing role in the national liberation struggle (Egypt, Palestine, Iraq, Algeria, Tunisia, etc.). In some countries, following their

destruction the trade-union organizations of the working class are in the process of formation or restoration, although the majority of them are in the hands of the national reformists. Labor strikes, demonstrations, active participation of the workers in the struggle against imperialism, the withdrawal of some strata of the working class from the national reformists, are a signal that the young Arab working class has entered upon the struggle for its historic role in the anti-imperialist and agrarian revolution, in the struggle for national unity. In several countries, Communist parties have already been organized and are in the process of formation.

The world industrial and agrarian crisis, in one way or another, has enveloped all the Arab countries, having hit with particular force the workers and the peasant masses. The decline in earnings and unemployment is worsening the poor living standards of the proletariat, which are bad enough without that, and this drives it along the road to revolutionary class struggle. The ruined poor and middle peasants and workers, who are perpetually in need, and who are laid off, the representatives of the urban pauper class and the broad strata of the *petite bourgeoisie*, who are at present greater in number than heretofore, feel the yoke of imperialism and begin to rise for the struggle in the name of national liberation. Imperialism endeavors to cast on their shoulders all the consequences of the crisis and to square accounts at their expense. However, the new wave of peasant indignation against the unbearable claims of the landowners, usurers, and agents of imperialism, tends to unite the workers in their struggle for their daily bread; in protest against the imperialist yoke, all Arab countries dismembered by English, French, Italian and Spanish jackals of capital are uniting in the struggle for national unity and national independence. Under these conditions, the growing struggle of the Arab masses against imperialism is, together with the revolutionary struggle in China, India, Indo-China, etc., in Latin America, and Black Africa, the most important moment in the crisis of the entire imperialist colonial system.

In Syria, Palestine, and Egypt, where the working-class movement has more or less taken shape, where Communist parties have been organized, where the peasant movement has reached an appreciable degree of maturity, where further development of the anti-imperialist struggle is unthinkable without a consistent and systematic struggle against national reformism—there the urgent and immediate task of the Communist parties is an agrarian peasant revolution and the organization of their work in accordance with the aims of anti-imperialism and anti-feudalism. The overthrow of the imperialist yoke, the confiscation of all concessions, enterprises, constructions, plantations, and other possessions of the imperialists, complete national political independence (plus the abolition of the monarchy in Egypt and the restoration of political unity in Syria), the confiscation of the land of all feudal landowners and colonial usurpers who live on unearned income, an eight-hour working day, and social insurance of workers at the expense of capitalists, freedom of organization for the toilers, and a workers' and peasants' government, a struggle for the liberation of the Arab peoples and their free and voluntary union— such are the main demands which define the content of the anti-imperialist and anti-feudal revolution. The delimitation of and struggle against national reformism must be based on such a foundation. Among the partial demands which should be set forth are the following: the reduction of the working day to eight hours, an increase in wages, unemployment insurance at the expense of the capitalists, freedom of workers' and peasants' organizations, annulment of the indebtedness of poor and middle peasants to usurers, landowners, and banks, discontinuation of payments for leasing land, withdrawal of all the armed forces of the imperialists, and a free popular vote on the question of political self-determination (in Egypt, about the monarchy and the Anglo-Egyptian Treaty; in Syria and Palestine, about the mandate of the League of Nations). In more backward countries, such as Iraq, Tunisia, Tripoli, Morocco, the existing Communist groups there must endeavor to organize and to bring about the spontaneous rise and growth of the anti-imperialist movement, connecting it with the struggle against the top reactionary feudal lords and national reformists, with the struggle of the workers and peasants for their everyday needs. In Algeria, which is a completely enslaved French colony, the center of gravity of the work must be shifted to the development of a struggle for the organization of Arab workers against starvation, colonial norms of pay and general labor conditions, and to a struggle against colonial plunder of Arab lands. The unifying slogans of the anti-imperialist struggle for all the Arab countries must be: (1) Down with imperialism in Arab lands; (2) Complete national political independence of Arab countries, and free decision by them on the question of their political system and boundaries; (3) A voluntary federal union of the liberated Arab peoples within the framework of an All-Arab workers' and peasants' federation of the Arab peoples, on the basis of a union of the working class, the toilers of the city, and the peasantry.

The slogan of the All-Arab Workers' and Peasants' Federation of the Arab peoples could and should be set forth, not in the sense that the working class makes as the condition for its participation in the anti-imperialist national liberation struggle the outright victory of the working class and the basic masses of the peasants. It should be interpreted in the sense that, by waging a struggle for national liberation under all and any circumstances with greater firmness and consistency, the proletariat at the same time explains to the masses that there can be no lasting victory for national and political independence without an agrarian peasant revolution and the establishment of a workers' and peasants' government, at least in the more developed Arab countries (Syria, Palestine, Egypt, and Algeria). The Communist parties will be able to lead the broad masses of workers against the bourgeoisie, the peasant masses against the imperialist usurpers, landowners, and usurers; they will be able to elicit the support of the poor in the city and the masses of the *petite bourgeoisie* only when they simultaneously act as leaders and organizers of the struggle against imperialism for the national liberation of the Arab countries. Hegemony over the working class cannot be realized without a persistent proletarian struggle for Arab national independence and freedom.

The Communists are duty bound to wage a struggle for national independence and national unity, not only within the narrow and artificial boundaries created by imperialism and the dynastic interests of certain Arab countries, but on an all-Arab scale, for the national unification of the entire East. In overcoming the artificially created boundaries, the anti-imperialist revolutionary movement must find its strength, must achieve a genuinely revolutionary range, must become the center of gravitation for the broadest masses. This will also facilitate the struggle against the influence of the reactionary clergy. No such situation should be allowed as the isolated outbreak of a revolutionary anti-imperialist movement in Egypt, Palestine, or in any other Arab country, without the support of the other Arab countries. The Communist parties are called upon to act as organizers in the struggle for national liberation and for an anti-imperialist revolution on an all-Arab scale.

The relationship with the *petite bourgeoisie* and national revolutionary groups which wage, albeit with great hesitation, a struggle against imperialism, must follow the rule: To proceed separately, but to strike together. Occasional temporary agreements with them for militant action are permissible, provided their vacillation and inconsistency are criticized, thereby preserving the complete ideological and organizational independence of the Communist movement. The Communist parties must try to attract to the side of the anti-imperialist struggle not only the workers and peasants, but also the broad strata of urban *petite bourgeoisie*. Besides taking stock of all specific conditions of the struggle, the Communist parties must bear in mind the fact that the sharpening of contradictions among imperialists, which inevitably leads to world conflict, creates a particularly favorable soil for a new upsurge of the Arab national and revolutionary movement. Both the strategic position of the Arab countries and the efforts of the imperialists to make use of the Arab peoples as cannon fodder for a new world carnage, and for the intervention against the U.S.S.R.—all this lends a special significance to the anti-imperialist struggle of the Arab masses.

6. A bold and resolute setting forth of the slogan for the national liberation of all Arab peoples is especially necessary because, in spite of the quite firm and clear decisions of the Communist International, the questions of the struggle for the liberation of the Arab masses from the yoke of imperialism, both English and French, as well as world imperialism in general, have not yet occupied their proper place in the work

of the Communist parties of Syria, Palestine, and Egypt. Some Communist groups and individual Communists in Iraq, Algeria, and Tunisia are devoting even less attention to this question of primary importance. Opportunism, especially Rightist opportunism, which capitulates before the great powers and the national bourgeoisie on the national question, is one of the main handicaps to the development of the Communist movement in Arab countries. In Palestine, the Communist party experienced its gravest crisis in connection with the Arab uprising in 1929, when the Party found itself isolated from the Arab masses, as a result of Zionist deviation, which hampered the Arabization of the Party. It took one and one-half years to secure the indispensable prerequisites for the Bolshevization of the Party, and even so it did not occur without opportunistic efforts, under anti-Bolshevik slogans, to block the Arabization of the Party. In Egypt, the Party found itself completely isolated from the masses, at the very time the mighty, spontaneous outbreak of the mass movement was in full swing. Not only was it unable to expose the traitorous counterrevolutionary conduct of the Wafd and to create a revolutionary counterpoise to it, but it even permitted the crudest anti-Bolshevik errors on the matter of the irreconcilable struggle against imperialism and its reactionary monarchial agency by detaching itself from the mass anti-imperialist movement. In Syria, the Rightist opportunistic elements openly rose up in opposition to any declaration by the Communist party to the workers' and peasants' masses as to its mere existence, and to the fact that the Communist party began, under its own banner, the struggle against French imperialism. In Tunisia and Algeria, by the way, the Communist organizations are also growing weak, because of the fact that the Communists have been unable to present to the masses the question of the struggle against French imperialism. Without overcoming opportunism, and especially arrant Rightist opportunism on the Arab national question, Communist parties cannot develop in Arab countries.

Leaving in force the decisions concerning the tasks of the Communists in any one Arab country, the following steps are necessary in order to strengthen the activities of the Communists in all Arab countries:

1. To develop an extensive mass campaign as to the aims and tasks of the anti-imperialist Arab national liberation movement, tying it in with the regular tasks of the workers' and peasants' movement in the corresponding countries.

In waging a struggle for the overthrow of the imperialist yoke in each separate country, it is necessary to weave in this slogan with the struggle for a free decision by the Arab popular masses on the question of national self-determination, and along with this, for the Communists to carry on propaganda for national unity in the form of an all-Arab workers' and peasants' federation.

2. For this purpose, it is necessary to hold large and small meetings,

and wherever possible demonstrations, to issue special leaflets, to organize anti-imperialist committees to assume the initiative in the struggle, whose representatives are chosen from the factories and foundries, and from the rural and urban working population.

3. To create a general press organ, for the time being, for the Communist parties of Egypt, Syria, Palestine, and the Communists in Iraq.

To establish a more regular and lasting contact for the exchange of experience and to coordinate the work in the early stages among the Communist parties of Egypt, Syria, Palestine, and the Communists in Iraq, bearing in mind the fact that in the future it will be necessary to secure the over-all collaboration of the Communists of Tripoli, Tunisia, Morocco, and Algeria. Having taken special measures to organize and to unify the Communists in Algeria, Tunisia, and Morocco, the future course must be to detach the organization of all these countries from the French Communist party and make them independent units.

46. Joseph Vissarionovitch Stalin

(1879-1953)

THE BIOGRAPHICAL SKETCH PRESENTED BELOW reflects the changed attitude toward Stalin following Khrushchev's exposure of his "shortcomings" at the Twentieth Congress of the Communist Party in 1956. The Soviet government obviously attempted to distinguish between Stalin's many constructive services to the Party and his departure from Leninist principles, especially during the closing years of his rule.

Translated from *Bol'shaya Sovetskaya Entsiklopediya,* Second edition, 1957, Vol. XL, pp. 419-424.

Stalin (Dzhugashvili), Joseph Vissarionovitch (21 December, 1879 - 5 March, 1953): a prominent figure in the Russian and international revolutionary movement, the Communist Party of the Soviet Union and the Soviet state, and an outstanding theoretician of Marxism-Leninism. He was born in the city of Gori, Tiflis Gubernia, into the family of a shoemaker, subsequently a worker in a shoe factory. In 1894 he completed his parish school education and entered the Tiflis Orthodox Divinity Seminary. At the end of the 19th century the workers' movement expanded in Russia and disseminated Marxism. The Petersburg "Alliance for the Struggle of the Liberation of the Working Class," founded by V. I. Lenin in 1895, gave a strong impetus to the development of the Social-Democratic movement throughout the country, including the Transcaucasus. Under the influence of Russian and Georgian Social Democrats J. V. Stalin, while still in the Seminary, began to take part in the revolutionary movement, became a member of a Marxist circle, and studied the works of K. Marx, F. Engels, V. I. Lenin, and G. V. Plekhanov; in 1898 he entered the Tiflis organization of the RSDWP [Russian Social-Democratic Workers' Party] and began to conduct propaganda among the workers at the Tiflis iron works. In 1899 J. V. Stalin was expelled from the Seminary for Marxist propaganda, became an outlaw, and a professional revolutionary. About this time he began to collaborate with the prominent revolutionary Marxists, V. Z. Ketskhoveli and A. G. Tulukidze. V. K. Kurnatovsky, a student and collaborator of V. I. Lenin, who arrived in Tiflis in the fall of 1900, played a very important role in the dissemination of Lenin's ideas in the Transcaucasus. J. V. Stalin was associated with Kurnatovsky in revolutionary work. In September, 1901, with the participation of V. Z. Ketskhoveli and J. V. Stalin, the Social Democratic newspaper, *Brdzola (Bor'ba)*, modelled after *Iskra*, began to appear. J. V. Stalin had several articles in it.

At the end of 1901 the Tiflis Committee dispatched J. V. Stalin to Batum, where he carried on revolutionary activity among the workers, participated in the founding of the Batum Social-Democratic organization, and was one of the organizers of the huge political demonstration of Batum workers in March, 1902. In April, 1902, J. V. Stalin was arrested. In exile he learned about the divergence of opinion between the Bolsheviks and Mensheviks at the Second Congress of the RSDWP and he sided with the Bolsheviks. In the fall of 1903, J. V. Stalin was exiled to the village of Novaya Uda, Balagansky County, in Irkutsk Gubernia. In January, 1904, he escaped from exile and illegally returned to the Caucasus where, along with M. G. Tskhakaya, S. G. Shaumyan, V. M. Knun'yats, F. I. Makharadze, and others who were members of the Caucasian United Committee of the RSDWP, he helped to edit the newspaper *Proletariatis Brdzola (Bor'ba Proletariata)*, and took part in the struggle of the Bolsheviks for the summoning of the Third Congress of the Party.

During the first Russian Revolution, 1905-1907, J. V. Stalin, as one of the leading Party figures of the Transcaucasus, carried on extensive organizational and ideological work; in his articles, published in Bolshevik newspapers and brochures, he defended the Lenin idea of the hegemony of the proletariat and the armed uprising, and opposed the opportunistic tactics of the Mensheviks and anarchists. J. V. Stalin took part in the work of the First All-Russian Bolshevik Conference in Tammerfors (1905), the Fourth ("United") Congress of the RSDWP (Stockholm, 1906), and the Fifth ("London") Congress of the RSDWP (1907). At the Fourth Congress of the RSDWP, J. V. Stalin defended the Bolshevik line on revolution, but in the discussion of the agrarian question he was among the "dissenters" who, at variance with Lenin, advanced a program for the nationalization of the land and defended the erroneous demand for the division of the landlords' land among the peasants.

From June, 1907, while living in Baku, J. V. Stalin, along with S. G. Shaumyan, P. A. Djaparidze, G. K. Ordjonikidze, M. Azizbekov, S. S. Spandaryan, K. E. Voroshilov, I. T. Fioletov, and others, worked in the Baku Party organization, took an active part in Bolshevik newspapers published in Baku, and carried on the struggle with the Mensheviks.

In March, 1908, J. V. Stalin was arrested and exiled to Sol'vychegodsk, in Vologordsky Gubernia; in June, 1909, he escaped from exile and returned to Baku. In February, 1910, Stalin's article, "Letter to the Caucasus," in which he supported the Lenin line of struggle against the liquidators and conciliators, was published in the central Party press (as a supplement to the newspaper, *Social-Democrat*). In March, 1910, J. V. Stalin was arrested again and exiled to Sol'vychegodsk. In January, 1912, at the CC [Central Committee] elected by the Sixth All-Russian ("Prague") Party Conference, J. V. Stalin was admitted *in absentia* to membership in the CC and the Russian Bureau of the CC. In February, 1912, he escaped from exile and continued to take part in Party work, contributed to the Bolshevik newspaper, *Zvezda (Star)*, and helped to prepare the first number of the newspaper, *Pravda* [April 22, May 5]. In April, 1912, J. V. Stalin was arrested in Petersburg and exiled to the Narymsky Territory; in September, 1912, he again escaped from exile to Petersburg where, along with Ya. M. Sverdlov, V. M. Molotov, M. S. Ol'minsky, and others, he took part in editing *Pravda* and in Bolshevik leadership for the election campaign for the Fourth State Duma. In December, 1912, J. V. Stalin took part in the CC sessions with Party workers in Cracow. Based on the theory and program of the Bolshevik Party on the national question drafted by Lenin, J. V. Stalin at the end of 1912 and the beginning of 1913 wrote the well-known work, *Marxism and the National Question*, which was highly regarded by Lenin. In this work, J. V. Stalin subjected to sharp criticism the opportunistic national program of the Austrian Social Democrats and their followers in Russia —the Bundists and Menshevik-Liquidators, and defended the Bolshevik program on the national question. In February, 1913, he was arrested in Petersburg, and exiled to Turkhansky Territory.

After the February bourgeois-democratic revolution, March 12, 1917, J. V. Stalin returned to Petrograd. He became a member of the Presidium of the CC Bureau and also one of the editors of *Pravda*. During this period, J. V. Stalin assumed an erroneous position on the question of peace and the role of the Soviets, defended the already discarded slogan about revolutionary-democratic dictatorship of the proletariat and peasantry, and defended the policy of "pressure" by the Soviets on the Provisional government. ". . . This was a profoundly erroneous position," said Stalin subsequently, "for it produced a pacifist illusion, helped to keep the mills of the defenders of capitalism running, and hampered the revolutionary education of the masses. I shared this erroneous position then with other Party comrades and did not completely abandon it until the middle of April, when I accepted the Lenin thesis" (*Sotch.*, Vol. 6, p. 333). At the Seventh (April) All-Russian Conference of Bolsheviks (1917), J. V. Stalin supported the Lenin course on socialist revolution and reported on the national question. During this period, the Bolshevik Party under the leadership of Lenin launched tremendous work among the workers, soldiers, and peasants, and carried on the struggle for the transformation of the bourgeois-democratic revolution into a socialist revolution. J. V. Stalin took an active part in the work of the Party for the organization and political education of the masses.

In July and August, 1917, the Sixth Congress of the Bolshevik Party was held in Petrograd. V. I. Lenin directed the preparation and running of the Congress from the underground through Ya. M. Sverdlov, J. V. Stalin, V. M. Molotov, G. K. Ordjonikidze. Since V. I. Lenin could not be present at the Congress, the Central Committee delegated J. V. Stalin to make the Party CC report and the report on the political situation. The Lenin line on the preparation and carrying out of the socialist revolution was developed in these reports. In conclusion, J. V. Stalin issued a rebuttal to the statements of E. Preobrazhensky and others, who regarded the victory of the revolution in Russia as impossible without the victory of revolution in the West. "Without denying," said J. V. Stalin, "that Russia itself is the country that is paving the road to socialism . . . it is necessary to abandon the antiquated conception that only Europe can show us the way" (Sotch., Vol. 3, pp. 186-187). The Congress accepted the Lenin positions on armed uprising and on the achievement of the dictatorship of the working class.

At the historic session of the Party CC on October 10 (23), 1917, the written and proposed resolution of V. I. Lenin on the necessity of beginning the armed uprising in the immediate future was accepted. The political center for the direction of the uprising—the Political Bureau of the CC, headed by Lenin—was created. On October 16 (29), 1917, the CC in a broad session ratified the resolution on an armed uprising accepted at the previous session, and created a military-revolutionary center, the members of which were Ya. M. Sverdlov, J. V. Stalin, F. E. Dzerzhinsky, A. S. Bubnov, and M. S. Uritsky. V. I. Lenin directed the activity of this center.

At the Second All-Russian Congress of Soviets, October 26 (November 8), 1917, J. V. Stalin was elected a member of the All-Union Executive Committee and confirmed as People's Commissar of Nationalities. From March, 1919, Stalin also served as People's Commissar for State Control, reorganized later into the People's Commissariat of Worker-Peasant Inspection. During the foreign War of Intervention and the Civil War, J. V. Stalin was a member of the Revolutionary Military Council of the Republic and he carried out the tasks set by the Central Committee of the Party and Soviet government on several fronts (the Tsaritsyn part of the Southern Front, the Eastern, Southern, and South-Western Fronts).

After the rout of the interventionists and the end of the Civil War when, in connection with the transition to peaceful economic construction, the anti-Party groups launched a struggle against the Party line worked out by Lenin, J. V. Stalin upheld the Lenin line against the anti-Party groupings and fractions (Trotskyites, "Workers' Opposition," Decists [Democratic-Centralists]). At the Tenth Congress of the Party, (1921), J. V. Stalin made the "Report on the Regular Tasks of the Party on the National Question." After the Eleventh Party Congress (1922), the plenary session of the CC of the Party elected J. V. Stalin Secretary-General of the CC.

Under the direction of V. I. Lenin, in this period the Party carried out the big task of creating the Union of Soviet Socialist Republics. V. I. Lenin thought that the USSR must be a voluntary union of equal and sovereign allied republics. On this question, J. V. Stalin at first held an erroneous position, advocating the project of so-called "autonomization," i.e., of the entry into the RSFSR of other Soviet republics with the rights of autonomous units. V. I. Lenin opposed this proposition, criticizing Stalin's error in carrying out the national policy and his compromise on the manifestations of great-power chauvinism. The Lenin principles were accepted by the Central Committee and laid the foundation for the formation of the Union of Soviet Socialist Republics. Due to the illness of Lenin, the report to the First [All-Union] Congress of Soviets of the USSR on the formation of the Union of Soviet Socialist Republics (1922), was delegated by the CC of the ACP (b) to J. V. Stalin.

After the death of V. I. Lenin, the Communist Party under the direction of the Central Committee firmly and convincingly led the Soviet people along the path to the realization of Lenin's legacy, along the road to the building of socialism. At this time, J. V. Stalin worked in various capacities, work which had great significance for the defence and propaganda of Leninism, and for the ideological defeat of the currents hostile to Leninism. In this respect, a big role was played by J. V. Stalin's work, *The Foundations of Leninism* (1924), in which were presented the basic problems of Leninism and the discovery of what V. I. Lenin had added to Marxism. In the struggle against the Trotskyites, Stalin, along with other Party figures, defended the Lenin theory on the possibility of the victory of socialism beginning in each country separately and on the possibility of the victory of socialism in the USSR under conditions of capitalist encirclement.

Proceeding from the instructions of V. I. Lenin, who worked out a scientific program for the building of socialism in the USSR, the Party pursued the course of the socialist industrialization of the country. This line was laid down in the political report of the Central Committee made by J. V. Stalin at the Fourteenth Party Congress (1925). The report, which emphasized that the essence of industrialization consists predominantly in the development of heavy industry and, above all, of machine building, revealed the basic difference between socialist industrialization closely connected with the improvement of the material position of the toilers, and the capitalistic which follows the path of the colonial usurpers and rapacious and merciless exploitation of the toilers. At the beginning of 1926 appeared J. V. Stalin's book,. *Problems of Leninism,* which emphasized criticism of the opportunistic views of the Zinovievites, who had fallen into the ideological positions of Trotskyism. At the Fifteenth Party Conference (November, 1926), J. V. Stalin reported on "The Social-Democratic Deviation in Our Party," and at the Seventh Broad Plenary Session of the Executive Committee of the Communist International (December, 1926) he reported on "Once Again on the Social-Democratic Deviation in Our Party." These two reports played an important role in the consolidation of Party ranks under the banner of Lenin's ideas, in the exposure of the Trotskyites, their capitulation before capitalism, and their disorganizing activities.

Relying on the successes of socialist industrialization and guided by the Lenin cooperative plan, the Fifteenth Congress of the ACP (b) (1927) set forth as the most important immediate task of the Party and Soviet people the collectivization of agriculture. These questions were clarified in the political report of the Party made by Stalin at the Congress. During this period the anti-Party group of Right opportunists—Bukharin, Rykov, Tomsky, and others—came out openly against the general Party line. J. V. Stalin's reports on "The Industrialization of the Country and the Right Deviation in the ACP (b)" (1928), "The Right Deviation in the ACP (b)" (1929), and others, exposed the line of the Right opportunists, who expressed the ideology of the kulaks.

At the Sixteenth Congress of the ACP (b) (1930) and the Seventeenth Congress of the ACP (b) (1934), J. V. Stalin reported on the work of the Party's Central Committee. During this period the Communist Party and the Soviet state launched socialism's attack against the capitalist elements. In the midst of the tense international situation the country surmounted enormous difficulties in order to put an end to technical-economic backwardness in the shortest possible time. Pursuing a course of priority for the development of heavy industry, the Party achieved decisive successes in the socialist industrialization of the country and in the collectivization of the agricultural economy.

In 1938 J. V. Stalin wrote *Dialectical and Historical Materialism,* in which he gave a concise clarification of the fundamentals of the Marxist-Leninist philosophy, pointing out its significance for the practical activity of the Party.

The Eighteenth Congress of the ACP (b) took place in March, 1939. In his CC report to the Congress, J. V. Stalin explained the program worked out by the Central Committee for the struggle of the Party and Soviet people for the completion of the building of a socialist society and the gradual transition from socialism to communism.

On May 6, 1941, J. V. Stalin was appointed Chairman of the Council of People's Commissars of the USSR. At the beginning of the Great Patriotic War of the Soviet Union, J. V. Stalin was appointed Chairman of the State Committee of Defence, People's Commissar of Defence, and Commander-in-Chief of the Armed Forces of the USSR, in which posts he remained until the end of the war. The great victory over the Hitlerite coalition was won by the Soviet people under the guidance of the Communist Party and its Central Committee, headed by Stalin.

During the war J. V. Stalin, as head of the Soviet government, took part in the conferences of the leaders of the three powers—the USSR, the USA, and Great Britain—in Teheran (1943), in Yalta and Berlin (1945). During these years J. V. Stalin carried on a daily correspondence with the President of the USA and the Prime Minister of Great Britain, in which he persistently fought to strengthen the anti-Hitlerite coalition and consistently safeguarded the national interests of the peoples of countries subjected to Hitlerite aggression.

In the postwar period J. V. Stalin published *Marxism and the Problems of Linguistics* (1950) and *The Economic Problems of Socialism in the USSR* (1952), in which important questions of Marxist-Leninist theory were discussed. *The Economic Problems of Socialism in the USSR* exerted great influence on the working out of certain theses of the political economy of socialism. J. V. Stalin emphasized the objective character of the economic laws under socialism; relying on the pronouncements of the classics of Marxism-Leninism, he formulated the basic economic law of socialism, the law of planned, proportionate development of the national economy. He noted the significance for the expansion of socialist production of the priority of the growth of the means of production. At the same time, the work contains a series of erroneous and controversial postulates (for instance: the affirmation that trade exchange was beginning to hamper the development of the productive forces of the country and the indispensability of a gradual transition toward exchange of products; underestimation of the action of the law of costs in the sphere of production, especially in regard to the means of production; the assertion of the inevitability of the reduction of the scale of capitalist production after the Second World War and the inevitability under existing conditions of wars among capitalist countries).

The Nineteenth Congress of the CPSS was held in October, 1952. J. V. Stalin spoke at the closing session of the Congress. The plenary session of the CC, meeting after the Congress, elected Stalin a member of the CC Presidium and Secretary of the CC of the Communist Party of the Soviet Union.

J. V. Stalin's outstanding activity was highly valued by the Soviet government. He was awarded the titles, Hero of Socialist Labor (1939), Hero of the Soviet Union (1945), and Generalissimo of the Soviet Union (1945). He was awarded three Orders of Lenin, the Order of Victory, of the Red Banner, of Suvorov First Class, and medals.

On March 5, 1953, following a severe illness, J. V. Stalin died.

Over a period of many years, Joseph Vissarionovitch Stalin conducted leading Party and government work. Prominent as a proletarian revolutionary, he played a huge role in the organization of the struggle of the Russian proletariat against Tsarism, against the landlords and bourgeoisie, in the preparation and carrying out of the socialist revolution in Russia, in the struggle with the White Guards and interventionists during the Civil War, in the realization of the Lenin plan for the industrialization of the USSR and the collectivization of the agricultural economy, and in the struggle for the building of socialism, the independence of the Soviet country, and the reinforcement of peace. J. V. Stalin deserves great credit for the ideological struggle against the foes of Leninism— the Trotskyites, the Right opportunists, bourgeois nationalists, and various revisionists. In his theoretical works, J. V. Stalin advocated Leninism, creatively developed the Marxist-Leninist theory in conformity with the building of socialism in the USSR, which had great significance for the entire international workers' and communist movement. By his dedication to the working class, his selfless struggle for socialism, and for Marxism-Leninism, J. V. Stalin acquired a world-wide reputation and tremendous authority in the Party and among the people. Under such conditions, the cult of Stalin's personality took shape and developed little by little.

To understand how this could happen, it is necessary to bear in mind the objective, concrete historical conditions under which the building of socialism in the USSR was proceeding, as well as certain negative personal qualities of Stalin himself. For a long time the Soviet country was a besieged fortress. Over it hung the threat of imperialist attack. This threat increased after the advent of fascism to power in Germany (1933). The building of socialism took place in the midst of a savage class struggle. The opposition of the exploiting classes had to be overcome and a ruthless struggle had to be developed against the enemies of Leninism. The complex international and domestic situation demanded iron discipline, strong centralization of leadership, and gave rise to the necessity for the separate restriction of Soviet and also of internal Party democracy. These limitations were inevitable during the savage struggle with the class enemy and his agency, and during the war against the German-fascist aggressors. Stalin began to erect the norm of intra-Party and state life. He violated the norms worked out by Lenin for Party life and the principle of collectivism in leadership, manifesting intolerance toward everything at variance with his opinion. While the activity of local Party organizations was proceeding normally, in conformity with Party rules, the Plenums of the Central Committee and Party Congresses were held irregularly and later were not summoned at all for many years. Stalin actually proved to be above criticism.

As early as the end of December, 1922, and the beginning of January, 1923, V. I. Lenin wrote "Letter to the Congress." Lenin considered it necessary to bring this letter to the attention of the next Fourteenth

Party Congress. He pointed out in the letter that J. V. Stalin had concentrated immense power in his own hands. Lenin expressed anxiety lest Stalin should not always be sufficiently cautious in the exercise of such power. Lenin noted that Stalin was rude, capricious, disloyal, and paid too little attention to his comrades. Lenin proposed the replacement of Stalin in the post of Secretary-General by another comrade, on the ground that Stalin's shortcomings could in the future lead to serious consequences for the Party and the country. After his death, V. I. Lenin's letter was made public at meetings of delegates to the Thirteenth Party Congress (May, 1924). Between the Twelfth and Thirteenth Congresses, especially after the death of Lenin, the anti-Leninist groups became more active. The opposition led by Trotsky came out in the open against the general Party line. The delegates to the Thirteenth Congress and subsequently those to the CC plenary session, discussing V. I. Lenin's letter in the light of the extreme intra-Party struggle, took into account the great theoretical and organizational work conducted by Stalin in the fight against the Trotskyites and other opposition groups, and on the assumption that he would conscientiously carry out his pledge about overcoming the shortcomings that occasioned Lenin's serious anxiety, spoke out in favor of Stalin's retention in the post of Secretary-General of the CC.

Immediately after the death of Lenin, J. V. Stalin took cognizance of the critical reproofs. Later, however, especially after the Seventeenth Party Congress (1934), having grossly overestimated his services J. V. Stalin came to believe in his own infallibility. The successes achieved by the Party and the Soviet country and the adulation addressed to him turned Stalin's head.

In the final years, there appeared in the activity of J. V. Stalin a sharp discrepancy between word and deed, between theory and practice. His works contained correct, profound Marxist theses about the people as the maker of history, and about the role of the Party and its Central Committee as the collective leadership. In practice, however, in the last years of his life Stalin departed from these Marxist-Leninist principles and spread the cult of his own personality. This was reflected in the *Short Course on the History of the ACP (b)* (1938), and in the second edition of Stalin's biography (1946), edited by Stalin himself.

J. V. Stalin correctly emphasized the need to strengthen the Soviet state, to conduct a relentless struggle against the class enemy, and to be on guard against counter-revolutionaries. In 1937, however, he set forth the mistaken thesis that in proportion as the Soviet state progressed toward the building of socialism the class struggle in the country must become ever more and more intensified. The class struggle in the Soviet Union reached its peak during the period when the question, "Who is who?" was decided, when the struggle for the building of the foundations of socialism was in full swing. But later, as the exploiting classes were liquidated and Soviet society achieved solid moral-political unity, the thesis about the inevitability of the further sharpening of the class struggle was erroneous. J. V. Stalin made use of this thesis to justify the resort to mass repressions in connection with the political rout of ideological opponents, which, under the new conditions, was already unnecessary. In this situation, the sworn enemies of the Party and the people—Yagoda, Yezhov, and Beria, worming their way into J. V. Stalin's confidence, slandered and exterminated many honest and dedicated Party people. The Lenin principles on national policy were likewise violated. The exposure and rout in 1953 of Beria's criminal band provided an opportunity to unmask and to liquidate the violations of socialist legality perpetrated by this band.

J. V. Stalin made an important contribution to the defence of the country and to the struggle against fascism. However, on the eve of the Great Patriotic War he was mistaken in his evaluation of the international situation. Having exaggerated the significance of the Soviet-German non-aggression treaty, Stalin refused to believe the facts about the direct preparation of the German-fascist forces for invasion of the territory of the USSR. He rejected all proposals about the necessity for military preparedness on the part of Soviet forces close to the frontier areas. This was one of the reasons why the invasion of the Hitlerite armies surprised the Soviet troops in the Western regions. The Soviet forces covering the state boundary displayed heroic resistance to the invaders, but being inadequately prepared to repulse the attack and forced to accept battle under very disadvantageous circumstances, they sustained heavy losses in men and military equipment which led to a sharp change in the correlation of forces to the enemy's advantage. In the direction of certain important military operations, J. V. Stalin sometimes made decisions without consulting the CC members involved in military work and failed to clarify the actual position, which adversely affected the course of military action during the first period of the war.

During the war the Party and the government organized military production on a broad scale in the eastern regions of the country. Thanks to the great advantage of the socialist system, the availability of a highly developed industry, and the selflessness of the peoples of the Soviet Union, in a short time it was possible to achieve superiority over the enemy in the quantity and quality of weapons, to frustrate fascist plans for a "Blitzkrieg," to insure a change for the better in the course of the war, and to prepare conditions for the defeat of the Hitlerite invaders. The Communist Party and its Central Committee were the organizing and directing forces of the heroic, nation-wide struggle against the German-fascist invaders. The Communist Party united and directed the activity of all Party, Soviet, economic, and social organizations and military organs. The members of the Party CC, outstanding Soviet military leaders, and local Party and Soviet organizations developed tremendous organizing, political, economic, and military work. Thanks to the stoicism and heroism of the Soviet fighters, the activities of the outstanding Soviet Army commanders were prepared and the projected military operations which culminated in complete victory over the enemy were carried out on an unprecedented scale with skill and courage.

During the postwar years, J. V. Stalin often made erroneous decisions on economic questions unilaterally and obviously vetoed urgent new measures and proposals emanting from CC members. This was detrimental to the economic development of the country, especially in the sphere of agriculture. Stalin also made serious mistakes on certain questions of the foreign policy of the Soviet state (for instance, the rift with Yugoslavia).

The Party with Lenin-like directness and decisiveness censured Stalin's mistakes in the last years of his activity in order to exclude the possibility of their repetition in the future. The Party subjected to sharp criticism the violations of the Lenin norms of Party life, the departure from the Lenin principles of collective leadership and intra-Party democracy, and the violation of socialist legality. The liquidation of these violations strengthened the Communist Party of the Soviet Union, raised its authority still higher among the toiling masses, and created all the conditions for the strengthening and further development of socialist democracy in the USSR.

The ideologists of imperialism and the other enemies of socialism, striving to avert the workers of their own countries from socialism, tried to prove that the cult of personality, with all its consequences, is a natural outgrowth of the socialist social and state system. Actually, the cult of personality is in fundamental opposition to the Soviet socialist system and to Marxist-Leninist theory. This explains why the Communist Party of the Soviet Union itself, on its own initiative, launched a decisive struggle for the liquidation of the cult of personality and its consequences.

The Stalin cult of personality and the mistakes he made in the final years of his life undoubtedly impeded to a certain extent the development of Soviet society, but it could not halt this development, especially as it could not change the nature of the Soviet system.

The Soviet people and the Communist Parties of all countries supported and approved the decisions of the Twentieth Party Congress, which mapped out the program for the building of communism and the steady rise of the living standards of the toilers of the USSR, pointed out the line of consistent struggle for the preservation and consolidation of peace, for the strengthening of the unity of the socialist countries, for strengthening the fraternal international connections among the Communist and workers' parties of all countries.

The decisions of the Twentieth Party Congress thus disclosed the harm done to the Party and government by the Stalin cult of personality and pointed out the path to the overcoming of its consequences.

For a long time J. V. Stalin occupied the leading position in the membership of the Central Committee of the Communist Party. All his activity was connected with the realization of the great socialist transformation in the Soviet country. The Communist Party and the Soviet people will remember Stalin and will render him his due. His name is inseparable from Marxism-Leninism, and it would be the grossest distortion of historical truth to disseminate the mistakes Stalin made in the final years of his life over all his many years of Party and state activity. The campaign undertaken by reactionary imperialist circles against the "Stalinism" they invented is actually a campaign against the revolutionary workers' movement. The pronouncements of the revisionists against so-called "Stalinism" is likewise in essence a form of struggle against the fundamental theses of Marxism-Leninism.

47. Stalin: on overcoming

Russian backwardness

CONFRONTED IN 1931 BY THE FACT that the First Five-Year Plan (1928-1933) was already lagging behind schedule, Stalin exerted heavy pressure on Soviet business executives to maintain a "Bolshevik tempo," and extracted pledges from them to complete the Plan in four years. In the Soviet Union, everything was subordinated to the battle for production. Stalin urged the development of Soviet specialists to free the country from its dependence on foreigners. At this time he issued his famous warning that the USSR had only ten years in which to bridge the fifty to one hundred year gap between it and the advanced capitalist nations or go down to defeat. Ten years later the Soviet Union, on June 22, 1941, was invaded by Nazi Germany.

Stalin's speech, "The Tasks of Business Executives," delivered at the First All-Union Conference of Leading Personnel of Soviet Industry, February 4, 1931, excerpts from which are presented below, reveals the climate of emergency in which the First Five-Year Plan was being carried out. From J. Stalin, *Works*, Vol. 13 (Moscow: Foreign Languages Publishing House, 1955), pp. 39-41.

... We must ourselves become experts, masters of the business; we must turn to technical science—such was the lesson life itself was teaching us. But neither the first warning nor even the second brought about the necessary change. It is time, high time that we turned towards technique. It is time to discard the old slogan, the obsolete slogan of non-interference in technique, and ourselves become specialists, experts, complete masters of our economic affairs. . . .

This, of course, is no easy matter; but it can certainly be accomplished. Science, technical experience, knowledge, are all things that can be acquired. We may not have them today, but tomorrow we shall. The main thing is to have the passionate Bolshevik desire to master technique, to master the science of production. Everything can be achieved, everything can be overcome, if there is a passionate desire for it.

It is sometimes asked whether it is not possible to slow down the tempo somewhat, to put a check on the movement. No, comrades, it is not possible! The tempo must not be reduced! On the contrary, we must increase it as much as is within our powers and possibilities. This is dictated to us by our obligations to the workers and peasants of the U.S.S.R. This is dictated to us by our obligations to the working class of the whole world.

To slacken the tempo would mean falling behind. And those who fall behind get beaten. But we do not want to be beaten. No, we refuse to be beaten! One feature of the history of old Russia was the continual beatings she suffered because of her backwardness. She was beaten by the Mongol khans. She was beaten by the Turkish beys. She was beaten by the Swedish feudal lords. She was beaten by the Polish and Lithuanian gentry. She was beaten by the British and French capitalists. She was beaten by the Japanese barons. All beat her—because of her backwardness, because of her military backwardness, cultural backwardness, political backwardness, industrial backwardness, agricultural backwardness. They beat her because to do so was profitable and could be done with impunity. You remember the words of the pre-revolutionary poet [Nekrasov]: "You are poor and abundant, mighty and impotent, Mother Russia." Those gentlemen were quite familiar with the verses of the old poet. They beat her, saying: "You are abundant," so one can enrich oneself at your expense. They beat her, saying: "You are poor and impotent," so you can be beaten and plundered with impunity. Such is the law of the exploiters—to beat the backward and the weak. It is the jungle law of capitalism. You are backward, you are weak—therefore you are wrong; hence you can be beaten and enslaved. You are mighty—therefore you are right; hence we must be wary of you.

That is why we must no longer lag behind.

In the past we had no fatherland, nor could we have had one. But now that we have overthrown capitalism and power is in our hands, in the hands of the people, we have a fatherland, and we will uphold its independence. Do you want our socialist fatherland to be beaten and to lose its independence? If you do not want this, you must put an end to its backwardness in the shortest possible time and develop a genuine Bolshevik tempo in building up its socialist economy. There is no other way. That is why Lenin said on the eve of the October Revolution: "Either perish, or overtake and outstrip the advanced capitalist countries."

We are fifty or a hundred years behind the advanced countries. We must make good this distance in ten years. Either we do it, or we shall go under.

That is what our obligations to the workers and peasants of the U.S.S.R. dictate to us. . . .

48. the treason trials

ALTHOUGH THE LEADERS OF THE SOVIET REGIME had no compunction about plotting the overthrow of other governments, as indicated earlier by their program for the Arab countries, they reacted strongly to plots against their own security by instituting the purges of 1936-1938, which had widespread repercussions at home and abroad. The purges, which began during the final stages of the preparation of the Stalin Constitution of 1936, represented the culmination of a split in the Communist Party between the supporters of the exiled Trotsky and those of Stalin, who had undertaken to implement socialism in one country instead of concentrating on world revolution. The first victims of the purge were Kamenev and Zinoviev in 1936. The famous "Trial of the 17," from which excerpts are provided below, was held in January, 1937. It was followed by the secret trial and execution in June of several prominent Red Army leaders, led by Marshal M. N. Tukhachevsky, and by the last great public trial of Right-wing Communists Bukharin and Rykov in March, 1938. The purges inside the USSR led to the defection of many Communists and Communist-sympathizers abroad, who henceforth attacked the Stalin regime. The purge of top army officers convinced foreign governments, including that of Nazi Germany, of the military weakness of the Soviet Union. Some victims of the notorious Stalin purge trials have been posthumously rehabilitated under the Khrushchev regime.

The excerpts from the "Trial of the 17" presented below include a passage from Karl Radek's "confession," and parts of Procurator Andrei Vyshinsky's summation of the accusations against the accused. Radek, one of the most brilliant of the Soviet leaders, and Sokolnikov received ten-year prison terms. Pyatakov, Serebryakov, and eleven others were condemned to be shot. Vyshinsky, better known to Americans for his bitter invective as Soviet representative at the United Nations, had demanded the death penalty for all those accused.

From *Report of Court Proceedings in the Case of the Anti-Trotskyite Centre Heard Before the Military Collegium of the Supreme*

Court of the U.S.S.R., Moscow, January 23-30, 1937 (Moscow: People's Commissariat of Justice of the USSR, 1937), pp. 443-445; 477-478; 514-516.

... *Vyshinsky:* Accused Radek, tell us, did a certain person visit you at your country house near Moscow?

Radek: As I have already testified, in the summer of 1935 I was visited by that very diplomatic representative of that Central European country who first sounded me in his conversation with me in 1934.

Vyshinsky: Did he arrive and converse with you in anybody's presence, or were you alone?

Radek: No, Bukharin was with me at the time. We were sitting on the veranda when a car drove up and through the window I saw this gentleman whom I knew, and two other persons unknown to me. As I had not received any previous warning of this visit I was surprised. He began to explain his visit by stating that he had been visited by two persons who would probably interest me, a professor at the Königsberg University and the adviser to one of the leaders of one of the provinces of that country, who ought to interest me because the attitude of Königsberg towards Russia is different than, say, Rosenberg's because Prussia is afraid of Poland, does not trust her and that is why she is more interested in active relations with the U.S.S.R.

I listened to all he said and as we had agreed not to enter into any negotiations with these representatives here except to give our visa to Trotsky's mandate, and as I could not tell him why, the only thing I could do was to start to make fun of him. We started a wrangle over the race question. Then, these representatives, realizing that we did not intend to enter into the conversation for the sake of which they had come to see me, departed.

This visit had a sequel. Either the diplomatic agent could not understand why he was received in this way, or the persons at the back of him wanted to find out what this meant, whether any change had taken place in the attitude of the *bloc* towards that country. Several months later, approximately, November 1935, at one of the regular diplomatic receptions, the military representative of that country....

The President: Do not mention his name or the country.

Radek: ... approached me and began to complain about the complete change of atmosphere between the two countries. After the first few words he said that during Mr. Trotsky's time the relations between the armies of the two countries were better.

He went on to say that Trotsky had remained true to his old opinion about the need for Soviet-German friendship. After speaking in this strain for a little while longer he began to press me hard as one who had formerly pursued the Rappalo line. I replied to this by uttering the same formula which I had uttered when I was first sounded, namely, that the realist politicians of the U.S.S.R. appreciate the significance of Soviet-German friendship and are prepared to make the necessary concessions in order to ensure this friendship. To this he replied that we ought at last to get together somehow and jointly discuss the details, definitely, about ways of reaching a rapprochement.

I told him that when the circumstances permitted I would be glad to spend an evening with him. This second conversation revealed to me that there was an attempt on the part of military circles to take over the connections which Trotsky had established with certain circles in Germany, or that it was an attempt to verify the real content of the negotiations that were being conducted. Perhaps, also, it was an attempt to ascertain whether we knew definitely what Trotsky had proposed.

Vyshinsky: Did you ever speak to Pyatakov, or with someone else, about the date when the possible war would approach?

Radek: When Pyatakov returned from Oslo I put a number of questions to him concerning foreign policy. He informed me that, first, Trotsky had told him that it was not a matter of a five-year period, not a matter of five years, but of one year, or, at most, of two years. It was a matter of war in 1937. Then I asked Pyatakov: "Did Trotsky tell you this as his own assumption?" Pyatakov replied: "No, Trotsky said that he had got this in his conversation with Hess and other semi-official persons in Germany with whom he had dealings." Hence it was a directive giving an orientation for a very definite date.

I asked him: "So it is a matter of a separate war against the U.S.S.R.?" To this Pyatakov replied that Trotsky had spoken about war in 1937 in general without separating the attack on the U.S.S.R. from the general developments. And when I asked Pyatakov how did Trotsky exactly picture to himself the development of events, Pyatakov replied that Trotsky had said: Military preparations had been completed and now it was a matter of securing to Germany the diplomatic means. That would take a year. And he said that the object of these diplomatic strivings were, first, to secure British neutrality. Secondly, either Germany would come to an arrangement with France, or, relying upon the growing fascist movement which would weaken the democratic government of France, she would be able, under favourable circumstances, to put France out of action for a long time by a swift blow, and strike at the U.S.S.R. with concentrated forces. This was the second fact communicated by Pyatakov.

The third point that emerged from Trotsky's conversation with Pyatakov was that Germany demanded complete freedom of action for the advance of Germany to the Balkan and Danube countries. This is also a very important fact.

Vyshinsky (to Pyatakov): Did you say that? Do you confirm that?

Pyatakov: Yes. Radek is relating it very exactly. It is all quite true.
Vyshinsky: I have no more questions. . . .
. . . Radek is one of the most outstanding, and, to do him justice, one
of the most able and persistent Trotskyites. While Lenin was alive he
fought Lenin, and after Lenin's death he fought Stalin. His quality as
a social danger, as a political danger, is in direct proportion to his personal ability. He is incorrigible. In the anti-Soviet, Trotskyite centre he
is the holder of the portfolio of foreign affairs. On Trotsky's instructions
he carries on diplomatic negotiations with certain foreigners or, as he
expresses it, "puts a visa" on Trotsky's mandate. Regularly, through, so
to speak, his own diplomatic courier, Romm, he corresponds with Trotsky
and receives from him what he here grandiloquently calls "directives."
He is one of the men who is most trusted by and intimate with the
big chief of this gang, Trotsky. . . .
. . . I accuse the people who are sitting here before us of having, in
1933, on Trotsky's instructions, organized what they called a "parallel"
centre consisting of the accused in the present case Pyatakov, Radek,
Sokolnikov and Serebryakov, but what was really the operating active
Trotskyite centre; that this centre, on Trotsky's instructions, through the
medium of the accused Sokolnikov and Radek, entered into communication with representatives of certain foreign states for the purpose of
organizing a joint struggle against the Soviet Union; and that this centre
undertook, in the event of its coming into power, to grant these states
a number of political and economic privileges and territorial concessions;
that this centre, through the medium of its members and other members
of the criminal Trotskyite organization, engaged in espionage on behalf
of these states, supplying foreign intelligence services with extremely
important and extremely secret materials of utmost state importance;
that for the purpose of undermining the economic power and defence
capacity of our country this centre and its accomplices organized and
carried out a number of diversive and wrecking acts which resulted in
the loss of human life and caused considerable damage to our Soviet
state.
   Of this I accuse the members of the "parallel" anti-Soviet Trotskyite
centre: Pyatakov, Radek, Sokolnikov and Serebryakov, that is to say, of
crimes covered by Articles 58[1a] of the Criminal Code of the R.S.F.S.R.,
viz., treason to the country; 58[6], *viz.,* espionage; 58[8], *viz.,* terrorism;
58[9], *viz.,* diversion; 58[11], *viz.,* forming secret criminal organizations. I
accuse all the other accused: Livshitz, N. Muralov, Drobnis, Boguslavsky,
Knyazev, Rataichak, Norkin, Shestov, Stroilov, Turok, Hrasche, Pushin
and Arnold, of being guilty of the same crimes as members of this
organization, bearing full and joint responsibility for these crimes, irrespective of the distinctive features of the criminal activities which characterize the crimes of each one of them, that is to say, of crimes covered
by the same Articles of the Criminal Code.

Comrade Judges, the principal charge that is made in the present trial is that of treason to the country. The penalty for treason to the country is indicated in Article 58[1a] of the Criminal Code of the R.S.F.S.R. It describes treason to the country as acts committed to the damage of the military power of the Union, of its state independence and its territorial inviolability, such as: espionage, disclosing military and state secrets and desertion to the enemy. All these elements, except the last—flight abroad—are present in this case. On those who have committed this grave state crime, which our great Stalin Constitution justly calls the worst of crimes, the law imposes the severest penalty. The law demands that, in the event of the guilt of the criminals being proved, they be sentenced to be shot, permitting clemency only under extenuating circumstances.

Comrade Judges, in your conference chamber you will have to reply to the question—are there for these accused, for each one separately, individual and definite circumstances which would permit you to mitigate the penalty which the law holds out for them? In my opinion there are no such extenuating circumstances. I accuse the defendants on the basis of the Articles of the Criminal Code indicated in the indictment in their full scope.

I am not the only accuser! Comrade Judges, I feel that by my side here stand the victims of the crimes and of these criminals: on crutches, maimed, half alive, and perhaps legless, like Comrade Nagovitsina, the switch-girl at Chusovskaya Station, who appealed to me, through *Pravda,* today, and who, at 20 years of age, lost both her legs in averting a train disaster organized by these people! I do not stand here alone! I feel that by my side here stand the murdered and maimed victims of these frightful crimes, demanding of me, as the State Prosecutor, that I press the charge on all points!

I do not stand here alone! The victims may be in their graves, but I feel that they are standing here beside me, pointing at the dock, at you, accused, with their mutilated arms, which have mouldered in the graves to which you sent them!

I am not the only accuser! I am joined in my accusation by the whole of our people! I accuse these heinous criminals who deserve only one punishment—death by shooting! . . .

49. the German invasion
of the USSR (1941)

ALTHOUGH THE SOVIET GOVERNMENT HAD BEEN WARNED of the coming Nazi invasion of the USSR, Soviet leaders disregarded these warnings, in the belief that they were part of a design to worsen Soviet-German relations. The invasion therefore came as a surprise to the Soviet government, which was ill-prepared to meet it. It was Molotov, not Stalin, who addressed the nation on June 22, 1941, in a manner strongly reminiscent of Tsar Alexander I's appeal to the Russian nation, July 18, 1812, against the Napoleonic invasion of Russia. Molotov's address revealed the extent of Soviet surprise at the breach of the ten-year Nazi-Soviet non-aggression pact signed in Moscow on August 23, 1939. Not until July 3, 1941, did Stalin himself publicly address the nation and its armed forces. In this apologetic appeal Stalin, who in Soviet eyes could do no wrong, sought to justify the Soviet pact with Nazi Germany on the ground that the USSR thereby gained time to prepare for the onslaught. It was in this address that Stalin called for all-out national resistance to the invader and for a scorched-earth policy whenever retreat became necessary. Nikita Khrushchev, in his secret report to the Twentieth Congress of the Communist Party in 1956, denounced Stalin for failing to heed the mounting evidence of an imminent Nazi invasion and held him "criminally responsible" for the wholesale Red Army retreat.

Below are to be found the radio addresses of Molotov and Stalin to the nation, delivered on June 22, 1941, and July 3, 1941, respectively. From *Soviet War Documents,* issued by the Embassy of the Union of Soviet Socialist Republics, Washington, D.C., December, 1943.

1. Radio Address of Vyacheslav M. Molotov

Vice Chairman of the Council of People's Commissars of the USSR and
People's Commissar of Foreign Affairs

Citizens of the Soviet Union:
 The Soviet Government and its head, Comrade Stalin, have authorized
me to make the following statement:
 Today, at four a.m., without any claims having been presented to the
Soviet Union, without a declaration of war, German troops attacked our
country, attacked our borders at many points and bombed from their
airplanes our cities—Zhitomir, Kiev, Sevastopol, Kaunas and some
others—killing or wounding over 200 persons. There were also enemy
air raids and artillery shelling from Rumanian and Finnish territory. This
unheard-of attack on our country is perfidy unparalleled in the history
of civilized nations. The attack on our country was perpetrated despite
the fact that a treaty of non-aggression had been signed between the
USSR and Germany and that the Soviet Government has most faithfully
abided by all the provisions of this treaty. The attack on our country
was perpetrated despite the fact that during the entire period of the
operation of this treaty the German government could not find grounds
for a single complaint against the USSR as regards observance of the
treaty. The entire responsibility for this predatory attack on the Soviet
Union falls fully and completely upon the German-fascist rulers.
 At five-thirty a.m., that is, after the attack had already been perpetrated, Schulenburg, the German Ambassador in Moscow, made a
statement on behalf of his government, to me as People's Commissar of
Foreign Affairs, to the effect that the German government had decided
to launch a war against the USSR in connection with the concentration
of Red Army units near the eastern German frontier. In reply to this I
stated on behalf of the Soviet Government that until the very last
moment the German Government had not presented any claims to the
Soviet Government, that Germany had attacked the USSR despite the
peaceable position of the Soviet Union, and that for this reason fascist
Germany is the aggressor. On the instruction of the Government of the
Soviet Union, I must also state than at no point had our troops or our
air force committed a violation of the frontier and that therefore the
statement made this morning by the Rumanian radio to the effect that
Soviet aircraft allegedly had fired on Rumanian airdromes is a sheer lie
and provocation. Likewise a lie and a provocation is the whole declaration
made today by Hitler, who is trying belatedly to concoct accusations
charging the Soviet Union with failure to observe the Soviet-German
pact.

Now that an attack on the Soviet Union has already been committed, the Soviet Government has ordered our troops to repulse this predatory assault and to drive the German troops from the territory of our country.

This war has been forced upon us not by the German people, not by the German workers, peasants and intellectuals whose sufferings we well understand, but by the clique of bloodthirsty fascist rulers of Germany who have enslaved Frenchmen, Czechs, Poles, Serbians, the people of Norway, Belgium, Denmark, Holland, Greece and other nations. The Government of the Soviet Union expresses its unshakable confidence that our valiant Army and Navy and the brave falcons of the Soviet Air Force will acquit themselves with honor in performing their duty to the fatherland, to the Soviet people, and will inflict a crushing blow upon the aggressor. This is not the first time that our people have had to deal with an attack by an arrogant foe. At the time of Napoleon's invasion of Russia our people's reply was a patriotic war, and Napoleon suffered defeat and met his doom. It will be the same with Hitler, who in his arrogance has proclaimed a new crusade against our country. The Red Army and our whole people will again wage a victorious patriotic war for country, honor and liberty.

The Government of the Soviet Union expresses the firm conviction that the whole population of our country, all the workers, peasants and intellectuals, men and women, will conscientiously perform their duties and do their work. Our entire people must now stand solid and united as never before. Each one of us must demand of himself and of others the discipline, organization, and self-denial worthy of real Soviet patriots, in order to provide for all the needs of the Red Army, Navy and Air Force and to ensure victory over the enemy.

The Government calls upon you, citizens of the Soviet Union, to rally still more closely around our glorious Bolshevik Party, around our Soviet Government, around our great leader, Comrade Stalin. Ours is a righteous cause. The enemy will be defeated. Victory will be ours.

II. Radio Address of Joseph V. Stalin

Chairman of the Council of People's Commissars of the USSR and Chairman of the State Committee of Defense

Comrades! Citizens! Brothers and Sisters! Men of our Army and Navy! I am addressing you, my friends!

The perfidious military attack on our motherland begun on June 22 by Hitler Germany is continuing. In spite of the heroic resistance of the Red Army, and although the enemy's finest divisions and finest air-force units have already been smashed and have met their doom on the field of battle, the enemy continues to push forward, hurling fresh forces into the attack. Hitler's troops have succeeded in capturing Lithuania, a considerable part of Latvia, the western part of Byelorussia, and part of the Western Ukraine. The fascist air force is extending the range of operations of its bombers, and is bombing Murmansk, Orsha, Mogilev, Smolensk, Kiev, Odessa and Sevastopol. A grave danger hangs over our country.

How could it have happened that our glorious Red Army surrendered a number of our cities and districts to the fascist armies? Is it really true that the German-fascist troops are invincible, as is ceaselessly trumpeted by boastful fascist propagandists? Of course not! History shows that there are no invincible armies and never have been. Napoleon's army was considered invincible but it was beaten successively by Russian, English and German armies. Kaiser Wilhelm's German army in the period of the first imperialist war was also considered invincible, but it was beaten several times by the Russian and Anglo-French forces and was finally smashed by the Anglo-French forces. The same must be said of Hitler's German-fascist army today. This army had not yet met with serious resistance on the continent of Europe. Only on our territory has it met serious resistance. And if as a result of this resistance the finest divisions of Hitler's German-fascist army have been defeated by our Red Army, it means that this army too can be smashed and will be smashed, as were the armies of Napoleon and Wilhelm.

As to part of our territory having nevertheless been seized by German-fascist troops, this is chiefly due to the fact that the war of fascist Germany on the USSR began under conditions favorable for the German forces and unfavorable for the Soviet forces. The fact of the matter is that the troops of Germany, as a country at war, were already fully mobilized, and the 170 divisions hurled by Germany against the USSR and brought up to the Soviet frontiers were in a state of complete readiness, only awaiting the signal to move into action, whereas the Soviet troops had still to effect mobilization and to move up to the frontiers.

Of no little importance in this respect is the fact that fascist Germany suddenly and treacherously violated the non-aggression pact she concluded in 1939 with the USSR, disregarding the fact that she would be regarded as the aggressor by the whole world. Naturally, our peace-loving country, not wishing to take the initiative in breaking the pact, could not have resorted to perfidy. It may be asked: how could the Soviet Government have consented to conclude a non-aggression pact with such treacherous fiends as Hitler and Ribbentrop? Was this not an error on the part of the Soviet Government? Of course not! Non-aggression pacts are pacts of peace between two states. It was such a pact that Germany proposed to us in 1939. Could the Soviet Government have declined such a proposal? I think that not a single peace-loving state could decline a peace treaty with a neighboring state, even though the latter was headed by such fiends and cannibals as Hitler and Ribbentrop. But that, of course, only on one indispensable condition, namely, that this peace treaty does not infringe either directly or indirectly on the territorial integrity, independence, and honor of the peace-loving state. As is well known, the non-aggression pact between Germany and the USSR was precisely such a pact.

What did we gain by concluding the non-aggression pact with Germany? We secured our country peace for a year and a half and the opportunity of preparing its forces to repulse fascist Germany should she risk an attack on our country despite the pact. This was a definite advantage for us and a disadvantage for fascist Germany. What has fascist Germany gained and what has she lost by treacherously tearing up the pact and attacking the USSR? She has gained certain advantageous positions for her troops for a short period, but she has lost politically by exposing herself in the eyes of the entire world as a bloodthirsty aggressor. There can be no doubt that this short-lived military gain for Germany is only an episode, while the tremendous political gain of the USSR is a serious and lasting factor that is bound to form the basis for the development of decisive military successes of the Red Army in the war with fascist Germany.

That is why our whole valiant Army, our whole valiant Navy, all our falcons of the air, all the peoples of our country, all the finest men and women of Europe, America and Asia, finally all the finest men and women of Germany, condemn the treacherous acts of the German fascists and sympathize with the Soviet Government, approve the conduct of the Soviet Government and see that ours is a just cause, that the enemy will be defeated, that we are bound to win.

By virtue of this war which has been forced upon us, our country has come to death grips with its most malicious and most perfidious enemy— German fascism. Our troops are fighting heroically against an enemy armed to the teeth with tanks and aircraft. Overcoming innumerable difficulties, the Red Army and Red Navy are self-sacrificingly disputing every inch of Soviet soil. The main forces of the Red Army are coming into action armed with thousands of tanks and airplanes. The men of the Red Army are displaying unexampled valor. Our resistance to the enemy is growing in strength and power. Side by side with the Red Army, the entire Soviet people is rising in defense of its native land.

What is required to put an end to the danger hovering over our country, and what measures must be taken to smash the enemy?

Above all, it is essential that our people, the Soviet people, should understand the full immensity of the danger that threatens our country and abandon all complacency, all heedlessness, all those moods of peaceful constructive work which were so natural before the war, but which are fatal today when the war has fundamentally changed everything. The enemy is cruel and implacable. He is out to seize our lands watered with our sweat, to seize our grain and oil secured by our labor. He is out to restore the rule of the landlords, to restore Tsarism, to destroy the national culture and the national state existence of the Russians, Ukrainians, Byelorussians, Lithuanians, Letts, Estonians, Tatars, Uzbeks, Moldavians, Georgians, Armenians, Azerbaijanians and the other free peoples of the Soviet Union, to Germanize them, to convert them into slaves of the German princes and barons. Thus the issue is one of life or death for the Soviet State, of life or death for the peoples of the USSR; the issue is whether the peoples of the Soviet Union shall remain free or fall into slavery.

The Soviet people must realize this and abandon all heedlessness, they must mobilize themselves and reorganize all their work on new, wartime lines, when there can be no mercy to the enemy. Further, there must be no room in our ranks for whimperers and cowards, for panic-mongers and deserters. Our people must know no fear in the fight and must selflessly join our patriotic war of liberation, our war against the fascist enslavers. Lenin, the great founder of our State, used to say that the chief virtue of the Bolshevik must be courage, valor, fearlessness in struggle, readiness to fight together with the people against the enemies of our country. This splendid virtue of the Bolshevik must become the virtue of the millions and millions of the Red Army, of the Red Navy and of all the peoples of the Soviet Union.

All our work must be immediately reconstructed on a war footing, everything must be subordinated to the interests of the front and the task of organizing the demolition of the enemy. The peoples of the Soviet Union now see that there is no taming German fascism in its savage fury and hatred of our country, which has insured all working people labor in freedom and prosperity. The peoples of the Soviet Union must rise against the enemy and defend their rights and their land.

The Red Army, the Red Navy and all the citizens of the Soviet Union must defend every inch of Soviet soil, must fight to the last drop of blood for our towns and villages, must display the daring, initiative and intelligence that are inherent in our people. We must organize all-round assistance to the Red Army, insure powerful reinforcements for its ranks and the supply of everything it requires, we must organize rapid transport of troops and military freight, and extensive aid to the wounded.

We must strengthen the Red Army's rear, subordinating all our work to this cause. All our industries must be put to work with greater intensity to produce more rifles, machine guns, artillery, bullets, shells, airplanes; we must organize the guarding of factories, power stations, telephone and telegraph communications, and arrange effective air-raid protection in all localities. We must wage a ruthless fight against all disorganizers of the rear, deserters, panic-mongers, rumor-mongers, we must exterminate spies, diversionists and enemy parachutists, rendering rapid aid in all this to our destroyer battalions.

We must bear in mind that the enemy is crafty, unscrupulous and experienced in deception and the dissemination of false rumors. We must reckon with all this and not fall victim to provocation. All who by their panic-mongering and cowardice hinder the work of defense, no matter who they are, must be immediately hailed before the Military Tribunal.

In case of forced retreat of Red Army units, all rolling stock must be evacuated, the enemy must not be left a single engine, a single railway car, not a single pound of grain or gallon of fuel. Collective farmers must drive off all their cattle and turn over their grain to the safe-keeping of State authorities for transportation to the rear. All valuable property, including non-ferrous metals, grain and fuel, which cannot be withdrawn, must be destroyed without fail. In areas occupied by the enemy, guerrilla units, mounted and foot, must be formed, diversionist groups must be organized to combat the enemy troops, to foment guerrilla warfare everywhere, to blow up bridges and roads, to damage telephone and telegraph lines, to set fire to forests, stores and transports. In the occupied regions conditions must be made unbearable for the enemy and all his accomplices. They must be hounded and annihilated at every step, and all their measures frustrated.

This war with fascist Germany cannot be considered an ordinary war. It is not only a war between two armies; it is also a great war of the entire Soviet people against the German-fascist forces. The aim of this national war in defense of our country against the fascist oppressors is not only elimination of the danger hanging over our country, but also aid to all European peoples groaning under the yoke of German fascism. In this war of liberation we shall not be alone. In this great war we shall have loyal allies in the peoples of Europe and America, including the German people who are enslaved by the Hitlerite despots. Our war for the freedom of our country will merge with the struggle of the peoples of Europe and America for their independence, for democratic liberties. It will be a united front of peoples standing for freedom and against enslavement and threats of enslavement by Hitler's fascist armies.

In this connection, the historic utterance of the British Prime Minister, Mr. Churchill, regarding aid to the Soviet Union, and the declaration of the United States Government signifying its readiness to render aid to our country, which can only evoke a feeling of gratitude in the hearts of the peoples of the Soviet Union, are fully comprehensible and symptomatic.

Comrades! Our forces are numberless. The overweening enemy will soon learn this to his cost. Side by side with the Red Army, many thousands of workers, collective farmers and intellectuals are rising to fight the enemy aggressor. The masses of our people will rise up in their millions. The working people of Moscow and Leningrad have already commenced to form vast popular levies in support of the Red Army. Such popular levies must be raised in every city which is in danger of enemy invasion, all the working people must be roused to defend our freedom, our honor, our country, in our patriotic war against German fascism.

In order to insure rapid mobilization of all the forces of the peoples of the USSR, and to repulse the enemy who has treacherously attacked our country, a State Committee of Defense has been formed in whose hands the entire power of the State has been vested. The State Committee of Defense has entered on its functions and calls upon all our people to rally around the Party of Lenin-Stalin and around the Soviet Government so as self-denyingly to support the Red Army and Navy, demolish the enemy and secure victory.

All our forces—for the support of our heroic Red Army and our glorious Red Navy!

All forces of the people—for the demolition of the enemy!

Forward, to our victory!

50. private enterprise and profits spur production

DURING THE YEARS OF RECONSTRUCTION following World War II, the Soviet government was forced to resort to private initiative to expedite reconstruction and to increase production. Ever since the NEP, the USSR when confronted by economic emergency has resorted to capitalist tools. By way of contrast, when the United States is confronted by economic difficulties, there is a demand for government aid to private enterprise. Because of drastic housing shortages stemming from widespread destruction in European Russia during the war and from the opening up of new industrial areas in Siberia, one of the greatest concessions made by the Soviet government was in the direction of private housing construction, for which substantial loans were advanced to individual workers.

Another drastic departure from Marxism was the introduction of the profit element into the Soviet economy. To promote increased production, every industry was expected to show a profit. To accelerate this program there was re-emphasis on cost accounting to reduce expenses and on the payment of bonuses to managers and workers whose enterprises showed a profit. Thus the Soviet economy made the transition from state socialism to something akin to state capitalism.

The two articles below are among the first in the Soviet press to emphasize the above-mentioned policies. They also reflect "self-criticism" of Soviet production methods. They are reprinted from *Soviet Press Translations,* published by the Far Eastern Institute, University of Washington and edited by Ivar Spector, Vol. III (No. 16, September 15, 1948), 503-504; and Vol. IV (No. 1, January 1, 1949), 22-25.

I. Greater Private Housing Construction*

The program for housing construction which is being carried into effect in our country is imbued with Stalinist concern for human beings, and for raising the material and cultural level of the life of the Soviet people. The scale of this program is enormous: we must replenish the housing reservoir destroyed during the years of the war and develop new construction on a scale that will insure a substantial improvement in the housing conditions of the workers. Indeed, only the Soviet state, for which the interests and needs of the people are pre-eminent, is a match for such a task.

Not only is the Soviet state itself constructing buildings for the workers; in addition to this, it is extending great aid to the residents of cities and workers' settlements who are erecting their own private dwellings. The law on the Five-Year Plan provides that individual tenant-builders, with the aid of state credits, will construct buildings representing a total living space of 12,000,000 square meters during the five-year period.

This task is being performed vigorously. Let us recall that in the past year alone, houses with a living space of 4,000,000 square meters, constructed by the population itself, have been made available for occupation. Tens of thousands of coal miners, metallurgical workers, oil workers, and machine builders—workers and employees in the most varied industries—moved into new dwellings that they had constructed with the help of state credits.

Today there are many opportunities for developing private construction still more extensively. From year to year the Government has been granting large funds for financing individual tenant-builders. Nearly 1,500,000,000 rubles have been earmarked for this purpose during the present year. This generous help from the state must be used intelligently and economically.

This depends to a large degree upon the directors of the Ministries and enterprises. Indeed, it is not only a matter of granting state loans to workers or employees. Tenant-builders need help from many quarters and in many forms. It is no accident that many collective contracts contain clauses obligating the administrations to cooperate with tenant-builders in acquiring materials, supplying transportation, and arranging for technical consultation.

Where these pledges are not only set down on paper, but fulfilled to the letter and on time, fine results have been achieved.

At Mine No. 4 of the *Skuratovugol* Trust, nearly 200 miners are

* Editorial, *Trud,* July 6, 1948.

building their own houses this year. This work is progressing successfully, since the administration is extending effective aid to the miners: the component parts of the future homes are prefabricated and processed in special workshops, and experienced construction foremen help the tenant-builders assemble them on a previously prepared site. All this building is being carried out in accordance with a special construction curve, which is calculated in such a way that the miners will be able to celebrate Miner's Day in their new quarters.

According to their collective contract, the administration of the Kara-kubsk Mine Board (Stalinsk Region) must supply a large quantity of various materials for private construction. This pledge is being strictly observed. The miners' committee of the trade-union is constantly on the alert to see that not a single request of the tenant-builders goes unheeded. And it is quite understandable that, with such a working arrangement, more dwellings than were scheduled by the collective contract should have been erected here last year, and that the plan should be over-fulfilled this year.

Such achievements are numerous. But there must be many more; private construction must be pushed with considerably more speed and success. Meanwhile, the utilization of funds allotted for the financing of this all-important work is still proceeding very slowly at the present time. The situation in the enterprises of the Ministry for the Oil Industry of the Southern and Western Districts is especially unsatisfactory.

In some enterprises private construction is still regarded as a task of minor importance, one whose performance may be postponed because it is a secondary issue. Is it necessary to demonstrate the impropriety and harmfulness of such a viewpoint?

Helping the worker to provide himself with his own house and substantially improving housing conditions will insure the creation of permanent cadres in industrial enterprises.

Active aid to workers and employees who are constructing their own homes is the duty of the trade-unions. A vast field of activity has been opened here for each *zavkom*[1] and for each trade-union organization. A check must be made from day to day as to how the administration is fulfilling the pledges contained in the collective contract, and as to whether everything possible is being done so that tenant-builders may receive loans, plots of ground, materials, and technical aid on time.

Genuine concern for the needs and demands of the tenant-builders is the decisive factor for success in this work. The directors of the Karl Marx Mine *(Ordzhonikidzeugol* Trust) are pledged to supply the latter with motor transportation, according to the collective contract. This pledge is being ostensibly fulfilled—the vehicles are being supplied. It has been decided, however, to charge the miners 28 rubles per hour for their use—more than double the operating costs. The mine committee

[1] Factory Committee, eds.

of the trade-union (headed by Comrade Shchepanenkov), through its vigorous intervention, was quite right in securing the revocation of this improper order.

Careful control must be maintained over the utilization of credits granted by the state. Unfortunately, by no means all factory and plant committees have organized such control. As a result there are frequent cases in which funds earmarked for financing private construction are being utilized by enterprises for quite different purposes. It happens that persons are found among the tenant-builders who obtain loans without intending to build a house, and spend them for other needs.

What is this vicious practice leading to? To a delay in the circulation of state funds and, hence, to a situation in which workers who actually need credit for construction cannot receive it in due time. The same thing is also caused by a delay in repaying loans received from the state; bank workers who permit great indebtedness on the part of tenant-builders are to blame for this.

The third quarter has arrived—the time of greatest activity for individual tenant-builders. Not a single day must be lost at the height of the season. Indeed, it must be recalled that in most enterprises the first months of the year have been spent primarily in adjusting credits and in completing construction held over from last year. The main work lies ahead, and it must be conducted in an exact and organized manner, without delay.

A mass check on the fulfillment of collective contracts is presently in progress. The strictest attention must be given to pledges for the development of private construction. To see that tenant-builders receive the full measure of aid that the administration is pledged to extend them is a matter of honor for trade-union organizations. In this way, they will assist in a more rapid and successful solution of the housing problem, and will contribute to further improvement in the living conditions of the workers.

II. Intraplant Cost Accounting*

Three years have passed since the Molotov Urals Plant changed over to the manufacture of civilian products. During this period the workers of the plant have introduced into production more than twenty types of new products necessary for the restoration and development of our national economy. Among these products are such complicated units as power shovels for construction; rock-loading machines, cranes, and drills for our

* Based Upon the Experience of the Molotov Urals Plant By A. Bykhovsky, Hero of Socialist Labor and Director of the Molotov Plant, from *Pravda*, October 18, 1948.

miners; pipe drills, drill couplings, weighted drill pipes, and torpedo drills for the oil industry; hydroturbines for *kolkhoz* electric power stations; shafts and axle bearings for railroad transportation; and harpoon guns and harpoons for the whaling industry. Prior to the war, the plant had never known such production on such a scale, in such variety, and with such organization. The manufacture of machinery completely new to the plant has also occasioned changes in the character of our metallurgical production. All this has made special demands on the directors of production, and on the technology and economics of production.

Intraplant cost accounting has been a most powerful economic lever in improving the operation of the enterprise. It serves as a basic means in the struggle for profits. The economical phase of the work of the enterprise is evoking the most lively interest throughout the collective. The economy of the plant was the subject of discussion at technical conferences in September 1947 and in March 1948. Our report on cost accounting was discussed at the Regional Conference for Scientific Production. This has helped the workers of the plant to feel out both the strong and weak spots in our system of cost accounting.

The most important thing in organizing intraplant cost accounting, as our experience has shown, is the norms that form the basis for the *tekhpromfinplan*[2] of the shop, section, and brigade. Cost accounting cannot be reduced to a superficial planning of expenditures and the comparison of these expenditures with the actual cost of production. The *tekhpromfinplan* must be based upon technically computed, mean progressive norms, guaranteeing the systematic reduction of production costs.

The working out of the proper technical norms is the first and basic prerequisite for the organization of cost accounting at a plant. The working out of such norms and the system of control over changes in them is decentralized in our plant. In the metallurgical shops the norms for the consumption of all materials, by units, grades of steel, shape, and dimensions are prepared by the chief metallurgist of the plant; the chief mechanic of the plant works out the norms for materials necessary for the exploitation of equipment and repairs to equipment; the head of tool production prepares the norms for tool consumption; etc. The norms for working time consumed in the manufacture of individual products are worked out by the labor and wage section, together with norm specialists in the shops, on the basis of documents supplied by the chief technologists. Three-quarters of the norms in effect at the plant are technically computed norms. It is on them that the cost-accounting operations of the shops are based.

Norms do not remain static. In proportion as production becomes more perfect—and it is being steadily perfected—the norms for the

[2] Technical Industrial Financial Plan, eds.

expenditure of materials are reduced. This year they have been reduced by from 6 to 20 percent on different products in comparison with 1947. These changes were immediately reflected in the plans of the shops. In May we completed a new revision of all the norms for basic and auxiliary materials, and established such norms where they were absent for some reason or other. These new norms make it possible for the plant to reduce, on a technical basis, the expenditure of materials by an average of 10 percent in 1948, as compared with last year.

Overhead expenses constitute a very important factor in the cost of production. The ability to plan these expenses for different items on the basis of exact accounts is a great art. Step by step, our plant is mastering this art. Expenditures for current repairs to equipment, and for the consumption of tools, as well as of all types of power, are rigorously normalized. Transportation expenses in the shops are also strictly regulated. There was an especially large number of repair operations in the first machine shop. Expenditures for repairs to equipment were allocated to this shop on the basis of data reported concerning expenditures during the preceding period in accordance with the so-called mean statistical method. The shop was advanced 55,000 rubles per month. Today, expenditures for repair operations are planned on the basis of computed norms established by the plant's chief mechanic. These expenditures have been reduced to 32,000 rubles for this shop at the present time. Expenditures for tools were reduced by 10 percent at the same shop with a change-over to computed norms.

It is also necessary to continually improve and simplify the organizational structure of the shops and divisions. Even with an increase in the technical equipment of an enterprise and with a change in its economy, backwardness in the organizational structure of production may be reflected negatively in the results achieved. The successful incorporation into production of certain new products has made it possible for us to simplify the organizational structure of the shops, and to merge some of them.

In 1948 we have merged two shops engaged in the manufacture of small parts, and two forging shops, and consolidated a number of minor parts and sections. Thanks to the mechanization of auxiliary operations, and the merging of parts and sections, the number of auxiliary workers has been reduced by 7 percent as compared with last year. All this has resulted in considerable savings for the plant in overhead expenses. The average percentage of shop overhead expenses also has been sharply reduced throughout the plant. Thus, at the small forging shop (headed by Comrade Smirnov), the overhead expenses were reduced by 168 percent last year. This was achieved through more economical use of steam and a reduction in the number of sections, which released a number of engineering and technical workers.

The technical growth of production, the introduction of speed methods of manufacture, high production equipment, and the mechanization of labor processes—all these are leading to a systematic reduction of labor consumption per unit product.

Last year labor expenditure was reduced on an average of 20 percent per product as compared with 1946, and by an additional 23 percent during the first eight months of this year. We have considerably reduced the time for the manufacture of all new products. Labor expenditures in the manufacture of power shovels were reduced by 28 percent during the current year, by 33 percent in the manufacture of rock-loading machinery, and by 27 percent in the manufacture of drills.

The technical measures being carried out at the plant are making it possible to reduce production costs systematically. In 1947 the plant reduced production costs by 29.6 percent, as compared to an 18.8 percent plan. During the first eight months of this year, production costs were reduced by 23.3 percent—4.9 percent greater than planned.

Intraplant cost accounting is carried on at our plant only in connection with expenditures relating to the shop. In other words, we take into consideration the utilization of the wage fund (according to wage rates, bonus payments, and overtime), deviations from technology, wastage through the fault of the shop, special expenditures for equipment, and shop expenditures. Thus, changes in the cost of materials and unfinished products received from a neighboring shop are not reflected in the results of the work of a given shop. The total result of the cost-accounting activities of the shop—savings or over-expenditure—is determined by a comparison of the actual expenditures of the shop with the tasks included in the plan. The head of the shop enjoys independence in his operations within the limits of the approved plan given him. He directs the daily loading of equipment, and the disposition of manpower, establishes bonuses for leaders in production (within limits established by special regulations), and presents plans for cost accounting to the sections and brigades.

During the war years cost accounting in sections and brigades was relaxed at the plant. Today we are restoring and extending it. This year cost accounting for each furnace unit has been organized at the open-hearth furnace shop. Here the results are tallied for each smelting every twenty-four hours, showing the quantity and cost expended in materials and fuel, the quantity of metal going for scrap, etc. This experiment has justified itself. An open-hearth furnace that lagged behind in 1947 has already effected more than 1,000,000 rubles in savings today.

In the struggle for the so-called "small savings," that is, immediately at the work location—in grams of lubricants, fuel, and auxiliary materials—the initiative of the Komsomol organization has been of great help. The Komsomol youth brigades have introduced proposals which, if carried out, can effect savings up to 4,000,000 rubles per year.

Intraplant cost accounting demands precise calculation of all indices of the *tekhpromfinplan* of the shop, section, and brigade. A written form for monthly accounting of the results of the work of the shop, which has been established at the plant, fully meets this requirement. It reflects all the factors involved in the cost of goods production for trade, and planned and reported production costs on the principal products of the shop per month. The form is prepared by the ninth of each month on the basis of the bookkeeping figures of the shop's economist, and is verified and signed by the head of the shop. Subsequently, a controlled verification of cost-accounting data is performed in the planning and production section of the plant. The accomplishment of this form has required no increase in staff.

Qualified workers for planning and accounting are necessary for the consolidation of intraplant cost accounting. Such specialists, having a secondary and higher specialized education, are literally few and far between. We have organized special one-year courses for training economists, but these personnel are still less qualified than the graduates of the technical colleges for economics and of the *vuzi*. Other enterprises of the region are also experiencing a severe shortage of economists. Practical experience itself is demanding the organization, at our regional center, of a special school of economics under the State University, as well as the opening of a technical college for industrial economics, which formerly existed and produced satisfactory cadres of planners and economists.

Literature dealing with questions of economics and accounting is also necessary. It must be said that there is very little of such literature—there are no serious works on intraplant cost accounting other than a few pamphlets.

The publication of planned price indices on materials should be centralized. The publication of the latter separately at each plant is very expensive and has not always been successful from the standpoint of quality.

Material encouragement is an important stimulus in the struggle for economy. Today, without the reduction of production costs, bonuses for the overfulfillment of the production program could not be paid. In determining the amount of the bonus, however, we have not taken into account the amount of the savings effected for the shop. One month the shop headed by Comrade Melnikov, which effected the negligible saving of one-tenth of one percent, received the same bonus as the shop of Comrade Oparin, which reduced production costs by 4.6 percent. This is not as it should be. The extent of the reduction of production costs over and above the plan should necessarily be taken into account in encouraging workers by bonus payments. Then material interest in the active carrying out of cost accounting will increase, and additional sources of economy will be revealed.

The question of bonus payments for the reduction of production costs in sections and, especially, in brigades, is not sufficiently clear. This is having the effect of allowing managers of shops to neglect changing over sections and brigades to cost accounting.

These are the questions which have been raised by the practical experience of intraplant cost accounting at our enterprise.

The Molotov plant is coping successfully with its program, is overfulfilling its plans for the reduction of production costs, and is effecting savings over and above the plan. The nine-month plan for goods production has been fulfilled by 105 percent.

The collective of the plant, having accepted the challenge of the Muscovites, has pledged itself to effect a saving of 10,000,000 rubles this year through the reduction of production costs over and above the plan.

The attention of the entire collective has been focused on cost accounting, and herein lies the great contribution of the plant's Party organization. Upon the initiative of the plant's Party Committee, two technical conferences of the Party were convened, which have played an important role in developing the campaign for profits. The Party Committee has repeatedly discussed the questions involved in carrying out the decisions of the technical conferences of the Party. In March of this year, the cost accounting activities of two shops were discussed, while in May those of three shops were discussed. In July, the report of Comrade Kudryavtsev, the chief engineer of the plant, on how to effect the transition to a profit basis was discussed at a session of the Party Committee. The Party organization is rallying the efforts of the workers, specialists, and managers of production around the questions of cost accounting, and are contributing day by day to its consolidation.

Intraplant cost accounting is the true course toward, and the essential prerequisite for, profits at an enterprise and increased socialist accumulations.

51. the Soviet family

THE STATUS OF THE SOVIET FAMILY has undergone many changes since the October Revolution of 1917. Under the impetus of war, revolution and civil war, the family in the early years of Soviet power faced disintegration. Although Lenin and some other Bolshevik leaders sought to stem the tide of social anarchy, Marxist theory envisaged the "withering away" of the family, at least as a legal and economic institution. The first step in this direction was the secularization of family law. The reaction against the loosening of family ties, encouraged by easy marriage and divorce laws, came in the 1930's. Since that time, the Soviet government has re-emphasized the family as an indispensable Soviet institution, and has enacted legislation to preserve and strengthen it.

The article below traces the evolution of the Soviet attitude on marriage from 1917 to 1944. It provides the reader with a Soviet interpretation of the basic changes effected during this period. The editors have appended supplementary material to bring Soviet legislation pertaining to the family up-to-date.

The article, "The Development of Soviet Family Law," by G. M. Sverdlov, was published originally in *Sovietskoye Gosudarstvo i Pravo* (No. 10, October, 1947), and appeared in English translation in *Soviet Press Translations,* published by the Far Eastern and Russian Institute, University of Washington, Vol. III (No. 16, September 15, 1948), pp. 490-502. The article has been slightly abridged, with most of the footnotes eliminated.

> Women in the USSR are accorded equal rights with men in all spheres of economic, government, cultural, political and other public activity.
> The possibility of exercising these rights is ensured by women being accorded an equal right with men to work, payment for work, rest and leisure, social insurance and education, and by state protection of the interests of mother and child, state aid to mothers of large families and unmarried mothers, maternity leave with full pay, and the provision of a wide network of maternity homes, nurseries and kindergartens."
>
> —Article 122, USSR Constitution

Immediately following the Great October Revolution, the first socialist state in the world began to carry out one of its historic tasks—the reorganization of family and marriage relations upon new foundations.

On December 19 and 20, 1917, the Gazette of the Provisional Workers' and Peasants' Government published the first two historic decrees of the Soviet regime concerning marriage and the family—the decree on "The Dissolution of Marriage", and the decree on "Civil Marriage, Children, and Registration of Status."[1]

These two decrees occupy a special place in the history of Soviet law. The era of Soviet family legislation begins with them. They formulate for the first time the most important and most fundamental principles of the Soviet family and marriage, which have remained basically unchanged throughout the subsequent history of our legislation, and which are fully reflected in the operation of our law. V. I. Lenin on many occasions pointed out the enormous importance of these decrees in his speeches and articles.

What then do these first decrees of the Soviet state concerning marriage and divorce represent? What was V. I. Lenin's estimate of them?

Pre-Bolshevik Legislation

The family legislation of Tsarist Russia exhibited all the basic features characteristic of all bourgeois legislation. While distinguished from other bourgeois legislation by its repudiation of civil, secular marriage, and by a more intimate and obvious intermingling of its provisions with those of canon law, pre-Revolutionary family legislation was based, fundamentally, on the inequality of the woman, the despotism of the husband and father, and the age-old principles of domination and subjugation.

Many crude and archaic precepts, which occasionally may be traced back to the Code of Decorum,[2] may be found in Tsarist laws concerning marriage and the family. In effect, however, the latter was pervaded by the same ideas as was the legislation of other countries at that time. . . .

In addition to these provisions relating to family law, which are to a greater or lesser degree characteristic of any system of bourgeois law, Tsarist legislation also contained provisions reflecting relationships that

[1] The first undated decree was published in Number 36 of the above-named Gazette for December 19, 1917. See S.U., 1917, No. 10, Art. 152. The second decree, dated December 18, 1917, was published in Number 57 of the above-named Gazette for December 20, 1917. See S.U., 1917, No. 11, Art. 160.

[2] Such as the famous Articles 106 and 107 of Vol. X of the Code of the Russian Empire, with their notorious definitions of the wife's obligation to abide with her husband ". . . in absolute obedience, and to offer him all compliance . . . ," of the husband's obligation "to excuse her faults and lighten her infirmities," etc.

had arisen at earlier, prebourgeois stages of social development. Pre-Revolutionary Russian law took polygamy under its protection in the case of those peoples among whom this manifestation represented survivals of earlier tribal custom. For the peoples of Transcaucasia, and for the nomad peoples of Eastern Siberia it allowed the marriage of minors, etc.

It would appear that the elimination of the gross inequality of women which pervaded Tsarist family and marriage legislation, and the liquidation of the survivals of previous social structures, in which this law abounded, should have been the most pressing and immediate task of the bourgeois democracy, with its bombastic slogans upholding various "liberties" and every sort of "equality," that came to power in Russia following the February Revolution.

But the "Revolutionaries" and "Democrats" of the Provisional Government did not set about solving such problems. . . . Even a minimum reform program required that the marriage legislation should be at least reorganized in accordance with the principles of secular, civil marriage. But the secularization of marriage found no place among the tasks of the Provisional Government. It is well-known for example, that the draft of a law on "freedom of conscience," drawn up by the Ministry of Internal Affairs of the Provisional Government in June 1917, contained no provision for transferring to the state the registration of marriages, as in the case of other acts relating to civil affairs.

In May 1917, the Provisional Government made an attempt "to reform" divorce legislation. A "special council" was set up, which was to draft a suitable law. Consisting of prominent bourgeois professors, doctors, and jurists, among whom was, in particular, the well-known Cadet, Professor Petrazhitsky, this council was headed by a representative of the Church (Archpriest Filonenko, a member of the State Duma). The draft of the law, which this council was commissioned to prepare, was thereupon to have been submitted to the judgment of the Ruling Synod and promulgated in the name of the Provisional Government. The council deliberated zealously over a period of two weeks, and eventually drafted a law on "grounds for divorce," which somewhat enlarged the number of the latter, as compared with the previous state of affairs, but which left the system of ecclesiastical consistory divorce suits completely untouched. But even this apocopated "reform" of the marriage law got lost somewhere in the departmental shambles, and everything in the field of Tsarist marriage and family legislation remained just as it was right up to the October Revolution. . . .

Soviet Legislation, 1917

The socialist revolution, in its very first decrees, eliminated the survivals of serfdom in the field of family law. "Over a period of some *ten weeks,* beginning on October 25 (November 7), 1917, up to the dissolution of the Constituent Assembly (January 5, 1918)," as V. I. Lenin said, "we performed a thousand times more in this field than the bourgeois democrats and liberals (Cadets), and the petty bourgeois democrats (Mensheviks and S.R.'s) *during the eight months* of their power."[3]

The December decrees of 1917 proclaimed in a brief but expressive manner the secularization of marriage: "The Russian Republic henceforth recognizes only civil marriages." They freed marriage from any restrictions whatsoever imposed by guardianship, religion, and social station—the consent or permission of parents or authorities was no longer needed in order to enter into marriage, while the question of adherence to this or that religion was no longer of any importance. In spite of the slanderous insinuations and heartrending shrieks, which came flying from every nook and cranny of the bourgeois press, to the effect that the Bolsheviks were bringing with them the "nationalization of women," the abolition of marriage, promiscuous sexual intercourse, etc., etc., the decrees clearly and firmly proclaimed monogamy as the basis of Soviet marriage. In making civil marriage obligatory, the decree stated that marriage applications were not to be accepted by the Soviet ZAGS[4] from persons already married.

The December decrees proclaimed the full equality of men and women in the sphere of marriage and the family, completely removed the distinction between illegitimate children and children born in wedlock, and eliminated "a source of bourgeois filth, dejection, and debasement" [Lenin]—the pre-Revolutionary divorce procedure, by establishing free divorce. Such was the basic content of these first two decrees of the Soviet regime concerning marriage and divorce.

Here it is appropriate to note an interesting circumstance. The final adoption and promulgation of these decrees was preceded by the publication of a draft of one of them in the press. On November 21, 1917, that is, less than one month after the October Revolution, the "Draft of the Decree Concerning Civil Marriage, Children, and Registration of Status" was printed in No. 231 of the Gazette of the Provisional Workers' and Peasants' Government. At that time, of course, there could be no broad discussion of these questions: the situation was then unfavorable. But the draft of the marriage decree, printed in the yellowed pages of the newspapers of that time, formed a basis, as it were, for a certain tradition which has characterized the procedure followed in promulgating the most important legislation in the field of family law. Thus, in 1925 the draft of the Code of Laws on Marriage, the Family, and Guardianship ... was submitted for wide discussion by the working masses, and in 1936 a draft of the law prohibiting abortions was submitted for similar wide discussion. ...

[3] Lenin, *Works,* Vol. XXVII, p. 25

[4] Registry Office

The 1918 Code

The December decrees of 1917 performed the initial house cleaning in the field of marriage and family relations, without which it would have been impossible to begin the creation of the new socialist family. At the same time they defined the basic outlines of the regulation of this new family. But at this particular time they still did not, and could not, supply an answer to the numerous concrete legal questions which were inevitably to arise in the course of putting the principles of the new socialist law into practice.

This was accomplished by the Code of 1918, which was adopted at the Session of the Fifth Convention of the All-Russian Central Executive Committee.

The first Code of Laws on civil status, marriage, the family, and guardianship was not only the first codification of our family legislation, it was in general the first Soviet Code of Laws. . . . It was not only a codification of the laws preceding it, but also a general application of the practical experience of the judicial organs and the organs of the ZAGS, already considerable by that time. The report by Comrade Kursky at the session of the ACEC drew attention to this circumstance.

What new elements were introduced by this Code, as compared with the decrees of 1917? First of all, it gave a negative answer to the question, very important in both its practical and theoretical aspects, as to whether the new law recognizing only secular marriage had retroactive force. Marriages concluded before the promulgation of the new revolutionary laws were dealt with in the same fashion as registered marriages (note to Art. 52).

The question of the treatment of ecclesiastical marriages concluded after the Revolution was formulated differently than in the decree of 1917. Without repeating the already indefinite and incomplete phraseology of the decree of 1917 to the effect that "church marriage . . . is the private affair of the contracting parties," the Code gave the question of ecclesiastical marriages a strictly definite, legal form and proclaimed very categorically: " . . . ecclesiastical marriage does not engender any rights or obligations for persons entering therein. . . ."

But the first sentence of the decree of 1917 stated that "the Russian Republic henceforth recognizes only civil marriages." It is interesting to note here the fate of this provision. During discussion of the draft of this decree at a meeting of the ACE[5] on December 12, 1917, a proposal was introduced that apparently attempted to confine itself to

[5] See Minutes of the Session of the A.C.E.C., Convention I, 1918, pp. 142-143.

a recognition of civil marriage, but not to attribute to the latter the importance of an exclusive form, and the only form recognized by the state. It was proposed to eliminate the work "only," in the proposal cited above. By this "editorial" amendment, and by eliminating only one tiny word, it was apparently designed to define the relation of the Soviet state toward the form of marriage on the same pattern followed in a number of bourgeois countries, where the secularization of marriage exists peaceably side by side with the legal recognition of church marriages (as, for example, in England), and where the secular and ecclesiastical forms of marriage are optional, and legally effective in an equal degree.

The ACEC rejected this amendment, and the idea of recognizing only civil marriage and of recognizing no other, remained in full force.

The Code of 1918 phrased this provision somewhat differently. In Article 52 it directed that "only civil (secular) marriage, registered at a civil registry office, engenders rights and obligations for the partners. . . ." This provision emphasized, with greater force and expressiveness than was the case in the decree of 1917, the organic union established by the legislator between the concept of civil marriage and registration. Marriage does not exist outside of registration—this is the quite clear and straightforward position adhered to in this Code. Hence the provisions of the Code, which refer, not to a "legalization" of marriage at the ZAGS, as was the case in the subsequent Code of 1926, but to the fact that marriages "are concluded" at organs of the ZAGS (Arts. 53, 54, 55, 57, and others). Hence the provisions that lend to marriage registration itself the significance of legality. Hence, however, since acts of registration are invested with legal force, appears the necessity for special provisions which would indicate the procedure and principles to be followed in nullifying the legal effectiveness of this registration, in the event that the marriage is concluded in violation of the law. In this Code we see a minutely worked-out section "Concerning the Annulment of Marriage" and the procedure for determining this annulment.

The question of the rights and obligations of the spouses was worked out in greater detail in this Code as compared with the decrees of 1917. Provisions to the effect that a change in the residence of one spouse does not create an obligation for the other to follow him, that marriage does not make the property of the spouses community property, and that the spouses themselves may enter into all proprietary and contractual relations permitted by law, were introduced in our family law for the first time. The idea of equal rights for men and women in marriage and the family has progressively taken deeper root and is becoming more and more firmly established. It is interesting to note the following detail in this connection. The Decree of 1917, among the obligations imposed by marriage, made reference to the obligation of a husband to support his wife, if the latter is incapacitated. The Code of 1918 no longer referred to this unilateral obligation of the husband toward his wife. Following a consistent policy as regards the equality of men and women, it declares that "a needy (i.e., not possessing a living wage and incapacitated) spouse has the right to receive maintenance from the other spouse, in the event that the latter is in a position to support him."

The Code of 1918 settled in detail the question of determining paternity, while the question of the rights and obligations of parents and children was worked out from every angle, in any event much more completely than in the decrees of 1917. The idea of equal rights for women was also reflected in the establishment of equal rights for the mother and father. It was proclaimed, in particular, that "parental rights are to be exercised by the parents conjointly," and that "in case of disagreement on the part of the parents, the question at issue is to be decided by the local court with the participation of the parents." This provision of the Code, like some others, clearly "conflicted" with the age-old concepts of bourgeois law, which missed no opportunity to emphasize the priority of the father in all matters concerning the children.

The idea of subordinating parental right to the interests of the children was proclaimed for the first time in our legislation: "Parental rights are to be exercised exclusively in the interests of the children, and in the event that they are exercised inequitably, the court is given the authority to deprive the parents of these rights."

The reciprocal obligation of the children ". . . to provide maintenance for their parents, if the latter are incapacitated and in need . . ." was also established by law for the first time.

It must be noted that the Code of 1918 formulated for the first time the subsidiary obligation to provide alimony for needy and incapacitated (subsidiary in the sense that it comes into force only in the event that the above-mentioned persons are unable to secure maintenance from their parents, children, or spouses). Thus, the Code of 1918 offered a wider concept of the scope of the family, not confining it solely to spouses, parents, and children.

Finally, let us also note that the Code of 1918, for the first time following the October Revolution, regulated questions of guardianship. The decree of November 10, 1917, concerning the abolition of estates and civil ranks, did away with the pre-Revolutionary institutions of guardianship along with other class institutions, while no new institutions of guardianship were created. The Code of 1918 defined the principles and concrete forms of Soviet guardianship.

The transition to the New Economic Policy placed on the agenda the question of a partial revision of the marriage and family laws issued during the first months following the October Revolution, and of certain changes in these laws in the direction of increased protection of women's and children's rights in the family.

The most important thing at that time was the question of the form of marriage and the legal significance of marriage registration.

The increased emphasis given to the registration of marriages in the organs of the ZAGS as a factor bound up with the establishment of conjugal rights and obligations, was very specific at the time our first legislative acts concerning family law were adopted (1917-1918). This acuteness as to the question of marriage registration arose from the necessity for opposing civil, secular marriage to ecclesiastical marriage, which at that time was still the predominant form of marriage, especially in the rural areas. The remarks made by V. I. Lenin at the Congress of Women Workers on November 19, 1918, are well-known: "This law concerning the complete freedom of marriage is taking hold very well in our cities and at our factory and plant sites, but in the rural areas it very frequently remains on paper. Ecclesiastical marriage has predominated there until now." These words were uttered just as the Code was being adopted in the autumn of 1918. The provisions of our legislation of 1917-1918, which set up civil marriage, concluded at the ZAGS as a counterbalance to church marriage and placed under the special protection of the law, proved to be one of the means for strengthening the status of civil marriage in the struggle against the influence of religion on family relations.

But the posing of the question of the implications of marriage registration in this emphatic manner simultaneously solved another question, which during this period did not have the immediate importance that it acquired subsequently. The attachment of legal consequences to marriage registration gave a negative answer to the question of the legal consequences of so-called *de facto* marriage: according to the Code of 1918, *de facto* marriage enjoyed no protection whatsoever, and created no rights or obligations. During this period there could not have been any other approach to *de facto* marriages. The recognition and protection of any consequences whatever resulting from *de facto,* unregistered marriage relations under conditions arising at a time when a bitter struggle for civil marriage was being waged, would have meant in effect that the new law was taking a course leading to the recognition of ecclesiastical marriages. For the law to take such a course would have meant, at that time, coming into conflict with one of the basic tasks of the Code—to promote the liberation of marriage from religious influence. Naturally, the Code did not take this course.

But practical experience quickly raised, in a rather acute form, the question of some sort of safeguard for unregistered marriage relations. The extension of legal effectiveness only to registered marriage achieved its positive goal and promoted the weakening of religious influence. But at the same time this system reflected negatively, during this period, on the interests of women from the working strata of the population. The economic disorder following the imperialistic and civil wars, the economic difficulties of the first years of the New Economic Policy, unemployment, and the as yet low material standard of living, very frequently placed the working woman in a difficult and materially dependent position in relation to the economically stronger partner. "Short-term marriages," which were extremely prevalent during the first years of the NEP among the *kulaks* and *nepmen,* the so-called "seasonal marriages," and the open exploitation of women admitted to the household in the guise of *"de facto* wives" with a premeditated desire to avoid marriage registration, which imposed specific obligations—all these phenomena could not help, of course, but attract the attention of the Party, the Government, and broad Soviet public opinion. Voices began to be heard with increasing frequency at meetings and in the press in favor of offering legal protection also to *de facto* marriage relations.

The considerable successes already achieved by that time in the task of reinforcing the principles of the new way of life and in the consolidation of civil, secular marriage also contributed to this orientation of thought. At the Second Session of the Twelfth Convention of the ACEC in October 1925, data from the Moscow ZAGS were cited, for example, according to which seventy-one per cent of the marriages had been performed without the observance of church rites.

To be sure, these data referred to Moscow, the most progressive proletarian center, and doubtless they were different in the rural areas. But nevertheless it cannot be doubted that by the time the question of the necessity for protecting the interests of women suffering injury due to the lack of protection for *de facto* marriage relations had become urgent, considerations to the effect that safeguarding unregistered marriages would strengthen church influence could no longer play a decisive role.

A heated discussion flared up around the question of the value of marriage registration and whether it was necessary or not to protect *de facto* marriage. It began long before the final draft of the Code was discussed at the Third Session of the Twelfth Convention of the ACEC in November 1926. Thus, for example, even four years prior to this, when the draft of the Civil Code of the RSFSR was being debated at the Fourth Session of the Ninth Convention of the ACEC in October 1922, the question of revising the Family Code of 1918 was raised, while the necessity for recognizing *de facto* marriages was advanced as one of the arguments.

From this time on, the question of the attitude to be taken toward *de facto* marriages, among other problems of family law, was constantly in the pages of the newspapers and magazines and on the agenda of every sort of meeting and debate over a period of several years until, finally, following prolonged and heated debate at the Third Session of the Twelfth Convention of the ACEC on November 19, 1926, the viewpoint favoring legal recognition of *de facto* marriage gained the upper hand.

The 1926 Code

In accordance with the exact terms of the Code of the RSFSR of 1926, *de facto* marriage relations and registered marriage relations were not wholly on a par with one another. This Code was concerned only with the mutual maintenance of the partners and matters associated with property acquired during marriage. But judicial practice and later legislation pursued a course leading to complete equality in every respect between *de facto* marriage and registered marriage.

The Code of 1926 solved, in a new way, not only the question of the form of marriage, but also a number of other essential questions.

Thus, a substantial change was introduced in dealing with the question of marriageable age. As compared with the Code of 1918, the marriageable age of the woman was raised to 18 years (from 16 years, as set by the Code of 1918). A change was introduced in the regulation of the property relations of the spouses. The Code of 1918 had established complete separation of the property of the husband and wife, stating in Article 105: "Marriage does not create common ownership of the property of the partners." This provision was aimed against the inequality of women's rights, and against bourgeois conceptions that asserted the supremacy of the husband in governing the property relations of the spouses. But it soon became clear that this one provision was insufficient, since the declaration of this principle alone frequently acted counter to the interests of the working woman, by unjustly denying her her right to property acquired by the spouses during marriage. This was amended in the Code of 1926, according to Article 10, by which "property belonging to the partners prior to entry into marriage, remains the separate property of each. Property acquired by the partners in the course of marriage is regarded as the common property of the partners."

The provision dealing with the question of the maintenance of the spouses was changed. The Code of 1918 did not limit a spouse's obligation to pay alimony to a definite term following discontinuance of marriage, and after divorce alimony could be recovered for life. The Code of 1926 eliminated the possibility of life-long maintenance, by limiting the term for payment of alimony to one year after dissolution of marriage.

The mutual relations of parents and children were defined somewhat more fully and minutely in the new Code. The divorce procedure was changed. According to the Code of 1918, divorce was carried out by a court, and in the event that both parties desired divorce, it could be performed by an organ of the ZAGS, without recourse to a court. The Code of 1926 abolished the court procedure for effecting divorce, and established a procedure of registration through the ZAGS for all cases.

Adoption

Finally, let us consider the question of adoption. As is well-known, the Code of 1918 did not permit adoption. As stated in Article 183 of the latter, adoption performed subsequent to the issuing of the Code, "... does not engender any obligations and rights for the foster parents or for the adopted." How may we explain the negative attitude of the Code of 1918 toward this institution?

We must recall the situation in 1918, when the Code was adopted. This was a period during which *"petit bourgeois* elements predominated in the country's economy. Millions of small businessmen in the cities and rural areas constituted the soil for the growth of capitalism. These small businessmen did not recognize either labor discipline or state discipline, and they did not submit either to accounting or to control. The *petit bourgeois* element of speculation and commercialism, and the attempts of small businessmen and merchants to enrich themselves at the expense of the people's needs presented a special danger at this critical moment."[6]

Such a situation could not, of course, but influence the solution of the question at issue. During this period there were very real and well-founded fears that the institution of adoption would be used by the *"petit bourgeois* element" for the purpose of exploiting the labor of the adopted—waifs, orphans, and the children of poor peasants, farm hands, and workers—"to enrich themselves at the expense of the people's needs." In addition, it must be considered that at that time there were still no organs of Soviet guardianship at all in many places, and where they already existed, they were still too feeble and inexperienced to insure proper state control over every case of adoption.

There was also another consideration that played a role in the prohibition of adoption by the Code of 1918. By the time it was issued, the law of 1918 concerning the abolition of inheritance was already in effect. There was a very real fear that the *petit bourgeois* element of innumerable "small businessmen," who did not submit "either to accounting or control," would likewise make use of the institution of adoption for the evasion of this law.

From the above account it is apparent that the repudiation of adoption was associated with the conditions of the class struggle in our country during the first years of the Revolution, and with the distribution of class forces during this period. But nothing at all resembling the incompatibility in principle of the institution of adoption with the system of socialist law is to be inferred from all this, as was represented in our

---

[6] *A Brief Survey of the History of the ACP (b)*, p. 211.

literature at one time. On the contrary, only the reverse conclusion as regards the temporary nature of the prohibition of adoption by the Code of 1918 may be drawn from the above account. And, in fact, this institution underwent a vigorous development in Soviet law with the recession of the conditions of class struggle of the first period of the Revolution, which had prevented its being put into effect. The Code of 1926 already contained an entire and well developed chapter entitled "Adoption" (Arts. 57-67), which was put into force even before the Code was adopted in its entirety.

This represents, basically, the new material introduced by the Code of 1926, as compared with the Code of 1918.

The Constituent Republics

We are unable here to consider in detail the development of the family and marriage legislation of all the Republics. The comparative study of the legislation of all the Union Republics is a subject for independent research, in which, it is hoped, the scientific workers of these Republics will undoubtedly play the decisive role. Let us but mention in general that at first the Code of 1918 was adopted by all the other Union Republics. In a number of these Republics, the new Soviet provisions had to encounter not only bourgeois attitudes in the sphere of marriage and the family, but also attitudes arising from still earlier structures— survivals of tribal government in the form of various ancient customs— the bride price, polygamy, marriages of minors, etc. These peculiarities were reflected in the marriage and family laws of a number of Republics. But the basic questions of marriage and family relations were dealt with in all the Republics in the same manner as in the RSFSR Code of 1918. Thus, at the initial stage of its development, this branch of the legislation of the Union Republics was more or less uniform.

But in 1926 the renovation of family and marriage legislation began, not only in the RSFSR, but in all the other Republics. New family codes were issued in the Ukraine, in Byelorussia, Azerbaijan, Armenia, and Uzbekistan from 1926 to 1928; in Georgia, in 1930; and in Turkmenia, in 1935. With the publication of the new Codes in the Republics of the Soviet Union, a considerable divergence began among the systems of legislation of the Republics, to which our literature has already often drawn attention. To be sure, these systems of legislation did not differ from one another basically and essentially—the liberating ideas introduced by the Great October Socialist Revolution received equally clear expression in all the systems of legislation of the Republics. The equality under family law of the woman, both as wife and mother and as regards both person and property, the secular and free character of marriage, and state protection of the rights of children—all these principles of Soviet marriage and family legislation formed the basis of all the codes of the Republics. But nevertheless, divergences in dealing with questions of no little practical importance (relating to certain rights and obligations imposed by marriage, marriageable age, the scope of maintenance, etc.) make their appearance in the systems of legislation of the Union Republics. Many of these differences were really determined by the peculiarities of the economy, climates, and national character, while the wisdom of, and necessity for, the existence of others is subject to doubt.

The 1936 Legislation

Ten years have elapsed since the adoption of the RSFSR Code on Marriage, the Family, and Guardianship. During this time the country achieved decisive successes in the task of socialist construction. *In A Brief Survey of the History of the ACP (b)* we read: "By 1936 the economy of the USSR had changed completely. By this time the capitalist elements had been completely liquidated—the socialist system had been victorious in all spheres of the national economy. . . .The exploitation of man by man had been abolished forever. Public, socialist ownership of the means of production had been established as the stable foundation of the new socialist order in all branches of the national economy. Depressions, poverty, unemployment, and bankruptcy had disappeared . . . from the new socialist society. Conditions had been created for a comfortable and cultured life for all the members of Soviet society."

Under these conditions there likewise appeared the opportunity and necessity to consider fully the question of strengthening the family as a social nucleus, capable of fulfilling highly useful social functions under the conditions of socialism. With the appearance of a material basis for the strengthening of the family, intolerance toward looseness in the mutual relations of men and women, and toward a casual attitude in regard to children, the family, and family obligations, became ever more deeply and firmly rooted in the consciousness of the masses.

". . . In connection with the increased welfare of the masses," we read in *A Brief Survey of the History of the ACP (b)* in the pages relating to the period described, "the Government has issued a law prohibiting abortions." In addition to prohibiting abortions, the decree of the CEC and the SPC of the USSR of June 27, 1936,[7] considerably extended the material basis for the protection of mother and child, for the first time introduced state bonuses for mothers with many children, and introduced essential changes in the legal regulation of a number of

[7] SZ, 1936, No. 34, p. 309.

questions relating to marriage and the family, which were aimed at increasing responsibility for maintenance and at suppressing easy divorces. As this law itself pointed out, the changes in the marriage legislation were dictated by the aim of ". . . combatting the casual attitude toward the family and family obligations."

Wartime and Postwar Legislation

The treacherous attack of fascism on the Soviet Union disrupted peacetime socialist construction and inflicted enormous injury on millions of Soviet families. But even while the war was in progress, when the cannon still roared on the battlefields, and when fierce battles were still being waged on the soil of Byelorussia and the Ukraine, our people, Government, and Party, never for a minute in doubt of ultimate victory, set about solving a number of problems relating to postwar peacetime socialist construction. The problem of the further strengthening of the family was one of the first among these tasks. The Decree of the Presidium of the Supreme Soviet of the USSR appeared on July 8, 1944, a decree which, by its significance, will go down in the history of the Soviet state as one of the most outstanding legislative acts.

The existence in this Decree of the aim of strengthening the family does not require proof in the form of any special analysis of its provisions. . . . This aim is formulated in the text of the Decree itself as one of its guiding ideas. Let us recall the introductory words of this legislative act: "Concern for children and mothers and for the strengthening of the family has always been one of the most important tasks of the Soviet state. In safeguarding the interests of the mother and the child, the state extends great material assistance to pregnant women and to mothers for the maintenance and rearing of their children. During and following the war, when there will be greater material hardships for many families, the further extension of measures of state assistance will be required."[8]

This "concern for children and mothers and for strengthening the family" occasioned, above all, a new and enormous expansion of the material basis and legal guaranties for the protection of mothers and children.

[8] Decree of the Presidium of the Supreme Soviet of the USSR of July 8, 1944, "Concerning the Increase of State Assistance to Pregnant Women, to Mothers with Large Families, and Unwed Mothers; the Improvement of Infant-and-Maternity Welfare; and the Establishment of the Honorary Title 'Heroic Mother', the 'Order of Maternal Glory,' and the 'Maternity Medal.' " (*Vedomosti Verkhovnogo Sovieta SSSR*, July 16, 1944, No. 37).

Bonuses for Large Families

State assistance was considerably expanded in the form of bonuses for large families, which were introduced in our country as early as 1936. This expansion was reflected not only in the increased amount of each actual bonus payment, but also in the fact that the number of children entitling mothers to a bonus was lowered, and thus the number of mothers receiving this bonus was increased several times. At this time the bonus began to be paid after the birth of the third child, whereas before it had become payable upon the birth of the seventh. Changes in the operation of this bonus brought it closer to the vital needs of the family—the amount of the bonus was increased in proportion to the number of children, not only single annual bonus payments, but monthly payments were established, and the procedure as to bonus payments itself was simplified. State bonuses for unmarried mothers were introduced which were payable upon the birth of the first child, as well as the right of the mother to place the child in a state children's institution entirely at the expense of the Government.

New labor safeguards for pregnant women and nursing mothers were introduced.

Reflecting the esteem and respect with which the Soviet land surrounds motherhood, the Decree introduced high awards of glory and heroism for mothers bearing and rearing a specific number of children.

But the "concern for children and mothers and for strengthening the family" also led our legislators to make substantial changes in legislation previously in force in the sphere of the legal regulation of marriage and family relations. These changes related to the following three questions: the legal value of marriage registration, forms of protection for the unwed mother and her offspring, and divorce.

As we have seen above, our legislation recognized two solutions of the question of marriage registration prior to the publication of the Decree of July 8, 1944: one, established by the Code of the RSFSR of 1918, ascribed exclusive significance to the above; the other, contained in the codes of a number of Union Republics in effect prior to the publication of the Decree of July 8, 1944, held the legal value of registration at a minimum. But both of these solutions were occasioned by the specific historical circumstances in which they were adopted. In the one case, this solution was occasioned by the historical problem, very pressing at that time, of overcoming the influence of the church on marriage; in the other case, it was occasioned by the problem of protecting the woman from exploitation, which had manifested itself somewhat under the conditions arising from a certain revival of capitalist elements during the years of the NEP. These problems in themselves were very important and urgent in their time. But it is not difficult to see that, viewed in the perspective of the entire movement of the country toward socialism, these tasks were temporary and transient. The liquidation of the last remains of the capitalistic classes, which was achieved by the country in its progress toward socialism, the mass attraction of women to socially productive labor, and the successes in the sphere of her real emancipation, as well as the increased standard of cultural and ethical requirements exacted from every person by the country, especially in questions relating to the family—all this made it possible to formulate the question of the state's attitude toward so-called *de facto* marriages in a different manner. The circumstances that had at one time been grounds for protection of the latter have disappeared. Today, entry into unregistered, *de facto* relations under the new conditions of life in our country is, on the whole, no longer necessary at all.

Meanwhile the system of obligatory marriage registration, a system under which marriage registration has acquired a constitutional legal significance, offers the state the opportunity of exerting its active influence on the mode of life in the direction of a further consolidation of socialist principles, and in the direction of a further strengthening of the family. And inasmuch as there are no longer grounds for not taking advantage of these opportunities—grounds which existed at an earlier stage of socialist construction, the state is introducing the principle throughout the territory of the USSR by virtue of which "... only registered marriage engenders rights and obligations for the partners" (Art. 19 of the Decree).

Divorce

The changes introduced by the Decree of July 8, 1944, dealing with the question of divorce, are also intimately related to the question of marriage registration. Just as with the conclusion of marriage, the state likewise in this case seeks to insure its opportunity to exert active influence on marriage relations, in order to restrain the thoughtless dissolution of the latter. Whereas before, prior to the Decree of July 8, 1944, the role of the state in divorce was confined to a passive act of registration, today the desire of one or even of both parties to obtain divorce must coincide with the recognition by the state of the necessity for dissolving this marriage. Today, marriage is dissolved, as stated in Article 26 of the Decree of July 8, 1944, only "... in the event of recognition of the necessity to dissolve the marriage." The judicial procedure is being established; two stages of the court examination (arbitration in a people's court, and the decision of a divorce case by a higher court having jurisdiction in this field), obligatory deposition by the parties and ascertainment of the motives for divorce by the court, the summoning of witnesses to the arbitration, and public trial of the case are being introduced; and the fees associated with divorce are being raised. While by no means introducing the principle of the indissolubility of marriage, leaving the principle of free divorce in force, and allowing divorce if serious grounds exist therefore, the state is introducing certain restraints in order to prevent the abuse of liberty in regard to this question, and to prevent groundless divorces.

Thus, just as in the question of marriage registration, the new procedure for divorces can only mean the increased cultural and educational influence of the socialist state on the mode of life in the direction of strengthening the family and in the direction of strengthening socialist principles.

Unmarried Mothers and Their Children

Lastly, the Decree of July 8, 1944, introduced substantial changes in dealing with the question of protecting the unmarried mother and her offspring. Having abolished the mother's right, which previously existed, to institute an action for the establishment of paternity and for recovery of alimony for maintenance of a child fathered by a person with whom she had not been registered, the Decree at the same time considerably increased state assistance to the unwed mother and established for her the right (even if she possesses but one child) to obtain state compensation or to place the child in a children's institution entirely at state expense. In addition, the Decree provided for prosecution for insult and injury to the dignity of the woman and mother, including the unwed mother (Art. 31 of the Decree).

By liberating the unmarried mother from the often difficult situation in which she found herself in connection with the establishment of paternity and the recovery of alimony, and extending assistance to her for the rearing of her child, the state has at the same time created a more normal situation for the child as well, by no longer placing the latter in dependence upon the possibly accidental outcome of a paternity case.

This new formulation of the question arose from the need for really effective protection of the interests of the child of the unwed mother, and from the need for creating favorable conditions for bringing the child to maturity as a healthy and sound individual.

Thus, while motivated by the need for the overall consolidation of a stable and amicable family, founded on the basis of registered marriage, the Decree is at the same time doing everything possible toward extending the necessary material and moral support to the extra-marital child and its mother.

The Decree of the Presidium of the Supreme Soviet of the USSR of March 14, 1945, contained a number of very important provisions relating to the procedure for the application of the Decree of July 8, 1944, in relation to children, the marriage of whose parents is not registered. This Decree also introduced an important provision permitting the subsequent equality of status through marriage and recognition of paternity, of the children of the unwed mother and children born in marriage (Art. 3).

Trend Toward Uniformity

As we have seen above, our legislation, beginning in 1936, embarked on a policy of regulating marriage and family relations on an All-Union scale. Aside from the Decrees of the CEC and SPC of the USSR of June 27, 1936, and the Decrees of the Presidium of the Supreme Soviet of the USSR of July 8, 1944, and March 14, 1945, already referred to, we may further mention the Decrees of the Presidium of the Supreme Soviet of the USSR of September 8, 1943, "Concerning Adoption," and of November 10, 1944, "Concerning the Procedure for Recognizing *De Facto* Marriage Relations in the Event that One of the Partners Dies or Is Missing at the Front", and the Decree of the SPC of the USSR of November 27, 1944, relative to the establishment by the NKU of the USSR of an order "Concerning the Procedure for the Examination by the Courts of Cases Involving the Dissolution of Marriage."

Such All-Union acts as the "Regulation Concerning the Procedure for the Fixing and Payment of State Bonuses and the Extension of Exemptions to Pregnant Women, Mothers with Large Families, and Unmarried Mothers", ratified by the SPC of the USSR on August 18, 1944, and the Decree of November 14, 1945, "Concerning Heirs, Legal and Testamentary," are likewise very intimately related to questions of family law.

This tendency toward uniformity of legal standards in such an important sphere of social life as the family is quite natural and in conformity to principle. During discussion of the status of the Committee on Legislative Proposals, at the Third Session of the Supreme Soviet of the USSR, it was pointed out quite correctly that "the uniformity of the socioeconomic and political basis in all the Republics of our Soviet Union warrants and urgently requires uniformity of the legal standards founded on this basis."

Drawing upon the practical legislative experience of the Soviet Union, which "... has promulgated certain basic laws concerning marriage and the family, which have a guiding significance for the legislation of all the Union Republics," the Revisory Commission for the Introduction of Additions and Amendments in the Text of the Constitution of the

USSR, as is well-known, proposed at the above-mentioned session of the Supreme Soviet to delegate the establishment of the principles of marriage and family legislation to the jurisdiction of the USSR.

This proposal by the Supreme Soviet of the USSR was adopted, and at the present time Article 14 of the Constitution of the USSR contains a provision to the effect that "the establishment of the principles of marriage and family legislation" is likewise subject to the jurisdiction of the USSR.

The establishment by the Constitution of the practice of All-Union legislative regulation of marriage and the family once more testifies to the great significance for the state attributed in our country to this sphere of social relations.

Editors' Supplement

On October 4, 1959, there appeared in *Izvestia,* the official organ of the Soviet government, an article entitled "Soviet Ritualism". It criticized the somewhat perfunctory process of marriage registration amid drab surroundings as unbefitting the celebration of such a memorable event in the life of the Soviet citizen. The need for a glamorous Soviet ritual was emphasized. In 1960, the city of Leningrad took the initiative in meeting this need by the establishment of a Palace of Weddings. Within a few months Moscow and many other Soviet cities followed suit.

The new emphasis on Soviet wedding ritual stemmed in part from the improved standard of living in the USSR in the 1950's. It was also introduced to offset a growing trend among Soviet young people to seek an elaborate church wedding ceremony following the unromantic process of civil registration. The Soviet ritual, in other words, was essentially a substitute for church ritual.

In the Soviet Palace of Weddings, music, flowers, champagne, photographs and a fifteen-minute ceremony provide a more romantic setting for the bride and groom than the Registry office. Dressed for the occasion, they march into the marriage hall to the sound of Tchaikovsky's music, *Auld Lang Syne,* or whatever tune may seem appropriate to the occasion. They are greeted by a smiling woman official of the city Soviet, who reminds them of the solemnity of the occasion, the responsibilities they are about to assume and asks them if they have given due consideration to the significance of the step they are about to take. The couple exchange rings, sign the wedding register and receive official congratulations, together with a marriage certificate. In an adjoining room, Soviet champagne and refreshments are available to the bridal party on payment of catering costs. The wedding fee itself, paid by the groom, amounts to 1.50 rubles. Not all Soviet marriages take place at a Palace of Weddings. The institution is sufficiently popular so that reservations ordinarily must be made several weeks in advance.

A rising tide of Soviet criticism in regard to certain aspects of the 1944 marriage legislation led to the publication on February 16, 1964, of recommended reforms in family law pertaining to illegitimate children and divorce. Under the provisions of the law of 1944, the paternity suit was abandoned, the state contributed to the support of a child born out of wedlock until the age of twelve, and the father's name was omitted from the birth certificate. The growing expense of this procedure is indicated by the fact that 3.3 million mothers received monthly allowances from the state in 1957, as compared to 280,000 in 1945. Under the new proposals, the name of the unmarried father will be entered in the birth certificate, thereby removing what came to be regarded as a stigma on the child. It is assumed that the father, as in the early Soviet period, will henceforth be expected to contribute to this child's support.

The forthcoming reforms make provision for the trial of a divorce suit directly before a people's court, thereby substantially reducing expenses stemming from the 1944 legislation. The 1944 law, which was designed to strengthen family ties, had required a petition to a people's court (costing 10 rubles) for purposes of reconciliation, and, when that failed, a divorce suit before a higher court, where the fees sometimes amounted to three months' salary.

References

BERMAN, HAROLD J., *Justice in the U.S.S.R., An Interpretation of Soviet Law*, Revised and Enlarged Edition. Cambridge: Harvard University Press, 1963. Chapter 14, "Law and the Family," pp. 330-344.

FITZSIMMONS, THOMAS, *et al., eds., USSR: Its People, Its Society, Its Culture.* (Survey of World Cultures Series.) New Haven: Hraf Press, 1960.

52. the establishment of boarding schools in the USSR

IN 1956 BOARDING SCHOOLS WERE ESTABLISHED in the Soviet Union. In its initial stage, this move evoked opposition from some parents and educators. To many it suggested the creation of a privileged class of "gifted children." The main purpose, as expressed in the articles presented below, was to create a well-disciplined corps of Communist leaders for the building of the new Soviet society. The lives of these students were to be regulated from dawn to dusk. The program involved sacrifices on the part of students and parents, who were to be separated for the greater part of the year. The perpetuation of Communism appeared to depend on the rearing of children in a "collective" environment, under carefully supervised ideological instruction.

Below are two articles: "Boarding Schools" (*Pravda,* June 28, 1956. Complete Text), and "Some Questions of Establishing Boarding Schools" (By I. Kairov, President of the Russian Republic Academy of Pedagogical Sciences. *Utchitelskaya gazeta,* June 27, 1956, p. 2. Condensed Text). 1956, *The Current Digest of the Soviet Press* (Vol. VIII, no. 27, August 15, 1956, pp. 5-6), published weekly at Columbia University by the Joint Committee on Slavic Studies appointed by the American Council of Learned Societies and Social Science Research Council. Reprinted by permission.

Boarding Schools

During the current five-year plan and in accordance with the decisions of the 20th Party Congress, universal secondary education will be in the main established in the U.S.S.R., the educational and material facilities of schools will be reinforced, polytechnic instruction will be organized and a network of new schools, kindergartens and nurseries will be extensively developed. Moreover, the Congress stated that it would be advisable to begin organizing a new type of educational institution—boarding schools —which would solve, at a higher level, the tasks of training comprehensively developed and educated builders of communism.

The 20th Party Congress decision to establish a new state system for bringing up children has received extensive support from the Soviet public, from parents and teachers. The basic idea of boarding schools, distinguishing them from ordinary schools, is that the educational influence of teachers embraces the entire life of children from early childhood, when they no longer need direct maternal care, until maturity. The Leninist requirement of combining education with socially productive work must be fully met at these institutions.

Boarding schools will have all the conditions necessary for proper organization of children's meals, a rational living schedule, education, work, physical and esthetic development and leisure. The children's permanent residence at boarding schools will create the prerequisites for developing independent activity, physical culture and sports for the most complete satisfaction of the students' most varied requirements.

Thanks to this, boarding schools will be able to give pupils truly lasting and sound knowledge on a secondary school level, a broad polytechnical outlook, a knowledge of the fundamentals of industrial and agricultural production, good labor training, physical hardening and thorough spiritual development.

Our country's boarding schools must become the basic form of general secondary and polytechnical education of the younger generation. The general school as it now exists will be converted into a boarding school, that is, it will be enlarged by well-built and well-equipped dormitories, dining rooms, workshops and physical culture gymnasiums.

At present, with the new system of education in its initial stage, efforts should be focused on sending children aged seven to 17—the most impressionable age—to boarding schools. Of course, this does not mean that we will not have complete boarding schools, including nurseries, kindergartens and schools in the first stage of our work. Such institutions will exist but there will be comparatively few of them at first.

Since boarding schools should become schools for all children, they should be built to meet the needs of various territories, on the basis of small school districts, in direct contact with the population.

Here we should remember that general schools have occasionally been located in unfavorable conditions. The boarding schools which are to replace them must therefore be located in healthier and more favorable places. Several boarding schools can be located in one place, in one children's settlement. In this case a single material base can be set up for several children's institutions, which are independent in terms of education work. This would improve care of the children and reduce its cost.

Vacancies at boarding schools must be filled on a voluntary basis. Children who live with their parents can and must be taught along with boarding school pupils in a school which is part of the boarding school system.

At the beginning of May, 1956, the Party Central Committee held an extended conference of practical personnel of schools and children's homes and of personnel of Party and Young Communist League agencies, Ministries of Education and public education departments on questions of boarding school organization. At the conference sharp criticism was levelled at many directors of public education agencies who have tried in every way to delay the establishment of boarding schools.

Unfortunately, conclusions have not always been drawn from the work of this conference and from this criticism. Not enough work in establishing boarding schools has been done in many republics and provinces of the country. For example, the plan to begin opening boarding schools in Stalingrad and Omsk in the 1956-1957 academic year has been completely abandoned. The Tatar Autonomous Republic Ministry of Education and the Tyumen and Chkalov Province Public Education Departments have in fact adopted the same position.

Many places are not really working out plans for establishing boarding schools in the coming years of the five-year plan.

The U.S.S.R. State Planning Commission and the U.S.S.R. Ministry of Finance are actually ignoring this matter. So far they have not defined their attitude toward boarding school plans made by public education agencies. They have also not decided upon the funds which must be spent for the construction of boarding schools from capital investments for housing and the communal economy.

The Russian Republic Academy of Pedagogical Sciences is lagging in the examination of a number of questions about the organization of boarding schools. Programs for training boarding school teachers are now very necessary; teaching materials on a great variety of questions concerning the organization of educational and training work at boarding schools are also needed. There is a growing demand for books on the experience of work at children's homes and boarding schools. But the Academy of Pedagogical Sciences and its institutes have not yet provided any materials on these questions.

Boarding schools are a new development. They require the most vigorous and constant support from Party agencies, as does any new and important matter which breaks with old and accustomed practice.

The various economic ministries and agencies cannot remain aloof from the work of establishing boarding schools. They must use the funds, materials and manpower of their building organizations and participate in the construction both of new boarding schools and of dormitories for existing schools in accordance with the plan of the Ministries of Education.

Collective farms are displaying a great deal of interest in establishing boarding schools. For example, 19 collective farms in Uzbekistan have expressed the wish to build boarding schools at their own expense. It is important to support and develop this initiative of collective farms in every way.

The task of establishing boarding schools is of tremendous importance. The primary obligation of local Party and Soviet agencies is to supervise this work diligently, to provide real support for public education agencies in implementing it and to guarantee the rapid establishment of boarding schools.

Some Questions of Establishing Boarding Schools

The decision of the 20th Party Congress on organizing boarding schools has been warmly supported by the Soviet people.

More than 200 boarding schools are scheduled to open in 1956 in the Russian Republic. Moscow has decided not to wait until standard buildings are erected but to open 13 new educational institutions this autumn, adapting existing school buildings and buildings under construction for this purpose.

When complete, the boarding schools will include a nursery, a kindergarten and a general polytechnical school. At the first stage of development these new educational institutions can have a kindergarten and a school, or just a school. The schools will have five or seven classes, depending on existing conditions. Children whose parents cannot provide the necessary conditions for a good upbringing must be given preference in admission.

The general and polytechnical education in these schools will in the main correspond to the training in the general schools. In the first years they will work on the basis of the study plan, programs and textbooks established for the general schools. Improved study plans, programs and textbooks will be set up for them in the next year or two.

Until the Statutes on Boarding Schools are approved, the Russian Republic Academy of Pedagogical Sciences recommends that public education departments be guided by the following in organizing boarding schools.

Education in the boarding schools should be combined with production work. Labor in all its forms should occupy an important place in the student's daily life. Classroom studies, personal care and work in school gardens and shops, at enterprises and on collective and state farms develop industriousness.

It is possible to train pupils in boarding schools for participation in various branches of work. This is done on the basis of a general and polytechnical education. Students can, in accord with their own wishes, study in special groups for a given occupation, such as that of lathe operator, milling-machine operator, electrician, plant laboratory assistant, field expert, livestock specialist, horticulturist, farm machine operator, etc. Training is offered in applied arts, stenography, typing and sewing. The organization of such groups will depend on the needs of the local economy and cultural work and on the school's production surroundings. The Councils of Ministers of autonomous republics and territory and province executive committees assign enterprises, state farms and Machine and Tractor Stations to boarding schools for production practice. One month out of the year should be set aside for production practice for secondary and senior students. The graduates of boarding schools receive a diploma stating their acquired production training.

The pupils will remain in the boarding schools, making it possible to make these schools the true center of communist upbringing. The Academy of Pedagogical Sciences considers it possible to offer certain advice on organization of the children in these schools.

The students will constitute a single group, in which the leading role should belong to the Young Communist League and Young Pioneer organizations. . . .

The academy recommends approximately the following structure for the student body and its elected organizations. At the head of the student body stands the Student Council, elected by open vote at a general meeting of the students. It is comprised of nine to 15 members and is accountable to the general assembly of students. The Student Council elects a chairman, vice-chairmen and committee secretaries and chairmen. It examines and decides all current questions concerning the day-to-day life of the student body, enlisting the broad *aktiv* of the students in discussion and decision of the most important problems. . . .

The primary groups of the boarding school are organized on the basis of grades, residence in houses and sections of the boarding school, study and production work and sports. A primary group elects leaders from among its members (monitors, brigade leaders, etc.) and determines their rights and duties. The monitors and brigade leaders form a permanent *aktiv* which functions under the leadership of the Student Council.

The Student Council has the right to adopt encouragement measures with respect to the students and primary groups—such measures as expression of gratitude, mention on the Honor Roll or in the Book of Honor, certificates of merit, challenge banners, awards, etc. The Council can take punitive measures against students who do not meet their obligations or abide by the rules of the boarding school; it can reprove, censure, reprimand, deny the right to participate in commercial projects and issue strict warnings.

The activity of the elected organizations of the student body can develop successfully only if the directors of the institution, the entire teaching staff and the Y.C.L. and Pioneer organizations enhance their authority among the students in every way. The Y.C.L. organization should play the leading role in the elected organizations of the student body, see to it that the most active, conscious and disciplined students are elected to the organizations and exercise general supervision over their work.

The teachers must guide the work of the student organizations, exercising the necessary tact and not permitting highhandedness or too much supervision.

In order to avoid parallelism in the activity of the various student organizations, it is wise to focus the Student Council's attention on such questions as organization of students' study work, living conditions, labor and leisure, the duty system, observance of order and schedules, etc.

It is very important to establish a proper daily schedule in boarding schools. Here the daily routine should take into account the age and individual characteristics of the pupils and should provide a strict, definite time schedule for studies, labor and creative activity; five meals a day; enough time for sleep and active relaxation in the fresh air; gymnastics, games and sports; personal care and socially useful daily work....

There is no doubt that cadres will largely decide the success of this new undertaking. In order to set up work correctly in this new type of school, it is necessary to enlist the most experienced people, expert teachers. Persons who have experience in administrative work and organizational abilities should be appointed directors of boarding schools.

The heads of academic sections and the instructors should also be selected from among the most qualified teachers in the mass schools, teachers who know their subject perfectly, who are experts at teaching and who love their profession. It will be most difficult to select the people for upbringing work. The Academy of Pedagogical Sciences proposes that the director be authorized to select these people and that he be required to appoint persons with higher education for this work, persons capable of organizing the collective activity of the children, of combining their love for children with intelligent demands on them and of exercising a favorable influence on their charges by their own personal example. Such persons may be permitted to conduct no more than six hours of classroom work a week.

According to the Academy of Pedagogical Sciences, the boarding school staff should have a supervisor of practice farming (agronomist and teacher), a supervisor of production shops and production practice (engineer and teacher), an instructor of production training and laboratory assistants. The director entrusts supervision of the physics, chemistry, biology, mechanical and freehand drawing departments and departments and laboratories for production subjects to the most experienced teachers.

The establishment of boarding schools changes the role of the family and the form of parental participation in the upbringing of children who live in boarding schools. The participation of parents in the educational work of the school should be carried on in an organized manner through parents' committees, established for constant and prolonged ties between the teaching staff on the one hand and the Soviet public and the parents on the other. Representatives of local public organizations and patrons should be drawn into parents' committees.

Can the parents take the child from the boarding school under certain circumstances? The voluntary principle in placing children in boarding schools answers this question in the affirmative. However, in order not to disturb the system of upbringing, schedules and order in the boarding schools, it would be better to establish that children can be handed over to parents only during vacations and at the end of a school year.

The boarding school should maintain constant contact with the broad public. It is important to decide who will be the patron of a school as soon as it is opened. It would be desirable for large industrial enterprises or agricultural production units (state farms or M.T.S.) to be the patrons of boarding schools.

The establishment of the new system of upbringing is an exceptionally complex and difficult question. It can be successfully solved if the departments of public education adopt an attitude of great responsibility toward the opening of the new type of school and if the broad Soviet public helps in this undertaking.

53. Soviet archeology:

ancient Khorezm*

FOREMOST AMONG THE ACHIEVEMENTS OF SOVIET ARCHEOLOGICAL science is the truly gigantic work done by Soviet research experts in studying the history of the Central Asiatic peoples. One of the most important centers of world civilization was located here in ancient times, and it exerted a tremendous influence upon the history of surrounding countries—Iran, Afghanistan, India, Eastern Turkestan, Mongolia, China, Siberia, and Eastern Europe. Mighty states of antiquity grew up here: those continually mentioned in ancient and Oriental sources—Bactria, Sogdiana, Parthia, and Khorezm. But the history of the economy, the culture, and the art of these states has remained almost entirely unknown.

Local chronicles, about the existence of which we have direct evidence, were destroyed by fire during the stormy events of the Arab invasion of the seventh and eighth centuries A.D., and until recent times all our knowledge was drawn from meager scraps of information in the works of foreign historians and geographers—Greeks, Romans, Chinese, and later on Arabs and Persians. The sole means of reconstructing the life of the Central Asiatic peoples in the remote past has been the findings of extensive archeological research. But thirty years ago this work was in a rudimentary stage. Only the Great October Socialist Revolution, which opened the road wide for the national rebirth of the former colonies of Tsarist Russia, made possible the archeological study of Central Asia, which has assumed truly gigantic proportions in the thirty years of our era.

The prerequisites created by the Soviet regime for the planned state organization of research projects and for excellent technical facilities for the latter, were combined with the new advanced methodology of the Soviet scientific Marxists. The systematic study of vast territories and attention to the monuments of the labor of the people, who are the real creators of world civilization, were rewarded by extremely important discoveries and historical conclusions of paramount significance. They

* By S. P. Tolstov, Director of the Ethnographical Institute and Chief of the Khorezm Archeological and Ethnographical Expedition of the USSR Academy of Sciences, in *Ogonyok*, No. 50, December, 1947

have now made it possible for us to interpret in an entirely new fashion the ancient history of the Central Asiatic peoples, with due regard for its significance to neighboring countries—both near and far—and the ancient history of the whole world.

To us, the workers of the Khorezm Expedition of the USSR Academy of Sciences, has fallen the great honor of being one of the detachments of this army of Soviet archeologists, who are engaged in a campaign to uncover the monuments of the ancient history of our motherland that have been hidden in the earth and buried in the sands of the desert.

This year the Khorezm Expedition marks the completion of a decade of work. During the period from 1937 to 1947 more than 12,000 kilometers of exploratory routes have been surveyed in the deserts surrounding the Khorezm oasis, where the territories of the Uzbek SSR, the Kara Kalpak ASSR, the Turkmen SSR, and the Kazakh SSR meet, as well as in the Kara Kum, the Kzyl-Kum, the Ust Urt Plateau, and along the ancient beds of the Amu-Darya and Syr-Darya rivers.

In 1946 and 1947 aviation was used in these surveys for the first time in the history of Soviet archeology, which enabled the expedition not only to discover numerous sites almost inaccessible by land, not only to decipher the history of the ancient irrigation system, but also to discover the great roads of antiquity, which in the early Middle Ages connected Khorezm with the countries of Eastern Europe, Khazaria, Volga Bulgaria, and Rüs, and to solve at last the problem of when the ancient Caspian bed of the Amu-Darya—the Uzboi—which had long excited the interest of scientists, functioned.

More than six hundred previously unknown monuments were discovered in the desert surrounding Khorezm, dating from the fourth millenium B.C. up to the seventeenth and eighteenth centuries of our own era. Fifteen of these sites were selected for systematic excavation. On the whole, this work has enabled us to reconstruct the ancient Korezm civilization, which was utterly unknown ten years ago, from its origin in the villages of primitive hunters and fishermen of the Neolithic Age, who built their communal reed dwellings on the islands in the ancient delta of the Amu-Darya, up to the flowering of that remarkable culture in the medieval Khorezm Empire of the twelfth and thirteenth centuries, which was cut short by the catastrophe of the Mongol invasion.

In investigating the ancient beds of long-defunct canals, which stretch for dozens of kilometers through the desert, and the ruins located on their banks—ruins of cities, fortresses, castles, and a whole series of once-blooming rural districts; in carefully analyzing the layout of dwellings and settlements, the products of the crafts and domestic trades, the workers of the expedition penetrated step by step into the inmost secrets of history and those processes in the development of the material productive forces and the organization of production that lie at the basis of the historical process. The investigation of the ruins of fortresses on the borders of Khorezm, of fortified points on the ancient trade and strategic routes, and of coins, minted by the rulers of Khorezm in various eras, have all revealed to us many aspects of the political history of the ancient Khorezm state.

A study of the various monuments of art and architecture discovered by the expedition, the innumerable castles, palaces, simple farmhouses, terra cotta statuettes, seals, gems, finely worked inscriptions on coins, outwardly well-preserved in desert conditions, a study which has been crowned in 1946-1947 by the discovery of decorative frescoes and monumental sculptures in a Khorezm palace of the third century A.D. in the ruins of an ancient Khorezm city now know as Toprak-Kala (in the Kara Kalpak ASSR), has thrown light upon the history of the artistic culture of ancient Khorezm. This country must be regarded as one of the outstanding artistic centers of the Hellenistic East, as one occupying a worthy place alongside Syria, Egypt, the north Black Sea coast, northern India, and Afghanistan.

Our work, as well as the work of other collectives of Soviet archeologists, has demonstrated how utterly without foundation were the ideas held by bourgeois historians concerning the perpetual stagnation of society in the ancient East. These researches have revealed the utter groundlessness of the claims of reactionary historians, who have asserted that the ancient arena of historical development was confined only to Western Europe at a time when the East was doomed for a thousand years to revert in a vicious circle to a sort of prehistoric feudalism. The history of Khorezm is unfolded before us today as a history of transition from a primitive communal society to an ancient slave-owning society, which took place about the seventh and eighth centuries B.C.— about the same time that the ancient state of Greece was formed— by the establishment of the mighty state of Khorezm.

We now see that ancient Khorezm, having reached its zenith in the third and fourth centuries A.D., entered in the fifth and sixth centuries upon a period of profound social crisis, connected with the downfall of the slave-owning society. These events are clearly reflected in the monuments: this is proved by a reduction of the irrigation system and the decline of the cities and trades, which took place at that time; by a shift in the center of gravity of social life to the village; by reinforced fortifications for private dwellings; by the demolished and gutted castles and estates. In some of these we have discovered arrows driven into the walls, and on the shattered floors huge stones that had been shot from catapults.

We see that in Khorezm, as well as in Europe, the fifth and sixth centuries opened a new epoch in history, the medieval and feudal period, when the whole tenor of life, the whole character of culture, utterly changed. Passing from monument to monument, we observe, step by step, how a new period of economic and cultural revival succeeded the deep barbarism of the early middle ages from the tenth century on, how the canals were rebuilt, how the cities were reborn, how handicrafts and trade flourished, how in the twelfth century the requisite conditions were created for the emergence of Khorezm from the period of feudal disintegration and its transformation into the nucleus of one of the earliest and mightiest feudal monarchies of the Orient, the Empire of the Shahs of Khorezm, which sustained the first blow from the hordes of Genghis Khan, sharing with Rüs the great service of shedding its blood to save European civilization. Studying the latest monuments we see what a high price Khorezm paid for its role in these terrible events. Wandering in the dead silence of the desert among ruins deserted after the invasion of Genghis Khan, past the dead oasis of Kavat-Kala, among sandy hills on which stand the ruins of houses and castles dating from the beginning of the thirteenth century and almost untouched by the passage of seven centuries, you are involuntarily transported back to that tragic epoch, which cut short the mighty flourishing of the Khorezm renaissance. By the eighteenth century Khorezm was transformed into one of the most wretched holes in an otherwise backward Central Asia, known as the Khivan Khanate.

Our expedition has solved with absolute certainty the problem of why vast areas that were once irrigated and settled regions in various countries of the Near East and Central Asia have dried up, a question which has interested scientists for many decades. By means of material from Khorezm, which has been substantiated by materials from other expeditions, we have been able to prove that it was not natural historical forces (as many have thought) that were involved here. It was not the "drying-up of Central Asia," not a shift in the courses of the rivers, not an invasion by the sand, not the salting of the soil, that explains this phenomenon. Its explanation is rooted in the processes of social history: the transition from an ancient to a feudal society, and the accompanying conquests by barbarians, the subsequent feudal dissension, and the attacks of nomads —which was the solution to this problem, predicted by the genius of Marx and now proved by documentary evidence. But that which man has destroyed, he can restore. The history of contemporary Khorezm is striking evidence of this. . . .

54. the Mitchurin biological

science: a historic controversy

AFTER WORLD WAR II, under the Stalin regime, the growing breach between the East and the West manifested itself in a controversy over genetics which had widespread repercussions inside the USSR and abroad. In 1948, Academician Trofim D. Lysenko, who represented the Mitchurin school of biological science, emerged triumphant over those Soviet scientists who upheld Western concepts on genetics, as developed by J. G. Mendel, August Weissmann, and Thomas H. Morgan, the American biologist. Outstanding Western scientists, such as H. J. Muller, President of the Genetics Society of America, and Henry Dale, President of the Royal Society of Great Britain, who regarded "Lysenkoism" as wholly unscientific, resigned in protest their memberships in the USSR Academy of Sciences. In the Soviet Union, the controversy was not solely one of genetics. Lysenko and his supporters appeared ready to subordinate and distort long-established scientific knowledge in a supreme effort to substantiate the principles of dialectical materialism. Under the Khrushchev regime, although Lysenko and his doctrines have continued to receive official support, some of his opponents have been rehabilitated and appear to be teaching orthodox genetics. One reason for this modicum of tolerance may be that the anticipated transformation of Soviet agriculture, as based on the implementation of the Lysenko doctrine, has not materialized. On the contrary, in 1963 and 1964 the USSR was forced to purchase abroad large quantities of grain to meet the needs of the Soviet population.

The articles presented below, from Soviet and American sources, present two sides of this historic controversy. The Soviet articles are reprinted from *Soviet Press Translations,* Vol. III (No. 22, December 15, 1948), 686-694; Vol. IV (No. 2, January 15, 1949), 47-48; and Vol. IV (No. 3, February 1, 1949), 78-79.

I. The Triumph of Mitchurin Biological Science*

We have before us a bulky, beautifully printed scientific work. This is the Stenographic Record of the session of the Lenin All-Union Academy of Agricultural Sciences. The Record contains a report by Academician T. D. Lysenko on "The State of Biological Science," and complete stenographic accounts of the discussion on this report. Taking part in the debates were fifty-six participants in the session of the Academy—regular members of the Academy, scientific workers from agricultural and scientific research institutes, professors of agricultural colleges and biological institutes, agronomists, mechanization experts and managerial personnel from the Ministry of Agriculture of the USSR and the Ministry for *Sovkhozi* of the USSR.

The session of the Lenin All-Union Academy of Agricultural Sciences was one of the major events in the ideological life of the Soviet people. The report by Academician T. D. Lysenko and the numerous statements by our scientists on the subject of this report elicited enormous interest from the scientific public, practical workers in socialist agriculture, and Party workers. This is quite understandable. Biology, as a science of the laws of the origin and development of life, is one of the important elements of the natural scientific basis of the Marxist-Leninist world outlook. In this field of science an intense ideological struggle is in progress between materialism and idealism on questions pertaining to knowledge and the changing world. Biology is immediately bound up with the solution of the historic problem of creating an abundance of products in our country.

The Stenographic Record of the session is of enormous scientific value. The profound theoretical report by T. D. Lysenko and the detailed comments by Mitchurin scientists have breathed new life into our science. The report and the comments on it sum up many years of theoretical struggle between the Mitchurinites and the Weismannites, as well as the practical achievements of progressive Mitchurin biological science. The record not only enriches the reader's understanding with the most recent discoveries in one of the most important fields of natural science, but testifies graphically to the enormous role that science plays in the building of communism when this science serves the people.

In his report, Academician T. D. Lysenko has shown the existence of two diametrically opposed trends in biological science: the progressive

*By I. Laptev in *Pravda,* September 11, 1948. (On the publication of the book *The State of Biological Science.* Stenographic Record of the session of the V. I. Lenin All-Union Academy of Agricultural Sciences, from July 31 to August 7, 1948. OGIZ—Selkhozgiz, 1948, 536 pp., price: 12 rubles, 200,000 copies. Editorial Board: V. N. Stoletov, A. M. Sirotin, G. K. Obyedkov.)

and materialistic, as represented by the *Mitchurin* school, named after its founder, I. V. Mitchurin, the outstanding Soviet naturalist and great transformer of nature, and the reactionary, idealistic, represented by the *Weismann* (Mendel-Morgan) school, founded by Weismann, the German biologist; the monk Mendel, an Austrian biologist; and Morgan, the American biologist.

The history of biological science has always been an arena for ideological struggle. Charles Darwin (1809-1882) laid down the principles of scientific biology in his work *The Origin of the Species*, published in 1859. With his theory of natural and artificial selection, Darwin gave a scientific explanation of the origin and development of life and thereby refuted the idealistic and theological explanation, which had prevailed up to his time, of the origin of plants, animals, and man himself. The classic writers of Marxism-Leninism set a high value on this contribution of Darwin. "While setting a high value on the importance of the Darwinian theory," says T. D. Lysenko, "the classical writers of Marxism at the same time pointed out the errors admitted by Darwin. The Darwinian theory, while indisputably materialistic in its basic features, contains a number of substantial errors. Thus, for example, it was a serious blunder when Darwin introduced reactionary Malthusian ideas into his theory of evolution side by side with materialistic principle. In our time this serious blunder is being made worse by reactionary biologists" (page 8).

The English parson, Malthus, propagated the reactionary idea of "an eternal, natural law," to the effect that living beings multiply more rapidly than the quantity of food at their disposal permits. In this way he explained the impoverishment of the working class under conditions of capitalism.

This Malthusian scheme, which Darwin borrowed in order to explain the struggle for existence in nature, radically contradicted the materialistic principles of his own doctrine. But Darwin was unable to free himself from the errors he admitted. They were revealed and pointed out by the classical writers of Marxism.

The reactionary biologists made every effort to discard the materialistic elements of Darwinism, and, conversely, to develop the erroneous aspects of Darwinian theory, based on the Malthusian scheme of overpopulation, together with the struggle within the species allegedly following therefrom. Our country, unfortunately, has had its proponents of Weismannism and Morganism—I. I. Schmalhausen, B. M. Zavadovsky, A. R. Zhebrak, N. P. Dubinin, and others. Truckling to the reactionary biologists, they propagated the doctrines of the latter and were guided by these doctrines in their own scientific work.

The founders of reactionary, idealistic biology, proclaiming themselves as "Neo-Darwinists," completely denied, in effect, the materialistic side of Darwinism and dragged idealism and metaphysics into biology.

Reactionary, idealistic biology is based on a denial of the effect of environment on the development of the organism and on a denial of the inheritance of the features and characteristics acquired by plants and animals under the influence of changing conditions of life. The Weismannites regard the body as isolated from the environment in which it exists. They divide the living organism in a mechanical fashion into two basically different entities: the inherited substance in the nucleus (genes, chromosomes), which according to their theory is the bearer of heredity, and the body, which is supposed to have no relation to heredity.

They regard the inherited substance as immortal, as never reproducing itself, while the living body is only the repository, the culture medium. T. D. Lysenko has exposed these reactionary views and has subjected them to minute and scientifically founded criticism. He points out:

> An immortal, hereditary substance, independent of the qualitative peculiarities of the development of the living body; controlling the perishable body, but not produced by it—such is Weismann's conception, openly idealistic and mystical in its essence, which he brought forward in the guise of a discussion of "Neo-Darwinism" (page 12).

These idealistic views of the Weismannites and Morganites led them to the idea of the incomprehensibility of the inherited substance, to a denial of the laws of development of life, and to the recognition of a divine principle in the origin of plants and animals. For example, the physicist, E. Schrödinger, applauding the Weismann theory in his book *What is Life from the Viewpoint of Physics?*, came to the conclusion: "... A private, individual soul is equal to an omnipresent and omniscient soul." This conclusion, he says, is "... the most that can be offered by the biologist who attempts to prove at one stroke both the existence of God and the immortality of the soul." If not all the adherents of Weismannism and Morganism speak so frankly, they only exhibit their inconsistency.

Unequipped with a comprehension of the laws of the animate world, the Weismann-Morganites have been powerless to offer anything in the way of methods for its transformation. A characteristic feature of reactionary biology is its divorce from practice and from the requirements and demands of the people. T. D. Lysenko has shown the sterility and worthlessness of the practical and theoretical work of the Weismannites by the example of the work of Professor N. P. Dubinin, Corresponding Member of the Academy of Sciences of the USSR, who "labored" for many years to ascertain the differences between the cell nuclei of fruit flies in the city and in the country. During the war, when Soviet scientists were contributing all their efforts to the task of our people's struggle against the German usurpers, this learned man was investigating ... the influence of the war upon chromosome changes in fruit flies!

The pseudo-scientific character of Weismannism-Morganism is furthermore to be found in the fact that it denies the possibility of consciously planned influence upon the development of plant and animal organisms. But a science that does not offer clear perspectives nor practices the power of orientation and certainty in achieving a set goal is unworthy of being called a science.

The idea of the independence of the organism's inherited characteristics from the conditions of the environment has led the Weismann-Morganites to the assertion that characteristics due to heredity are dependent upon accident. It was not by accident that I. V. Mitchurin called Mendel's laws "pea-brained."

The Weismann-Morganites look upon animate nature as a chaos of accidents and unrelated phenomena. But a science that does not recognize the laws of nature yields its place in the comprehension of the latter . . . to Providence. It does not equip practical workers in the struggle for the transformation of the world. As a result it becomes fortune-seeking and quackery. "We must steadily keep in mind that *science is the enemy of accidents,*" says T. D. Lysenko (page 521), recalling one of the basic theses of Marxism-Leninism.

The consistent defense and development of the materialistic principles of Darwinism represent the enormous contribution of the progressive representatives of Russian biological science. The outstanding Darwinian biologists, I. I. Metchnikov, I. M. Setchenov, A. N. Severtsov, and, in particular, K. A. Timiryazev, waged an irreconcilable struggle against reactionary biology in all its various forms, while defending and developing Darwinism.

I. V. Mitchurin, the great transformer of nature, laid the foundations for a new school of biology, legitimately named after him the Mitchurin school. Mitchurin biological science is the most advanced and progressive biological science, because it has dialectical materialism as its firm foundation, the all-conquering power of which has been verified by the entire experience of history, in all fields of the social sciences and in the natural sciences. "Dialectical materialism," writes Comrade Stalin, "is the philosophy of life of the Marxist-Leninist Party. It is called dialectical materialism because its approach to natural phenomena, and its method of investigating natural phenomena, and its method of comprehending these phenomena is *dialectical,* while its interpretation of natural phenomena, its conception of natural phenomena and its theory are *materialistic.*" The report by Academician T. D. Lysenko on "The State of Biological Science" is clear example of the application of dialectical materialism in the struggle against reactionary and idealistic theories in biology, in the comprehension of the laws of development of the animate world, and in its active transformation.

Mitchurin biological science proceeds from the basic thesis of dialectical materialism, which states that the conditions of life determine the origin and development of the living organism, changes in its heredity, and the acquisition by it of new features and characteristics, which are thereupon transmitted through heredity. It completely refutes the basic thesis of Weismannism-Morganism of the complete independence of the properties of heredity from the conditions of life of plants and animals. It does not recognize the existence of a special substance in the organism governing heredity. The entire organism possesses the properties of heredity. A change in the conditions of life leads to a change in the organism, and to the acquisition by the latter of new features and characteristics, i.e. to a change in its heredity. The organism and the conditions of life necessary to it represent a unit. This is a unit of form and content, in which the organism represents the form while the conditions and sources of life represent its content. The form changes with a change in the content. Quantitative changes become qualitative. This transition proceeds irregularly. The old heredity is exploded, so to speak. New properties of heredity appear. *"Changes in the conditions of life,"* says T. D. Lysenko in his report, *"compel even the type of development of plant organisms to change. The mutated type of development is, thus, the original source of change in heredity.* All those organisms which cannot change in conformity with changed conditions of life do not survive and do not leave descendants" (page 29).

The strongest side of the Mitchurin theory is its effectiveness, its close association of theory and practice, and its enrichment of practice with scientific generalizations drawn from practice itself.

On the pedestal of the monument to I. V. Mitchurin has been cut his famous maxim: "Man can and must create new forms of plants better than nature."

Developing this Mitchurin thesis, T. D. Lysenko says: *"The scientific solution of practical problems is the truest path to a profound comprehension of the laws of development of the animate world"* (page 37). These principles of Mitchurin biological science comprise one of those radically new theses that has placed it above Darwinism.

In their scientific research the Mitchurinites proceed from Darwinian theory. But Darwin's theory is by no means sufficient to solve the practical problems of socialist agriculture. Darwinism is a science that *explains,* preëminently, the history of the organic world. Mitchurin biological science is a further development of Darwinism as a science directed toward the practical and revolutionary *alteration* of the world. "Darwinism," says T. D. Lysenko, "has not only been purged of faults and errors, has not only been raised to a higher level, but has to a considerable degree undergone alteration in a number of its theses. From a science which *explained,* preëminently, the past history of the organic world, Darwinism has become a creative, *effective* medium for planned mastery, from the viewpoint of practice, of the animate world" (page 38).

Mitchurin went farther than Darwin in the development of biological science. Mitchurin biology not only embodies everything better and progressive that the leading scientists of the whole world have contributed to biology, but is a new and higher stage in the development of biological science. Mitchurin biology has become the most progressive in the world.

T. D. Lysenko's great contribution is that he has raised the banner of Mitchurin biology aloft, has successfully defended it in the struggle against Weismannism-Morganism, surreptitiously introduced into our country by certain Soviet scientists truckling to Weismann, Mendel, and Morgan, has developed the teachings of I. V. Mitchurin theoretically, and has embodied them extensively in the practice of socialist agriculture.

Agrobiology, an outstanding work by Academician T. D. Lysenko, and a number of his other studies, have set forth the theoretical principles of Mitchurin genetics and have made available to the public the enormous experience gained during the struggle for an increased yield of agricultural crops. The theory of the development of plants by stages, worked out by T. D. Lysenko, made it possible to discover the laws of the development of plant organisms, to control the conditions of their existence, and to create and alter, in a controlled manner, varieties possessing the heredity that we need. The conversion of spring wheat to winter wheat, for example, is of great theoretical and practical importance.

The vernalization of grain crops according to the method of T. D. Lysenko has made it possible to extend varieties of spring wheat to more northerly regions and to guarantee a considerable increase in their yield. This year plantings of vernalized seed have been earmarked for an area totalling 7,000,000 hectares. Summer plantings of potatoes, which have eliminated degeneration of plantings in southern regions, are taking place over an area of hundreds of thousands of hectares. Academician T. D. Lysenko has made a great contribution to the scientific basis of seed culture in our country. He has worked out new measures for cultivating rubber plants, such as, for example, cluster sowing of kok-saghyz. The system of agrotechnical measures for increasing the crop yield of millet, worked out by T. D. Lysenko, has made it possible to obtain more than fifteen centners of this valuable crop per hectare over an area exceeding 1,000,000 hectares in 1947. Topping of cotton plants, which insures this plant protection against dropping of the ovaries, and which increases the pre-frost yield, is practiced over an area totalling 85 to 90 per cent of all cotton plantings.

This is by no means a complete list of T. D. Lysenko's scientific discoveries, which have been extensively incorporated in the practice of socialist agriculture—testimony to the great vital power of the Mitchurin teaching.

The session showed that Mitchurin science in our country can be justly proud of its achievements. This is clearly evident from the statements of our Mitchurin scientists.

Academician I. G. Eichfeld spoke on the work of the All-Union Institute of Plant Culture. In their day the Weismann-Morganites attempted to convert this Institute into their own stronghold, which impeded the development of creative work. Its scientific collective has achieved great successes on the basis of Mitchurin teaching. "The practical significance of the new approach in the study of universal complexes (seeds—I. L.)," says Eichfeld, "is evinced by the indisputable fact that the Institute directly produced more than 170 new varieties under the difficult conditions of war and the postwar period, while in 1949 this number will reach 200" (page 55). During the war years the Institute did a great deal in consolidating the foodstuff base for industry in the Urals. On the basis of its studies, agriculture has been advanced great distances in the Far North and in the arid regions of the Soviet Union.

The Weismann-Morganities, such as Academician Schmalhausen, Professor N. P. Dubinin, and certain others, for example, have repudiated vegetative hybridization stubbornly and without evidence. Nevertheless, it is known that I. V. Mitchurin developed more than 300 varieties of fruit and berry crops by means of vegetative hybridization. Mitchurin gardens extend throughout the entire country, S. I. Isayev pointed out that the vegetative hybrid between apple and pear trees, for example, has become widely distributed in nineteen regions of the Soviet Union.

In his speech Academician P. N. Yakovlev stated that

numerous investigators working under the direction of Academician T. D. Lysenko in diverse localities of the Soviet Union have conducted brilliant studies during the last eight or ten years on the vegetative hybridization of annual herbaceous plants with sharply contrasting features. Over a period of eight or ten years this school has obtained more facts concerning vegetative hybridization than have been obtained throughout the world during the last 150 years (page 86).

Academician A. A. Avakyan spoke of the wide application of the hybridization method in selection work, telling of the crossbreeding of winter varieties of common wheat with branchy wheat, while Academician P. P. Lukyanenko spoke on wheat and couch grass hybrids, citing the experience of the Krasnodar Selection Station in creating high-yielding and high-standard varieties of winter wheat for the Kuban. The wide application of the hybridization method of selection work with winter wheat at the Krasnodar Station, points out P. P. Lukyanenko, has shown the extraordinary effectiveness of the Mitchurin principle of crossing varieties of different geographical origin. All the hybrid varieties of winter wheat developed by the Krasnodar Station and widely introduced in the production scheme were obtained on the basis of the application of this principle of selecting pairs during crossing. *Novoukrainka-83*, in particular, a high-yielding variety of winter wheat, was developed by crossing *Ukrainka* with *Marquis,* a Canadian variety of spring wheat.

Doctor of Agricultural Science I. A. Minkevitch cites telling figures on the achievement of Mitchurin teaching in the field of olive crops. "Suffice it to say," he points out, "that 70 percent of the area of the Soviet Union sown in olive crops is being planted with varieties selected by the Institute for Olive Crops" (page 94). The studies of this Institute have proved that free cross-pollination between high-yielding varieties resistant to broom rape is an extremely promising method for obtaining new starting material in selection work on the sunflower.

Academician E. I. Ushakova subjected the idealistic views of the Morgan-Mendelites to sharp criticism and justly expressed surprise in regard to the fact that our philosophers, for incomprehensible reasons, have tolerated these views. In contrast to the Morgan-Mendelites, who have never set themselves the task of developing new varieties, she demonstrated the achievements of the Gribov Selection Station, where new kinds of tomatoes, eggplant, pepper, and sugar peas have been created, and muskmelons and watermelons have been raised for mass cultivation in the *kolkhozi* of the Moscow Region.

G. P. Vysokos, the director of the Siberian Scientific Research Institute for Grain Culture, speaks of the promising experiment of introducing seedings of winter wheat in Siberia. In the course of many decades neither science nor practice had been able to solve the problem of the freezing of this crop under Siberian conditions. Academician T. D. Lysenko was the first to discover the reason for this. He explained the winter destruction of winter wheat in Siberia as due to a mechanical injury to the subsoil portion of the plants and their leaves when the soil froze. He discovered that in the steppe portion of Siberia receiving little snowfall winter wheat can survive the winter very nicely if it is sowed in the completely uncultivated stubble fields of spring crops and with strict observance of the agrotechnical measures recommended by him. "Our institute and the Karagandinsk *sovkhoz*," says G. P. Vysokos, "have been cultivating winter wheat for six years, obtaining abundant harvests in recent years. Last year the Omsk *Obkom* of the ACP(b) and the *Oblispolkom,* taking note of the positive experience of our institute, projected the necessary measures for introducing winter wheat in the *kolkhoz* field" (page 173).

Academician D. A. Dolgushin severely criticizes the followers of Weismannism-Morganism, who have held up the development of our work on selection and seed culture. His report on experiments with branch wheat have given rise to special interest. Branchy wheat yields up to ten grams of grain per ear as compared with two grams per ear of ordinary wheat raised under the best conditions. Given a corresponding agrotechnical level, branchy wheat can yield harvests on the order of 80 to 100 centners per hectare! "I think that I am not wrong in saying that we stand today on the threshold of a new era in our seed culture," says D. A. Dolgushin (page 209).

Enormous vistas are unfolding before socialist agriculture in connection with the wide introduction of the Dokutchayev-Williams complex, that is, with the introduction of rationalized crop rotation, the planting of windbreaks, etc. Academicians I. V. Yakushkin and S. F. Demidov; agronomists I. I. Khoroshilov, A. V. Krylov, director of the Dokutchayev Agricultural Institute for the Central Black-soil Belt; V. S. Dmitriev, director of the Agricultural Planning Board of the *Gosplan* of the USSR; and others, spoke of achievements in this field.

I. I. Khoroshilov showed the enormous role played by the proper system of agriculture in the experience of the *kolkhozi* of the Millerov MTS and the Stalin *kolkhoz* of the Salsk District, Rostov Region. In the face of the unusual drought of 1946, this *kolkhoz* achieved a yield of grain crops equaling fourteen centners per hectare. In 1947, which was still less favorable for this region, the yield of grain crops equalled 16.2 centners per hectare. It is characteristic that at the Stalin *kolkhoz* the total yield of grain per able-bodied worker equaled fifty-seven centners as compared with thirty-nine centners on an average throughout the *kolkhozi* of the Salsk District; correspondingly, the monetary income of each able-bodied worker equaled 4,470 rubles as compared with 1,656 rubles, while the milk yield per forage cow equaled 1,857 liters as compared with 1,297 liters (page 195). The introduction of the Dokutchayev-Williams complex has created a high standard in agriculture and has increased the welfare of the *kolkhoz* peasantry.

Socialist agriculture is the most highly mechanized agriculture. The speech by Academician I. F. Vasilenko is of great interest. He spoke of the strong bond between progressive Mitchurin agrobiology, which is based on the works of Timiryazev, Dokutchayev, Williams, Kostytchev, Mitchurin, and Lysenko, and all branches of agricultural science and mechanical engineering, in particular. Proceeding from the requirements of Mitchurin agrobiology, Soviet scientists have created machines of such design that they can aid the workers of agriculture to influence nature and to increase the fertility of the soil in a planned manner. Today our factories manufacture only plows with colters, which insure high-standard plowing, while Soviet combines work on a low cut. The situation in the USA, says Academician Vasilenko, is quite different. There, agronomy is divorced from biology. Plows with colters are not used. During threshing in the USA a high cut is used on the plants, only the grain is gathered, while the straw is strewn about the field by a special whirligig. An enormous quantity of weed seeds is thrown to the ground together with the chaff and straw. Shallow ploughing of stubble fields is not practiced. As a result the USA is among the first countries in the world in point of view of potential contamination of the soil.

The achievements of Mitchurin biology are also to be found in the field of cattle breeding. "Our zootechnical science and practice," said T. D. Lysenko in his report, "proceeding from the state plan for obtaining products of animal husbandry of the requisite quantity and quality, must align their work in accordance with the principle: *select and perfect breeds in accordance with feeding, maintenance, and climatic conditions, and at the same time, create feeding and maintenance conditions corresponding to breeds, which is inseparably connected with this"* (page 35).

V. A. Shaumyan, director of the State Pedigree Breeding Farm for Long-Horned Kostroma Cattle, spoke of the experience in developing a new native breed of cattle—the Kostroma breed. The collective of the Karavayevo *sovkhoz* and the *kolkhozniki* of the leading farms have succeeded in making every cow in the best herds of the new Kostroma breed produce from 4,800 to 6,300 kilograms of milk a year. There are dozens and dozens of cows that produce from 10,000 to 14,000 kilograms of milk. "These many years of work," says V. A. Shaumyan, "confirm the fact that no law of the inalterability of hereditary traits and instincts exists" (page 217).

Academician L. K. Greben threw light on the work at Askania-Nova, where new breeds of livestock, surpassing foreign livestock in many ways —the Askanian Rambouillet, producing up to twenty-one kilograms per ram per shearing, the Ukrainian white steppe hog, which produces up to eleven pigs per farrowing on an average, and the Ukrainian speckled steppe hog—developed on the basis of methods worked out by Academician M. F. Ivanov. E. M. Tchekmenev, USSR Vice-Minister for *Sovkhozi,* noted that K. D. Filyansky, S. F. Pastukhov, G. R. Litovtchenko, N. A. Vasilyev, and Balmont had created valuable breeds of finewooled sheep on the basis of the progressive Mitchurin school of animal husbandry. At the same time he cited a number of facts serving as evidence that the Weismann-Morganites, Serebrovsky, Glembotsky, and others, were impeding the rate of qualitative improvement of the various breeds of livestock in our country and were inflicting serious economic damage upon animal husbandry.

The comments by the followers of reactionary Weismann biology again demonstrated the shameful bankruptcy of Weismannism-Morganism. As a consequence of their theoretical paucity and practical sterility, they could say nothing rational in defense of their views, nor could they demonstrate anything of practical value from their studies.

Academician I. I. Schmalhausen, who is considered to be the leader of the Weismann-Morganites in our country, attempted to prove in his statement that he is a follower . . . of I. V. Mitchurin. Actually, however, Academician I. I. Schmalhausen cleaves to the principles of Weismannism-Morganism on the basic questions of biology in his study *Factors in Evolution* and in many of his other works, as a number of the statements showed. S. I. Alikhanyan attempted to prove that the Weismann chromosome theory of heredity is not idealistic and that "Mendel's laws" allegedly do not contradict the teaching of I. V. Mitchurin. The pedantic speech by B. M. Zavadovsky boiled down to the statement that "we must not think of throwing Mendelian genetics out of our Soviet science" (page 288). He asserted that "the Mitchurin school cannot alone replace, exhaust, and eliminate all those schools of thought that we possess alongside the Mitchurin school" (page 291), and attempted to contrast the works of T. D. Lysenko with the teaching of I. V. Mitchurin. All the "scientific arguments" of B. M. Zavadovsky amounted, in the end, to a mere juggling of citations, inadmissible for the scientific worker. Academician V. S. Nemtchinov rose to the complete defense of the Weismann-Morganites in his speech, and in particular to the defense of those who have been pursuing their studies at the Timiryazev Agricultural Academy. In setting forth his position, he stated, to the accompaniment of noise and laughter in the chamber, that "the chromosome theory of heredity has become part of the gold reserve of the science of humanity" and that this had been allegedly proved . . . by statistics (page 472).

The comments by Academicians M. B. Mitin, I. I. Prezent, P. P. Lobanov, as well as the address by V. N. Stoletov (now director of the Timiryazev Academy), in all of which the Weismann-Morganites were subjected to detailed criticism, are of great interest.

Academician M. B. Mitin criticized Y. A. Filiptchenko, N. K. Koltsov, I. I. Schmalhausen, and other followers of Mendelism-Morganism. He recalled that the Party had condemned Menshevik idealism in philosophy and natural science as early as 1931. In his interpretation of the teaching of I. V. Mitchurin he emphasized the importance of Soviet patriotism in science.

> We can be proud that our Soviet scientist, I. V. Mitchurin, discovered and gained mastery of the laws of conscious control of the development of organisms. Let all the cosmopolites of science assert that "questions of priority in science are of no importance." But we cannot avoid being filled with a legitimate pride at the fact that this enormous contribution to biological science is the work of a Soviet Russian scientist (page 231).

Academician I. Prezent began his address with an exposition of the history of the struggle of progressive-materialistic biology against reactionary, idealistic biology—a struggle that has continued for several decades. He exposed the attempts by the followers of Mendelism-Morganism, such as, for example, B. M. Zavadovsky, and S. I. Alikhanyan to mold Mitchurin science along the lines of Morganism, and thus reconcile the irreconcilable. Such a falsification of Mitchurin ideas has met a determined rebuff. I. Prezent also exposed the ridiculous attempts by Academician Zhukovsky to deny the existence of vegetative hybrids. The Mitchurinites, by the actual demonstration of vegetative hybrids of various plants at the session itself, proved by facts the absurdity of such assertions. Having convincingly proved the theoretical inanity and the practical sterility of a number of other Morganites, I. Prezent states:

Today Darwinism is not what is was in Darwin's day. The law of selection is not formulated in the light of Mitchurin theory as Darwin himself formulated it. This law of selection must include the role of the environmental conditions, and when we consider artificial selection, it now emerges on a Mitchurin basis, as planned, environmental selection. Darwinian science was ignorant of this level of selection . . . . (page 507).

V. N. Stoletov devoted his address to exposing the Morgan-Mendelites, their sterility, and their divorce from practice. He demonstrated by striking facts that A. R. Zhebrak, M. S. Navashin, B. M. Zavadovsky, and I. A. Rapaport, in spite of their boastful promises that the Morganites would allegedly bless humanity in the future with great discoveries, were in effect barren fig trees. V. N. Stoletov states:

> All the investigations of T. D. Lysenko and the Mitchurinites are subordinated to the solution of this or that important practical problem. On this basis Mitchurin science is growing in stature and strength.
> A vital cause is the foe of formalism. In the light of the vital Mitchurin cause which is gaining strength in our country, the scholasticism, metaphysical nature, and sterility of Morganism have become especially apparent. And this has therefore proved a deterrent for the Morganites. They do not desire to occupy themselves with a vital cause that would quickly cure them of their formalism. But the investigation of worthless questions, such as those that interest Dubinin . . . only intensifies this formalism.
> Science is the vital organism by which truth develops, said Herzen in his day. Soviet science is all the more vital an organism in that it is the science of the people. And this vital, healthy organism will find a way to free itself from defunct, reactionary Weismannism.
> Evidence of this is to be found at the present session of the Academy that bears the name of the immortal Lenin; an Academy watched over by the paternal care of our great Stalin (page 485).

At the end of the deliberations of the session, P. M. Zhukovsky, S. I. Alikhanyan, and I. M. Polyakov, in the face of the indisputable achievements of Mitchurin biological science, declared that they renounced their erroneous views and would continue their work in the future from the standpoint of progressive, Mitchurin biological science. Practical experience will show the extent to which their statements are sincere.

The addresses by the representatives of progressive, Mitchurin biology showed that it has become inseparably incorporated in the practice of socialist agriculture; has become a close ally of the *kolkhozniki* and the workers of the *sovkhozi;* and is raising the level of our agriculture to unprecedented heights, inaccessible to the countries of capitalism.

Mitchurin biological science is a powerful force aiding the Soviet people to create an abundance of products in our country and to make it the richest country in the world.

Before passing to his concluding remarks, Academician T. D. Lysenko made the following statement:

One of the notes asks me what the attitude of the CC of the Party toward my report is. My reply is that the CC of the Party has examined my report and has approved it (page 512).

This statement evoked a storm of applause which became an ovation. All rose to their feet, greeting with enormous enthusiasm the great friend and coryphaeus of science, our leader and teacher, Comrade Stalin.

The session revealed the complete triumph of the Mitchurin school over Morganism-Mendelism. It represented an historic landmark in the development of biological science. In the letter to Comrade J. V. Stalin cited in the Stenographic Record, the participants of the session wrote:

> In continuing the work of V. I. Lenin you have rescued the teachings of I. V. Mitchurin, the great transformer of nature, for progressive, materialistic biology; and you have elevated the Mitchurin school of biology before all science as the only true and progressive school of all branches of biological science. This has, at the same time, further consolidated the natural-scientific foundations of the Marxist-Leninist world outlook, the all conquering power of which has been confirmed by the whole of historical experience.

At the conclusion of the Stenographic Record, the decisions of the session are cited, which emphasize the importance of Mitchurin science as a new and higher stage of materialistic biology and which condemn the idealistic, metaphysical Weismann school of biology. The session appealed to the workers of agricultural science to present a united front, under the leadership of the Party of Lenin and Stalin, in developing Mitchurin science, which is capable of successfully solving the problems involved in the future development of agriculture.

II. The Destruction of Science in the USSR

The wilful destruction of science in the USSR by politicians is a tragedy of the greatest significance. It is quite evident that the Soviet politicians, being uneducated in modern natural science, and having proved themselves unwilling or unable to grasp the exacting technicalities involved in genetic reasoning, have through motives of their own taken a dislike to its conclusions, and have accordingly maneuvered to have it cast into

NOTE: In this article H. J. Muller, professor of zoology at Indiana University and one of the foremost American geneticists discusses the significance of the assault on science by the Soviet government. Dr. Muller was senior geneticist at the Institute of Genetics in Moscow for four years (1933-1937) and has known the leading Soviet geneticists as a co-worker and friend . . . . His experiments in genetics have won him a Nobel laureate in physiology, presidency of the Genetics Society of America, and presidency of the Eighth International Congress of Genetics held in Stockholm in the summer of 1948. From *The Saturday Review of Literature,* Vol. 31 (December 4, 1948), 13-15, 63-65. By permission.

limbo. This aim they have accomplished by the use of the same combination of flagrant misrepresentation and calculated brutality which has marked their dealings with their political opponents. Hardly four months ago, as a case in point, the Central Executive Committee of the Communist Party of the Soviet Union officially repudiated the entire science of genetics and approved in its stead a group of superstitions that hark back to ancient times.

This amazing act is of the greatest significance not only for geneticists, nor for scientists alone, but for everyone. For despite the pretenses of Communist officials and their followers, this matter is not a controversy between scientists or a dispute over the relative merits of two scientific theories. It is a brutal attack on human knowledge.

And, ironically, the great majority of the geneticists who have been purged were thoroughly loyal politically; many were even ardent crusaders for the Soviet system and leadership, as the writer well knows through personal contact with them.

Unhappily, it is necessary to confess that there no longer seems any chance of saving the core of biological science, in that section of the world, short of a political overturn. Nor could what has been lost be restored in one generation. All that we can now hope to do is to conduct an autopsy, in the hope of discovering ways to check the already dangerous spread of infection to countries outside the Soviet sphere, and to make clear to the people of those countries the important lessons for civilization and humanity involved in it.

What has happened to genetics during the past few months in the USSR is only the dramatic culmination of a campaign which has been ruthlessly waged against this section of science and the workers engaged in it for more than a dozen years. In 1935 genetics had reached a very high state of advancement in the USSR, and many eminent scientists were working in it. In that year the Soviet Communist Party, unable to find a single reputable scientist willing to take part in its attack on genetics, began systematically to build up the reputation of an alleged "geneticist," a peasant-turned-plant-breeder named Trofim Lysenko. Lysenko had achieved some dubious success in applying, by trial-and-error proceedings an early American discovery about pretreating seeds in order to influence the time of maturation of certain crops; but this gives him no more claim to being a geneticist than does the treatment of dogs for worms. To a scientist, Lysenko's writings along theoretical lines are the merest drivel. He obviously fails to comprehend either what a controlled experiment is or the established principles of genetics taught in any elementary course in the subject.

The role of USSR's second great so-called "geneticist" was assumed by a suave and unscrupulous juggler of words, the dialectical materialist "philosopher," I. Prezent. His authoritarian sophistries have been calculated to lend an aura of profundity that at the same time confuses and impresses the earnest lay disciple of the Party line. However, like Lysenko's work, his writings are thoroughly unscientific in method, and fail to stand up under either theoretical analysis or the test of objective results. These two careerists have been represented to the public as bona fide scientists. They have been pushed forward, ahead of conscientious experimentalists, as proponents of what is supposed to be a valid scientific theory, but is actually a naive and self-contradictory party dogma. Although taking the name of Darwinism, or, more specifically "Michurinism," this dogma actually represents a reversion to a pre-Darwinian era all but forgotten by modern scientists.

That Lysenko and Prezent are not, as they are made to appear, self-constituted leaders of the rebellion against science, but are merely the tools of the highest political power, is shown by a number of telling facts. For one thing, long before Lysenko and Prezent had risen to their present eminence, not a few geneticists of high standing were individually martyrized on various pretexts. Only a deep-seated antagonism to genetics on the part of the higher authorities can explain why, in 1933 or thereabouts, the geneticists Chetverikoff, Ferry, and Ephroimson were all, on separate occasions, banished to Siberia, and Levitsky to a labor camp in the European Arctic, or why, in 1936, the Communist geneticist Agol was done away with, following rumors that he had been convicted of "Menshevik idealism" in genetics.

Again, in 1936, the Medicogenetical Institute, which with its numerous staff of biologists, psychologists, and more than 200 physicians constituted a shining example, unmatched anywhere in the world, of the possibilities of research in human genetics, was vilified and misrepresented in *Pravda,* and then dissolved. One of the charges made against the Institute was that it had been attempting to exalt heredity as against environment. Everyone conversant with the Institute's work knows that actually it had been entirely objective in its gathering of data, but that in its interpretations it had leaned as far as possible—if not even too far—in the environmentalist direction. Under pressure Solomon Levit, founder and director of the Institute, made a "confession" of scientific guilt, which he later admitted to the writer was entirely false and given only because loyalty to the Communist Party demanded it. Immediately afterwards he was abstracted from the scene, and has not been heard from since.

Both Agol and Levit spent the year 1931-32 in Texas, working on Rockefeller Foundation fellowships under the writer's direction. They were able then to express themselves freely in private conversation without fear of reprisals. Yet the writer can vouch that both of them went out of their way on every occasion to defend the Soviet regime, the policies and person of Stalin, and the orthodox philosophy of dialectical materialism, and that they made rather a nuisance of themselves in magnifying the importance of environmental influences even where the pertinent evidence was weak or absent. In short, they were convinced Stalinists but, being scientists with dangerous knowledge and data, the government sacrificed them.

Further evidence of the machinations of the Party to build up the reputation of Lysenko, Prezent, and their hangers-on, may be found in an affair that occurred in December 1936. A carefully prearranged and widely publicized "genetics controversy," was held in Moscow before a packed auditorium of invited spectators, with Lysenko appearing as the main speaker for what may be called the prosecution. It was obvious that the Party administrators, who presided over the session, paid no attention to the painstaking scientific arguments of the geneticist defendants, but rejoiced at every crude slander dropped by the attacking clique. The scientifically-educated portion of the audience sided completely with the geneticists; however, the administrators and the organs of publicity, though they did not yet dare to damn them completely, thundered dire warnings. The addresses of this congress were heavily expurgated when printed in book form; yet within a few months even this emasculated volume was placed on the banned list.

Still more evidence of the Party's hostility to genetics is offered by the case of the Seventh International Congress of Genetics, that was scheduled to be held in Moscow during the summer of 1937. This meeting was called off after the Party had first toyed with the idea of allowing it to be held with the provision that all papers on evolution and human genetics be omitted—in spite of the fact that many foreign geneticists had intended in their papers to attack the Nazi racist doctrines! In 1939, when Edinburgh finally acted as host to the Congress, all forty Soviet geneticists who had submitted papers to it were at the last moment refused permission to attend. At the same time the world-renowned and widely-beloved president of the Congress, Nicolai Ivanovich Vavilov, the Soviet's leading bona fide geneticist, sent to Edinburgh a discourteous letter of resignation, which, according to information in my possession, had been written for him.

During 1939 another public "genetics controversy" was staged in Moscow, and this time the now exalted Lysenkoists were made to appear as the clear-cut victors, while Vavilov and the other real geneticists were publicly shamed. At about this time, Vavilov's important posts as president of the Lenin Academy of Agricultural Sciences, head of the Institute of Plant Production, and head of the Institute of Genetics were turned over to Lysenko. In 1940, during the period of the Soviet-Nazi liaison, Vavilov was arrested and sentenced to death on the charge of being a British spy. After the Nazi attack on the USSR, he was sent to far northeastern Siberia, where he died in 1942. It is reported that after his death his invaluable collection of thousands of economically important agricultural plants, together with its great reservoir of genes, which he and his fellow-workers had painstakingly collected all over the world, was allowed to disintegrate.

Meanwhile, the Soviet attack on other geneticists and the science of genetics in general continued. Owing to war conditions, the imposition of internal secrecy, and censorship on news leaving the country, it is impossible to learn the real causes of the death of such distinguished geneticists as Karpechenko, Koltzoff, Serebrovsky, and Levitsky. Certain it is, however, that from 1936 on Soviet geneticists of all ranks lived a life of terror. Most of those who were not imprisoned, banished, or executed were forced to enter other lines of work. The great majority of those who were allowed to remain in their laboratories were obliged to redirect their researches in such a way as to make it appear that they were trying to prove the correctness of the officially approved anti-scientific views. During the chaotic period toward the close of the war, some escaped to the West. Through it all, however, a few have remained at work, retained as show pieces to prove that the USSR still has some working geneticists.

Late last year these remaining geneticists, and those biologists in related fields who still had the temerity to support the genetic viewpoint, were caught in a carefully laid trap. They were invited to express their views in the columns of the *Moscow Literary Gazette*. Several of them took advantage of this seeming return to freedom of scientific discussion by restating the case for genetics. Lysenko and Prezent thereupon replied in their characteristic style. The discussion furnished an excuse for a new Soviet "conference" on genetics, held in Moscow this past July. Presumably this affair was Russia's substitute for the Eighth International Congress of Genetics in Stockholm. At Moscow last July the real and the spurious scientists debated once again. At length Lysenko announced that the Communist Central Committee had in fact prejudged the case, and had already decided in his own favor. This decision by a non-scientific political body of course settled the question.

Party members among the geneticists attending the conference hastened to recant their "heresies" publicly. The presidium of the Academy of Sciences, headed by the obedient physicist Sergei Ivanovitch Vavilov, brother of the great geneticist who had been done to death, toed the Party line by removing from their posts in utter disgrace the greatest Soviet physiologist, Orbeli, the greatest Soviet student of morphogenesis, Schmalhausen, and the best remaining Soviet geneticist, Dubinin. Dubinin's laboratory, long known for the admirable work done there by numerous careful investigators, was closed down.

It is significant that although Orbeli and Schmalhausen were biologists in fields other than genetics, they recognized the fundamental place genetic principles occupy in the biological sciences. Now that the real Russian geneticists are gone, scientists in kindred subjects are more open to attack. Indeed, the attack has already begun; recently *Pravda* reported that at the meeting of the Academy of Medical Sciences this September a whole group of leaders in physiology, microbiology, epidemiology, psychiatry, etc., were being severely criticized for "supporting Mendelian views."

Although it has been a long time since the teaching of genetics was permitted in the USSR, the Academy of Agricultural Sciences has ordered the revision of textbooks and courses in biology to remove all traces of genetic doctrines. In September the minister of higher education, Kaftanov, confessed that his department had been too lax in the past and promised that all university teachers and research workers infected with the "reactionary theory"—the phrases are his—of "Mendelism-Morganism" would be eradicated. The publishing houses were to be purged likewise.

These developments have been given wide publicity in the Soviet press, and popular feeling is being deliberately stirred against the scientists. At the same time, the scientific academies are making public obeisances to Stalin himself, thanking him for his direction and his "daily assistance to scientists," and pledging themselves to correct their errors. Malenkov, Deputy Premier of the Soviet Union, and since Zhdanov's death widely considered as the most likely successor to Stalin, is now specifically mentioned in press dispatches as considering Lysenko one of his most important protégés.

Nowhere in the world today do laymen—either politicians or ordinary citizens—have the kind of education which would fit them to judge the merits of a theory in natural science. In appealing to them the anti-scientist has the advantage of being able to make whatever assertions he likes and to play upon emotion and prejudice. On the other hand, the scientist's meticulous statements of the details of his evidence and of the often intricate steps of his reasoning are likely to fall upon deaf ears. But if he simply resorts truthfully to calling his opponent an ignoramus or fakir he is himself suspected of prejudice.

It would be unfair to genetics to give the impression that we could state the case for that science in the space of a magazine article. However, certain of its cardinal accomplishments, which have been denied by the Lysenkoists, should be pointed out here so that we may understand the issues involved.

One of the fundamentals of the science of genetics is the demonstration of the existence in all forms of life of a specific genetic material, or material of heredity, which is separate from the other materials of the body. This genetic material is composed of thousands of different kinds of ultramicroscopic particles, called genes, of which each cell has two whole outfits (one derived from each parent). Most genes are contained in microscopically visible bodies, called chromosomes, and are inherited according to definite rules discovered in the last century by the Czech Mendel. The other materials, making up the body as we see it, have been developed as a result of the coordinated activity of the genes, and in this process of development, both in embryo and in adult, environmental influences play a very considerable role in helping to determine just what kind of product, i.e. what bodily traits, shall be formed. Moreover, the developmental reactions started and guided by the genes are so adjusted that, in many cases, a given kind of modification in the environment results in an especially suited, or "adaptive," modification of these other materials of the body, so as to cause it to function better under the given conditions.

The genes themselves, however, are not changed in any directed or adaptive way by influences outside of themselves. Although they are relatively stable, they do sometimes undergo sudden inner changes in their chemical composition, called mutations. These mutations occur as a result of ultramicroscopic accidents. But order does emerge from these accidents. For the relatively frequent individual who inherits a mutated gene that is detrimental to life tends to die out, whereas the rare one who inherits a gene that chanced to change in a beneficial way tends to live and multiply. Thus, under natural conditions, a population may, in the course of ages, become ever better adapted in its characteristics, i.e., it may evolve. In this way has modern genetics implemented Darwin's theory of natural selection and given it a firm basis.

The gene theory, then, gives us a unit on a lower level than the cell, and in a sense more fundamental than the cell, and even more necessary for a comprehension of all biological sciences, including agriculture and medicine. It is indispensable for a rational interpretation of the origin of life, of the relation between inanimate and animate, of the way in which organisms have undergone change in the past, and of how they may become changed, either in the course of natural breeding or in response to artificial manipulations, in the future. Moreover, through analysis of the genes of an organism, and of how they operate, we may hope to unravel ever more of the tangled web of biochemical processes which constitute its development, its physiology, and its pathology—studies which are already well under way. Finally, this knowledge must affect our whole philosophical outlook, and many phases of the anthropological, psychological, and social sciences.

Lightly waving away the amassed evidence for this coherent modern conception of living things, Lysenko and Prezent deny the very existence of genes or of a separate genetic material, ignore the all-important distinction between heredity and individual development, and offer—in the name of Darwin!—a return to pre-Darwinian days that had been all but forgotten by modern biologists. They would have the heredity itself respond in a directly adaptive way to outside influences, and would also have it able to incorporate the directly adaptive changes which the body may have undergone in its development. Thus, instead of explaining in a rational way the origin of the body's adaptive structures and reactions, they force upon the germ cells themselves (1) the ability to give that type of response which is to be to the advantage of the future body, and (2) the ability somehow to mirror changes already incurred by the body that contains them. This leaves entirely unexplained the origin and the *modus operandi* of the germ cells' assumed ability to respond adaptively, and hence it also fails to explain the origin of the body's own adaptive abilities. The Lysenko-Prezent doctrine therefore implies a mystical, Aristotelian "perfecting principle," a kind of foresight, in the basic makeup of living things, despite the fact that it claims in the same breath not to be "idealistic" at all. And, though verbally accepting natural selection as playing some role, it fails to make use of it for the solution of the main problem, that of why organisms do have adaptability.

In support of these fantastic claims, Lysenko and his followers offer no properly documented, controlled, or repeatable factual evidence. Mainly they attempt to convince by citation of authority, and quote two in particular. The more important of these is Darwin. Under the influence of the current opinion of his day, Darwin accepted to some extent the old doctrine of inheritance of acquired characters, which had been brought into prominence not long before by Lamarck. However, Darwin ascribed to this now disproved doctrine only a secondary role. His own most distinctive contribution was the theory of evolution through the natural selection of accidental changes in heredity, and this has, as we have seen, been abundantly substantiated in the present century. Yet it is mainly the erroneous feature borrowed by Darwin from Lamarck which the Lysenko group insists upon as "Lysenkoism." Moreover, Lysenkoists rely heavily on the work of the old practical plant breeders, especially the Russian Michurin and the American Burbank, who produced new varieties by trial-and-error crossing and rule-of-thumb selection. Despite the usefulness of some of these varieties, however, the writings of these men contributed nothing to our understanding of the biological principles concerned. On the contrary, they adopted the same grave theoretical misconceptions as were usual among laymen of their day. Yet the importance of Michurin as a scientist has been insisted on by Stalin himself, so that the Lysenko group often refer to themselves as "Michurinists."

As this militant mysticism spreads, it is certain to have dire repercussions in every branch of intellectual activity within the USSR and the countries in its growing sphere of influence. This one important falsehood, persisted in, will poison more and more of the structure of knowledge, affecting its practice and theory.

One curious effect of the Lysenko doctrine has been on the Communist conception of the nature of man and of racial and class differences. In the official view, individuals or populations which have lived under unfavorable conditions and have therefore been physically or mentally stunted in their development, would tend, through the inheritance of these acquired characteristics, to pass on to successive generations an ever poorer hereditary endowment; on the other hand, those living under favorable conditions would produce progressively better germ cells and so become innately superior.[1] In a word, we should have innate master and subject races and classes, as the Nazis so blatantly insisted.

True, the Russian theory differed from that of the Nazi in certain ways. For example, the stocks of supposedly inferior heredity would, according to the Russians, have become inferior because of their worse conditions of living, while according to the Nazis, their assumed hereditary inferiority was primary and their lower economic status was a result of this. Moreover, according to the Russians, but not the Nazis, this hereditary inferiority, although an accumulated effect of many generations of poorer conditions, would nevertheless be remedied by "two or three generations" of bettered conditions. No explanation is offered of why the improvement should occur so much more readily than the deterioration. Yet, on both views alike, genetics is so perverted as to make inevitable the conclusion that the races and classes of mankind today are arranged in hereditary hierarchies corresponding to the economic hierarchies. From this it would follow that if a child were transferred at birth from one group to another, its inborn biological handicap or advantage could not be cancelled in its generation.

Modern geneticists, on the other hand, realizing the tremendous role physical and social environment play in the development of human mental traits, would not assume that culturally or economically less developed peoples are *ipso facto* inherently less capable. Indeed, the noninherited effects of cultural differences on mental *development*—as contrasted with innate *endowment*—are so great that no valid conclusions concerning hereditary differences in mentality between existing human populations may be drawn at all.

This similarity between the Nazi and Communist theories was of course the reason why the Russians were reluctant to allow Western geneticists to come to the 1937 International Genetics Congress to attack the Nazi racial fallacies. It explains why the Communists did not want to allow any discussions concerning man—or even evolution in general—to be held at that Congress. It shows why they expunged all mention of man from the published proceedings of their 1936 "genetics controversy."

In the light of modern scientific knowledge, Lysenkoism must be termed a superstition, as much a superstition, as belief that the earth is flat. It is an exceedingly dangerous superstition, for it not only leads to an entirely false conception of the nature of living things and to erroneous methods in the attempt to control other organisms, but it

---

[1] The writer was told in 1936 that this was the "official" doctrine of the Communist Party, i.e., held by the Party peerage, by Yakovlev, head of agriculture in the Party. Yakovlev was later purged, but this does not affect the validity of his testimony.

leads to social and medical policies which would, in the end, degrade rather than advance humanity.

III. A Rebuttal from the Presidium of the Academy of Sciences of the USSR.

1. Reply to Professor H. J. Muller by the Presidium of the Academy of Sciences of the USSR in *Pravda,* December 14, 1948

Professor H. J. Muller of Indiana University, USA, sent the president of the Academy of Sciences of the USSR a letter, also published in the American press, in which he expresses disagreement with recent decisions of the Presidium of the Academy of Sciences of the USSR on questions relating to biological science and announces his resignation as a member of the academy.

The contents of this letter bear witness that Professor Muller, in defining his position on scientific questions, is not guided by the interests of science, and by the interests of truth.

He attempts to accuse the Academy of Sciences of the Soviet Union to the effect that, in the dispute between the followers of the views of Weismann-Morgan and the adherents of the genuine Darwinian theory, which has been elevated to a new and loftier level in the works of the outstanding Russian scholar, Mitchurin, it has definitely adopted the position of the Mitchurin biology. In this connection, Muller is far from acting as behooves an objective investigator, examining the reasons and arguments advanced by the opponents of the Weismann school. He has ignored the well-known dictum of Pavlov that "facts are the air of the scholar," and preferred to reject the analysis of numerous new experimental data obtained by Soviet investigators. Such conduct can hardly be regarded as a sample of scientific courage and objectivity.

The Academy of Sciences of the USSR, in defining its position, proceeded on the basis of experimental work, which clearly showed the erroneous concepts of Weismann-Morgan and the triumph of the ideas of Mitchurin. Mitchurin and his successor, Academician T. D. Lysenko, rejected the teaching of a special "hereditary subtance," independent of the rest of the organism and of its conditions of life. Having discovered the link between heredity and the living conditions of organisms, the Mitchurin biology advanced concrete methods for a conscious, controlling influence over the organic world, and pointed out the way to transform the nature of organisms in the direction necessary to man. Mitchurin biology rejects the power of accidents, of blind elemental forces, in one of the most important spheres of human activity—in the process of producing new types of plants and new breeds of animals.

The Mitchurin teaching is a further stage in the development of Darwinism. Having imbibed the huge wealth of ideas of Darwin, as well as the leading, progressive views of other biologists, including Lamarck, having further cast aside their fallacies, the teaching of Mitchurin and his followers has raised biology to a new and higher level.

Profound indignation is aroused by the assertion of Muller to the effect that Mitchurin biology allegedly leads to racist conclusions, inasmuch as it allegedly follows that the living conditions of culturally backward peoples must determine hereditary incapability of adopting a higher culture. This nonsense has nothing in common with Mitchurin science.

Soviet scholars categorically reject the attempts to apply biological laws to social life, including the conclusions of Mitchurin biology. The development of society is subject not to biological but to higher, social laws. Every attempt to extend the laws of the animal world to mankind means an attempt to lower man to the level of a beast.

Not Mitchurin biology, but Morgan genetics, is being used in every way possible by reactionaries to substantiate racial theories. It was so in fascist Germany and it is being done now in America. And Professor Muller, president of the Genetics Society of America, some time ago came out against eugenics, and is now a propagandist of man-breeding, and has joined forces with the most avowed racists and reactionaries in science.

Professor Muller expresses his disdain for "so-called dialectical materialism," which is inseparably bound up with the Mitchurin teaching. It should be recalled here that in 1934 Muller expressed other views and called upon geneticists "to rid themselves of antimaterialistic and antidialectical propensities." We do not believe in the sincerity of these words. However, Soviet science, not in words but in reality, is mastering the method of dialectical materialism, for this method is the most reliable weapon of scientific research. Regarding everything as in motion, in development, in interrelationship, dialectical materialism rejects the existence of certain unchangeable substances, such as an "hereditary substance," affirms the closest connection between the organism and the environment. Perhaps it is precisely this which Muller does not like.

Muller declares that in its decision on the biological question the Academy of Sciences was motivated by political goals, that science in the Soviet Union is subject to politics.

We, the Soviet scientists, are convinced that the entire experience of history teaches that there does not exist and cannot exist in the world a science divorced from politics. The fundamental question is with what kind of politics science is connected, whose interests it serves—the interests of the people or the interests of the exploiters.

Soviet science serves the interests of the common people; it is proud of its connection with the policy of the Soviet state, which has no other aims but the improvement of the welfare of the workers, and the strengthening of peace and the progress of democracy. The close, creative collaboration of Soviet biological science with the policy of the state is demonstrated more clearly than anything else in the practical work of increasing the yield in agricultural crops, livestock breeding, and in realizing plans unprecedented in scope and marvelous in concept against drought by planting thousands of kilometers of forests.

Soviet scientists regard with feelings of the warmest sympathy those foreign scientists who honestly and sincerely strive to serve the interests of peace, progress, and democracy. However, it is impossible to shut one's eyes to the fact that in capitalistic countries the bourgeoisie subordinates scientific research to its interests, in pursuit of the goals of profit, oppression of the working masses, and suppression of democracy. At the present time, it is common knowledge that there is taking place in the United States the militarization of science, the subjection of science to the usurping, aggressive plans of American imperialism.

One wonders why Professor Muller does not come out against the utilization of scientific achievements by American imperialists for the purpose of the mass destruction of people and cultural treasures, but rather against Mitchurin biological science, which pursues the task of the speediest possible advancement of the people's welfare.

The successes of the Soviet people in building a new communist society, the flourishing of culture, science, and art in the USSR, depend on the ever-growing authority of and profound respect for the Soviet land on the part of all the progressive people of the world. On the other hand, these successes evoke malice and hatred on the part of the enemies of genuine science and progress—the imperialists and their hirelings.

Professor Muller was once known as a progressive scientist. This is a very uncomfortable position in present-day America. Having come out against the Soviet Union and its science, Muller has won the enthusiasm and recognition of all the reactionary forces of the United States.

The Academy of Sciences of the USSR without any feeling of regret parts with its former member, who betrayed the interests of real science and openly passed over into the camp of the enemies of progress and science, peace and democracy.

Presidium of the Academy of Sciences of the USSR

2. Reply to Professor Henry Dale by the Presidium of the Academy of Sciences of the USSR in *Pravda*, December 26, 1948

In 1942, the English physiologist, Henry Dale, who was at that time president of the British Royal Society, was elected by the Academy of Sciences of the USSR as an honorary member. The Academy of Sciences of the USSR recently received a letter in which Henry Dale announced his resignation from the staff of the Academy of Sciences of the USSR, because of his disagreement with the decisions of the Academy concerning questions in biology. Long before the receipt of Professor Dale's letter by the Presidium of the Academy of Sciences, passages from this letter were widely publicized in the press of Great Britain and the United States for purposes obviously hostile to the Soviet Union.

In his letter, Henry Dale affirms that the victory of the Mitchurin trend in Soviet biological science was not the result of an honest and open conflict of scientific opinions. This assertion is obviously at variance with the facts and testifies that Professor Henry Dale has either forgotten or consciously ignores certain basic facts in the history of biological science.

The conflict of scientific opinions, of which Henry Dale speaks, has been developing in biology for decades. As early as the beginning of the century, the Russian scientist, K. A. Timiryazev, a faithful watchdog of Darwinism, passionately defended the Darwin theory against Weismann, Mendel, and Bateson. Timiryazev decisively opposed the theory about immutable germ plasma and the various metaphysical ids and genes.

The Darwinian doctrine has received exceptional circulation and further profound development in the Soviet Union. The "monkey trials" that have taken place in America could not occur in our country. As a result of the work done by our researchers, new chapters have been written in the materialistic doctrine of Darwinism, and in this field the greatest contribution was made by I. V. Mitchurin.

In his time, Darwin pointed out that he inadequately developed the question of the influence of external environment upon the rise of mutability in organisms. This focal question concerning the laws of development of organic nature has received thorough clarification in the works of Mitchurin. He demonstrated how the characteristics of organisms originate and mutate under the influence of environmental conditions, and how these mutations become fixed by means of heredity. No malice on the part of the obscurantists can refute Mitchurin's discoveries, as they are based on the materials obtained in numerous experiments and have received extensive practical application. Lenin, the creator of our socialist state, discovered Mitchurin, in the real sense of the word, and provided him with every means of support and all requisites for the development of his work.

The great physiologist, Pavlov, came to the analogous conclusion, on the basis of his world-renowned physiological investigations, that environmental conditions are of foremost importance for organisms in their individual and historical adjustment. Speaking at the International Congress of Physiologists in Groningen as early as 1913, Pavlov declared: "It can be accepted that certain newly formed conditioned reflexes are later converted into fixed reflexes by means of heredity."

Mitchurin's motto—"We cannot wait for favors from nature; they must be taken from her; this is our task"—has become the motto of all progressive Soviet scientists laboring for the welfare of the people. The

Mitchurin teaching, developed by Academician Lysenko, provides a key to the deliberate transformation of the properties of plants and animals in the direction necessary to man. And it is because of this that the Mitchurin teaching finds enthusiastic support from the Soviet state and the Communist Party, which have for their task the over-all development of the welfare of society.

The long-standing dispute between the adherents of genuine creative Darwinism, raised to a higher level in Mitchurin's works, and the adherents of the Mendel-Morgan doctrine has ended in our country with the defeat of the latter. This defeat was inevitable, as inevitable as the defeat of all unscientific doctrines blocking the path of scientific development.

The unscientific nature of the views advanced by Mendel and Morgan has been demonstrated with particular clarity in recent events. It is by no means an accident that this doctrine was used as the basis of Hitler's theory and that it has become the theoretical basis of all the abominations and bloody nightmares of Nazism. Professor Dale must know that this doctrine is being used at the present time to justify the persecution of Negroes in America and the oppression of colonial peoples, and as a basis of American claims for the establishment of world domination. All sincere advocates of progress and democracy must welcome the defeat of this doctrine.

It is difficult to accuse Professor Dale of ignorance of certain basic facts in the history of biological science. We can only assume that in composing his letter he was influenced by forces having no relation to science. Professor Dale takes the liberty of manipulating unverified facts —such as work in genetics in the USSR being subject to restriction— though it is known that this work has acquired unprecedented scope due to the victory of the Mitchurin doctrine. All this attests to the fact that Henry Dale's letter has no connection with the scientific dispute, but has become a weapon in the political campaign of slander against all democracy, including the USSR. This campaign is inspired by the enemies of true science and democracy, by aggressive, antidemocratic forces in America and England.

Professor Dale, who has consented to become the obedient tool of the antidemocratic forces, can only arouse the pity of all honest scientists throughout the world.

The Presidium of the Academy of Sciences, after judging Professor Henry Dale's letter to be detrimental to science and democracy, passed a resolution depriving Henry Dale of his title of honorary member of the Academy of Sciences of the USSR, and it presents this resolution for confirmation by the General Assembly of the Academy of Sciences of the USSR.

NOTE: In November 1964, following the overthrow of Khrushchev, a veritable avalanche of criticism was unleashed in the Soviet press and in scholarly periodicals against Lysenko's theories on genetics. The revolt against Lysenkoism spread to the Institute of Genetics of the USSR Academy of Sciences, of which Lysenko himself was the director. On the Moscow radio and in the Government newspaper, *Izvestia*, Lysenko's foes propounded the principles of molecular biology, the basis of recent Western achievements in genetics. One of the allegations levelled against Khrushchev, who supported Lysenko, was that he had "ignored the findings of science applied primarily to biological and agricultural research." — Editors.

References

LYSENKO, T. D., *Soviet Biology. A Report to the Lenin Academy of Agricultural Sciences, Moscow, 1948*. London: Birch Books Limited (n.d.).

OLSHANSKY, M., "Biological Science and Agricultural Production," *Kommunist* (No. 4, March, 1963). Translated in *Current Digest of the Soviet Press*, Vol. XV (No. 16, May 15, 1963), pp. 23-25, 38 (Condensed text).

"The Theoretical Principles of Directed Changes of Heredity in Agricultural Plants," *Pravda* and *Izvestia* (January 29, 1963). Translated in *Current Digest of the Soviet Press*, Vol XV (No. 5, February 27, 1963), pp. 3-10.

55. the launching of the first

artificial earth satellite (Sputnik)

THE ARTICLE BELOW (*Pravda,* October 16, 1957), by a leading Soviet scientist provides a summation of Soviet scientific research which paved the way for the launching of *Vostok I,* the first Sputnik. 1957, *The Current Digest of the Soviet Press* (Vol. IX, No. 40, November 13, 1957, pp. 3-5), published weekly at Columbia University by the Joint Committee on Slavic Studies appointed by the American Council of Learned Societies and Social Science Research Council. Reprinted by permission.

A Great Victory of Soviet Science*

October 4, 1957, will occupy a special place in the history of mankind. On this red-letter day the first artificial earth satellite appeared in the sky. This satellite was created by Soviet scientists, designed and launched by Soviet engineers and technicians, and it took the orbit exactly indicated by the Soviet people.

The world press is paying a great deal of attention to this event. But apart from enthusiastic comment, many bourgeois newspapers and magazines cannot conceal their alarm over this remarkable new achievement of Soviet science and technology. Impartial people see this as a major victory for socialism in the competition with capitalism. The foes of the Soviet Union, trying to minimize the importance of this event, are terming it accidental and insignificant.

Is the earth satellite, launched in our country for the first time in world history, an isolated achievement of science and technology, an accidental success? No! Such a success is unthinkable for separate, isolated branches of science and technology. Scientific and technical progress in our country takes place on a broad front.

* By Academician A. Topchiyev, Chief Academic Secretary of the Presidium of the USSR Academy of Sciences

Socialism Opened Broad Horizons for Scientific Development. By bringing about fundamental political and economic changes in our country, the Great October Socialist Revolution opened up broad horizons for the flourishing of science. . . .

V. I. Lenin paid great attention to scientific development, displaying truly paternal concern about Soviet scientists, about providing them with the most favorable conditions for their scientific work. The Party and government have not spared funds or resources to aid scientists in every way and to create and train new cadres of a scientific and technical intelligentsia.

Science has played a large role in the entire constructive process of building socialism. Its importance has increased many times in the period of the building of communism in our country. The Communist Party's general line for industrialization, for the preponderant growth of the production of the means of production, for accomplishment of the U.S.S.R.'s main economic task and for achievement of a higher labor productivity than under capitalism necessitated the comprehensive development of theoretical and practical research in all branches of knowledge and maximum application of the results of scientific exploration. Each step in the development of socialist industry provides food for science and sets new tasks before it. Science, in turn, influences technology and production.

The successful launching of the first artificial earth satellite is the natural result of Soviet scientific and technical development under socialist conditions, the natural victory of socialism over capitalism. What, then, are the achievements of our science and technology that made possible this success, this well-deserved triumph of our people?

Achievements of Soviet Physicists. In the last quarter of a century, physics has forged way ahead in the natural sciences. Developing a rapid pace, physical research has had results of striking importance.

Speaking of the achievements of theoretical physics, we must note above all the further development by Soviet scientists of the theory of relativity, particularly with respect to the nonstationary solution of Einstein's equation of gravitation and the problem of the law of the movement of the system of bodies.

Soviet physicists have made a large contribution to the development of modern quantum mechanics. A major landmark in this direction was V. A. Fok's approximation method of resolving problems of the quantum mechanics of many particles. The theory advanced by Soviet scientists that nuclear forces arise as the result of the exchange of light particles and the creation by our physicists of the liquid-drop model of the atomic nucleus had a substantial influence on the further development of the theory of nuclear forces.

The discovery of the Vavilov-Cherenkov effect was of great importance. The theory of this effect was worked out by I. Ye. Tamm and

I. M. Frank. They have solved the problem of the radiation of an electron moving in a given medium at a velocity greater than that of light.

L. D. Landau's works on thermodynamics and static physics and P. L. Kapitsa's discovery of the superfluidity of liquid helium, which made it possible to predict the phenomenon of the second sound in helium, subsequently discovered in experiments, are also major achievements of Soviet theoretical physics.

Experimental physics, especially nuclear physics, has achieved large successes. Begun back in 1924, the research on cosmic rays by means of the Wilson chamber developed into a series of experiments for studying the properties of elementary particles, artificially splitting the atomic nucleus and studying artificial radioactivity and the mechanism and law of the formation of positrons. In 1940 the spontaneous fission of uranium nuclei was discovered in the Soviet Union. Soon afterwards it was established that by a small enrichment of a natural mixture of uranium isotopes with uranium -235 a chain process of fission was possible with the use of ordinary water as a retarding agent.

In recent years Soviet science has achieved results in the peaceful use of atomic energy which have brought it to the fore in world science.

V. I. Veksler's method of "autophasing" charged particles made it possible to build powerful accelerators. The world's largest, 10,000,000,000-electron-volt accelerator put into operation in 1957 is based on this method, which is now used all over the world.

In building accelerators—the basic instrument for studying the properties of elementary particles—our scientists and technicians have reached the highest energies ever obtained in the world's research laboratories. Research and designing work is now being done to construct a still more powerful, 50,000,000,000-electron-volt accelerator, which will be another mighty impetus to the development of nuclear physics.

Extensive research in the physics of nuclear reactors and reactor building is being done in the Soviet Union. One result of this work is our atomic power plant, the first in the world. The successful operation of this power plant has been the basis for planning the construction of several larger atomic power plants in the next few years. Work is now being done to build atomic motors for transport purposes, and an atomic icebreaker is under construction.

The construction of nuclear reactors has also made it possible to organize the production of radioactive isotopes, which are extensively used in research laboratories and at the country's industrial enterprises as radiation sources and as "tracer" atoms. Radioactive isotopes helped to disclose the nature of several complex processes occurring in nature and technology. They have made it possible, for instance, to obtain a wealth of new data on the mechanism of photosynthesis, the displacement and absorption of nutritive substances in plants, the biochemistry of the higher nervous activity and several other biological problems.

Among the studies of fundamental importance for the use of nuclear energy mention should be made of the work done to achieve a controlled thermonuclear reaction by means of high-energy impulse discharges. This enabled us to obtain temperatures of more than 1,000,000 degrees C. in laboratory conditions for the first time in the world. The study of high-energy gas discharges brings us closer to solution of the general task of present-day science—the creation of a reactor capable of operating on heavy and superheavy hydrogen (deuterium and tritium) rather than on uranium fuel. The work of I. V. Kurchatov, M. A. Leontovich, L. A. Artsimovich, and other scientists is tremendously important for accomplishment of these tasks.

There would have been no satellite without the present-day achievements of radio engineering, the beginning of which is linked with the name of the Russian scientist A. S. Popov. In the hard years of the Civil War and postwar chaos V. I. Lenin, the founder of the Soviet state, supported the remarkable scientist M. A. Bonch-Bruyevich, who in his Nizhny Novgorod laboratory enriched radio engineering with his research on radio-instrument making. In 1922 he built a 12-kw. radiotelephone station, which at that time was the most powerful in the world. The first radio concert in the world was broadcast in the Soviet Union. Radio engineering in the U.S.S.R. is steadily improving and is now solving new and greater problems.

Communication with the satellite would be impossible without a knowledge of the laws of the propagation of radio waves, particularly in the ionosphere. The earth is blanketed by a layer of air the atoms of which become ionized as a result of bombardment by cosmic rays. This layer—the ionosphere—is "transparent" only for radio waves of a definite frequency; waves of other frequencies are reflected back from this layer. Academician M. V. Shuleikin was among the first to devote his energies to a study of the propagation of radio waves in the ionosphere.

For 25 years now work has been done continually in the Soviet Union to "sound" the ionosphere by means of several dozen special ionosphere stations. All this made it possible to choose the correct radio-wave frequencies for communication with the satellite. In 1930 Academicians L. I. Mandelshtam and N. D. Papaleksi theoretically substantiated and actually carried out the phase methods of measuring distances by means of radio waves. The stations now observing the satellite are based on these methods.

Radar was the first means enabling man to peer into outer space for the first time long before the first earth satellite was launched. I am speaking of the measurement of the distance to the moon with the help of radar. The theoretical basis for this was provided by Academician N. D. Papaleksi. Radio astronomy, a new branch of science, developed as a result of the successes gained in developing antenna engineering and in increasing the sensitivity of radio receiving equipment. Radio telescopes are now used to study the sun and so-called "radio stars."

Research in the field of semiconductors has become widespread. Considerable success was achieved in studying thermoelectric phenomena. This work, done under A. F. Ioffe, resulted in the building of thermoelectric generators, which transform heat energy into electric power.

A great future lies ahead for semiconductor photocells, which transform the energy of various types of radiation into electricity. Silicon photocells convert the energy of sunlight into electricity.

The semiconductor laboratories of the P. N. Lebedev Physics Institute and the Institute of Physics and Engineering worked out the theory and studied the electrical properties of semiconductors and on this basis designed Soviet models of semiconductor radio apparatuses—diodes and triodes. The use of semiconductor devices in radio equipment makes it possible to build apparatuses that are small and have other advantages over equipment employing tubes.

Some Achievements in Mathematics and Chemistry. The rapid development of present-day physics and technology has confronted mathematicians with fundamentally new tasks. Soviet scientists continuing the glorious traditions of Russian mathematicians have introduced many new elements in the development of both theoretical and applied methematics. Our mathematicians—Academician I. M. Vinogradov, A. N. Kolmogorov, S. L. Sobolev, M. V. Keldysh, M. A. Lavrentyev and others—enjoy well-deserved fame in the U.S.S.R. and abroad.

The new tasks which have arisen before mathematics have brought about such trends as the theory of information, the theory of programming and the theory of computing machines. Mathematical logic has found important application. Today no sphere of theory or practice can get along without using a complex mathematical apparatus. Rapid computing machines that solve various problems in nuclear physics, aerodynamics, radio engineering, astrophysics, etc., have been built in this country.

Soviet chemistry occupies an important place in the general achievements of Soviet science that have made it possible to solve major problems of technical progress. A substantial contribution to the development of both theoretical and applied chemistry has been made by Soviet chemists under the guidance of Academicians A. N. Nesmeyanov, N. N. Semyonov, A. Ye. Arbuzov, A. P. Vinogradov, B. A. Kazansky, A. N. Frumkin, M. M. Dubinin, I. I. Chernyayev and others.

An outstanding achievement of Soviet chemistry, for instance, is the theory of chain ramified reactions, founded by N. N. Semyonov and his school, a theory of great importance for world science. A study of a large number of model reactions has made it possible to disclose the basic laws of chain processes and to outline ways of studying the various elementary stages of the process and, what is particularly important, ways of controlling a developing chain reaction.

An exceptionally important role in the creation of industrial radium and natural radioactive elements and in the artificial radioactive elements industry belongs to the research done by V. G. Khlopin and his students. It was under his direction that the first preparation of Soviet radium was obtained. V. G. Khlopin discovered the law of quantitative co-precipitation, which makes it possible to calculate theoretically and work out new methods for the isolation of radioactive substances.

The achievements in such new fields of chemistry as biochemistry, biophysics, organic chemistry of elements and others are of great importance. A major achievement in the field of the chemistry of organic compounds of elements is the method of obtaining organic compounds of metals by means of diazo compounds, a method discovered by A. N. Nesmeyanov. The theoretical and experimental studies of A. N. Nesmeyanov and his school have led to the creation of new methods in the organic synthesis of metals and elements and the production of a number of valuable new types of substances.

K. E. Tsiolkovsky's Ideas Are Being Carried Out. Solution of one of the greatest tasks ever undertaken by mankind—the task of overcoming the force of gravitation and entering cosmic space—would have been impossible without the creation of rapid flying machines. In this field, too, Soviet scientists and designers have achieved big successes. Fast jet planes are now flying on international air routes, evoking the admiration of specialists throughout the world.

Russian science has remarkable traditions in rocket building. More than half a century ago, when no airplanes yet existed, K. E. Tsiolkovsky for the first time in the history of science laid the foundations for the theory of jet propulsion and proposed a design for a rocket to travel in cosmic space. But it was only with the victory of the Great October Socialist Revolution that Tsiolkovsky's ideas won the recognition of the Soviet government and the scientific community.

At the end of the 1920's there appeared in this country groups of engineers who carried out research in a number of concrete problems of the physics and technology of jet propulsion. Tirelessly continuing his research on the dynamics of rockets, which he had started at the beginning of the century, K. E. Tsiolkovsky by this time had arrived at the conclusion that a single rocket using chemical fuel could not achieve cosmic speed (eight to 11 km. per second). In searching for a solution to the problem of achieving high speeds, he arrived at the idea of building multistage rockets, an idea which has proved to be so fruitful.

Thanks to the concern of the Communist Party and the Soviet government, research in the field of jet propulsion in this country was included, even during the first five-year plans, in the group of special studies of state importance. This made it possible at the beginning of the 1930's, long before similar work was done abroad, to carry out stand tests of jet engines and, in 1933, to launch the first rocket, designed by the engineer M. K. Tikhonravov for meteorological observations.

In the postwar years we began to build ballistic and guided long-range rockets. Rocket technology was developed and perfected both in the interests of the country's defense and for scientific purposes.

Since 1947 instruments lifted into the air by rockets have been used regularly for studying the upper layers of the atmosphere and the processes occurring beyond its boundaries. The X-ray radiation of the sun has been discovered; information has been obtained on the chemical composition of the atmosphere at heights of more than 100 km.; a study has been made of the concentration of free charges in the ionosphere, which plays a highly important role in shortwave distant radio communications; observations have been made of the state of a living organism in a weightless condition, arising when a rocket begins its free flight; and a number of other valuable studies have been conducted that broaden the horizons of scientific cognition and prepare the conditions for the cosmic flight of man.

Our instrument-making industry played an extremely important role in preparing the launching of the artificial earth satellite. The work of such eminent scientists as D. S. Rozhdestvensky, S. I. Vavilov, G. S. Landsberg and A. A. Lebedev laid the foundation for the Soviet optical industry. This industry has provided our astronomical observatories with the most modern optical equipment. It managed in a short time to equip the optical stations for carrying on observations of the satellite. It is now boldly competing with American industry in the construction of giant telescopes. Yet there was a time when we imported even opera glasses from Germany! The designers and workers of the instrument industry have done a great deal to help make the satellite.

The artificial earth satellite was launched in the U.S.S.R. as part of the program for the International Geophysical Year. Our country is participating in this program by a large number of other measures also, of course; these are being carried out under the coordinated plan of international studies and in collaboration with scientists abroad. In this work the prestige of Soviet science as the advanced science of the world has been enhanced as never before.

The victory of Soviet science, which was expressed in the launching of the first artificial earth satellite—an event noted with great satisfaction by all progressive mankind—is the result not of individual record achievements of Soviet science but of the creation of a single broad front of Soviet science, the creation of its basis—socialist industry. The socialist system has made science in the U.S.S.R. mighty, the most progressive science in the world, capable of carrying out its lofty mission—that of serving the cause of building communism.

The strength of Soviet science lies in its ties with practice, with life. Its basic features are collectivism, a wide scope of scientific work, contact with industry and selfless devotion to the interests of the people, who are building socialism. Soviet scientists are participating with great enthusiasm in the grandiose program of communist construction outlined by the 20th Party Congress.

In September, 1957, the Party Central Committee and the Council of Ministers found it necessary to draw up a long-range plan for developing the U.S.S.R. national economy over a longer period and instructed the U.S.S.R. State Planning Committee, the Union-Republic Councils of Ministers, the economic councils and the U.S.S.R. ministries and agencies to draft a plan for national economic development for 1959-1965. This decision states: "A major condition for accomplishing the main task of the long-range plan is an all-around increase in labor productivity on the basis of uninterrupted technical progress and the mastering and extensive introduction, in all branches of production, of the discoveries of advanced science and technology. The new draft long-range plan should offer broad prospects for the development of all branches of science, theoretical research and major new scientific discoveries."

Thus, the Communist Party and the Soviet government are providing a new stimulus for the creative work of our scientists and opening up broad new prospects for scientific creative work for the good of our country.

56. the Siberian Division, USSR Academy of Sciences

AS ONE PHASE OF ITS PROGRAM to accelerate the development of Siberia, the Soviet government in 1957 established the Siberian Division of the USSR Academy of Sciences. This program has included the construction of a "Science City" in the vicinity of Novosibirsk. The new science center is of strategic, as well as of economic and educational significance.

Below is an interview with Academician A. N. Nesmeyanov, President of the USSR Academy of Sciences (*Pravda,* June 8, 1957, p. 3, condensed text). 1957, *The Current Digest of the Soviet Press* (Vol. IX, No. 23, July 17, 1957, p. 30), published weekly at Columbia University by the Joint Committee on Slavic Studies appointed by the American Council of Learned Societies and Social Science Research Council. Reprinted by permission.

New Scientific Center in the East

... The Communist Party and the Soviet government show great concern for the development of the productive forces in the eastern part of our country and are taking energetic measures to put the inexhaustible resources of this remarkable region to work serving the people. Science has an enormous role to play in the development of the economy and culture of the eastern regions. An initiative of Academicians M. A. Lavrentyev and S. A. Khristianovich has acquired great importance in this connection. They and their colleagues expressed a wish to move to permanent posts in Siberia and to found a mighty science center there. This initiative evoked a widespread response in Soviet society. Many of our scientists declared themselves ready to follow this patriotic example.

On June 7th a meeting of the Presidium of the U.S.S.R. Academy of Sciences was held at which the Chief Academic Secretary of the Presidium, A. V. Topchiyev, reported that the government had approved the proposal of Academicians M. A. Lavrentyev and S. A. Khristianovich for the founding of a mighty science center in Siberia. He read the decision of the U.S.S.R. Council of Ministers on this question. The chairman of the organizational committee of the Siberian Division of the U.S.S.R. Academy of Sciences reported on the work that is to precede the establishment of the new scientific center in Siberia and acquainted the gathering with the plan of development. The Presidium prepared to carry out the government decisions to establish a Siberian Division of the U.S.S.R. Academy of Sciences and outlined several measures connected with this.

In an interview with a *Pravda* correspondent A. N. Nesmeyanov, President of the U.S.S.R. Academy of Sciences, said:

"The organization of the Siberian Division of the U.S.S.R. Academy of Sciences is all the more important because it coincides with the country's current reorganization of the management of industry and construction and with the extension of the role of local organizations in the development of socialist industry.

"Included in the Siberian Division will be the scientific institutions of the West Siberian branch of the U.S.S.R. Academy of Sciences. The East Siberian, Yakut and Far Eastern branches of the Academy and the Coordinated (Kompleksny) Research Institute and Physics Institute of the U.S.S.R. Academy of Sciences in Krasnoyarsk will also be subordinated to this division. The staffs of these research institutions have made an important contribution to the development of science and their work has made possible many successes in many fields of knowledge. The creation of the Siberian Division opens up still broader avenues of scientific work. Unification of the creative powers of local scientists and scientists who will take up permanent posts there beginning in 1957 will mutually enrich their scientific work, raise the level of research and relate research more closely to production.

"The principal task of the Siberian Division is to use all means to develop theoretical and experimental research in the physical, technical and natural sciences and in economics, research that is oriented toward the solution of highly important scientific problems and toward solutions that will make possible a more successful development of the productive capacity of Siberia and the Far Eastern Region.

"The government has ruled that the Siberian Division will be subordinated to the U.S.S.R. Academy of Sciences and to the Russian Republic Council of Ministers. An organizational committee including many well-known scientists has been set up to perform duties preparatory to the organization of the division.

"A scientific settlement is to be built on the banks of the Ob river near Novosibirsk to house the Siberian Division of the U.S.S.R. Academy of Sciences. It is to consist of buildings for the scientific institutions and comfortable housing for the personnel. A total of 700 hectares has been allotted to the scientific settlement.

"Party and Soviet organizations of Novosibirsk Province and scientists working in the eastern part of the country are cooperating actively in the organization of the new scientific center. The Novosibirsk City Soviet Executive Committee has already set aside a large number of comfortable apartments for the staff of the new division.

"The Presidium of the U.S.S.R. Academy of Sciences has accepted the proposal of the organizational committee of the Siberian Division concerning the establishment of several new institutes in the scientific settlement. To supplement the Chemical and Metallurgical Institute, the Transport and Power Institute and other institutes of the West Siberian branch of the U.S.S.R. Academy of Sciences already existing in Novosibirsk, the following institutes will be founded: a Mathematics Institute, with a computation center, a Mechanics Institute, a Hydrodynamics Institute, a Physics Institute, an Automation Institute, a Geology and Geophysics Institute, a Thermodynamics Institute, an Institute of Experimental Biology and Medicine, a Cytology and Genetics Institute and an Economics and Statistics Institute.

"Besides these, the Presidium of the U.S.S.R. Academy of Sciences will consider adding to the institutes of its East Siberian branch at Irkutsk and also to the number of institutions concerned with chemistry.

"The problem of the transfer of several institutes, departments, laboratories and individual groups of scientists from other cities to the Siberian Division must be decided very soon. Measures must also be worked out to provide help for the newly organized institutes. Plans for building modern laboratories in the institutes are being considered.

"Academician M. A. Lavrentyev has been appointed chairman of the Siberian Division of the U.S.S.R. Academy of Sciences. The Vice-Chairmen for Scientific Questions are Academician S. A. Khristianovich and Prof. T. F. Gorbachev. The Vice-Chairman for Organizational Questions is S. Kh. Dadayan. . . .

"The U.S.S.R. Academy of Sciences will use the experience acquired by the Siberian Division for the further developing of science in parts distant from the center of our country. There is no doubt that our higher educational institutions will also be able to benefit by this experience."

57. three Soviet literary works

of historical significance

The Silent Don, BY MIKHAIL SHOLOKHOV, *The Russian Question,* by Konstantin Simonov, and *Doctor Zhivago,* by Boris Pasternak have been selected for consideration in this work because of their historical significance. The first two passages are representative of Soviet literary criticism. In the third, Boris Pasternak speaks for himself in excerpts translated from *Doctor Zhivago.*

I. *The Silent Don,* by Mikhail Sholokhov

Mikhail Alexandrovitch Sholokhov (1905-   ) is a literary phenomenon, not only in Soviet but in Russian literature. The Ukrainian Cossacks produced Gogol (1809-1852), but Sholokhov is the first great writer to appear among the Don Cossacks. His monumental work, *The Silent Don* (1926-1940), is an epic of the Cossacks on the eve of the Russian Revolution of 1917, during that Revolution, and in the Civil War that followed. It is perhaps the most popular work in Soviet literature, more than six million copies having been printed in the USSR by 1960. This novel has been translated into many foreign languages.

The remarkable fact about *The Silent Don* is that it emerged unscathed by Soviet censorship under the Stalin regime. Possibly it was because he was the first to depict the class struggle among his people that Sholokhov was permitted to write as a free Cossack. In any event, his hero, Grigory Melekhov, who fought first on one side and then on the other in the Civil War, emerged disillusioned with both the Whites and the Reds. The article on Sholokhov by a Soviet literary critic, which is presented below, is equally remarkable for its objectivity, if we bear in mind that it was produced under the Stalin regime. Its publication in a Soviet literary periodical astonished American literary critics.

420

The article is from *Soviet Press Translations,* edited by Ivar Spector and published by the Far Eastern and Russian Institute, University of Washington, Vol. IV (No. 10, May 15, 1949), pp. 301-315.

The Realism of Sholokhov*

Mikhail Sholokhov is justly acknowledged to be a classic in Soviet literature, and *The Silent Don,* his remarkable epic on the fate of the Don Cossacks during the October Revolution and the Civil War, is the best novel of the last thirty years.

Much serious work has been devoted to Mikhail Sholokhov: books by Lezhnev, Hoffenshafer, Yermilov, Kirpotin, and others. In 1940 heated discussion in regard to the destiny of Grigory Melekhov flared up in the pages of *Literaturnaya Gazeta.* A multitude of controversial, and at times non-controversial, ideas were expressed about the works of Sholokhov. And if we were now to analyze these numerous and varied statements, one thing would be clear: discussion of Sholokhov, regardless of the divergent conclusions as to his creative work, leads to a solution of our most vital literary problems.

There is not one research study which has not raised the following questions in regard to Sholokhov in one connection or another: Sholokhov and the traditions of classical Russian literature, the problem of the hero in Sholokov, *narodnost* in Sholokhov, and nature in Sholokhov.

And all these questions taken together touch upon one basic and cardinal problem: the new kind of realism in our literature.

In this article I do not propose to give a consistent account of Sholokhov's creative path. This has already been done more than once in adequate detail. Using *The Silent Don,* for the most part, as an example, I should merely like to point out the uniqueness and novelty of Sholokhov's realism and the rare quality and perspective that Sholokhov has brought to Soviet literature. For whereas it is legitimate to speak of the classic traditions in the works of Sholokhov, the time has now come to raise the question of Sholokhov himself as a living tradition, a tradition extraordinarily fruitful for our prose.

Sholokhov is one of the few writers who know how to avoid repeating the same material in their work, and who at the same time remain true to their creative method. Sholokhov is absolutely characteristic and recognizable in his gigantic epic *The Silent Don;* in his story of collectivization, *Virgin Soil Upturned;* in the fragments of the broadly conceived epic novel, *They Fought for Their Motherland;* in his semi-journalistic sketches; in the *Science of Hatred,* a story of the war years; and in *The Motherland.* But *The Silent Don* is particularly significant, merely due to the fact that it is the only complete work of Sholokhov. It

* By Tamara Khmelnitskaya . . . *Zvezda,* No. 12, December 1948

embraces a history-laden decade in the life of the Don Cossacks. During this decade the destinies of its heroes unfold before our eyes and are treated according to their continual mutations. People are portrayed in their searchings, in their fallacies, in their frustrations, in their contradictions, and in their struggle. The growth and development of these heroes coincide with the growth and development of Sholokhov's creative method. The novel embraces a whole decade in the life of these heroes, and work on the novel occupied fourteen years altogether in the life of its author.

This novel was conceived in 1926, and its final section was written as late as 1940. The creative growth and the mature mastery of Sholokhov are revealed with particular force, especially in these last two parts of the novel—in the fourth volume.

At first Sholokhov contemplated beginning his narrative at the height of the Civil War on the Don. "I began," said Sholokhov, "with a description of the Kornilov campaign, with the second volume of *The Silent Don* as it exists today, and I wrote whole sections of the novel. Then I saw that this was not what I needed to begin with, and I put away the manuscript. I started anew, beginning with the old Cossack life, and wrote the three parts of the novel which constitute the first volume of *The Silent Don*. And when the first volume was completed and I had to write further—of Petrograd and the Kornilov campaign—I returned to the earlier manuscript and used it for the second volume. It was a shame to throw away work that had already been done."

It is precisely in this "work that had already been done" that we find a very great number of relatively weak spots in the novel—some that are dry chronicle, some that give a pale and biased portrait of Communist Buntchuk, and some that are excessively naturalistic or simply superfluous. In the war sections of the novel it would be easy, and, it must be said, beneficial for the thing as a whole, to delete the notebook of the slain Cossack, which consists chiefly of unsavory and excessively physiological details in connection with Lisa, the depraved daughter of the merchant Mokhov. On the contrary, the very beginning of the novel, which was written later, includes some of its best pages.

It embodies, in superb epic sweep, the traditional customs and features of the patriarchal life of the well-to-do Don Cossacks; and it projects vividly and with talent the characters of the chief heroes—Grigory Melekhov, Aksinya Astakhova, and Natalya Korshunova.

Whereas it is possible to find much that is episodic, casual, and petty in the war sections of the novel, and oftentimes material that burdens the epic with nonessential details, the beginning and the final sections of *The Silent Don* unroll before us in severe and concise narrative lines, organically essential to the entire development of the plot.

The language of the novel and its descriptions of nature reveal with particular clarity the evolution of Sholokhov's style. The language of the central parts of the novel is profusely larded with the dialect of the Don Cossacks—not only the speech of the characters, but frequently the author's narration as well. His linguistic colors are laid on very thick. Every few words his speech glitters with repetitions of *azhnik, kubyt, khutch, vovzyat, do sye, zaraz; kritchat*—instead of *plakat; shumet*—instead of *kritchat; gutarit*—instead of *govorit* (not to mention such unfamiliar expressions in Russian as *sepetit, teleshit, tchikilyat, potchunet,* etc.). By the end of the novel dialect is used only to embellish the speech of the characters, and it is sparing, expressive, and appropriate.

In the central parts of the novel, the descriptions of nature are excessively lavish, overladen with figures of speech, enumerations, and comparisons, and they abound with names of local grasses and flowers. The minute, local details are combined with the somewhat oleographic prettiness of deliberately employed "poetical" diction, such as *marevo, son, metchta,* etc.

By the end of the novel, the descriptions of nature become cleaner, more precise, and more compact. Sholokhov attains the utmost conciseness and tremendous generalized expressiveness in the famous scene where Grigory, having buried that which was dearest in life to him, Aksinya, "saw above him the black sky and the blinding flash of the sun's black disk." The whole depth of Grigory's grief and despair is reflected here, and this image is a new and lively expression of the usual hackneyed formula: "everything turned black before his eyes."

And not only in its landscape, but also in the revelation of the souls of its characters, does Sholokhov's novel penetrate ever deeper into the essence of life, toward an understanding of what is fundamental and general. A multitude of events—everyday and important events, casual and decisive events—fills the lives of these characters, in the course of which is revealed the true meaning and truth of this life. Proceeding from this vital truth, Sholokhov creates not merely a description of life but the destiny of a hero. This destiny unfolds naturally from the social and personal character of the hero—this is what is limned in epic fullness toward the end of Sholokhov's novel. But before referring specifically to the features of Sholokhov's treatment of the problem of destiny, we shall first dwell upon a very essential question in the creative work of Sholokhov—his connection with the classical traditions of Russian literature and, in particular, with Tolstoy.

The Silent Don has often, and not without foundation, been compared with Tolstoy's *War and Peace,* with emphasis, furthermore, upon all the diversities of the two epochs and upon the scale of the artistic and philosophical design. What is common to both is a very tangible crisscrossing of the historical and the personal: the great events of the folk epic plus the detailed, individualized, daily course of the private lives of the heroes. With Tolstoy, as with Sholokhov, the historical novel exists in conjunction with the psychological family novel: the Patriotic War of 1812 and the history of the Rostov and Bolkonsky families in Tolstoy; and the October Revolution, the Civil War, and the history of the Melekhov, Korshunov, and Astakhov families in Sholokhov. This is the basic principle of composition in both novels.

But this likeness would be less striking if it were not for certain peculiarities in the depiction of the characters of the heroes—details insistently repeated and emerging each time with the appearance of Tolstoy's and Sholokhov's favorite heroes. The lustrous eyes and heavy gait of Princess Marya, the down on the short upper lip of Princess Bolkonsky in Tolstoy; and the curls on the chiseled neck of Aksinya, the gliding gait and arched brows of Darya, the wife of Petro, the kindly calf's eyes of Prokhor Zykov in Sholokhov.

In his voluminous book on Sholokhov, Lezhnev devotes much space to this tradition of clearly Tolstoyan detail. Sometimes his examples are convincing, but frequently, in pursuit of coincidences, he resorts to strained and unnecessary interpretations, which not only fail to confirm, but rather compromise, the very principles of comparison between Sholokhov and Tolstoy. Thus Lezhnev makes endless references to the proud but shameful head of Aksinya, comparing it with references to the proud but shameful head of Anna; and he makes the most trifling analogies between the mother love of the Countess Rostova for her sons in *War and Peace* and that of Ilyinishna in *The Silent Don;* between the symbolic dreams of Anna and Vronsky and the dreams of Grigory Melekhov, between the feminine friendship of Natasha and the Princess Marya and the tacit, mutual understanding between Dunyashka and Aksinya. The principle of similarity, which in some cases is obvious and requires no proof, is reduced to absurdity due to Lezhnev's excessive zeal, when in reality the most far-fetched coincidences mentioned are nothing other than the quite differently revealed feelings of mother love, feminine friendship, etc. Lezhnev makes obtrusive and reiterated reference to traditions and influences. It is surprising that along with the Tolstoyan and Sholokhovian details compared, he did not think to mention Karenin's ears, which were hateful to Anna, and Stephan Astakhov's ears, which moved repulsively when he ate.

Yes, there are doubtless common points of comparison between Sholokhov and Tolstoy in their psychological method of depicting characters, in their selection of repetitious characteristic detail, and in their crossing of the historical and family novel. But these comparisons reflect only the most superficial and obvious likenesses. They do not exhaust in any degree and do not define the Tolstoy tradition in Sholokhov. Therefore it is important not merely to note the similarity of elements, but to understand why Sholokhov derived this or that principle of writing from the creative heritage of Tolstoy.

Such an understanding of his affinity to and inheritance from Tolstoy coincides with the very attitude toward the classical heritage expressed by Sholokhov himself: "There are writers whom Tolstoy and Pushkin did not influence. . . . So help me God, all good writers have influenced me. Each is good in his own way. Take Tchekhov, for instance. Would it seem that there is anything in common between me and Tchekhov? But Tchekhov, too, has influenced me! And it is my misfortune and that of many others that they did not influence us more."

Sholokhov is right when he takes up arms against writers "who do not remember their origins," and deliberately impoverish themselves by rejecting the enormous resources of the classical heritage. Of course, Sholokhov is not speaking of the outright borrowing of specific features and principles, but of a feeling of affinity to and adaptation of the entire literary culture of the past, of the broad and untrammeled selection of creative principles fruitful for our time. It is no wonder that the classical traditions of Sholokhov are not drawn from Tolstoy alone. A very distinct and simultaneous combination of the Gogolian and Tolstoyan traditions is characteristic of Sholokhov—a combination extremely essential to our literature.

And, of course, Tolstoy was not dear to Sholokhov because of his repetition of details in depicting character. This coincidence is most superficial and mechanical, and therefore least binding.

The Tolstoyan principle in Sholokhov's creative work bears fertile fruit, chiefly in his ability to depict how man is moulded and altered, in his understanding of the multiplicity and inconsistency of human nature in its entirety, it would seem, and at times in its elementariness. Sholokhov, following Tolstoy, decisively rebelled against rigid and strict consistency in character depiction. There is no character of any human worth in *The Silent Don* that Sholokhov has not depicted in the process of development and mutation, which is sometimes unexpected. And in these unexpected revelations of astonishing and seemingly inappropriate traits lie the great psychological wealth and creative daring of Sholokhov. The truth of life is discerned in all its contradictions and mutations, and not once and for all in some established pattern.

We have before us the supposedly simple character of Natalya Korshunova—the unloved wife of Grigory Melekhov—which is well defined from the very first chapters of the novel. The whole pathos and the whole tragedy of Natalya lie in her unrequited and unchanging emotion for Grigory. Throughout the novel she passes as an unloved and deceived wife. This determined her destiny, drove her to her first unsuccessful attempt at suicide and to her fatal attempt to have no more children by Grigory. The hopeless constancy of her love shattered and destroyed this reserved, modest, proud, and patient woman with her secret passions. But how many shades of feeling does Grigory reveal for this unloved wife, how often stubborn indifference turns into its counterpart, pity and warm, compassionate remorse! He regards Natalya as the

mother of his children—a modest, submissive wife, hiding the sorrow of
her frustrated emotions—and grateful tenderness toward her bursts forth
in scenes marked by the subtlest psychological lyricism.

> She was with him, his wife and the mother of Mishatka and Polyushka.
> For him she had decked herself out and washed her face, hurriedly throw-
> ing on a kerchief so that it could not be seen how ugly her head had
> become since her illness. She sat there with her head tilted slightly to one
> side—so sad, so plain and yet nevertheless so beautiful, shining with some
> pure, inward beauty. She always wore high collars in order to hide from
> him the scar that had once disfigured her neck. All this because of him.
> . . . A mighty wave of tenderness filled Grigory's heart. He wanted to say
> something warm and caressing to her, but he could not find the words and
> silently drawing her close to him, he kissed her white, sloping brow and
> sorrowful eyes.

And Natalya's death was not a welcome deliverance for Grigory,
untying his hands, but a real sorrow, an agonizing and unforgettable
recrudescence of the deepest pangs of conscience. Thus Sholokhov enriches his portrait of the unloved wife.

But Natalya Korshunova is a character endowed with the frank sympathy of the author. Let us take another example—a clearly negative
character. Stepan Astakhov is a crude and brutal man, who exercised
the worst traditional rights of Cossack society—the right to treat his
wife as his property, to chastise and torment her whenever he took it into
his head. After his wedding Stepan treated the seventeen-year-old Aksinya brutally, knowing that he was not first with her. Stepan sadistically
beat Aksinya half to death because she honorably informed him of her
liaison with Grigory, and every day he tormented and tortured her; and
no one intervened in her behalf, for such is the legal right of the husband
"to teach" his wife.

And in the course of time, this same Stepan discovers in himself a real
and sincere feeling for Aksinya. This is not merely the possessive passion
of the lord and master. He loves Aksinya with a strong and deep human
love, despite her treachery and open desertion, despite the fact that he
knows that she returned to him not from love but from sorrow. Sholokhov
conveys the whole depth of Stepan's feelings and his unexpected delight
at the daring of Aksinya's truthful confessions, in the remarkable scene
of the accidental meeting between Stepan and Grigory at Veshki.

There is no need to speak here of how the relations between Grigory
and Aksinya became involved and developed. The strong and invincible
physical passion embodied in the first part of the novel is transformed, as
the narrative moves and develops, into a great and very human love, a
love that is fostered and is the product of suffering, filled with concern,
apprehension, and tenderness. It is a deep, lasting, and inextinguishable
love between two people, a love that endured much and more than once
tasted of sorrow, a love that wearied from constant loss, ruin, and part-
ing; it is the love of people engulfed in the maelstrom of tremendous,

historic upheavals that they do not understand, who vainly seek peace, who mutually desire only a stable refuge in life. The ruin of Aksinya is the peak of the tragic culmination of the fate of Grigory. The light fades out of his eyes. "Like a burned-off clearing in the steppe, life became black for Grigory. He had lost everything dear to his heart." "With the death of Aksinya he lost his wit and his former daring." And in all its merciless clarity, he sees that his life is spent, and that his course had been false and aimless, rejected by the people and by the times.

The aspect of the world changes, and thereby the aspect of the heroes inhabiting this world. The emotions and characters of people are not depicted once and for all in immobile and unchanging terms. In the novel they grow, develop, and live in all their aspects, in all the complex contradictions of life.

The ability to portray this mutation of human emotions and characters, the ability to depict destiny in all its facets, is the most convincing trait in Sholokhov's realism.

An unusually true and precise reflection of the historic conflict in the soul and life of the heroes, as well as the concrete and truthful form that this conflict takes, is a peculiarity that is characteristic of Sholokhov as a genuine Soviet artist. This comes not from tradition, but from his contemporary perception of reality. But Sholokhov's mastery of the subtlest psychological mutations, and his art in endowing preconceived characters with a multitude of diverse facets were derived from Tolstoy. And this is much more important than the obvious and conventional "Tolstoyan" repetition of detail in character depiction.

But it is not without reason that Sholokhov speaks of the diverse classical traditions existing for him. What is characteristic for each writer is not so much the individual masters of the past that inspired him, as the selection of these traditions. Thus, it is precisely the conjunction of the Tolstoyan and Gogolian traditions in the works of Sholokhov that has extreme importance and significance for Soviet prose. Whereas Tolstoy inspired Sholokhov to a profound analysis of emotions and thoughts, Gogol furnished him many examples of marvelous, everyday humor and pathetic lyricism, in which the author's voice asserts itself.

The Silent Don is a thing of deep poetry. It is not only a historical and psychological novel; it is a lyric epic. Whereas the flowing, emotional digressions of a general nature in *Dead Souls* earned the whole novel the title of a poem in prose, that is likewise applicable in the same degree to *The Silent Don.*

It was primarily the image of Russia that inspired Gogol in his emotional digressions. The author's winged flights of imagination are imbued with ardent patriotism. Likewise, Sholokhov's lyric flights are always marked by warm, filial love for the motherland, for his native silent Don, for the people who give their lives for their native soil. All the "Gogolian patches" in Sholokhov's novel, all the emotional digressions are based primarily upon this fiery patriotism and are imbued with images from the native soil. Let us merely recall Sholokhov's ardent and moving hymn to the steppe in Part VI of *The Silent Don:*

> Beloved native steppe! The bitter wind that settles on the manes of the mares and stallions! The dry muzzle of the horse is salty from the wind, and the horse, sniffing the bitter, salty smell, chews his silky gums and neighs, tasting therein the tang of the wind and the sun! Beloved native steppe under the low Don sky! The forked ravines; the dry valleys; the steep red clay banks; the expanse of feather grass with its beaten-down, nest-like traces of horses' hoofs; the mounds in wise silence, guarding their buried Cossack glory! . . . I bow low and filially kiss thy fresh earth —the Don Cossack, stainless, blood-soaked steppe!

During the course of the eight parts of *The Silent Don,* there are not many of these clearly "Gogolian patches," not more than five or six. But they enter into the fabric of the novel in an absolutely organic union, and they lend lyric wings to the strict objectivity of the narrative, imbuing it with warm, patriotic feeling.

In Gogol these moving digressions are highly emphasized, as if deliberately elevated above "the lowly prose of everyday existence." The living soul of the author, as it were, soars upward from the base and confined world of "dead souls."

Sholokhov packs the pathos of his own speech with the utmost realism. In an excerpt resembling the people's lament for their slain warriors, he paints a heart-rending picture of the bitter lot of a poor, widowed Cossack woman:

> My own, my dear one, tear open the collar of your last shirt! Tear your hair, grown thin from the joyless burden of life; bite your lacerated lips until they bleed; wring your work-scarred hands and beat your head upon the ground on the threshold of your empty hut! For now there is no master in your house, no husband for you, no father for your children. Remember that now there is no one to caress you, nor your orphans, no one to deliver you from poverty and excessive toil; no one to press your head to his breast at night, as you drop overcome with weariness; and no one to say to you as he once said: "Don't worry, Aniska—we'll live through it!" You will never get a husband, for toil, poverty, and children have withered you and made you ugly! Your half-naked, sniveling children will never know a father; you will drag the plow yourself, panting from excessive strain; you will toss the hay from the mower, throw it into the wagon, lift heavy bundles of wheat on your pitchfork, feel something tearing low in the belly. You will then writhe in agony, cover yourself with rags, and bleed to death.

This realistic picture of peasant poverty, blended with the most moving emotions, is characteristic of Sholokhov alone. But the coalescence of the Gogolian and Tolstoyan traditions is, in itself, significant for our literature. Can we not find just this coalescence in Fadeyev's *The Young Guard?* Let us recall the lyrical digression on the hands of the mother which is so reminiscent of the Gogol note.

The romantic patriotism of *Taras Bulba* embellishes Gorbatov's *The Invincibles*. The relations between Taras and his sons in *The Invincibles* are treated on an absolutely new and different basis, as the modern parallel to Taras Bulba, Ostap, and Andrei.

Sholokhov is not alone in his selection of classical traditions. And it is quite characteristic of our time that Gogol's lyric pathos is being perceived primarily as patriotic emotion. And it was Sholokhov, and none other, who set the example in so utilizing Gogol for our literature.

Sholokhov employs the classical traditions neither blindly nor mechanically; he chooses those which most fruitfully and effectively serve to epitomize and give meaning to contemporary reality. And whereas Sholokhov himself has become a living tradition for our literature, our literature must learn from him to select the principles that most enrich the realistic representation and revelation of our life.

It is necessary, in this sense, to mention still another characteristic of Sholokhov's realism that deepens the traditions of classical Russian prose. This is the organic relation of the hero to the world in which he lives. This is not merely the environment, the customary way of life, or the social and ideological relations of the hero—not merely the very obviously embellished atmospheric language. It is rather his perception of the natural coalescence of the hero and the whole world around him, the world of nature in particular.

The life of the Cossack farm, its traditional ceremonies, its peculiar features of daily labor, which are specifically Cossack, including not only peasant but likewise military training, are all plunged into the vast and living world of nature, which is known to Sholokhov's hero in the most minute detail. Apart from this organic unity between the hero and the surrounding world, there is no valid and comprehensive realism.

Sholokhov, with all the richness, psychological complexity, and historical significance of the problem he raises, never ignores the problem of the work, but always integrates it with the entire environment of his world. And if we are to trace the traditions of Sholokhov, this art must be learned first of all.

It is a curious fact that in *The Silent Don* we often encounter the word "world" in the most varied context. "The world had opened before Aksinya in its innermost pulsation." "They live shut off from the whole *blue world* by shutters bolted from within and from without." "This was all that remained to him in life, all that still rooted him to the whole vast world, shining under the cold sun."

For Sholokhov, the world is not an abstract or decorative, poetic word. The world is the organic unity of man with nature, with the environment, with the constantly regenerative currents of life.

It is characteristic that those who "live shut off from the whole blue world" are not real people, but the merchants Mokhov in their degenerate environment; they are not representatives of the great world, but the dying remnants of the dim and stuffy microcosm of the past. And the world "in its innermost pulsation" is revealed to none other than Aksinya, the most striking and inspired heroine of the novel.

Likewise Grigory Melekhov, who loves and understands nature, who knows how to find its secret life and beauty, is in constant communion with the world around him. Grigory's tragic rejection at the end of the novel is emphasized in the image of the world, shining with blinding splendor under the cold sun. The world became cold for Grigory, who had lost the truth of life. The tragedy of Grigory during the entire course of the novel is revealed as his conflict with the historic, progressive movement of the people, and is epitomized in this breach between the hero and the world, which had grown cold for him.

Sholokhov's perception of the world as a unit is concretely revealed in his penetrating portrayal of the natural environment of his heroes.

Entire studies by Hoffenshafer and Kirpotin are devoted to Sholokhov's landscape, to his method of depicting nature in his creative work. Likewise all authors of works on Sholokhov have much to say about this. Each one in his own way underscores the organic bond between nature and life in Sholokhov's heroes. But however we classify Sholokhov's landscapes, whether parallel to the thoughts and experiences of the heroes, or in sharp contrast to them, this task has little value. All these parallels and contrasts must inevitably be mechanical or superficial. The important thing is not whether the emotional storms come from a clear sky or accompany similar, violent manifestations of nature. It is not that each stirring of the soul is necessarily coincidental with a similar commotion in the life of nature. The thing is that with Sholokhov nature is primarily the real embodiment of lifegiving forces, that nature is creative, triumphing over death, decay, and loss, and over the dust and devastation brought into life by war.

This perception of life as eternally creative and eternally regenerative, as vanquishing the tragedies of each personal destiny, lends special power and majesty to Sholokhov's books. The conclusion of Part V of *The Silent Don* is very characteristic of Sholokhov. This part ends with a description of the modest grave of the Red Army soldier Valet, who had been killed by the Whites.

> In the course of a fortnight, the small mound was overgrown with plantain and young wormwood; ears had begun to form on the wild oats; the rape beside it turned a striking yellow; the sweet clover drooped its double clusters; the wild thyme, spurge, and honeysuckle sweetly scented the air . . . and in May the bustards darted near the shrine, beat out a small patch in the blue wormwood, flattened the green flood of ripening couch grass, fighting for the female, for the right to live, to love, to multiply. And a little later, right there beside the shrine, beneath the mound, under the oleaster-like cover of the old wormwood, the female bustard laid nine speckled, smoky-blue eggs and sat on them, warming them with the heat of her body and protecting them with her glossy, feathered wings.

Sholokhov more than once returns to this contrast between poverty, war devastation, and the wantonly blooming, eternally revitalizing and regenerating forces of nature. So Grigory buries Grandfather Sashka beside the grave of his daughter.

> Overwhelmed with memories, Grigory lay down on the grass, not far from this little cemetery so dear to his heart, and for a long time gazed at the majestic expanse of blue sky above him. Somewhere up there, in the heights of that boundless expanse, the winds were frolicking and chilly clouds, gleaming in the sun, were drifting; and on the earth which had just received Grandfather Sashka, that merry ostler and drunkard, life seethed as furiously as ever; on the steppe, creeping like a green flood to the very edge of the orchard, in the thicket of wild hemp beside the poles of an old threshing floor, there sounded the low, incessant clucking of a quail fight, the marmots were whistling, the bumblebees were buzzing, the grass caressed by the wind was rustling, skylarks were singing in the fitful light, and somewhere far off along the dry valley, a machine gun chattered steadily, angrily, and hollowly, in affirmation of the majesty of man's place in nature.

"The majesty of man," as affirmed by the machine gun, by senseless destruction and death, sounds mournfully ironic in this context. But the leitmotif of the epic *The Silent Don* abounds in many tragic fates; this is the pathos of life which cannot be conquered and destroyed, of life which bursts through and exists in spite of carnage and bloodshed, of life in whose name this blood is shed.

Immediately following this scene of ruin, murder, and death, Sholokhov gives us his apotheosis of the exultant springtime regeneration of nature. Immediately after the shocking scene of the humiliation and terrorism inflicted upon the Red Army prisoners is heard Sholokhov's favorite motif of the regeneration of life.

At the very height of the Civil War, when the roads of the steppe were poisoned by the sickeningly sweet stench of corpses from a multitude of wagons with dead bodies, the same motif of the great regenerative power of life again appears in its own right: "Invisible life, fertilized by spring, mighty in its seething throb, unfolded on the steppe."

This leitmotif of eternally revitalized and regenerated life makes even the most tragic of Sholokhov's pages not hopeless but profoundly optimistic.

To speak of Sholokhov's heroes apart from the vast world of nature embellishing and brightening their entire lives would be an utter negation of the very essence of his creative perception of the world. For Sholokhov, the life of man is always one manifestation of the bond between this life and the world as a whole. In this world grandiose historic and social upheavals take place in the life of the people. It is precisely to these decisive and crucial moments in history, disrupting the established way of life, that Sholokhov invariably turns in his work. This process of the disruption of the old and the formation of a new awareness always engrosses the attention of the writer. And *The Silent Don* is the great epic of the Great October Revolution and the Civil War.

The Civil War became the theme of the best books of Soviet literature in the early period. It suffices to mention *Tchapayev* and *Myatezh* by Furmanov; *Zhelezny Potok* by Serafimovitch; *Razgrom* by Fadeyev; *Khozhdenie Po Mukam*[1] by A. N. Tolstoy. Each of these books raises creative problems decisive for the new epoch.

In regard to material, Sholokhov, as it were, chose a comparatively limited task—to depict the Civil War as it occurred among the Don Cossacks. But on the basis of this unique material, he boldly tackled the complex problem of creating a great synthesis of ideological significance.

In tsarist Russia, the Don Cossacks were particularly well-to-do and were granted a number of class privileges; in temper they were considerably more reactionary than the peasantry of Central Russia. It is no wonder that the Don region was called the Russian Vendée. The usual complex class structure of the village—the kulak, the middle-class peasant, and the pauper—was here combined with ideas of Cossack honor, which had been grafted upon them during the centuries, ideas of class prerogative and independence for the Cossacks. Lenin, in speaking of the Don Cossacks, more than once emphasized their reactionary temper. Lenin wrote about the "land of the Cossacks as cut off from all Russian democracy" (Vol. XXI, p. 204), about "the most patriarchal localities with a stratum of the most prosperous farmers as the most class-conscious" Vol. XXIII, p. 52). In his speech at the Extraordinary All-Russian Congress of Railroad Workers in 1918, Lenin, speaking of the victory of the Soviet régime and the defeat of the White Army in the most backward localities, singled out the Don for special attention: "Even on the Don, where more than anywhere else, well-to-do peasants live by hired labor, exploit the labor of others, and engage in a constant struggle with the new peasant settlers ... even there where the peasantry is most exploitive, the people are up-in-arms against this organization of junkers, officers, and property owners" (Vol. XXII, pp. 231-232).

It was on the Don that the Civil War assumed particularly brutal and bloody aspects. The cleavage began in each family. Brother rose up against brother, son against father; the kulaks murdered their sons who had embraced the revolutionary movement of the people.

This direct and brutal aspect of the Civil War on the Don is embodied in the early *Stories of the Don* by Sholokhov: "Lazorevaya Steppe," "Smertny Vrag," "Tchervotototchina," "Prodkomissar," "Semeiny Tchelovek." The naked and intense drama of these stories, with their merciless verisimilitude in depicting the brutalities of the class struggle on the Don, portended a great artist. But the struggle in these early stories was still portrayed in a one-track manner. The heroes have only one trait. They

[1] Translated in the United States as *The Road to Calvary*, eds.

act more than they think and feel. The conflict of ideas is portrayed without any shading. On the one hand are the kulaks, the bitterest enemies of the Soviet régime; on the other the Communists, the poor peasants. There is much bloodshed in these stories and many descriptions of brutal murders and physiological nudity. This is struggle in its most effective expression. The struggle of the old and the new in the conscience, revealed in the difficult and cróoked paths of vaccilation, errancy, and quest for the right path, as an inner contradiction in the soul of a man not yet mature enough to understand the laws of history—this is the theme which Sholokhov has epitomized with real profundity in *The Silent Don*.

Here Sholokhov has set himself an extremely daring and difficult task— to endow the hero with a clearly positive role in regard to character and mental qualities, but, historically, to make him play a negative role.

The Silent Don is a broad historical canvas. And the fate of the Don Cossacks in the Civil War is portrayed in extremely minute and varied detail. Here is the White Cossack officer class, reared in the monarchist traditions—young Listnitsky; here are the big kulaks—the Korshunovs, for whom the Revolution constitutes a threat to their property, and whose attitude toward it was unreservedly hostile; here are adventurers such as Fomin, who were ready to serve any régime, if only to save their lives, ready to plunder the people under any flag; here is the Cossack middle class—the Astakhovs, Anikushka, Prokhor Zykov, and the Melekhov family. The latter had no fierce hatred of the Soviet régime, as had the kulaks; but they, too, zealously guarded their small property and adhered to the Whites, without indulging in any deep political reasoning in this connection. The logic of history—the victory of the Soviet régime—can overcome the resistance of these people and, in the very end, win them to its side.

The Communist agitator among the workers—metal worker Stockman —and the Bolsheviks from the milieu of Cossack paupers—Valet, Kot-lyarov, and Koshevoy—also play their role in *The Silent Don*. The political and ideological line of each of these is drawn with adequate clarity and consistency in this novel.

And Sholokhov, from this varied array of participants in the Civil War on the Don, chooses a hero from the milieu of the well-to-do Don Cossacks, and forces him to tread a difficult and devious path, a path of quest, error, frustration, and lapse.

Turgenev wrote as follows to Slutchevsky in regard to *Fathers and Children*: "My whole story is aimed against the nobility as the leading class. Look closely at Nikolai Petrovitch Kirsanov, Pavel Petrovitch, and Arkady . . . esthetic feeling has compelled me to take the very best representatives of the nobility, thereby to prove my thesis more adequately. If the cream is bad, what of the milk?[2]"

In the person of Grigory, Sholokhov, too, takes the very cream of the

[2] *The First Collection of I. S. Turgenev's Letters,* St. Petersburg, 1885, p. 105.

middle class Cossacks. Grigory is a man endowed with an innate sense of his own worth and a thirst for justice. His participation in the first imperialistic war aroused in him from the beginning a depressing anguish and shame. The first Austrian that he killed obsessed his tortured conscience because he did not understand why he was fighting; he did not see in whose "name" it is worth while to exterminate people. Grigory was instinctively aware of the senselessness of imperialistic carnage. and shortly thereafter in the hospital, Garanzha opened his eyes to the exploitive nature of the war of 1914, to the fact that it was waged in the interests of the ruling clique, while the people in it were merely cannon fodder and cattle fattened for the slaughter, as the tipsy old railroad worker, with bitterly ironic tenderness, informed the men going up to the front. Grigory parted from Garanzha "with open eyes and malevolent," as he put it.

The officers of the tsarist army aroused in Grigory a feeling of anger, contempt, and proud repugnance, from his very first days in the service. He abruptly dismissed the ugly insolence and harsh shouts of officers of any rank in the old army, both when he served as a mere private, and when he had earned, by fraudulent means, his dubious military fame, and he himself commanded a division of the insurgent army. As a private, he decisively rebelled against rough treatment by non-commissioned officers and sergeants major. When, as a division commander, he was called before General Fitzhelaurov, Grigory at once put the irate general in his place, as the latter tried "to dress him down."

Grigory, despite his high rank, always felt like an alien among the officers of the White Army. "With the Whites, at their headquarters, I was an alien, and they always distrusted me. Indeed, how could it be otherwise? The son of a peasant, an illiterate Cossack, how could I be their equal?"

Grigory returned more than once to these thoughts and expressions of his irrevocable alienation among the White officer corps. When Kopylov said he "resembled a Bolshevik," reproached him for his illiteracy, his ignorance of military science, and disdainfully called him a "blockhead," Grigory answered with a veiled threat which he soon carried out:

> "So I'm a blockhead to you. Just wait, give me time; I'll go over to the Reds, and there I'll be worth my weight in gold. Then you had better not cross my trail, you well-mannered and educated loafers. I'll rip out your soul along with your guts."

Grigory regarded the Bolsheviks with interest and a veiled sympathy and respect, even during the time when, because of his own political blindness, he was a commander in the White Army. He was more than once torn with doubts; he more than once inquired painfully of himself if he were not leading his soldiers against the people. More than once he regretted that he had cast his lot with the Whites, with the Cadets, with those who had betrayed the people and flooded the motherland with foreign troops.

Grigory's organic patriotism evokes the natural reaction of indignation when he sees English soldiers treacherously brought into Russia by the White Guardsmen.

> "I see why you hate Fitzhelaurov," Kopylov said to him, "but why this Englishman? Don't you like his helmet?"
> "At Ust-Medveditsa there was something about it I didn't like; he should have worn it somewhere else; I wouldn't let them set foot on our soil."

Grigory's outburst of patriotic feeling, of the true spirit of the people, is revealed with the wonderful humor characteristic of Sholokhov, in the remarkable scene depicting Grigory's nighttime drinking bout with a White officer and the English lieutenant. Grigory listens with interest and sympathy to the Englishman's stories about the Reds, who attacked tanks in their bast shoes. Grigory inquired insistently why it was that Campbell respected the Reds and why he thought that they would beat the Whites. And when Grigory, who was feasting with Campbell in a peaceful and friendly fashion, burst out with his farewell greeting, which seems rather unexpected, coming from an officer of the White Army, we hear the real voice of a Russian man of the people:

> "Go home quick, while you still have your head on your shoulders. I say this to you from the bottom of my heart. Understand? There's no need for you to meddle in our affairs."

Many places can be found in the novel where Grigory Melekhov stands before us as a true son of his people, as a man who commanded an undoubted place in the ranks of those who fought for the Soviet regime. Twice we see Grigory enrolled in these ranks—at the beginning of the Revolution, and later in Budenny's army, where he successfully commanded a squadron; and each time Grigory's seemingly natural participation in the struggle for independence and the rights of his people ended in retrogression, frustration, and desertion to the counter-revolutionary camp.

What prevented Grigory from being a true people's hero? It has been said repeatedly that Grigory's ideological vacillation arose out of the contradictions of his class position, which were typical of the middle-class peasantry. The struggle between the toiler and the property owner engrossed the soul of the middle-class peasant, and ideological inertia and blindness sometimes prevailed at a certain point. Grigory, with an intuitive sense of justice and a keen awareness of his own human worth, embarks upon a quest for reality and seeks new paths, but Garanzha's influence, nevertheless, proved indecisive.

> "Your Cossack, sucked upon his mother's milk and nurtured during his whole life, won the upper hand over the great human truth."

The provocative rumors spread by the Whites, that the Bolsheviks were encroaching upon what was from time immemorial Cossack land, as well as upon the traditional ideas of Cossack honor, which must be relinquished for the sake of the new *muzhiks* who were coming to the Don to take away the Cossacks' fertile land, were the factors that induced Grigory to take his false step. He turned aside from the true path and joined the Whites, deluded by the illusory dream of an independent Cossack state.

The inert, animal attitude of the property owner is echoed in Grigory's argument with the Cossack paupers Valet and Koshevoy.

> "With you, it's another matter," Grigory said to Valet. "You've got nothing ahead of you, nothing behind you—you can just get up and take off. Once Valet, always Valet! You've got nothing but the shirt on your back!"

And Grigory, deceived by the provocative speeches of the White Guardsmen, joined their ranks to defend his land. "We will fight for it as we would for our sweethearts," he thought.

And though Grigory says that war is not decided by science but by the cause for which you are fighting, he himself did not, in essence, understand just what cause he was fighting for, first on one side and then on the other. In reality—and this is the most horrible thing about the mistakes and oscillations of Grigory—he is indifferent to the aims of one side or the other. He is tired of war; he avidly desires peace, his family, his own plot of land, which he wants to cultivate with his own hands. Grigory is obsessed with an almost physical craving to work on the land.

Grigory dreamed so passionately and blindly of this farm labor on his own land that he utterly forgot the times in which he lived; he forgot that the social hurricane had not yet ceased to rage, that the battle continued, and that his beloved land must still be won from the enemy.

A perfect foil for him is Mikhail Koshevoy, who during this time, while working on the land and reveling in the happiness of being with his beloved young wife, himself cuts short this placid and blissful existence, because his duty as a citizen calls him, because he feels a deep sense of responsibility to the Party and to the people. He understands that there must still be a long struggle for the victory of the people's régime.

> "I started farming a little too early; I was in too much of a hurry," thought Mishka in vexation, reading the regional newspaper reports from the fronts, or listening to the tales of demobilized Cossack Red Army men in the evenings.

But Grigory, in his reckless and elemental yearning for the land, became indifferent to the outcome of the Civil War. Both the Reds and the Whites seemed to him equal obstacles to a peaceful life.

"I've served my time. I don't want to serve anybody any more. I've fought too much in my life, far too much, and I am utterly exhausted in spirit. I'm fed up with it all—with the revolution and the counter-revolution. I want to live near my children, to work on my farm—that's all."

And each time that Grigory wishes to remain on the sidelines of the struggle, life inexorably hurls him into the very thick of events, to his shame and ruin.

Grigory himself said: "You must either join the Whites or the Reds. You can't stay in the middle—you'll be crushed." But in life, he attempted to remain in the middle, and he was morally crushed.

A feeling of maladjustment and perplexity always obsesses Grigory when he finds himself on the side of the Whites. His innumerable confessions are sprinkled throughout the entire novel:

"I drift like a snowstorm on the steppe."

"War has taken everything out of me. I am afraid of myself. Look into my soul; there is a blackness there, like an empty well."

"I have always envied such men as the younger Listnitsky, or even our Koshevoy . . . . To them everything was clear from the very beginning, but even now nothing is clear to me. Both of them had straight roads before them, their goals were in sight; but ever since 1917 I have been going round in circles, reeling like a drunkard. I left the Whites, but I didn't join the Reds. I have been drifting like dung in a hole in the ice."

Grigory recognizes his own duality, but he cannot overcome it. And when the decisive step is needed, when the time comes for him to answer to the Soviet régime for his former treacheries, he, in his own words, feels his blood "turn to water on the day of reckoning."

Though he understands the utter hopelessness of the White movement, the moral filth and avowed criminality of Fomin's gang, he nevertheless joins it with hidden loathing and the secret hope of leaving at the slightest opportunity.

Sholokhov is implacable toward his favorite hero. He forces him to endure this shame too, since the bandit gang is the final and inevitable stage on the path of errancy and apostasy.

It was the height of moral punishment for Grigory to encounter the condemnation and hatred of the people, when the old Cossack woman looked at him with open revulsion as an accomplice of Fomin's band of thieves.

"There's no getting rid of you, damn you!" He hears the malevolent farewell words of the old woman. "They're right," he thought. "Why the devil do they need us! Nobody needs us; we keep everyone from working and living in peace."

"And to think that I have cast my lot with such people," he thought, gripped by longing, sorrow, and anger at himself, at his whole hateful life.

Grigory flees from Fomin's band and joins Aksinya, but retribution is inevitable. Fate deprives Grigory of much more than life. It deprives him of Aksinya, for whom he has lived, and who is dearest and most important to him. The death of Aksinya, which has turned the sun black—the symbol of Grigory's implacable sorrow—consummates his tragic fate.

Grigory Melekhov's end is much disputed—whether Sholokhov did the right thing in bringing his favorite hero to such a morally hopeless dénouement or whether some other outcome was possible for him.

If we take the actual historical fate of the middle-class Cossack, disregarding the artistic design of the novel, his outcome was certainly otherwise. Grigory Melekhov, as a representative of the middle-class Cossacks, could have taken a very different road and could have ended his life on either side of the conflict. He could have come to ruin by remaining with the Whites, as did his brother Petro, or he could have died as a heroic fighter for the Soviet régime, as did Kotlyarov, Valet, or Podtelkov. He could have found the courage to answer to the Don *Tcheka,* instead of riding off to Fomin's band. He might not have encountered such a one-track mind as that of Mikhail Koshevoy, who dismissed him abruptly and impatiently in Nagulnov's manner, failing to discern Grigory's great human value, which would make it worth while to inculcate and develop in him true love for, and confidence in, the Soviet régime.

It is known that the path of the middle-class Cossack in the Civil War was extremely complicated and tortuous. After a series of errancies and frustrations, the majority of the middle-class Cossacks came over to the Soviet régime.

I repeat that Grigory's real-life destiny could have been compounded in many ways. But the destiny of Grigory Melekhov as the hero of *The Silent Don* could and should have been shaped only as Sholokhov embodied it. This is because the character of Grigory Melekhov is much more than a mere empirical representation of the path of the middle-class Cossack in the Civil War.

The fate of Grigory Melekhov personifies the tragic path of a man who did not perceive the progressive movement of history, who did not understand that in an epoch of world-shaking upheavals it is impossible to stand aloof from events, impossible to defend one's own personal and property rights when they are at variance with the interests of the entire life of the people.

Sholokhov has newly raised and solved the problem of the tragic in our literature. Whereas in bourgeois literature the tragedy of the hero is always the tragedy of a man who became the victim of society or who outstripped his age and was misunderstood by it, a man who enters into conflict with the old reactionary world outlook, the tragedy of a hero who contends with society—in the literature of victorious socialism, it is the tragedy of errancy, the tragedy of a man who has divorced himself from the purposeful, progressive path of the future.

Sholokhov chose a character imbued with human charm, force, justice, subtlety of feeling, and spiritual purity; and he led this hero along the paths of errancy.

Lenin, in speaking of the gigantic social upheavals which the Revolution brought to the world, made repeated reference to the fact that the traditionally entrenched ideas of an entire way of life were being demolished.

Sholokhov has portrayed this demolition for us with tremendously tragic force. Sholokhov has carried the struggle of the outworn versus the new, the reactionary versus the progressive, into the conscience and soul of his hero, and he has interpreted this struggle as a tragic struggle. But in contrast to the tragedy of the old bourgeois art, the tragedy of the hero does not coincide with a tragic and hopeless attitude toward the world.

If the tragic hero is the victim of society and of his epoch, all reality portrayed by the author is tragic.

If the tragedy is presented as the tragedy of an erring man who does not understand the progressive movement of history, this man alone is doomed to tragic ruin. The false path which brought him to ruin is condemned. But reality itself, from which he detached himself, is still progressive and forward-looking, still an affirmation of life.

This new form of tragedy is, in itself, the highest form of affirmation, of a creative and perspective concept of reality. The personal tragedy of Grigory Melekhov is tremendous. The losses in the great struggle between the new and the old are incalculable. But even through the tragic sorrow of these losses, which are portrayed with such mastery, emerges the novel's exultant leitmotif—the victorious verity of the people, the verity of history.

Sholokhov furnishes a daring and profound revelation of all the hardships of this struggle, both in action and in consciousness. This form of hero portrayal is more conducive to the affirmation of progressive ideas than any schematic demonstration of these ideas with stereotyped characters to illustrate them.

The tragedy of errancy is a psychologically complex and dialectically focused method of depicting the conflicts of life. Sholokhov has endowed it with all the daring and truthfulness inherent in socialist realism.

Through the character of Grigory, Sholokhov was one of the first to epitomize a problem which, up to the present time, is still one of the most essential ideas of our literature. This problem is the relation between the personal and the social—the private and the historical—the awareness of the fact that man, in an epoch of great historical upheaval, must fight for the right cause; otherwise he is doomed to moral extinction.

It is a curious fact that this vital bond between the personal and the historical was formulated with amazing insight and rare foresight by Belinsky: "If the whole purpose of our life consisted only in personal happiness and our personal happiness consisted in one love alone, life would actually be as dreary as a desert heaped with coffins and broken hearts; it would be a hell, before the horrible existence of which the poetic images of the earthly inferno sketched by the genius of the stern Dante would pale into insignificance. . . . But . . . in addition to the inner world of the heart, there still remains for man the great world of life, the world of historical contemplation and social activity—that great world where thought becomes a cause and high feeling a feat, and where the two opposing banks of life—the *here* and the *there*—merge into one solid firmament of historical progress and historical immortality. . . . This is the world of unremitting labor, of unending conception and creation— the world of eternal struggle between the past and the future."[3]

In this struggle Grigory remained on the side of the past, and the world of the future rejected him.

Still one more feature attesting to Sholokhov's great artistic skill is characteristic of him. Sholokhov ends not with a period but with a multitude of periods. He does not bring the life of his hero to its physical conclusion. The line of errancy and apostasy is ended. Grigory himself brought it to an end; he threw down the weapon criminally turned against the Soviet régime, and returned "to answer for his actions." He does have a blood tie with the future—his son Mishatka, whose fate will be different. He does have a chance to purge himself and to earn the forgiveness and confidence of the Soviet régime. There is also the grievous but deserved possibility that he will confess his crimes and answer for them with his life.

Such a hero, about whom and for whom we desire to think, has much about him that is good and substantial.

Any continuation of Grigory's destiny, whether it be death or moral regeneration, would prove, in photographic terms, to be "overdeveloping." In the novel it is not Grigory Melekhov's life, but the whole tragic course of his errancy that comes to an end.

The power of Sholokhov's realism consists in the fact that the character of Grigory Melekhov is not a rationalistic idea, not a transparent symbol, but a self-contained human being, embodied in a living character —in all the truly vital contradictions of life, in all the psychological complexity of inner motivation. It consists in great and striking individuality set off in sharp relief against a broad social and historical background.

Sholokhov's thought is never crystallized in set formulas. It is infused in all the life it epitomizes.

Sholokhov is profoundly historical, despite the fact that his historical heroes proper—Krasnov, Kaledin, and Kornilov, as well as the specific

[3] V. G. Belinsky, *Works in Three Volumes,* Vol. III. Goslitizdat, Moscow, 1948, pp. 266-67.

historical episodes in the Civil War on the Don, are considerably less successful than his fictional heroes and scenes.

The character of Grigory Melekhov was unusually fruitful in illustrating the great and tragic psychological disintegration that occurred in the epoch of the Civil War. The daring and difficult experiment of portraying a hero, positive in his own human charm but negative in the historical role that he played, was appropriate for precisely that period.

It is quite clear that by the 1930's, in the period of the new, organic disintegration of the village, during the time of collectivization, it would be historically wrong to choose a hero such as Grigory Melekhov. At this time a morally positive hero could not have been posited upon such a low political level. In the 1930's a man opposed to the Soviet régime could have been none other than an avowed class enemy, such as Polovtsev or Ostrovtsov in *Virgin Soil Upturned.* In this epoch a positive hero could not have followed a deliberately perverse, reactionary path. But he might have chosen the wrong method of performing his allotted tasks. He might have used wrong methods in the struggle for the right cause.

Sholokhov's keen sense of reality prompted him to create the remarkable character of Nagulnov—a man of upright and passionate nature, possessed by a revolutionary pathos ("I am altogether committed to world revolution"), but devoid of flexibility and tact in working with people, and capable of carrying a needed and useful idea to the point of absurdity, through his one-track policy.

The character of Nagulnov is depicted in vivid contradiction. On the one hand, he desires in the purity and warmth of his heart to be useful to the Party and the people; on the other hand, he is irascible, unable to grasp actual circumstances. Nagulnov is prepared to give his life for the idea of collectivization. But, at the same time, he is capable of having an ignorant peasant shot because the latter slaughtered his cattle. He has a crude idea of collectivization. Upon his initiative, the peasants not only give their cattle to the *kolkhoz,* but also their fowl, down to the last cock.

The mistakes and failures of Nagulnov are portrayed through the prism of humor. Humor is a powerful weapon in the hands of a great artist like Sholokhov. He, like few others, understood that humor, as well as tragedy, is one of the most expressive instruments of art in depicting the contradictions of life. If something is funny, it means that something is not right; and for this purpose the merciless form of satire is not always necessary. Humor is good precisely where you have overall sympathy or love for the characters and events depicted, and you see their weaknesses; where you have the pervasive tolerance of an affectionate person and you poke fun at their foibles.

In *Virgin Soil Upturned,* Nagulnov's weakness in Party tactics, his deviations from the correct line, and the anecdotal form used are also portrayed by Sholokhov through the prism of humor. Witness the wonderful scene in which the collectivized roosters fight in the *kolkhoz* barn, and the crowd of village idlers arranges cock fights on *kolkhoz* land.

Nagulnov's asceticism, his desire to rule out private life altogether, until socialism is victorious throughout the world, is also humorously portrayed.

And in conjunction with this, Sholokhov attains the true heights of tragedy in the scene depicting Nagulnov's expulsion from the Party, in his portrayal of the prejudiced and bureaucratic attitude that prevails toward a living human being who is in need of timely guidance, but who is the soul of honor and ardently devoted to the cause of the Party.

In *Virgin Soil Upturned,* Sholokhov, with the power and insight of a great and intelligent artist, is not satisfied to depict the bare externals of the struggle between the new and the reactionary—with events alone. Here, as in *The Silent Don,* he depicts this struggle in terms of conscience.

Kondrat Maidannikov, a typically honest, middle-class peasant who accepted the Soviet régime in toto and understood the usefulness and the necessity of *kolkhozi,* but who had not yet expunged the feeling of the property owner from his soul, replaces the great and tragic figure of Grigory Melekhov. Kondrat suffers because his bulls, his property that he has cared for with his life's blood, do not belong unreservedly to him, but have become the common property of the *kolkhoz.* Kondrat, who cannot overcome his particular weakness for his own "property," is a living character, who aptly personifies the actual contradictions of reality.

Sholokhov depicts life in flux and in crisis, emphasizing what is difficult and contradictory, at times even what is morbid; but he never loses his sense of perspective toward the realistic, progressive trend of the historical process.

In *Virgin Soil Upturned,* rural collectivization is portrayed not only in the general form of the tense, dramatic conflict for the *kolkhozi,* but also in the concrete form of practical business affairs. We readily perceive the direct and practical task undertaken by Sholokhov. To a certain extent, *Virgin Soil Upturned* is a graphic and exemplary handbook on how and how not to organize *kolkhozi.*

And this practical, professional approach has not impoverished, but on the contrary, has enriched the art of Sholokhov. He discovered a new quality, a quality typical of our literature. He speaks of processes that prevail in our life—in particular, the process of rural collectivization —with businesslike precision, attention, and exactitude.

His representation of the tasks implicit in labor, construction, and organization, and his close attention to the methods employed in their solution have provided the material and the pathos not only for a production blueprint but for a great artistic canvas as well. And in this sphere, too, the creative work of Sholokhov is a vital and fruitful tradition for our time.

The theme of the Great Patriotic War against fascism is embodied in Sholokhov's story *The Science of Hatred,* and in the yet unfinished, epically conceived canvas *They Fought For Their Motherland.*

It is really too early to speak of this work, because we have seen only isolated fragments and episodes from it; and we cannot trace the cardinal feature of Sholokhov's art, the portrayal of man in his movement, mutation, and development. But even these isolated episodes testify to the power of Sholokhov's talent, to his skill in portraying with majestic simplicity the deep tragedy of the people, their supreme heroism and deep-rooted love for the motherland, and their exceptional courage and endurance in battle.

Ordinary Russian people figure in this epic of Sholokhov's: the peasant Zvyagintsev, the agronomist Streltsov, and the miner Lopakhin. They pass through the bitter "science of hatred" in the grim and tragic situation at the beginning of the war—in the period of retreat. They survive it as a personal sorrow, as a grievous error, for which each one is responsible. With characteristic power, Sholokhov depicts the scene in which the people, personified by the stern and angry old woman, pass judgment upon the retreating army, and, as exactingly as a parent or a master, rebuke its soldiers.

"You're in this fight, so fight as you should, you sinners; don't drag the enemy after you through the whole country. Don't expose your old mother to shame before the people."

And thereupon Sholokhov graphically portrayed with what zeal and tenacity, with what passion and concentration our people fought—how great was their vital power and love for their native soil, how great was their faith that they would be victorious despite all obstacles.

On every page Sholokhov portrayed the heroism and inflexible determination of the Russian people, not only in scenes of battle but in scenes of everyday life during the war. The people displayed their true temper in battle, on the operating table in the hospital, in fording rivers, on long marches, in digging entrenchments, and in their brief rest periods. They are bound together by strong soldierly friendship, spiced with salty, dirty jokes, and at times with profanity. Through the external crudity of their relations emerge their exceptional warmth, their humanity, and their skill in helping a comrade at a difficult moment. They are ready to sacrifice themselves for the common cause.

After being seriously wounded, Streltsov voluntarily left the hospital and returned to the front, because he knew how precious each man is in battle, and how the ranks of his unit had been decimated.

These people, in contrast to Grigory Melekhov and many participants of World War I, know full well why they are fighting.

Even at the height of the war and the devastation, these people think of construction, of the harvest, and of life. In a begrimed and scorched ear of wheat growing alone at the edge of a fire-blackened field, the peasant Zvyagintsev sees the embodiment of all the criminal and destructive work of the enemy.

> During the long months he spent at the front, Zvyagintsev saw much of death, of the people's grief and suffering; he saw villages demolished and razed to the ground; blasted factories, formless piles of brick and rubble where cities had recently stood; he saw orchards crushed to death by tanks and mangled by artillery fire; but on this day he chanced to see for the first time during the whole war the warm ripe grain on the vast expanse of the steppe, and his soul was filled with yearning.

This is the organic, typically Sholokhovian bond between man and the soil, between man and the life-giving forces of nature. The leitmotif of viable nature blooming in defiance of death and devastation emerges more than once in Sholokhov's epic.

The full-blooded and very human humor, invariably inherent in Sholokhov, likewise serves in this epic as an affirmation of life and of the invincible spirit of the heroes defending their motherland. This is evidenced not only in the strong, friendly jokes which almost constantly salt the dialogue of the heroes, but also in Sholokhov's art of selecting comic detail which reveals with particular mirth the hardiness and tenacity of the characters he has depicted.

The thing that is new to Sholokhov in this war epic, in comparison with *The Silent Don* and even with *Virgin Soil Upturned,* is the fact that historic events of tremendous importance are portrayed not only in the growth and mutation of the principal heroes emerging against the background of the whole narrative, but in a series of typical pictures and episodes revealing the character of the people as a whole— as it was manifested in this greatest of world wars.

The most precious thing for contemporary literature in the works of Sholokhov is the realistic daring and profundity of his depiction of reality, his skill in selecting the most crucial and historically decisive moments in the life of our country and in portraying these in all their multiplicity of aspect, contradiction, and complexity of human relations. It is his skill in depicting the organic bond between man and the surrounding world; it is his powerful and creative affirmation of life which is convincing and tangible precisely because Sholokhov paints for us the most difficult, and at times the most tragic and tense, moments of life, from which the people, at the cost of enormous losses, grit, and tenacity, finally emerge victorious.

ii. The Russian Question, by Konstantin Simonov

Konstantin Simonov (1915-   ), already well known for his wartime play, *The Russian People* (1942) and for his novel, *Days and*

Nights (1945) about the battle of Stalingrad, attracted much attention in 1947 with his controversial play, *The Russian Question.*

The significance of *The Russian Question* is that it marks the advent in Soviet Literature of the "Cold War" between the Soviet Union and the United States. Although the plot was undoubtedly conceived by the author during his visit to the United States in 1946, its publication and performance were manifestations of Soviet retaliation against the "Truman Doctrine" of March 2, 1947.

Below is a translation of a review of *The Russian Question,* which demonstrates not only the content of the play but also official Soviet reaction to it. The review is from the trade-union organ, *Trud,* April 3, 1947.

The Russian Question*

Konstantin Simonov, as a writer, is distinguished by a remarkable feeling for the pulse of the times, that profound sense of reality, which arises only from the complete identification of the writer with his age. Simonov's last play, presented in the Lenin *Komsomol* Theatre, describes the morality of the American capitalistic press, its back-alley gossip, its lies, and slanders. This is not a new theme in literature. The renowned American writer, Upton Sinclair, wrote a book dealing with his country's press, and called it *The Brass Check.* The brass check is a pin which the guest of the American house of prostitution receives upon payment of several dollars for the use of its facilities. Romain Rolland termed the capitalistic press "a monster, a new Minotaur, to which the whole world pays tribute."

Thus, in his play, our author describes secrets which have long ceased to be secrets. The significance of this play does not consist alone in its exposé of the methods of slander and systematic deceit employed by the reactionary press.

Following the horrible trials of the recently concluded war, the people of the entire world are reflecting upon social orders, upon the meaning of personal and social freedoms, and upon what may prove beneficial or detrimental to mankind. And this is not an abstract interest in ethical problems, but a conviction born from bloody experience that today's post-war world must be put in order and rebuilt on real democratic principles. Simonov's play also touches upon personal problems and personal freedom, or more specifically, the lack of freedom in the capitalistic world.

Who are these journalists, Preston, Hardy, and Murphy? They are

* Play by K. Simonov on the Stage of the Lenin Komsomol Theatre by M. Tcharny

mute slaves. They are allowed to open their mouths only in order to utter that which is profitable to the newspaper owners, McPherson and Hearst. Preston, Hardy, and Murphy are identical in their slavery, but Simonov also reveals their human diversity. Hardy is not entirely similar to Preston, and Preston differs from Murphy.

Hardy is definitely a low, bankrupt journalist. For the ten dollars necessary to feed his family, he is ready to pen any slander. He is not so stupid that he does not comprehend the villainy of what he is doing. But this man is already accustomed to a world in which everything is bought and sold, and he has reached such a state of cynicism that he regrets only his lack of personal talent, which prevents him from selling himself at a higher price.

Preston, the editor of the foreign department of a McPherson newspaper, is a Philistine, but somewhere in the depths of his soul there gnaws the worm of doubt, and he is troubled by his outraged conscience. Preston endeavors to console himself with the fact that if his boss removed him from his job and put another in his place, neither the Soviet Union, which is defamed by this newspaper, nor anyone else "would benefit."

Murphy is a straight-forward, good-natured, disinterested man in his personal affairs, but he is on the staff of a newspaper of the notorious Hearst. His friends half-jokingly refer to him as "the bandit of the pen," but these are bad jokes: working for Hearst certainly means abetting banditry. Murphy realizes this, but does not have the strength to tear himself away from the Hearst clique. He considers himself a hopeless case, begins to drink, and embarks on desperate adventures in which he almost consciously seeks death.

Simonov's play is written with obvious sympathy toward the American working class, with compassion for the good people who are placed in circumstances which unmercifully kill all the better elements in them. This play's best personification of the noble qualities of the American people is the journalist, Smith. Smith was a correspondent in the Soviet Union during the worst years of the war. Together with our soldiers, he lay in the trenches at Gzhatsky. He saw Stalingrad, and wrote a fine, truthful book on what he had witnessed. This book was published in due time, and enjoyed great success. American readers remembered Smith as an objective author. And now when the war has ended, when the American monopolists are concerned with the expansion of their influence over the entire world, when they have again brought into the limelight the banal Goebbels bugaboo of a Bolshevik threat, McPherson changes his course. He wishes to exploit the good name of journalist Smith for his slanderous attacks upon the USSR. With this objective in mind, he engages Smith to go to the USSR and write a book on the subject: "Why the USSR Wants Another War."

For such a book, Smith is promised $30,000. The advance enables him to buy a suburban home on the installment plan, and to furnish it according to Jessie's taste, Jessie who has long dreamed of family comfort and who now marries Smith.

The plot of the play is built upon the fact that Smith, having accepted McPherson's offer, does not write a slanderous book but rather gives an honorable, truthful account of the USSR. Indeed, can the American, Smith, permit himself the luxury of being honorable? Of course! Of course! is the reply. Think what you wish, write what you wish, but who will publish it for you? The press belongs to the McPhersons, and they have their own ideas. The editor of a liberal newspaper who is in sympathy with Smith, but frightened by the all-powerful monopolists, is also compelled to reject Smith's articles.

Everything that Smith possesses is taken away from him—the home, which he did not have time to pay for in full, the car, the furniture. Even his wife, Jessie, deserts him. She supposedly loves Smith, but she loves luxury and comfort even more. Smith is left alone. But it is made clear that his solitude is imaginary, for many, perhaps the majority of the American people, sympathize with him.

The play ends with the words of Smith himself, which express confidence that he will find his place, not in the America of McPherson and Hearst, but in another America, the America of Abraham Lincoln and Franklin Roosevelt. For there are two Americas.

Thus, "the Russian question" becomes a question which tests the honesty of many people, not only in America, but also in other capitalistic countries.

Smith is not a Communist; he says this himself. But to people with the interests and psychology of McPherson, it seems incredible and suspicious that a man should turn down the dollar for the sake of his honor. What politics is this! Saltikov-Schedrin once wrote: "Many believe that if a man is able to snatch a handkerchief out of his neighbor's pocket unnoticed, this is allegedly enough to establish his political reputation." The McPherson ideology and practice are based on the art of adroitly filching from all the neighbors' pockets that which is most valuable. They are so accustomed to these "politics"—and have so prospered by them, that of course they regard their manner of living as the ideal system in the human dormitory. And here is this Smith . . .

No, there is actually nothing extraordinary in this. The McPhersons regard Smith's action, not as the mere eccentricity of one man, but as a revolt against all their morality, against their whole system of domination over the individual and over society. This is why "the Russian question" becomes the proving ground for many problems in capitalistic America, problems which would seem to have no direct bearing on the Russian question.

The Lenin *Komsomol* Theatre properly understood this play (staged by S. Birman) as a completely realistic work, and interpreted it in this manner. The Americans of "The Russian Question" are average middle-class people, and it is easy to imagine that under other conditions their lives would have been different. Under favorable conditions, their fine natural traits would have been developed and not suppressed.

I. Bersenev's portrayal of McPherson is very convincing. This man, with his simple and even gentle manners, is far removed from the typical, bourgeois villain. Nevertheless, the actor conveys the feeling of the brutality and cynicism of this capitalist, who is surfeited with wealth and power.

The characterizations of Hardy, the reporter of scandalous gossip (by A. Shatov), and the correspondent of the Hearst newspaper, Bob Murphy (V. Bragin), are successful. A. Shatov, in his minor role, depicts Hardy not only as a contemptible creature who would sell himself, but also as a victim. Bragin in the role of Murphy, has created an extremely lively, interesting portrayal of a good-natured, clever man, who is finally ruined by the unprincipled and mercenary atmosphere of the bourgeois press. The old publisher, Kessler, appears in the play merely to deliver one monologue. He does not act, but merely talks while sitting in a chair. Nevertheless, actor V. Maruta succeeded in presenting this narrative so as to create a most colorful character, who fits into the production as a natural and indispensable element.

A. Pelevin plays the most important role of Smith with great restraint, achieving great expressiveness at times, but the restraint of Pelevin's acting often makes his performance static. There is little movement in his Smith. He plays the role as if everything were known to Smith beforehand, not only McPherson's reaction to his book, but also Jessie's departure, and in general, everything that happens, from the first scene to the conclusion. He is such a wise, skeptical philosopher, almost indifferent in his awareness of what goes on about him.

It seems to us that there should be a great deal more warmth, spontaneity, and more of a feeling of indignation in Smith; for in the end, it was not he who deceived McPherson, but McPherson who deceived Smith, with his natural ideas and expectations. It is not without purpose that Smith states that for a long time he naïvely believed that there was only one America. "Now he knows there are two Americas." Smith reaches this conclusion as the result of a trying experience. We would like to see this emotional experience more clearly expressed in the production.

The role of Jessie, Smith's wife, is extremely interesting in concept. V. Serova provides sympathetic portrayal of a woman tired of an unsettled life and restless feelings, who yearns for true love and family comfort. Nevertheless, Jessie's departure upon the disclosure of the collapse of Smith's material security, and her entire farewell scene, with its completely theatrical fainting, seems to lack sufficient artistic preparation. The author, perhaps, shares the blame for these unconvincing scenes.

It seems that A. Kozlova has extracted everything possible from her incidental role as the stenographer, Meg. Gould, one of the editors of a McPherson newspaper, is, according to the author's concept, an extremely singular figure. This former labor-union "leader," renegade and traitor is even more unprincipled and rapacious than McPherson. He considers it profitable to pose as a "man of the people." In the actual performance, something else is conveyed. B. Plotnikov portrays him as a neurasthenic, with sad eyes, unsuccessful in business and love, more easily injured than able to injure others. This interpretation makes Gould appear as a transient character, "a passerby."

But these are particulars which will perhaps be overcome in the theatre in the process of further work on the play. But, on the whole, "The Russian Question" at the Lenin *Komsomol* Theatre is a performance of great cultural content, interest, and significance, pertinent to the issues of the day.

III. *Doctor Zhivago,* by Boris Pasternak

The publication in the Western world (1957-1958) of the novel, *Doctor Zhivago,* by Boris Pasternak (1890-1960), had strong repercussions both inside and outside the Soviet Union. Rejected by the magazine, *Novyi Mir* for publication in the USSR, it appeared first in Italy (Giangiacomo Feltrinelli Editore, Milano, Italy), and shortly thereafter in many other languages. Although Pasternak was awarded the Nobel Prize in Literature, in October 1958, ostensibly for his poetry, the Soviet furore evoked by this timely recognition forced him to decline the honor.

The reasons for the rejection of *Doctor Zhivago* in the Soviet Union are not far to seek. In the first place, forty years after the October Revolution of 1917 he states unequivocally that Russia's only salvation and that of the world lies in Christianity. Second, he attacks collectivism, in which the individual is submerged, labelling it (gregariousness) "a haven for mediocrity." Third, Pasternak defines the Soviet revolution as a soldiers' revolt led by professional revolutionaries (Bolsheviks) who are only at home in turmoil and chaos. On the other hand, he commends the Revolution of 1905 as an "idealized university-type revolution," to which he would like to return. In the October Revolution, he suggests that the end failed to justify the means.

Below are excerpts translated from *Doctor Zhivago* (Ann Arbor: The University of Michigan Press, 1958). A complete English translation was published in the United States in 1958 (New York: Pantheon).

"There are talented people," said Nikolai Nikolayevitch. "But groups and societies of every sort are in fashion nowadays. Any kind of gregariousness is a haven for mediocrities, whether it is founded on Soloviëv or Kant or Marx. Only individuals seek the truth, and they sever relations with everyone who doesn't love it well enough. Is there anything left in this world that deserves our loyalty? Very little. I think one should be loyal to immortality, which is another word for life, a stronger word. One must remain true to immortality—one must be true to Christ! Ah, you're grimacing, my poor man. Again you've failed to understand a thing."

"Hmm," roared Ivan Ivanovitch. Thin, blonde, unstable as quicksilver, with a small insidious beard that made him look like an American of the days of Lincoln (he was constantly grabbing it in his hand and nibbling the tip). "Of course, I have nothing to say. As you know, I look at these things quite differently. While on the subject, tell me how they unfrocked you? I have wanted to ask you for a long time. I bet you were frightened? They didn't pronounce anathema on you, did they?"

"Why change the subject? However, why not? Anathematize me? No, they don't do that nowadays. It was unpleasant, and there were consequences. For instance, I was banned from the civil service for a long time, and I was not permitted to go to the capitals. But these are matters of no significance. Let us return to the subject under consideration. I said, one must be true to Christ. Now I'll explain. You don't understand that one can be an atheist, not know whether or not there is a God, or why there should be one, and at the same time realize that man does not live in a state of nature, but in history, and that history as we understand it today began with Christ, and that the Gospels are its foundation. What is history? It is the product of centuries of systematic effort to solve the mystery of death and to overcome it in the future. That's why people discover mathematical infinity and electromagnetic waves; that's why they write symphonies. You can't make progress in this direction without something to uplift you. For these discoveries, you must have spiritual equipment. The basic facts of this equipment are contained in the Gospels. Here they are: In the first place, love for one's neighbor, which is the supreme form of vital energy. Once it fills the heart of man it must overflow and spend itself. Moreover, the chief components of contemporary man, without which he is unthinkable, are, namely, the idea of freedom of the individual and the idea of life, as sacrifices. Mind you, all this is still exceedingly new. There was no history in this sense among the ancients. Theirs was the bloody swinishness of the cruel and pockmarked Caligulas, who had no realization of how inferior every slaveholder is. Theirs was the boastful dead eternity of bronze monuments and marble columns. Time and the generations of mankind only began to breathe freely after the coming of Christ. Only after His advent did men begin to live for their progeny. Man does not die in the street any more under the fence, but in his own home in history, while he works at full swing for the conquest of death. He dies dedicated to this theme. Ouf! How worked up I am, as they say. But I might as well be hitting my head against a wall."

"Metaphysics, my dear fellow. My doctors have forbidden it, my stomach won't digest it." . . .

. . . "Just think, what a time we are living in! [Zhivago] And you and I are living in these days. Such an unprecedented thing happens only once in a century. Think of it, the whole of Russia has had its roof ripped off, and we and all the people are out under the open sky! And there's nobody to spy on us. Freedom! Real freedom, not just in words and demands, but it has dropped from heaven, beyond all expectation. Freedom by accident, by mistake.

And how tremendously at sea everyone is! Have you noticed? As if crushed by his own weight, by the discovery of his own power.

"I say, go on ironing. Keep quiet. You aren't bored? I'll change the iron for you.

"Last night I observed a meeting. An astonishing sight! Mother Russia is on the move, she can't stand still, she's on the go and she can't stop, she's talking and she can't cease. And it isn't as if only people are talking. Stars and trees come together and converse, flowers philosphize at night, stone houses hold meetings. It is strongly reminiscent of the Gospel, isn't it? Just as in the days of the Apostles. You remember what St. Paul says? You will speak with tongues and prophesy. Pray for the gift of understanding."

"I know what you mean about stars and trees holding meetings. I know what you want to say. I myself have experienced it."

"Half of it was due to the war, the rest to the revolution. The war was an artificial break in life—as if existence could be postponed for a time (what nonsense!). The revolution burst forth involuntarily, like a sigh suppressed too long. Everyone was revived, reborn, experienced a change and a transformation. You might say that everyone has been through two revolutions—one, his own personal revolution—the other, the general revolution. It seems to me that socialism is a sea—the sea of life, the sea of originality—into which these separate, individual revolutions must flow like rivers. I said the sea of life, the life that can be seen in pictures, transformed by genius, creatively enriched. But now people have decided to experience it, not in books, but in themselves, not abstractly, but in practice." . . .

. . . The same group [of Zhivago's thoughts] also included loyalty to the revolution and admiration for it. This was revolution in the sense in

which it was accepted by the middle classes and in which it was understood by the students, followers of Blok, in 1905.

In this group, these familiar, long-held ideas also included the symptoms
of something new, promises and omens which had appeared on the horizon
before the war, between 1912 and 1914, in Russian thought, Russian art
and Russian destiny, the destiny of all Russia and his own, Zhivago's.

After the war, one could wish to return to these ideas, in order to
renew and continue them, just as one longs to return home after being
absent.

In the second group, the subject of his thought was also new, but how
different, how unlike the first! These new things were unfamiliar, the past
did not pave the way for them, they were involuntary, realistically prescribed, new, sudden as an earthquake.

Such a new thing was the war, with its bloodshed and horrors, its
homelessness and savagery. New, too, were the experiences and worldly
wisdom that the war taught. New, too, were the remote towns to which
the war carried one and the people with whom the war brought one
into contact. The revolution itself was new—not the idealized university-
type revolution of 1905, but this one, the present one, born of the war,
bloody, a soldier's revolution, which did not give a hoot for anyone, led
by professionals who understood this elemental movement, namely, the
Bolsheviks. . . .

. . . "During the third year of the war people became convinced that
sooner or later the line of demarcation between the front and the rear
would vanish, that the sea of blood would rise until it reached everyone
of us, and that it would submerge those sitting out the war, as well as
those in the trenches. This flood is the revolution.

"During its course it will seem to you, as it seemed to us in the war,
that life has stopped, that everything personal has come to an end, that
nothing happens in the world anymore but killing and dying; and if we
live long enough for the records and memoirs of this time to appear, and
read these reminiscences, we shall be convinced that in these five or ten
years we have experienced more than others have in a whole century.

"I don't know whether the people themselves will rise and sweep forward like a tide or whether everything will be done in their name. No
dramatic proof of such a tremendous event is required. I'll be convinced
without this. It is of little value to dig into the causes of Cyclopean
events. There are none. Family quarrels have their own genesis, and after
people pull each other's hair and smash the dishes they are at their wits'
end to figure out who was the first to start it. All that is truly great has
no beginning, like the universe. Suddenly it is present, without any origin,
just as if it had always been there or had dropped from heaven.

"I also think that Russia is destined to become the first socialist state
in the world. When this happens, we'll be stunned for a long time, and
after awakening we'll never retrieve even half of our lost memories.

We'll forget what preceded what and we'll not bother to look for a non-existent explanation. The newly established order will surround us with the habitualness of a forest on the horizon or the clouds overhead. It will encircle us from every quarter. There will be nothing else." . . .

"You saw Strelnikov?" she asked quickly . . . "They say he is not a Party member."

"Yes, I think that's true. What is it about him that draws people to him? He is doomed. I think he'll come to a bad end. He will atone for the evil he has brought about. Revolutionaries who take the law into their own hands are horrifying, not as evil doers, but because they are like a mechanism out of control, like derailed trains. Strelnikov is as mad as all of them, although his madness did not emanate from books, but was a product of his experience and suffering. I don't know his secret, but I'm certain he has one. His alliance with the Bolsheviks is an accident. As long as they need him and he goes along with them, they will tolerate him. But the moment the need is past, they will cast him aside without compunction and trample him, as they have done before with many military experts."

"You think so?"

"Absolutely."

"And is there no way out for him? By running away, for instance?"

"Where, Larisa Fedorovna? This was customary at one time under the Tsarist regime. But just try to do it now."

"It's a pity. By your tales, you make me feel sorry for him. And you've changed. You used to judge the revolution less harshly, without irritation."

"That's just the point, Larisa Fedorovna. There are limits to everything. After all this time, something should have been accomplished. But it turned out that those who inspired the revolution understand nothing but turmoil and change, and no matter how much bread you feed them, they want something on a global scale. The building of new worlds, transitional periods, are for them an end in themselves. They are not trained for anything else, they don't understand anything else. And do you know why these eternal preparations are so useless? Due to the lack of specific, ready-made abilities and to mediocrity. Man is born to live, not to prepare for life. And life itself, the phenomenon of life, the gift of life, is so excitingly serious! So why substitute for it a childish harlequinade of immature devices, with the Chekhovian flights of schoolboys to America? But enough of this. Now it's my turn to ask questions. We were approaching the city on the morning of your revolution. Were you involved in it?"

"Oh, I should think I was! Of course. There were fires all around us. We ourselves were almost burned to death. I told you how the house swayed! There's an unexploded shell in the yard by the gate to this day. Looting, bombardment, outrages, as is the case with any changeover of power. About that time we were already schooled and accustomed to it. It was not the first time. And the things that went on under the Whites! Murders on the sly for personal revenge, extortions, an outright orgy! Yes, but I haven't told you the main thing. Our Galiullin! He turned out to be an unusually big shot under the Czechs. A sort of Governor-General."

"I know. I heard about it. Did you see him?"

"Very often. How many lives I saved, thanks to him! How many I concealed! One must be fair to him. He acted irreproachably, chivalrously, not like all those underlings, Cossack captains, and village policemen. But at that time it was the small fry that set the tone and not the decent people. Galiullin helped me a great deal, and I am thankful to him. We are old friends. As a young girl, I often visited the yard where he grew up. Railroad workers lived in the house. In my childhood I had a close-up view of poverty and hardship. As a result, my attitude toward revolution is different from yours. It's closer to me. It's so much a part of me. But all of a sudden he became a colonel, this boy, the son of a yard-keeper. Or even a White general. I am of civilian background and don't know much about the ranks. And by profession I'm a history teacher. Yes, that's how it was, Zhivago. I helped many people. I used to go to see him. We talked about you. I have always had connections and protectors in every government, and grievances and losses under every regime. It's only in bad books that the living are divided into two camps and never come into contact with one another. But in real life everything is so interwoven! What a hopeless nonentity one would have to be to play only one role in life, to occupy only one place in society, always to stand for one and the same thing! Ah, so this is where you are?" . . .

. . . "But first, the ideas of a social perfection, as they have come to be understood since the October Revolution, do not enthuse me. Second, all this is still far from being put into practice, and merely talking about it has cost such seas of blood that possibly the end does not justify the means. Third, and this is the main thing, when I hear about the transformation of life. I lose my self-control and succumb to despair.

"Transformation of life! Only people who, although they may be worldly wise, have never understood life, have never felt its spirit, its soul, can reason in this fashion. For them existence is a lump of coarse material which has not been ennobled by their touch, which stands in need of processing. But life can never be a material, a substance. Life, if you want to know, continually renews itself, perenially remakes itself, constantly changes and transforms itself; it is much superior to our stupid theories."

"And yet if you attended the meetings and mingled with our remarkable, splendid people, I make bold to state that it would raise your spirits. You would not suffer from melancholia. I know where it comes from. You are depressed because we are being pummeled and you do not see a ray of light ahead. But, my friend, one should never succumb to panic. I know about things that are far more terrible, which have happened to me in person—temporarily they cannot be told—and yet I do not lose heart. Our reverses are purely temporary. Kolchak's ruin is inevitable. Mark my words. You'll see, we'll be victorious. Cheer up."

"No, this is impossible!" thought the doctor. "What childishness! What shortsightedness! I repeat time and again that our views are diametrically opposed; he seized me by force, and holds me against my will, and he imagines that his reverses must disturb me and that his calculations and hopes imbue me with cheerfulness. What blindness! The interests of the revolution and the existence of the solar system are for him one and the same thing."

Yuri Andreyevitch was convulsed with pain. He said nothing in reply and only shrugged his shoulders, without trying to conceal the fact that Liveria's naïveté exhausted his patience, and he controlled himself with difficulty. Nor did Liveria fail to notice this.

"Jupiter, you are angry, which means that you're not telling the truth," he said.

"Will you understand, understand once and for all, that all this means nothing to me: "Jupiter," "don't succumb to panic," "whoever says A must say B," "The Moor has done his work, the Moor can go." All these clichés, all these expressions, mean nothing to me. I will say A, but I won't say B, even if you tear yourself to pieces and burst. I'll admit that you are the torchbearers and liberators of Russia, that without you she would perish, wallowing in poverty and ignorance. Nevertheless, I have no respect for any of you and I spit on you, I hate you, and you can all go to the devil.

"Those who mold and shape your thinking are sinning with proverbs, but they've forgotten the main one, that they cannot force someone to like them, when they've gotten into the habit of liberating and conferring happiness especially on those who do not ask for this. Most likely you think that for me there is no better place in the world than your camp and your society. Very likely I should even bless you and thank you for keeping me in bondage, for liberating me from family, son, home, business, from everything I hold dear, and that makes life worth living." . . .

58. Nikita Sergeyevitch

Khrushchev (1894-   )

THE FOLLOWING BIOGRAPHICAL SKETCH of Nikita Khrushchev appeared in the *Bol'shaya Sovetskaya Entsiklopediya,* Second Edition, Vol 46 (1957), pp. 390-391.

KHRUSHCHEV, NIKITA SERGEYEVITCH (born April 17, 1894): An outstanding figure in the Communist Party and Soviet government, a loyal disciple of V. I. Lenin, member of the Presidium of the Central Committee [CC] of the Communist Party of the Soviet Union [CPSU], First Secretary of the CC of the CPSU. Member of the Presidium of the Supreme Soviet of the USSR.

N. S. Khrushchev was born into a miner's family in the village of Kalinovka, Kursk Gubernia. From his early years he worked as a hired shepherd and later as a machinist in the factories and mines of the Donbas [Donets Basin]. In 1918, N. S. Khrushchev joined the Communist Party. He took an active part in the Civil War on the Southern Front. Following the Civil War, he worked in a Donbas mine, and later studied in the workers' faculty of the Donets Industrial Institute. N. S. Khrushchev engaged in active Party work in the regiment, in the mine, and in the workers' faculty, and was more than once elected Secretary of the Party cell. After completing the workers' faculty, N. S. Khrushchev became a leading Party worker in the Donbas, and later in Kiev. In 1929 he enrolled at the J. V. Stalin Industrial Academy in Moscow, where he was elected Secretary of the Party Committee.

From January, 1931, N. S. Khrushchev was Secretary of the Bauman, and later of the Krasnaya Presnya, Party District Committee in the city of Moscow. From 1932 to 1934 N. S. Khrushchev served first as the Second, and later as the First Secretary of the Moscow City Party Committee and then as Second Secretary of the Moscow Provincial Party Committee; in 1935 he was elected First Secretary of the Moscow Provincial and City Party Committees, where he worked until 1938. During these years, N. S. Khrushchev carried on extensive organizational work in connection with the implementation of Party and government plans for the socialist reconstruction of Moscow, for the organization of public services and amenities in the capital, and for the improvement of the living conditions of workers and employees.

In January, 1938, N. S. Khrushchev was elected First Secretary of the CC of the Communist Party of the Ukraine; from March to December, 1947, he served as Chairman of the Council of Ministers of the Ukrainian SSR, and in December, 1947, he was re-elected First Secretary of the CC of the Communist Party of the Ukraine, where he worked until December, 1949. Having headed the Ukrainian Party organization for twelve years, N. S. Khrushchev played an outstanding role in rallying the Communists of the Ukraine for the solution of the tasks of the development of the national economy and culture, and in improving the welfare of the workers.

During the Great Patriotic War, 1941-1945, N. S. Khrushchev was in the active army and carried on extensive work at the front, was a member of the Military Council of the Kiev Special Military District, Southwest Command, of the Stalingrad, Southern, and First Ukrainian fronts. N. S. Khrushchev actively participated in the defence of Stalingrad and in the preparations for the rout of the Fascist-German troops at Stalingrad.

Simultaneously with his work on the front lines, N. S. Khrushchev, as Secretary of the CC of the Communist Party of the Ukraine, carried on extensive work for the organization of a nationwide partisan movement in the Ukraine against the Fascist-German usurpers.

In the postwar period, N. S. Khrushchev conducted important work in organizing the struggle for the reconstruction and further development of the national economy.

From December, 1949, to March, 1953, N. S. Khrushchev was Secretary of the Party Central Committee and First Secretary of the Moscow Provincial Party Committee.

Since 1934, N. S. Khrushchev has been a member of the Party Central Committee. In 1938 he was elected an alternate member of the Politburo of the Party CC, and in 1939, after the Eighteenth Party Congress, a member of the Politburo of the Party's Central Committee. At the Nineteenth Party Congress (1952), N. S. Khrushchev delivered the report, "Changes in the Statutes of the All-Union CP (b)." At the Congress he was elected a member of the CC of the CPSU, and at the plenary session of the CC, a member of the Presidium of the CC of the CPSU and Secretary of the CC of the CPSU. In March, 1953, the joint plenary session of the CC of the CPSU, the USSR Council of Ministers, and the Presidium of the Supreme Soviet of the USSR deemed it necessary that N. S. Khrushchev should concentrate on the work of the Central Committee of the CPSU, in view of which he was relieved of his duties as the First Secretary of the Moscow Provincial Committee of the CPSU.

In September, 1953, a plenary session of the CC of the CPSU elected

N. S. Khrushchev First Secretary of the Central Committee of the Communist Party of the Soviet Union.

At the Twentieth Congress of the CPSU (1956), on February 14th, N. S. Khrushchev delivered the report of the CC of the CPSU, and on February 25th, at a closed session of the Congress, he reported on "The Cult of the Individual and Its Consequences." At the Twentieth Party Congress, he was elected a member of the CC of the CPSU and at the plenary session of the CC a member of the Presidium of the CC of the CPSU and First Secretary of the CC of the CPSU.

N. S. Khrushchev is Chairman of the Bureau of the CC of the CPSU of the RSFSR.

The trips of N. S. Khrushchev, together with other leading figures of the USSR, to the Chinese People's Republic, the Polish People's Republic, Yugoslavia, India, Burma, Afghanistan, Great Britain, and other countries, and his participation in the Geneva four-power conference of the heads of state [July, 1955], were important landmarks toward strengthening peace and friendship among peoples.

For great services in directing economic construction and also for successful fulfillment of Party and government tasks in the Great Patriotic War, N. S. Khrushchev has been awarded three Orders of Lenin, the Orders of Suvorov First and Second Class, the Order of Kutuzov first Class, The Order of the Patriotic War First Class, the Order of the Red Banner of Labor, and three medals.

By a decree of the Presidium of the Supreme Soviet of the USSR, April 16, 1954, for outstanding services to the Communist Party and Soviet people, N. S. Khrushchev was awarded the title of Hero of Socialist Labor and presented the Order of Lenin and the "Hammer and Sickle" gold medal on his sixtieth birthday.

NOTE: The following supplement to Krushchev's biographical sketch appeared in the BSE's *Yezhegodnik (Yearbook)*, 1962, pp. 620-621..

In 1957 N. S. Khrushchev was awarded the Order of Lenin and a second "Hammer and Sickle" medal for outstanding service in working out a plan and implementing measures for the reclamation of the virgin lands.

In 1959 he was awarded the International Lenin Prize for strengthening peace among peoples.

At the Twenty-Second Congress of the CPSU in 1961 Nikita Sergeyevitch Khrushchev was elected to the CC of the CPSU. In 1961 he was awarded the Order of Lenin and a third "Hammer and Sickle" gold medal for outstanding service in guiding the creation and development of the rocket industry, science and technology, and for the successful accomplishment of the world's first cosmic flight of a Soviet man on the sputnik *Vostok,* which opened a new era in the conquest of outer space.

59. Khrushchev's visit to the United States (September 1959)

KHRUSHCHEV'S TOUR OF THE UNITED STATES in September, 1959, has never been adequately evaluated. From his own speeches, it is clear that he was by no means correctly informed on conditions in this country. His visit marked a turning point in his outlook on East-West relations. The impression is given that Khrushchev was America-struck, and that he has never been the same since that visit. Just as Peter the Great opened a window to Europe, history may yet record that Khrushchev opened a window to America. The American impact on the Soviet Union noticeably increased. Khrushchev has continued to recommend to his own people that they should adopt methods and techniques in agriculture and industry that have proved so successful in the United States. Since to Red China the United States was Enemy Number One, Khrushchev's visit to this country undoubtedly imperilled Sino-Soviet relations on the eve of the tenth anniversary of the Red Chinese victory over Chiang Kai-shek, and helped to produce the rift in the "indestructible" alliance. In the United States, the main theme of Khrushchev's speeches was coexistence and the relaxation of cold-war tensions.

Below are excerpts from one of Khrushchev's speechs in the United States and from his address to the people of Moscow on his return to the Soviet Union. These are from *World Without Arms. World Without Wars,* by N. S. Khrushchov[*sic*], Book 2 (Moscow: Foreign Languages Publishing House, 1959), pp. 95, 100, 104, 319-320, 320-321.

Speech on Arrival in Washington, September 15, 1959

...All nations are deeply interested in preserving and consolidating peace, in peaceful coexistence. War augurs no good to anyone. Peace is of benefit to all peoples. That, in our opinion, is the cardinal principle which statesmen of all countries should act upon, in order to meet the hopes of the peoples.

We have come to you with an open heart and with good intentions. The Soviet people want to live in peace and friendship with the American people. There is nothing to prevent the relations between our countries from being built up as relations between good neighbours. The Soviet and American peoples, as well as other peoples, fought well together against the common enemy during the Second World War, and crushed him. In peacetime we have more grounds and greater opportunities for friendship and co-operation between the peoples of our countries. . . .

. . . We should like to reach an understanding with your Government on questions of vital importance. Such questions are many. But I should above all like to mention the questions of relaxing international tension and eliminating the "cold war," of disarmament, a German peace treaty, world trade and better relations between our countries.

I think the main subject of our talks with the President will be the problem of eliminating the "cold war" and promoting peace, of easing international tension. Recently your President said that thought should be given to the question of how much longer the arms race and the state of tension in international relations could continue and whether the world had not reached a point where there might be an explosion. We fully share the dissatisfaction with the existing state of world affairs and the concern voiced in that statement. . . .

. . .The Soviet Union is for the development of international relations along the principles of peaceful coexistence. These principles were bequeathed to us by Vladimir Ilyich Lenin, the great founder of the Soviet state. And we are faithful to these principles. We hold that differences in world outlook should not impair relations between countries. Close economic and cultural contacts should be established between all countries. That will help nations and statesmen to know and understand each other better. It will facilitate the establishment of mutual trust and peaceful co-operation. . . .

Speech at the Mass Meeting in Moscow
On Return From the United States
September 28, 1959

. . .Our time can and must become the time of the triumph of great ideals, the time of peace and progress. *(Prolonged applause.)*

The Soviet Government has long since perceived this. And that is why we have repeatedly proposed to the Great Powers to organize a meeting between Heads of Government in order to exchange views on urgent international issues. When we made these proposals, we believed in the power of human reason. We believed that with a rational approach, representatives of different political views, of states with different social systems, could, in the interests of peace, find a common language in order to arrive at correct solutions to the problems agitating all humanity today. In our age of tremendous technological progress, in circumstances when there exist states with different social systems, international problems can be successfully solved only on the basis of the principles of peaceful coexistence. There is no other way. Those who say that they do not understand what peaceful coexistence is, and are afraid of it, are wittingly or unwittingly helping to further the "cold war," which is bound to spread unless we intervene and stop it. It will reach such a point of intensity when a spark may at any moment set off a world conflagration. In that war much will perish. It will be too late to discuss what peaceful coexistence is when such terrible means of destruction as atomic and hydrogen bombs, and ballistic missiles, which are practically uninterceptible and can carry nuclear weapons to any point on the globe, go into action. Not to reckon with this means to close one's eyes and stop one's ears, to hide one's head in the sand as the ostrich does at the approach of danger. If we humans imitate the ostrich and hide our head in the sand, then, I ask you, what is the use of having a head if it is incapable of averting the danger to life? *(Prolonged applause.)*. . . .

. . . From this lofty rostrum, before you Muscovites, before my whole people, my Government and Party, I must say that President Eisenhower displayed wise statesmanship in appraising the present world situation, displayed courage and determination. (Stormy applause.) Notwithstanding the complex situation prevailing in the United States, the President, a man who enjoys the absolute confidence of his people, proposed an exchange of visits between the Heads of Government of our two countries. We give him due credit for this important initiative aimed at strengthening the cause of peace. *(Prolonged applause.)* In taking this step, he was confident that we would accept the hand he proffered us, inasmuch as we have repeatedly addressed both President Eisenhower and other Heads of Government to that effect. And the President was not mistaken. *(Applause.)*

Dear comrades, it gives me great satisfaction to report to you that we have fulfilled part of our arrangement with President Eisenhower concerning the exchange of visits. At the President's kind invitation we have visited the United States of America, where we have had some important meetings and talks. . . .

60. the University of the

Friendship of Peoples

TO PROMOTE SOVIET INTERESTS in the developing countries
of Asia, Africa, and Latin America the University of the Friendship
of Peoples was founded in Moscow in 1960, with Professor Serge
Rumyantsev, Doctor of Technical Sciences, as Rector. The first public announcement of this inter-cultural propaganda project was made
by Khrushchev at the Indonesian National University, during his visit
to Southeast Asia (*Pravda,* February 24, 1960). The new university
was located in a former military academy, which the further demobi-
lization of the Soviet armed forces made available. In some respects,
the project is reminiscent of Stalin's Communist University of the
Toilers of the East, established in 1922 under the Commissariat of
Nationalities and designed to train Communist cadres for revolution
in Asia. Friendship University was renamed the Patrice Lumumba
University in 1961, after the assassination of the pro-Soviet Congo-
lese leader lent considerable propaganda value to his name.

It is still too early to tell whether the University of the Friendship of Peoples will prove to be any more permanent and successful
than Stalin's project of the twenties. Most of the students accepted by
Lumumba University would not have been eligible for scholarships
in Western universities or for enrollment at other Soviet institutions
of higher learning. All of them required preliminary linguistic and
academic training before they could qualify for specialized study—
undoubtedly one reason for their so-called "segregation" in a separate
institution. The Soviet government has displayed unusual sensitivity
in regard to Lumumba University, especially since 1963, when friction
between Soviet and African students evoked charges of racial dis-
crimination and led to much adverse comment abroad. Lumumba
University is nevertheless an ambitious and expensive project through
which the USSR hopes to train, both scientifically and ideologically,
many of the future leaders of Asia, Africa, and Latin America.

The article below, by L. Tachalin, written before the trouble occurred, is from *Soviet Union* (No. 146, 1962), p. 33.

Friendship University: Two Years Old

The Asian, African and Latin American countries need college-trained personnel to carry through economic and cultural development and to build a new life. With training facilities at home deplorably short so far, knowledge has to be acquired abroad.

Young people of Africa, Asia and Latin America who wanted a higher education and could afford it set out for London, Paris, Heidelberg or New York. It took a lot of money. Two years ago a new address appeared. Thousands of letters from all parts of the world bore it: "Patrice Lumumba Friendship University, Moscow, USSR." This institution is unique among the higher schools of the world.

"It was very hard at first. On all sides I heard a language I did not understand at all. I thought I would never be able to learn it. But in three months, with the help of the teachers, I could already express myself in Russian and understand it when spoken. Now I am a student in the department of agriculture. The first semester has ended, the first exams have been passed."

Thus writes G. D. Senasinghe, a first-year student from Ceylon, in his department's newspaper, "Agrobiologist."

Patrice Lumumba University was founded in 1960 with the chief object of helping the countries of Asia, Africa and Latin America to train their own specialists. A non-governmental institution, it is sponsored by such organizations as the Union of Soviet Societies for Friendship and Cultural Relations with Foreign Countries, the Central Council of Trade Unions and the Soviet Afro-Asian Solidarity Committee.

The first applicants came to Moscow two years ago (1960). Their fare to the USSR was paid by the University. Tuition at the University is free. Besides, the students are given a monthly grant, free textbooks, free medical treatment and free accommodation at holiday homes and health resorts.

Some 1,300 young men and women from seventy-six countries are enrolled in the University's seven departments. They spend the first year in the preparatory department, studying Russian and subjects from the secondary school course. Students who have not had a regular school education go through a somewhat longer preparatory period. Then the student chooses which department he wishes to enter: engineering, history and philology, agriculture, medicine, physico-mathematical and natural sciences, economics and law. The course is five years for medical students and four years for the others.

What demands are made of the student? Only one: that he study diligently. That is what Premier Khrushchev said in his speech at the opening of the University. "Study diligently, don't waste a single day, don't miss a single opportunity to acquire knowledge, to study science and engineering."

The University has an experienced teaching staff. Among the professors and assistant professors there are twenty-three holding Doctor's degrees and seventy with Candidate's degrees. As the students advance into the senior years the teaching staff will be enlarged considerably. Professors will be invited from abroad to lecture and conduct seminars. A post-graduate department is to be opened.

Lectures and classes start at nine in the morning. As a rule, the students have three subjects a day. Here is a day's schedule in the engineering department:

9 to 10:45 (with 10-min. break): Technology of metals.
Classroom work in groups of 15 to 20.
11 to 12:45 (with 10-min. break): Higher mathematics.
Lecture, to audience of 100 to 150.
13 to 14:45 (with 10-min. break): Russian
Classes of three or four students.

At three in the afternoon classes end, but many students stay on in the University buildings. Some visit the library (which already has more than 80,000 volumes), others go to study rooms or laboratories (where they will always find a teacher to give them any help they need). We came across Clovis Vilanova, a student from Brazil, of the physics and mathematics department, finishing a technical drawing. "My ambition," he told us in excellent Russian, "is to become a physicist." He has been in Moscow a year and a half. "Naturally, I'm very pleased. Brazil has few specialists in physics."

Perhaps the most characteristic thing about the students at Friendship University is their zeal, one might even say their obsession, for acquiring knowledge. They sit up late in the laboratories. The experimental workshops are never empty; virtually a machine-building factory in miniature, they have the facilities for building a motor car, if need be.

Another feature is that the students do not limit their interests to any narrow speciality, bearing in mind that their underdeveloped countries need personnel with versatile knowledge and skills.

One should not get the impression, however, that the students are bookworms interested only in lectures and seminars. They go in for sports, attend the theatre and visit recreation centres. They spend their winter and summer vacations in a variety of ways. Bsaes Mohamed Abdel-majid, a medical student from Tunisia, made a two-week trip with friends to the Ukrainian city of Kharkov last winter. He was greatly impressed by what he saw in one of Kharkov's largest factories, at the Polytechnical Institute, and in the city in general. Young Kharkovites showed him about;

together with them he spent some of the time relaxing in the surrounding countryside. Meanwhile, at holiday homes near Moscow, several dozen of Mohamed's colleagues were playing table tennis, learning to ski, watching television, and dancing.

The students have founded associations of compatriots—for example, the Association of Latin American Students—and regional organizations. Yet all the young people proudly call themselves Muscovites, and they have made many friends in the city's factories, offices and schools.

There are various, self-government bodies: the councils of the University, the departments, the hostels and the club, and the board of the athletics society. The councils, elected bodies made up of students and members of the teaching staff, decide on matters relating to studies and recreation. For instance, on the initiative of the council of the phsyico-mathematics department it has been decided to set up a science club.

The spirit of internationalism is something not included in the University curriculum but the students learn it fast. The young people from different countries and of different races are like brothers. "Patrice Lumumba Friendship University is a good instrument of mutual understanding between nations of the world," says Tamrat Endailalu of Ethiopia, a future geologist.

What prospects lie ahead?

The number of applicants is tremendous. As many as 43,000 applications were filed for the 500 places available in 1960. A new complex of University buildings is in the blueprint stage. A student town—an international town of learning—will arise.

In a few years the first graduates will go out into life with their Friendship University diplomas.

NOTE: Attendance at Lumumba University has increased steadily since 1960. In 1966, the university had a teaching faculty of 900 members, and an enrollment of 3,600 students from 82 countries in Asia, Africa, and Latin America. The first class of 228 students from 46 countries was graduated in 1965 and another class of 470 students from 59 countries was graduated in 1966. In 1966 over 55% were studying engineering or medicine, fields of vital importance to emerging nations. These foreign students receive handsome stipends from the Soviet government: 80 rubles per month in the preparatory school; 90 rubles per month during regular academic training; 125 rubles per month for those with superior academic records; and 150 rubles per month for graduate students. This exceeds the stipend to Soviet students enrolled there, which ranges from 50 to 70 rubles per month.

61. no coexistence in ideology and the arts

FOLLOWING STALIN'S DEATH IN 1953, the process of de-Stalinization was accompanied by a relaxation of the rigid controls over literature and the arts characteristic of the Zhdanov period. The Khrushchev regime was soon confronted by a dilemma resulting from the application of the principle of ideological coexistence to the arts, as well as to international relations. This threatened to undermine the whole ideological structure on which the Communist Party was based. From time to time, Khrushchev found it necessary to prescribe limits to the freedom of expression of writers, artists, and musicians, many of whom proved ready and willing to abandon the Party line. He also found it advisable to bar unrestricted criticism of the Stalin era.

One of Khrushchev's most effective pronouncements, from which the excerpts below are taken, was his speech of March 8, 1963, at a Meeting of Party and Government Leaders With Workers in Literature and the Arts (*Pravda* and *Izvestia,* March 10, 1963, pp. 1-4). 1963. *The Current Digest of the Soviet Press* (Vol. XV, No. 10, April 3, 1963, pp. 7-13; and No. 11, April 10, 1963, pp. 6-12), published weekly at Columbia University by the Joint Committee on Slavic Studies appointed by the American Council of Learned Societies and Social Science Research Council. Reprinted by permission.

...The Building of Communism and the Tasks of Artistic Creativity. The activity of writers, artists, composers, sculptors and film and theater workers is constantly in the field of vision of the Party and the people. And this is fully understandable. We live in a time when literature and art, as Vladimir Ilych Lenin foretold, have become an inseparable part of the affairs of the entire people. . . .

Communism is being built by the labor and only by the labor of millions. That is why the Party exerts every effort so that the entire Soviet people—workers, collective farmers, engineers, designers, technicians, teachers, physicians, agronomists, scientists, and those engaged in all branches of culture, literature and art—will participate in the construction of communism in a single monolithic labor collective. . . .

In the battle for communism that we are waging, the education of people in the spirit of communist ideals is of the greatest importance. And this constitutes the main task of our party's ideological work at the present time. We must bring forward in combat order all the types of the Party's ideological weapons, among which belong such powerful means of communist education as literature and the arts. *(Applause.).* . . .

The literature and art of socialist realism has attained great heights of artistic creation, has a rich revolutionary tradition and enjoys world renown. In all the Soviet republics wonderful works, great spiritual values, have been created in which the peoples of our country justly take pride. . . .

Remember how in its time our people armed themselves with Demyan Bedny's poetry. During the Civil War years, when the Soviet people were defending the world's first socialist workers' and peasants' state in bitter combat with world imperialism, the Red Guards, Red Army soldiers and partisans went into battle with Demyan Bedny's songs on their lips. Those songs were accessible to all, were comprehensible to everyone, even the illiterate peasants, in the ranks of the Red Army. . . .

Only outstanding works of great revolutionary, creative enthusiasm reach to the depths of the soul and consciousness of a person and arouse in him lofty civil feelings and a determination to devote himself to the struggle of the people's happiness. The authors of such works deserve and are worthy of the people's gratitude. It is to the creation of works of such high ideological content and artistic impact on the minds and feelings of people that the Communist Party calls writers, artists, composers and film and theater workers. *(Prolonged applause.)*

Our people need a militant revolutionary art. Soviet literature and art are called upon to re-create in bright artistic images the great and heroic time of the building of communism, to reflect truthfully the assertion and victory of new, communist relations in our life. The artist must be able to see the positive elements, to rejoice at these positive elements that form the essence of our reality and to support them; at the same time, it goes without saying, he must not overlook negative manifestations, all the things that hinder the birth of the new in life.

Everything, even the very best thing, has its shadowy side. And the very best person can have flaws. The whole issue is how life's phenomena are approached and from what positions they are evaluated. As they say, you find what you look for. An unbiased person who actively participates in the conscious activity of the people will see both the good and the negative in life objectively, will correctly understand and accurately evaluate these phenomena and will actively support the advanced, the major things, those that have decisive significance for social development.

But he who regards our reality from the point of view of an observer

on the sidelines cannot see and re-create a truthful picture of life. Unfortunately, it happens that some of the representatives of art judge
reality only by the smell of the latrines, depict people in a deliberately
ugly way, paint their pictures in dark colors that can only plunge people
into despondency, ennui and hopelessness, and portray reality in conformity with their own preconceived, distorted, subjective imagination of
it, according to their own far-fetched, anemic concepts. . . .

The makers of the film ("Ilyich's Zastava") orient the viewer toward
the wrong segment of youth. In their life, their labor and struggle our
Soviet young people are continuing and enlarging the heroic tradition of
the preceding generation, which proved its great devotion to the ideals of
Marxism-Leninism in the years of peaceful construction and at the fronts
of the Patriotic War. Our youth are well portrayed in A. Fadeyev's novel
"The Young Guard." And it is a great pity that S. Gerasimov, who made
a film from this novel, did not advise his pupil, M. Khutsiyev, to show in
his picture how the wonderful tradition of the Young Guards lives and
is being developed in our youth. . . .

*Party Spirit and Kinship With the People Are the Most Important
Principles of Our Art.* In recent years writers and artists have devoted
great attention in their creative work to the period in the life of Soviet
society connected with the Stalin cult. All this is fully understandable
and proper. Works have appeared in which Soviet reality in those years
was illuminated truthfully from Party positions. One can cite as example
A. Tvardovsky's poem "Horizon Beyond Horizon," A. Solzhenitsyn's
story "One Day in the life of Ivan Denisovich," some of Ye. Yevtushenko's verses, G. Chukhrai's film "The Clear Sky" and other works.

The Party supports genuinely truthful artistic works no matter what
negative sides of life they may deal with, if they help the people in their
struggle for a new society and consolidate and strengthen their forces. . . .

Indeed, the years of the cult of the individual left grievous consequences. Our party has told the people the whole truth about this. But in
addition, it should be borne in mind and remembered that these years
were not a period of stagnation in the development of Soviet society, as
our enemies imagine. Under the leadership of the Communist Party and
under the banner of the ideas and precepts of the great Lenin, our
people were successfully building and did build socialism. By the efforts
of the Party and the people, the Soviet Union was turned into a powerful
socialist state that withstood the severest trials of war and victoriously
completed battles unprecedented in history with the utter defeat of the
fascist hordes. *(Stormy applause.)*

Therefore we say that those writers who treat the evaluation of that
stage in the life of our country extremely one-sidedly, trying to present
almost all events in a gloomy light, to paint them in dark colors, are
acting incorrectly. There are still plenty of writers who prefer to
draw their material from rubbish heaps and issue such works as truthful

illuminations of the life of the people. The advocates of this point of view regard all works that speak of the achievements of our people, of the positive element in life, as "varnishing" works. It is impossible to agree with such assertions. It is known that there was prettification in some works, and the Party has stated its negative attitude to this phenomenon. But certainly not everything in those times was bad; the people showed heroism in that period of socialist construction too, and therefore we cannot smear tar on everything.

It is necessary to rebuff those who like to stick the tag of "varnisher" on the writers and artists who portray what is positive in our life. And what should be the name for those who pick out only the bad in life and describe everything in dark colors? Obviously, they should be called tarrers. The good in life should be properly reflected in literature and art. . . .

When you read I. G. Ehrenburg's memoirs, you are struck by the fact that he depicts everything in somber shades. Comrade Ehrenburg himself was not subjected to persecution or restrictions during the period of the cult of the individual. The fate of such a writer as, for example, Galina Serebryakova, who spent many years in prison, was quite different. But despite this she maintained fortitude of spirit and fidelity to the cause of the Party, and immediately after her rehabilitation she joined creative life, took up her weapons and created works needed by the people and the party. *(Stormy applause.)* . . .

The question is often raised now as to why the violations of legality and abuses of power were not disclosed and halted during Stalin's lifetime and whether this could have been done then. Our viewpoint on this question has been fully and quite clearly explained more than once in Party documents. Unfortunately, there are still people, including some in the arts, who try to present events in a distorted light. Therefore today we must concern ourselves once again with the Stalin cult.

It is asked, did the leading cadres of the Party know of, let us say, the arrests of people at the time? Yes, they knew. But did they know that people who were innocent of any wrongdoing were being arrested? No. This they did not know. They believed Stalin and did not admit the thought that repression could be applied against honest people devoted to our cause. . . .

The Party has implacably condemned and condemns the gross violations of Leninist norms of Party life, the arbitrariness and abuse of power, committed by Stalin. For all this, however, the Party renders Stalin's services to the Party and the Communist movement their due. We believe even today that Stalin was devoted to communism; he was a Marxist, and this cannot and must not be denied. His fault was that he committed gross mistakes of a theoretical and political nature, violated Leninist principles of state and Party leadership and abused the power entrusted to him by the Party and the people.

At Stalin's funeral many people, myself among them, had tears in their eyes. They were sincere tears. Although we did know of some of Stalin's personal shortcomings, we still believed him. . . .

In the last years of his life Stalin was a profoundly sick man who suffered from suspiciousness and persecution mania. The Party has told the people extensively how Stalin created such "cases" as the "Leningrad case," the "doctors' case" and others. . . .

Our respected Mikhail Alexandrovich Sholokhov raised his voice in the spring of 1933 in protest against the arbitrariness then going on in the Don. Recently two letters from Mikhail Alexandrovitch to Stalin and Stalin's replies to the letters were discovered in the archives. It is impossible to read without emotion Sholokhov's truthful words, written from the bottom of the heart, on the outrageous conduct of the people who were committing criminal acts in Veshenskaya and other districts of the Don. . . .

Stalin's abuses of power and the arbitrary acts he committed became known to us only after his death and the unmasking of Beria—that hardened enemy of the Party and the people, spy and vile provocateur. . . .

The poet R. Rozhdestvensky spoke here. He took issue with N. Gribachev's poem "No, Boys!" Comrade Rozhdestvensky's speech betrayed the idea that it is only the group of young writers that expresses the mind of all our youth, that they are the mentors of youth. This is not so at all. Our Soviet young people have been reared by the Party, they follow the Party and regard it as their educator and leader. *(Stormy applause.)*

I should like to set before the young poet R. Rozhdestvensky the example of a poet-soldier who has a keen eye and who hits the ideological enemy without a miss, the poet-Communist N. Gribachev. *(Applause.)* We live in a period of sharp ideological struggle, a period of struggle for the minds, for the re-education of people. This is a complex process, considerably more difficult than reconstructing machine tools and factories. You—the writers and artists—are, figuratively speaking, the blacksmiths for re-forging human psychology. You possess powerful tools, and these tools of yours should always be employed in the interests of the people. *(Applause.)*

Strictly speaking, nonpartisanship *(bespartiinost*—literally, "non-party-ness") actually does not exist in society. And he who advertises his nonpartisanship is doing so in order to cover his disagreement with the views and ideas of the Party so that he can attract supporters. . . .

In the fire of the cruel struggle with the counterrevolutionaries and interventionists, the working people of our country went through a school of political education, learned their political ABCs through harsh experience and decided whom they were for, whose side they should support, and they became Bolsheviks.

This is very well and convincingly shown in D. Furmanov's story

"Chapayev" and the film made from it, in A. Serafimovich's novel "Iron Torrent," and in A. Fadeyev's novel "The Rout," in N. Ostrovsky's novel "How the Steel Was Tempered" and in other works by our Soviet revolutionary writers. Their works, which are imbued with Party spirit, play a great role even now and are weapons for our party in its ideological work. It is no accident that "How the Steel Was Tempered" enjoys great popularity in Cuba and a number of other countries that are struggling for their freedom and independence. . . .

We Are Against Peaceful Coexistence in the Sphere of Ideology. Historical experience teaches us that in the ideological struggle one must not trust words and declarations, one must know how to recognize who is issuing them and what they are being issued for. To do this it is first of all necessary to be a Marxist-Leninist, a convinced Communist who has devoted all his life and talent to the struggle for the happiness of the earth's working people.

One cannot consider oneself a fighter for the interest of the working people and still stand midway between the combatant sides "accepting both good and evil with equanimity." . . .

. . . Comrade Ehrenburg once visited V. I. Lenin in Paris and, as he writes in his account of the meeting, received a friendly welcome. Comrade Ehrenburg even joined the Party, but then he left it. He did not participate directly in the socialist revolution but rather took the position of an uninvolved observer. I think that it would not be a distortion of the truth to say that in his memoirs "People, Years, Life," Comrade Ehrenburg evaluates our revolution and the entire succeeding period of socialist construction from this same position. . . .

A notable example of patriotic, Party-oriented understanding of the tasks of the artist is to be seen in the works of our outstanding writer Mikhail Alexandrovich Sholokhov. Take his novels "The Silent Don" and "Virgin Soil Upturned," the story "The Fate of a Man," or the chapters from the novel "They Fought for Their Country." These are highly artistic works of enormous power and revolutionary enthusiasm, filled with Communist Party spirit and the spirit of the class struggle of the workers and peasants of our country for the victory of the revolution and socialism. Comrade Sholokhov himself took an active part in the struggle during the Civil War, during the liquidation of the kulaks as the last exploiter class, and in the Patriotic War against the fascist predators. He took part in these battles not as an observer but as a fighter, and in peacetime he remains a fighter for the happiness of the working people. *(Stormy applause.)* . . .

In the example of Mikhail Alexandrovich Sholokhov's work everyone sees that the writer's Communist Party spirit not only does not limit the expression of his artistic individuality but, on the contrary, actively promotes the flowering of his talent and raises his works to the level of the highest social importance.

We adhere to class positions in art and are resolutely opposed to the peaceful coexistence of socialist and bourgeois ideologies. Art belongs to the sphere of ideology. Those who think that in Soviet art there can be peaceful cohabitation of both socialist realism and formalist, abstractionist tendencies will inevitably slip into the position of peaceful coexistence in the sphere of ideology, a position that is alien to us. . . . Unfortunately, this bait has been taken by some Communist writers and artists, and even some officials of creative organizations. At the same time it should be noted that some non-Party people, such as Comrade Sobolev, for instance, staunchly defend the Party line in literature and art.

At the last meeting Comrade I. Ehrenburg said that the idea of coexistence had been stated in a letter as a joke. Let us say that this was the case. But if so, it was a vicious joke. One should not joke thus in the field of ideology. . . .

I have already had occasion to say that peaceful coexistence in the field of ideology is treason against Marxism-Leninism and betrayal of the cause of the workers and peasants. Soviet society is now at a stage in which there has been achieved full and monolithic unity of all the socialist nations of the country and all strata of the people—workers, collective farmers and the intelligentsia—who are successfully building communism under the guidance of the Leninist Party.

Our people and party will not tolerate any encroachments on this monolithic unity. One of the evidences of this phenomenon is the attempt to force us to accept peaceful coexistence of ideologies. This is why we are directing our fire both against these pernicious ideas and against those who hold them. It is my hope that we are all together on this point. (Prolonged applause.)

Abstractionism, formalism, which some of its advocates are suggesting should be given the right to exist in socialist art, is one of the forms of bourgeois ideology. One must regret that some people, including creative workers made wise by life experience, do not understand this. . . .

Perhaps some will say that Khrushchev is calling for photographic portrayal, for naturalism in art. No, comrades! We call for vivid works of art that truthfully portray the real world in all its diversity of colors. Only such art will give people joy and pleasure. Man will never lose the capacity for artistic talent and will not allow dirty daubs that any donkey could paint with his tail to be foisted on him in the guise of works of art. (Applause.). . . .

In music, as in other arts, there are many different genres, styles and forms. No one places any ban on a single one of these styles and genres. But we wish nevertheless to set forth our attitude to music, to its tasks and to the trend in composition.

To put it briefly, we stand for melodious, meaningful music that stirs people's souls and inspires strong emotions, and we oppose any cacophony. . . .

There are also serious shortcomings in composition. The apparent preoccupation with jazz music and jazz bands cannot be considered normal. Do not think that we oppose all music for jazz bands, there are various kinds of jazz bands and various kinds of music for them. Dunayevsky was able to write good music for jazz bands as well as for others. I like some songs as played by the jazz band conducted by Leonid Utyosov. But there is some music that turns your stomach and gives you a pain. . . .

Music that does not have melody evokes nothing but irritation. They say this comes from failure to understand. And indeed there is jazz music of a kind that defies understanding and is repulsive to hear.

Some so-called modern dances, brought into our country from the West, call for objections. I have had occasion to travel widely about the country. I have seen Russian, Ukrainian, Kazakh, Uzbek, Armenian, Georgian and other dances. They are beautiful dances and it is pleasant to watch them. But what is called modern fashionable dancing is simply some kind of indecency, frenzy, devil knows what! They say that one can see such indecency only among the Shaker sects. I cannot confirm this, for I have myself never attended Shaker revivals. *(Laughter in the hall.)*

It seems that among workers in the arts one finds young people who strive to prove that melody in music has lost its right to existence and in its place is coming "new" music—"dodecaphony," a music of noise. It is hard for a normal person to understand what the word "dodecaphony" means, but in all likelihood it is the same thing as is meant by cacophony. Well, we are completely sweeping out this here cacophony music. Our people cannot take this garbage into their ideological arsenal. . . .

The Guidance of the Leninist Party Is the Guarantee of All Our Successes. Among certain people one can hear talk about some kind of absolute freedom of the individual. I do not know what they have in mind, but I believe that there will never be absolute freedom of the individual, even under full communism. . . . And under communism the will of one man must be subordinated to the will of the entire collective. Unless this is so, anarchic self-will will sow dissension and disorganize the life of society. . . .

Under contemporary conditions we must conduct a stubborn struggle against vestiges of the past within the country and repulse the attacks of the organized class enemy in the international arena. We do not have the right to forget this even for one minute. But some people are attempting to push us onto the path of peaceful ideological coexistence, to palm off on us the rotten idea of "absolute freedom." If each person were to impose his subjectivist views on society as rules for everyone and were to try to achieve their realization contrary to the generally accepted norms of socialist society, this would inevitably lead to the disorganization of the normal life of the people, the activity of society. Society cannot permit anarchy and self-will on the part of anyone, whoever it may be.

The Communist Party of the Soviet Union is the guiding figure of socialist society. It expresses the will of the entire Soviet people, and the goal of its activity is the struggle for the vital interests of the people. The Party enjoys the people's confidence, which it has earned and is earning with its struggle, with its blood. And the Party will remove from the path of Communist construction everything that stands in the way of the people's interests. *(Prolonged applause.)* ...

We should like our principles to be well understood by all, especially by those who are trying to impose on us peaceful coexistence in the field of ideology. There can be no joking in politics. He who preaches the idea of peaceful coexistence in ideology is objectively slipping down into the positions of anti-communism. The enemies of communism would like to see us ideologically disarmed. And by propagandizing the peaceful coexistence of ideologies, by calling on the help of this "Trojan horse" that they would be happy to wish upon us, they are attempting to achieve this insidious goal of theirs. ...

But it must be said that books also are appearing that in our opinion give an imprecise or, to speak more correctly, an incorrect, one-sided interpretation of events and phenomena connected with the cult of the individual and of the essence of those fundamental, radical changes that have taken place and are taking place in the social, political and spiritual life of the people since the 20th Party Congress. I would place Comrade Ehrenburg's novel "The Thaw" among these books.

With the concept of thaw is associated the idea of a time of instability, inconstancy, incompleteness, of temperature fluctuations in nature, when it is difficult to foresee how and in what direction the weather will develop. It is impossible to formulate by means of such a literary image a correct opinion of the essence of those fundamental changes that have taken place in the social, political, production and spiritual life of Soviet society since Stalin's death.

62. Khrushchev on anti-semitism

FROM THE SPEECH BY N. S. KHRUSHCHEV, March 8, 1963, at a Meeting of Party and Government Leaders With Workers in Literature and the Arts. (*Pravda* and *Izvestia,* March 10, 1963, pp. 1-4). 1963. *The Current Digest of the Soviet Press* (Vol. XV, No. 11, April 10, 1963, p. 11), published weekly at Columbia University by the Joint Committee on Slavic Studies appointed by the American Council of Learned Societies and Social Science Research Council. Reprinted by permission.

. . . Letters are being received in the Party Central Committee expressing concern over the fact that some works give a distorted view of the position of Jews in our country. The bourgeois press, as you know from the exchange of letters between the English philosopher Russell and myself,[1] is even conducting a slanderous campaign against us.

At our meeting in December we already touched upon this question in connection with the poet Yevtushenko's "Babi Yar." Circumstances require us to return to this question.

Why is this poem criticized? For the fact that its author did not succeed in truthfully showing and condemning the fascist, specifically fascist, criminals for the mass murders they committed in Babi Yar. The poem presents the matter as though only the Jewish population fell victim to the fascist crimes, whereas many Russians, Ukrainians and Soviet people of other nationalities died there at the hands of the Hitlerite executioners. It is evident from this poem that its author did not manifest political maturity and disclosed ignorance of the historical facts.

Who needed to present matters as though the population of Jewish nationality in our country is mistreated by someone, and why did they need to present them thus? This is untrue. From the days of the October Revolution the Jews in our country have had equality with all other peoples of the U.S.S.R. in all respects. We do not have a Jewish question, and those who dream it up are singing a foreign tune.

---

[1] *Current Digest of the Soviet Press,* Vol. XV, No. 4, pp. 3-5.

As for the Russian working class, before the Revolution also it was the resolute foe of any national oppression, including anti-Semitism.

In prerevolutionary times I lived among the miners. The workers stigmatized those who participated in the Jewish pogroms. The inspirers of the pogroms were the autocratic government, the capitalists, the landholders and the bourgeoisie. They needed the pogroms as a means of diverting the working people from revolutionary struggle. The organizers of the pogroms were the police, the gendarmerie, the Black Hundreds who recruited hoodlums from the dregs of society, from declassed elements. In the cities many janitors were their agents.

For example, the famous Bolshevik revolutionary Comrade Bauman, who was not a Jew, was killed in Moscow by a janitor at the assignment of the gendarmerie.

Gorky's wonderful novel "Mother" superbly showed the internationalism of the working class of Russia. In the ranks of the revolutionary workers are representatives of various nationalities. It is enough to recall the Russian worker Pavel Vlasov and the Ukrainian Andrei Nakhodka.

I spent my childhood and youth in Yuzovka, where many Jews lived at the time. For a while I worked at the factory as apprentice to the fitter Yakov Isaakovich Kutikov. He was a skilled worker. There were other Jews too among the workers at the factory. I remember that a Jew worked as a foundryman pouring copper, and this was then considered a very high skill. I often saw this foundryman; he was evidently a religious man and did not work Saturdays, but since all the Ukrainians, Russians and others worked on Saturdays, he used to come to the foundry and spend the whole day there, although he did not take part in the work.

Russians, Ukrainians, Jews, Poles, Latvians, Estonians and others worked at the factory. Sometimes no one even knew the nationality of one or another worker. Relations were comradely among the workers of all nationalities.

This is class unity, proletarian internationalism.

When I was in the United States of America and was riding in a car in Los Angeles, a man sat down in the car and introduced himself as the deputy mayor of the city. He spoke Russian, not very pure Russian but quite fluent. I looked at him and asked:

"How do you know Russian?"

"I lived in Rostov, my father was a merchant of the second guild."

Such persons lived in Petersburg and wherever they wished.

The Jew Kutikov, with whom I worked at the factory, could not live wherever he chose in tsarist times, you see, but such a Jew as the father of the deputy mayor of Los Angeles could live where he wished.

That was how the tsarist government viewed the national question; it too treated it from a class point of view. Therefore Jews who were big merchants, capitalist, had the right to live everywhere, but the Jewish poor shared the same lot as the Russian, Ukrainian and other workers;

they had to work, to live in hovels and carry the burden of forced labor, like all the peoples of tsarist Russia.

Different people behaved differently in the period of the Patriotic War against the fascist invaders also. In those days no little heroism was displayed, including heroism by Jews. Those of them who distinguished themselves were awarded the title Hero of the Soviet Union, many were awarded orders and medals. I shall mention as an example Hero of the Soviet Union General Kreizer. He was deputy commander of the Second Guards Army during the great battle on the Volga, he took part in the fighting for liberation of the Donets Basin and the Crimea. General Kreizer is now in command of troops in the Far East

There were also instances of treason on the part of people of various nationalities. I can cite the following fact. When Paulus's grouping was surrounded and then crushed, the 64th Army, commanded by General Shumilov, took part in capturing Paulus's headquarters, and General Z. T. Serdyuk was a member of the Military Council. He telephoned me and said that among the prisoners taken at Paulus's headquarters was Kogan, formerly an instructor of the Kiev City Young Communist League Committee. I asked:

"How could he get there? Aren't you mistaken?"

"No, I'm not mistaken," said Comrade Serdyuk. "This Kogan was interpreter at Paulus's headquarters."

A mechanized brigade commanded by Colonel Burmakov took part in capturing Paulus. The commissar of this brigade was Comrade Vinokur, a Jew by nationality. I knew Vinokur back in 1933, when I had worked as Secretary of the Bauman Borough Party Committee in Moscow and he had been secretary of the Party cell at the butter and milk plant.

It turns out thus: One Jew serves as interpreter at Paulus' headquarters, another in the ranks of our troops takes part in capturing Paulus and his interpreter.

People's acts are judged not from a national but from a class standpoint.

It is not in the interests of our cause to dig up out of the rubbish heaps of the past examples of discord among the working people of various nationalities. It is not they who bear the responsibility for inflaming national hatred and national oppression. This was the work of the exploiting classes. And as for the traitors to the interests of the revolution—the hirelings of tsarism, of the landowners and of the bourgeoisie recruited them everywhere and found venal souls among people of various nationalities. . . .

63. the Soviet-Chinese polemic:

Suslov's speech

AFTER KHRUSHCHEV'S DENUNCIATION of the Stalin "cult of personality" at the XXth Congress of the Communist Party of the Soviet Union (CPSU), February 24-25, 1956, relations between the USSR and Red China began to cool off. Within the next two years it became apparent that the Chinese were acting alone in Asia, especially in non-Muslim Asia, rather than in close cooperation with the Soviet Union. The rift between the two chief members of the Communist orbit was exacerbated by Khrushchev's trip to the United States in the fall of 1959. Mao Tse-tung and his followers bitterly resented Khrushchev's effort to improve Soviet-American relations, at a time when the United States as Red China's chief enemy blocked Chinese expansion in the Pacific and the entry of the Chinese People's Republic (CPR) into the United Nations. Since Red China was in no position to compete economically with the USSR in aid to the developing nations of Asia and Africa, as the struggle for power and prestige between the two powers increased in the 1960's Red Chinese leaders injected the racial issue into the conflict in an attempt to eliminate the Soviet Union from Asian-African affairs on the ground that it was a European and not an Asian power. The Red Chinese also resorted to the use of Communist ideological tools to achieve strictly national objectives, as in their border dispute with India. For several years, the Soviet government tried to cover up its growing estrangement from its Chinese ally and to call a halt to the ideological polemics involved. By 1964, however, even the Soviet leaders could no longer conceal the fact that the rift was basic rather than superficial.

M. A. Suslov, member of the Presidium and Secretary of the Central Committee of the Communist Party of the Soviet Union, made an extensive report, "On the Struggle of the C.P.S.U. for the Solidarity of the International Communist Movement," to the Central Committee's plenary session in February, 1964, which summed up the ideological and political controversy between the USSR and Red China. This report was finally published in *Pravda,* April 3, 1964. The excerpts from this address presented below cover 1. The Background of the Rift and 2. Soviet Aid to Red China.

1964. *The Current Digest of the Soviet Press* (Vol. XVI, No. 13, April 22, 1964, pp. 3-16; and No. 14, April 29, 1964, pp. 3-17), published weekly at Columbia University by the Joint Committee on Slavic Studies appointed by the American Council of Learned Societies and Social Science Research Council. Reprinted by permission.

i. The Background of the Rift

The new evaluations and conclusions worked out as a result of the collective efforts of the fraternal parties on the basis of the creative application of the principles of Marxism-Leninism to the conditions of our epoch — on the role of the world socialist system, on the paths of the construction of socialism and communism, on the possibility of averting a world war, on the peaceful coexistence of countries with different social systems, on the necessity for a struggle against the ideology and practice of the cult of the individual, on the forms of the transition to socialism in the developed capitalist countries and the countries that have liberated themselves from colonialism—all this is being distorted and in effect cast aside by the Chinese leadership.

Having virtually cast aside the Declaration and Statement collectively worked out by the Communist and Workers' Parties, the C.P.C. [Communist Party of China] leaders are proposing to the fraternal parties their own notorious "25 points," the true sense of which in effect reduces to: denial of the increasingly decisive influence of the socialist system on the course of world development; a disdainful attitude toward the struggle of the working class in the capitalist countries; the counterposing of the national-liberation movement to the world system of socialism and the international workers' movement; adventurism in foreign policy and the maintenance of the atmosphere of the "cold war"; sectarianism and putschism in questions of revolution; the defense and preservation of the methods and practices of the cult of the individual that have been condemned by the Communist movement; and justification of the factional struggle within the Communist movement. . . .

Whereas a short time ago Chinese propaganda aimed its attacks largely at the foreign-policy course of the C.P.S.U., our internal policy is now being subjected to open attacks. The C.P.C. leadership is endeavoring in every way to discredit the line of the 20th C.P.S.U. Congress

(1956) on all questions, to declare the struggle against the Stalin cult a mistake and to cast aspersions on the Program of the C.P.S.U.

Reviving practices and methods already applied by the Trotskyites, the Chinese leaders are attempting to place the Soviet people, Soviet Communists, in opposition to the leadership of the Party, the leadership of the country. Matters have come to such a pass that the Chinese press and radio are appealing to Soviet people to fight against the Central Committee of our party and the Soviet government.

What is this? A struggle for the "purity" of Marxism-Leninism? No, it is the most outright rejection of the elementary norms of mutual relations between Communist Parties, rejection of Marxist-Leninist principles of relations between socialist countries, a transition to a position of open anti-Sovietism.

The C.P.C. leaders no longer limit their actions to the sphere of ideology. They have carried over ideological differences to interstate relations, to the realm of the practical policies of the socialist countries and the Communist Parties. Striving to weaken the unity and solidarity of the socialist commonwealth, the C.P.C. leadership is permitting itself every kind of maneuver and contrivance to undermine the economic and political relations between the socialist countries, to introduce discord into their actions in the international arena. The undermining, schismatic activity of the Chinese leaders in the world Communist movement has recently been sharply stepped up. There is no longer any doubt that Peking has plotted a course toward a split in the Communist Parties, toward the creation of factions and groups hostile to Marxism-Leninism. . . .

. . . It is becoming increasingly clear that under the cloak of ultra-revolutionary phrases and slogans, the C.P.C. leadership is now waging a furious attack upon the gains of world socialism, concentrating its main fire not against the imperialists but predominantly against the C.P.S.U. and other Marxist-Leninist parties. . . .

They trumpet about unity, but all their actions pursue another purpose: To disorganize and split the socialist camp, to undermine the ideological foundations and the organizational and political principles that rally and unite the peoples of the socialist commonwealth. They are striving to impose on the socialist countries a "Sinicized" socialism, an adventurist course in foreign and domestic policy, and the ideology and practice of the cult of the individual. . . .

An editorial in *Jenmin Jihpao* and *Hung Chi* on October 22, 1963, says: "The national-liberation revolution in Asia, Africa and Latin America is today operating as the most important force dealing direct blows at imperialism."

The Marxist teaching about the historical role of the working class is obviously being revised here and the workers' movement in the developed capitalist countries is being belittled. As for the world socialist system, the Chinese theoreticians assign to it the role of a mere "support base" for bolstering and developing the revolution of the oppressed nations and peoples of the whole world. It goes without saying that such a position can bring nothing but harm to both the socialist system and the national-liberation movement, the great cause of the struggle of the international proletariat.

According to the view of the Chinese theoreticians, it seems that the world socialist system is not only failing to render increasingly decisive influence on the entire course of world development but is not even playing an independent role in the revolutionary struggle of the masses against imperialism.

Such a treatment of the role and importance of the world system of socialism does not conform to the actual correlation of forces in the world and directly contradicts the conclusions drawn in the 1960 Statement of the fraternal parties. . . .

While attaching great significance to the national-liberation movement, Marxist-Leninists hold at the same time that the chief content, the chief direction and the chief features of the historical development of human society in the modern epoch are determined by the world socialist system, the forces fighting against imperialism and for the socialist reorganization of society. It is precisely on this beachhead that the most highly organized class forces are concentrated, and primarily the basic masses of the working class—the most advanced class of modern society, the one that, as our teachers Marx, Lenin and Engels pointed out, is the gravedigger of capitalism. . . .

It would not occur to a single Marxist-Leninist to assert that peaceful economic competition "can replace the struggle for liberation on the part of the peoples of different countries," that the victory of socialism in economic competition will "automatically" lead to the downfall of capitalism and will save the peoples the need to wage a class and national-liberation struggle. Such myths are being circulated from Peking expressly to discredit the idea of economic competition between the two systems. In fact, Marxist-Leninists see the revolutionary importance of the victories of socialism in economic competition precisely in that they stimulate the class struggle of the working people and make them conscious fighters for socialism. Peaceful economic competition not only does not doom the masses to passive waiting but, on the contrary, kindles their revolutionary activeness. The imperialists are well aware of this; they are afraid of successes in the development of the socialist countries and strive to restrain their progress.

As you see, comrades, in essence the question of peaceful economic competition is far from being an economic one alone. It contains a profound political idea: To win out over capitalism economically means seriously to facilitate the struggle against imperialism by all revolutionary forces. And it now becomes a political question.

Our party sees its chief task to lie in strengthening the economic and defensive might of the U.S.S.R. and the world socialist system as a whole, in intensifying its influence on the entire revolutionary process. We shall continue to pursue unswervingly and persistently a line aimed at fulfilling the C.P.S.U. Program for the construction of communism—the most just social system—in our country. Communist construction is the greatest contribution to the fulfillment of the internationalist duty of the Soviet people. This path was outlined by the great Lenin. Nothing and no one will ever turn us from this Leninist path. . . .

The Chinese-Albanian alliance is not accidental. It arose on the soil of opposition to the Leninist course of the 20th Congress of the C.P.S.U., on the soil of a hostile attitude toward the liquidation of the consequences of the Stalin cult. As in China, the Albanian leaders' defense of the cult of the individual is linked with the fact that for many years they themselves have been implanting a cult of the individual and resorting to the most vicious methods of guiding the party and the country. . . .

A comprehensive analysis of the correlation of forces in the international arena has enabled the Communist and Workers' Parties to draw the highly important conclusion that it is possible to avert a world war even before the complete victory of socialism on earth and to emphasize once again that the Leninist principle of the peaceful coexistence of states with different social systems is the unshakable foundation of the foreign policy of the socialist countries.

These postulates, as is known, were set forth in the Declaration and Statement of the 1957 and 1960 Moscow conferences. The experience of recent years not only has failed to shake but, on the contrary, has confirmed the vital need for a policy of peaceful coexistence. It is thanks to the persistent implementation of this policy by the socialist countries, supported by hundreds of millions of people throughout the world, that it has been possible to disrupt the schemes aimed against peace by imperialist reaction. The fact that mankind today enjoys the blessings of peace is not a gift from the gods. It is the real result of the persistent struggle of all peace-loving forces against attempts to unleash a thermonuclear war, the result of the growth in the might of the Soviet Union and the other socialist countries, as well as of the correct policy of the Communist Parties, which have raised aloft the banner of the struggle for peace and have united all progressive mankind under this banner. . . .

In waging their struggle against the Leninist course of peaceful coexistence and counterposing to it the path of "prodding" revolution through war, the C.P.C. leaders have gone so far as to assert that war is an acceptable and even, in essence, the only means for resolving the contradictions between capitalism and socialism. Ignoring the experience of the whole world Communist movement, they are setting forth the path of the victory of revolution in China as an absolute, trying to elevate it to an immutable truth for all countries and peoples. Chinese propaganda, relevantly and irrelevantly, quotes Mao Tse-tung's statements on questions of war and peace made as long ago as the 1930s, during the period of the civil war in China. . . .

. . . Attempts to depict Marxist-Leninists in the role of pacifists of some kind look simply ridiculous. The 1957 Declaration noted that as long as imperialism exists, the soil for aggressive wars is preserved. However, the Communist Parties have not drawn from this the conclusion that a world war is fatally inevitable. They have shown that although the nature of imperialism, its predatory essence, remains unchanged, the correlation of forces in the world arena *has* changed, the place and role of imperialism in world economics and world politics has altered and the opportunities for its influence on the course of world events is diminishing. All this compels the imperialists to accede to peaceful coexistence.

The point, consequently, is not that the imperialists have become more "peace-loving" and more "complaisant" but that they cannot refuse to take the growing strength of socialism into account. The imperialists know that the Soviet Union and the socialist countries possess formidable weapons and are capable of giving a devastating rebuff to any aggressor. The imperialist cannot but reckon with the strength of the mighty workers' and the democratic movements in the capitalist countries, with the enormous scale of the peoples' national-liberation struggle. The truth that should the imperialist madmen unleash a world war capitalism would be swept away and buried is becoming increasingly clear in the camp of our class enemies. . . .

By coming out on July 31, 1963, with hysterical attacks on the Moscow treaty banning nuclear weapons tests in three environments and thus turning up in the company of the most aggressive circles of imperialism, the Chinese leaders have even further exposed themselves as adversaries of the policy of the struggle for peace and peaceful coexistence of states with different social systems. The enemies were heartened by this, and friends could not but condemn it.

The Chinese leaders sensed that they had gone too far, and in order to extricate themselves from this situation they began to turn their propaganda around, as they say, 180 degrees. A flood of "peace-loving" declarations has recently begun to gush forth from Peking, and the representatives of the Chinese government are hastening to sign documents having to do with the struggle for peace and fidelity to the policy of peaceful coexistence. This is precisely the nature of many of the statements made by Chou En-lai during his tour of the countries of Africa and Asia. . . .

. . . Everyone knows the sharply negative reaction of the Chinese leaders to the efforts the Soviet Union and the other socialist countries have been making to normalize and improve economic and other relations with the capitalist countries, including the United States of America. The question arises involuntarily: why should the normalization of relations between the two great nuclear powers—the U.S.S.R. and the U.S.A., on whom the relaxation of international tension largely depends—evoke such opposition on the part of the Chinese government? With an obstinacy worthy of better application, the Chinese leaders are striving to prevent the improvement of Soviet-American relations, representing it as "collusion with the imperialists." At the same time, the C.P.R. government is exerting feverish efforts to establish relations with Britain, France, Japan, West Germany and Italy. It is obvious from all this that they would not reject an improvement in relations with the U.S.A. as well but cannot so far see suitable conditions for this.

Never before have so many businessmen, political leaders and statesmen from the capitalist countries come to Peking. C.P.R. representatives have been conducting negotiations with them and concluding agreements on trade, credits, scientific and technical aid, and even political problems.

Do we want to reproach the C.P.C. leaders for such activity? Of course not. This is a normal procedure, constituting an organic element of the policy of peaceful coexistence. All socialist countries will inevitably have to do business with people from the bourgeois states, including not only friends but representatives of the ruling imperialist circles. But the whole trouble is that the Chinese leaders feel that when they themselves develop such activity, it is the policy of true "revolutionaries," while when other socialist countries do the same thing, it is allegedly "revisionism" and "betrayal." . . .

In the light of the Chinese leaders' practical activities in recent years, the true political meaning of the slogan they have advanced—"The wind from the East is prevailing over the wind from the West"—has become especially clear. As long ago as the 1960 conference, this slogan was subjected to resolute criticism as being nationalistic, one that substitutes for the class approach a geographical and even a racist one. It plainly bespeaks a belittling on their part of the role of the world socialist system, the working class and popular masses of Western Europe and America. . . .

The Chinese leaders attack the C.P.S.U. because it is pursuing a line toward raising the people's well-being. They call the improvement of the life of the Soviet people "bourgeoisification"; the principle of material incentive, in their opinion "leads to people's pursuit of personal profit, money-grubbing, desire for gain, the growth of bourgeois individualism, harm to the socialist economy and even its corruption" *(Jenmin Jihpao,* Dec. 26, 1963).

Is there not concealed beneath these strident words a profound contempt for man's vital needs, for the principles and ideals of a socialist society? . . .

Yes, comrades, it must be said openly: The entire conglomeration of the theoretical and political views of the leaders of the Communist Party of China is largely a rehash of Trotskyism, which was discarded long ago by the international revolutionary movement.

What in fact are the Chinese leaders' views on problems of war and peace? They are nothing but a restatement in new conditions of the Trotskyite slogan "Neither peace nor war."

Or take the active opposition of the leadership of the C.P.C. Central Committee to economic competition with capitalism. Is this a new statement of the question? No, it is a reiteration of the old Trotskyite postulate about rejecting peaceful economic construction and going over to the tactic of "revolutionary war," of "prodding" a world revolution with weapons in hand.

Everyone knows that the true sense of Trotsky's theory of "permanent revolution" lay precisely here. The struggle against Trotskyism on this question was of historic importance. The destinies of the world's first socialist country, the destinies of the entire world revolutionary movement depended on its outcome. What would have happened if our party had adopted such a course? It would have proved defenseless in the face of world imperialism, it would have been easy prey for it in the event of armed attack. . . .

The facts indicate that nationalism is gaining increasing ascendancy in the entire policy of the Chinese leadership and is becoming the mainspring of their actions. This was manifested back during the period of the "great leap," which was obviously conceived as an attempt to catch up to all the socialist countries "in one jump," to seize a dominant position in the world socialist system. More recently these tendencies have become even more intense. This has found reflection in such acts of the Chinese government as the artificial stirring up of nationalist passions over border questions, the behavior of the C.P.C. leaders during the Caribbean crisis, and the Chinese government's position on the nuclear question. . . .

For many years now Chinese propaganda has been persistently suggesting to everyone that the ideas of Mao Tse-tung are the "supreme incarnation of Marxism-Leninism" and that our epoch is "the epoch of Mao Tse-tung." Asserting that the generalization of the historical tasks of modern times has fallen wholly on the shoulders of Mao Tse-tung alone, Chinese propaganda is representing matters as though the ideas of Mao Tse-tung are the Marxism-Leninism of our epoch, "the scientific theory of socialist revolution and the building of socialism and communism."

It is now perfectly clear that the C.P.C. leadership is striving to spread the Mao Tse-tung cult to the entire world Communist movement, so that the C.P.C. leader, like Stalin in his time, might be elevated like a god above all the Marxist-Leninist parties and might decide all questions of their policy and activities according to his whims. The ideology and practice of the cult of the individual largely explain the appearance of the Chinese leaders' hegemonic schemes.

However, history does not repeat itself. And what was once a tragedy can seem a mere farce the second time. The C.P.C. leaders should know that the Communist movement will never permit a repetition of the practices of the cult of the individual, which are alien to Marxism-Leninism and for which it paid such a high price in the past. The Communist movement and the cult of the individual are incompatible. . . .

But it can be seen that it is precisely this aspect of Stalin's activity that has captivated the Chinese leaders; therefore they identify his incorrect methods of leadership with the dictatorship of the proletariat. Despite the fact that many instances of Stalin's abuses of power during the period of the cult of the individual have become generally known and despite Stalin's deviation from Leninist principles on a number of important questions, the Chinese leaders have put Stalin on a pedestal, representing him as the "great continuer" of Lenin's cause. The Chinese leaders write and speak about the mass repressions during the cult of the individual as though they were merely a question of petty "excesses." . . .

Marxist-Leninists and the peoples fighting for national independence consider it their task to bring the anti-imperialist, democratic revolution to completion, to create and consolidate the national front, and to struggle for the formation of national democratic states, for the non-capitalist path of development.

The Chinese leaders are sidestepping the essence of the present stage of the national-liberation revolution, do not see the differences in the situations of individual countries and are offering the peoples of all countries the same recipe—armed struggle and the establishment of the dictatorship of the proletariat. Such postulates can lead in practice to the undermining of the national front and a strengthening of the positions of the colonialists and neocolonialists. . . .

II. *Soviet Aid to Red China*

. . . Our party and the Soviet people know the scope and nature of the economic aid the Soviet Union has given China. The U.S.S.R. helped the Chinese People's Republic construct in a short time more than 200 major industrial enterprises, shops and other projects, furnished with the most modern equipment. With the Soviet Union's help, entire branches of industry that did not previously exist in China have been created in the C.P.R.: aircraft, motor vehicle and tractor building; power, heavy and precision machine building; instrument making; radio-technology; and various branches of the chemical industry.

Enterprises built or reconstructed with the aid of the Soviet Union provide China with 8,700,000 tons of iron, 8,400,000 tons of steel and 32,200,000 tons of coal and shale a year. Enterprises created with our country's assistance account for 70% of the total output of tin, 100% of the synthetic rubber, 25%•30% of the electric power and 80% of the trucks and tractors. Defense enterprises built with the technical assistance of the Soviet Union were the basis for the creation of China's defense industry.

During the period 1950-1960 more than 10,000 Soviet specialists were sent to China for various periods. In the years 1951-1962 some 10,000 Chinese engineers, technicians and skilled workers and about 1,000 scientists underwent instruction, scientific training and practice in the U.S.S.R. During this time more than 11,000 students and higher-degree candidates graduated from Soviet higher educational institutions.

Soviet-Chinese cooperation achieved its greatest development after 1953, when, on the initiative of the C.P.S.U. and Comrade N. S. Khrushchev personally, the elements of inequality on the mutual relations between our countries that had been one of the phenomena of the Stalin cult were eliminated. In 1957 Mao Tse-tung said, "The credit for eliminating all the unpleasantness and accretions in the Chinese question belongs to N. S. Khrushchev."

In 1959 the extent of Soviet-Chinese economic ties was almost double the 1953 figure, and the volume of deliveries for construction projects grew eightfold during this same time. In the period 1954-1963 the Soviet Union gave China more than 24,000 complete sets of scientific-technical documents, including designs for 1,400 major enterprises. This documentation embodied the enormous experience of the Soviet people and its scientific and technical intelligentsia. All this scientific and technical documentation was, in essence, given to China free.

The Soviet Union granted the Chinese People's Republic 1,816,000,000 rubles in long-term credits on favorable terms.

The C.P.S.U. Central Committee and the Soviet government exerted strenuous efforts in order that China might firmly occupy the position of a great socialist power in the international arena, and they unswervingly strove for the restoration of the C.P.R.'s rights in the United Nations. We kept the C.P.R. leadership constantly informed of all the Soviet Union's most important foreign-policy actions and strove to coordinate the foreign policies of our countries....

In 1950 a treaty of friendship, alliance and mutual aid was signed between the Soviet Union and the Chinese People's Republic, and it became an important factor not only in the development of multifaceted relations between our countries but in the strengthening of peace in the Far East....

Unfortunately, however, starting in 1958 the C.P.R. government began with increasing frequency to take various steps toward undermining Soviet-Chinese friendship, and through its uncoordinated actions in the international arena to create difficulties not only for the Soviet Union but for other socialist countries as well.

Soviet-Chinese relations became especially bad after the C.P.C. leaders went over from individual unfriendly acts to the sharp curtailment of economic and cultural ties with the Soviet Union and other socialist countries. Even on the eve of the 1960 Moscow conference of fraternal parties, the Chinese government demanded from the U.S.S.R. a revision of all the previously concluded agreements and protocols on economic and scientific-technical cooperation, refused a considerable part of the planned deliveries of Soviet equipment and reduced the volume of Soviet-Chinese trade to a minimum.

Although the Soviet government knew that by such a course the Chinese leaders would bring harm to the friendship and cooperation between the U.S.S.R. and the C.P.R., it had no choice but to consent to this. As a result, by 1962 the total volume of economic cooperation between the Soviet Union and the C.P.R. (including trade and technical assistance) had fallen to 36.5% of the 1959 level, while deliveries of sets of equipment and materials stood at only one-fortieth the 1959 figure. The volume of economic cooperation and trade declined even further in 1963. . . .

Now, having apparently "forgotten" its earlier explanations, the C.P.R. government is asserting that the Soviet-Chinese ties were curtailed on the initiative of the Soviet Union and that precisely this is the reason for the grave situation in which the Chinese national economy has found itself in recent years.

Now the Chinese leaders are bending over backwards to prove that, in general, Soviet aid to China never existed, that there were only ordinary trade operations. Striving to erase Soviet aid from the memory of the people, the Chinese are not even shrinking from knocking the plant trademarks from Soviet machine tools and machines and from concocting the slander that the Soviet Union allegedly delivered obsolete equipment to China. And this is said despite the fact that not only the Chinese themselves but even the foreign press has asserted that such enterprises as the Changchun Motor Vehicle Plant, the Harbin Electrical Equipment Plant, the Loyang Tractor Plant and many others that were built with the aid of the Soviet Union are excellent examples of modern industry. . . .

Despite the openly hostile actions of the C.P.C. leadership, our country, conscientiously fulfilling its earlier commitments, even now continues to assist China in the construction of 80 industrial enterprises, and engineering and technical workers, scientists and students from the C.P.R. are undergoing production practice and instruction in the U.S.S.R. as before. The Soviet Union responded in a fraternal way to the economic difficulties that arose in China in 1960 and 1961. During the period when the C.P.R. was experiencing an especially acute food shortage, the C.P.S.U. Central Committee and the Soviet government offered the C.P.C. leadership a loan of 1,000,000 tons of grain and 500,000 tons of sugar. At that time the Soviet Union granted the C.P.R. five years to liquidate 288,000,000 rubles of its indebtedness in commercial accounts. . . .

NOTE: *The New York Times* (Harry Schwartz, May 17, 1964, p. 20) listed the following key Chinese exports to the USSR: 100,000 tons of lithium concentrates, 34,000 tons of beryllium concentrates, 51,000 tons of borax, 270,000 tons of tungsten concentrates, 32.9 tons of piezoelectric quartz, 7,730 tons of mercury, 39 tons of tantalum-niobium concentrates, 37,000 tons of molybdenum concentrates and 180,000 tons of tin. A number of these minerals, especially lithium, the Chinese claim were essential to the development of the most advanced branches of Soviet science and to the manufacture of rockets and nuclear weapons.

Pacific Books Paperbounds

Prices subject to change without notice.

PACIFIC BOOKS, *Publishers*

P. O. Box 558, Palo Alto, California 94302